I0818432

# VIET NAM

ANAÏS CA DAO VAN MANEN

# VIET NAM

## THE COOKBOOK

# INTRODUCTION

Born in France to Vietnamese parents, I grew up speaking French as my first language, even after my parents returned to Vietnam with me when the country reopened in the early 1990s. Though I could barely speak Vietnamese at the time, I could definitely eat Vietnamese, whether during family meals at home or when I snuck out to street vendors in the evening with my saved pocket money. Vietnamese food became my primary connection to my culture, and I realized I wasn't alone. Many second- and third-generation kids living overseas, where they absorb their host cultures, will still eat Vietnamese food at home. Whenever I speak to other people who grew up with blended cultures, I find that it is almost always through food that they have found a connection to their heritage, just as I did. I believe this is true for most diaspora communities.

When I moved abroad, cooking Vietnamese food for myself and my friends was my solution to homesickness. After a failed attempt at becoming a graphic designer in Paris, I realized that my passion and sense of focus lay in cooking. This realization led me on the path towards becoming a chef, which took me to London, Bogotá and other cities. While working in various restaurants and introducing my own version of Vietnamese food through various pop ups, I was fortunate to meet many chefs, including Leandro Carreira, who put me in touch with Phaidon, which would soon become my publisher. My pitch was simple: if Anthony Bourdain loved Vietnam, we must write a book about it.

What began as a straightforward, and maybe naive, idea evolved into an incredibly rewarding journey of discovery about Vietnamese food and culture. However, initially, the project intimidated me. We Vietnamese are very opinionated about food, and rightfully so. While restaurants and master chefs define French gastronomy, Vietnamese cuisine begins in the home kitchen, with family as its foundation. Food becomes deeply personal here, playing a crucial role in relationships. We ask each other whether we've eaten yet as a sign of affection: often an older person will greet a younger person with, 'Con ăn cơm chưa?' meaning, 'Have you had rice yet?'.

At the age of thirty, I understood that Vietnamese cooking is something that must be experienced firsthand, learned through watching and doing, and most importantly, from our elders who carry generations of knowledge. While living abroad for a decade, I had tried to maintain my connection with Vietnam through calls with my mother, who still lived there, and by researching online and in libraries, but I knew that to truly understand our cuisine, I needed to go there, to learn directly from those who could teach me. This realization led my husband and I to make the life-changing decision to move to Vietnam, where I could fully immerse myself in the food.

Today's Vietnam has emerged from the shadow of its history, transforming into one of Asia's most dynamic nations. Home to a young population, with 20.1 per cent under the age of 24 (2019), it has become one of Southeast Asia's most exciting places to live. Vietnamese food is transmitted through stories, folk songs and word of mouth, starting from the home. With 54 distinct communities, each with their own customs and stories, and strongly regional cuisines, capturing it all in one book seemed daunting.

I was fortunate to learn from chị Nguyễn Thị Thu Ba, a talented home chef who shared her wealth of home-style cooking knowledge, and from countless individuals I met during my travels. Yet I realize there's still so much to discover. Food is malleable; each family brings their own touch, different cultures use the same ingredients differently, environments dictate diets, and history has its own version of everything. Authenticity is difficult to find when everybody claims it, but I realized, that wasn't necessarily what I was looking for. What mattered were the stories of the people who make up Vietnam, each with their own unique relationship with food and cooking.

Between testing dishes in my home kitchen and opening my first restaurant in Vietnam, I spent an entire year travelling across the country, learning from its myriad communities. I was welcomed everywhere from the mountains of Hà Giang to Trà Vinh in Southern Vietnam, and through the coastal province of Nghệ An; the unique city of Huế; Kon Tum province in the Central Highlands; and the beautiful beaches of Phan Rang in Ninh Thuận province. While in Kon Tum, in the Central Highlands, I ended up on national TV promoting the region's sustainable tourism. In Bản Luốc, Hà Giang province, I was invited to a wedding hosted by a couple from the Nung community: a wild evening spent between karaoke and shots of homemade rice liquor infused with foraged herbs. Waking up to nature the following morning, with the sight of green rice fields and buffaloes ploughing right in front of me, will stay in my memory forever.

With the help of generous friends and guides, I discovered techniques, dishes and ingredients I had never heard of before: from black pigs in Hà Giang to crickets and various edible worms. We caught river prawns (shrimp) in Bảo Lộc and made fermented jackfruit in Nghệ An. In Hanoi, we visited a district specializing in young green rice (*cốm*). This district comes alive in autumn during the harvest season when they process this rice by removing the skin, toasting it and then pounding it in a giant stone mortar: the aroma of this whole process fills the streets. When the vendors dispatch to sell freshly roasted young green rice as snacks across the city, it's clear that autumn has settled in, bringing with it a unique flavour and atmosphere.

Through the many meals I shared with my hosts, I learned about the values of a family meal, the subtle regional differences, and the multiple customs of different cultures living in Vietnam. In Hà Giang, when I stayed with cô Mui, a homestay owner from the Red Dao community, we would pick our daily vegetables from her garden, play with her grandchildren and cook on her wood fire stove, something rarely seen in a city kitchen. I learned that in the Red Dao culture, you should always serve two spoonfuls of rice to your guests and yourself, as serving a single spoonful is done only for the ancestors.

Beyond discovering new ingredients and techniques, this journey opened my eyes to the environmental challenges facing Vietnam today: climate change, pollution and increasing soil salinization among them. Yet if there's one thing I know about Vietnamese people, it's our resilience. I believe we'll face these challenges head on, finding solutions for generations to come.

While phở and bánh mì have brought worldwide attention to Vietnamese cuisine, it extends far beyond these dishes. As I recount all the recipes we discovered over the past two and a half years of immersion, and the ones we have yet to cook or eat, I realize how lucky I am to call this country my home.

In this book, I've tried to compile as varied a collection as possible to give you a taste, from snacks you can get from street carts to seafood dishes usually served at *quán ốc* (snail eateries), and to the pillar of it all: the family meals from the few communities I was lucky enough to meet. Consider this an introduction to Vietnamese food; it is not a complete reference but an invitation to come and learn more.

## ACKNOWLEDGEMENTS

This book is the result of two and a half years of intensive research, cooking, travelling, interviewing, writing, photographing and editing across Vietnam. It would not have been possible without the generosity and kindness of so many people who shared their knowledge, skills and stories with me.

In Vietnamese culture, we use specific pronouns to address people that reflect our relationship and show respect, particularly to elders. *Chị/Anh* for those like an elder sister/brother, *Cô/Chú* for those around our parents' age, *Bác* for those older than our parents, and *Bà/Ông* for those of our grandparents' generation. As you'll notice throughout these acknowledgements, most of the people mentioned are my elders, and it is through their experience that I was able to learn and write this book.

I am deeply grateful to chị Nguyễn Thị Thu Ba and cô Vương Thị Minh Hiếu, who shared countless recipes with me. Chị Thu Ba, a force of nature, spent a year and a half cooking and testing recipes with me, making everything from scratch. Cô Hiếu, who cooked for me since childhood, instilled in me a passion for Vietnamese food that has never wavered.

The book took shape thanks to Nguyễn Khánh Huyền, who helped organize my kitchen thoughts into coherent words and recipes, and handled Vietnamese–English translations. The photography, captured by Phương Bích Phạm and Pan Nguyễn with assistance from Nguyễn Thu Hương, required six months of travel throughout Vietnam, from shooting in the rain in Bảo Lộc to catching perfect sunrises in Phan Rang.

Before my travels began, I spent a year researching Vietnam's history, geography and people, guided by Charlotte Looram, Michel Galey, Dr Nguyễn Thị Mai Hương, Dr Lê Thị Liên and Dr Vũ Hồng Liên. The staff at the University of Social Sciences and Humanities (USSH-VNUHCM) in Ho Chi Minh City, particularly anh Nguyễn Trọng Hùng and anh Bùi Việt Thành, generously shared their personal collections of books on Vietnamese food.

Throughout my travels, I was welcomed into homes and kitchens across Vietnam. In Trà Vinh, my friend Nguyễn Thanh Tuấn introduced me to Villa Basi and cô Sa Quan, who shared Khmer specialties and made enough of them to feed a whole village.

In Hanoi, journalist anh Nguyễn Đình Thiên Ý connected me with culinary artist Nguyễn

Thị Lâm and her family in Bát Tràng, while cô Nguyễn Thị Ngọc Bích and cô Vũ Hằng Nga taught me the intricacies of Hanoian cooking in their own home.

In Huế, thanks to Denise Thao's coordination and Đào Hữu Quý's daily guidance, I learned about imperial cuisine and local eating traditions. They introduced me to cô Công Huyền Tôn Nữ Bích Hà and Nguyễn Ngọc Quang, who shared their amazing crispy rice cake recipe. In the ancient village of Phước Tích, bác Phan Thị Hồng Thanh, bác Trần Thị Hoa, chị Trịnh Thị Thu and bác Nguyễn Thị Thủy taught me the craft of traditional cake-making, which is slowly disappearing.

My two trips to Hà Giang were transformative, opening my eyes to the mountain produce and spices that would influence this book and my own cooking. The Red Dao, Tày and Nùng communities shared not just their food but also their culture, from Red Dao baths to wedding celebrations. I'm grateful to anh Triệu Tà Phẩu, Chu Đặng Thanh Tùng, cô Bôn Xà Chằm, anh Triệu Văn Kính, chị Triệu Mùi Pú, cháu Triệu Thùy Dung, cháu Triệu Chí Kiên, chị Triệu Mùi Chiều and family, and cô Mùi from Chán Mủi Homestay in Hồ Thầu.

I am forever grateful to cô Lê Thi Xuân of Quan Sa restaurant in Hoang Su Phi, who welcomed a stranger into their home, shared their tradition of making smoked sausages and buffalo, and sent me off with carefully prepared food. Through their kindness, I learned first hand that Vietnamese cuisine is as much about the warmth of its people as it is about the flavours on the plate.

In Ninh Thuận, my dear friend Nguyễn Ngọc Thảo Nhi took me to her hometown, where my obsession with Phan Rang-style rice paper rolls began. Through Nhi, I met bà Lượng Thị Dánh, chú Kiều Anh, cô Đạo Thị Tuyết, and chị Kiều Thị Hồng Vân and Kiều Maily, who taught me about Chăm culture as I experienced the Kate Festival for the very first time.

In Kon Tum, cô Y Sểnh and chị Y introduced me to young cassava leaves and wild edible plants. In Đắk Lắk province, chị H Duyên Êban and chị Nguyễn Thị Hải Vân amazed me with their use of golden ants in cooking, while bác Đinh Công Đông, bác Đinh Thị Như Thoa and chị Đinh Thị Thanh Đan taught me to appreciate the subtle bitterness prized in Mường cuisine.

In Nghệ An province's Quỳ Châu district, cô Sầm Thị Bích and chị Sầm Thị Lương showed me their Thai home museum and a vision of sustainable tourism. In Vinh, I'll never forget chu Nguyễn Như Hồng pounding dried buffalo skin, cô Lê Thị Hải Yến teaching me to clean eels for soup, and cô Nguyễn Thị Hằng introducing me to what would become one of my favourite snacks: sugar-coated sticky (glutinous) rice flour balls. Throughout this process, I'm grateful to friends like Marion Bhasin and Marie Ke who tested recipes and shared their perspectives and insights.

I'm grateful to the Phaidon team – Emilia Terragni, Ellie Smith, Clare Churly, João Mota and Claire Rogers – for bringing this project to life.

Ana Teodoro and James Brown of Cantina have been my greatest design supporters since my London days, and I'm thankful to work with them again.

Feroz Gajia has been proofreading every essay I've written. Thank you.

Finally, this book would not exist without the unconditional support of my mother, Trần Ngọc Thanh Trúc, and my husband Peter Van Hoesen.

# A BRIEF HISTORY OF VIETNAMESE CUISINE

The food of any nation is shaped by the forces of its history. Vietnamese cuisine, as we know it today, is the culmination of countless transformations: ancient kingdoms rising and falling, migrations of peoples, cultural exchanges both peaceful and forced, and the gradual formation of what we now call Vietnam. While Vietnam's turbulent history is often reduced to its modern conflicts, the ways people have grown, cooked and eaten food in these lands have been evolving for millennia. What follows is my attempt to trace this rich history through the lens of its food.

### FROM HUNTER-GATHERER TO AGRICULTURIST (PALEOLITHIC–2000 BCE)

Traces of human life have been found in Northern Vietnam as early as the Paleolithic Age. Excavations in the Hòa Bình province in Northern Vietnam reveal that between 12,000 to 10,000 BCE, the Hoabinhian hunter-gatherers subsisted on mainly nuts, foraged plants, tubers, molluscs, shellfish and mountain snails. Meat was eaten sparingly through hunting, and rice was discovered, although its cultivation would come later.

The beginning of the Neolithic Age marked the start of primitive pottery, new cobblestone tools, and the use of tree bark and bamboo shoots to preserve and cook rice (Rice in Bamboo Tubes, page 240). From 2500 BCE, sea levels receded in the Red River Delta and conditions became favourable for farming. Humans progressively moved towards the Delta in the north and further south to An Sơn, along the Vàm Cỏ Đông River.

Sea fishing increased with the expansion of settlements. By the end of the late Neolithic period, the Việt ancestors of today's ethnic Kinh (Vietnamese, who make up about 85 per cent of Vietnam's current population), Mường, Thổ and Chứt peoples had domesticated dogs, pigs, chickens and buffaloes. They started their journey into rice cultivation through slash-and-burn methods, gradually replacing foxtail millet as the primary grain, though foraging still played a significant role in the Việt diet.

The development of agricultural skills and domestication led to irrigation along waterways for rice production, fostering the creation of sedentary communities. This period also marks the beginning of Vietnamese oral history through legends and myths.

The *Lĩnh Nam Chích Quái*, a collection of Vietnamese folklore from this era, reveals that the Việt produced rice alcohol, made food using palm trees, ate cassava roots, preserved meat, fish and prawns (shrimp), and used ginger roots to make salt. Marriage was consummated after the couple shared sticky (glutinous) rice, and newborns were presented on banana leaves. This anthology provides insights into the origins of Việt civilization and culinary practices, including the legend of Square Sticky Rice Cakes (page 388) and Pounded Sticky Rice Cakes (page 394).

Notably, the modern Vietnamese diet still reflects these ancient customs. Rice and its variations remain the primary carbohydrate source in daily meals, seafood and snails are widely consumed and Vietnamese meals always include a plate of *rau sống* (herb salad).

### A THOUSAND YEARS OF CHINESE COLONIZATION (111 BCE–938 CE)

In 207 BCE, Chinese forces invaded the north, establishing the Nan Yue kingdom. It was divided into two commanderies: Giao Chi, covering the Red River Delta region, and Cửu Chân, situated around the Mã and Cả rivers to the south. When the Han dynasty incorporated the Nan Yue kingdom 93 years later, it marked the beginning of nearly a millennium of Chinese administration and attempted cultural assimilation of Northern Vietnam.

As a settlement of the Chinese Empire, Giao Chi depended on tributes to China to maintain trade and diplomatic relations. According to historical books like *An Nam Chí Lược* and *Sanguo Zhi*, local lords were required to send their finest produce, including seashells, pearls, spices, salt, honey and sugars, like sugar candy (*shimi*), maltose (*kẹo mạch nha*) and sugar cane syrup (*tang*). The Chinese widely appreciated these offerings, as it was said that sugar cane could reduce the effects of wine.

Historical records show that Giao Chi provided tributes to China that included ginger, turmeric, galangal, cinnamon, pepper and cardamom. The abundance of these products in Giao Chi made it an important source for the Chinese imperial court, particularly for medicinal and culinary purposes.

During this period, Vietnamese rice agriculture underwent drastic development and change, from the use of fertilizers to the introduction of iron ploughshares drawn by buffaloes. New policies increased rice harvests to twice per year. Three major belief systems entered Vietnam through different channels during Chinese rule: Confucianism through administrative officials and schools, Buddhism via travelling monks and temples, and Taoism through Chinese settlers and merchants in local communities. These would become the three pillars of Vietnamese culture, known as *Tam Giáo đồng nguyên*. While Confucianism stayed within the upper class, Taoism and Buddhism spread to smaller villages and communities, subsequently influencing the Viets' way of eating.

New methods of cooking and eating developed, from the use of woks and chopsticks to the doctrine of the five flavours (sweet, salty, bitter, sour and spicy – the latter also described as pungent). However, despite the subjugation of Chinese customs, local rites and heroes were still widely celebrated, and traditional practices like teeth lacquering and betel chewing persisted.

The Việt diet, while following the Chinese doctrine of the five flavours, was and remains very different from that of China. The latter has a culture of eating cooked vegetables and greens due to the early introduction of human fertilizers and the associated risks of contamination. In contrast, a Vietnamese meal always includes fresh herbs or raw vegetables, a practice so ingrained in the culture that it is passed down through Vietnamese proverbs, or *ca dao tục ngữ*. For example, the proverb, '*Cơm không rau, đau không thuốc*,' teaches us that 'rice without vegetables is like pain without medicine'.

In 938 CE, Vietnam gained independence, marking the beginning of what would become the Ngô dynasty (939–965 CE) and the Đại Việt kingdom. This did not, however, mark the end of the relationship between Vietnamese and Chinese food; to say that Chinese food had influenced Vietnamese food would be both wrong and right, as Chinese cuisine itself was, and still is, highly regional. The most direct influence had come from southern China, where similarities can still be found in the use of shrimp pastes, fish sauce and flat rice noodles (*ho fen* or *bánh phở*).

This exchange would not be one-way either; Vietnam would later introduce sweet potatoes to China in the sixteenth century. Legend has it that while exporting sweet potatoes was forbidden in Vietnam, a Chinese doctor Lin Hualian saved the life of a Vietnamese princess and was offered cooked sweet potatoes. He asked for raw ones, which he hid in his vest to bring back to China.

While neighbouring regions would later become fully Chinese, rebellions, resistance and a new cultural self-awareness would allow Northern Vietnam to forge and retain its own identity and food culture. Chinese direct influences on Vietnamese cuisine would become more apparent in the early seventeenth century when Chinese traders harboured in Hoi An. The appearance of terms like 'tofu' and 'lap xuong' would occur only after the first trilingual Vietnamese–Portuguese–Latin dictionary was published in 1651.

It is always challenging to define who played what role in the development of a food culture and to analyse how history has forged people's palates. While modern times allow for faster sharing of foods and knowledge, it is essential to step back from generalizations and misconceptions.

## FUNAN AND KHMER KINGDOMS: THE FOUNDATIONS OF SOUTHERN CULTURE (1ST–15TH CENTURY CE)

While the north was under Chinese rule, the south developed differently through maritime trade. The Funan kingdom emerged in the Mekong Delta, with its port city Óc Eo. Located in present-day An Giang province, it became a crucial hub connecting Rome, India and China. The Funan people were very skilled in water management, creating an extensive network of canals and irrigation systems that allowed them to achieve remarkable agricultural productivity.

Chinese envoy reports from 240 CE provide valuable insights into Funan's agricultural prosperity: farmers would sow once but harvest three times yearly. Beyond rice, they cultivated vegetables, beans, sugar cane, cotton and raised silkworms. Historical records also mention the cultivation of fruit trees including oranges, pomegranates and coconuts, as well as pepper and abundant areca palms.

Funan was also a significant producer of crafted goods. Archaeological evidence from Óc Eo reveals sophisticated workshops producing gold ornaments, glass beads and various jewellery, transforming raw materials from India and other regions into finished products. Analysis of stone grinding tools shows evidence of turmeric, ginger, fingerroot, sand ginger, galangal, clove, nutmeg and cinnamon.

The use of spices in modern Southeast Asian cuisine presents interesting parallels to these ancient trading patterns, for instance, the presence of cloves in Southern-style Phở (page 186) contrasting with its absence in the northern version (page 182). Another intriguing example is the use of fingerroot in the traditional Khmer Noodle Soup *bún num bò chóc* (*num banh chok* in the Khmer dialect) (see page 212), Though establishing direct historical connections would require further research, it is intriguing to consider how these ancient spices may have influenced the flavours and dishes of Vietnamese cuisine as we know it today.

As Funan declined due to both external factors and environmental challenges, the Chenla kingdom rose to power before giving way to the Khmer Empire. The Khmer Empire continued Funan's sophisticated water management traditions, developing extensive hydraulic systems that would later influence agricultural practices in the region. The cultural and culinary practices of the Khmer people left lasting marks on southern cuisine through the use of coconut milk, fish sauce and palm sugar.

While both modern Cambodian and southern Vietnamese cuisines share preparation methods for dishes like sour soups, each developed their own distinct interpretations. The Khmer shared certain dishes with their Cham neighbours, as seen in variations of coconut rolls (Khmer-style Coconut Rolls, page 438) that appear in both cultures.

## THE CHAMPA KINGDOM: TRADE, AGRICULTURE AND CULTURAL EXCHANGE (2ND–17TH CENTURY CE)

While northern Vietnam was ruled by the Chinese and the Funan kingdom ruled the Mekong Delta, the Cham people, descendants of the Sa Huỳnh culture with Austronesian origins, established the Champa kingdom along the central coast by the second century CE. Their network of coastal kingdoms stretched from modern-day Quảng Bình to Bình Thuận.

The challenging terrain between the mountains and sea led the Chams to develop remarkable irrigation systems, particularly evident in the plains of Phan-Rang, Phan-Ri and Phan-Thiết, where they cultivated an impressive variety of crops including rice, legumes, sesame and aromatic plants. They also maintained orchards of fruits and trees such as tamarind, which remains significant in the region today.
The Chams shared their territories with various highland peoples, including the Randaiy (predecessors of today's Êde people) between Khánh Hoà and Phú Yên, and the Mada (ancestors of modern Djarai) in Bình Định. Their most significant agricultural innovation was the development of drought-resistant, early ripening rice varieties. These hundred-day rice varieties would later transform agriculture in Song dynasty China after their introduction in 1012. This type of rice, known as Champa rice, was incredibly adaptable and could grow well in many different environments.

The Chams were skilled traders, establishing extensive networks that connected Chinese, Arab, Persian and Indian merchants. Their ports handled precious woods, aromatic resins and spices. Historical sources indicate their development of various fermented fish preparations, including early forms of *mắm nêm* and possibly *mắm ruốc*, which remain essential components in central Vietnamese dishes such as Rice Noodles with Pork and Fermented Thick Fish Sauce (page 216).

Jesuit missionary Christoforo Borri's observations from 1617–1622 provide a valuable snapshot as Cham influence was waning. He describes *balachiam* (likely an early form of *mắm*), a fermented fish sauce so essential that households stored it in barrels, like wine in Europe. His accounts document foods unique to the region at that time, including pineapples not yet seen in the north, and the consumption of chameleons, which were considered a delicacy but are rarely eaten today.

By 1693 the Champa kingdom had merged into the larger state that would become Vietnam. Today, their descendants primarily reside in Ninh Thuận and Bình Thuận provinces, divided between Brahmin Cham and Cham Bani (Muslim) communities. Modern Cham cuisine, as seen in dishes like Chăm-style Mixed Rice (*cơm trộn – lithei jrau* in the Cham dialect – page 266), demonstrates the importance of fermented fish preparations and fresh herbs in their cooking, elements which resonate throughout Vietnamese cuisine.

## NAM TIẾN: THE FORMATION OF REGIONAL CUISINES (15TH–19TH CENTURY CE)

In the north, following independence from Chinese rule in 938 CE, the Việt focused on strengthening agriculture in their Red River Delta homeland. Each year, kings of the Lý dynasty (1009–1225 CE) and later the Trần dynasty (1225–1400 CE) performed a symbolic ploughing ceremony honouring the God of Agriculture. Laws severely punished those who stole or killed water buffalos, recognizing these animals as essential to rice cultivation and the kingdom's prosperity.

The gradual expansion southwards, known as *Nam tiến*, accelerated after the 1471 conquest of Champa territories under Lê Thánh Tông (r. 1460–1497), emperor of Đại Việt. Chinese merchants, primarily from Fujian and Guangdong, established five distinct communities in Hội An by the early seventeenth century. Their presence influenced local cuisine, as seen in dishes like Hội An Chicken Rice (page 263). The origins of Hội An's famous *cao lầu* noodles remain debated, while its noodles and cooking techniques show Chinese influences, the dish requires specific local ingredients: noodles made with ash from particular trees and water drawn from the ancient Ba Le well, built by the Cham over five centuries ago.

In 1698, Nguyễn Hữu Cảnh (1650–1700), a military commander and key administrator for the Nguyễn Lords, established Vietnamese administrative control over Saigon, previously primarily Khmer territory. This marked the final stage of the southward expansion and created the geographical outline of modern Vietnam.

The establishment of Huế as the capital at the start of the Nguyễn dynasty (1802–1945) marked a crucial development in Vietnamese culinary history. Under Emperor Tự Đức (r. 1847–1883), royal cuisine reached unprecedented levels of refinement. Each royal meal required fifty specialist cooks to prepare thirty-five to fifty distinct dishes. Provinces sent their finest products to the palace, white rice selected grain by grain, bird's nests from islands, and various local specialties. Fresh earthen pots were used only once for cooking the emperor's rice, then broken, and new bamboo chopsticks were provided daily.

Yet this imperial splendour existed alongside persistent food insecurity. Severe famines struck different regions throughout the early nineteenth century, affecting North Central Vietnam in 1823–1824, the Red River Delta in 1827, and Central Vietnam in 1835. Despite the Nguyễn emperors' attempts to establish culinary conformity across their realm, regional variations persisted, reflecting the complex history of Vietnamese expansion and adaptation.

## THE FRENCH CENTURY (1859–1954)

The consolidation of Vietnamese territory was completed just as French influence began to grow. The French colonial period brought significant changes to Vietnam's food landscape, though these changes occurred gradually and unevenly. Initially, French colonists largely rejected local cuisine, preferring imported canned goods or attempting to recreate French dishes.

The French administration established monopolies on key commodities including salt, opium and alcohol, creating a back-breaking tax system that affected traditional food production and trade. However, they also introduced new ingredients and techniques gradually adapted by Vietnamese cooks. Early French influence can be seen in the development of Puff Pastry Meat Pies (*pa tê sô*, from French *pâté chaud*, page 419), which seems to make an appearance in adverts published in Vietnamese newspapers around 1910 as French products became more widely available.

While colonizing Vietnam, the French paradoxically sought to escape it by establishing Đà Lạt and Sa Pa in the highlands as remedy stations: these retreats built in the cooler mountainous climate were designed with French-style architecture to cure their tropical malaise and homesickness. Đà Lạt became particularly significant for introducing new vegetables to Vietnamese cuisine. Đà Lạt's early colonial agricultural experiments yielded mixed results. While sheep farming failed, by 1903 the region successfully produced green beans, strawberries, potatoes, carrots, celery, beetroots (beets), parsley, tomatoes and onions. These vegetables, initially grown for exclusively French consumption, gradually entered Vietnamese cooking. Several of these colonial-era crops have been thoroughly integrated into modern Vietnamese food culture. Đà Lạt continues to supply vegetables to the rest of the country, with certain products like artichoke tea or soup having become local specialties.

New ingredients like tomatoes, first known as *ca-tô-mâch* then as *cà chua*, became essential to Vietnamese cooking, particularly in sour soup. French terms entered Vietnamese culinary vocabulary – *rô ti* (roasted) remains common in dishes like Roasted Chicken Leg (page 284). By 1932, western cookbooks, such as *Sách Nấu Đồ Tây* (*Book of Western Cooking*) by Lê Thị Tuyền, were teaching Vietnamese cooks French culinary techniques.

Meanwhile, Saigon was developing its own distinct culinary identity through another significant migration: Chinese immigrants establishing *Chợ Lớn* (Chinatown). These newcomers brought their own cooking techniques and ingredients, creating a fusion of Vietnamese, French and Chinese influences that would characterize southern urban cuisine. Chinese immigrants played crucial roles as intermediaries between Vietnamese and French culture, particularly in food preparation and trade.

This period of cultural exchange, while rooted in colonialism, resulted in lasting culinary innovations. Vietnamese cooks selectively adopted and adapted French ingredients and techniques, creating distinctive dishes that reflect both resistance to and selective acceptance of colonial influence.

## FROM SCARCITY TO ABUNDANCE (1940–PRESENT)

Vietnam's modern culinary identity was forged through periods of profound hardship. The Second World War's impact reached Vietnam through devastating famines, particularly in the north where French colonial policies prioritizing industrialization over agriculture led to the deaths of a million Vietnamese people between 1940 and 1945. The situation worsened when Japanese occupation forces commanded rice supplies, leaving Vietnamese farmers unable to access their own harvests.

In the decades that followed, Vietnamese cooks developed innovative techniques to adapt to scarcity. Rice was extended with root vegetables, as seen in Sweet Potato Rice (page 258), and new cooking methods emerged from necessity. Smokeless cooking techniques were developed to avoid detection, while MSG was introduced as a way to enhance simple broths and stretch limited ingredients. The Vietnamese term for MSG's flavour (*ngọt*) describes a particular kind of sweetness distinct from sugar, closer to the natural sweetness of long-simmered meat stocks. These ingenuities are just another proof of the spirit of this country: resourcefulness and resilience.

Food rationing continued through reunification in 1975 as Vietnam rebuilt itself. The Đổi Mới economic reforms of 1986 marked a turning point, opening Vietnam to international trade and sparking rapid culinary evolution. Today, while seasonal ingredients are available year-round and international brands compete with Vietnamese food companies, regional cuisines maintain distinctive characteristics shaped by this complex history.

# REGIONAL CUISINES

Vietnam stretches across 15 degrees of latitude, encompassing both subtropical and tropical zones. This geography, with Vietnam's 3,260-km/2,026-mile coastline and two major river deltas, has created a water-rich environment averaging more than 1 km/3,280 ft of streams and water bodies per square kilometre/3,280 ft of land. There are more than 700 species of fish in Vietnam, making it a very seafood-centric country. The country's fifty-four ethnic communities, belonging to five distinct language families, have each contributed to Vietnam's unique food landscape through centuries of migration, interaction and adaptation. Its complex history allowed Vietnam to develop a unique food landscape with rich and varied culinary traditions.

## NORTHERN VIETNAM

Northern Vietnam encompasses two main regions: the Red River Delta and the Northern Highlands. The Red River Delta serves as Vietnam's cultural cradle. As the homeland of the Việt people, who form the majority community, the region embodies traditional ways of eating and cooking, focusing on distinctive flavours with minimal sugar use. Influenced by Confucianism and Taoism, the cuisine follows more structured eating rules and etiquettes than in the south. The region's relatively flat terrain and dense river system enable intensive rice cultivation, accounting for 20 per cent of national food production.

Northern cooking follows seasonal rhythms. Winter brings dishes like Meat Aspic (page 102), while summer introduces cooling dishes like Morning Glory Boiled Water (see page 354) made with dracontomelon, a fruit that announces summer's arrival through its seasonal availability. Even simple ingredients like mustard greens change their culinary role through the growing cycle – young leaves for soup, mature leaves for stir-frying, and late-season specimens for pickling. Traditional Northern dishes persist in villages like Bát Tràng, known for specialties such as Bát Tràng Bamboo Shoot and Squid Soup (page 379).

The Northern Highlands maintain four distinct seasons but with cooler temperatures. Communities like the Hmong, Dao, Nung and Tay have developed sustainable lifestyles combining farming and foraging. The region's ingredients like *mắc khén* (Indian prickly ash), *thảo quả* (black cardamom) and the prized *hạt dổi* (magnolia seeds) give distinctive flavours to dishes like Grilled Pork Skewers with Indian Prickly Ash (page 150). On top of these unique spices, they often use *lợn đen lũng pù*, an indigenous black pig raised naturally by families, giving it a unique flavour compared to the bland, industrial pork we've grown accustomed to. Seasonal foraged ingredients appear in autumn dishes like Bamboo Worms Fried with Lime Leaves (page 344). The region's cuisine also balances fresh and fermented ingredients, from *cơm mẻ* (fermented rice) in Tay cuisine to fermented wild bamboo shoots and mountain mustard greens. Like elsewhere in Vietnam, food and medicine intertwine here. *Củ ấu tẩu*, an indigenous taro variety from the *Aconitum* genus, requires precise preparation to transform from poison to food or medicine, as in *cháo ấu tẩu* (bitter acconitum congee), a medicinal porridge that helps relax muscles after work. While Vietnam is often considered rice-centric, the Hmong people traditionally relied on maize as their staple grain. However, this is changing as agricultural practices shift. Government programs now promote wet rice cultivation, marking a significant transition in highland diet.

## CENTRAL VIETNAM

Central Vietnam comprises three distinct regions: North Central Coast, South Central Coast and Central Highlands. The coastal regions experience dramatic climate variations, with hot, dry summers from May to August, followed by a heavy monsoon season from September to December. This unstable weather pattern, marked by frequent typhoons and floods, has historically shaped its people known for their '*chịu thương chịu khổ*' (endurance through hardship) and their cuisine. The region's agricultural practices have adapted to these harsh conditions, favouring hardy root crops and plants that could potentially withstand powerful storms and flooding, unlike the silt-based cultivation methods seen in the fertile Mekong Delta.

The coastal cuisine's characteristically salty and spicy flavours developed from the environment as well as out of necessity. Saltier dishes mean more rice is consumed, an age-old piece of kitchen wisdom for making food go further in difficult times, a reality that has shaped Vietnamese cooking for generations, regardless of the region. Each area developed distinctive preserved foods – Nam Dan in Nghệ An province is known for *Tương Nam Đàn* (soybean sauce), which is used for cooking fish or as a dipping sauce or is served simply with rice. Along the coast, *Cá Mắm*, made by salting whole fish directly on fishing boats, helps sustain communities through difficult seasons. As the coastline narrows from north to south, regional cuisine increasingly features fermented products, from *mắm ruốc* and *mắm nêm* to fish sauce in Phan Thiết, and even fermented meat like *nem Bình Định* (fermented pork roll). Each coastal province has developed distinctive seafood dishes. Phú Yên is known for Phú Yên Fish Noodle Soup (page 202) made with local fish and indigenous chives. The region's resourceful cooking is exemplified in dishes like *Mắt Cá Ngừ Phú Yên*, a poached tuna eye soup that originated when fishermen, after selling the prized meat of the tuna, made meals from the leftover parts of fish, such as head, eyes and intestines. What began as a dish of necessity has evolved into a local delicacy. Another remarkable aspect of Vietnamese culture: the ability to transform anything into a dish.

Despite being the imperial capital for surprisingly less than 150 years, Huế, the former seat of the Nguyễn dynasty, still stands distinctly apart. The city's cuisine reflects its royal heritage through formal dining customs, elaborate presentation and smaller portions. This sophistication appears in its rich cake culture, from Royal Flower-shaped Cakes (page 432) to street food like Huế-Style Clear Prawn Dumplings (page 402). Huế cuisine is also shaped by its unique ingredients. Baby basket clams (*hến*) from Cồn Hến, a small island in the Hương River (Perfume River), feature in many dishes including Baby Basket Clam Rice (page 268).

The Central Highlands feature characteristic plateau terrain and basalt red soil, with two distinct seasons and cooler temperatures than the coastal regions. The area's agricultural production ranges from rubber and coffee plantations to tropical fruits like avocado and durian. In Đà Lạt, French colonial influence may have brought the cultivation of Western vegetables like artichokes, unique to this area, but the Vietnamese have since made it their own terroir.

The region is home to several communities including the Ja Rai, Êde and Bahnar – collectively known as Montagnards by the French. As predecessors of the land before the Viets, their cuisine reflects a deep knowledge of local plants and their medicinal properties. Before the widespread use of lime, the Êde used golden ants for sourness, as in Sour Soup with Golden Ants (page 370). Traditional ingredients include young cassava leaves, seen in Stir-fried Cassava Leaves with Steamed Mackerel (page 332). Papaya flowers are prized for their medicinal properties, and *lá é*, lemon basil, is used for its distinctive aroma. These ingredients, along with wild herbs, reflect the region's rich biodiversity, a natural wealth now threatened by intensive farming and environmental challenges.

Traditional seasoning here differed from that used in the coastal regions. Instead of fish sauce, communities relied on wild herbs, peppers and bamboo ashes for flavouring. Before modern borders existed, salt first came in large blocks through trade with neighbouring Laotian. When cooking, these blocks of salt would be dipped in dishes to season them.

## SOUTHERN VIETNAM

Southern Vietnam's distinctive food culture emerged during the Khẩn Hoang period – a time from the sixteenth century onwards when people cultivated new land and established communities, gradually transforming the region's wild terrain into agricultural land. During this formative period, unlike Northern Vietnam's predominantly Confucian and Taoist influences, southern cuisine emerged through adaptation to the environment. Stretching from the edge of Central Vietnam to An Giang province, this area encompasses the southeast region and the Mekong Delta, benefitting from fertile soil and a two season climate: dry and monsoon. The region produces tropical fruits, vegetables and both marine and freshwater seafood throughout the year. Settlers developed simple cooking methods using any available ingredients from rivers and fields, as seen in dishes like *Cá Lóc Nướng Trui* (grilled snakehead fish with straw) or Stir-fried Frogs' Legs (page 283).

Ho Chi Minh City (formerly Saigon) serves as a melting pot, blending regional cuisines, modernity and outside influences. In its neighbourhood of Chợ Lớn, which is also Vietnam's largest Chinatown, the Chaozhou community's influence appears in dishes like Venison Noodles with Chilli and Lemongrass Oil (page 232).

With two distinct seasons, the Mekong River Delta produces fruits, vegetables and herbs all year round. The abundance of herbs defines the region's eating culture. A hotpot dish like Goby Fish Hotpot (page 176) in Miền Tây may be served with more than fifteen different herbs. In Bến Tre, coconut makes constant interesting appearances in different forms, from *Kẹo dừa* (coconut candy) and coconut rice (see page 258) to Coconut and Thick Noodle Soup (page 200). Often oversimplified by its sweet reputation, southern food has a complexity that extends far beyond palm sugar and coconut.

Less formal and strict than Red Delta River cuisine in the north, southern cuisine continues to evolve through adaptation and creation, shaped by its environment and the various communities who have settled here.

These regional differences extend to language, too – a rice bowl becomes '*bát*' (Northern), 'đọi' (Central) or '*chén*' (Southern), while a ladle is known as '*muôi*', '*môi*' and '*vá*', respectively. The beauty of Vietnamese cuisine lies not solely in uniformity, as it is sometimes misinterpreted, but in how these distinct regional flavours, traditions and cultures live together and create a Vietnamese meal.

# AT THE VIETNAMESE TABLE

In Vietnam, the word '*ăn*' (eat) extends far beyond just consuming food. It appears before many activities: '*ăn uống*' (eating and drinking), '*ăn mặc*' (dressing), '*ăn chơi*' (having fun), as if life's experiences must first be digested to be fully understood. This primacy of eating in Vietnamese culture is captured in the proverb, '*Học ăn, học nói, học gói, học mở*,' (learn to eat, learn to speak, learn to wrap, learn to open). Learning to eat comes first because it encompasses understanding taste, manners, traditions and community.

This deep relationship with food reveals itself in even daily language. '*Ăn cơm*' (eating rice) is used to describe any meal, whether you're having noodles, soup or rice, which reflects how central rice is to Vietnamese cuisine and culture.

Understanding Vietnamese eating means understanding a complex inventory of flavours and textures beyond the traditional five flavours (sweet, sour, salty, bitter, spicy/pungent). It ranges from astringent (*chát*) to the toasty rich flavour of roasted nuts (*bùi*). But the true sophistication lies in how these flavours are coupled – salty-sweet (*mặn-ngọt*), sour-sweet (*chua-ngọt*) – creating unique combinations and layers in any meal.

The way we eat directly reflects history, geography and culture. Vietnam has been able to pick and choose from different cultures and knowledge, shaping them to its own unique character. Like a traveller adapting to new lands, the Chinese yin-yang principle shed its original form, reimagining itself in the vibrant palette of Vietnamese culture. This concept is based on the fundamental belief that every ingredient has a natural temperature essence – some foods cool the body, while others warm it, creating a dynamic balance of internal energy. For instance, river fish and duck are considered 'cold' foods, so they're paired with 'hot' ginger in dipping sauces; and balut (duck embryo) is balanced with Vietnamese coriander (*rau răm*), a 'hot' herb.

Food is also medicine in Vietnam. All communities have their own medicinal plants, whether sourced from home gardens or foraged, that feature in daily meals and traditional remedies. For example, the Mạ people of Bảo Lộc use Gnetum gnemon leaves (*Lá bép*) in dishes like Rice and Gnetum Gnemon Leaf Soup (page 338), which is believed to help new mothers produce milk.

While it's nearly impossible to learn all the different ingredients' effects, we instead learn through folk songs (*ca dao*) from older generations how to cook and eat them correctly. On a personal note, it is why my mother named me Ca Dao, as to remember the folk songs and wisdom from her grandmother teaching her the ways of life.

Consider this folk song:

> *Con gà cục tác lá chanh,*
> *Con lợn ủn ỉn mua hành cho tôi.*
> *Con chó khóc* đứng*, khóc ngồi,*
> *Mẹ* ơi đi *chợ mua tôi* đồng *riềng.*
>
> (The chicken squawks in the lemon leaves,
> the pig grunts, 'Buy me some green onions.'
> The dog cries, sitting and standing,
> 'Grandma, go to the market and buy me
> some galangal!')

This playful verse carries deep culinary wisdom: chicken pairs with lime leaves, pork with spring onions (scallions), and so on. These proverbs balance humour with practical knowledge, making them perfect teaching tools that have endured through generations.

### KEY INGREDIENTS OF VIETNAM

Beyond the intriguing philosophy of Vietnamese cuisine, several key characteristics define our way of eating. Seasoning is deeply personal – while regions have their distinct styles, meals often feature communal dipping sauces that allow individuals to adjust flavours to their taste. In a country bordered by the sea, seasoning takes many forms, from fish sauce to various fermented seafood pastes. Each region has its specialties: Huế and Central Vietnam are known for their fermented shrimp paste (*mắm ruốc*) and thick fish paste (*mắm nêm*), while Hanoi favours its own type of shrimp paste (*mắm tôm*).

.

Modern times have brought new ingredients including all-purpose seasoning (*hạt nêm*), MSG and soup powder (*bột canh*). These ingredients have sparked modern discussions, and their use, like anything, depends on moderation and understanding. In this book, I've provided base seasonings that match my family's taste. Feel free to adjust them as you layer flavours in your own kitchen.

Vegetables reign supreme in Vietnamese cuisine, appearing as boiled sides, in salads or as fresh herbs and greens (*rau thơm* and *rau sống*). Aromatic mixed herbs (*rau thơm*) range from spearmint to Vietnamese balm and coriander (cilantro). When combined with leafy greens or shredded vegetables like banana blossoms, salad greens or cabbage, they become *rau sống*. While certain pairings are traditional, and I suggest combinations that go well with certain recipes, I encourage you to follow these principles with whatever herbs and vegetables you have available. The core idea is to bring freshness to every meal.

Rice in Vietnam transcends its basic form. Beyond regular and sticky (glutinous) rice, it transforms into fresh and dried noodles, and various types of rice paper. These come in different sizes and thicknesses, with regional variations adding to their diversity. Thin rice papers are great for wrapping, rolling and frying, while thicker versions, sometimes studded with sesame seeds, are perfect for grilling.

## THE VIETNAMESE FAMILY MEAL

Vietnamese food starts in the family home. A typical family meal centres around several dishes accompanying rice: first the 'mains', usually protein-based, followed by sides often featuring stir-fried or boiled vegetables, and always a soup (*canh*) to aid digestion. The table comes alive with dipping sauces, a plate of fresh herbs and vegetables, and perhaps some pickles.

Each region expresses this basic structure differently. A family meal in Central Vietnam, for example, might feature Braised Tuna with Pineapple (page 276), Cucumber Salad (page 135) and Clam Soup with Star Fruit (page 382), while in the south you might find Braised Goby Fish and Pork Belly (page 274), Sweet and Sour Soup (Mekong Delta Style) (page 368) and simple boiled vegetables. Seasonal changes also influence meals: in the summer, boiled and simple dishes like Poached Pork Belly with Shrimp Paste (page 300) combat the heat of the kitchen, while there is something so rewarding and satisfying in eating 'sizzling' pancakes (see page 415) during the rainy seasons.

Once you understand the underlying principles of the Vietnamese family meal, substitutions will start to become intuitive: courgette (zucchini) can replace gourd, stocks (broths) can be made with any protein, and sourness can come from lime, tamarind or even young pineapple. The essence can remain unchanged even as ingredients are adapted.

Shared meals extend beyond the everyday. In Vietnam, gatherings happen for death anniversaries, Lunar New Year (*Tết*), weddings and any excuse to eat and drink together. These gatherings reflect our way of life, respecting elders even after they've passed, treating everyone as family. While each person has their own bowl of rice, we share dipping sauces and dishes, offering the choicest pieces to our elders. Even the heavens respect mealtime, as expressed in the saying, '*Trời đánh tránh bữa ăn*,' (even the heavens avoid bothering people during meals).

Meals become increasingly elaborate for traditional events, such as the kitchen god's farewell ritual at the lunar year's end, where a full meal is cooked for the ancestors and gods and later eaten by the family. The ritual sends the kitchen god to heaven to report on our yearly behaviour, though we cleverly include sticky rice in the offerings, hoping it might seal the god's lips from revealing too much!

Vietnam's eating habits evolved with urbanization and modernization. While shared meals remain important, we have less time to cook, more dining choices and flourishing street food scenes. Cities particularly showcase this adaptation: with everyone rushing to work, breakfast becomes whatever is quick and satisfying. Sticky rice offers an affordable, filling option; noodle soups (*phở*, *bún*) provide fast comfort; *bánh mì* (Vietnamese baguette) presents a convenient grab-and-go choice.

Lunch is adapted similarly, with one-plate dishes like Crispy Fried Chicken with Fried Rice (page 264) or Broken Rice (page 270) serving as convenient alternatives to full meals. Rice shops (*Cơm Bình Dân*) represent a modern take on family-style dining, where customers choose from various pre-cooked dishes to create their own combinations.

When friends gather, food and drink flow together. Beer culture, introduced by the French in the nineteenth century, has become intrinsically Vietnamese. Gatherings typically feature snail dishes, beer garden food (*quán nhậu* specialties), grilled items or hotpots.

Opposite, I've suggested some recipe combinations for different occasions. Some are classic combinations, some are regional combinations and some are my personal favourites. If you are unfamiliar with Vietnamese food or a less confident cook, I recommend starting with the everyday family meals and salads. As you become more familiar with Vietnamese home cooking, you can progress into other dishes like seafood, snacks and desserts.

Finally for those who wants a little bit of challenge, cakes are your perfect opponent. These aren't your average baked goods, which explains why they're usually the proud territory of professional artisans, or grandmothers (and a few very persistent home cooks and professional chefs who refuse to be defeated by them).

## MEAL COMBINATIONS FOR DIFFERENT OCCASIONS

### *Everyday Family Meals*

- Tamarind Glazed Pork Ribs (page 298), Papaya Soup with Baby Shrimp (page 372) and Beef and Celery Stir-fry (page 322).
- Braised Pork Belly with Eggs (page 303), Pickled Mustard Greens (page 467), and Chayote and Shrimp Soup (page 383).
- Braised Goby Fish and Pork Belly (page 274), Sweet and Sour Soup (Mekong Delta Style) (page 368) and a plate of herb salad (*rau sống*).
- Grilled Aubergines with Spring Onion Oil (page 158), King Oyster Mushrooms Stir-Fried with Lemongrass and Chilli (page 332) and Squash and Peanut Soup (page 358).

### *Meals for Time-pressed Days*

- Boiled cabbage with Dipping Sauce for Boiled Vegetables (page 471) and hard-boiled eggs.
- Minced Pork Omelette (page 348) and Chive Soup with Tofu and Minced Pork (page 374), with a small bowl of light soy sauce and slices of cucumber.

### *Meals for Festivals and Family Gatherings: Lunar New Year Feast*

- Square Sticky Rice Cakes (page 388), spring rolls (pages 114 and 152), Pork Roll (page 462), Beef Stew (page 316) and Pickled Chinese Onions (page 466).

### *Meals for Festivals and Family Gatherings: Kitchen God's Farewell*

- Steamed Chicken with Lime Leaves (page 283), Steamed Momordica Sticky Rice (page 242), Sweet Floating Rice Dumplings (page 444), Meat Aspic (page 102) and Kohlrabi Salad (page 136).
- Crispy Rice Cake with Steamed Rice Dumplings (page 400) and Huế Beef Noodle Soup (page 204).
- Chicken and Banana Blossom Salad (page 128) with Chicken Phở (page 194).

### *Food for Gatherings with Friends*

- Vinegar-dressed Lettuce Salad (page 135), Stir-Fried Beef with French Fries (page 350) and Lemon Basil Fried Rice (page 260).
- Tamarind Fried Crabs (page 84), Grilled Ark Clams with Spring Onion Oil (page 99) Steamed Clams with Lemongrass (page 86).
- Sweet and Sour Beef Salad (page 108), Grilled Beef in Piper Lolot Leaves (page 144) and Beef in Vinegar Hotpot (page 168).

## A CULINARY ADVENTURE

I hope this book inspires you to cook Vietnamese food for yourself, your family and your friends. The recipes offer a foundation, but like any living cuisine, they invite adaptation and personalization. As so many of my hosts would say while I chased them around their kitchens with measuring spoons and cups in hand: 'Cooking is about feeling; you put a bit of this and a bit of that, you taste and you adjust.' There's nothing quite like trying to keep up with a mother or grandmother as they effortlessly season by instinct! Vietnamese cooking isn't about rigid rules; it's about understanding the principles of balance, in flavours, textures and nutrition.

# LEGEND

| | |
|---|---|
| \|V\| | vegetarian |
| \|VE\| | vegan |
| \|DF\| | dairy-free |
| \|GF\| | gluten-free |
| \|≤5\| | 5 ingredients or fewer |
| \|≤30\| | 30 minutes or less |

# SNACKS

## Món ăn vặt

From morning to evening, from street vendors to street carts to stalls, snacking is a quintessential activity in Vietnam. It can take many forms, from crunching on simple toasted melon seeds while having drinks with friends, to having a plate of rice paper salad after school, or eating a summer roll during office hours.

*Quán ăn vặt*, dedicated stalls specializing in snack dishes, can be found in every city, and they cater particularly to young crowds who tend to go for their own combinations or sometimes invent something new. The snack options available in Vietnam seem limitless, evolving constantly with each generation.

This chapter is a small collection of snacks that are seen often in Vietnam and that can be recreated in your own kitchen; the roll recipes also serve as an introduction to Vietnamese rolls that you can explore further with the ingredients that are available to you. Other snacks, especially the hot ones, are served often alongside a beer in *quán nhậu*, Vietnam's famous beer halls. Drinking in Vietnam is always accompanied by eating – whether it's braised chicken feet or fried tofu with spring onion (scallion) sauce.

Overall these dishes can work equally well as starters (appetizers) for gatherings with friends. While not present in this chapter, sweet soups (*chè*) and the majority of savoury cakes can also be served as snacks.

## SHAKEN MANGO WITH CHILLI

Xoài Dầm/Xoài Lắc

Mangoes are enjoyed in Vietnam at all stages of ripeness, from green and tart to bright yellow and sweet. This street food snack utilizes slightly underripe, yellow mangoes that still have a sour and tangy flavour. In contrast to simply eating mangoes with Roasted Chilli Salt (page 479), this dish seasons the mango slices with a bit of fish sauce. The mango pieces are then traditionally 'shaken' (*lắc*) in the sauce, often served in a plastic takeaway cup. While this snack can now be found across Vietnam, it is a relatively recent creation. The dish was apparently invented by a street food vendor in 2016 and quickly went viral, with local newspapers reporting it as one of the most searched-for Vietnamese dishes between 2016 and 2017.

Serves 2–3
Preparation time: 15 minutes
Cooking time: 5 minutes

| DF | ≤5 | ≤30 |

- 1 mango, not too ripe and preferably a bit tangy (approx. 570 g/1 lb 4 oz)
- 20 g/¾ oz rock sugar
- 2 tablespoons plus 1 teaspoon fish sauce
- 25 g/1 oz large chilli, deseeded and coarsely chopped
- ½ teaspoon MSG, optional

Using a sharp knife, peel the mango and cut the flesh into 2–3-cm/about 1-inch cubes. You should have approximately 435 g/15 oz of mango cubes. Set aside.

In a small saucepan over a medium heat, combine the rock sugar, the 2 tablespoons fish sauce and 1 tablespoon of water. Bring to a simmer and cook for about 5 minutes, or until the mixture thickens to a glaze-like consistency. You'll know it's ready when the sauce coats the back of a spoon.

Meanwhile, put the chilli in a mortar and pound with a pestle until coarsely crushed but not completely paste-like.

Once the sauce has thickened, remove it from the heat and stir in the crushed chilli and remaining 1 teaspoon of fish sauce. Mix well to combine.

Place the mango cubes in a large mixing bowl. Pour the warm chilli glaze over the mango and gently toss to evenly coat. If using MSG, sprinkle it over now and toss again to combine.

Serve immediately in small bowls, or cover and refrigerate for 2–3 hours to allow the flavours to develop further. The mango can be served chilled or at room temperature.

# COCONUT COATED PEANUTS

## Đậu Phộng Ca Dá Cốt Dừa

This old-school vegan snack, once a favourite of the previous generation, is now commonly sold pre-packaged but can still be made at home. The peanuts are meticulously coated with a flour mixture using coconut milk as a binder, resulting in a crunchy, flavourful snack.

Makes 300 g/10½ oz; serves 6 as a snack
Preparation time: 30 minutes
Cooking time: 15–20 minutes

| V | VE | DF |

- 150 g/5½ oz (1 cup) peanuts with skin, young if possible
- 100 g/3½ fl oz (⅓ cup) coconut milk
- 45 g/1½ oz (¼ cup packed) light brown sugar
- 1 teaspoon salt
- 150 g/5½ oz (1 cup) plain (all-purpose) flour
- 30 g/1 oz (scant ¼ cup) rice flour
- 30 g/1 oz (scant ¼ cup) cornflour (cornstarch)
- 250 ml/8 fl oz (1 cup) coconut oil
- 125 ml/4 fl oz (½ cup) vegetable oil

Using a sieve, sift through the peanuts to remove any loose skins or broken pieces that could burn during frying. Set aside only the whole peanuts.

In a bowl, combine the coconut milk, brown sugar and salt. Stir until the sugar and salt are completely dissolved.

In another bowl, sift together the plain (all-purpose) flour, rice flour and cornflour (cornstarch) to remove any lumps.

Place the cleaned whole peanuts in a large, wide mixing bowl.

You are now ready to coat the peanuts, which is a gradual process. Drizzle 1 tablespoon of the coconut milk mixture over the peanuts while continuously rotating the bowl in a circular motion. Using a fine-mesh sieve, sprinkle 1½ tablespoons of the flour mixture over the peanuts while continuing to rotate the bowl. Using clean hands, gently separate any peanuts that stick together. Repeat this process, alternating between coconut milk and flour, until all the coconut milk mixture is used and the peanuts are evenly coated and round. Each peanut should be individually coated and separate from the others.

In a deep, heavy pot, combine the coconut and vegetable oils. Heat to 175–180°C/345–350°F. If not using a thermometer, test the oil temperature by inserting wooden chopsticks into the oil - it should bubble vigorously around them.

Working in batches to avoid overcrowding, carefully add the coated peanuts to the hot oil. Wait 30 seconds before gently stirring with a skimmer or wooden chopsticks. Fry for 3–4 minutes until golden brown, stirring occasionally to ensure even cooking. Remove with a skimmer or slotted spoon and drain on paper towels. Let cool completely before serving.

Once cooled, transfer to an airtight container; they will keep for about a week, or until it they soften (depending on humidity). Serve as an afternoon snack or as an accompaniment to drinks.

# PORK BLOOD SAUSAGES

## Dồi Huyết

These blood sausages are often eaten as a drinking snacks or alongside Pork Organ Congee (page 256) or Rice Noodles with Fried Tofu and Shrimp Paste (page 207). The recipe varies by region, with local cooks adapting the seasonings based on available herbs and pig parts, showcasing the spirit of nose-to-tail cooking in Vietnam.

Serves 6–8
Preparation time: 30 minutes
Cooking time: 20 minutes

| DF |

315 g/11 oz pig's small intestines
865 g/1 lb 15 oz fresh pig blood
½ teaspoon salt
400 g/14 oz minced (ground) pork (preferably fatty, like from the leg)
1 teaspoon MSG
1 tablespoon fish sauce
35 g/1¼ oz shallots, finely chopped
35 g/1¼ oz sawtooth coriander (culantro), thinly sliced
25 g/1 oz spring onions (scallions), chopped
20 g/¾ oz Vietnamese coriander/cilantro (rau răm), leaves picked and coarsely chopped

*To serve*
50 g/1¾ oz Vietnamese coriander/cilantro (rau răm)
Ginger Dipping Fish Sauce (page 474) or Seasoned Fermented Shrimp Paste Dipping Sauce (page 476)

Soak the intestines in cold salted water for 10 minutes to clean. Scrub thoroughly under cold running water, removing as much outer fat and inner mucosa lining as possible. Set aside.

In a large bowl, combine the fresh pig blood with the salt, stirring until well mixed, then set aside to slightly coagulate.

In a separate bowl, combine the minced (ground) pork with the MSG and fish sauce. Let marinate for 5–10 minutes.

Add the shallots, sawtooth coriander (culantro), spring onions (scallions) and Vietnamese coriander/cilantro to the blood mixture. Stir well. Add the marinated pork to the blood mixture and thoroughly combine.

To prepare the casing, tie one end of the intestine securely with kitchen string. If using a sausage stuffer, attach the cleaned intestine to the nozzle, then slowly feed the mixture through.

Alternatively, you can stuff using the neck of a plastic bottle: cut off the top portion of a clean plastic drinking bottle, turn it upside down to create a funnel, then wrap the intestine around the bottle neck. Add the mixture through the wide end and use a chopstick to carefully push the mixture down.

Whichever method you use, gently squeeze the filled intestine to ensure even distribution, then tie off the end securely with string.

To steam the sausages, place the sausages in a steamer with cold water. Place over a low heat and steam for 30 minutes, checking periodically to ensure the sausages aren't bursting. Do not pierce the casings as this will release the juices.

Alternatively, you could steam for 15 minutes as above, let cool slightly, then pan-fry until golden brown on all sides, about 5 minutes over a medium heat.

Let the sausages rest for 5 minutes before slicing and serving with Vietnamese coriander and dipping sauce.

***Note:*** Feel free to add other parts such as throat or crunchy bits, and additional herbs like in Pork Cartilage Sausages (page 148).

# SMASHED RICE CRACKER

## Bánh Đập

*Bánh đập* is a unique snack originating from the Quảng Nam region of Vietnam. This simple yet flavourful dish showcases a perfect balance between textures and tastes. The name comes from the action of smashing the rice cracker between your hands, to pull apart and dip it in the anchovy sauce. The dish combines the subtle, textural elements of fresh, soft rice paper and grilled rice paper with a pungent anchovy sauce. The contrast between the soft and crispy textures, paired with the range of flavours from mild to tangy and pungent, makes *bánh đập* a delightful sensory experience.

Serves 1
Preparation time: 10 minutes
Cooking time: 2–3 minutes

| **DF** | ≤30 |

- 1 sheet of medium-thick rice paper (bánh tráng or bánh tráng gạo để nướng - for grilling)
- 1 sheet of thin rice paper (bánh ướt), store-bought or homemade (see page 403)

*For the thick fish sauce*

- 10 g/¼ oz garlic, minced
- 5 g/⅛ oz long red chilli (or any hot chilli), finely chopped
- 1 tablespoon sugar
- 1 teaspoon lime juice
- 1 tablespoon fermented anchovy sauce (mắm nêm)
- 1 teaspoon hot water

Preheat a barbecue grill to low (embers) if cooking traditionally, or preheat an oven grill (broiler) to 170–180°C/340–350°F, or have a griddle (grill pan) ready.

To prepare the thick fish sauce, in a small bowl, combine the garlic, chilli, sugar, lime juice, fermented anchovy sauce and the measured hot water. Stir well until the sugar completely dissolves, about 30 seconds.

If using a barbecue or oven grill, place the medium-thick rice paper on the barbecue or on the top rack under the grill (broiler) for 1 minute 30 seconds until opaque and crispy; you might have to test 1 or 2 sheets to find the best setting for your barbecue or oven grill. If using a pan, heat over a medium heat, then when the pan is hot (water droplets should sizzle), place one sheet of the dry rice paper flat on the surface and, watching carefully, grill for 60–90 seconds until the paper starts to bubble and turn opaque. Using tongs, carefully flip and cook for another 30–45 seconds until crispy and lightly golden. Remove from the heat. Transfer to a plate and set aside.

Serve immediately while the grilled rice paper is still crispy, with the thick fish sauce in a small dipping bowl.

To eat, break off small pieces of the layered sheets and dip into the fish sauce.

# RICE PAPER SALAD

## Bánh Tráng Trộn

This popular Vietnamese street food snack traces its origins to Trảng Bàng, Tây Ninh province, where it started as a way to utilize leftover scraps from rice paper-making. Initially a simple mix of shredded rice paper and Tây Ninh shrimp salt, it has since evolved considerably. Vendors are known for their creative additions like quail eggs, beef jerky, chilli oil, and most importantly, their signature sauces, like in this recipe, which has been shared by chị Nguyễn Thị Thu Ba, who once used to sell this. Nowadays, ingredients are readily available at specialist supply shops, from different types of shredded rice paper to dried beef liver and its sauce. If you can't find dried beef liver and its sauce, I've included an alternative sauce recipe that replicates the same flavour. Any type of beef jerky works well as a substitute.

Serves 6
Preparation time: 1 hour
Cooking time: 25 minutes

| DF |

- 300 g/10½ oz rice paper
- 60 g/2¼ oz (scant ½ cup) Toasted Peanuts (page 459)
- 3 teaspoons salted shrimp powder
- 18 quail eggs, boiled and peeled
- 1 young mango (around 450 g/1 lb), peeled and shredded
- 60 g/2¼ oz Vietnamese coriander/cilantro (rau răm)
- 150 g/5½ oz dried beef liver or beef jerky (khô bò đen), marinated with 3 teaspoons of the black sauce that comes with it, or any kind of beef jerky, marinated with 3 teaspoons of the Homemade Dried Beef Liver Sauce, below)
- 90 g/3¼ oz dried squid
- 3 teaspoons Chilli and Lemongrass Oil (page 457)
- 30 g/1 oz chilli sauce

*For the dried shrimp flakes*
- 100 g/3½ oz dried baby shrimp (tép)
- 2 tablespoons vegetable oil
- 1 tablespoon Annatto Oil (page 457)
- 15 g/½ oz garlic, coarsely chopped
- 1 teaspoon sugar
- ½ teaspoon salt

*For the spring onion oil*
- 65 ml/2 fl oz (¼ cup) neutral oil
- 120 g/4¼ oz spring onions (scallions), finely chopped

*For the homemade dried beef liver sauce (khô bò đen), optional*
- 1 tablespoon dark soy sauce
- 2 tablespoons oyster sauce
- 60 ml/2 fl oz (¼ cup) light soy sauce
- 2 tablespoons brown sugar
- ½ teaspoon garlic powder
- ½ teaspoon ground ginger
- ¼ teaspoon black pepper
- ¼ teaspoon chilli powder
- ½ teaspoon ground cinnamon
- ½ teaspoon star anise
- 2 tablespoons honey

*For the beef sauce*
- 1 tablespoon Annatto Oil (page 457)
- 1 tablespoon neutral or vegetable oil
- 12 g/½ oz peeled shallot
- 12 g/½ oz peeled garlic
- 250 g/5½ oz dried beef liver sauce (pre-prepared or see above)
- 35 g/1¼ oz tamarind paste
- 2½ teaspoons sugar

For the dried shrimp flakes: Rinse the dried baby shrimp and soak in cold water for 5 minutes. Drain well.

In a frying pan or skillet over a medium-low heat, warm the vegetable and annatto oils. Add the garlic and fry for 3 minutes, or until golden brown, stirring occasionally. Add the drained shrimp, sugar and salt. Continue frying for 20 minutes, or until the shrimp are fragrant and semi-dry, stirring occasionally to prevent sticking.

For the spring onion (scallion) oil: In a small saucepan, heat the vegetable oil until it begins to shimmer (about 180°C/350°F). Place the chopped spring onions in a heatproof bowl. Pour the hot oil over the spring onions and stir to combine. Let cool completely.

For the homemade dried beef liver sauce: In a small saucepan, combine all the sauce ingredients with 60 ml/2 fl oz (¼ cup) water. Bring to a simmer over a medium-low heat and cook for 5–7 minutes until slightly thickened and fragrant, stirring occasionally. Remove from heat and let cool completely.

For the beef sauce: In a medium saucepan over a medium heat, warm both the oils. Add the shallot and garlic, and fry for 1 minute, or until fragrant. Add the dried beef liver sauce, tamarind paste and sugar. Simmer for 3–4 minutes, or until well combined and slightly thickened. Remove from the heat.

To assemble each portion, in a large mixing bowl, combine 50 g/1¾ oz of the rice paper, 10 g/¼ oz (1 tablespoon) of the toasted peanuts, ½ teaspoon of the salted shrimp powder, 3 of the boiled quail eggs, halved, 10 g/¼ oz of the dried shrimp flakes mixture, 35 g/1¼ oz (about 3 tablespoons) of the shredded mango, 10 g/¼ oz of the Vietnamese coriander/cilantro, 10 g/¼ oz (1 tablespoon) of the spring onion oil, 25 g/1 oz of the dried beef liver or beef jerky, 15 g/½ oz of the dried squid, ½ teaspoon of the chilli and lemongrass oil, 1 teaspoon of the chilli sauce and 25 g/1 oz (1½ tablespoons) of the beef sauce. Using clean hands or tongs, gently toss all the ingredients together until well combined. Serve immediately.

# ĐÀ LẠT-STYLE GRILLED RICE PAPER

## Bánh Tráng Nướng Đà Lạt

While grilling rice paper is a traditional cooking method in Vietnam, this specific popular street snack gained prominence in Đà Lạt, the capital of Lâm Đồng province. Now found throughout the country and nicknamed 'Vietnamese pizza' by tourists, this modern version features various toppings on a crispy grilled rice paper base. Though this recipe provides the more basic preparation with egg, spring onions (scallions) and chilli sauce, vendors often customize their version with toppings like cheese spread, beef jerky, sliced frankfurters or pork floss, showcasing their unique modern take on this simple snack. If you want a simpler alternative, the Phan Rang's version has only quail egg, raw spring onions and a spread of seasoned *mắm ruốc*, a type of fermented shrimp paste: a local speciality.

Serves 10
Preparation time: 30 minutes
Cooking time: 20 minutes

| GF |

*For the fried shrimp*
- 50 g/1¾ oz dried shrimp
- 2 tablespoons neutral oil
- 20 g/¾ oz garlic, minced
- ½ teaspoon salt
- 1 teaspoon sugar

*For the minced pork*
- 2 tablespoons neutral oil
- 200 g/7 oz minced (ground) pork
- ½ teaspoon salt
- 2 teaspoons sugar
- ½ teaspoon black pepper
- 30 g/1 oz spring onions (scallions), chopped

*For grilling*
- 10 medium thickness rice paper sheets (or yellow rice paper with sesame seeds/ bánh tráng mè vàng)
- 10 teaspoons melted butter or margarine
- 20 raw quail eggs
- 100 g/3½ oz (scant ½ cup) Fried Shallots (page 458)
- 50 g/1¾ oz spring onions (scallions), chopped
- chilli sauce, for drizzling
- mayonnaise, for drizzling

Soak the shrimp in a bowl of warm water for 10 minutes, then drain well.

Heat the oil in a small pan over a medium heat. Fry the garlic in the oil for 1–2 minutes until golden, stirring constantly to prevent burning. Add the drained shrimp, salt and sugar and stir-fry for 5 minutes, or until fragrant and slightly crispy. Transfer to a small bowl and set aside.

To prepare the minced (ground) pork, heat the oil in a pan over a medium-high heat. Add the minced pork, salt, sugar and black pepper. Stir-fry for 7–8 minutes until cooked through, breaking up any lumps so the meat evenly cooks. Add the spring onions (scallions) at the end. Adding them late retains their colour and freshness. Set aside and keep warm.

To charcoal grill (the traditional method), place a grill rack on nearly burned-out embers in a barbecue. You don't want excessive heat, as the rice paper will burn really easily.

Position a piece of rice paper on the rack. Rotate the paper clockwise continuously to prevent burning: this is crucial, as rice paper can burn within seconds.

Add the toppings in the following order: spread 1 teaspoon of the melted butter over evenly. Crack 2 of the raw quail eggs directly onto the rice paper, then use a spoon or fork to beat them and spread evenly across the entire surface. Spread 1 tablespoon of the minced pork in an even layer. Add a sprinkle of fried shallots for crunch. Spread 1 teaspoon of the fried shrimp evenly on top. Sprinkle over some of the spring onions.

Alternatively, in a bowl, combine 3 of the beaten quail eggs, 2 teaspoons of the chopped spring onions (scallions), 2 tablespoons of the cooked minced pork and 1 teaspoon of the melted butter to create a more uniform topping that's easier to manage on the grill. Spread this mixture on the grilled rice paper instead of adding toppings separately. Then add a sprinkle of fried shallots, fried shrimp and spring onions on top.

Whichever topping method you choose, continue rotating the rice paper, for it to cook evenly.

When the rice paper is opaque and the egg set, add a drizzle of chilli sauce and mayonnaise in a zigzag pattern, then fold it in half using tongs.

Serve immediately while hot and crispy.

*Note:* An alternative to the traditional cooking method is to grill (broil) the rice paper. Preheat the grill (broiler) to 190°C/375°F. Place a piece of rice paper on the highest rack. Grill for 1 minute, or until it starts to bubble slightly. Add the toppings as per the instructions above (either one at a time or all together) and grill for another 1 minute. Drizzle with chilli sauce and mayonnaise, fold in half, and grill for 30 more seconds.

# SHREDDED PORK SKIN ROLLS

Bì Cuốn

A favourite snack across Southern Vietnam, these shredded pork skin rolls are particularly significant in the Mekong Delta region during *Tết* (Lunar New Year), when they're first presented at the ancestral altar before being shared by the family. Though more economical than *gỏi cuốn* (Fresh Summer Rolls, page 40), as they use shredded pork skin with just a small amount of meat, what makes these rolls special is the nutty toasted rice powder and abundance of fresh herbs. The sweet and sour fish sauce brings all the flavours together.

Makes 10 rolls; serves 3–4
Preparation time: 30 minutes

| DF | ≤5 | ≤30 |

600 g/1 lb 5 oz Shredded Pork Skin Seasoned with Toasted Rice (page 460)
1 head of lettuce, leaves separated
150 g/5½ oz aromatic mixed herbs (rau thơm – spearmint, perilla, Vietnamese basil, fish mint, coriander/cilantro), leaves picked and sorted, large ones torn
10 sheets of medium-size dry rice paper
Sweet and Sour Fish Sauce (page 471), to serve

Divide the shredded pork skin mixture into 10 equal portions (about 60 g/2¼ oz each).

Sort through the lettuce leaves, selecting 10 similar-size pieces.

Divide the herbs into 10 small bundles (about 15 g/½ oz each).

To assemble each roll, dip one rice paper sheet in warm water for 2–3 seconds until just pliable. Place on a clean, damp tea towel (or a plate), then layer in this order: 1 lettuce leaf, 15 g/½ oz mixed herbs, 60 g/2¼ oz shredded pork skin mixture. Roll up the rice paper tightly like a spring roll, tucking in the sides as you go, then place seam-side down on a serving plate. Repeat with the remaining ingredients to make 10 rolls.

Present the rolls immediately, with individual small bowls of the sweet and sour fish sauce for dipping.

# VEGAN PORK SKIN ROLLS

Bì Cuốn Chay

This vegan adaptation of Shredded Pork Skin Rolls (above) uses fried tofu and vermicelli to replicate the texture of pork and skin, while maintaining the signature roasted rice seasoning. A combination of at least 3–4 different herbs is essential, as their varied aromatics create the depth that makes Vietnamese rolls distinctive.

Makes 8 rolls; serves 3–4
Preparation time: 20 minutes
Cooking time: 15 minutes

| V | VE | DF |

65 ml/2 fl oz (¼ cup) neutral oil, or more as needed
200 g/7 oz firm tofu, cut into 5-mm × 10-cm/¼ × 4-inch sticks
15 g/½ oz dried rice vermicelli noodles (bún tàu)
40 g/1½ oz Toasted Rice Powder (page 459)
8 sheets of 22-cm/8½-inch-long square rice paper (bánh tráng mỹ tho)
100 g/3½ oz herb salad (rau sống – lettuce, fish mint, peppermint, Vietnamese basil)

*For the sesame salt*
1 teaspoon white sesame seeds
½ teaspoon salt

*For the spring onion oil*
1 tablespoon neutral oil
30 g/1 oz spring onions (scallions), finely chopped

*To serve*
Seasoned Vegetarian Fish Sauce (page 472) or Dipping Sauce for Summer Rolls (page 477)
Pickled Daikon and Carrots (page 468)

To prepare the sesame salt, heat a small pan over a medium heat. Add the sesame seeds with the salt and toast for 30–60 seconds until fragrant, stirring constantly to prevent burning. Transfer to small bowl and let cool.

To make the spring onion (scallion) oil, heat the oil in a small pan over a medium heat. Add the spring onions and fry until fragrant but still bright green, about 1 minute. Remove from the heat and set aside.

To prepare the filling, heat the oil in pan to about 170°C/340°F. If not using a thermometer, test the oil temperature by inserting wooden chopsticks into the oil – small bubbles should form rapidly around them.

Add the tofu and fry over medium-low heat for 7–8 minutes until golden and crispy. Remove the tofu and drain on paper towels.

To the same oil, still over the heat, add the vermicelli and fry for about 30 seconds until puffed. Remove immediately when white and puffy to prevent burning. Strain immediately.

In a large bowl, combine the fried tofu and puffed vermicelli, then add the toasted rice powder. Mix in the sesame salt and spring onion oil, then toss gently until well combined.

To make the rolls, dip the rice paper briefly in room temperature water, then place on a clean surface. When the paper becomes pliable (about 30 seconds), add a layer of the mixed herbs and a portion (about 3 tablespoons) of the tofu mixture. Roll the paper tightly from the bottom up, tucking in the sides as you go, then place seam-side down on serving plate.

Serve immediately with dipping sauce and the pickled vegetables.

# SUMMER ROLLS WITH CHINESE SAUSAGES, OMELETTE, JICAMA AND DRIED SHRIMP

## Bò Bía Mặn

This dish reflects the history of the Teochew; originally from eastern Guangdong province in China, they formed significant communities throughout Southeast Asia, like in Singapore, Thailand and Vietnam since the eighteenth century, adapting their traditional *popiah* to local ingredients and tastes. While the original version uses wheat flour pancakes as wrappers, the Vietnamese adaptation uses *bánh tráng* (dry rice paper) – a quintessential local ingredient. The filling maintains its Teochew roots with Chinese sausage (*lạp xưởng*) but incorporates Vietnamese herbs, showcasing how immigrant communities adapted their cuisine while preserving their culinary heritage.

Makes approx. 20 rolls; serves 4–5
Preparation time: 1 hour
Cooking time: 30 minutes

| DF |

- 130 g/4½ oz Chinese sausage (lạp xưởng)
- 3 eggs
- 2 tablespoons neutral oil
- 25 g/1 oz shallots, minced
- 550 g/1 lb 4 oz peeled jicama (600 g/1 lb 5 oz before peeling), cut into thin matchsticks (julienned)
- 1 teaspoon sugar
- ½ teaspoon salt
- ½ teaspoon fish sauce
- 25 g/1 oz spring onions (scallions), chopped
- ½ teaspoon black pepper
- 20 rice paper sheets
- 115 g/4 oz herb salad (rau sống – lettuce, fish mint, Vietnamese basil, peppermint)
- 35 g/1¼ oz (2 tablespoons) Fried Shallots (page 458)
- 25 g/1 oz Toasted Peanuts (page 459)

*For the seasoned dried shrimp (ruốc)*

- 2 tablespoons neutral vegetable oil
- 20 g/¾ oz shallots, minced
- 10 g/¼ oz garlic, minced
- 50 g/1¾ oz dried shrimp (con ruốc), soaked for 30 minutes and drained
- ½ teaspoon salt
- 2 teaspoons sugar
- 1 tablespoon Annatto Oil (page 457)

*For the dipping sauce (makes 20 bowls)*

- 250 g/9 oz jar fermented soybean sauce (tương hột), beans and liquid separated (you should have 150 g/5½ oz beans plus 100 g/3½ oz liquid)
- 100 g/3½ oz (⅓ cup) hoisin sauce
- 1 tablespoon neutral oil
- 10 g/¼ oz peeled shallot
- 1 teaspoon tapioca flour
- 65 ml/2 fl oz (¼ cup) coconut water
- 1 tablespoon coconut milk
- 2 teaspoons sugar

Bring a large saucepan of water to the boil. Add the sausage and cook for 10 minutes, or until firm when pressed. Transfer to a chopping (cutting) board and slice diagonally into 3-mm/⅛-inch-thick pieces. Set aside.

In a bowl, whisk the eggs until well combined.

Heat a non-stick frying pan or skillet over a medium heat. Pour in one-third of the egg mixture to make a thin omelette, swirling to coat the pan. Cook for 1–2 minutes until set but not browned. Repeat with remaining egg mixture, then roll each omelette and slice into 5-mm/¼-inch strips. Set aside.

Heat the oil in a pan over a medium heat. Add the shallots and fry for 1 minute. Add the jicama and stir-fry for 2 minutes. Add the sugar, salt and fish sauce, and cook for another 6 minutes. Add the spring onions (scallions) and black pepper and stir-fry for another 30 seconds. Set aside.

To prepare the seasoned dried shrimp: heat the oil in a small pan over a medium-low heat, add the shallots and garlic and fry for 2 minutes. Add the soaked dried shrimp, salt and sugar and cook for another 2 minutes, then add the annatto oil and stir-fry for 2 more minutes. Set aside.

To make the dipping sauce, add the beans from the fermented soybean sauce to a blender and blend until fine. Add the liquid from the soybean sauce and the hoisin sauce, then blend for 10 seconds.

Heat the oil in a small pan over a medium-low heat. Add the shallot and fry for 1–2 minutes. Add the blended beans, bring to the boil, then simmer for 6 minutes.

Mix the tapioca flour with the coconut water, then add to pan. Add the coconut milk and sugar. Cook for 3 minutes.

To assemble the rolls, on each sheet of rice paper, place 4–5 g herb salad, 1 tablespoon (15 g/½ oz) of stir-fried jicama, 5 g/⅛ oz omelette, 5 g/⅛ oz Chinese sausage (about 2 slices) and ½ teaspoon (4–5 g) of the seasoned dried shrimp. Roll tightly, either tucking in the sides or not, as you prefer. Repeat with the remaining ingredients.

For each serving, provide 30 g/1 oz of the dipping sauce topped with 1 teaspoon of the fried shallots and 1 teaspoon toasted peanuts.

# FRESH RICE NOODLE ROLLS

## Phở Cuốn

In Vietnam, phở noodles are usually made daily by specialist shops and delivered to phở shops in the early mornings. The noodles are made by steaming rice batter into large sheets, which are then cut into strips of varying thickness. When shopping, phở noodle sheets should not be confused with *bánh ướt* (rice paper sheets), which look similar but are thinner. Whole phở noodle sheets can typically be found at local Vietnamese shops or wet markets, or alternatively, *cheung fun* sheets (thin steamed rice noodle sheets used in Cantonese cuisine) can be used as a substitute. *Phở cuốn* are usually served as a starter (appetizer) or snack, and sold alongside Deep-fried Phở Nest with Egg (page 188) in dry phở specialist food stalls.

Makes 12 rolls; serves 3–4
Preparation time: 30–45 minutes
Cooking time: 10 minutes

| DF |

- 300 g/10½ oz beef tenderloin (or any cut suitable for quick stir-frying), thinly sliced
- 10 g/¼ oz garlic, minced
- 10 g/¼ oz shallot, minced
- ¼ teaspoon black pepper
- 2 teaspoons fish sauce
- ½ teaspoon oyster sauce
- 2 tablespoons neutral oil
- 12 phở noodle sheets, about 12 × 10 cm/4½ × 4 inches each, or pre-prepared cheung fun
- 1 head of lettuce, leaves separated
- 12 g/½ oz coriander (cilantro), bottom stalks removed, keeping about 4 leaves per stalk

*To serve*
Northern-style Fish Sauce (page 471)
Pickled Kohlrabi and Carrots (page 469)
Hanoi-style Chilli Sauce (page 477)

In a bowl, combine the beef slices with the garlic, shallot, black pepper, 1 teaspoon of the fish sauce and the oyster sauce. Let marinate for 30 minutes at room temperature.

Heat the oil in a large pan over a high heat until very hot. Add the beef and stir-fry until just cooked, 1–5 minutes, depending on your pan. You don't want it to overcook and become chewy. Remove from the heat, then add the remaining fish sauce. Mix well and let cool slightly.

To assemble each roll, place a phở sheet on a clean surface. Layer on the sheet in the following order: a lettuce leaf, 4 coriander (cilantro) leaves and about 2 tablespoons of the cooked beef. Roll tightly from one end to the other. (Unlike the fresh summer rolls on page 40, there's no need to tuck the edges inside.) Continue rolling the remaining sheets until all the ingredients have been used.

Serve immediately with: Northern-style Fish Sauce, Pickled Kohlrabi and Carrots and Hanoi-style Chilli Sauce

FRESH RICE NOODLE ROLLS

# FRESH SUMMER ROLLS

## Gỏi Cuốn

In Vietnamese markets, you'll find bundles of *rau thơm* (aromatic mixed herbs), which are an essential element of Vietnamese dining where fresh herbs accompany most meals. While finding all these herbs might be challenging outside Vietnam, their combination is crucial for these rolls. Each herb plays its part in building the layers of flavour that make this dish complete.

Makes 15 rolls; serves 4–5
Preparation time: 45 minutes
Cooking time: 30 minutes

| DF |

- 1 tablespoon fish sauce
- 1 teaspoon salt
- 350 g/12 oz pork belly (side)
- 310 g/11 oz (about 15) prawns (shrimp)
- 150 g/5½ oz aromatic mixed herbs (rau thơm – fish mint, mint, perilla, Vietnamese basil, coriander/cilantro, Vietnamese balm, spearmint)
- 15 rice paper sheets
- 15 lettuce leaves
- 75 g/2¾ oz bean sprouts
- 375 g/13 oz fresh thin rice noodles, at room temperature
- 30 g/1 oz Chinese chives (lá hẹ)
- Dipping Sauce for Summer Rolls (page 477) or Sweet and Sour Fish Sauce (page 471), to serve

Combine 900 ml/30 fl oz (3¾ cups) of water with the fish sauce and salt in a large pot, then add the pork belly (side). Bring to a simmer, then cook until tender, about 20 minutes. Let cool completely.

Slice the pork belly thinly, against the grain (see note), then set aside.

Bring a pot of water to the boil. Cook the prawns (shrimp) in the boiling water until pink, about 7 minutes.

Meanwhile, prepare a bowl of iced water. When cooked, transfer the prawns to the iced water to stop them cooking any further (shock).

Peel and devein the prawns, then slice each prawn in half lengthways. Pat dry with paper towels.

Sort the herbs into individual piles and prepare a bowl of room temperature water.

To assemble each roll, dip the rice paper briefly in the water, then place on a clean surface. When the paper becomes pliable (about 30 seconds), layer next to each other, from the bottom of the paper to the top in the following order: 1 lettuce leaf, 5 bean sprouts, 10–15 aromatic herb leaves, about 25 g/1 oz of the rice noodles, sliced pork belly and 2 shrimp halves, pink-side down. To roll, fold the bottom edge over the filling, fold in the sides, add 2 Chinese chives, then tightly roll upwards. Place seam-side down on a serving platter. Repeat for the remaining rolls.

Dip your fresh summer rolls with your chosen dipping sauce.

***Note:*** To find the direction of the grain in meat, look for the parallel lines of muscle fibre running through the meat – these lines are the 'grain'. You can see them more clearly on some cuts than others. Think of it like wood grain or the fibres in celery. Cutting against the grain, will make your meat much easier to bite.

# PHAN RANG-STYLE RICE PAPER ROLLS WITH GRILLED PORK AND FISH CAKE

Chả Cuốn Phan Rang

This speciality from Phan Rang features multiple textures: crispy fried rice paper contrasting with fresh herbs, grilled meat and softened rice paper wrappers. The dish uses a specific local rice paper: large 31-cm/12½-inch squares dotted with white sesame seeds, which creates distinct layers unlike the more common *gỏi cuốn*. While traditionally made with *chả cá* (fish cake, page 463) and *nem nướng* (grilled pork patties, page 142), you can substitute with other grilled meats. You can use the same sauce as in the Nha Trang-style Grilled Pork Patties recipe (page 142) or make this simpler version below.

Makes 8 rolls
Preparation time: 45 minutes
Cooking time: 20 minutes

| DF |

*For the fried rice paper*
- 8 sheets thin black sesame rice paper (bánh tráng mè đen) (15–20 cm/6–8 inches; see note)
- neutral oil, for frying

*For the sauce (makes 240 ml/8 fl oz/1 cup)*
- 40 g/1½ oz Toasted Peanuts (page 459)
- 25 g/1 oz toasted sesame seeds
- 1 tablespoon neutral oil
- 2 tablespoons fish sauce
- 15 g/½ oz deseeded long red chillies
- 1½ teaspoons Annatto Oil (page 457)
- 2 tablespoons light brown sugar
- ¼ teaspoon salt
- 1 teaspoon tapioca starch
- ½ teaspoon MSG, optional
- 1 teaspoon rice vinegar

*To serve*
- 8 sheets thin white sesame rice paper (bánh tráng gạo mè trắng) (31-cm/12½-inch square or the largest you can find; see notes)
- 160 g/5½ oz herb salad (rau sống – lettuce, perilla, Vietnamese balm, fish mint)
- 80 g/2¾ oz cucumber, cut into thin matchsticks (julienned)
- 120 g/4¼ oz Pickled Daikon and Carrots (page 468)
- 8 hard-boiled duck eggs, cooked for 8 minutes
- 160 g/5½ oz fried Tuna Fish Cake (page 463), cut into slices
- 200 g/7 oz Grilled Pork Patties (page 142, about 8 grilled skewers) or other grilled meat

For the fried rice paper: Take a sheet of black sesame rice paper and lightly brush with water to soften. Roll into a rectangle shape and let dry for 15 minutes.
Fill a pan with the oil and heat over a medium-high heat to 180°C/350°F. If not using a thermometer, test the oil temperature by inserting wooden chopsticks into the oil – it should bubble vigorously around them.

Carefully add the dried rice paper and fry for 2–3 minutes until crispy inside and out – it will become opaque when ready. Carefully remove from the oil and drain on paper towels.

For the sauce: In a blender, combine the peanuts, sesame seeds, oil, 1 tablespoon of the fish sauce, 2 tablespoons of water and the chillies. Blend for 30 seconds. Add 4 tablespoons of water and blend until smooth, about 1 minute.

Heat the annatto oil in a small pan over a medium heat. Add the blended paste, brown sugar and 100 ml/3½ fl oz (¼ cup plus 3 tablespoons) water. Season with salt. Simmer on low for 5 minutes, stirring occasionally.

Mix the tapioca starch with 1 tablespoon of water in a small bowl. Stir this into the sauce and cook for 30 seconds until slightly thickened. Remove from the heat and add the remaining fish sauce, the MSG, if using, and rice vinegar. The sauce should be loose enough to dip – thin with water if needed.

To assemble each roll, quickly dip a large white sesame rice paper in water (for about 5 seconds) and lay on a clean, damp cloth. Along the bottom third of the rice paper, arrange the herbs, cucumber and pickled vegetables. Add sliced duck egg, tuna fish cake and grilled pork patty. Place a piece of fried rice paper on top of the filling. Fold the bottom edge over the filling, tuck in the sides, and roll tightly to seal.

To eat, first dip the roll into the sauce, then eat the first bite. Afterwards, use a teaspoon to spoon the sauce into the rest of the roll. Doing so this way will prevent the filling from falling out.

***Note:*** If using a smaller rice paper to roll this dish, remember to adjust the amount of filling accordingly. While black sesame rice paper is traditional and provides better texture for this dish, you can also fry the same rice paper used for wrapping. Or any rice paper you have.

# SWEET AND SOUR PICKLED PIG'S EARS

## Tai Heo Ngâm Chua Ngọt

Pickled meats are a common preparation for *Tết* (Lunar New Year), as they keep well during the holiday period. While traditionally these pig's ears were left at room temperature for one to two nights to develop sourness, this recipe uses refrigeration for food safety. When properly stored, these pickles can keep for up to six months in the refrigerator. This is best served with fresh herbs, rice paper, and Seasoned Fermented Thick Fish Sauce (page 476) or can just be eaten as a snack.

Serves 6–8 as a starter/appetizer or side dish
Preparation time: 45 minutes
Cooking time: 20 minutes, plus cooling and pickling time

| DF |

- 810 g/1 lb 12 oz pig's ears (about 2 ears), cleaned and hair removed
- 1 lemongrass stalk (35 g/1¼ oz)
- 10 g/¼ oz shallot, thinly sliced
- 1 tablespoon fish sauce
- 250 ml/8 fl oz (1 cup) white vinegar
- 100 g/3½ oz carrots, peeled
- 30 g/1 oz garlic, sliced
- 50 g/1¾ oz red shallots, sliced
- 20 g/¾ oz long red chilli, sliced diagonally

*For the pickling liquid*

- 300 ml/10 fl oz (1¼ cups) white vinegar
- 1 tablespoon fish sauce
- 175 g/6 oz (¾ cup plus 2 tablespoons) sugar
- 1 teaspoon salt

In a large pot, bring 1 litre/1¾ pints (4¼ cups) of water to the boil. Add the pig's ears, lemongrass, shallot and fish sauce. Cover and cook for 15 minutes, turning the ears occasionally. Remove from the heat but keep covered for 5 minutes.

Meanwhile, prepare a bowl of iced water.

Transfer the ears to the ice bath. Let cool completely, about 15 minutes.

Trim the cooled ears, then thinly slice at an angle (you should have about 760 g/1 lb 10 oz), then place in a bowl and cover with the vinegar. Let stand for 15 minutes to remove any excess gelatine, then drain well in a fine-mesh sieve and set aside.

To make the pickling liquid, in a saucepan, combine the vinegar, fish sauce, sugar and salt with 70 ml/2½ fl oz (scant ⅓ cup) water. Bring to the boil, stirring to dissolve the sugar, then remove from the heat and set aside.

Using a small sharp knife or mandoline, cut the carrots into thin, decorative flowers (as instructed in the aspic recipe on page 102). You can make 5 flowers out of this.

To assemble the pickle, layer the sliced pig's ears, garlic, red shallots, chilli and carrot flowers in sterilized glass jars. Pour the hot pickling liquid over to completely cover the ingredients, then let cool to room temperature, about 1 hour.

Seal the jars and refrigerate for at least 1 hour before serving. Once opened, they will keep refrigerated for up to 2 weeks.

# BEEF SHIN IN FISH SAUCE BRINE

## Bắp Bò Ngâm Mắm

This is a traditional Vietnamese dish that preserves beef shin (shank) in fish sauce. The beef is marinated with garlic, chilli, cinnamon and star anise, though spices vary by family and region. This dish is a cherished preparation for *Tết* (Lunar New Year), as it can be kept and served through the festivities. The ideal cut is *bắp hoa bò* (beef round heel muscle) – the centre portion of the shin that resembles a flower. However, any part of the shin rich in connective tissue, which transforms into gelatine during cooking, works well for this dish.

Serves 6–8
Preparation time: 30–40 minutes, plus at least 3 days pickling time
Cooking time: 1 hour 15–1 hour 30 minutes

| DF |

2.23 kg/5 lb beef shin (shank) (bắp hoa bò)
40 g/1½ oz piece fresh ginger, peeled and thinly sliced (keep the peel)
4 lemongrass, trimmed to 12-cm/4½-inch long (about 15 g/½ oz per stalk), then cut into 3 pieces (keep the trimmings)
45 green bird's eye chillies (40 g/1½ oz/ scant ½ cup)
50 g/1¾ oz (⅓ cup) whole green peppercorns
45 g/1½ oz garlic, thickly sliced
45 g/1½ oz shallots, thickly sliced
1 carrot (about 125 g/4¼ oz), peeled and cut into 1.5-cm/¾-inch-thick flowers (see step 2, page 102)

*For the poaching water*
125 ml/4¼ fl oz (generous ½ cup) fish sauce
lemongrass trims (reserved from above)
ginger peel (reserved from above)
2 star anise
5 g/⅛ oz cinnamon stick
1 black cardamom pod (thảo quả)

*For the pickling liquid*
835 ml/28 fl oz (3½ cups) fish sauce
1 kg/2 lb 4 oz (4½ cups) rock sugar (brown or white)

Pat the beef dry with paper towels. Roll tightly into a log shape, then secure the ends and middle with kitchen string and tie like a porchetta or roast beef, spacing the string about 4 cm/1½ inches apart, to keep it round and beautiful.

Bring 1.9 litres/3¼ pints (8 cups) of water to the boil in a large pot. Add the wrapped beef, then cook for 2–3 minutes until the surface of the meat turns grey. Carefully remove and then rinse under cold running water. Pat dry thoroughly.

To prepare the poaching liquid, in a large pot, combine 2.5 litres/ 4½ pints (10½ cups) of water with the fish sauce. Add the lemongrass trimmings and ginger peel. Bring to the boil over a medium heat.

Heat a pan over medium-low heat, then add the star anise, cinnamon and black cardamom and toast in the dry pan until fragrant (1–2 minutes). Add the toasted spices to the pot.

Add the blanched beef to the simmering liquid, then reduce the heat to low. Simmer for 60–80 minutes to slowly poach it, skimming the surface regularly to remove scum. (The cooking time may vary depending on the size of your shins/shanks.)

Prepare a bowl of iced water, then test the beef for doneness by inserting a chopstick into the meat: the juice should run clear, not pink. (You should have about 1.3 kg /2 lb 14 oz of cooked meat.) Transfer the meat immediately to the ice bath and let it cool completely, about 30 minutes, then remove the string.

To make the pickling liquid combine the fish sauce, rock sugar and 600 ml/1 pint (2½ cups) of water in a pot. Bring to the boil, stirring to dissolve the sugar. Remove from heat and cool completely.

In a large, sterilized jar or container, layer the cooked beef with the sliced ginger, trimmed lemongrass, bird's eye chillies, green peppercorns, garlic, shallots and carrot flowers. Pour the cooled pickling liquid over the layered ingredients, ensuring everything is fully submerged.

Seal the jar or container and refrigerate for at least 3 days to allow the flavours to develop.

Thinly slice the pickled beef shin before serving.

***Note:*** While we use beef shin (shank) here, pork belly (side) can also be brined.

# CHICKEN FEET PICKLED IN CALAMANSI AND LEMONGRASS

Chân Gà Sả Tắc

This dish is a great snack to prepare in advance for Lunar New Year celebrations. It's a perfect accompaniment for drinking sessions, known as '*nhậu*' in Vietnamese. The chicken feet can be stored in the refrigerator for up to a week, allowing the flavours to deepen over time. You'll enjoy the crunchy, gelatinous texture of the chicken feet, coated in a sweet, spicy and tangy sauce that pairs wonderfully with Vietnamese draft beer.

There's also a variation of this dish called *thịt ba rọi lắc sả tắc* that uses leftover crispy pork belly (Roasted Pork Belly, page 161) instead of chicken feet. Unlike this recipe, the pork version is more of a fresh salad and doesn't require overnight marination. It's a quicker dish that captures the flavours of calamansi and lemongrass.

Serves 6–8 (4–5 pieces per person)
Preparation time: 45 minutes, plus 24 hours pickling time
Cooking time: 20 minutes

| DF |

250 ml/8 fl oz (1 cup) coconut water
¾ teaspoon salt
1 teaspoon fish sauce
35 g/1¼ oz lemongrass trimmings
45 g/1½ oz piece fresh ginger, peeled and sliced
1 kg/2 lb 4 oz chicken feet (approx. 18), halved horizontally
40 g/1½ oz long red chillies (about 3), de-seeded and thinly sliced
95 g/3½ oz shallots, thinly sliced
5 lemongrass stalks, trimmed, cut into 15-cm/6-inch lengths, then thinly sliced
2 tablespoons sugar
Handful of ice

*For the sauce*
2 tablespoons caster (superfine) sugar
16 g/½ oz (3½ teaspoons) rock sugar
85 ml/3 fl oz (⅓ cup) vinegar
2 teaspoons fish sauce
½ teaspoon salt

*For pickling*
195 g/6¾ oz calamansi (about 18), halved
35 g/1¼ oz garlic, minced
2 teaspoons fish sauce

Combine 250 ml/8 fl oz (1 cup) of water with the coconut water, salt, fish sauce, lemongrass trimmings and ginger in a pot. Bring to a simmer over a medium heat, add the chicken feet, then stir for 1 minute. Add the chillies, shallots and lemongrass, then cover and cook for 15 minutes over a medium-high heat, stirring every 3 minutes for even cooking.

Meanwhile, prepare the sauce. In a small saucepan, combine all the ingredients with 250 ml/8 fl oz (1 cup) of water. Place over a medium-low heat until the sugar dissolves. Simmer for 1 minute, then remove from the heat and allow to cool completely. Set aside.

To prepare the pickling mixture, put all the ingredients in a large bowl and mix by hand, gently squeezing the calamansi to release their flavour. Set aside.

After the chicken feet have finished cooking, leave the feet in the cooking liquid for 3 minutes, then drain. Transfer to a bowl with the ice and 1 tablespoon of the sugar. Let soak for 5 minutes for crunchy skin, then drain well.

Add the cooled chicken feet to the pickling mixture. Pour in the cooled sauce, mix thoroughly and add the remaining sugar.

Transfer to an airtight container and refrigerate for 24 hours before eating. It will keep for 1 week in the refrigerator.

Serve chilled as a starter (appetizer) or snack.

CHICKEN FEET PICKLED IN CALAMANSI AND LEMONGRASS

# BRAISED CHICKEN FEET WITH CHILLI AND LEMONGRASS OIL

Chân Gà Rim Sa Tế

This is a popular snack that can often be found in *quán nhậu* (beer halls). Cooking it twice makes the meat/collagen fall off easily from the small bones. It is an acquired way of eating, to gnaw on small bones, but one that is quite familiar to Vietnamese people. You can even find a packed version of this at the convenient shop as snacks for kids.

Serves 2–3
Preparation time: 30 minutes
Cooking time: 45 minutes

| DF |

1 tablespoon fish sauce
7 lime leaves
1 lemongrass stalk, smashed and tied into a knot
12 chicken feet, nails clipped off
¼ teaspoon ground turmeric
2 tablespoons vegetable oil
1 tablespoon fish sauce
1 tablespoon sugar

*For the spice mixture*
30 g/1 oz lemongrass, minced
12 g/½ oz garlic, finely chopped
10 g/¼ oz shallot, finely chopped
1 long red chilli, finely chopped
10 g/¼ oz (2 teaspoons) Chilli and Lemongrass Oil (page 457)

*To serve*
1 handful Vietnamese coriander/cilantro (rau răm), leaves picked
2 lime leaves, thinly sliced

In a large pot, combine 500 ml/18 fl oz (2 cups) water with the fish sauce, lime leaves and knotted lemongrass. Bring to the boil over a high heat. Add the chicken feet, reduce the heat to low, cover and simmer for 10 minutes. Remove from the heat but keep the pan covered for 20 minutes to continue gently cooking.

Using a slotted spoon, remove the chicken feet from the cooking stock (broth) and let cool completely. For the best results, refrigerate the feet until they are fully chilled, about 1 hour.

Measure 70 ml/2½ fl oz (scant ⅓ cup) of the cooking stock and stir in the ground turmeric. Reserve the remaining stock for soups.

In a small bowl, combine all the spice mixture ingredients.

Heat the vegetable oil in a wok or deep frying pan over a medium heat. Add the spice mixture and stir-fry for 1–2 minutes until fragrant and golden, stirring constantly to prevent burning. Increase the heat to medium–high, add the cooled chicken feet, and stir-fry for 2–3 minutes, turning frequently. Add the fish sauce, sugar and turmeric-infused stock. Reduce the heat to low, cover and braise for 15 minutes, or until the sauce has reduced and the chicken feet are glazed.

Transfer to a serving plate, arrange the Vietnamese coriander/cilantro leaves around the edge, and scatter with the sliced lime leaves. Serve hot.

# FRIED TOFU WITH SPRING ONION SAUCE

Đậu Tẩm Hành

This Hanoian dish showcases Northern Vietnam's tofu-making craft, a skill dating back to the tenth century through Chinese influence and the arrival of Buddhism. While simple, it demands two things: one, fresh firm tofu made on the day; two, perfectly fried tofu – crisp and golden outside, soft and silky inside. When dipped, the tofu soaks up just enough of the spring onion (scallion) sauce. You'll find it in *quán nhậu* (beer halls) as a snack, or as a side dish in larger meals. If you don't have any fresh tofu, you can buy pre-packaged firm tofu.

Serves 4–6 as side dish
Preparation time: 10 minutes, plus 30 minutes drying time
Cooking time: 8–10 minutes

| DF |

400 g/14 oz firm tofu
oil, for deep-frying

*For the sauce*
60 ml/2 fl oz (¼ cup) fish sauce
180 ml/6 fl oz (¾ cup) boiling water
1½ teaspoons sugar
½ teaspoon MSG
1 teaspoon vinegar
40–50 g/1½–1¾ oz small spring onions (scallions), thinly sliced

Cut the tofu into uniform 3 × 5 × 3-cm/1¼ × 2 × 1¼-in cubes (size consistency is important for even cooking). Leave the tofu on paper towels or on a grill rack to dry for 30 minutes.

Fill a wok one third full with oil (enough to submerge the tofu). Heat the oil over a medium–high heat. Carefully add the tofu and fry for 7–8 minutes until the edges are crispy. Remove and drain on paper towels.

To make the sauce, combine the fish sauce, the measured boiling water, the sugar and MSG in a bowl. Stir until the sugar dissolves. Add the vinegar and thinly sliced spring onions (scallions).

Dip each piece of fried tofu in the spring onion sauce, place on a serving plate, then spoon extra spring onions and sauce over the top. Serve immediately.

# BALUT (FERTILIZED DUCK EGGS)

Hột Vịt Lộn

*Hột vịt lộn* is a popular snack in Vietnam and other Southeast Asian countries. Fertilized duck eggs are prized for their high protein content and reputed benefits for blood circulation. In Vietnamese culture, these eggs are believed to have cooling properties and are often served with *rau răm* (Vietnamese coriander/cilantro) to balance their effects. It's recommended to choose younger fertilized eggs for softer egg whites and a smaller formed duck embryo. Balut should be served while still warm for the best experience.

Serves 4
Preparation time: 5 minutes
Cooking time: 15 minutes

| DF | GF | ≤5 | ≤30 |

- 12 fertilized duck eggs
- 350 ml/12 fl oz (1½ cups) coconut water
- ½ teaspoon salt
- 50 g/1¾ oz Vietnamese coriander/cilantro (rau răm)
- 2–3 tablespoons Salt and Pepper Seasoning Mix (page 480)

In a saucepan that can comfortably fit all the eggs in a single layer, combine the fertilized duck eggs, coconut water and salt. Place the pan over a medium heat and bring the liquid to a simmer. You'll see small bubbles consistently rising to the surface, but the water should not be rapidly boiling. Reduce the heat to maintain a gentle simmer and cook the eggs for 15 minutes. Use a timer to ensure precise cooking time.

Using a slotted spoon, carefully remove the eggs from the cooking liquid. If desired, strain and reserve the cooking liquid. Let the eggs cool for 2–3 minutes until they're comfortable to handle but still warm.

Place each egg in an egg cup, then using the back of a spoon, gently tap and crack the wider end of the egg. Carefully peel away a small portion of the shell and membrane to create an opening 2–3 cm/about 1 inch wide.

Provide each person with: 3 warm balut eggs, 12–15 g/½ oz Vietnamese coriander/cilantro and 1 portion of Salt and Pepper Seasoning Mix in a small bowl.

To eat traditionally, you first, carefully sip the warm broth from inside the egg. Then, using a small spoon, eat the egg contents with the fresh Vietnamese coriander leaves, dipping both the egg and coriander in the seasoning mix as desired.

# STIR-FRIED BALUT WITH TAMARIND SAUCE

Hột Vịt Lộn Xào Me

In Vietnam, tamarind comes in dense cubes and is 100 per cent pure tamarind. Elsewhere, you are most likely to buy tamarind paste, a diluted version that is easier to use and keep. This recipe uses the diluted paste, so the amount of tamarind used serves as a base for you to adjust depending on the type of tamarind you use. If it's too sour, balance it with more sugar, or if it's not sour enough, balance it with lime juice or calamansi juice.

Serves 1–3
Preparation time: 15 minutes
Cooking time: 8 minutes

| DF | ≤30 |

- 1 teaspoon neutral oil
- 10 g/¼ oz garlic, coarsely chopped
- 3 cooked balut from Balut (Fertilized Duck Eggs) (above), peeled
- ½ teaspoon fish sauce
- ½ teaspoon sugar
- 15 g/½ oz (1½ tablespoons) Toasted Peanuts (page 459), crushed
- 5 g/⅛ oz Vietnamese coriander/cilantro (rau răm), leaves picked

*For the tamarind sauce*

- 20 g/¾ oz (1½ tablespoons) tamarind paste
- ¼ teaspoon salt
- 1½ teaspoons sugar
- ½ teaspoon cornflour (cornstarch)

To prepare the tamarind sauce, in a small saucepan, combine the tamarind paste, salt and sugar with 70 ml/2½ fl oz (scant ⅓ cup) of water. Place over a medium heat and bring to a simmer, stirring occasionally.

In a small bowl, mix the cornflour with 1 tablespoon of cold water until smooth. Add to the simmering sauce and cook for 1–2 minutes until thickened. Remove from the heat and set aside.

Heat a frying pan or skillet or wok over a medium heat. Add the oil and garlic, and stir-fry for about 1 minute until the garlic turns golden brown, stirring constantly to prevent burning. Add the peeled balut eggs to the pan. Season with the fish sauce and sugar and cook for 30 seconds, gently turning the eggs to evenly coat them. Pour in the prepared tamarind sauce and cook for 2 minutes, occasionally spooning the sauce over the eggs, until they are well coated and heated through.

Transfer to a serving bowl and top with the crushed peanuts and Vietnamese coriander/cilantro leaves. Serve immediately.

STIR-FRIED BALUT WITH TAMARIND SAUCE

# STIR-FRIED CORN WITH SPRING ONION OIL

Bắp Xào Mỡ Hành

Historically it is said that the first corn was introduced to Northern Vietnam by scholar Phùng Khắc Khoan in the sixteenth century after his travels to China. Today, corn has become a versatile and essential crop in Vietnam, used in everything from wine production to livestock feed. In the northern mountainous regions like Hà Giang, Yên Bái or Sơn La provinces, the H'Mông people notably use corn as their primary carbohydrate instead of rice. While various corn varieties are cultivated throughout Vietnam, for this particular dish, *bắp nếp* (sticky corn) is recommended for its glutinous texture.

Serves 1–2
Preparation time: 10–15 minutes
Cooking time: 10–15 minutes

| DF | ≤30 |

- 285 g/10 oz corn cobs (bắp nếp/sticky corn or sweetcorn)
- 1 teaspoon lard, plus an extra 1 teaspoon lard or butter
- ½ teaspoon unsalted butter
- 1 teaspoon fish sauce
- ½ teaspoon sugar
- 20 g/¾ oz spring onions (scallions), chopped
- ¼ teaspoon MSG, optional
- 5 g/⅛ oz (1 teaspoon) Fried Shallots (page 458)
- ¼ teaspoon salt or fish sauce, or to taste

Bring a large pot of water to the boil over a high heat. Add the corn cobs and boil for 5 minutes, or until tender when pierced with a fork. Remove the corn from the water and let cool until comfortable to handle, about 5 minutes.

Using a sharp knife, carefully cut the kernels from the cob, working from top to bottom. You should have approximately 160 g/5½ oz (1 cup) of kernels.

Heat a 15-cm/6-inch frying pan or skillet or wok over a medium-low heat. Add the lard and butter, letting them melt together. Add the corn kernels to the pan and stir-fry for 3 minutes, stirring frequently to prevent them from sticking. Add the fish sauce and sugar and continue to stir-fry for 1½ minutes until the corn starts to slightly caramelize. Add the spring onions (scallions) and stir-fry for 1 minute more, or until the onions are bright green and fragrant. Add the extra teaspoon of lard or butter and the fried shallots and stir to combine. Season to taste with either salt or fish sauce. Stir well to combine.

Transfer to a serving dish and serve immediately.

STIR-FRIED CORN WITH SPRING ONION OIL

## FRIED QUAIL IN BUTTER

Chim Cút Chiên Bơ

During Vietnam's colonial period, the French introduced canned butter, which introduced this ingredient to the Vietnamese palate. This butter-inspired seasoning adds a distinctive sweet note that has become synonymous with many Vietnamese dishes. In this recipe, coating the naturally lean quail in butter or margarine creates a rich, flavourful exterior that perfectly complements the meat.

Serves 2–3
Preparation time: 40 minutes
Cooking time: 30 minutes

- 250 ml/8 fl oz (1 cup) coconut water
- ½ teaspoon salt
- 5 quails (550 g/1 lb 4 oz), spatchcocked, front open
- 250 ml/8 fl oz (1 cup) vegetable oil
- 40 g/1½ oz (3 tablespoons) butter or margarine
- Salt and Pepper Seasoning Mix (page 480), to serve

*For the marinade*

- 1 teaspoon black pepper
- 1 tablespoon light soy sauce
- 1 teaspoon Annatto Oil (page 457)
- ¼ teaspoon salt
- ¼ teaspoon Vietnamese five-spice powder (ngũ vị hương)
- ½ teaspoon sugar
- 1 teaspoon oyster sauce
- 10 g/¼ oz shallot, minced
- 10 g/¼ oz garlic, minced

In a large bowl, combine the coconut water and salt. Add the spatchcocked quails and let them marinate for 30 minutes at room temperature. Remove the quails from the coconut water and pat thoroughly dry with paper towels.

In a bowl, combine all the marinade ingredients until well mixed. Coat the quails evenly with the marinade, ensuring it gets into all the crevices. Let marinate for 10 minutes at room temperature.

Heat the vegetable oil in a wok or deep frying pan over a medium-high heat until it reaches 170–180°C/340–350°F. If not using a thermometer, test the oil temperature by inserting wooden chopsticks into the oil – it should bubble vigorously around them. Carefully add the marinated quails and fry, turning partway through, for 2–3 minutes until lightly golden. Remove with a slotted spoon and place in a bowl with 25 g/1 oz of the butter. Toss gently to coat.

Pour the oil through a fine-mesh sieve and return it to the wok. This step prevents the garlic and shallot particles from burning.

Return the wok to medium-low heat. Add the butter-coated quails and cook for 20 minutes, turning occasionally to ensure even cooking. Increase the heat to high and fry for a final 2–3 minutes, or until the skin is crispy and golden brown. Transfer the quails to a bowl, add the remaining butter and toss to evenly coat.

Transfer to a serving plate and serve immediately while hot, accompanied by the seasoning mix.

## HALONG BAY FRIED SQUID PATTIES

Chả Mực Hạ Long

Halong Bay, in northeast Vietnam, is known for its squid patties made from locally caught squid, which can weigh up to 2 kg/ 4½ lb. While traditional recipes use these large local squid, any fresh squid or cuttlefish works well. You can pre-fry the patties for 2 minutes and then freeze them at this stage if desired; then fry them again until golden and warm when ready to eat.

Makes 12 patties; serves 4–6
Preparation time: 30–40 minutes
Cooking time: 10–12 minutes

**| DF |**

- 600 g/1 lb 5 oz large squid (mực nang), cleaned and skinned (420 g/15 oz cleaned weight)
- 60 g/2¼ oz onion, finely chopped
- 20 g/¾ oz shallots, finely chopped
- 2 tablespoons sticky (glutinous) rice flour
- 1 teaspoon all-purpose seasoning (hạt nêm)
- ¼ teaspoon black pepper
- ½ teaspoon sugar
- oil, for frying and shaping
- chilli sauce, to serve

Coarsely chop 320 g/11½ oz of the squid for making the paste. Dice the remaining 100 g/3½ oz of the squid into 5-mm/¼-inch cubes, then set aside.

In a food processor, combine the chopped squid, onion, shallots, rice flour, all-purpose seasoning, black pepper and sugar. Blend for 1–1½ minutes until a paste forms.

Combine the paste with the reserved diced squid.

Fill a small bowl with oil, then wearing oiled gloves to make shaping easier, form the mixture into 12 balls. Flatten to form patties.

Fill a pot with oil and heat the oil to 170°C/340°F. If not using a thermometer, test the oil temperature by inserting wooden chopsticks into the oil – small bubbles should form rapidly around them. Carefully add the patties to the oil and then fry for 4–5 minutes, flipping every minute to ensure even cooking, until puffed and golden. (Do this is batches if needed.) Remove when they are just cooked but not browned. Drain on paper towels.

Serve immediately with chilli sauce.

# CRISPY FRIED CHICKEN CARTILAGE

## Sụn Gà Chiên Giòn

In Vietnam there are two types of chicken cartilage that you can eat: one comes from the soft middle breast bones, and one comes from the mid-point of the wings or legs. While unfamiliar to the West, these crunchy bits are quite popular again as a snack while drinking. This version is great for beginners, as you fry the cartilage in a crispy batter, and it's seasoned with an addictive salt and pepper mix.

Serves 3–4
Preparation time: 20 minutes
Cooking time: 15–17 minutes

| DF |

400 g/14 oz chicken knee cartilage
1 teaspoon fish sauce
¼ teaspoon black pepper
¼ teaspoon salt
15 g/½ oz peeled shallot
15 g/½ oz peeled garlic
3 tablespoons rice flour
1 tablespoon cornflour (corn starch)
15 g/½ oz spring onions (scallions), finely chopped
500 ml/18 fl oz (2 cups) neutral oil, for frying
1.5 g lime leaves (3 leaves)

*For the seasoning mix*
½ teaspoon black pepper
1 teaspoon salt
½ teaspoon sugar
¼ teaspoon MSG, optional

*To serve*
Vietnamese coriander/cilantro (rau răm)
sliced tomatoes
chilli sauce

In a large bowl, combine the chicken cartilage with the fish sauce, black pepper and salt. Mix well and set aside.

Put the shallot and garlic in a mortar and pound with a pestle until they form a fine paste. Place the paste in a piece of muslin (cheesecloth) or a fine-mesh sieve and squeeze the liquid into the marinated cartilage. Reserve the solid paste.

Add the rice flour, cornflour (corn starch) and spring onions (scallions) to the marinated cartilage. Mix thoroughly to coat evenly.

Heat the oil in a wok or deep frying pan over a medium heat to 150°C/300°F. If not using a thermometer, test the oil temperature by inserting wooden chopsticks into the oil – it should gently bubble around them. Add the reserved garlic and shallot paste to the oil and fry for 1–2 minutes until fragrant and golden. Remove with a fine-mesh sieve and set aside.

Increase the heat to reach 175°C/345°F. (It should bubble vigorously around the chopsticks). Working in batches to avoid overcrowding, fry the cartilage for 8–10 minutes until golden brown and crispy. Remove any floating pieces of spring onion with a strainer to prevent burning. Ensure the frying temperature remains about 175°C/345°F.

In the last 30 seconds of the last batch of frying, add the lime leaves to the oil. Remove both the cartilage and lime leaves with a skimmer and drain on paper towels.

For the seasoning mix: In a small dry frying pan or skillet over a medium heat, combine the salt, black pepper, sugar, and MSG (if using). Toast for 2½ minutes, or until hot and fragrant, stirring constantly to prevent burning.

Transfer the fried cartilage to a large bowl, sprinkle with the hot seasoning mixture, and toss well to evenly coat.

Arrange on a serving plate, garnish with Vietnamese coriander/cilantro leaves and sliced tomatoes. Serve immediately with chilli sauce on the side.

# FRIED CHICKEN CARTILAGE WITH FISH SAUCE

## Sụn Gà Chiên Nước Mắm

This dish follows the same preparation method as Fish Sauce Fried Chicken Wings (page 110) but uses chicken cartilage instead. It's a practical dish that demonstrates the efficient use of chicken parts in Vietnamese cooking, where various cuts and textures are appreciated. This is commonly served as a beer snack (*món nhậu*), and it's usually paired with *rau răm* (Vietnamese coriander/cilantro) to freshen up the sweetness of the glaze. You can either dip it in Salt and Pepper Seasoning Mix (page 480) or even Green Chilli Salt (page 480).

Serves 2–3
Preparation time: 15 minutes
Cooking time: 10–12 minutes

| DF | ≤30 |

- 300 g/10½ oz chicken knee cartilage
- 1½ teaspoons fish sauce
- ¼ teaspoon black pepper
- 60 g/2 oz garlic, half finely minced, half chopped
- 1 tablespoon rice flour
- ½ teaspoon cornflour (cornstarch)
- 500 ml/18 fl oz (2 cups) neutral oil, for frying
- 1.5 g lime leaves (3 leaves), thinly sliced
- 145 g/5 oz onion, thinly sliced
- Vietnamese coriander/cilantro (rau răm), to serve

*For the sauce*

- 1 tablespoon fish sauce
- 1½ teaspoons sugar
- 1½ teaspoons black pepper
- 30 g/1 oz garlic, chopped

In a bowl, combine the chicken cartilage with the fish sauce and black pepper. Mix well and set aside.

Press the finely minced garlic through a fine-mesh sieve to extract the liquid, or use a garlic press. Add the garlic liquid to the marinated cartilage.

In a small bowl, mix together the rice flour and cornflour (cornstarch). Coat the marinated cartilage evenly with this mixture.

Heat the oil in a large frying pan or wok over a medium-high heat to 170–180°C/340–350°F. If not using a thermometer, test the oil temperature by inserting wooden chopsticks into the oil – it should bubble vigorously around them. Working in batches if necessary, carefully fry the coated cartilage for about 7 minutes, or until golden brown and crispy, turning occasionally. Remove with a skimmer and drain on paper towels.

Using the same oil, quickly fry the chopped garlic until golden, about 30 seconds. Remove with a fine-mesh sieve and add to the fried cartilage.

Add the lime leaves and onions to the hot oil and fry for 30 seconds, or until the onion is just softened. Remove and add to the cartilage mixture.

In a small bowl, combine all the sauce ingredients with 1 teaspoon of water, stirring until the sugar dissolves.

Transfer the fried cartilage mixture to a large bowl, pour over the sauce and toss well to evenly coat.

Transfer to a serving plate and garnish with Vietnamese coriander/cilantro leaves.

Serve immediately.

# FRIED STICKY RICE

## Xôi Chiên

Unlike traditional steamed sticky (glutinous) rice, this version is cooked in a rice cooker or pot to achieve extra moisture and stickiness. This results in a 'sandwich' that becomes crispy on the outside while remaining soft inside when fried. The shaped rice must be fried immediately or kept covered with clingfilm (plastic wrap) at room temperature; refrigeration will dry it out. In terms of the filling, this recipe is the most basic version, some people would add pork floss to the dish or jicama to the stir-fried pork.

Makes 7–8 rice sandwiches; serves 7–8
Preparation time: 30 minutes, plus overnight soaking time
Cooking time: 35–40 minutes

| DF |

300 g/10½ oz sticky (glutinous) rice
¾ teaspoon salt
300 ml/10 fl oz (1¼ cups) neutral oil, for frying

*For the filling*
300 g/10½ oz minced (ground) pork
1 teaspoon sugar
½ teaspoon black pepper
1 tablespoon fish sauce
1 tablespoon neutral oil
30 g/1 oz shallots, minced
½ teaspoon salt

Rinse the rice under running water three times.

Combine 375 ml/13 fl oz (1⅔ cups) water and the salt in a pot and bring to the boil. Add the rice and cook over a low heat for 30 minutes or until it is fully cooked and the water has evaporated, checking to ensure the pot doesn't burn on the bottom. Alternatively place 375 ml/13 fl oz (1⅔ cups) water, the salt and the washed rice in a rice cooker and cook.

Meanwhile, make the filling. Place the minced (ground) pork in a bowl with the sugar, black pepper and fish sauce and set aside to marinate.

Heat the oil in a pan over a medium heat. Add the shallots and fry for 1½ minutes. Add the marinated pork and fry for 4 minutes over a low heat. Add the salt, then continue frying for 5 minutes until the pork is fully cooked. Let cool completely.

To make plain rice discs: either brush some oil on some small dipping bowls or jar lids (about 3 cm/1¼ inches deep) or line with clingfilm (plastic wrap). Press the rice into the bowls or lids while hot. Press firmly to compact the rice.

Flatten a portion of rice into a disc, place 1 tablespoon of the cooled filling in the centre, cover with another portion of rice, then seal the edges completely.

Heat the oil in a shallow pan over a medium heat to 170–180°C/340–350°F. If not using a thermometer, test the oil temperature by inserting wooden chopsticks into the oil – it should bubble vigorously around them. Carefully add the rice discs and fry for 3 minutes, flipping halfway through, until lightly golden (avoid over-frying to prevent hardening).

For plain discs, split and fill after frying; or for filled discs, serve immediately after frying.

***Note:*** For leftover unfried portions, brush with oil and wrap in clingfilm (plastic wrap) to maintain their moisture. They will keep in the refrigerator for up to 2 days.

# FRIED STUFFED BUNS

Bánh Bao Chiên

While steamed buns are widely known, these fried versions are particularly popular as a student snack in Vietnam. This recipe features a traditional filling of jicama, minced (ground) pork and quail egg. Modern food stalls now offer creative variations, including durian and salted egg fillings.

Makes 14–15 buns
Preparation time: 30 minutes, plus 1 hour–1 hour 30 minutes proving time
Cooking time: 10–15 minutes per batch

- 350 g/12 oz (2⅓ cups) plain (all-purpose) flour, plus extra for dusting if needed
- 25 g/1 oz (⅓ cup) milk powder
- 4 g (approx. 1 teaspoon) fast-action (active) dried yeast
- 4 g (1 teaspoon) salt
- 15 g/½ oz (1 tablespoon) oil, plus extra for greasing if needed
- 25 g/1 oz (4 teaspoons) condensed milk
- 300 g/10½ oz Minced Pork and Jicama Filling (page 464, see note)
- 15 quail eggs, boiled and peeled
- vegetable oil, for deep-frying

In the bowl of a stand mixer fitted with a dough hook (or a large bowl if mixing by hand), combine the flour, milk powder and yeast.

In a separate bowl, whisk together 200 ml/7 fl oz (¾ cup plus 1 tablespoon) of water with the salt, oil, and condensed milk.

Add the liquid mixture to the dry ingredients, then mix on medium speed (or mix with your hands) until the dough comes together. Rest for 5 minutes.

Knead on high speed for 2 minutes, or until smooth (or knead in the bowl with yours hands until smooth).

Shape the dough into a ball, then place in a bowl, cover with clingfilm (plastic wrap) and let prove for 1 hour–1 hour 30 minutes, or until doubled in size.

Divide the dough into 40 g/1½ oz portions (14–15 pieces). Lightly flour or oil a clean work surface, then roll out each portion into a circle.

Place 20 g/¾ oz of the filling and one quail egg in the centre of each. Gather the edges over the top, folding the top edge in a zigzag like a concertina to make it look nice if you like, and pinch to seal.

Remove any excess dough (5–9 g/⅛–¼ oz) from the top where you have pinched it for even cooking, then let the shaped buns rest for 10 minutes.

Heat the oil to 160°C/320°F. If not using a thermometer, test the oil temperature by inserting wooden chopsticks into the oil – it should gently bubble around them. Working in batches if needed, to avoid overcrowded, carefully add the buns, then fry for 8–10 minutes, stirring and rotating for even cooking. Remove when golden brown and drain on paper towels.

Serve hot for the best texture and flavour.

*Notes:* You can customize the filling with more shiitake mushrooms or dice in some vermicelli if desired.

Be careful when deep-frying and maintain the oil temperature to ensure the buns cook evenly without absorbing too much oil.

# SAUTÉED WAXY BANANA WITH COCONUT MILK

## Chuối Xào Dừa

This snack from the south of Vietnam features *chuối sáp*, a variety of banana that is less sweet and more chewy than common bananas. Often called 'waxy banana', it develops a texture similar to plantain when cooked. These days, you can find frozen *chuối sáp* in many Asian supermarkets. Interestingly, even though it is a sweet dish, this recipe contains spring onion (scallion) because it is known to cut through the richness of the coconut milk, and give the dish a distinct flavour and aroma. An alternative method is to peel, smash and grill the bananas directly over hot coals; it would then be *chuối đập nước cốt dừa* (smashed banana with coconut milk).

Serves 4
Preparation time: 15 minutes, plus overnight soaking and chilling times
Cooking time: 30 minutes

| V | VE | DF | GF |

600 g/1 lb 5 oz waxy bananas (chuối sáp) (about 1 palm-size bunch/16–20)
30 g/1 oz (3 tablespoons) Toasted Peanuts (page 459), coarsely crushed, to garnish

*For the seasoned coconut milk*
20 g/¾ oz (2 tablespoons) tapioca pearls (bột báng)
210 g/7¼ oz (scant 1 cup) coconut milk
7 g/¼ oz pandan leaves (2–3 leaves), tied up
1 teaspoon sugar
1 teaspoon tapioca flour
2 tablespoons warm water
3 g spring onion (scallion), chopped

The day before serving, bring a pan of water to the boil and simmer the whole bananas for 20 minutes. Remove from the water and refrigerate overnight to make them very waxy and tasty.

Soak the tapioca pearls in a bowl of cold water overnight.

The next day, peel the chilled bananas and cut each into 3–4 vertical slices.

To prepare the seasoned coconut milk, in a pan, combine the coconut milk, pandan leaves and sugar, bring to a gentle simmer and cook for 2 minutes.

In a small bowl, mix the tapioca flour with the measured warm water. Stir the tapioca mixture into the simmering coconut milk, and cook for another 2 minutes.

Drain the tapioca pearls, add to the pan and simmer for 2–4 minutes until the pearls are translucent. Stir in the spring onion (scallion).

Arrange the banana slices flat on each serving bowl or plate. Pour the hot coconut sauce and pearls over the bananas and top with the crushed peanuts.

Serve immediately.

# MASHED SWEET POTATO AND BEANS

## Khoai Xéo

This Central Vietnamese snack combines dried sweet potato batons with black beans, peanuts and sticky (glutinous) rice. The name '*khoai xéo*' comes from the way the ingredients are mashed (*xéo*) together with chopsticks at the end of cooking. In Nghe An province, where sweet potatoes grow in abundance, locals created this preservation method to enjoy them year-round.

Serves 6–8
Preparation time: 30 minutes, plus 2–3 days dehydrating and overnight soaking times
Cooking time: 45 minutes

**| V | VE | DF | GF | ≤5 |**

350 g/12 oz white sweet potatoes, peeled and cut into 5–6-cm/2½-inch-long, 1-cm/½-inch-thick batons
200 g/7 oz (1 cup) black beans
150 g/5½ oz (1 cup) dried skin-on peanuts (or fresh peanuts)
200 g/7 oz (1 cup) sticky (glutinous) rice
120 g/4¼ oz (⅔ cup) sugar
¼ teaspoon salt

To prepare the sweet potato using the preservation method, lay the sweet potatoes on a tray (I use a woven tray to allows air flow) and set under direct sunlight to dehydrate for 2–3 days until hard. Alternatively, you can do this in a dehydrator. Store in an airtight container for year-round use.

In separate bowls, soak the black beans, peanuts (if using dry ones) and rice for at least 6 hours or overnight, rinsing twice during the soaking time.

Soak the sweet potato batons for 30 minutes–1 hour, rinsing several times.

To pre-cook the beans and peanuts, place in separate pans, cover with 2.5 cm/1 inch of water and bring to a simmer. Cook the peanuts, covered, for 10 minutes. Cook the beans, covered, for 4 minutes. Drain both separately.

In a large pot, combine the sweet potato batons with 1 litre/1¾ pints (4¼ cups) of water. Bring to a simmer over a high heat, cover, and cook for 5 minutes. Add the drained peanuts and beans without stirring. Cover and simmer over a medium heat for 5 minutes. Layer the rice on top without stirring. Cover and cook for 10 minutes.

Gently check the vegetables with a wooden spoon, and lightly stir to release some steam. Continue cooking on very low heat for 12 minutes, watching carefully to prevent burning. Add the sugar and salt, remove from the heat and stir gently to combine until the texture is soft, chewy and slightly sticky.

Line a container with baking (parchment) paper or lightly oil it to prevent sticking. Then press the mixture firmly into the container to form a solid block. Once cooled, cut into bite-size pieces for serving.

It is best served at room temperature, but it will keep for 1 week in the refrigerator. It can be reheated gently if desired.

# FRIED RICE FLOUR CAKE WITH EGGS

## Bột Chiên

A beloved street food in Ho Chi Minh City, *bột chiên* showcases the cultural fusion in Vietnamese cuisine. Originally introduced by the Chinese-Vietnamese community, this dish has evolved to become distinctly Vietnamese with the addition of green papaya salad as an accompaniment. It is known in Vietnamese food philosophy that papaya will help digest greasy food thanks to the enzyme papain present in it.

Serves 3
Preparation time: 30 minutes, plus overnight cooling time
Cooking time: 30 minutes

| V | DF |

- 200 g/7 oz (1⅓ cups) rice flour, sifted
- ½ teaspoon salt
- 455 ml/15 fl oz (scant 2 cups) boiling water
- 10 g/¼ oz spring onion (scallion), chopped
- 1 egg
- 2 tablespoons neutral oil, plus extra for greasing

*To serve*

- 225 g/8 oz young papaya, shredded
- 1 quantity sauce from Steamed Chive Dumplings (page 395)

In a small pot, whisk together the sifted rice flour and salt. Gradually add the measured boiling water while stirring constantly with a wooden spoon to prevent lumps from forming. Cook over a low heat for 7 minutes, or until the mixture thickens to a smooth, paste-like consistency, stirring continuously.

To steam the rice cakes, line an 18-cm/7-inch pan or mould with baking (parchment) paper and lightly oil the surface. Pour the hot batter into the prepared pan and smooth the surface with a spatula. Brush the top lightly with oil. Place a clean dish towel between the steamer lid and the pot to prevent condensation drips. Steam over a medium heat for 20 minutes, or until firm to the touch. Remove from heat, keep covered and let cool completely in the refrigerator overnight.

Remove the rice cake from the mould and cut into rectangles approximately 1 × 3 × 4 cm/½ × ¾ × 1½ inches. Place the cut pieces on a plate and let them air dry for 10 minutes at room temperature.

In a separate bowl, combine the chopped spring onion (scallion) with 1 beaten egg.

Heat a heavy frying pan or cast iron skillet over a medium heat. Add 1 tablespoon of the oil. Add the rice cake pieces and fry for 5 minutes, or until golden and crispy on all sides, turning occasionally. Add the remaining 1 tablespoon of oil, then pour in the egg mixture. Cook for 1–2 minutes until the egg is set .

Serve immediately with shredded young papaya, accompanied by the sauce.

# BREAD AND SANDWICHES

## Bánh mì

The French may have brought the baguette to Vietnam, but we turned it into our own version pretty quickly. The bread itself is light and crispy. The bread-making process was adapted to Vietnam's tropical climate, local ingredients and eating culture. You can recreate the bread with the recipe in this chapter, but do keep an eye on your environment, as this factor greatly affects your results. Remember, Vietnam is a humid tropical country with temperatures often around 30°C/86°F.

*Bánh mì* can be eaten simply with condensed milk for breakfast, as a side to dishes like 'Sizzling' Beef Steak (page 72) or stuffed and turned into a sandwich. In Vietnam, each *bánh mì* cart has their signature toppings, sauces, fried patties or original pâté – like the famous *pa tê cột đèn Hải Phòng* (Hai Phong lamp-post pâté).

To explore the realm of *bánh mì*, follow this basic combination: start with fat on the bottom (such as butter or mayonnaise), add your protein of choice, then add a sauce (such as meat sauce, soy sauce or seasoned fish sauce), followed by herbs, vegetables and pickles. Finish by adding some heat with freshly sliced chillies or chilli sauce.

# VIETNAMESE BAGUETTE

## Bánh Mì

As food historian Erica J. Peters documents in *Appetites and Aspirations in Vietnam*, bread making in colonial Vietnam began in the 1860s when the French military trained local workers to bake for their troops. What started as military provisions eventually spread through cities as Vietnamese and Chinese bakers opened their own *boulangeries*, making bread increasingly accessible to the local population. Over generations, bakers adapted the craft to local conditions. Nowadays, this has become a staple in the Vietnamese breakfast diet, and can also come in different shapes from rounded *bánh mì cóc* or long and thin *bánh mì que*.

Making these baguettes in Vietnam's tropical climate requires specific adjustments to flour types and attention to humidity levels. Nowadays, it is not uncommon to use bread improver to keep the bread consistent. If used, add 2.5 g to the recipe.

Makes 8
Preparation time: 15 minutes, plus 45 minutes proving and 8½ hours chilling times
Cooking time: 16 minutes

| V | ≤5 |

500 g/1 lb 2 oz (3⅓ cups) 13 per cent protein flour
5 g/⅛ oz (approx. 1½ teaspoons) fast-action (active) dried yeast
315 g/11 oz (1⅓ cups) refrigerator-cold water
10 g/¼ oz butter, plus 2 teaspoons for scoring
2 × 250 mg vials ascorbic acid
¼ teaspoon salt
oil, for greasing

In a stand mixer fitted with the dough hook, combine all the ingredients except the salt. Mix for 1–2 minutes on medium speed. Add the salt and knead for 1 more minute. Increase to high speed and mix for 2–3 minutes until the dough reaches 25°C/77°F.

Lightly oil a large bowl. Remove the dough from the mixer and transfer to the bowl. Cover with clingfilm (plastic wrap) and let rest for 30–40 minutes at room temperature (cooler climates will need the longer proofing time).

Divide the dough into 8 pieces (100 g/3½ oz each). Lightly oil the top of each piece. Cover with clingfilm and rest for 5 minutes.

To shape into baguettes, flatten each piece, roll tightly and taper the ends, then place on a baking sheet. Cover the shaped rolls and refrigerate for 8½ hours or overnight.

Remove the dough from the refrigerator 15 minutes before baking, leaving it uncovered. Using a bread knife or sharp blade, make a curved slash on the top of each baguette, then add a small piece of butter in the scored line.

Preheat the oven to 240°C/475°F/Gas Mark 9 with a tray on the bottom. Fill a spray bottle with water and set aside.

Place the bread in the oven, fill the tray on the bottom with 60–100 ml/2–3½fl oz (¼–⅓ cup) of water and then spray the bread with the water from the spray bottle 10 times. Reduce the heat to 170°C/340°F/Gas Mark 3½ and bake for 9 minutes. Remove the tray, increase the heat to 190°C/375°F/Gas Mark 5, and then bake for 5 more minutes or until golden brown. Flip the rolls over and bake for 2 more minutes on the other side. Alternatively, bake for 9 minutes, reduce the heat to 170°C/340°F/Gas Mark 3½ and bake for 7 more minutes. Remove from the oven and eat hot, fresh out of the oven or let cool for a sandwich. The baguettes will keep for up to 5 days.

# CARAMELIZED PORK SANDWICH

## Bánh Mì Thịt Khìa

While *bánh mì* is now known worldwide, it actually just means 'bread' or 'baguette'. The full name of this sandwich is '*bánh mì thịt (khìa)*', and it features caramelized pork. If you used only cold cuts of meat instead, it would be called '*bánh mì thịt nguội*'. It is also worth mentioning how interestingly this dish evolved when the Vietnamese diaspora brought it to France. There, they would use French baguette, which is a little bit denser than the Vietnamese counterpart, and most would make only pickled shredded carrots, shredded much finer, very much like the beloved French dish *carottes râpées* (grated pickled carrots).

The *thịt khìa* itself, pork slowly caramelized in coconut water until glazed, is also a key ingredient in *cơm tấm Long Xuyên* (Long Xuyen broken rice), where the pork is cut into matchsticks and served over broken rice.

Serves 1
Preparation time: 20 minutes
Cooking time: 50 minutes

*For the caramelized pork (thịt khìa) (makes enough for 6–8 sandwiches)*

- 500 g/1 lb 2 oz pork (thịt đầu rồng heo – the part connecting the chump/ham and the loin), with skin, or pork belly (side)
- 1 tablespoon Annatto Oil (page 457)
- 30 g/1 oz shallots, coarsely chopped
- 15 g/½ oz garlic, coarsely chopped
- 2 tablespoons fish sauce
- ¼ teaspoon salt
- 350 g/12 oz (1½ cups) coconut water
- 1 teaspoon sugar
- 60 g/2¼ oz onion, halved
- ⅛ teaspoon Caramel Braising Sauce (page 456)

*For the baguette (bánh mì)*

- 1 Vietnamese Baguette (page 66)
- 1 teaspoon Mayonnaise for Vietnamese Baguettes (page 478)
- 15 g/½ oz Pork Liver and Minced Pâté (page 81)
- 30 g/1 oz Caramelized Pork (see above), sliced
- 30 g/1 oz Vietnamese-style Cold Cuts (page 80)
- 25 g/1 oz Pork Roll (page 462)
- 30 g/1 oz cucumber, sliced
- 25 g/1 oz Pickled Daikon and Carrots (page 468)
- 5 g/⅛ oz coriander (cilantro)
- soy sauce (I use Maggi)
- sriracha sauce
- 2 slices of long red chillies
- salt and pepper

Bring 1 litre/1¾ pints (4¼ cups) of water to the boil in a large pot. Add the pork to the pot (cut the pork into large chunks, if needed to fit the pot). Stir gently and blanch for 2–3 minutes until the surface of the meat turns white. Remove the pork immediately using tongs, then rinse under cold running water. Pat completely dry with paper towels, then cut into 3 equal pieces (approximately 165 g/5¾ oz each). Let rest at room temperature while preparing the other ingredients.

In a pan over a medium heat, heat the oil. Add the shallots and garlic and sweat for 3 minutes. Add the pork chunks and stir-fry for 1 minute. Add the salt and fish sauce and stir-fry for another 1 minute. Add the coconut water, sugar, onion and caramel braising sauce, then bring to a simmer. Cover, reduce the heat to low and cook for 20 minutes.

Uncover and remove 75 ml/2½ fl oz (⅓ cup) of the sauce; reserve this for your sauce for the baguette.

Continue simmering for 30 minutes to reduce the sauce and caramelize the meat. Remove from the heat when the sauce has reduced and the meat is a brown caramel in colour. It should be nearly dry, with the glaze completely sticking to the meat. Cover the meat with clingfilm (plastic wrap) and store in the refrigerator for 3–4 days.

To assemble the baguette, use a sharp knife to split the baguette lengthways. Spread the mayonnaise and pâté on one side of the bread. Layer the caramelized pork slices, Vietnamese-style cold cuts, and pork rolls, then add the cucumber slices, pickled daikon and carrots and coriander (cilantro). Season with a pinch of salt and pepper, a dash of soy sauce, and a dash of sriracha. Top with chilli slices and drizzle with the reserved caramelized pork sauce.

Close the sandwich and serve.

# VIETNAMESE BAGUETTE WITH ROASTED PORK BELLY

Bánh Mì Thịt Heo Quay

Originally a Cantonese dish, roasted pork belly (side) is now found throughout Vietnam. In *bánh mì*, its rich crispiness contrasts with Vietnamese coriander/cilantro and pickles. If desired, substitute coriander (cilantro) for Vietnamese coriander, or make a mix of both.

Serves 1
Preparation time: 10 minutes

| ≤30 |

*For the sauce (bánh mì heo quay) (makes enough for 4–6 baguettes)*
- 25 g/1 oz peeled garlic
- ½ teaspoon neutral oil
- ½ teaspoon black pepper
- 50 g/1¾ oz (3½ tablespoons) light soy sauce
- 3 tablespoons water
- 2 teaspoons sugar

*For the baguette*
- 1 Vietnamese Baguette (page 66)
- 25 g/1 oz cucumber, thinly sliced
- 25 g/1 oz Pickled Daikon and Carrots (page 468)
- 50 g/1¾ oz Roasted Pork Belly (page 161), cut into thin slices with skin intact
- 10 g/¼ oz Vietnamese coriander/cilantro (rau răm), leaves picked
- 4–5 slices long red chilli, sliced diagonally
- 1–2 teaspoons sauce (bánh mì heo quay, see above)

Combine all the sauce ingredients in a small pan. Bring to a simmer and cook for 3 minutes. Set aside to cool.

Using a sharp knife, cut the baguette lengthways, leaving one side connected (like a hinge), creating a pocket for the filling.

Hold the baguette open and layer the ingredients in the following order: cucumber, pickled vegetables, roasted pork belly (side) pieces and Vietnamese coriander/cilantro. Finally, add the chilli slices and spread a layer of the sauce.

Close the sandwich and serve immediately while the bread is still crispy.

# VIETNAMESE BAGUETTE WITH SHREDDED PORK SKIN

Bánh Mì Bì

My childhood favourite, *bánh mì bì*'s appeal lies in its shredded pork skin coated with toasted rice powder, which adds a nutty flavour. Spring onion oil and fish sauce complement the meat, keeping this sandwich from being dry.

Serves 1
Preparation time: 10 minutes

| ≤5 | ≤30 |

- 1 Vietnamese Baguette (page 66)
- 5–10 g/⅛–¼ oz Spring Onion Oil with Fried Pork Fat (page 458)
- 50 g/1¾ oz Shredded Pork Skin Seasoned with Toasted Rice (page 460)
- 25 g/1 oz Pickled Daikon and Carrots (page 468)
- 4–5 slices long red chilli, sliced diagonally
- Sweet and Sour Fish Sauce (page 471)

Using a sharp knife, cut the baguette lengthways, leaving one side connected (like a hinge), creating a pocket for the filling.

Hold the baguette open and layer the ingredients in the following order: drizzle both sides of bread with the spring onion oil with fried pork fat; spread the shredded pork skin evenly over; layer the pickled vegetables on top of the pork; arrange the chilli slices evenly over it all; then drizzle with the sweet and sour fish sauce.

Close the sandwich and serve immediately while it is still crispy.

## VIETNAMESE BAGUETTE WITH GRILLED PORK SKEWERS

Bánh Mì Thịt Xiên Nướng

This *bánh mì* is a common sight on Hanoi streets and across Northern Vietnam, especially early mornings in front of schools and markets. You can choose how many skewers you want, and the vendor uses the bread to pull the meat off. Traditionally, the skewers are grilled over charcoal with the bread warmed alongside, but I've adapted this recipe for a home oven.

Serves 2
Preparation time: 10 minutes, plus 20 minutes marinating time
Cooking time: 15–20 minutes

¼ teaspoon Vietnamese (or Chinese) five-spice powder (ngũ vị hương)
½ teaspoon fish sauce
½ teaspoon oyster sauce
½ teaspoon honey or sugar cane syrup
¼ teaspoon black pepper
½ teaspoon Annatto Oil (page 457)
½ teaspoon all-purpose seasoning (hạt nêm)
¼ teaspoon Caramel Braising Sauce (page 456)
200 g/7 oz pork belly (side), skin removed, cut into 4–5-cm/1½–2-inch-thick slices, then uniform 5-mm/¼-inch cubes

*For the baguettes*
2 Vietnamese Baguettes (page 66)
50 g/1¾ oz cucumber, thinly sliced
50 g/1¾ oz Pickled Kohlrabi and Carrots (page 469)
20 g/¾ oz coriander (cilantro), leaves picked
Hanoi-style Chilli Sauce (page 477)

Soak 4–6 bamboo skewers in water for 30 minutes, then pat dry before using.

In a mixing bowl, combine the five-spice powder, fish sauce, oyster sauce, honey/sugar cane syrup, black pepper, annatto oil, all-purpose seasoning and caramel braising sauce. Mix until well combined. Add the pork cubes to the marinade and mix thoroughly to coat, then cover and refrigerate for 20 minutes.

Remove the pork from the refrigerator 5 minutes before grilling.

Thread 5–6 pork cubes onto each skewer, leaving small gaps between pieces. Make 4 even-size skewers. Reserve any remaining marinade for basting.

Preheat the grill (broiler) to 190°C/375°F or heat a barbecue grill and let the flames reduce so you have amber coals (medium heat).

Place the skewers on a rack in a pan and place under the grill or on the barbecue grill. Turning every 5 minutes (or every 1 minute on the barbecue) and basting with the remaining marinade, cook for 10–15 minutes until golden brown on all sides and thoroughly cooked through.

To assemble the baguettes, use a sharp knife, cut the baguettes lengthways, leaving one side connected (like a hinge), creating a pocket for the filling. Layer the cucumber and pickled vegetables. Remove the grilled pork from the skewers and arrange along the length of each baguette. Add the coriander (cilantro) leaves and finally the Hanoi chilli sauce to taste.

Close the sandwiches and briefly place under the grill or on the barbecue grill to crisp it. Serve immediately.

## VIETNAMESE BAGUETTE WITH FISH CAKE

Bánh Mì Chả Cá

This recipe uses mackerel for its elasticity, while the more traditional version, Fried Strabismus Fish Cake (page 463), uses freshwater fish and is often served with noodles. Traditionally these fish cakes were shaped into round patties and then thinly sliced. A new style has emerged, where the batter is pressed into long 'noodles' directly into hot oil for crispier edges. I like to add Pickled Daikon and Carrots (page 468) to this *bánh mì*.

Makes 1 baguette
Preparation time: approx. 30 minutes
Cooking time: 7–8 minutes

| ≤5 | ≤30 |

1 Vietnamese Baguette (page 66)
soy sauce (I use Maggi) or Sweet and Sour Fish Sauce (page 471), for drizzling
hot sauce, for drizzling
40–50 g/1½–1¾ oz Tuna Fish Cake (page 463), piped before cooking (see note)
4–5 chilli slices
25 g/1 oz cucumber, sliced
10 g/¼ oz Vietnamese coriander/cilantro (rau răm)

Using a sharp knife to split the baguette lengthways.

Layer the ingredients in the following order: sauce of your choice, hot sauce, fish cake pieces, chilli slices, cucumber and, Vietnamese coriander/cilantro.

***Note:*** To make piped fish cakes, heat the oil as in the recipe on page 463, then put the fishcake mixture into a piping (pastry) bag and pipe directly into the hot oil. Alternatively, you can make the fish cake into patties as in the tuna fish cake recipe and then cut it into pieces to serve.

## 'SIZZLING' BEEF STEAK

Bò Né

The name comes from the way this beef steak is served. The dish arrives on a sizzling small cast-iron frying pan with hot oil still bubbling and spattering, forcing you to lean back or dodge to avoid getting splashed. Now a favourite for breakfast, you can order it with one or two fried eggs on the same sizzling pan to go with a *bánh mì* (Vietnamese Baguette, page 66). *Bò né* is often served with crusty bread, fried eggs, and pâté on the side. You can also add a small bowl of soy sauce or fish sauce for dipping or scoop up 1–2 tablespoons of the cooking sauce for a dip.

Serves 3
Preparation time: 5 minutes, plus 10–15 minutes marinating time
Cooking time: 10 minutes

| DF | ≤30 |

- 200 g/7 oz beef rump (sirloin), cut into 3 pieces (9 × 9 cm/3½ × 3½ inches; 1.5-cm/¾-inch thick)
- ½ teaspoon oyster sauce
- 2 teaspoons light soy sauce
- 10 g/¼ oz garlic, minced
- 10 g/¼ oz shallot, minced
- 90 g/3¼ oz white onion, quartered
- 95 g/3½ oz (⅔ cup) cherry tomatoes, halved, or bull's heart tomatoes, quartered
- 3 Vietnamese Baguettes (page 66), to serve

Make shallow slits on the surface of each beef piece. Using a meat mallet, flatten each piece of beef.

Mix the oyster sauce, light soy sauce, minced garlic and minced shallot in a bowl. Coat the beef pieces in this mixture and let it sit for 10–15 minutes.

Heat a cast iron pan frying pan or skillet over a medium–high heat. Cook the marinated beef for about 5 minutes until fully cooked, flipping once. Add the quartered onions and the tomatoes to the pan with the beef. Cook for an additional 1–2 minutes until the vegetables are slightly charred but still crisp.

To serve, transfer the hot cast iron pan directly to the table. Serve immediately, while the pan is still sizzling, with warm baguettes.

## VIETNAMESE BAGUETTE WITH COMBO PAN

Bánh Mì Chảo

The name of this dish literally means 'bread with pan', as all the toppings and sauces are served on a sizzling pan. Think of it as Vietnam's answer to a full English breakfast. While this recipe includes basic toppings, street vendors offer customization options from cheese spread to frankfurters and various cold cuts. The best way to serve this is on a small sizzling cast-iron frying pan, as it will keep everything warm as you eat.

Serves 1
Preparation time: 5 minutes, plus 15 minutes marinating time
Cooking time: 10 minutes

| ≤30 |

- 20 g/¾ oz butter
- 20 g/¾ oz onion, sliced
- 1 teaspoon oyster sauce
- ½ teaspoon light soy sauce
- 1 egg
- 2 meatballs plus 3–4 tablespoons sauce from Pork Meatballs with Tomato Sauce (page 305)
- 35 g/1¼ oz Pork Liver and Minced Pâté (page 81)
- ½ frankfurter, optional

*For the marinated beef*

- 80 g/2¾ oz beef tenderloin, thinly sliced
- ½ teaspoon light soy sauce
- 1 teaspoon oyster sauce
- 5 g/⅛ oz garlic, chopped
- ¼ teaspoon black pepper

*To serve*

- 5 g/⅛ oz coriander (cilantro), optional
- Salt and Pepper Seasoning Mix (page 480)
- 1 Vietnamese Baguette (page 66)
- 30 g/1 oz Pickled Daikon and Carrots (page 468)
- 3–4 slices cucumber
- 25 g/1 oz Pork Roll (page 462), sliced

Prepare the marinated beef: in a small bowl, combine the sliced beef, light soy sauce, oyster sauce, garlic and black pepper. Mix well and marinate for 15 minutes at room temperature.

Heat a pan over a medium heat. Add the butter and let it completely melt. Add the onion and sauté for 2–3 minutes until translucent. Add the marinated beef to the pan and stir-fry for 2–3 minutes until the beef is just cooked. Add the oyster sauce and light soy sauce, then pour in 1 teaspoon of water to create a glaze. Stir to combine.

Push the beef and onions to one side of the pan, then crack the egg into the empty space. Cook to your desired doneness (I recommend sunny-side up).

Add the meatballs, pâté and frankfurter (if using) to the pan and heat through for 1–2 minutes.

To serve, arrange all the pan components on a serving plate. Garnish with coriander (cilantro) leaves, if desired, add a sprinkle of the salt and pepper mix and serve with a warm baguette, pickled vegetables, sliced cucumber, pork roll. You can add additional condiments, such as soy sauce, hot sauce and mayonnaise, if liked.

# ĐÀ LẠT-STYLE MEATBALLS

## Xíu Mại Đà Lạt

These meatballs became a Đà Lạt speciality, perhaps because the mountain city's cool weather makes hot broth dishes especially enticing. While the rest of Vietnam goes through periods of heatwave, it seems like Đà Lạt is always cool, like spring in Europe. For this reason, it was an attractive place to French colonists and their families to go on holiday; with the French-inspired architecture and being reminiscent of the French Alps, it was the perfect location for homesick colonists to settled.

From early morning, vendors serve these meatballs with slices of pork skin alongside freshly grilled bread. You can also eat *bánh mì* with the more traditional *xíu mại* (Pork Meatballs with Tomato Sauce, page 305).

Serves 4–5
Preparation time: 30 minutes
Cooking time: 35–40 minutes

| **DF** |

1 tablespoon Annatto Oil (page 457)
10 g/¼ oz garlic, minced
20 g/¾ oz shallots, minced
100 g/3½ oz onion, sliced
60 g/2¼ oz pork skin, blanched and cut into 2–3-cm/1-inch cubes
650 ml/22 fl oz (2¾ cups) Basic Pork Stock (page 464), or 650 ml/22 fl oz (2¾ cups) water mixed with 1 teaspoon fish sauce and ¼ teaspoon sugar
1 teaspoon fish sauce
1 quantity meatball base from Pork Meatballs with Tomato Sauce (page 305)

*For the sauce*
400 g/14 oz tomatoes, roughly cut into 2-cm/¾-inch chunks
½ teaspoon salt
1½ teaspoons sugar
2 tablespoons neutral oil
2 teaspoons Annatto Oil (page 457)
25 g/1 oz shallots, coarsely chopped
20 g/¾ oz garlic, coarsely chopped
90 g/3¼ oz onion, sliced

*To serve*
30 g/1 oz spring onions (scallions), chopped
10 g/¼ oz coriander (cilantro) leaves, leaves roughly picked
15 g/½ oz Vietnamese basil, leaves picked
4–5 Vietnamese Baguettes (page 66)
Shrimp, Chilli and Lemongrass Oil (page 457) or Chilli and Lemongrass Oil (page 457), to taste

In a large pot, heat the annatto oil over a medium heat. Add the garlic and shallots and fry for 2–3 minutes until softened and fragrant. Add half the onion and the pork skin and continue frying for 1 minute, or until the onion starts to soften. Add the stock (broth) (or water with additional seasonings) and the fish sauce, then bring to a gentle simmer.

Gently drop the prepared meatballs into the simmering broth. Cook for 20 minutes, maintaining a gentle simmer. Occasionally skim any foam that rises to the surface.

Meanwhile, prepare the sauce. In a bowl, combine the tomatoes with the salt and sugar and set aside.

Heat the neutral oil and annatto oil in a separate pan over a medium-low heat. Add the shallots and garlic and fry for about 3 minutes, or until softened. Add the seasoned tomatoes and onion and cook over a medium heat for 10 minutes, stirring occasionally, until the tomatoes break down.

To combine and finish, pour the tomato sauce into the meatball broth. Simmer for 1–2 minutes to combine the flavours.

Ladle the meatballs and broth into bowls. Garnish with the spring onions (scallions), remaining onion, coriander (cilantro) leaves and Vietnamese basil leaves. Serve hot with warm baguettes, with chilli and lemongrass oil on the side for diners to add to taste.

# STEWED PORK TONGUE WITH PÂTÉ

Lưỡi Heo Hầm Pa Tê

This stew incorporates Pork Liver and Minced Pâté (page 81) with pork tongue, an underappreciated and economical cut of meat. The pâté adds depth to the braising liquid while tenderizing the tongue.

Serves 5–6
Preparation time: 30 minutes
Cooking time: 1 hour 20 minutes

- 900 g/2 lb pork tongue
- 15 g/½ oz peeled garlic
- 20 g/¾ oz peeled shallots
- 1 tablespoon Annatto Oil (page 457)
- 340 g/12 oz Pork Liver and Minced Pâté (page 81)
- 1 heaped teaspoon oyster sauce
- ½ teaspoon salt
- 1 tablespoon fish sauce
- 500 ml/18 fl oz (2 cups) coconut water
- 225 g/8 oz carrots, peeled and cut into 1-cm/½-inch-thick flowers (see note)
- 5–6 Vietnamese Baguette (page 66), to serve

Bring a large pot of 500 ml/18 fl oz (2 cups) of water to a rolling boil. Add the pork tongue, ensuring it is fully covered by the water, and boil for 2–3 minutes to blanch. Remove and plunge into cold water. When cool enough to handle, peel off the outer skin using a small knife (it should slip off easily now). You should have about 800 g/1 lb 12 oz after peeling. Cut the peeled tongue into 4-cm/1½-inch chunks.

Put the garlic and shallots in a mortar and pound with a pestle to a fine paste.

Heat the oil in a stockpot over a medium heat until shimmering. Add the pounded garlic and shallot paste, then fry for 1–2 minutes until fragrant and lightly golden. Add the diced tongue and the pâté, then add the oyster sauce and stir-fry for 2 minutes, evenly coating the meat. Add the salt and fish sauce, then stir well. Pour in the coconut water. Bring to a simmer and cook for 15 minutes, stirring occasionally. Add the carrot flowers and 300 ml/10 fl oz (1¼ cups) of water, then return a to simmer. Cook, uncovered, for 1 hour, or until the tongue is tender when pierced, skimming any foam that rises to surface.

To serve, divide the stew between 5–6 bowls. Serve hot with warm baguettes.

*Note:* To make carrot flowers, make small V-shaped notches around the circumference.

# PORK OFFAL STEW IN FIVE-SPICE SAUCE

## Phá Lấu

Originally a Teochew dish, *phá lấu* has become a local favourite in Saigon, especially in district 5, Saigon's own Chinatown. This dish has evolved since arriving in Vietnam: while keeping the Chinese red-braising technique with five-spice powder and soy sauce, local cooks add distinctly Vietnamese elements like lemongrass and coconut water, creating a unique hybrid of two culinary traditions. You can either dip the bread in the stew, or make a sandwich with the offal (variety meats). It often pairs with *rau răm* (Vietnamese coriander/cilantro).

Serves 6–8
Preparation time: 45 minutes
Cooking time: 1 hour 45 minutes

| DF |

- 60 g/2¼ oz lemongrass, crushed
- 30 g/1 oz piece fresh ginger (about 6 cm/2½ inches), crushed
- 3 teaspoons salt
- 450 g/1 lb pork tongue
- 450 g/1 lb pig's ears, cleaned and hair removed
- 600 g/1 lb 5 oz pig stomachs
- 200 g/7 oz pig large intestines

*For the braising sauce*

- 30 g/1 oz (2 tablespoons packed) light brown sugar
- 50 g/1¾ oz light soy sauce
- 20 g/¾ oz (1 heaping tablespoon) Chilli and Lemongrass Oil (page 457)
- ¼ teaspoon black pepper
- 3 tablespoons neutral oil
- 40 g/1½ oz garlic, minced
- 40 g/1½ oz shallots, minced
- 20 g/¾ oz lemongrass stalks
- 1 tablespoon fish sauce
- ½ teaspoon Vietnamese five-spice powder (ngũ vị hương)
- 300 ml/10 fl oz (1¼ cups) coconut water
- 1 teaspoon oyster sauce

*To serve*

- 30 g/1 oz Vietnamese coriander/cilantro (rau răm)
- 150 g/5½ oz cucumber, sliced
- Salt and Pepper Seasoning Mix (page 480), optional

*For the salt, pepper and lime dip (muối tiêu chanh), optional*

- 4 teaspoons light soy sauce
- 1 teaspoon Chilli and Lemongrass Oil (page 457)
- 1 teaspoon sugar
- 1 teaspoon lime juice

In a large pot, bring 2.5 litres/4½ pints (10½ cups) of water to a simmer with the crushed lemongrass and ginger and the salt. Add all the meats except the ears. Boil for 10 minutes to blanch. Drain and rinse thoroughly with salted water multiple times to remove any strong odours.

For the tongue: while still hot, use a small, sharp knife to carefully scrape off the entire outer surface – you'll see the rough, white outer skin layer separate from the meat underneath. Start from the thick end and work towards the tip.

To prepare the braising sauce, in a pot, combine the brown sugar, soy sauce, chilli and lemongrass oil and black pepper. Set aside.

In a separate pan, heat the neutral oil over a medium–low heat. Add the garlic and shallots and fry for 10 minutes.

Add these fried aromatics to the sauce mixture, then add all the blanched meats and the ears to the sauce. Add the lemongrass stalks, fish sauce, ¼ teaspoon of the five-spice powder and the coconut water. Cover and simmer over a low heat for 45 minutes to release the meat juices. Carefully remove the meats, and let cool slightly.

Thinly slice the tongue across grain. Cut the ears into thin strips. Cut the stomach and intestines into bite-size pieces.

Return all the meat to the pot. Add the remaining five-spice powder and the oyster sauce. Simmer for an additional 30 minutes, stirring occasionally to coat the meat with the sauce.

To prepare the salt, pepper and lime dip, if using, combine all the ingredients in a bowl. Alternatively serve with the salt and pepper seasoning mix.

Arrange the sliced meats in a small bowl. Garnish with the Vietnamese coriander/cilantro. Serve with the cucumber slices and your chosen dipping sauce.

# STEAMED BAGUETTES

## Bánh Mì Hấp

In Vietnam, stale bread finds new life in two different dishes: *bánh chuối nướng* (Baked Banana Cake, page 422) or *bánh mì hấp*, in which the bread is steamed to restore its moisture. While topping combinations vary between households, they often start with stir-fried minced (ground) meat and spring onion (scallion) oil. These steamed slices are served wrapped in fresh herbs and lettuce, then dipped in Basic Dipping Fish Sauce (page 470).

Makes 10; serves 4–5
Preparation time: 45 minutes
Cooking time: 25 minutes

5 stale Vietnamese Baguettes (page 66), halved lengthways and then halved widthways to make little boat shapes

*For the pork*
3 tablespoons neutral oil
400 g/14 oz lean minced (ground) pork,
25 g/1 oz garlic, coarsely chopped
1 tablespoon fish sauce
½ teaspoon black pepper

*For the fried shallots and onions*
4 tablespoons neutral oil
50 g/1¾ oz shallots, thinly sliced
1 small onion, sliced into rings

*For the jieama*
375 g/13 oz jicama (approx. 310 g/11 oz after peeling), peeled and cut into 3-mm/⅛-inch-thick dice (brunoised)
1 tablespoon fish sauce
¼ teaspoon black pepper

*For the spring onion oil*
5 tablespoons neutral oil
45 g/1½ oz Crispy Fried Pork Fat (page 459)
145 g/5 oz spring onions (scallions), diced
½ teaspoon fish sauce

*To serve*
25 g/1 oz spring onions (scallions), chopped
70 g/2½ oz Pickled Daikon and Carrots (page 468)
Basic Dipping Fish Sauce (page 470)
1 butterhead lettuce (150 g/5½ oz), optional
150 g/5½ oz aromatic mixed herbs (rau thơm – basil, fish mint, coriander/cilantro, spearmint), leaves picked, optional

To prepare the pork, heat the oil in a large frying pan or skillet over a medium heat. Add the minced (ground) pork and garlic and season with fish sauce and black pepper. Fry until the pork is thoroughly cooked, 8–10 minutes, then set aside.

Set up a steamer and bring the water to the boil. Arrange the baguette pieces in the steamer basket, set over the boiling water and steam for 10 minutes, or until softened. Remove and keep warm.

To prepare the fried shallots and onions, heat the oil in small pan over a medium-low heat. Add the shallots and fry until golden brown, 5–6 minutes. Add the onion rings, and cook until translucent, 3–4 minutes. Remove with a slotted spoon and drain on paper towels.

To cook the jicama, using the same pan and oil from the shallots and onion, heat over a medium heat, then add the jicama, and season with the fish sauce and black pepper. Cook until tender but still crisp, 5–6 minutes, then set aside.

To make the spring onion oil, heat the oil and crispy fried pork fat to 180°C/350°F. If not using a thermometer, test the oil temperature by inserting wooden chopsticks into the oil – it should bubble vigorously around them.

Place the spring onions (scallions) in a heatproof bowl. Carefully pour the hot oil over the spring onions. Add the fish sauce and stir. Set aside.

To assemble, set up the steamer and bring the water to the boil over a low heat. Top each baguette piece with a portion of cooked pork, a portion of fried shallots and onions and a portion of the cooked jicama. Place in the steamer basket, set over the boiling water and steam for 2 minutes. Then remove from the heat.

Drizzle the steamed baguettes with the spring onion oil. Arrange on a serving platter and garnish with the chopped spring onions. Serve immediately with the pickled vegetables and dipping sauce on the side. Wrap with butterhead lettuce and herbs, if you like.

# VIETNAMESE-STYLE COLD CUTS

Thịt Nguội

One of many Vietnamese cold cuts of meat essential to *bánh mì*, this preparation combines various cuts of pork, including pork skin. While traditionally wrapped in banana leaves, like in Pork Roll (page 462), it can also be prepared using the French ballotine technique, wrapped tightly in clingfilm and then in aluminium foil before steaming.

Serves 8–10
Preparation time: 1 hour 15 minutes
Cooking time: 1 hour

| DF |

- 1 lemongrass stalk
- 500 g/1 lb 2 oz pork skin
- 535 g/2 lb 3 oz pork loin
- 515 g/1 lb 2 oz pork fillet/tenderloin (thịt thăn chuột)
- 120 ml/4 fl oz (½ cup) neutral oil
- 50 g/1¾ oz garlic, coarsely chopped
- 50 g/1¾ oz shallots, coarsely chopped
- 320 g/11¼ oz Pork Paste (page 461)
- 1 teaspoon Cantonese cooking wine (rượu mai quế lộ)
- 4 teaspoons fish sauce
- 3 g (½ teaspoon) shiitake all-purpose seasoning (hạt nêm)
- 15 g/½ oz (1½ tablespoons) tapioca starch
- 15 g/½ oz (1½ tablespoons) cornflour (cornstarch)
- 5 g/⅛ oz (1 teaspoon) salt
- 10 g/¼ oz (2½ teaspoons) sugar
- 5 g/⅛ oz black pepper
- about 20 whole peppercorns

*For wrapping*

- banana leaves, blanched (see step 3, page 390), cut into 2 squares of 35 cm/14 inches and 1 square of 28 cm/11 inches

Bring a pot of salted water with the lemongrass to the boil, add the pork skin, then cook for 10 minutes, or until tender but still firm. Remove and let cool before thinly slicing.

Cut the pork loin and tenderloin into 8 × 7 × 4-cm/3 × 2¾ × 1½-inch chunks, then thinly slice each chunk.

In a small pan, heat half the oil over a medium-low heat. Add the garlic and fry for about 5 minutes until just before golden. Transfer the garlic and oil to a small bowl. Separate 1 tablespoon of the garlic oil and set aside separately, for brushing the leaves.

In the same pan, heat the remaining oil over a medium-low heat. Add the shallots and fry for 4–5 minutes until golden.

In a large bowl, combine the sliced pork skin, loin and tenderloin with the remaining ingredients and the fried garlic and shallots with their oil. Mix thoroughly, then marinate for 30 minutes at room temperature.

Set up a steamer and bring the water to the boil.

Clean and dry the banana leaves thoroughly. Brush the reserved garlic oil over all the leaves.

On a work surface, layer the larger leaves first, then the smaller leaf on top. Place 500 g/1 lb 2 oz of the meat mixture in the centre of the leaves. Roll tightly into a log shape. Secure the ends and middle with kitchen string. Tie like a porchetta or roast beef, spacing the string about 4 cm/1½ inches apart.

Place the wrapped meat in the steamer basket, set over the boiling water and steam for 45 minutes. Remove and let cool to room temperature. Refrigerate overnight.

To serve, remove from refrigerator and thinly slice.

# PORK LIVER AND MINCED PÂTÉ

## Pa Tê

Hải Phòng, a port city in northeastern Vietnam, is renowned for its pâté. Story has it that the spread first arrived in the 1890s with French chefs on ships. While initially served in colonial restaurants, it gradually became used more widely, evolving towards local tastes and techniques. Without home ovens, Vietnamese cooks developed their own methods, typically steaming the pâté or cooking it directly in the pan. Today, this spread appears not just in *bánh mì* (Vietnamese Baguette, page 66), but also in dishes like *xôi mặn* (Savoury Sticky Rice, page 248) and *lưỡi heo hầm pa tê* (Stewed Pork Tongue with Pâté, page 76).

Serves 10; makes 2 trays
Preparation time: 30 minutes, plus overnight soaking time
Cooking time: 45 minutes–1 hour 30 minutes

- 500 g/1 lb 2 oz pork liver
- 100 g/3½ oz Vietnamese Baguette (page 66)
- 2 eggs
- 120 ml/4 fl oz (½ cup) milk, plus extra for soaking the liver
- 50 g/1¾ oz (3½ tablespoons) butter
- 220 g/7¾ oz onion, diced
- 150 g/5½ oz pork fat, diced
- 50 g/1¾ oz shallots, coarsely chopped
- 30 g/1 oz garlic, coarsely chopped
- 350 g/12 oz minced (ground) pork (20–30 per cent fat)
- 2 tablespoons fish sauce
- 1¼ teaspoons black pepper
- 1 teaspoon sugar
- ½ teaspoon salt
- ¼ teaspoon Vietnamese five-spice powder (ngũ vị hương)
- 10–14 rashers (slices) bacon, optional

The night before, prepare the liver: slice the liver into 2.5-cm/1-inch pieces. Place in a bowl and cover with milk. Soak overnight in the refrigerator. Drain and pat dry before using.

Tear the baguette into small pieces. Place in a bowl and combine with the eggs and milk. Let stand for 10 minutes, or until the bread softens.

Melt 30 g/1 oz (2 tablespoons) of the butter in a large pan over a medium heat. Add the onion, then cook for 3 minutes, or until softened. Add the pork fat, then cook for 5 minutes to render. Add the shallots and cook for 1 minute. Add the garlic and cook for another 3 minutes, or until fragrant. Add the minced (ground) pork, then season with 1 tablespoon of the fish sauce and ½ teaspoon of the black pepper. Cook for 2–3 minutes until the meat changes colour. Remove from the pan and set aside.

In the same pan, melt the remaining butter. Add the liver and quickly sear for 1 minute. The liver should still be pink inside.

In blender, combine the cooked meat mixture, seared liver and soaked bread mixture. Blend for 30 seconds, or until smooth. Add the remaining 1 tablespoon of fish sauce and ¾ teaspoon of black pepper, with the sugar, salt and five-spice powder. Blend again until well combined.

If using bacon, line two 13 × 25 × 6-cm/5 × 10 × 2½-inch rectangular pans or two 15 × 7-cm/6 × 2¾-inch round pans with the bacon. Fill with the pâté mixture, then cover tightly with aluminium foil.

To cook, either steam or cook in the oven. To steam: steam for 45 minutes per batch. Check the internal temperature reaches 71°C/160°F.

To cook in the oven, preheat the oven to 160°C/325°F/Gas Mark 3. Place the pans in one or two larger pans. Fill half-full with water, then place in the oven. Bake for 45 minutes, or until internal temperature reaches 71°C/160°F.

Allow to cool completely in the pans. Refrigerate for a minimum of 4 hours or overnight.

Unmould when completely chilled. Slice and serve chilled as needed.

NT91144TS
1.6
1.2

# SEAFOOD AND SNAILS

## Món ốc và món hải sản

As Vietnam is a coastal country, seafood plays a big role in the Vietnamese diet. While some seafood like Venus clams are commonly prepared at home, most seafood is enjoyed at *quán ốc* – eateries specializing in fresh live seafood and snails. Along with sea snails, we also eat river snails like *ốc bươu* (apple snails), especially in northern regions.

At a *quán ốc*, you first select your fresh seafood and its weight, then you choose how you want it prepared. Each region has its signature *quán ốc* utilizing local specialties – like the famous *ốc nhảy* (jumping snails) in Vinh Hy Bay. The freshness is key: sea snails should be alive and actively moving, clams should be tightly closed and crabs should feel heavy for their size.

The dishes in this chapter represent classic preparations found in *quán ốc* across Vietnam. I've included several essential sauces that you can mix and match with the different types of seafood available to you. While some preparations may seem complex, the fundamental technique lies in preserving the natural sweetness of the seafood by not overcooking it, and in adding a complementary sauce.

# TAMARIND FRIED CRABS

## Cua Rang Me

Traditionally, meaty live crabs called '*cua thịt*' are used for this dish, with those from the Ca Mau province in the Mekong Delta region being especially sought after. If unavailable, you can substitute with live Dungeness, mud or brown crabs. This dish is best served with fresh Vietnamese coriander/cilantro (sometimes called hot mint) and a toasty *banh mi* (Vietnamese Baguette, page 66) on the side for mopping up the sauce. The sauce needs to be tangy with a bit of sweetness; you can adjust your level of sweetness to taste.

Serves 2–3 as a starter (appetizer)
Preparation time: 30 minutes
Cooking time: 20–25 minutes

| DF |

550 g/1 lb 4 oz live crabs (about 2 small crabs)
50 g/2 oz (¼ cup) lard or cooking oil
35 g/1¼ oz garlic, minced
45 g/1½ oz shallots, minced

*For the sauce*
110 ml/3¾ fl oz (scant ½ cup) boiling water
50 g/1¾ oz tamarind pulp with seeds
3 tablespoons light brown sugar
1½ tablespoons fish sauce
½ teaspoon black pepper
½ teaspoon cornflour (cornstarch)
20 g/¾ oz calamansi juice

*To serve*
30 g/1 oz Crispy Fried Pork Fat (page 459)
1 bunch Vietnamese coriander/cilantro (rau răm)
Freshly ground black pepper

Place the crabs in the freezer for 30 minutes before preparing the rest of the ingredients.

To make the sauce, pour the measured boiling water over the tamarind pulp in a bowl. Let infuse for 10–15 minutes, then strain to obtain 60–70 g/2¼–2½ oz tamarind paste. Mix with the sugar, fish sauce and black pepper. Set aside.

In a separate bowl, combine the cornflour and calamansi juice with 4 tablespoons of room temperature water. Set aside.

Remove the crabs from the freezer. Place the crabs bottom-side up on a chopping (cutting) board. Find the small hole near the rear (near the tail flap) and the slight depression near the front (thoracic and cerebral ganglia); with a spiking tool or sharp-pointed knife, spike all the way through the hole near the rear, then through the slight depression near the front.

Working over a bowl to catch the yellow crab head juice (tomalley) from the top shell, cut off the abdominal flap and split the top shell (carapace) from the belly of each crab, then split the bottom widthways to make it easier to fry. Reserve the yellow crab head juice in the bowl for the sauce.

To cook the crabs, heat the lard or oil in large wok over a medium heat. Add the crab halves and top shells (carapaces), and stir-fry for about 5 minutes until the colour of the shells changes completely. Add the minced garlic, then fry 2–3 minutes until golden. Lower the heat, add the shallots and cook for another 2 minutes until translucent.

To finish the sauce, add the reserved crab head juice and tamarind mixture to the wok, then stir-fry for 3–4 minutes to combine the flavours. Stir the cornflour mixture in its bowl and then slowly add to the wok. Cook for about 1 minute, or until the sauce becomes glossy and slightly thickened. Remove from the heat and stir in the fried pork fat.

Coat the fried crabs with some of the sauce, then arrange on a bed of Vietnamese coriander/cilantro, reassembled with the top shells arranged on top, and finish with freshly ground black pepper. Serve with the remaining sauce mixture in a small bowl on the side.

TAMARIND FRIED CRABS

## SALT AND PEPPER FRIED CRABS

Cua Rang Muối

My nanny cô Vương Thị Minh Hiếu taught me how to make this dish, which is a staple at seafood eateries but is simple enough to make at home. Unlike Tamarind Fried Crabs (page 84), which comes with a sauce, this version is dryer, and comes with crispy garlic bits.

Serves 2
Preparation time: 10 minutes, plus 30 minutes marinating time
Cooking time: 15 minutes

| DF |

2 crabs (about 400 g/14 oz each)
neutral oil, for frying
Salt and Pepper Seasoning Mix (page 480) or Green Chilli Salt (page 480), to serve

*For the crab marinade*
¼ teaspoon salt
½ teaspoon MSG
1 teaspoon sugar
½ teaspoon all-purpose seasoning (hạt nêm)
½ teaspoon black pepper
1 teaspoon minced garlic

*For the sauce*
2 tablespoons neutral oil
2 tablespoons chopped garlic
½ teaspoon all-purpose seasoning (hạt nêm)
½ teaspoon salt
½ teaspoon sugar
1 teaspoon lemon juice
¼ teaspoon black pepper
20 g/¾ oz spring onion (scallion) greens, sliced

Place the crabs in the freezer for 30 minutes before preparing the rest of the ingredients.

Remove the crabs from the freezer. Place the crabs bottom-side up on a chopping (cutting) board. Find the small hole near the rear (near the tail flap) and the slight depression near the front (thoracic and cerebral ganglia); with a spiking tool or sharp-pointed knife, spike all the way through the hole near the rear, then through the slight depression near the front.

To clean the crabs, cut off the abdominal flap and remove the top shells from the belly of each crab; set aside the crab roe, if the crabs are female. Cut each crab belly in half (or quarters if large) to make it easier to fry.

Prepare the crab marinade: mix all the ingredients together in a bowl. Add the crab pieces and thoroughly coat, then let marinate for 30 minutes.

Heat enough of the frying oil to submerge the crabs in a large pan over a high heat. Add the crab pieces, then lower the heat to medium-low. Fry the crab pieces for 5 minutes on each side, then remove and drain excess oil on paper towels.

Crack the claws of the crabs, so they absorb more of the sauce.

To make the sauce, in another pan, heat the oil over a medium heat, add the crab roe and stir-fry for 1 minute. Add the garlic and fry for 30 seconds–1 minute until fragrant. Add the all-purpose seasoning, salt, sugar, lemon juice and black pepper. Add the fried crab pieces and cook for 2 minutes. Remove from the heat, then add the spring onion (scallion) greens.

Serve immediately while hot, with your chosen seasoning mix.

## STEAMED CLAMS WITH LEMONGRASS

Nghêu Hấp Sả

The clams are slowly cooked and steamed in their own juices, resulting in an extremely flavourful broth infused with lemongrass, lime leaves and chilli. It is best served with *mắm sả ớt nam/bắc* (Lemongrass and Chilli Dipping Sauce, Southern/Northern Style, page 472) or simply with Salt and Pepper Seasoning Mix (page 480).

Serves 2–3 as a starter (appetizer)
Preparation time: 5 minutes
Cooking time: 2–5 minutes

| DF | ≤30 |

500 g/1 lb 2 oz clams (nghêu)
sliced bird's eye chillies, for cleaning
½ teaspoon fish sauce
2 lemongrass stalks (minimum 30 g/1 oz), thinly sliced on an angle
10 g/¼ oz long red chilli (about ½ chilli), cut into thin rounds
1 lime leaf, coarsely shredded, optional
salt

Soak the clams in a bowl of salted water with the bird's eye chilli slices to purge impurities; the chilli and salt will make the clams open up and release all the sand stored inside.

To steam the clams, in a shallow, approximately 20-cm/8-inch, pot, combine the cleaned clams and fish sauce with 3 tablespoons of water. Add all the prepared aromatics. Cover with the lid. Place the pot over a medium heat. The cooking time will vary depending on your pot type: thinner-bottomed pots will take approximately 2 minutes, while cast-iron pots or pans may take longer, up to 5 minutes. Cook until all the clams have opened. Remove from the heat, discard any shells that have not opened and serve immediately while hot.

# APPLE SNAILS STUFFED WITH PORK

## Ốc Bươu Nhồi Thịt

Apple snails, a staple in Vietnamese cuisine, are commonly found in rice fields, freshwater ponds and rivers. They are particularly enjoyed as a starter (appetizer) at banquets and during celebrations. In this recipe, the snails are stuffed with a flavourful mixture of minced (ground) pork, mushrooms and pork paste, then steamed over lemongrass for added aroma. The pork paste gives the filling a delightful springy texture. You can enjoy this dish with Ginger Dipping Fish Sauce (page 474) or simply Salt and Pepper Seasoning Mix (page 480).

Serves 4–6 as a starter (appetizer)
Preparation time: 30 minutes
Cooking time: 40 minutes

| DF |

- 22 lime leaves
- 2 handfuls lemongrass trimmings and scraps
- 1 kg/2 lb 4 oz apple snails (ốc bươu) (approx. 24 snails)
- 24 lemongrass leaves, cut into 15-cm/6-inch lengths
- Ginger Dipping Fish Sauce (page 474) or Lemongrass and Chilli Dipping Sauce (page 472), to serve

*For the stuffing*

- 10 g/¼ oz dried wood ear mushrooms, soaked and finely chopped
- 25 g/1 oz lemongrass, finely minced
- 35 g/1¼ oz shallots, coarsely chopped
- 15 g/½ oz garlic, coarsely chopped
- 1 lime leaf, finely sliced
- 5 g/⅛ oz (2 teaspoons) whole peppercorns
- 170 g/5¾ oz minced (ground) pork
- 100 g/3½ oz Pork Paste (page 461)
- 1 tablespoon fish sauce

Bring a large pot of water to the boil. Add 2 of the lime leaves and one of the handfuls of lemongrass trimmings and scraps. Add the snails, bring to the boil, cover and cook for 7 minutes. Strain and let cool slightly.

With a small knife or pick, remove the operculums from the snails. Remove the snail meat from the shells, clean the shells thoroughly and set aside. Clean the snail meat by removing the guts located at the back. You should have about 260 g/9 oz of snail meat.

To prepare the stuffing, soak the wood ear mushrooms in a bowl of hot water for 20 minutes, then drain and finely chop.

Finely chop the snail meat, then place in a mixing bowl with the chopped mushrooms, lemongrass, shallots, garlic, lime leaf, peppercorns, minced (ground) pork, pork paste and fish sauce. Mix thoroughly, then marinate for 15 minutes.

Prepare a bowl of iced water. Bring a pot of water to the boil add the lemongrass leaves and blanch for 30 seconds, then plunge immediately into the iced water. Pat dry.

Split the remaining lime leaves in half.

Fill a piping (pastry) bag with the marinated meat mixture.

Place half a lime leaf at the back of each shell. This will add extra flavour to the dish and keep the stuffing from leaking into the back. Fold one blanched lemongrass leaf into each shell, leaving strips sticking out on both sides for easy removal after cooking. Pipe the meat mixture into the shells.

Fill a steamer with water, and add the remaining lime leaves and lemongrass trimmings to the water for extra aroma. Steam the stuffed snails for 30 minutes.

Serve hot with the Ginger Dipping Fish Sauce or Salt and Pepper Seasoning Mix.

***Note:*** You can substitute the pork paste with finely minced (ground) pork. If you do so, you might need to add additional seasoning.

# GRILLED SNAILS WITH GREEN PEPPER SAUCE

Ốc Bươu Nướng Tiêu Xanh

Vietnam, one of the world's largest pepper exporters, grows this spice from the mountains of Buon Ma Thuot in the Central Highlands to the sandy Phu Quoc island in the Gulf of Thailand. Unlike black pepper, which needs grinding, these green peppercorns are eaten whole with the snails. If desired, you can substitute the sauce with either Northern- or Southern-style Lemongrass and Chilli Dipping Sauce (page 472).

Serves 2–3 as a starter (appetizer)
Preparation time: 20 minutes
Cooking time: 25 minutes

| DF |

500 g/1 lb 2 oz apple snails (ốc bươu)
3 bird's eye chillies, sliced
2 lemongrass stalks, coarsely cut

*For the sauce*
20 g/¾ oz long red chillies
35 g/1¼ oz(¼ cup) green peppercorns
1 tablespoon pork fat
25 g/1 oz peeled shallots
¼ teaspoon salt
2 teaspoons sugar
2 tablespoons fish sauce
½ teaspoon all-purpose seasoning (hạt nêm)
4 g lime leaves (4–5 leaves), thinly sliced

Soak the snails in a bowl of salted water with the chillies for 20 minutes.

In a large pot, add 1 litre/1¾ pints (4¼ cups) of water and the lemongrass. Transfer the snails to the boiling water, cover with the lid, and cook for 7 minutes, then drain in a colander.

With a small knife or pick, remove the operculums from the snails. Working over a bowl to catch the juices, remove the snail meat from the shells. Remove the guts located at the back and discard. Return the meat to the shells, keeping the collected juice for the sauce.

To make the sauce, put the chillies in a mortar and pound with a pestle until fine, then add the green peppercorns.

Heat the pork fat in a non-stick pan over a medium heat, add the shallots and fry for 1 minute. Add the peppercorn-chilli paste from the mortar. Using a wooden spoon, stir in the salt, sugar, fish sauce and all-purpose seasoning with 3 tablespoons of water. Simmer for 2 minutes until saucy. Remove from the heat, then stir in the lime leaves. Set aside.

Preheat a barbecue grill to medium–high heat (or amber coals). Alternatively, preheat the oven grill (broiler) to 190°C/375°F and position the rack at the top level.

Arrange the prepared snails in a grill basket (for the barbecue) or a heatproof tray (for the oven grill). Add 1 teaspoon of the sauce to each snail, making sure there are 1 or 2 peppercorns per shell. Cook for 5–7 minutes until heated through and slightly charred, using tongs to check the charring.

Using tongs, arrange the grilled snails on a serving plate. Provide small picks or forks for eating, and small bowls for the dipping sauce. Serve immediately while hot.

## SALT-ROASTED SPOTTED BABYLON SNAILS

### Ốc Hương Rang Muối

The key technique in this dish is stir-frying the snails in a liquid salt mixture that gradually reduces to form a seasoned crust on the shells. The snails are then picked out with a cocktail stick or toothpick and can be dipped in your chosen seasoning mix.

Serves 2–3 as a starter (appetizer)
Preparation time: 10 minutes
Cooking time: 20 minutes

| DF | GF | ≤30 |

1 lemongrass stalk, bruised
400 g/14 oz spotted Babylon snails (ốc hương)

*For the salt mixture*
1 teaspoon salt or shrimp salt (muối tôm tây ninh)
1 teaspoon sugar
1 teaspoon MSG
20 g/¾ oz long red chilli
1 bird's eye chilli

*To serve*
1 bunch Vietnamese coriander/cilantro (rau răm)
Salt and Pepper Seasoning Mix (page 480) or Green Chilli Salt (page 480)

Bring a large pot of water with the lemongrass to the boil. Add the snails and blanch for 5 minutes. Drain, reserving 4 tablespoons of the blanching water. Set the snails aside.

To make the salt mixture, combine in a blender the salt, reserved blanching water, sugar, MSG and both chillies. Blend until smooth.

Heat a pan over a medium–low heat, then add the blanched snails and blended salt mixture. Cook, stirring continuously, for 10–14 minutes until the water evaporates and the salt mixture forms a coating on the snails.

Transfer to a serving dish and serve hot with the Vietnamese coriander/cilantro and your chosen seasoning mix.

## MUD CREEPER SNAILS IN COCONUT MILK

### Ốc Len Xào Dừa

*Ốc len*, commonly known as 'mud creeper', is a type of snail found in mangrove forests or muddy areas in Vietnam. This dish is particularly popular in the Central and Southern regions of Vietnam, where coconut milk is widely used. The richness of the coconut milk is balanced by the fresh flavours of Vietnamese coriander/cilantro, lemongrass and chillies. To help with eating, the tips of the snails are cut off, allowing air to flow and making it easier to enjoy the dish by sucking out the snail meat.

Serves 2–3
Preparation time: 15 minutes
Cooking time: 20 minutes

| DF | GF |

500 g/1 lb 2 oz mud creeper snails (ốc len)
2 bird's eye chillies, sliced
65 g/2¼ oz lemongrass stalks, smashed
20 g/¾ oz Vietnamese coriander/cilantro (rau răm), coarsely chopped
15 g/½ oz long red chilli, sliced at an angle

*For the sauce*
2 tablespoons neutral oil
50 g/1¾ oz garlic, coarsely chopped
50 g/1¾ oz lemongrass, sliced
220 g/7¾ oz (1 cup) coconut milk
1 tablespoon sugar
½ teaspoon salt

Cut off the tip of each snail with a heavy cleaver. Clean thoroughly and rinse well, then soak in a bowl of water with the chilli slices for 10 minutes. Rinse again after soaking.

Combine 500 ml/18 fl oz (2 cups) of water with the snails and smashed lemongrass in a pot. Bring to the boil, then reduce to a simmer and cook for 6 minutes. Drain and rinse the snails to remove impurities.

To make the coconut sauce, heat the oil in wok over a medium heat, add the garlic and fry until golden, about 2½ minutes. Add the snails and sliced lemongrass and stir-fry for 30 seconds. Pour in the coconut milk, add the sugar and salt, then reduce the heat and simmer for 6 minutes, stirring occasionally. If the sauce becomes too thick, thin it out with a few tablespoons of water. Add the Vietnamese coriander/cilantro and sliced chillies, then remove from the heat.

Transfer to serving bowls. To eat this, you can use a cocktail stick or toothpick to take the snails out, or like the locals, you can suck on the large opening until it comes out.

MUD CREEPER SNAILS IN COCONUT MILK

## TAMARIND ROASTED PERIWINKLE SNAILS

## Ốc Mỡ Rang Me

Vietnam's extensive coastline hosts thousands of marine species, including numerous varieties of sea snails. This dish features *ốc mỡ* (common periwinkle snails), named for their translucent, fat-like appearance in the water. Shell patterns vary by region, giving each coastal area its own distinct variety. If these snails are not available, the same preparation method works well with cockles or razor clams.

Serves 2–3 as a starter (appetizer)
Preparation time: 10 minutes, plus 1 hour soaking time
Cooking time: 9 minutes

| DF |

- 500 g/1 lb 2 oz common periwinkle snails (ốc mỡ)
- a few chillies, for brining
- 1 lemongrass stalk, bruised
- 1 tablespoon pork fat or neutral oil
- 20 g/¾ oz garlic, minced
- 1 teaspoon Chilli and Lemongrass Oil (page 457)
- 5 g/⅛ oz (1 teaspoon) Crispy Fried Pork Fat (page 459)
- 5 g/⅛ oz (1 teaspoon) Fried Shallots (page 458)
- 5 g/⅛ oz (1 teaspoon) Fried Garlic (page 458)
- salt

*For the sauce*

- 50 g/1¾ oz tamarind paste
- 2 teaspoons calamansi juice (or lime juice)
- 2 teaspoons sugar
- 2 teaspoons fish sauce

Soak the snails in a bowl of salted water with the sliced chillies for 1 hour to purge impurities. Drain thoroughly in a colander.

Bring a pot of water with the lemongrass to the boil, add the cleaned snails and blanch for 5 minutes, then drain and set aside.

To prepare the sauce, in a small bowl, combine all the ingredients and mix well until the sugar dissolves.

Heat the pork fat or oil in a wok over a medium heat, add the minced garlic, then fry for 2 minutes until golden. Add the blanched snails and stir-fry for 1 minute. Pour the prepared sauce over the snails, then stir-fry for 2 minutes until well-coated. Add the chilli and lemongrass oil, crispy fried pork fat, fried shallots and fried garlic, and stir for an additional 30 seconds to combine.

Transfer to a serving dish and serve immediately.

## RAZOR CLAMS WITH SALTED EGG SAUCE

## Ốc Móng Tay Sốt Trứng Muối

You can use either duck or chicken salted eggs for this dish. The sauce can also accompany deep-fried, battered or stir-fried prawns (shrimp) or fish. Although this recipe calls for the clams to be shelled, you can keep them in the shells, if preferred. This dish can be served either as a starter (appetizer) or with steamed rice

Serves 2–3 as a starter (appetizer)
Preparation time: 15 minutes, plus 20 minutes soaking time
Cooking time: 12 minutes

- 500 g/1 lb 2 oz razor clams (ốc móng tay)
- 3 bird's eye chillies, sliced
- 2 salted egg yolks, steamed and fully cooked
- 1 lemongrass stalk, bruised
- 2 teaspoons fish sauce
- 1 teaspoon sugar, plus extra to taste
- ½ teaspoon MSG
- 1 tablespoon milk
- 15 g/½ oz butter or margarine
- 1 tablespoon neutral oil
- 10 g/¼ oz long red chilli, deseeded and sliced
- salt

Soak the clams in a bowl of salted water with the bird's eye chilli slices for 20 minutes to purge impurities.

Meanwhile, set up a steamer and bring the water to the boil, place the salted egg yolks in small flameproof bowls in the steamer basket, then set over the boiling water and steam for 10 minutes. Set aside to cool.

Bring a pan of water to the boil with the lemongrass. Add the clams and blanch for about 7 minutes until they just open.

Remove the meat from the shells and rinse thoroughly.

Mix the cleaned clam meat with 1 teaspoon of the fish sauce and the sugar and MSG in a bowl. Set aside.

In a bowl, mash the steamed salted egg yolks with the milk until smooth.

Melt the butter or margarine with the oil in wok over a medium heat, add the marinated clams and stir-fry for 1 minute. Add the mashed salted egg and the remaining fish sauce. Stir-fry for 4 minutes, stirring constantly to ensure even coating and to prevent the eggs from burning. Add the sliced long red chili and some more sugar, if desired.

Transfer to a serving dish and serve hot.

# STIR-FRIED NOODLES WITH RAZOR CLAMS

## Mì Xào Ốc Móng Tay

This is the *plat de resistance*, the hearty dish ordered during a seafood meal. Usually, after a few plates of clams and snails, locals will order this to fill up and finish the meal. Its simplicity lies in the use of instant noodles, making it both satisfying and unfussy.

Serves 3–4
Preparation time: 25 minutes
Cooking time: 15 minutes

| **DF** |

- 2 packets Vietnamese instant noodles
- 1 kg/2 lb 4 oz razor clams (ốc móng tay)
- handful of lemongrass trimmings
- 2 tablespoons neutral oil
- 30 g/1 oz garlic, coarsely chopped
- 20 g/¾ oz shallots, coarsely chopped
- 1 tablespoon fish sauce
- 1 teaspoon light brown sugar
- 200 g/7 oz morning glory (rau muống) stalks, cut into 6–7-cm/2½–2¾-inch lengths
- 1 tablespoon Annatto Oil (page 457)
- 10 g/¼ oz (2 teaspoons) Fried Shallots (page 458)
- 20 g/¾ oz coriander (cilantro) and spring onion (scallion) mix, roughly chopped
- ¾ teaspoon nước tương sa tế (see note), to serve

In a large bowl, soak the noodles in room temperature water for 10 minutes.

Meanwhile, thoroughly clean the razor clams under running water several times to remove any sand.

In a large pot, bring 1 litre/1¾ pints (4¼ cups) of water to the boil with the lemongrass trimmings. Add the razor clams, cover with the lid and cook for 5 minutes. Remove the clams with a skimmer, carefully extract the meat from the shells and rinse thoroughly until completely sand-free.

Heat the neutral oil in a large wok over a medium heat. Add the garlic and shallots, then stir-fry for about 4 minutes until they are starting to turn golden, stirring with a wooden spatula to prevent them from burning. Add the cleaned clam meat to the wok, then season with the fish sauce and sugar. Stir-fry for 1 minute, using a spatula to toss the ingredients. Increase the heat to high, then add the morning glory stalks and stir-fry for 30 seconds.

Drain the noodles in a colander. Add to the wok along with the annatto oil, then stir-fry for 1–2 minutes until the noodles are heated through. Add the fried shallots and herb mix, then briefly toss.

Divide among serving plates and serve with the soy sauce with chilli and lemongrass oil on the side.

***Note:*** To make nước tương sa tế, mix 1 tablespoon of soy sauce with 1 teaspoon of Chilli and Lemongrass Oil (page 457).

## STIR-FRIED SPOTTED BABYLON SNAILS WITH CORN

Ốc Xào Bắp

While this recipe traditionally uses Spotted Babylon snails, small whelks make a good substitute. Whelks require an additional 5 minutes of boiling due to their thicker shells.

Serves 3–4
Preparation time: 15 minutes, plus 20 minutes soaking time
Cooking time: 20 minutes

- 500 g/1 lb 2 oz spotted Babylon snails (ốc hương)
- rice washing water or salt water, for cleaning
- 3 bird's eye chillies, sliced, plus extra, optional, to taste
- 50 g/1¾ oz lemongrass, cut 9-cm/3½-inch long, then halved lengthways
- 45 g/1½ oz (3 tablespoons) butter or margarine
- 235 g/8¼ oz (1½ cups) corn kernels (from about 330 g/11½ oz corn cobs)
- 3 teaspoons fish sauce
- 2 teaspoons sugar
- ¼ teaspoon MSG
- 1 tablespoon neutral oil or fat
- 30 g/1 oz garlic, chopped
- 35 g/1¼ oz shallots, chopped

Soak the snails in a large bowl with the rice washing water or salted water and the chillies for 20 minutes to purge impurities. Drain, then rinse thoroughly under cold running water.

Bring 2 litres/3½ pints (8½ cups) of water to the boil in a pot. Add the lemongrass and return to the boil. Add the cleaned snails to the pot and simmer for 5 minutes, until the operculum pops out. Remove from the heat, then drain and set aside. (You can remove the operculums, if you wish.)

Melt 25 g/1 oz (2 tablespoons) of the butter in pan over a low heat. Add the corn kernels, then season with 1 teaspoon of the fish sauce, 1 teaspoon of the sugar and the MSG. Increase the heat to medium. Stir-fry for 5 minutes, or until the corn is tender-crisp. Remove and set aside.

In the same pan, add the oil or fat over a medium heat, then add the garlic and shallots and some chilli slices, if using. Fry for 2 minutes until golden but not crispy, then remove and set aside.

Add the drained snails to the pan, cover and cook over a medium heat for 2 minutes 30 seconds. They should be just cooked through. Return the corn and aromatics to the pan, then add the remaining fish sauce and the remaining butter. Stir-fry for 5 minutes. Add the remaining sugar. Mix well to combine.

Serve immediately.

## STIR-FRIED SPOTTED BABYLON SNAILS WITH GARLIC

Ốc Xào Tỏi

This drier version of Stir-fried Spotted Babylon Snail with Corn (see above) allows the sauce to coat the shells. For a more glazed finish, add extra water with the fish sauce. This is delicious served with Ginger Dipping Fish Sauce (page 474), Green Chilli Salt (page 480) or Sweet and Sour Fish Sauce (page 471)

Serves 3–4
Preparation time: 20 minutes, plus 20 minutes soaking time
Cooking time: 10 minutes

| DF |

- 500 g/1 lb 2 oz spotted Babylon snails (ốc hương)
- rice washing water or salted water, for soaking
- 3 bird's eye chillies, sliced, plus extra to taste
- 50 g/1¾ oz lemongrass, cut to 9-cm/3½-inch long, then halved lengthways
- 3 tablespoons pork fat or neutral oil
- 40 g/1½ oz garlic, coarsely chopped
- 55 g/2 oz shallots, coarsely chopped
- 2 teaspoons fish sauce
- 1 teaspoon sugar
- ¼ teaspoon MSG
- ½ teaspoon salt, or to taste
- Vietnamese coriander/cilantro (rau răm), to serve

To prepare the snails, follow the first 2 steps in the recipe above.

Heat the pork fat or oil in a large pan over a medium heat, add the garlic and fry for 2–3 minutes until golden. Remove the garlic with a slotted spoon and reserve flavoured oil in the pan.

In the same pan, add the shallots and fry over a medium heat for 1–2 minutes until translucent. Add extra chilli slices if desired. Add the drained snails and stir-fry for a few minutes to coat with the oil. Add the fish sauce, sugar and MSG, then cover and cook for 3 minutes. Add the salt and stir well. Cover and cook for 2 minutes more. Add the reserved fried garlic and stir to combine.

Line a serving plate with Vietnamese coriander/cilantro, arrange the snails on top and serve immediately.

STIR-FRIED SPOTTED BABYLON SNAILS WITH CORN

# HUẾ-STYLE BABY SNAILS

## Ốc Gạo Kiểu Huế

Unlike other snail dishes that are cooked to order, this Huế-style dish is prepared in large batches and left to marinate. Due to their small size, these snails, *ốc gạo* (*Assiminea lutea*), are typically scooped and sold by weight at markets or served by the plate at *quán ốc* (snail eateries). The dish is distinguished by its spicier profile and the use of *mắm ruốc* (Huế-style fermented shrimp paste), a signature ingredient in Huế cuisine.

Serves 2–3 as a starter (appetizer)
Preparation time: 20 minutes, plus 20 minutes soaking time
Cooking time: 10 minutes

| DF |

- 500 g/1 lb 2 oz baby snails (*Assiminea lutea*/ ốc gạo)
- salt, for soaking water
- a few chillies, for soaking water
- 35 g/1¼ oz lemongrass
- 30 g/1 oz long red chilli, stemmed and half deseeded
- 5 g/⅛ oz bird's eye chillies (about 2 chillies), stemmed
- 2 tablespoons pork fat or oil
- 10 g/¼ oz garlic, minced
- ¼ teaspoon chilli powder
- 2 teaspoons sugar
- ¼ teaspoon salt
- 15 g/½ oz Huế-style fermented shrimp paste (mắm ruốc), mixed with 2 teaspoons water
- 20–30 g/1 oz Vietnamese coriander/cilantro (rau răm), leaves picked, to garnish
- Lemongrass and Chilli Dipping Sauce (Southern Style) (page 472) or Salt and Pepper Seasoning Mix (page 480), to serve

Soak the snails in a bowl of salted water with the sliced chillies to purge sand and impurities.

Prepare a bowl of iced water. Bring a pot of water to the boil. Add the snails for 20–30 seconds, then immediately transfer to the iced water, drain and set aside.

Finely chop 15 g/½ oz of the top of the lemongrass and set aside. Cut the remaining lemongrass into 4-cm/1½-inch pieces, put them in a mortar and smash with a pestle.

Place the deseeded portion of red chilli into a blender and blend.

Using the mortar and pestle, pound the remaining red chilli with the bird's eye chilli until a coarse paste forms.

Heat the fat or oil in a wok over a high heat. Fry the garlic, blended chilli, chopped lemongrass and chilli powder for 1 minute, or until fragrant. Add the snails, sugar and salt, then stir-fry for 2 minutes. Add the smashed lemongrass and continue cooking for 1 minute 30 seconds. Stir in the diluted shrimp paste, then fry for 30 seconds. Reduce the heat, add the pounded chilli mixture, then stir-fry for 1 minute, or until glossy.

Transfer to a serving dish, garnish with Vietnamese coriander/cilantro leaves and serve hot, with your chosen dipping sauce.

# CHEESE-GRILLED SCALLOPS

Sò Điệp Nướng Phô Mai

For most Vietnamese people, their first memory of cheese is The Laughing Cow spreadable cheese – a French colonial legacy that stayed popular because it's affordable, keeps well at room temperature and has a long shelf life. While cheese wasn't part of traditional Vietnamese cuisine, it became more common after *Đổi Mới* (economic reforms) in the early 1990s, when foreign ingredients became more accessible. Today, The Laughing Cow and other processed cheeses appear in modern interpretations of traditional dishes, from *bánh tráng nướng đà lạt* (Đà Lạt-style Grilled Rice Paper, page 35) to seafood dishes like these grilled scallops.

Serves 2–3 as a starter (appetizer)
Preparation time: 15 minutes
Cooking time: 10 minutes

| **GF** | ≤30 |

300 g/10½ oz scallops in half shells (about 6; ideally Vietnamese, see note)
1 slice of processed cheese, cut into 6 small squares

*For the cheese sauce*
70 g/2½ oz (⅓ cup) processed cheese spread (preferably The Laughing Cow)
10 g/¼ oz (1½ teaspoons) condensed milk
1 egg yolk
10 g/¼ oz (1½ teaspoons) mayonnaise
¼ teaspoon salt

Preheat the grill (broiler) to 200°C/400°F.

To prepare the cheese sauce, put all the ingredients in a bowl and whisk until completely smooth. Set aside.

Clean the scallops if needed, leaving them in their shells: open the shells with a pastry knife, or the back of a butter knife, then remove the frill and the stomach sack and discard, leaving just the white flesh and coral (if it has coral). Pat dry with paper towels, if necessary.

Arrange the scallops on a baking sheet. Top each with 1 teaspoon of the cheese sauce, then place a small square of processed cheese on top.

Place the scallops on the top rack of the oven and grill (broil) for 10 minutes, or until the cheese has melted and lightly golden.

Let cool briefly, about 1 minute, then serve immediately.

***Note:*** If you can't find Vietnamese scallops, you can use queenie scallops as they are the closest in size; and if that is not available, you can use normal scallops but you might have to increase the toppings.

# GRILLED ARK CLAMS WITH SPRING ONION OIL

## Sò Lông Nướng Mỡ Hành

In Vietnamese seafood restaurants, diners can order various clams, sea snails and seafood either grilled or sautéed with their choice of sauce. This dish is great on a live fire barbecue but can also be replicated at home under the oven grill (broiler). The clams used here are commonly known as *Anadara kagoshimensis* and can be replaced by any other clams from the ark clams family, such as scallops or even razor clams.

Serves 4 as part of a shared meal
Preparation time: 20 minutes
Cooking time: 15 minutes

| DF |

*For the spring onion oil (mỡ hành)*
- 75 g/2¾ oz spring onions (scallions), thinly sliced (white and green parts separated)
- 2 tablespoons fish sauce
- ¼ cup neutral oil
- 15 g/½ oz garlic, coarsely chopped
- 10 g/¼ oz shallot, coarsely chopped
- 65 g/2¼ oz Crispy Fried Pork Fat (page 459), optional

*For the clams*
- 1 kg/2 lb 4 oz large ark clams (sò lông)
- 1 lemongrass stalk, smashed and cut into chunks

*To serve*
- 50 g/1¾ oz (⅓ cup) peanuts, toasted and coarsely crushed
- 30 g/1 oz Vietnamese coriander/cilantro (rau răm)
- Calamansi Fish Sauce (page 474), for dipping

Place the spring onion (scallion) greens in a non-reactive bowl with the fish sauce, mix well and set aside.

Heat the oil in a pan over a medium-low heat. Sauté the garlic, shallot and spring onion whites in the pan until golden, 3–4 minutes. If using pork fat, add and cook for 30 seconds more.

Pour the hot oil mixture over the reserved greens, then stir to combine.

Rinse the clams in cold water, or soak for 5 minutes in very salty water.

Fill a large pot with 1 litre/1¾ pints (4¼ cups) of water and add the lemongrass, then bring to the boil. Add the clams and cook until the shells open, 2–4 minutes.

Meanwhile, prepare a bowl of iced water. Preheat the grill (broiler) to 210°C/410°F.

Transfer the clams to the iced water immediately, and discard any unopened clams. Remove the top shells from the clams.

Arrange on a baking sheet and top each with the spring onion oil. Grill (broil) for 5 minutes until fragrant.

Remove and sprinkle with the crushed peanuts. Serve immediately with the Vietnamese coriander/cilantro leaves and dipping sauce.

# STARTERS

## Món khai vị

The selection here is often seen at weddings, death anniversaries, celebrations and gatherings. I recommend pairing a starter (appetizer) with a noodle or grilled dish or a hotpot when having family or friends over, if you want to do something different from the usual family meal.

Some of these recipes are also made for *Tết* (Lunar New Year), as they can be kept for a few days, like Meat Aspic (page 102), or frozen and fried when needed, as with Crab/Prawn Spring Rolls (page 116), or even served cold as a starter or snack, like Pork Roll with Green Chilli and Shredded Pork Skin (page 117).

You can still prepare these appetizers for a family meal: some, like Crab Soup (page 121) make a perfect breakfast. Many of these dishes are also popular at *quán nhậu* (beer halls), where they pair well with drinking.

## SCORCHED RICE WITH CARAMELIZED FISH SAUCE

Cơm Cháy Kho Quẹt

One of my favourite childhood memories is eating the scorched rice from the bottom of the rice cooker, dipped in *kho quẹt* (Caramelized Pork Dip, page 475), watching the crispy rice absorb the rich sauce. Like Italian crudités paired with *bagna càuda*, this dish combines crispy rice and simple boiled vegetables, all elevated by the savoury *kho quẹt* sauce. It's also a great way to repurpose leftover scorched rice from the rice cooker.

Serves 3–4
Preparation time: 25 minutes
Cooking time: 20 minutes

| DF |

- 60 g/2¼ oz carrots, cut into 1.5-cm/⅝-in-wide rounds or batons
- 70 g/2½ oz daikon, cut into batons
- 95 g/3½ oz okra (about 7)
- 1 quantity Caramelized Pork Dip (page 475)
- ground black pepper

*For the rice*

- 580 g/1 lb 4 oz (2½ cups) cooked rice, cooled (you can also use leftover rice for this)
- ½ teaspoon salt
- 1 tablespoon lard
- ½ teaspoon neutral oil, for brushing the rice

To prepare the rice, put the cooled rice and salt in a bowl.

Heat the lard in a 25-cm/10-inch pan over a medium heat. Once hot, add half of the rice. Brush a spatula or fish slice with a bit of oil to prevent sticking and use to evenly press it down. Cook for about 8 minutes, continuing to press the rice to flatten it. After another 4 minutes, flip the rice. Brush a bit of oil on the rice and cook, still uncovered, for another 10 minutes, or until both sides are golden and crispy.

Meanwhile, in a 15-cm/6-inch pot, bring 150 ml/5 fl oz (⅔ cup) of water to the boil over a medium heat. Add the carrots, daikon and okra. Simmer for 8 minutes.

Spoon the caramelized pork dip into small bowls or sauce dishes, and sprinkle some ground pepper on top.

Break the crispy rice into small pieces and arrange them on a plate. Serve with the boiled vegetables and caramelized pork dip the side.

To eat, take a piece of crispy rice and dip it into the caramelized fish sauce.

## MEAT ASPIC

Thịt Đông

*Thịt đông* is a cold meat jelly (gelatin) often eaten during *Tết* (Lunar New Year) as it can be prepared in large quantities and has a long shelf life. Traditionally, meats are washed with salt water to remove any gaminess, especially when freshly butchered from wet markets. However, this step is unnecessary for meats purchased from supermarkets or butchers.

Makes 2.5 litres/4½ pints (10½ cups); serves 8–10
Preparation time: 30 minutes, plus overnight chilling time
Cooking time: 2 hours

| DF |

- 15 g/½ oz dried wood ear mushrooms
- 160 g/5½ oz carrots (about 2 medium), peeled
- 1.5 litres/2½ pints (6¼ cups) hot water
- 70 ml/2½ fl oz (scant ⅓ cup) fish sauce
- 15 g/½ oz (2 tablespoons) whole black peppercorns
- 35 g/1¼ oz whole peeled, small red shallots
- 530 g/1 lb 3 oz pig's trotter (foot), cut into small chunks (optional; can substitute with more pork shin)
- 1.4 kg/3 lb 2 oz pork shin (shank), cut into 3–4-cm/1¼–1½-inch chunks
- 300 g/10½ oz pork skin, sliced into 3 × 2-cm/1¼ × ¾-inch strips
- 1 pig's ear
- ½ teaspoon salt

*To serve*

- Pickled Mustard Greens (page 467) or Pickled Chinese Onions (page 466)
- fish sauce or Salt and Pepper Seasoning Mix (page 480)

Soak the wood ear mushrooms in a bowl of water for 10 minutes. Cut off the roots, then slice into 2-cm/¾-inch chunks. Set aside.

Make 5 V-shaped cuts around each carrot, pointing towards the centre, creating flower shapes, then cut into 1.5-cm/⅝-inch-thick rounds. Set aside.

Fill a large casserole (or Dutch oven) or stockpot with the measured hot water and add the fish sauce, peppercorns and whole shallots. Add the pig's trotter (foot), if using, and cook for 15 minutes. Add the remaining meat (pork shin/shank, skin and ear) and the salt. Cover, and simmer over a low heat for 1 hour 15 minutes, stirring regularly. Add the mushrooms, then place the carrot flowers on top. Cover, and simmer for an additional 20 minutes, then remove from the heat.

Remove the carrot flowers and place 1–3 in the bottom of each of 2–3 large serving bowls. Divide the meat and mushrooms among the bowls, then pour the hot gelatinous stock (broth) over the meat to fill the bowls. Leave to cool to room temperature, then cover with clingfilm (plastic wrap) and refrigerate overnight. They will keep in the refrigerator for up to 4 days.

Serve cold with the pickles and dipping sauce.

# PIG'S EAR SALAD WITH TOASTED RICE POWDER

## Tai Heo Trộn Thính

This starter (appetizer) can be eaten as it is, with its dipping sauce, or can also become a wrap and roll dish, with rice paper and a plate of *rau thơm* (aromatic mixed herbs).

Serves 4–6 as a starter (appetizer)
Preparation time: 25 minutes, plus 20 minutes cooling time
Cooking time: 30 minutes

| DF |

- 25 g/1 oz spring onion (scallion) whites
- 30 g/1 oz piece fresh ginger (about 6 cm/2½ inches), peeled, plus 25 g/1 oz piece fresh ginger (about 5 cm/2 inches), peeled
- 1 tablespoon salt
- 1 pig's ear (300 g/10½ oz)
- 20 g/¾ oz lemongrass
- ½ teaspoon fish sauce
- ½ chilli (10 g/¼ oz), thinly sliced
- 3 lime leaves, thinly sliced
- 15 g/½ oz garlic, minced
- ½ teaspoon salt
- 3 tablespoons Toasted Rice Powder (page 459)
- 5–10 g/⅛–¼ oz peppermint/Vietnamese basil leaves (húng cây/húng quế), coarsely chopped, to garnish

*To serve*

- Sweet and Sour Fish Sauce (page 471), to serve
- aromatic mixed herbs (rau thơm - perilla, peppermint, fish mint, Vietnamese balm), optional
- rice paper, optional
- sliced cucumber, optional

Prepare a bowl of iced water.

Bring 1 litre/1¾ pints (4¼ cups) of water to the boil. Add the spring onion (scallion) whites, the 30 g/1 oz piece of ginger and salt. Add the pig's ear and blanch for 2 minutes. Remove and immediately soak in the iced water for 5 minutes. Drain well.

In a pot, add 1.5 litres/2½ pints (6¼ cups) of water, the remaining ginger and the lemongrass, then bring to the boil. Add the blanched pig's ear and cook for 15–20 minutes.

Meanwhile, prepare another bowl of iced water.

When the pig's ear is cooked, remove and soak in the iced water for 15 minutes. Drain well, then thinly slice the cooled pig's ear.

Transfer the sliced pig's ear to a large mixing bowl, add the fish sauce and mix thoroughly, then add the chilli, lime leaves, garlic, salt and toasted rice powder and mix until well combined.

To serve, transfer the pig's ear salad to a serving plate. Garnish with the chopped herbs.

This dish is served as a starter (appetizer) in two ways: directly with the prepared dipping sauce; or wrapped in rice paper with the herbs and sliced cucumber and then dipped in the sauce.

# SAUTÉED BABY CLAMS WITH RICE CRACKERS

Hến Xúc Bánh Đa

Baby basket clams, a speciality from Quảng Nam province, appear in many dishes including *cơm hến* (Baby Basket Clam Rice, page 268) and *trứng chiên hến* (Baby Basket Clam Omelette, page 348) and this dish. They were once so abundant that every household in Huế had a pile of shells at their doorstep, which they sold to lime kilns, and children would even collect these shells for traditional games. These baby basket clams should be served with thick rice crackers sprinkled with black sesame seeds, and true to Central Vietnamese cuisine, with enough heat to give it a proper kick.

Serves 4–6
Preparation time: 30 minutes
Cooking time: 25 minutes

| DF |

- 2 kg/4 lb 8 oz fresh baby basket clams
- 20 g/¾ oz piece fresh ginger, sliced
- 75 g/2¾ oz (½ cup) peanuts with skin
- 2½ tablespoons Annatto Oil (page 457)
- ½ teaspoon salt
- 1 tablespoon neutral oil
- 15 g/½ oz shallot, chopped
- 15 g/½ oz garlic, chopped
- 1 tablespoon plus 2 teaspoons fish sauce
- 2 teaspoons Chilli and Lemongrass Oil (page 457)
- 1 onion, diced
- 80 g/2¾ oz Vietnamese coriander/cilantro (rau răm), leaves picked (30 g/1 oz leaves), then chopped
- 10 g/¼ oz spring onion (scallion), chopped
- 1½ teaspoons sugar
- 1½ tablespoons toasted sesame seeds
- 2 teaspoons lime juice

*To serve*

- 5 g/¼ oz Vietnamese coriander/cilantro (rau răm) leaves, chopped
- lime wedges
- crispy sesame rice crackers

Rinse the clams thoroughly in cold water at least 3 times.

Bring a large pot of water with the sliced ginger to the boil. Add the clams and cook until the shells open, about 5 minutes. Drain, reserving the cooking liquid.

Fill a large bowl with water, place the cooked clams in a colander smaller than the bowl and place in the bowl. Stir the clams in the colander, and the meat should begin to separate from the shells and float. Push the meat over the lip of the colander into the bowl; the shells should remain in the colander. Drain the meat and discard the shells. You should have 300 g/10½ oz of clam meat.

In a pan over a medium-low heat, add the peanuts, then slowly toast while constantly stirring. Add 2 tablespoons of the annatto oil and the salt. Continue stir-frying for another 2 minutes, then remove from the heat and set the peanuts aside.

In a large pan, heat the neutral oil over a medium heat. Add the shallot and garlic and fry for 2–3 minutes until golden brown. Add the clam meat, and stir-fry for another 1 minute. Season with 1 tablespoon of the fish sauce and 1 teaspoon of the chilli and lemongrass oil. Add the onion, then sauté for 2 minutes until fragrant.

Add half of the chopped Vietnamese coriander/cilantro leaves, all of the spring onion (scallion), the sugar and the toasted peanuts. Stir-fry for another 30 seconds. Add the remaining chilli and lemongrass oil, the remaining annatto oil and the remaining fish sauce, then stir-fry for another 30 seconds. Remove from the heat, then mix in the remaining Vietnamese coriander, 1 tablespoon of the sesame seeds and the lime juice.

To serve, arrange the clam mixture in the centre of a serving plate with raised edges. Garnish with the chopped Vietnamese coriander, the remaining sesame seeds and the fresh lime wedges.

Serve hot with the sesame rice crackers arranged around plate, and additional lime wedges on the side, if desired.

SAUTÉED BABY CLAMS WITH RICE CRACKERS

# PORK SHIN WRAPPED IN RICE PAPER

## Bắp Giò Heo Cuốn Bánh Tráng

This dish belongs to the many wrap-and-roll dishes from Central and Southern Vietnam, where eating with hands is common practice, and eating fresh rolled wraps to combat the year-round hot climate is a must. The thinly sliced poached pork is served alongside a full plate of fresh herbs, young mango and delicate rice paper. While the pork itself is subtle in flavour, it's traditionally paired with the bold Seasoned Fermented Thick Fish Sauce (page 476). This dish may appear to be simple in flavours, but it is all about the accompanying herbs. In western Vietnam, particularly Tây Ninh province, the usual plate of *rau thơm* (aromatic mixed herbs) is enhanced with *rau rừng* (wild herbs), which can have up to nine different herbs, including amberella and pomelo leaves.

Serves 4–6
Preparation time: 30 minutes
Cooking time: 1 hour 10 minutes

| DF |

- 1 kg/2 lb 4 oz pork shin (shank), deboned
- ½ teaspoon salt
- 1 tablespoon fish sauce
- 20 g/¾ oz onion, roughly smashed
- 10 g/¼ oz shallot, roughly smashed

*To serve*

- 1 head of lettuce, leaves separated
- aromatic mixed herbs (rau thơm – perilla, Vietnamese basil, coriander/cilantro, fish mint, Vietnamese peppermint, mint)
- wild herb salad from the west of Vietnam (rau rừng tây ninh)
- 1 cucumber, sliced into thin strips
- 115 g/4 oz (1 cup) bean sprouts, optional
- 1 star fruit, sliced
- 1 green mango, cut into thin matchsticks (julienned), optional
- rice paper sheets
- 150 g/5½ oz (1 cup) Toasted Peanuts (page 459), chopped, optional
- Seasoned Fermented Thick Fish Sauce (page 476)
- Pickled Daikon and Carrots (page 468)

Using butcher's string, tightly roll the deboned pork shin (shank) into a long, round shape. Tie securely to maintain the shape during cooking.

In a large pot, combine 2 litres/3½ pints (8½ cups) of water with the salt, fish sauce, onion and shallot. Bring the mixture to a simmer. Carefully add the rolled pork shin to the simmering liquid. Cover the pot and simmer for 1 hour 10 minutes, or until the pork is tender. Remove and leave to cool.

Slice the cooled pork into thin rounds. Arrange the sliced pork on a large plate in the centre of the table.

On large platters, arrange the lettuce, herbs, cucumber, bean sprouts, if using, star fruit and green mango, if using.

Place bowls of warm water around the table for softening the rice paper. Place stacks of rice paper sheets around the table. Put the chopped peanuts in a small bowl, if using, and serve the dipping sauce and pickles in individual small bowls for each diner.

To eat, take a rice paper sheet, quickly dip it in warm water to soften, then place the softened rice paper on a plate or directly on the table.

Add a piece of lettuce, some herbs, cucumber, bean sprouts and a slice or two of pork to the centre of the rice paper, then sprinkle some chopped peanuts over the filling.

Fold the bottom of the rice paper over the filling, then fold in the sides and roll tightly. Dip the roll in the dipping sauce and enjoy.

## SWEET AND SOUR BEEF SALAD

Bò Bóp Thấu

A popular starter (appetizer) in Southern Vietnamese cuisine, this dish is a staple at various celebrations, including weddings, birthdays and family gatherings. The appeal of this dish lies in the different layers of flavours. From the green star fruit bringing acidity and crunchiness, to the unripe banana, known for its tartness, this dish really represents the Vietnamese philosophy of balancing flavours and texture.

Serves 3–4
Preparation time: 30–35 minutes
Cooking time: 15–20 minutes

| DF |

2 tablespoons lime juice
190 g/6¾ oz green banana, peeled (about 130 g/4½ oz peeled)
5 g/⅛ oz (1 teaspoon) salt
165 g/5¾ oz sour star fruit
115 g/4 oz white onion, sliced
300 g/10½ oz beef, thinly sliced
2.5 g (½ teaspoon) black pepper
1 tablespoon fish sauce
10 g/¼ oz garlic, minced
15 g/½ oz shallot, minced
1 tablespoon neutral oil
250 g/5½ oz pineapple, cleaned, cored and cut into thin slices
50 g/1¾ oz mint (about 25 g/1 oz leaves), to garnish

*For the garnishes*
40 g/1½ oz (generous ¼ cup) peanuts
½ teaspoon salt
40 ml/1¼ fl oz (2½ tablespoons) neutral oil, for frying
45 g/1½ oz shallots, sliced

*For the dressing*
1 tablespoon fish sauce
2 tablespoons sugar
4 teaspoons lime juice

Fill a bowl with 480 ml/16 fl oz (2 cups) of water and add 1 tablespoon of the lime juice. Peel and slice the green banana thinly, then soak in the lime water.

Fill another bowl with 480 ml/16 fl oz (2 cups) of water and add the salt and the remaining lime juice. Trim and slice the star fruit thinly, then soak in salt-lime solution.

Soak the onion in a bowl of iced water until serving. This helps reduce the sharpness.

Put the beef in a bowl with the black pepper, fish sauce, and half the garlic and minced shallot and allow to marinate.

To make the garnishes: toast the peanuts with the salt in a small pan over a medium heat for 5 minutes. Transfer to a mortar and coarsely crush with a pestle. Set aside.

Put the oil in a frying pan or skillet and place over a medium heat, then add the sliced shallots and fry until golden and crispy, 5–6 minutes. Set aside.

Heat the oil in a pan over a medium heat. Add the remaining garlic and minced shallot and fry for 1–2 minutes until fragrant. Add the marinated beef, then stir-fry for 2–3 minutes until just cooked.

To assemble the salad, drain all the soaked ingredients well. In a large bowl, combine the cooked beef, drained fruits, drained onion and pineapple slices. Add the dressing ingredients and toss thoroughly to release the juices.

Transfer to a serving plate. Top with the crushed peanuts, crispy shallots and fresh mint leaves. Serve immediately.

## RARE BEEF IN LIME JUICE SALAD

Bò Tái Chanh

While raw meat dishes are uncommon in Vietnamese cuisine, bò tái chanh is a notable exception. Similar to Latin American ceviche, this dish uses lime juice to 'cook' the beef. For the best results, the dish requires fresh, lean cuts, like fillet (tenderloin). This salad is delicious garnished with Fried Shallots (page 458) and thinly sliced bird's eye chillies.

Serves 2
Preparation time: 20 minutes, plus 20 minutes marinating time
Cooking time: 1 minute

| DF |

½ teaspoon neutral oil
200 g/7 oz beef, thinly sliced
70 ml/2½ fl oz (scant ⅓ cup) lime juice
45 g/1½ oz onion, thinly sliced
15 g/½ oz shallot, thinly sliced
2 teaspoons fish sauce
1½ teaspoons sugar
¼ teaspoon black pepper
15 g/½ oz aromatic mixed herbs (rau thơm – perilla, basil, fish mint, Vietnamese balm), to serve

In a heavy pot, heat the oil until very hot. Using a paper towel, very carefully wipe the pot, leaving only a thin oil layer. Be careful, as the pot will be extremely hot.

Add the thinly sliced beef to the pot. Shake the pot for 20 seconds until the beef is barely cooked. Remove from the heat.

Transfer the beef to a mixing bowl, then add 40 ml/1¼ fl oz (2½ tablespoons) of the lime juice. Marinate for 10 minutes, then drain and discard the lime juice.

In a separate bowl, combine the onion and shallot with the remaining lime juice, 1 teaspoon of the fish sauce, the sugar and the black pepper. Let it marinate for 5 minutes.

Add the marinated onion mixture to the beef. Add the remaining fish sauce, then marinate for an additional 5 minutes.

Transfer to a serving plate. Top with the aromatic mixed herbs. Serve immediately.

# FISH SAUCE FRIED CHICKEN WINGS

## Cánh Gà Chiên Nước Mắm

This dish is one of my childhood favourites. It works equally well as a starter (appetizer) or main course with rice.

Serves 2–3
Preparation time: 30 minutes, plus 2–3 hours marinating time
Cooking time: 45 minutes

| DF |

- 6 chicken wings (about 670 g/1 lb 8 oz), cut through the joint to separate into wingettes (flats) and drumettes
- 2 tablespoons fish sauce
- 10 g/¼ oz shallot, coarsely smashed
- 20 g/¾ oz piece fresh ginger, coarsely smashed
- 25 g/1 oz onion, smashed
- 10 g/¼ oz garlic, smashed
- 1 teaspoon brown sugar
- ½ teaspoon salt
- 5 g/⅛ oz (1½ teaspoons) cornflour (cornstarch)
- 10 g/¼ oz (1½ tablespoons) rice flour
- 10 g/¼ oz (1½ tablespoons) plain (all-purpose) flour
- oil, for deep-frying

*For the sauce*

- 1 tablespoon neutral oil
- 15 g/½ oz garlic, chopped
- 1½ tablespoons light brown sugar
- 1½ tablespoons fish sauce
- ½ teaspoon black pepper

*To serve*

- fresh salad greens
- sliced cucumber
- sliced tomato, optional

In a bowl, marinate the chicken wings in the fish sauce for 2–3 hours, or longer in the refrigerator. Drain, reserving the marinating liquid.

In a large pot, combine 1.5 litres/2½ pints (6¼ cups) of water with the marinating liquid, smashed aromatics, sugar and salt. Bring to a simmer. Add the wings and bring to the boil. Cover, remove from the heat, then let stand for 15 minutes. Remove the wings, drain, then cool completely.

Mix the cornflour (cornstarch), rice flour and plain (all-purpose) flour in a bowl. Use to evenly coat the cooled wings.

Heat the frying oil to 190–200°C/375–400°F. If not using a thermometer, test the oil temperature by inserting wooden chopsticks into the oil – it should vigorously sizzle around them. Carefully add the wing tips and fry for 7–8 minutes, or larger pieces for 10 minutes, until golden brown. Carefully remove from the oil and drain on paper towels.

For the sauce, heat the neutral oil in a pan over a medium-low heat, then fry the garlic for 3–4 minutes until golden. Add the sugar, 3 tablespoons of water, the fish sauce and pepper. Reduce for 1 minute over a high heat.

Add the fried wings to the sauce and toss to evenly coat. Remove from the heat once well-coated.

Arrange the wings on a platter with the fresh salad greens, sliced cucumber and sliced tomato, if desired. Serve immediately.

# FRIED STUFFED SENTINEL CRAB

## Chả Ghẹ

This is a popular dish served at weddings or big celebrations, as the use of crab represents a sign of wealth. It is mixed with different ingredients to make a patty, then stuffed back in the shells and steamed, and when ready to serve, it is fried until golden. You can serve this with chilli sauce.

Serves 4 as a starter (appetizer)
Preparation time: about 1 hour
Cooking time: 35–40 minutes

| DF |

- 4 live male sentinel crabs (about 1.1 kg/2 lb 7 oz)
- 5 g/⅛ oz dried wood ear mushrooms
- 15 g/½ oz mung bean vermicelli
- 20 g/¾ oz garlic, finely chopped
- 40 g/1½ oz shallots, finely chopped
- 200 g/7 oz minced (ground) meat
- 200 g/7 oz Pork Paste (page 461)
- 1 uncooked salted duck egg
- 1 tablespoon light brown sugar
- ½ teaspoon black pepper
- 5 teaspoons fish sauce
- 1 heaped teaspoon oyster sauce
- 1 teaspoon Annatto Oil (page 457)
- oil, for deep-frying

Place the crabs in the freezer for 30 minutes before preparing the rest of the ingredients.

Soak the wood ear mushrooms in a bowl of warm water for 15 minutes, or until soft. Drain and finely chop. Set aside.

Soak the vermicelli in a bowl of warm water for about 15 minutes until soft. Drain, then cut into short lengths. Set aside.

Half-fill a pan with water, place a steamer basket on top and bring to the boil.

Remove the crabs from the freezer. Place the crabs bottom-side up on a chopping (cutting) board. Find the small hole near the rear (near the tail flap) and the slight depression near the front (thoracic and cerebral ganglia); with a spiking tool or sharp-pointed knife, spike all the way through the hole near the rear, then through the slight depression near the front.

Put the crabs in the steamer basket, cover with the lid and cook for 15 minutes until fully cooked. Remove from the steamer and let cool slightly until cool enough to handle.

Remove the top shell and set aside, and then use the back of a knife to crack open the claws. Pick the meat out of the claws and body (they should yield about 440 g/15½ oz of meat). Reserve the shells.

In a large mixing bowl, combine the garlic, shallots and minced (ground) meat. Mix thoroughly for 5 minutes. Add the softened vermicelli and mushrooms to the mixture and mix well, or blend if preferred. Add the pork paste, crab meat and salted egg. Combine thoroughly. Season with the sugar, pepper, fish sauce, oyster sauce and annatto oil. Mix until well combined.

Stuff the mixture into the reserved crab shells.

Fill a deep pan one-third full with the frying oil, then heat to 150–160°C/300–325°F. If not using a thermometer, test the oil temperature by inserting wooden chopsticks into the oil – it should gently bubble around them. Carefully add the stuffed shells and fry for 5–6 minutes on each side until golden and cooked through. Carefully remove from the oil and drain of paper towels. Serve hot.

# SMALL PRAWN FRIED ROLLS

## Ram Tôm Đất

This unique fried prawn (shrimp) roll features two key ingredients: *tôm đất* (small fresh prawns/shrimp) and *bánh ram Hà Tĩnh*, thin, square brown rice paper from Hà Tĩnh province. The rice paper gets its brown colour from a slight caramelization of sugar in the rice batter. Small prawns have edible shells when fried, adding a crunch to every bite. Small prawns can be substituted by medium size prawns, but those must be peeled and blanched.

Makes 30 rolls; serves 4–6 as a starter (appetizer)
Preparation time: 30 minutes
Cooking time: 7 minutes per batch

| DF |

30 small prawns (shrimp/tôm đất) or Mylor prawns
270 g/9½ oz minced (ground) pork,
20 g/¾ oz spring onion (scallion) greens, finely minced
55 g/2 oz shallots, finely minced
2 teaspoons fish sauce
¼ teaspoon black pepper
30 sheets of thin, square brown rice paper (bánh ram Hà Tĩnh) or spring roll sheets (18 × 18 cm/7 × 7 inches)
1 egg, beaten, for egg wash
oil, for deep-frying

*For the dipping sauce*
4 teaspoons sugar
10 g/¼ oz garlic, minced
7.5 g/¼ oz long red chilli (about ½), finely chopped
1 tablespoon vinegar
5 teaspoons fish sauce
1 tablespoon coconut water, optional

*To serve*
1 head of lettuce, or more as needed
100 g/3½ oz aromatic mixed herbs (rau thơm – spearmint, basil, mint, fish mint, perilla)
1 cucumber, sliced
Sweet and Sour Fish Sauce (page 471)

Using scissors, cut off the prawn (shrimp) heads. Clean and set aside. You should have about 280 g/10 oz of meat.

In a mixing bowl, combine the minced (ground) pork, spring onion (scallion) greens, shallots, fish sauce and pepper. Mix well.

Lay a sheet of rice paper on a clean work surface with the corner facing you. Brush with egg wash, then fold the left and right corners towards the middle to form a rectangle. Place a teaspoon of the pork mixture in the centre, then shape into a horizontal log. Place a prawn on top, with the tail peeking out. Roll up tightly from the bottom, keeping the tail visible. Repeat for the remaining rolls.

Mix all the dipping sauce ingredients in a small bowl until the sugar dissolves.

Half-fill a frying pan or skillet with oil and heat to 160–175°C/325–345°F. If not using a thermometer, test the oil temperature by inserting wooden chopsticks into the oil – it should bubble and crackle around them. Carefully add the rolls and fry for about 7 minutes until golden and crispy. Carefully remove with a slotted spoon and drain on paper towels.

Serve with the lettuce, herbs, cucumber, sweet and sour fish sauce and dipping sauce.

***Notes:*** If small prawns are unavailable, use regular prawns. Blanch, shell and de-head them before use.

The rolls can be frozen before frying. If frying from frozen, add 4 minutes to the frying time.

The square brown rice paper (bánh ram Hà Tĩnh) can be substituted with regular spring roll wrappers if unavailable.

# CRAB SPRING ROLLS

## Nem Cua Bể

Originally from Hải Phòng, a major port city in northeastern Vietnam, these crab spring rolls are wrapped into square pillows rather than the usual cylinders. You can make this as a starter (appetizer) or serve it with Hanoi-style Grilled Pork with Vermicelli (page 146).

Makes 10 spring rolls; serves 4–5
Preparation time: 30–40 minutes
Cooking time: 8 minutes per batch

| DF |

- 10 g/¼ oz dried mushrooms, soaked and finely chopped
- 250 g/5½ oz picked crab meat
- 200 g/7 oz minced (ground) meat (pork or chicken)
- 60 g/2¼ oz jicama, shredded and squeezed in a clean cloth to remove excess water (40 g/1½ oz after squeezing)
- 15 g/½ oz shallot, finely minced
- 1 teaspoon fish sauce
- ¼ teaspoon black pepper
- ½ teaspoon MSG
- 10 rice paper sheets (16 cm/6¼ inches square)
- bean sprouts (small amount for each roll)
- 5 cooked prawns (shrimp), halved
- vegetable oil, for deep-frying

*To serve*

- Northern-style Fish Sauce (page 471), optional
- lettuce leaves
- Vietnamese balm (kinh giới)
- Pickled Kohlrabi and Carrots (page 469)

Soak the dried mushrooms in a bowl of warm water for 15 minutes, or until soft. Drain and finely chop.

In a large mixing bowl, combine the crab meat, minced (ground) meat, chopped mushrooms, jicama and shallot. Add the fish sauce, pepper and MSG. Mix thoroughly.

Lay one rice paper sheet flat. Place a small amount of bean sprouts in the centre, top with a portion of filling mixture and one halved prawn (shrimp). Fold the rice paper into a tight square shape, ensuring the filling is completely sealed.

Heat the oil in deep pot or fryer to 175–180°C/345–350°F. If not using a thermometer, test the oil temperature by inserting wooden chopsticks into the oil – it should bubble vigorously around them. Working in batches, carefully fry the spring rolls in the oil for 8 minutes, turning occasionally, until golden brown and crispy. Remove with a skimmer and drain on paper towels. Let cool slightly before serving.

To serve, score the rolls into four sections, making them easy to pull apart, and serve with the fish sauce, if using, lettuce leaves, Vietnamese balm and pickles.

# CRAB/PRAWN SPRING ROLLS

Chả Giò Cua/Tôm

The secret to making great spring rolls, which was passed down to me by cô Vương Thị Minh Hiếu, my family nanny, lies in the ratio: always use three parts seafood to one part pork, allowing the crab or prawns (shrimp) to really shine. While some recipes incorporate dried vermicelli or sweet potato, in our family recipe, we use taro. It provides just enough starch to bind the filling perfectly, creating the ideal texture.

Makes 20–25 spring rolls; serves 4–5
Preparation time: 30–40 minutes
Cooking time: 7–8 minutes per batch

| DF |

15 g/½ oz dried mushrooms, rehydrated and finely chopped
50 g/1¾ oz carrot, shredded
80 g/2¾ oz jicama, shredded and squeezed in a clean cloth to remove excess water
100 g/3½ oz taro, finely diced
290 g/10 oz crab meat, picked and cleaned (or prawns/shrimp, see note)
100 g/3½ oz minced (ground) pork
25 g/1 oz shallots, finely minced
10 g/¼ oz garlic, finely minced
1 teaspoon all-purpose seasoning (hạt nêm)
1 teaspoon fish sauce
½ teaspoon sugar
½ teaspoon black pepper
20–25 sheets of 16-cm/6¼-inch-diameter circular dry rice paper (bánh tráng)
neutral oil, for deep-frying

*To serve*
Sweet and Sour Fish Sauce (page 471)
1 head of lettuce, leaves separated
aromatic mixed herbs (rau thơm – perilla, basil, fish mint, Vietnamese balm)

Soak the dried mushrooms in a bowl of warm water for 15 minutes, or until soft. Drain and finely chop.

In a large bowl, combine the mushrooms, carrot, jicama, taro, crab meat, minced (ground) pork, shallots and garlic. Add the all-purpose seasoning, fish sauce, sugar and pepper. Mix thoroughly.

Place a rice paper sheet on a dry surface. Add 2 tablespoons of the filling mixture near the edge. Roll tightly, folding the sides in. Seal the edge with a little water.

Half-fill a pan with oil and heat to 175–180°C/345–350°F. If not using a thermometer, test the oil temperature by inserting wooden chopsticks into the oil – it should bubble vigorously around them. Working in batches, carefully fry the rolls in the oil until golden brown, 7–8 minutes. Drain on paper towels.

Serve immediately with the fish sauce, lettuce and herbs.

***Note:*** If you don't have picked crab, you can boil some prawns (shrimp), then cut them into small pieces.

This dish can be served as a main starter (appetizer) or you can just make the rolls, freeze them and fry when needed to accompany for example Grilled Pork with Rice Noodles (page 145).

# PORK ROLL WITH GREEN CHILLI AND SHREDDED PORK SKIN

## Chả Lụa Bì Ớt Xiêm Xanh

This is a popular *Tết* (Lunar New Year) preparation that builds on the traditional pork roll used in Vietnamese baguette and *xôi* (steamed sticky/glutinous rice). Green chilli, small garlic cloves and pork skin are added for colour and texture. You can also use sliced pig's ear instead of pork skin if desired.

Makes approx. 700 g/1 lb 9 oz; serves 4–5
Preparation time: about 1 hour 30 minutes
Cooking time: 1 hour 15 minutes

| **DF** |

- 500 g/1 lb 2 oz lean minced (ground) pork (leg meat is best), frozen for 1 hour to make it super cold
- 2 tablespoons neutral oil
- ½ teaspoon baking powder
- 1 tablespoon (8 g/¼ oz) cornflour (cornstarch)
- 2 tablespoons fish sauce
- ½ teaspoon sugar
- 125 g/4¼ oz pork skin, boiled and shredded into 5-mm/¼-inch-thick slices
- 50 g/1¾ oz peeled garlic (choose tiny cloves, about 60)
- 20 g/¾ oz tiny green chillies, stalks removed (about 40 chillies)
- 2–3 banana leaves, blanched (see step 3, page 390), cut into 27-cm/10¾-inch squares (about 6)

In a food processor, combine the frozen minced (ground) pork, oil, baking powder, cornflour (cornstarch), fish sauce and sugar. Process for 3–4 minutes, scraping the bowl regularly, and keeping the mixture cold, until a paste forms.

Freeze the pork paste for 1 hour.

Return the pork paste to the food processor and process again for 3–4 minutes until completely smooth.

Mix the pork paste with the shredded pork skin, whole garlic cloves and chillies. Refrigerate for 1 hour minimum.

Lay the blanched banana leaves on a work surface, overlapping them to form a large rectangle. Spread the pork mixture evenly over the leaves, leaving a 5-cm/2-inch border. Roll tightly like a Swiss (jelly) roll, ensuring you have a compact, even roll. Tie with kitchen string at 2.5-cm/1-inch intervals and at the ends.

Set up a steamer and bring the water to the boil. Place the wrapped roll in the steamer basket, set over the boiling water and steam for 1 hour. Remove from the heat and let rest in the steamer for 15 minutes.

Remove from the steamer, and let cool completely before unwrapping and slicing into rounds.

Serve hot or cold. It can be served as a main dish, in a baguette or as part of a cold cuts platter.

# FIVE-COLOUR PORK ROLLS

## Chả Hoa Ngũ Sắc

Many celebratory Vietnamese dishes are created in the 'five-colour' style, symbolizing the five elements of yin-yang philosophy. In the north of Vietnam, it also represents unity between the different communities living together. This five-colour dishes are often eaten during important occasions like *Tết* (Lunar New Year) and other festive gatherings. Here we use different bright ingredients to reflect all the different colours, from carrots to salted egg yolks and green chillies.

Makes 2 large rolls; serves 6–8
Preparation time: about 1 hour 30 minutes
Cooking time: 1 hour 15 minutes

| DF |

**For the filling**
- 500 g/1 lb 2 oz lean minced (ground) pork (leg meat is best), frozen for 1 hour to make it super cold
- 2 tablespoons neutral oil
- ½ teaspoon baking powder
- 1 tablespoon cornflour (cornstarch)
- 2 tablespoons fish sauce
- ½ teaspoon sugar
- 25 g/1 oz peeled shallots
- 1 carrot (about 125 g/4¼ oz), peeled and diced into 5-mm/¼-inch cubes
- 10 green bird's eye chillies, cut into rounds

*For the rolls*
- 3 banana leaves, blanched (see note), cut into 27-cm/10¾-inch squares (about 6)
- neutral oil, for brushing
- 2 nori sheets
- 6 salted egg yolks

In a food processor, combine the frozen minced (ground) pork, oil, baking powder, cornflour (cornstarch), fish sauce and sugar. Process for 3–4 minutes, scraping the bowl regularly, and keeping the mixture cold, until a paste forms.

Freeze the pork paste for 1 hour.

Return the pork paste to the food processor and process again for 3–4 minutes until completely smooth.

In a separate batch, process the shallots until finely chopped, then add to the pork paste along with the carrots and chillies. Mix thoroughly to combine.

Divide the mixture into two equal portions.

Arrange 3 banana leaf squares, overlapping, on a work surface to form a rectangle shape; they should overlap to prevent tearing when wrapped tightly. Brush a thin layer of oil on the surface of the banana leaves to prevent the meat from sticking after cooking. Place a nori sheet on top, then spread one portion of pork mixture evenly on the nori. Place 3 of the salted egg yolks in the middle. Use both hands to roll the leaves into a cylinder and then tie string around the middle to secure. Fold over one end and stand the roll upright. Use two fingers to press the meat down firmly and fold over the top end. Tie the roll widthways and lengthways with string, ensuring it's secure but not overly tight, as the meat will expand slightly during cooking. Repeat with the remaining portion of pork mixture, banana leaves, nori and eggs.

Set up a steamer and bring the water to the boil. Place the wrapped rolls in the steamer basket, set over the boiling water and steam for 1 hour. Remove from the heat and let rest in the steamer for 15 minutes.

Remove from the steamer, and let cool completely before slicing for serving.

***Note:*** To soften the banana leaves, wash them and trim off the hard edges. Bring a pan of water to the boil and blanch the leaves for a few minutes to make them more pliable and durable. Alternatively, you can sun-dry the leaves until they wilt. Pat dry and set aside.

# CRISPY FRIED TINY SHRIMPS

## Tép Chiên Bột

In southern Vietnam's countryside, many families catch wild shrimps and small fish from their own ponds using nets set in the morning and collected in the afternoon. These fresh catches are then coated in crispy batter and served as a snack or starter (appetizer). Because of their size, locals usually eat these fish and shrimps whole, without gutting. You can adapt this recipe to any small seafood you have in hand, from brown shrimps to fresh tiny anchovies.

Serves 4–6
Preparation time: 15 minutes
Cooking time: 30 minutes

| DF |

- 75 g/2¾ oz (½ cup) rice flour
- 25 g/1 oz (2½ tablespoons) cornflour (cornstarch)
- ¼ teaspoon salt
- ½ teaspoon sugar
- ¼ teaspoon black pepper
- ⅛ teaspoon baking powder
- 1 teaspoon vinegar
- 100 ml/3½ fl oz (⅓ cup plus 1 tablespoon) cold water
- 20 g/¾ oz spring onions (scallions), finely chopped
- 250 g/5½ oz tiny shrimps or small fish
- oil, for frying

*To serve*

- 60 g/2¼ oz or 1 head of lettuce, leaves separated
- 40–50 g/1½–1¾ oz aromatic mixed herbs/herb salad (rau thơm/rau sống – perilla, fish mint, Vietnamese basil, peppermint, coriander/cilantro)
- pickled vegetables
- sliced cucumber
- Basic Dipping Fish Sauce (page 470)

In a large bowl, mix together the rice flour, cornflour (cornstarch), salt, sugar, pepper and baking powder. Add the vinegar and cold water and stir until smooth. Fold in the spring onions (scallions). Let the batter rest for 5 minutes.

Fill a non-stick pan with oil to a depth of 1 cm/½ inch. Heat to 175–180°C/345–350°F. If not using a thermometer, test the oil temperature by inserting wooden chopsticks into the oil – it should bubble vigorously around them.

Mix the tiny shrimps into the batter. Using a ladle, carefully slide portions of the shrimp batter into the hot oil. Fry for 3 minutes per side, or until golden and crispy. Remove using a skimmer, then drain on paper towels.

Alternatively, for make-ahead preparation, fry at lower temperature for 6 minutes, then before serving, refry at 180°C/350°F for 1–2 minutes until crisp.

Arrange on a serving plate with the lettuce leaves, mixed herbs, pickled vegetables, sliced cucumber, and dipping sauce.

Serve immediately.

# SUGAR CANE PRAWNS

Chạo Tôm

A starter (appetizer) often found at celebrations or get-togethers, this dish consists of a prawn (shrimp) and meat paste wrapped around sugar cane or lemongrass stalks. This recipe avoids salt to preserve the natural moisture of the prawns. To serve, slice the meat vertically, wrap one half in lettuce with *bánh hỏi* (fine rice vermicelli sheets) and fresh herbs, then dip in seasoned fish sauce.

Makes 20; serves 8–10 as a starter (appetizer)
Preparation time: 40 minutes
Cooking time: 25–30 minutes

| DF |

- 470 g/1 lb unpeeled prawns (shrimp)
- 180 g/6 oz Pork Paste (page 461) (see note)
- 300 g/10½ oz minced (ground) pork
- 2 tablespoons Annatto Oil (page 457)
- 80 g/2¾ oz onion, finely chopped
- 15 g/½ oz garlic, finely chopped
- 35 g/1¼ oz shallots, finely chopped
- 1 tablespoon fish sauce
- 1 teaspoon sesame oil
- 1 teaspoon all-purpose seasoning (hạt nêm)
- 1 teaspoon sugar
- 20 sugar cane or lemongrass stalks, cut into 15-cm/6-inch-long pieces

*To serve*

- 200 g/7 oz fine rice vermicelli sheets (bánh hỏi )
- aromatic mixed herbs (rau thơm – perilla, spearmint, coriander/cilantro, basil, Vietnamese balm, mint)
- 1 head of lettuce, leaves separated
- Sweet and Sour Fish Sauce (page 471)

Set up a steamer and bring the water to the boil. Place the prawns (shrimp) in the steamer basket, set over the boiling water and steam for 2–3 minutes until just pink. Remove from the steamer, carefully peel and let cool completely. You should have about 250 g/5½ oz meat.

Ensure all the ingredients are well chilled. In a food processor, combine the pork paste, minced (ground) pork, peeled prawns, annatto oil, onion, garlic and shallots. Process until smooth.

Transfer the mixture to a bowl. Add the fish sauce, sesame oil, all-purpose seasoning and sugar. Mix thoroughly with your hands.

Divide the mixture into 20 equal portions. Mould each portion around a sugar cane stalk to form a log shape.

Refill the steamer and bring the water to the boil. Place the assembled 'prawns' in the steamer basket, set over the boiling water and steam for 5–7 minutes to set the shape.

Heat a charcoal barbecue grill, then wait for the flames to die down until you have amber coals or place a frying pan or skillet over a medium heat. Grill or fry the steamed 'prawns' for 5–7 minutes, turning occasionally, until golden brown and cooked through.

Transfer to a serving plate. Serve with the rice vermicelli sheets, fresh herbs, lettuce leaves and sweet and sour fish sauce.

***Note:*** If pork paste is unavailable, substitute with the same quantity of minced (ground) pork.

# CRAB SOUP

## Súp Cua

While *súp cua măng tây* (crab and asparagus soup), similar to Chinese crab and sweetcorn soup (also called corn crab soup), is served at wedding banquets, this version is a breakfast staple found on the streets of Vietnam. The egg-drop technique helps stretch the expensive crab meat, while shredded chicken adds bulk and protein to the soup. The key lies in maintaining proper ratios – too many ingredients will overwhelm the soup's subtle flavours. It can also be served as a starter (appetizer) during family meals.

Serves 6–8
Preparation time: 30 minutes
Cooking time: 2 hours 15 minutes

| DF |

*For blanching the bones*
25 g/1 oz spring onion (scallion) whites
30 g/1 oz piece fresh ginger (about 6 cm/ 2½ inches), crushed
1 kg/2 lb 4 oz pork bones

*For the broth*
20 g/¾ oz (⅔ cup) dried shiitake mushrooms
500 ml/18 fl oz (2 cups) warm water
1 × 140 g/5 oz onion, peeled and halved
1 corn cob
15 g/½ oz peeled shallot
70 g/2½ oz chicken

*For the soup*
70 g/2½ oz crab meat
½ teaspoon MSG
1 teaspoon salt
½ teaspoon all-purpose seasoning (hạt nêm)
1 teaspoon sesame oil
1 egg (50 g/1¾ oz)
40 g/1½ oz (⅓ cup) cornflour (cornstarch)
¼ teaspoon black pepper
⅛ teaspoon white pepper
15 cooked and peeled quail eggs, optional

*For garnish*
coriander (cilantro), leaves picked
pinch of black pepper
fresh chilli slices
light soy sauce
vinegar

To blanch the bones, bring 1 litre/1¾ pints (4¼ cups) water to the boil with the spring onion (scallion) whites and ginger. Add the pork bones and blanch for 2 minutes, then drain and rinse the bones thoroughly.

To prepare the broth, soak the dried shiitake mushrooms in the measured warm water for 10 minutes. Drain, then slice and set aside.

Using tongs, carefully hold the halved onion over an open flame, turning until charred all over, 4–5 minutes. Alternatively, heat the grill (broiler) to high and char under the grill, turning frequently, for 4–5 minutes. Remove black spots, then set aside.

Separate the corn kernels from the cob. You should have about 180 g/6 oz (1 cup) kernels. (Keep any leftover kernels for another dish.)

To make the broth, in a large pot, combine 2.5 litres/4½ pints (10½ cups) water with the blanched bones, charred onion and shallot. Add the corn cob and 120 g/4¼ oz (⅔ cup) corn kernels with their liquid. Bring to the boil and simmer for 1 hour 45 minutes. Add the chicken and cook for 15 minutes.

Meanwhile, prepare a bowl of iced water.

When the chicken is cooked, remove the chicken from the broth, then immediately submerge in the iced water. When the chicken is cool enough to handle, shred. Strain the broth and reserve for the soup.

To make the soup, in a pan over a medium-low heat, add 60 g/ 2¼ oz (⅓ cup) corn kernels, the soaked mushrooms, all the shredded chicken and the crab meat to the strained broth. Season with the MSG, salt, all-purpose seasoning and sesame oil.

Crack the egg into a small bowl, then beat well.

Mix the cornflour (cornstarch) with 40 ml/1¼ fl oz (2½ tablespoons) of water, then add to the broth while stirring, to thicken.

Ensuring the soup is simmering, slowly pour in the beaten egg while stirring to create egg threads.

Add the black and white pepper and the cooked and peeled quail eggs, if using, and remove from the heat.

To serve, ladle the soup into bowls, garnish with coriander (cilantro) and a pinch of black pepper, and serve with chilli slices, soy sauce and vinegar on the side.

***Note:*** You can substitute the crab with prawns (shrimp).

# SALADS

## Món gỏi

With its diverse geography, Vietnam is abundant in tropical fruits, vegetables and herbs. During hot seasons, *gỏi* (salads, also known as *nộm* in the north) are a great way to counter the extreme heat. Both fruits and vegetables, from rambutans and mangoes to the recently trendy mangosteen, can be used in Vietnamese salads. These ingredients are paired with protein and a light, sweet, sour and sometimes spicy dressing. Oil is generally not used; the fattiness (*vị béo*) comes instead from toasted peanuts, sesame seeds or fried shallots and garlic. You can serve most of these salads with grilled rice crackers or prawn crackers.While more elaborate salads like Lotus Stem Salad (page 125) appear at gatherings and weddings, simple ones like Cucumber Salad (page 135) can be served alongside family meals.

The methodology is simple and adaptable to ingredients at your disposal: vegetables, fruits or a combination of both; protein, if desired, from poached meat to dried fish; herbs for aromatic notes; a light dressing from the selection in this chapter; and toasted nuts or fried aromatics. You can observe subtle flavour differences between Northern-style salads and Southern-style ones and tweak your own version to your taste.

# POMELO SALAD

## Gỏi Bưởi

As pomelo is the star of this salad, it must be ripe enough to be juicy, sweet and tangy at the same time. At my house, we usually use *bưởi năm roi* ('five spankings pomelo', a variety of white pomelo), which traditionally grew in Vĩnh Long province. Legend has it that the name comes from an early twentieth-century farmer who would give five spankings to any child caught stealing his pomelos – the name stuck thanks to the fruit's enduring popularity. According to cô Vương Thị Minh Hiếu, the best time to make this dish is during the fifth month of the lunar calendar, when the pomelos are at their biggest and juiciest.

Serves 4–6
Preparation time: 45 minutes
Marinating time: 30 minutes

| DF |

170 g/5¾ oz cucumber (1 medium)
160 g/5½ oz carrots, peeled and cut into thin matchsticks (julienned)
300 g/10½ oz tiny shrimps (or 8 medium prawns), boiled and peeled
450 g/1 lb Poached Pork Belly (page 463), thinly sliced
1 tablespoon sugar
1 tablespoon fish sauce
60 ml/2 fl oz (¼ cup) lime juice
370 g/13 oz pomelo flesh, in chunks

*For the dressing*
15 g/½ oz garlic, minced
5 g/⅛ oz long red chilli, deseeded and minced
4 teaspoons sugar
3 ½ teaspoons fish sauce
1 tablespoon lime juice

*For the dipping sauce*
20 g/¾ oz garlic, chopped
5 g/⅛ oz deseeded chillies
1 tablespoon fish sauce
3 teaspoons light brown sugar

*To serve*
60 g/2¼ oz (4 tablespoons) Fried Shallots and Garlic (page 459)
10 g/¼ oz long red chilli, thinly sliced
20 g/¾ oz Vietnamese coriander/cilantro (rau răm), coarsely chopped
15 g/½ oz Vietnamese basil (húng quế) or holy basil, coarsely chopped

Use a sharp knife or julienne peeler to cut the cucumber lengthways into 3; use a spoon to scoop out and discard the seeds, then cut into thin matchsticks (julienne).

In a large mixing bowl, combine the julienned cucumber, carrots, shrimps and pork belly (side). Add the sugar, fish sauce and lime juice. Stir to evenly coat the ingredients. Cover and marinate for 30 minutes, then drain any excess liquid.

For the dressing, in a small bowl, mix together the garlic, chilli, sugar, fish sauce and lime juice.

For the dipping sauce, in another small bowl, combine the garlic, chillies, fish sauce, sugar and 2 tablespoons of water. Stir until the sugar dissolves.

To assemble the salad, transfer the drained, marinated salad base to a serving bowl. Add the pomelo and drizzle the dressing over the top. Gently toss everything together until evenly coated.

To serve, top the salad with the fried shallots and garlic, sliced chilli, chopped Vietnamese coriander/cilantro and chopped Vietnamese or holy basil. Serve the dipping sauce on the side for additional seasoning as desired.

# LOTUS STEM SALAD

## Gỏi Ngó Sen

Lotus, the national flower of Vietnam, is a versatile ingredient in Vietnamese cuisine. The seeds can be toasted and eaten as snacks, the leaves can be used to wrap and steam ingredients, and the roots can be used for various preparations. This salad uses young, crunchy lotus stems, which are prepared in stages and assembled just before eating. A special technique is used to remove stringy bits from the stems for a better eating experience. This recipe makes a large sharing plate for a family.

Serves 6
Preparation time: 1 hour
Marinating time: 50 minutes

| DF | GF |

500 g/1 lb 2 oz young lotus stems (ngó sen)
juice of 1 lime, plus 50 ml/2 fl oz (3½ tablespoons) juice
100 g/3½ oz carrot, shredded
1 long red chilli, sliced
350 g/12 oz Poached Pork Belly (page 463), thinly sliced
14 prawns (shrimp), cooked and peeled (about 100 g)
50 g/1¾ oz (¼ cup) sugar
170 g/5¾ oz Basic Dressing for Salad (page 478), plus extra to serve

*For the pickled onion*
75 g/2¾ oz onion, thinly sliced
60 ml/2 fl oz (¼ cup) rice vinegar
1 tablespoon sugar

*To serve*
1 long red chilli, cut diagonally
5 g/⅛ oz Vietnamese coriander/cilantro (rau răm)
5 g/⅛ oz coriander (cilantro)
25 g/1 oz (1½ tablespoons) Fried Shallots (page 458)
25 g/1 oz (1½ tablespoons) Fried Garlic (page 458)
35 g/1¼ oz (¼ cup) Toasted Peanuts (page 459), crushed
prawn crackers

Using kitchen shears or a sharp knife, trim the ends of the lotus stems, then cut the lotus stems into 6-cm/2½-inch lengths.

In a large bowl, soak the lotus stem pieces in water with the juice of the whole lime for 30 minutes.

Using a pair of chopsticks or a spoon, stir the lotus stems in a circular motion, removing any stringy bits as they cling to the chopsticks. Continue this process until you don't see any more stringy bits. Drain the lotus stems, discarding the lime water, and use a clean dish towel to squeeze them dry.

To make the pickled onion, in a small bowl, combine the onion, vinegar and sugar. Let the onion marinate for 20 minutes.

In a large mixing bowl, combine the prepared lotus stems, carrot, chilli, sliced pork belly (side), prawns (shrimp), pickled onion and its liquid, sugar and the remaining lime juice. Let the salad marinate for 20 minutes, then discard any excess liquid. Add the basic dressing for salad and toss everything together.

Transfer the salad to a serving platter. Garnish with the long red chilli, Vietnamese coriander/cilantro, coriander (cilantro), fried shallots, fried garlic and crushed toasted peanuts.

Serve with prawn crackers and extra basic dressing for salad for dipping.

# FIG SALAD WITH PORK AND PRAWNS

## Gỏi Trái Vả Tôm Thịt

*Trái vả* (*Ficus auriculata Lour*), a fig relative, is a speciality of Quảng Nam province in Central Vietnam. The green fruit is traditionally served raw and thinly sliced alongside *bánh khoái* (Huế-style Savoury Pancakes, page 418), or as in this recipe, boiled and then stir-fried. This version comes from Trịnh Thị Thu, of the ancient village of Phước Tích, in Thừa Thiên-Huế province. She shared her family recipe that uses figs from her garden. Her personal tip is to avoid using fish sauce in the main preparation to prevent it from overpowering the delicate flavour of the figs. It should be served with *bánh đa mè đen* (crispy sesame rice crackers) as a large starter (appetizer) in a meal.

Serves 8–10 as a side
Preparation time: 1 hour
Cooking time: 1 hour

| DF |

- 1 kg/2 lb 4 oz green figs (trái vả)
- 300 g/10½ oz pork belly (side)
- 500 g/1 lb 2 oz whole prawns (shrimp)
- 3 tablespoons neutral oil
- 35 g/1¼ oz garlic, thinly sliced
- ½ teaspoon chilli powder
- 1½ teaspoons MSG
- 1½ tablespoons all-purpose seasoning (hạt nêm)
- 1 tablespoon sugar
- ½ teaspoon black pepper
- ½ teaspoon salt
- 45 g/1½ oz (⅓ cup) peanuts, toasted
- 3.5 g bird's eye chilli, thinly sliced
- 1½ tablespoons sesame seeds
- 30 g/1 oz (2 tablespoons) Fried Shallots (page 458)
- 25 g/1 oz Vietnamese coriander/cilantro (rau răm), leaves picked
- 35 g/1¼ oz spearmint, leaves picked
- 1 teaspoon lime juice, or more to taste

*To serve*
- 50 g/1¾ oz long red chilli, sliced
- crispy sesame rice crackers, optional

Bring a large pot of water to the boil. Add the green figs and boil for 55 minutes over a medium-high heat.

Meanwhile, bring a pot of water to a simmer. Poach the pork belly (side) in the simmering water for 15 minutes. Drain the cooked pork, then cut into dice.

At the same time, bring another pot of water to the boil. Add the prawns (shrimp) and boil for 11–14 minutes until fully opaque and cooked through. Drain the prawns and, when cool enough to handle, peel them.

Using a slotted spoon, transfer the boiled figs to a chopping (cutting) board. When cool enough to handle, peel the figs and thinly slice them, squeezing out any excess water. You should have 500 g/1 lb 2 oz of prepared fig slices. Do not rinse the figs.

In a wok, heat the oil over a medium heat. Fry the garlic in the oil for 2–3 minutes until golden brown, then remove the wok from the heat and stir in the chilli powder.

Add the diced pork and peeled prawns to the wok. Stir-fry briefly to coat everything in the chilli oil. Add the sliced figs to the wok and increase the heat. Season with the MSG, all-purpose seasoning, sugar, pepper and salt. Stir-fry for 2 minutes, then remove from the heat. Add half of the toasted peanuts and the bird's eye chilli. Stir to combine.

Heat a small dry frying pan or skillet over a medium heat. Toast the sesame seeds in the pan, stirring frequently, for a few minutes until golden.

In a large serving bowl, combine the fig salad mixture, the remaining toasted peanuts, the toasted sesame seeds, the fried shallots, the Vietnamese coriander/cilantro and spearmint leaves and the lime juice. Gently toss everything together until well combined.

Transfer the dressed salad to a large serving plate, garnish with the sliced long red chilli and serve immediately with a crispy sesame rice crackers, if you like.

FIG SALAD WITH PORK AND PRAWNS

# CHICKEN AND BANANA BLOSSOM SALAD

## Gỏi Gà Hoa Chuối

This versatile salad can be enjoyed as a starter (appetizer) with prawn crackers, served alongside Chicken Congee (page 254), or simply paired with plain white rice. At home, poaching a whole chicken provides both the meat for this salad and a flavorful stock for other dishes. While it's a common dish to eat at home, you'll also find it at weddings or gatherings as a starter, typically served with prawn crackers.

Serves 2–3
Preparation time: 45–60 minutes
Cooking time: 10 minutes

| DF |

125 g/4¼ oz pepper elder (rau càng cua), picked (80 g/3 oz leaves)
1 carrot (about 135 g/4½ oz)
100 g/3½ oz banana blossom (bắp chuối)
juice of ½ lime
120 g/4¼ oz shredded morning glory (rau muống)
10 g/¼ oz Thai holy basil, leaves picked
25 g/1 oz Vietnamese coriander/cilantro (rau răm), leaves picked
15 g/½ oz long red chilli (about 1), sliced
140 g/5 oz cooked chicken thighs, shred the chicken into bite-size pieces
50 g/1¾ oz (1/3 cup) Toasted Peanuts (page 459)
5 lime leaves, sliced

*For the pickled onion*
115 g/4 oz onion, thinly sliced
1 tablespoon sugar
60 ml/2 fl oz (¼ cup) vinegar
70 g/2½ oz ice

*For the fried shallots*
60 ml/2 fl oz (¼ cup) neutral oil
85 g/3 oz peeled shallots

*For the dressing*
5 tablespoons calamansi juice
30 g/1 oz (2 tablespoons) sugar
1 teaspoon fish sauce

*For the dipping sauce*
2 tablespoons fish sauce
2 tablespoons sugar
2 tablespoons calamansi juice
15 g/½ oz garlic, minced
5 g/⅛ oz long red chilli, deseeded and minced

Soak the pepper elder in a bowl of iced water for 5–10 minutes, then drain in a colander.

Cut the carrot into thin matchsticks (julienne) or shred it using a grater (shredder), Soak in another bowl of iced water for 5 minutes, then drain.

Using a knife, shred the banana blossom. Soak in a bowl of cold water with the lime juice for 15 minutes, then drain.

Meanwhile, soak the morning glory in another bowl of cold water for about 15 minutes, then drain in a colander.

To make the pickled onion, in a mixing bowl, combine the onion, sugar and vinegar, then leave to pickle for 20 minutes. Add the ice, then stir with a spoon. Set aside.

To make the fried shallots, heat the oil in small frying pan or skillet over a medium heat. Add the shallots, then fry for 5–7 minutes until golden. Remove with a skimmer and drain on a paper towel-lined plate.

To make the dressing, in a small bowl, whisk together the calamansi juice, sugar and fish sauce until the sugar has dissolved. Set aside.

To make the dipping sauce, in separate small bowl, combine the fish sauce, sugar, calamansi juice, garlic and chilli. Stir with spoon until blended, then set aside.

To assemble the salad, in a large mixing bowl, combine all the prepared vegetables, drained pickled onion, herbs and chilli.

Add the chicken and fried shallots. Pour the dressing over and gently toss with large spoons or your hands.

Transfer the salad to a serving platter and top with the toasted peanuts and sliced lime leaves. Serve with the dipping sauce in a small bowl alongside.

# POACHED DUCK AND CABBAGE SALAD

## Gỏi Vịt Bắp Cải

This dish works with either duck or chicken. Serve it as a salad with prawn crackers or alongside congee. The poaching stock can be used to cook rice, similar to Hội An Chicken Rice (page 263).

Serves 4–6
Preparation time: 15 minutes, plus 30 minutes marinating time

| DF |

320 g/11¼ oz Turkish cabbage, shredded
150 g/5½ oz onion, sliced into rounds
105 g/3¾ oz carrot, peeled and shredded
240 ml/8 fl oz (1 cup) Homemade Vinegar (page 456), or rice vinegar
ice cubes
50 g/1¾ oz Vietnamese coriander/cilantro (rau răm), leaves picked, plus 15 g/½ oz to serve
800 g/1 lb 12 oz poached duck (such as from Duck Congee, page 255), sliced with a cleaver

*For the dressing*
3 tablespoons calamansi juice
2 tablespoons sugar
1 tablespoon fish sauce
15 g/½ oz chilli (about 1), deseeded and diagonally sliced

*To serve*
20 g/¾ oz (2 tablespoons) Toasted Peanuts (page 459), coarsely crushed
20 g/¾ oz (4 teaspoons) Fried Shallots (page 458)
2 tablespoons Ginger Dipping Fish Sauce (page 474), for drizzling, plus a small bowl

Soak the shredded cabbage in a bowl of iced water to maintain its crispness.

Rinse the onion under cold water, then combine in a bowl with the carrot and vinegar and marinate for 30 minutes. Add ice cubes to maintain the vegetables' crispness, then drain well.

In a large bowl, combine the drained cabbage, marinated onion and carrot, and Vietnamese coriander/cilantro leaves. Add the duck to the vegetable mixture.

Combine the dressing ingredients in a small bowl and stir until the sugar dissolves. Pour the dressing over the salad, then toss thoroughly to combine.

Transfer the salad to a serving platter. Top with the crushed toasted peanuts and fried shallots, drizzle over 2 tablespoons of the ginger dipping fish sauce and garnish with the extra Vietnamese coriander.

Serve immediately with a small bowl of the ginger dipping fish sauce on the side.

# MANGO AND DRIED FISH SALAD

Gỏi Xoài Khô Cá Sặc

This salad combines the tangy flavour of green mango with the savoury taste of dried snakeskin gourami fish (*Trichopodus pectoralis*). This dish originates from the southern region near the Mekong Delta and Cà Mau, showcasing popular local ingredients. The fish used is typically a freshwater species that has been salted and sun-dried for preservation. Outside of Vietnam, it can be found in Asian supermarkets.

Serves 4–6
Preparation time: 30 minutes
Cooking time: 10 minutes

| DF |

- 1 young mango, peeled (620 g/1 lb 6 oz after peeling)
- boiling water, for soaking
- 255 g/9 oz dried salted snakeskin gourami (khô cá sặc) or any other dried fish
- 60 ml/2 fl oz (¼ cup) plus 2 tablespoons neutral oil
- 10 g/¼ oz shallot, coarsely chopped
- 35 g/1¼ oz garlic, coarsely chopped
- 425 g/15 oz cucumber
- 335 g/11½ oz Poached Pork Belly (page 463), sliced
- 1 quantity Tamarind Dipping Sauce (page 476)
- 25 g/1 oz Vietnamese basil (húng quế), leaves picked
- 20 g/¾ oz Vietnamese coriander/cilantro (rau răm), leaves picked
- 2 bird's eye chillies, thinly sliced, optional

Shred the mango using a grater. Soak in a bowl of iced water to maintain its crispness.

Pour boiling water over the dried fish to clean it. Drain thoroughly.

Heat the 60 ml/2 fl oz (¼ cup) of oil in a pan over a medium heat. Fry the fish for 4–5 minutes until golden. Remove the fish from the pan, let it cool, then shred into pieces.

In a separate pan, heat the remaining oil. Fry the shallot and garlic in the oil for 5–6 minutes until golden. Drain on paper towels.

Using a julienne peeler, peel the cucumber lengthways, alternating peeled and unpeeled sections so the cucumber looks like it has 'zebra stripes'. Discard the peel and slice the cucumber into rounds.

Drain the mango well. In a large bowl, combine the shredded mango, cucumber slices, poached pork belly (side), shredded fried fish, half the tamarind dipping sauce, the herbs and the chillies, if using.

Transfer the salad to a serving platter and top with the fried shallots and garlic.

Serve immediately with the remaining tamarind dipping sauce on the side.

# GREEN MANGO SALAD WITH DRIED SQUID

Gỏi Xoài Khô Mực

To choose the right mango for this dish, look for a mango that is firm and not completely ripe. The best are light yellow in colour, with a nice acidity. While I use dried squid for this recipe, you can replace it with sliced pork belly (side), pig's ear or even jellyfish. While ripe mangoes are eaten as fruit, the sour ones are perfect for salad or just to eat with a dipping salt like Roasted Chilli Salt (page 479).

Serves 3–4
Preparation time: 30 minutes
Cooking time: 20 minutes

| DF |

- 1 mango, not too ripe (570 g/1 lb 4 oz)
- 2 dried squid (60 g/2¼ oz), soaked in water
- 20 g/¾ oz Vietnamese coriander/cilantro (rau răm)
- 20 g/¾ oz chillies (1–2 chillies), deseeded and thinly sliced
- 25 g/1 oz (2½ tablespoons) roasted peanuts

*For the sauce*

- 15 g/½ oz peeled garlic
- 5 g/⅛ oz chilli (about ¼ chilli), deseeded
- 2 teaspoons sugar
- 1 tablespoon fish sauce
- 1 tablespoon lime juice

*For the fried shallots*

- 2 tablespoons neutral oil
- 50 g/1¾ oz peeled shallots

Peel the mango and shred it using a grater (shredder). You should have about 350 g/12 oz of shredded mango.

To create the sauce, put the garlic and deseeded and sliced chilli in a mortar and pound with a pestle until you have a fine paste. Mix this paste with the sugar, fish sauce and lime juice.

Heat a charcoal grill.

Drain the soaked squid, then grill for about 7 minutes, turning every 15 seconds to avoid excessive burn marks.

Roll the grilled squid widthways and smash it with the handle of a cleaver, then shred it and set it aside.

To make the fried shallots, heat the oil in a pan over a medium–low heat. Fry the shallots for about 9 minutes or until golden. Remove with a skimmer and set aside. Reserve the oil in the pan.

With the pan over a medium heat, quickly fry the shredded squid for 1 minute.

In a large bowl, combine the shredded mango, Vietnamese coriander/cilantro, sliced chillies, half the fried shallots, half the peanuts and the sauce.

Transfer the salad to a serving plate. Top with the remaining fried shallots and peanuts, and the fried squid.

Serve immediately.

# HERRING SALAD

## Gỏi Cá Trích

This dish comes from Phú Quốc, an island in Kiên Giang province known for its fishing waters, where herring, anchovies for fish sauce production and other seafood are caught daily. The fish must be impeccably fresh and properly filleted, removing head, bones and innards. In Vietnam, herrings are at their plumpest from September to November, considered the prime season for this dish.

Serves 4–6
Preparation time: 45 minutes
Cooking time: 5 minutes

| DF |

1 onion (110 g/3¾ oz), thinly sliced
300 g/10½ oz herring fillet
255 ml/8½ fl oz (1 cup) lime juice
40 g/1½ oz (scant ½ cup) desiccated (shredded) coconut
25 g/1 oz (2½ tablespoons) Toasted Peanuts (page 459), coarsely pounded

*For the dipping sauce*
30 g/1 oz (3 tablespoons) peanuts, finely pounded (not too pasty)
155 g/5½ oz (¾ cup) Basic Dressing for Salad (page 478), or more to taste

*For the fried garlic*
2 tablespoons neutral oil
20 g/¾ oz garlic, thinly sliced

*To serve*
5 g/⅛ oz watermint (húng lùi)
5 g/⅛ oz peppermint (húng cây)
5 g/⅛ oz Vietnamese coriander/cilantro (rau răm)
1 long red chilli, deseeded and thinly sliced
lime wedges, optional
lettuce leaves
dry rice paper (bánh tráng)

In a bowl, soak the onion in iced water for about 30 minutes to maintain its crispness. Drain the onions when ready to use.

For the dipping sauce, in a small bowl, mix together the finely pounded peanuts with 100 g/3½ oz (½ cup) of the basic dressing for salad until combined. Set aside for serving.

For the fried garlic, in a small skillet, heat the oil over a medium heat. Fry the garlic for 2–3 minutes until golden brown. Strain the fried garlic using a fine-mesh sieve or slotted spoon, reserving both the fried garlic and the infused oil. (The infused oil isn't needed for this dish but it can be saved for another use. It will keep in the refrigerator for up to 1 month.)

In a large mixing bowl, combine the herring fillet and the drained onion. Add the remaining 55 g/2 oz (¼ cup) of the basic dressing for salad and the lime juice. Mix everything together well. Add the desiccated (shredded) coconut and half of the fried garlic. Gently mix to combine.

Transfer the salad to a serving platter. Sprinkle the coarsely pounded toasted peanuts and the remaining fried garlic over the top of the salad. Garnish with the watermint, peppermint, Vietnamese coriander/cilantro and sliced chilli.

Serve the salad with the prepared dipping sauce, lime wedges, if using, lettuce leaves, and rice paper on the side.

## WHITE SARDINE SALAD

Gỏi Cá Mai

This raw sardine salad can be used in Phan Thiết-style 'Yin and Yang' Hotpot (page 178) or eaten like rolls in dishes with *bánh tráng* (rice paper) and herbs. This type of white sardine is typically caught by fishers from September to the beginning of March, in Bình Định, in the central coastal region of Vietnam.

Serves 3–4
Preparation time: 15 minutes

| DF | ≤30 |

10 g/¼ oz long red chilli, or more depending on your taste, sliced
½ teaspoon salt
½ teaspoon MSG
1 teaspoon sugar
4 teaspoons lime juice
1 teaspoon fish sauce
30 g/1 oz garlic, thinly sliced
30 g/1 oz piece fresh ginger (about 6 cm/ 2½ inches), peeled and cut into thin matchsticks (julienned)
250 g/5½ oz white sardine fillet
wedge of lime
15 g/½ oz (1½ tablespoons) Toasted Peanuts (page 459)
20–40 g/¾–1½ oz onion, sliced
1 quantity dipping sauce from Herring Salad (page 132), to serve

In a small mixing bowl, combine the chilli, salt, MSG, sugar, lime juice and fish sauce. Mix well. Add half of the garlic and half the ginger to the seasoning mixture and stir to combine.

Add the white sardine fillet and use your hands or a spoon to gently coat the fish with the marinade. Cover and let marinate for 30 minutes.

On a serving plate, arrange the marinated white sardine fillet. Top with the remaining garlic, the remaining ginger, a lime wedge, toasted peanuts and onion.

Serve the salad with the dipping sauce on the side.

## FERMENTED YOUNG JACKFRUIT SALAD FROM THANH CHUONG

Nộm Nhút Mít Thanh Chương

Fermentation transforms raw young jackfruit's texture, making it more versatile for dishes like this salad or stir-fries.

Serves 2–3 as a starter (appetizer)
Preparation time: 15 minutes

| V | VE | DF | GF | ≤30 |

95 g/3½ oz Fermented Young Jackfruit (Central Vietnamese Style) (page 470), squeezed to remove excess liquid
½ teaspoon MSG
1 teaspoon sugar
¼ teaspoon black pepper
40 g/1½ oz Vietnamese balm (kinh giới), roughly chopped
2 lime leaves, cut into thin matchsticks (julienned)
90 g/3¼ oz (⅔ cup) peanuts, skin removed, toasted and coarsely crushed
2 bird's eye chillies, or to taste, thinly sliced
40 g/1½ oz (¼ cup) black sesame seeds, toasted and crushed

Put the jackfruit, MSG, sugar and black pepper into a bowl and mix well to allow the seasonings to be absorbed into the jackfruit.

Add the chopped Vietnamese balm, lime leaves, peanuts, chillies and sesame seeds. Mix gently but thoroughly to combine all the ingredients.

Transfer the salad to a serving plate. This salad is best enjoyed immediately while the herbs are fresh.

## CUCUMBER SALAD

Nộm Dưa Chuột

This quick, simple salad is perfect for everyday family meals.

Serves 2–3
Preparation time: 10 minutes, plus 30 minutes marinating time

| V | VE | DF | GF |

350 g/12 oz cucumber
3.5 g (½ teaspoon) soup powder (bột canh) (1 per cent of cucumber weight)

*For the seasoning*
¾ teaspoon soup powder (bột canh)
1¼ teaspoons sugar
¼ teaspoon black pepper
¾ teaspoon lime juice
¼ teaspoon chilli, or to taste
¼ teaspoon MSG

*To garnish*
¼ teaspoon chopped garlic
15 g/½ oz Vietnamese balm (kinh giới), roughly chopped
15 g/½ oz Vietnamese basil (húng quế), coarsely chopped
30 g/1 oz (3 tablespoons) Toasted Peanuts (page 459), coarsely pounded

Use a sharp knife to halve the cucumber lengthways, then slice the halves horizontally into thin 2–3-mm/⅛-in slices to create semi-circles.

In a mixing bowl, combine the sliced cucumber with the of soup powder. Let this mixture marinate for 30 minutes to draw out excess moisture from the cucumber.

Use your hands to gently squeeze the marinated cucumber slices to remove excess liquid. You should have approximately 200 g/7 oz of squeezed cucumber.

In a separate mixing bowl, combine the squeezed cucumber with all the seasoning ingredients. Use your hands to thoroughly mix everything together.

Add the garlic, herbs and toasted peanuts to the seasoned cucumber salad. Gently toss everything together until well combined.

Serve the cucumber salad immediately as a side dish or starter (appetizer).

## VINEGAR-DRESSED LETTUCE SALAD

Xà Lách Trộn Dấm

While its origins may be European, this salad has become thoroughly Vietnamese and is often served alongside *bò né* ('Sizzling' Beef Steak, page 72) or *gà rô ti nước dừa* (Roasted Chicken Leg, page 284). It is believed to have emerged during the French colonial period in Đà Lạt, in the high plateaus of Central Vietnam. The region's cool weather made it coveted by French colonists for its ability to grow European vegetables, including salads, green beans, radishes, strawberries and lemons.

Serves 4
Preparation time: 15 minutes, plus 2 hours marinating time
Cooking time: 5 minutes

| DF |

1 small white onion (155 g/5½ oz)
240 ml/8 fl oz (1 cup) white vinegar
1 teaspoon sugar
275 g/9¾ oz iceberg or Cos (romaine) lettuce, torn or chopped into bite-size pieces
1 small tomato, sliced

*For the dressing*
4 teaspoons neutral oil
35 g/1¼ oz shallots, sliced
60 ml/2 fl oz (¼ cup) white vinegar
¼ teaspoon salt
2 teaspoons light brown sugar
½ teaspoon fish sauce
¼ teaspoon black pepper

Use a sharp knife to thinly slice the onion. Place the onion in a bowl and cover it with the vinegar. Allow to marinate for 2 hours.

Drain the vinegar from the onion, then add the sugar and stir to coat the onion. Refrigerate the marinated onion until ready to use.

To make the dressing, in a small frying pan or skillet, heat 3 teaspoons of the oil over a medium heat. Fry the shallots for 3–4 minutes until golden brown. Remove two-thirds of the fried shallots and set them aside to use as a garnish. Remove from the heat and let the pan slightly cool.

Add the vinegar to the pan with the remaining fried shallots. Stir in the salt, light brown sugar, fish sauce and pepper. Add the remaining oil and mix everything together well.

To assemble the salad, in a large mixing bowl, combine the lettuce, tomato, and the marinated onion. Pour the dressing over the salad and use tongs or salad servers to gently toss everything together until evenly coated.

Transfer the salad to serving plates or a large serving bowl and garnish with the reserved fried shallots.

## FIDDLEHEAD FERN SALAD

### Nộm Rau Dớn

Fiddlehead ferns grow abundantly along mountain slopes and riverbanks throughout Vietnam's highlands, where local households often forage them for their kitchens. During our time in Hà Giang province, Anh Triệu Vàn Kính, of the Red Dao community in the rural district of Hoàng Su Phì, shared his version of this salad, using homemade fermented chillies and sawtooth coriander (culantro) for a fresh kick.

Serves 3–4
Preparation time: 15 minutes
Cooking time: 1 minute

| DF | ≤30 |

- 300 g/10½ oz young fiddlehead ferns (rau dớn non)
- 1 × 10 g/¼ oz fermented chilli (ớt ngâm muối) or fresh chilli, chopped
- 10 g/¼ oz sawtooth coriander (culantro), chopped
- 50 g/1¾ oz (1/3 cup) Toasted Peanuts (page 459)

*For the dressing*

- 2 tablespoons lime juice
- 2 tablespoons light brown sugar
- 1 tablespoon fish sauce
- 1 teaspoon all-purpose seasoning (hạt nêm)

Prepare a bowl of iced water.

Bring a pot of water to the boil. Add the fiddlehead ferns and blanch for 1 minute. Immediately transfer the blanched fiddlehead ferns to the iced water to cool. Drain the ferns and use paper towels to pat them dry.

In a small mixing bowl, combine the dressing ingredients. Stir until the sugar has dissolved.

In a large mixing bowl, combine the blanched and cooled fiddlehead ferns, the chilli and the sawtooth coriander (culantro). Add the toasted peanuts.

Pour the prepared dressing over the salad ingredients and use tongs or salad servers to gently toss everything together until evenly coated.

Transfer the salad to a serving dish and serve immediately.

## KOHLRABI SALAD

### Nộm Su Hào

This salad is a north Vietnamese staple that can be bulked up with poached prawns (shrimp) or sliced pork belly (side).

Serves 2–3 as a side dish
Preparation time: 15 minutes

| V | VE | DF | GF | ≤30 |

- 200 g/7 oz kohlrabi, peeled and shredded
- 50 g/1¾ oz carrots, peeled and shredded
- 1 teaspoon soup powder (bột canh)
- ⅛ teaspoon MSG
- 4½ teaspoons sugar
- 4 teaspoons rice vinegar
- ½ teaspoon Hanoi-style Chilli Sauce (page 477)
- 5 g/⅛ oz mint, leaves picked
- 5 g/⅛ oz coriander (cilantro), leaves picked
- 10 g/¼ oz peanuts

Place the kohlrabi and carrots in a large mixing bowl, then add the soup powder, MSG, sugar, vinegar and chilli sauce to the vegetables. Using your hands or large spoons, mix thoroughly until well combined. Add the mint and coriander (cilantro) leaves, then toss gently to combine.

In a small dry frying pan or skillet over a medium-low heat, toast the peanuts for 5–6 minutes until fragrant and golden.

Put the toasted peanuts in a mortar and coarsely pound with a pestle.

Transfer the salad to a serving plate and top with the pounded toasted peanuts.

Serve immediately while the vegetables are crisp.

# GREEN PAPAYA SALAD WITH GOLDEN ANTS

## Gỏi Đu Đủ Kiến Vàng

This unique dish comes from the Ê Đê people of Đắk Lắk and Gia Lai provinces, where dense forests and mountains provide an abundance of natural ingredients. Before the introduction of MSG, they used to season their food using what grew around them (herbs, chilli and even ants). These golden ants are used for their natural acidity. This recipe was taught to us by Chị H Duyên Êban, of the restaurant Ẩm thực truyền thống CƯ H'LĂM, who showed us how traditionally no fish sauce is used, creating a lighter, more subtle dressing that reflects the Ê Đê love of bitter, acidic and spicy flavours. The juice released from the papaya salad can then be drunk at the end.

Serves 2–3
Preparation time: 15 minutes

| DF | GF | ≤30 |

2 lime leaves
5 g/⅛ oz green chilli (about ¼ chilli)
1 teaspoon salt
1 teaspoon MSG
½ teaspoon sugar
10 g/¼ oz golden ants (kiến vàng)
270 g/9½ oz green papaya, shredded
1 tablespoon lime juice

Put the lime leaves, chilli, salt, MSG and sugar in a mortar and pound with a pestle until they are well combined.

Add the golden ants to the mortar and continue pounding with the pestle until the ants are fully incorporated with the other seasonings.

Add the green papaya to the mortar. Use the pestle to lightly pound and bruise the papaya, helping it absorb the flavours of the seasonings.

Finally, add the lime juice and use the pestle to mix everything together thoroughly.

Transfer the salad to a serving plate and serve immediately.

# GREEN PAPAYA SALAD WITH PRAWN AND PORK

## Gỏi Đu Đủ Tôm Thịt

For this salad, choose a papaya with green skin, slightly orange flesh and black seeds. When the papaya has both orange flesh and black seeds, it's fully ripe and is better for eating or in smoothies. If the seeds are white, the papaya is too young and it is better suited for pickling, or shredding and eating with Fried Rice Flour Cake with Eggs (page 62).

Serves 4–6
Preparation time: 45 minutes
Cooking time: 20 minutes

| DF |

1 × 1.1 kg/2 lb 7 oz semi-ripe papaya
25 g/1 oz lemongrass stalks (2 stalks), smashed
1 tablespoon fish sauce
400 g/14 oz pork belly (side)
300 g/10½ oz uncooked prawns (shrimp)
100 g/3½ oz (2/3 cup) Toasted Peanuts (page 459)
20 g/¾ oz Vietnamese coriander/cilantro (rau răm)
30 g/1 oz (2 tablespoons) Fried Shallots (page 458)

*For the dressing*
20 g/¾ oz peeled garlic
15 g/½ oz long red chilli, destemmed (and deseeded if you prefer less spice)
30 g/1 oz brown sugar
2 tablespoons lime juice
2 tablespoons fish sauce

*For the dipping sauce*
20 g/¾ oz garlic, chopped
5 g/⅛ oz deseeded chillies, coarsely chopped
1 tablespoon fish sauce
3 teaspoons light brown sugar

Peel the papaya, then using a grater or shredder, shred the papaya. You should have 650 g/1 lb 7 oz shredded papaya. Place in a colander, wash under running water and drain, then refrigerate.

In a pot, combine 500 ml/18 fl oz (2 cups) of water with the lemongrass, fish sauce and pork belly (side). Bring to a simmer and cook for 10 minutes, then drain and leave to cool.

Bring a separate pot of water to the boil. Add the prawns (shrimp), and cook for 2–3 minutes until pink. Remove with a skimmer, and leave to cool on a plate.

Using a sharp knife on a chopping (cutting) board, thinly slice the cooled pork belly.

To make the dressing, put the garlic and chilli in a mortar and pound with a pestle to a fine paste. Add the sugar, lime juice and fish sauce. Mix until the sugar dissolves.

In a large mixing bowl, combine the sliced pork and prawns with the dressing. Marinate for 30 minutes.

Add the shredded papaya, toasted peanuts, Vietnamese coriander/cilantro, and fried shallots to the mixing bowl. Toss well with wooden spoons.

In a small bowl, combine the dipping sauce ingredients with 2 tablespoons of water and stir until the sugar dissolves.

Transfer the salad to a serving platter. Serve with the dipping sauce in a small bowl alongside.

# GRILLED

## Món nướng

Grilling is fundamental to Vietnamese cuisine. Traditionally, Vietnam was largely rural, with every home featuring a designated grill area or a wood fire stove in the kitchen. Some areas, like the southwestern Mekong River Delta, developed unique grilling techniques, such as wrapping freshly caught fish in hay and burning it to cook it, a method known as *cá nướng rơm*. Despite increasing urbanization and more people living in apartments, grilled food remains integral to Vietnamese diets, sustained by numerous street food carts and stalls.

The grilling principle remains the same: avoid using the 'first fire' to prevent burning the dish. Instead, wood or coal should burn for 30–45 minutes until amber embers form. You'll know they're ready when the flames have died down and the coals have turned ashen grey on the outside with a deep orange-red glow underneath; I would recommend to blow away the ash with a fan before starting to grill. This radiant heat provides a more subtle, even cooking method.

The dishes in this chapter range from simple side dishes like Grilled Aubergines with Spring Onion Oil (page 158) to street snacks such as Grilled Dried Squid (page 150), and larger shared plates like Grilled Chicken with Indian Prickly Ash (page 149).

# NHA TRANG-STYLE GRILLED PORK PATTIES

## Nem Nướng Nha Trang

Though named after Nha Trang, this street food originated in Ninh Hòa district, 30 kilometres/18½ miles north of Nha Trang City. This is another wrap and roll dish in which you have to assemble your own roll, wrapping the grilled pork patties, herbs and vegetables in rice paper. While other regions serve their own versions with varying herbs, noodles and sauces, Nha Trang's signature comes with a thick sticky (glutinous) rice sauce, fresh herbs, green mango and crispy fried rice paper that adds a crunch to each roll.

Makes 16 skewers
Preparation time: 30 minutes
Cooking time: 15–20 minutes

| DF |

- 20 g/¾ oz garlic, coarsely sliced
- 20 g/¾ oz shallots, coarsely sliced
- 500 g/1 lb 2 oz minced (ground) pork (20 per cent fat)
- 500 g/1 lb 2 oz Pork Paste (page 461)
- 1 teaspoon sesame oil
- 1 teaspoon fish sauce
- 1 teaspoon light brown sugar
- ½ teaspoon black pepper
- 1 teaspoon all-purpose seasoning (hạt nêm)
- 1 tablespoon Annatto Oil (page 457)

*To serve*

- Thin, square brown rice paper (bánh ram Hà Tĩnh) or other rice paper
- oil, for deep-frying
- 1 cucumber, sliced or shredded
- 100 g/3½ oz firm mango, peeled and shredded
- herb salad (rau sống – butter lettuce, basil, perilla, spearmint, peppermint)
- rice paper, for wrapping
- Sticky Rice and Pork Dipping Sauce (page 473)

Using a mortar and pestle, crush the garlic and shallots until they are finely minced. Continue crushing them together until the texture is as fine as the minced (ground) pork.

In a large mixing bowl, combine the minced pork, pork paste, crushed garlic and shallot mixture, sesame oil, fish sauce, sugar, pepper, all-purpose seasoning and annatto oil. Mix everything together thoroughly, pressing the mixture for 4–5 minutes to develop its elasticity.

Form the pork mixture into long sausages around 16 skewers, then rest in the refrigerator for about 2 hours to ensure the sausages keep their shape.

Preheat a barbecue grill to high or an oven grill (broiler) to 200°C/400°F.

Grill the pork skewers (over hot coals or under the grill), turning every 5 minutes, until they are cooked through, 10–15 minutes. Once cooked, let the skewers cool directly under/on the grill (move them to the colder side of the barbecue).

Meanwhile, cut the brown rice paper into 10-cm/4-inch squares, then brush lightly with water. Roll each square into a cigar shape and let it dry for 5 minutes.

Fill a pan with oil to about 170°C/340°F. If not using a thermometer, test the oil temperature by inserting wooden chopsticks into the oil – small bubbles should form rapidly around them. Carefully add the rolls and fry each for 1–2 minutes, while flipping, until crispy; as soon as the roll touch the oil it should start bubbling and changing from transparent to opaque right away. Drain on paper towels.

To serve, arrange the grilled pork skewers on a serving platter. Around the skewers, arrange the sliced cucumber, shredded mango, crispy rolled and fried brown rice paper and a plate of various fresh herbs.

Provide rice paper wrappers for guests to wrap the dish as follows: lay a sheet of rice paper on a flat surface; place a few slices of cucumber, some shredded mango and a few pieces of fresh herbs onto the centre of the rice paper; top with 1–2 pieces of crispy fried rice paper and a grilled pork skewer; wrap the rice paper around the filling to create a roll.

Serve with the sticky rice and pork dipping sauce on the side for dipping.

# GRILLED BEEF IN PIPER LOLOT LEAVES

Bò Nướng Lá Lốt

Despite being commonly named 'grilled beef in betel leaves' in English, this dish actually uses piper lolot leaves, not betel. The confusion stems from betel leaves being famous for betel nut chewing, a stimulant practice common among Vietnam's older generations. Piper lolot leaves, highly aromatic and easily grown in home gardens, are essential to this dish. Common throughout Southeast Asian cuisine, these leaves transform when grilled, releasing an intense fragrance that perfectly complements the beef. In Vietnam, they are often eaten in the evening, when it is a little bit cooler for grilling. You can also use piper lolot in another beef dish, this time a broth, Beef and Piper Lolot Leaf Soup (page 361), or it can be simply chopped and added to a fried omelette.

Makes 50–60 rolls
Preparation time: 1 hour 15 minutes–1 hour 30 minutes
Cooking time: 30–40 minutes

| **DF** |

500 g/1 lb 2 oz minced (ground) beef
50 g/1¾ oz lemongrass, minced
350 g/12 oz bunch piper lolot (lá lốt)

*For the fat blend*
45 g/1½ oz peeled garlic
45 g/1½ oz peeled shallots
200 g/7 oz pork back fat, diced

*For the marinade*
2 teaspoons oyster sauce
2 teaspoons fish sauce
½ teaspoon salt
¼ teaspoon white pepper
¼ teaspoon black pepper

*To serve*
50 g/1¾ oz Spring Onion Oil (page 458)
30 g/1 oz (3 tablespoons) Toasted Peanuts (page 459), crushed
120 g/4¼ oz aromatic mixed herbs (rau thơm – peppermint, fish mint, coriander/cilantro, perilla, Thai basil)
100 g/3½ oz cucumber, cut into strips
1 star fruit, sliced and soaked in water
1 green banana, peeled and sliced, then soaked in water
thin rice paper

To make the fat blend, in a food processor or blender, combine the garlic, shallots and pork back fat. Blend until a paste-like consistency is achieved.

In a large mixing bowl, combine the minced (ground) beef, the fat blend and the lemongrass. Mix everything together thoroughly until well incorporated.

To marinate the beef, add the oyster sauce, fish sauce, salt and peppers to the beef mixture. Mix everything together well to evenly distribute the marinade. Allow the mixture to marinate for at least 30 minutes.

Preheat a grill (broiler) or barbecue to medium-high heat.

Take one piper lolot leaf and place a portion of the marinated beef mixture in the centre. Fold the sides of the leaf over the filling, then tightly roll it up to form a neat little parcel. Thread this onto a skewer, then repeat so you have 3–4 per skewer. Repeat this process until all the beef mixture has been used, resulting in 50–60 rolls.

Grill the skewered beef rolls on/under the preheated grill for 4–5 minutes per side until they are cooked through and slightly charred.

Transfer the grilled beef rolls to a serving plate. Drizzle over the spring onion (scallion) oil and sprinkle the crushed toasted peanuts over the top.

Serve with a platter of the mixed herbs, cucumber strips, star fruit slices and green banana slices. Provide rice paper wrappers on the side for diners to assemble their own rolls.

# GRILLED PORK WITH RICE NOODLES

## Bún Thịt Nướng

This dish balances charred grilled pork, fresh herbs, pickled vegetables and roasted peanuts, dressed with sweet and sour fish sauce, with all the flavours absorbed by the fresh rice noodles. A great addition to this dish is a few rolls per portion of Crab/Prawn Spring Rolls (page 116), or even Grilled Beef in Piper Lolot Leaves (page 144). The grilled pork can also be served alongside Steamed Rice Rolls (page 403) and dipping sauce.

Serves 6
Preparation time: 45 minutes
Cooking time: 25 minutes

| DF |

950/2 lb 2 oz pork shoulder blade, cut into roughly 7 × 4-cm/2¾ × 1½-inch pieces, about 5 mm/¼ inch thick, removing any sinewy bits
45 g/1½ oz lemongrass (about 2 stalks), 10 g/¼ oz minced, the rest cut into 10-cm/4-inch length stalks and smashed
40 g/1½ oz garlic, minced
20 g/¾ oz shallots, minced
1 teaspoon all-purpose seasoning (hạt nêm)
1 teaspoon sesame oil
3 teaspoons fish sauce
1 teaspoon light brown sugar
1 teaspoon honey
1 tablespoon Annatto Oil (page 457)
½ teaspoon black pepper

*To serve*
600–700 g/1 lb 5–1 lb 9 oz fresh rice noodles (bún)
50 g/1¾ oz Spring Onion Oil (page 458)
50 g/1¾ oz (1/3 cup) Toasted Peanuts (page 459)
100 g/3½ oz Pickled Daikon and Carrots (page 468)
50 g/1¾ oz sliced cucumber rounds
1 head of lettuce, washed and shredded
aromatic mixed herbs (rau thơm – fish mint, perilla, Thai basil, coriander/cilantro, Vietnamese balm)
Sweet and Sour Fish Sauce (page 471)

Place the pork pieces and smashed lemongrass in a mixing bowl.

In another bowl, combine the minced lemongrass with the garlic and shallots. Add this mixture to the bowl with the pork.

To the pork, add the all-purpose seasoning, sesame oil, fish sauce, sugar, honey, annatto oil and pepper. Mix everything together well to evenly coat the pork with the marinade. Let the pork marinate for at least 30 minutes.

Preheat a barbecue grill to high or an oven grill (broiler) to 200°C/400°F, or heat a griddle (grill) pan over a medium heat.

Grill the marinated pork for 8–10 minutes per side, until cooked through and slightly charred.

Divide the fresh rice noodles evenly between 6 serving bowls, then top with the grilled pork, spring onion oil, toasted peanuts, pickled vegetables, sliced cucumber rounds, shredded lettuce and fresh herbs.

Serve the sweet and sour fish sauce on the side for dipping.

# HANOI-STYLE GRILLED PORK WITH VERMICELLI

Bún Chả

One of Hanoi's most beloved dishes, *bún chả* thrives on the balance between caramelized grilled meats and a light, slightly sour dipping sauce that absorbs the smoky flavours to become a richly flavoured broth. Traditional Hanoi *bún chả* was grilled using bamboo skewers rather than today's metal grill baskets; the meat would be sandwiched between a split bamboo stick, adding a subtle bamboo flavour to the seasoned meat.

Serves 4
Preparation time: 30 minutes
Cooking time: 20–30 minutes

| DF |

*For the meatballs*
65 g/2¼ oz pork back fat
470 g/1 lb pork, minced (ground)
½ teaspoon Caramel Braising Sauce (page 456)
2 teaspoons oyster sauce
20 g/¾ oz shallots, finely minced
40 g/1½ oz onion, finely minced
2 teaspoons fish sauce
½ teaspoon black pepper
10 g/¼ oz garlic, minced
10 g/¼ oz spring onion, chopped
oil, for greasing

*For the pork belly*
260 g/9 oz pork belly (side) (without skin) or pork shoulder (with layers of fat and meat), thinly sliced (2–3 mm/⅛ in thick)
1 teaspoon Annatto Oil (page 457)
1 teaspoon fish sauce
1 teaspoon oyster sauce
¼ teaspoon black pepper
20 g/¾ oz shallots, minced
5 g/⅛ oz garlic, minced

*For the dipping sauce*
40 g/1½ oz (3 tablespoons) sugar
½ teaspoon salt
2 teaspoons all-purpose seasoning (hạt nêm)
2 tablespoons fish sauce
1 tablespoon vinegar
a few bird's eye chilli slices
20 g/¾ oz garlic, minced

*To serve*
600 g/1 lb 5 oz fresh rice noodles or vermicelli (bún/bún tươi)
aromatic mixed herbs (such as mint, coriander/cilantro, perilla)
80 g/2¾ oz mint leaves
60 g/2¼ oz coriander (cilantro)
60 g/2¼ oz perilla leaves

To prepare the meatballs, place the pork back fat in a food processor and blend until it reaches a smooth consistency. Transfer to a large mixing bowl and add all the remaining meatball ingredients, except the oil. Using clean hands, mix thoroughly until all the ingredients are well combined. Divide the mixture into 20 equal portions (30 g/1 oz each), rolling each portion between your palms to form neat, round meatballs. Place the formed meatballs on a clean plate or tray.

To prepare the pork belly (side), combine all the ingredients in a mixing bowl. Mix well using tongs or your hands, ensuring the meat is evenly coated. Let the meat marinate for at least 15 minutes.

To prepare the dipping sauce, in a saucepan, bring 350 ml/12 fl oz (1½ cups) of water to the boil over a high heat. Add the sugar, salt and all-purpose seasoning. Using a wooden spoon, stir until the sugar has completely dissolved. Remove the saucepan from the heat, then add the fish sauce and vinegar, stirring to combine. Just before serving, stir in the chilli and garlic.

Preheat a charcoal grill or an oven grill (broiler) to 200°C/400°F.

Use a basting brush to lightly oil a grilling basket, or grill rack over a grill tray, to prevent sticking, then arrange the meatballs and marinated pork slices evenly on the basket/rack, leaving space between each piece. Place the basket on the grill, or place the meatballs on the highest rack in the oven grill, and cook, turning the basket/meatballs every 2 minutes for even cooking, for 15 minutes.

Open the basket and use the basting brush to apply a light coat of oil to all the meat. Close the basket and continue grilling for another 5–15 minutes until the meat is fully cooked and nicely charred. Carefully remove from the heat.

To serve, arrange 5 grilled meatballs and 65 g/2¼ oz of the grilled pork slices in each bowl. Ladle 100 ml/3½ fl oz (scant ½ cup) of the dipping sauce over the grilled meat. On a separate plate, arrange in neat sections 150 g/5½ oz of the fresh rice noodles and 50 g/1¾ oz of the mixed herbs.

To eat this, use chopsticks to pick up a small portion of rice noodles, dip the noodles into the bowl filled with grilled meat and dipping sauce and add some fresh herbs to the same bite.

# PORK CARTILAGE SAUSAGES

Dồi Sụn

The herbs in this sausage vary from region to region. Here, I use sawtooth coriander (culantro), Vietnamese basil and spring onions (scallions), though some cooks prefer *rau răm* (Vietnamese coriander/cilantro) in their mix. You'll find these sausages served as a snack or paired with Rice Noodles with Fried Tofu and Shrimp Paste (page 207).

Serves 6–8
Preparation time: 50 minutes, plus 30 minutes marinating time
Cooking time: 30–35 minutes

| DF |

- 410 g/14½ oz pork intestines
- 60 ml/2 fl oz (¼ cup) neutral oil for frying
- 100 g/3½ oz lemongrass, minced
- 440 g/15½ oz cartilage and meat mixture, or a mix of pig's ears or throat and meat (50:50 ratio of meat:cartilage)
- 340 g/12 oz fatty pork, minced (ground)
- 35 g/1¼ oz garlic, coarsely chopped
- 25 g/1 oz shallots, coarsely chopped
- 125 g/4¼ oz Pork Paste (page 461)
- 1 tablespoon fish sauce
- ½ teaspoon salt
- 5 g/⅛ oz (2 teaspoons) whole peppercorns, coarsely crushed
- 25 g/1 oz Vietnamese basil (húng quế), chopped
- 25 g/1 oz sawtooth coriander (culantro), chopped
- 15 g/½ oz spring onions (scallions), chopped
- 1 teaspoon sugar
- Seasoned Fermented Shrimp Paste Dipping Sauce (page 476), to serve, optional

*To cook*

- 900 ml/30 fl oz (3¾ cups) water or coconut water
- 20 g/¾ oz lemongrass
- 1 teaspoon salt
- 1 tablespoon fish sauce, plus extra for dipping, if desired

To prepare the intestines, soak them in cold salted water for 10 minutes to clean. Scrub thoroughly under cold running water, removing as much outer fat and inner mucosa lining as possible, and set aside.

Heat a small pan over a medium heat and add the oil. Once hot, add the lemongrass and stir-fry for 8–10 minutes until it turns golden and fragrant. Strain and set aside the fried lemongrass.

In a large bowl, combine the cartilage and meat mixture, fatty pork, fried lemongrass, garlic, shallots, pork paste, fish sauce, salt, peppercorns, herbs and the sugar. Mix well and let it marinate for at least 30 minutes.

Tie one end of the cleaned pork intestines securely with kitchen string. Fill it with the meat mixture using a sausage stuffer or plastic bottle (see step 6, page 32), packing it tightly to avoid air pockets. Tie off the end securely with string.

To cook the sausages, in a pot, combine the water or coconut water with the lemongrass, salt and fish sauce and bring to the boil. Add the filled sausage and gently poach for 8–10 minutes (see note). This helps to set the sausage and infuse it with additional flavour. Allow the sausage to cool to room temperature before grilling or frying.

Preheat a barbecue grill or oven grill (broiler) to medium, grill the sausage for 10 minutes, or until golden brown on both sides. Alternatively, bring a pan of oil 170°C/340°F and fry the sausages in the hot oil for about 12 minutes.

To serve, divide the cooked sausage evenly among 6–8 plates or a serving platter. Offer the dipping sauce in a bowl on the side, if desired.

***Notes:*** The sausages should be very gently poached to avoid them exploding; you can poke a couple of holes in the casing with a cocktail stick or toothpick, though this will lose some of the flavour.

If preparing these sausages to serve with Pork Organ Congee (page 256), you can poach them in the stock you prepare for the congee to give it extra flavour, or you can add them when the rice is added.

# ROASTED DUCK WITH FERMENTED TOFU

Vịt Nướng Chao

This dish can be made with either duck or goose. Without an oven, chop and stir-fry the meat instead. In the north, it's traditionally served with fresh rice noodles and sliced onions.

Serves 2–3
Preparation time: 10 minutes, plus 45 minutes marinating and 30 minutes resting times
Cooking time: 20 minutes

| DF |

700 g/1 lb 9 oz black Muscovy duck (½ duck), deboned
50 g/1¾ oz fermented tofu (chao)
20 g/¾ oz liquid from the fermented tofu (chao)
15 g/½ oz long red chilli, destemmed
15 g/½ oz piece fresh ginger, peeled
15 g/½ oz peeled shallot
30 g/1 oz peeled garlic
1 teaspoon sugar
1 tablespoon fish sauce
10 g/¼ oz (2 teaspoons) Chilli and Lemongrass Oil (page 457)

*To serve*
Fermented Tofu Sauce (page 477)
50 g/1¾ oz Pickled Daikon and Carrots (page 468)
50 g/1¾ oz sliced cucumber rounds
aromatic mixed herbs (rau thơm – fish mint, perilla, Thai basil, coriander/cilantro, Vietnamese Balm)

Place the duck in a bowl. Add the fermented tofu with its liquid. Toss to evenly coat the duck. Let it marinate for 30 minutes.

Preheat the oven to 210°C/410°F/Gas Mark 6.

In a food processor or blender, combine the chilli, ginger, shallot and garlic. Blend or pulse until finely minced.

Add the minced aromatics, sugar and fish sauce to the marinated duck. Mix well and let marinate for an additional 15 minutes.

Place the marinated duck, skin-side up, on a baking sheet or in a roasting pan. Roast for 10 minutes.

Reduce the oven temperature to 150°C/300°F/Gas Mark 2 and continue roasting for another 10 minutes. Turn off the oven, leaving the door slightly open, and let the duck rest to finish slowly cooking for 30 minutes. The duck should be roasted on the top but still juicy inside.

To serve, slice the roasted duck and divide it evenly among 2–3 plates. Accompany the duck with the fermented tofu sauce, pickled vegetables, sliced cucumber and mixed herbs.

# GRILLED CHICKEN WITH INDIAN PRICKLY ASH

Gà Nướng Mắc Khén

In Hà Giang province, I was introduced to a rustic grilling technique perfect for impromptu picnics. Split a sturdy branch in half lengthways, then sandwich a butterflied chicken between the halves. The meat is secured using thin strips peeled from branches as natural ties. Instead of grilling directly over the flames, the branch is propped at an angle next to the fire, letting the gentle heat slowly cook the chicken. Starting with the skin facing the fire and finishing with the meat side, this method produces perfectly cooked chicken with crispy skin.

Serves 4–6
Preparation time: 1–2 hours
Cooking time: 30 minutes (adjust for larger chickens)

| DF | GF |

10 g/¼ oz cardamom (2 pods)
15 g/½ oz Indian prickly ash (mắc khén)
5 g/⅛ oz MSG
10 g/¼ oz salt
2–5 g (½–1 teaspoon) dried chilli flakes, or to taste
35 g/1¼ oz oil
1 × 750 g/1 lb 10 oz chicken, spatchcocked

Pound the cardamom pods in a mortar with a pestle.

In a bowl, combine the pounded cardamom with the Indian prickly ash, MSG, salt, chilli flakes and oil. Rub this spice mixture all over the chicken, then cover and marinate for 1–2 hours in the refrigerator.

There are three ways to cook the chicken.

For the traditional method, split a bamboo pole in half lengthways. Place the marinated chicken inside the split bamboo and secure both ends of the bamboo with soft branches. Plant the bamboo next to a fire for indirect cooking.

For the charcoal grill method, grill the chicken over a medium-low heat for about 30 minutes, turning occasionally.

For the oven method, preheat the oven to 180°C/350°F/Gas Mark 4. Roast the chicken for about 30 minutes until fully cooked.

To check for doneness, use a meat thermometer to ensure the internal temperature of the chicken reaches 74°C/165°F.

Serve the grilled chicken hot.

*Note:* For larger chickens, add 15 minutes of cooking time per additional 300–400 g/10½–14 oz.

# GRILLED PORK SKEWERS WITH INDIAN PRICKLY ASH

## Thịt Xiên Nướng Mắc Khén

*Mắc khén*, or Indian prickly ash, is commonly used in Vietnam's northern mountains for its numbing, peppery flavour, similar to Sichuan peppercorns. While it's traditionally paired with pork, another local spice, black cardamom, is saved for chicken and fish dishes. This recipe also calls for *cơm mẻ* (fermented rice), a staple in local kitchens. Each family keeps their own jar, feeding it with leftover rice like a sourdough starter. Some even add a chicken bone for extra flavour. These days, you can find *cơm mẻ* in Vietnamese supermarkets, either in pre-prepared jars or, if you ask at the counter, from their own fermenting batch in the back.

Makes 4 skewers; serves 2–4
Preparation time: 30 minutes, plus 1 hour marinating time
Cooking time: 20–30 minutes (charcoal) or 1 hour (traditional wood fire)

| DF |

- 750 g/1 lb 10 oz pork (leg or lean meat)
- 1 tablespoon Indian prickly ash (mắc khén), ground
- 1½ magnolia seeds (hạt dổi)
- 60 g/2¼ oz galangal, peeled
- 1½ teaspoons all-purpose seasoning (hạt nêm)
- 30 g/1 oz fermented rice (cơm mẻ)
- 1 tablespoon fish sauce
- Northern Vietnamese Spice Mix (page 474), to serve

Cut the pork into 2 × 6-cm/¾ × 2½-inch pieces. Separate the lean meaty pieces and the fatty pieces.

Put the Indian prickly ash and magnolia seeds in a mortar and grind with a pestle. Add the galangal and pound everything together.

In a mixing bowl, combine the galangal mixture with the all-purpose seasoning, fermented rice and fish sauce. Add the lean and fatty pork pieces, mix everything together thoroughly and let marinate for 1 hour.

Soak 4 bamboo skewers in water for 5 minutes to prevent them from burning during grilling.

Thread the marinated pork pieces onto the 4 soaked bamboo skewers, alternating between the meat pieces and the pork fat pieces.

There are three grilling options.

For the traditional wood fire method, place the skewers on the side of the wood fire (away from the direct heat – prop them upright if needed so they aren't too close to the heat) and slowly grill for about 1 hour.

For the charcoal method, heat a charcoal barbecue grill to medium-high; grill the skewers for 20–30 minutes, turning regularly for even cooking and searing on all sides.

For the amber grill method, wait for the coals to burn out until they are red and glowing, then cook the skewers for 25–30 minutes.

To serve, place the grilled pork skewers on a platter and offer the northern Vietnamese spice mix as a dip on the side.

# GRILLED DRIED SQUID

## Khô Mực Nướng

In my youth, the smell of dried squid grilling over coal would drift through our neighbourhood on some evenings as vendors passed by. Though pungent, grilling transforms the dried squid, bringing out its sweetness and charred flavour. Traditionally eaten with pork lard to add richness, this snack might be less common now, but you'll still find vendors outside *quán nhậu* (beer halls), where it pairs perfectly with draft beer, and it is now more often sold with commercial chilli sauce.

Serves 2–3
Preparation time: 5 minutes, plus 10 minutes soaking time
Cooking time: 8–10 minutes

| DF | ≤5 | ≤30 |

- 2 dried squid (about 150 g/5½ oz)
- 330 ml/11 fl oz (1 1/3 cup) can beer (or water if you prefer to keep it alcohol-free)
- chilli sauce or pork lard (mỡ nước), to serve

Preheat a charcoal barbecue grill to medium (red embers) or an oven grill (broiler) to 180°C/350°F.

Keeping the dried squid whole and intact, place it in a bowl or on a tray. Pour the beer over the squid until it is fully submerged and soak for 10 minutes, turning occasionally to ensure even soaking. The beer will help tenderize the squid and enhance its sweetness after grilling. After 10 minutes, remove the squid from the beer. Pat dry with paper towels.

Clip the whole squid onto a grilling rack to keep them flat and ensure even cooking. Grill until cooked through and aromatic, 8–10 minutes, or until the squid meat turns opaque white but remains chewy.

Shred the grilled squid into thin strips across the grain and serve with chilli sauce or pork lard (for the traditional style).

GRILLED PORK SKEWERS WITH INDIAN PRICKLY ASH

# GRILLED FLATTENED SPRING ROLLS

## Chả Lụi

Originally from LaGi, a coastal city in Bình Thuận province, this dish has spread to neighbouring tourist destinations like the port cities Phan Thiết and Vũng Tàu. The key lies in the grilling technique: the meat-wrapped rice paper requires constant attention, with skilled vendors flipping the long flat skewers every few seconds to achieve a crispy crust without burning. Once grilled and cut into bite-size pieces, these rolls are served with various condiments and a sweet sauce, balanced by the nutty crunch of toasted peanuts.

Makes 20 flat rolls; serves 5–6 as a starter (appetizer)
Preparation time: 30 minutes
Grilling time: 15 minutes

| DF |

20 g/¾ oz peeled shallots
60 g/2¼ oz prawns (shrimp)
½ teaspoon Chilli and Lemongrass Oil (page 457)
1 teaspoon neutral oil
150 g/5½ oz minced (ground) pork
80 g/2¾ oz Pork Paste (page 461)
1 teaspoon Annatto Oil (page 457)
1 teaspoon fish sauce
½ teaspoon black pepper
½ teaspoon sugar
25 sheets thin, square brown rice paper (bánh ram Hà Tĩnh )

*To serve*
30 g/1 oz roasted peanuts (see note), finely pounded (not too pasty)
1 quantity Basic Dressing for Salad (page 478)
mixed herb salad (rau ghém – lettuce, Thai basil, watermint, fish mint)
thin rice paper (bánh tráng)
50 g/1¾ oz shredded mango

In a food processor or blender, blend the shallots, prawns (shrimp), chilli and lemongrass oil, and neutral oil until a paste-like consistency is achieved.

In a mixing bowl, combine the blended paste with the minced (ground) pork. Add the pork paste, annatto oil, fish sauce, pepper and sugar and thoroughly mix all the ingredients together.

Place one piece of brown rice paper on a clean work surface. Lightly moisten the rice paper with water. Place a portion of the meat mixture in the centre of the rice paper. Fold both ends of the rice paper inwards, then fold the mixture lengthways to form a 6-cm/2½-inch-long flat roll. Repeat filling and rolling until all the meat mixture has been used, making a total of 20 flat rolls.

Prepare a charcoal barbecue grill to medium (the charcoal should have red embers).

Carefully thread the flat rolls onto flat skewers, securing them in place.

Grill the skewered rolls over the hot charcoal for approximately 15 minutes, turning them every 5 seconds to prevent burning. Cook until they are golden brown and cooked through. Use a sharp knife to cut the grilled rolls in half diagonally.

In a small bowl, mix the finely pounded roasted peanuts with 100 g/3½ oz of the Basic Dressing for Salad to create a dipping sauce.

Serve the grilled flattened spring rolls with the dipping sauce, herb salad, thin dry rice paper and shredded mango.

*Notes:* It is recommended to use flat skewers, as it will maintain the rolls better.

To freshly roast peanuts, preheat the oven to 175°C/350°F/Gas Mark 4; place the peanuts on a baking tray and roast in the oven for 15–20 minutes until golden.

You can substitute the pork paste with the same amount of minced (ground) pork.

# GRILLED CHICKEN WITH CHILLI SALT

## Gà Nướng Muối Ớt

This grilled chicken with chilli salt pairs well with white rice or *xôi* (steamed sticky/glutinous rice). In Saigon's late afternoons, street vendors grill whole chickens over charcoal for the after-work crowd. The secret to their crispy skin lies in constant rotation and regular brushing with a signature glaze. While they use charcoal, I've adapted this recipe for the oven grill, making it easier to recreate at home.

Serves 4
Preparation time: 20 minutes, plus overnight marinating time
Cooking time: 45 minutes

790 g/1 lb 12 oz chicken, spatchcocked
½ teaspoon salt (for marinating)

*For the chilli salt mixture*
65 g/2¼ oz Vietnamese chilli flakes
10 g/¼ oz salt
15 g/½ oz (3½ teaspoons) sugar
1 teaspoon garlic powder

*For the glaze*
40 g/1½ oz golden (corn) syrup
2 teaspoons fish sauce
1 tablespoon Annatto Oil (page 457)
½ teaspoon fresh chilli, minced

*To serve*
Vietnamese coriander/cilantro (rau răm), optional
cucumber slices
Green Chilli Salt (page 480)

Cut the chicken at the knee joints and fold it back as shown in the photo. Season the chicken with the salt. Cover and marinate the chicken in the refrigerator overnight for best results.

Preheat the oven grill (broiler) to 190°C/375°F.

For the chilli salt mixture, in a small bowl, combine the Vietnamese chilli flakes, salt, sugar and garlic powder. Mix well and set aside.

In a separate bowl, prepare the glaze by mixing together the golden (corn) syrup, fish sauce, annatto oil and fresh chilli. Set aside.

Place the marinated chicken on the upper rack of the grill, skin side up, and grill (broil) for 15 minutes.

Remove the chicken from the oven and use a basting brush to thoroughly coat the entire chicken, including the cavity, with the prepared glaze.

Reduce the grill temperature to 150°C/300°F. Return the chicken to the grill and cook for an additional 7 minutes.

Remove the chicken, apply a second layer of the glaze, then return it to the grill for another 7 minutes.

Apply a final layer of glaze to the chicken and coat it thoroughly with the chilli salt mixture. Grill the chicken for a final 15 minutes.

To serve, present the grilled chicken with the Vietnamese coriander/cilantro, if desired, cucumber slices and the green chilli salt on the side.

***Note:*** The total cooking time for a 790 g/1 lb 12 oz chicken will be 45 minutes. Increase the cooking time proportionally for larger chickens.

GRILLED CHICKEN WITH CHILLI SALT

# GRILLED SNAKEHEAD FISH WITH POUNDED CHILLI AND HERBS

## Cá Lóc Nướng Giã Ớt và Lá É

This traditional Bahnar dish (called '*Ka chroah buh peh pơhăng păng hla ech*' in the Bahnar dialect) combines grilled snakehead fish with a local herb paste of *lá é* (lemon basil) and sawtooth coriander (culantro). Bác A Wơr and his family grills the fish in their garden over low coals, letting it dry completely before pounding it with the herbs. It feels like a mix between a salad and a condiment, with the heat and freshness of the herbs, and it pairs perfectly with plain rice or congee.

Serves 4–6
Preparation time: 15 minutes
Cooking time: 30–40 minutes

| DF |

- 2 whole snakehead fish (cá lóc) (630 g/1 lb 6 oz total), gutted and gills removed, then butterflied, keeping the back intact (as your fish supplier)
- ½ teaspoon salt
- ½ teaspoon MSG
- ¼ teaspoon all-purpose seasoning (hạt nêm)
- ½ teaspoon black pepper

*For the herb paste*

- 10 g/¼ oz bird's eye chillies, stemmed
- 60 g/2¼ oz lemon basil (lá é)
- 10 g/¼ oz sawtooth coriander (culantro)
- ¼ teaspoon sugar
- ½ teaspoon MSG
- ½ teaspoon all-purpose seasoning (hạt nêm)
- ½ teaspoon salt
- lime juice, to taste, optional

Preheat a charcoal grill.

Season both sides of the butterflied fish with the salt, MSG, all-purpose seasoning and pepper.

Place the fish in a Vietnamese-style grilling rack, or place on a standard grill rack. Starting belly side down, grill the fish over the hot charcoal embers for 7 minutes. Flip so the fish is skin side down and grill for 18 minutes. Flip once more to so it's belly side down and continue grilling over a low heat until fully cooked and dry, 5–15 minutes more; it should be dry because you need to pound it later. Let cool slightly.

When cool enough to handle, shred the fish by hand. Carefully remove all the bones. Set aside.

To make the herb paste, put the chillies in a mortar and pound with a pestle. Add the lemon basil and sawtooth coriander (culantro) and continue pounding. Season with the sugar, MSG, all-purpose seasoning and salt. Add 2 teaspoons of water and pound until a coarse paste forms.

To serve, mix the shredded fish with the herb paste. You can add some lime juice if you want extra acidity.

Serve immediately.

# GRILLED CARP

## Cá Chép Nướng

In Hà Giang's rice fields, small carp are released in May when the paddies are flooded. These fish feed on rice flowers, growing quickly and developing rich flavour. By late August, as fields are slowly drained for harvest, the well-fed carp are ready for cooking. When we visited, the Triệu family, of the Red Dao community in the rural district of Hoàng Su Phì, shared their tradition of pairing the fish with black cardamom, a local mountain spice that enhances its taste. This sustainable and smart practice is possible only in chemical-free rice fields, ensuring the carp's survival.

Serves 4
Preparation time: 10 minutes
Cooking time: 20–25 minutes

| DF | ≤5 |

- 1½ teaspoons black cardamom pods (thảo quả), ground
- 1 tablespoon fish sauce
- 1 teaspoon all-purpose seasoning (hạt nêm)
- 570 g/1 lb 4 oz carp (about 13 small fish), cleaned

In a large bowl, combine the cardamom, fish sauce and all-purpose seasoning. Mix well.

Use paper towels to pat the carp dry. Coat the cleaned and dried carp evenly with the spice mixture, then let rest for 5 minutes.

Preheat a barbecue grill to low heat or an oven grill (broiler) to 180°C/350°F.

Carefully place the marinated carp onto the preheated grill grates or under the oven grill. Grill the carp for 20–25 minutes, turning occasionally, until the fish are cooked through and lightly charred on the outside.

Serve the grilled carp hot, alongside other Vietnamese dishes.

## GRILLED PORK ROLLED IN MOUNTAIN MUSTARD GREENS

### Thịt Cuốn Rau Cải Nướng/Mèo

In Hà Giang, we discovered the distinctive taste of local black pigs, each household tending to these animals with corn and gourds from their own gardens. While this pork was traditionally shared only during important occasions like weddings and funerals, the availability of freezers now allows families to keep portions on hand year-round. The natural, rich flavour of this pork shines in simple preparations, whether boiled or grilled like these skewers, showing a clear difference from commercial meat.

Makes 20 rolls; serves 4
Preparation time: 20 minutes
Cooking time: 15–20 minutes

| DF | GF |

260 g/9 oz pork shoulder, thinly sliced
60 g/2¼ oz (⅓ cup) Mountain mustard greens or young mustard leaves (cải bẹ) (about 20 leaves)

*For the marinade*
1 teaspoon chilli flakes
¼ teaspoon MSG
½ teaspoon salt
1 teaspoon neutral oil
1 teaspoon Indian prickly ash (mắc khén)

*To serve*
herb salad/aromatic mixed herbs (rau sống/rau thơm – fish mint, stinkvine, pennywort)
Northern Vietnamese Spice Mix (page 474)

In a mixing bowl, combine all the marinade ingredients. Add the pork to the marinade and mix well. Let marinate for at least 15 minutes.

Cut or fold each mustard leaf into 5-cm/2-inch sections. Take each section of mustard leaf and place it on top of a slice of the marinated pork. Carefully roll the pork around the mustard leaf, enclosing the leaf inside the meat. Thread the rolled pork and mustard leaf bundles onto skewers.

Preheat a barbecue grill to medium (red embers) or oven grill (broiler) to 190°C/375°F.

Grill the skewered rolls over charcoal or on the top rack of the oven grill for 15–20 minutes, turning them occasionally to ensure even cooking. Cook the rolls until the meat is fully cooked through and the mustard greens are slightly charred.

Arrange the grilled pork and mustard leaf rolls on a serving platter and serve with the herb salad and the northern Vietnamese spice mix for dipping.

## PORK ROLLED WITH LIME LEAVES

### Thịt Cuốn Lá Chanh

This dish is popular in mountainous regions of Vietnam, where using leaves to enhance the flavours of meat is common. A similar version, *thịt lợn cuốn lá hồi*, uses star anise leaves wrapped around meat and fried until crispy.

Serves 4–5; makes 10–12 rolls
Preparation time: 20 minutes
Cooking time: 8–10 minutes per batch

| DF |

460 g/1 lb pork neck or shoulder, sliced diagonally into large pieces
20 g/¾ oz lime leaves (20–30 leaves)
neutral oil, for frying

*For the marinade*
1 teaspoon fish sauce
½ teaspoon MSG
½ teaspoon all-purpose seasoning (hạt nêm)
1 teaspoon Indian prickly ash (mắc khén)
½ teaspoon chilli flakes
¼ teaspoon magnolia seeds (hạt dổi)

In a mixing bowl, combine all the marinade ingredients. Add the pork to the marinade and mix well. Let the pork marinate for at least 15 minutes.

Fold each lime leaf in half. Place each folded lime leaf on top of a marinated pork slice, then roll the pork around the lime leaf. Thread 4–5 of the rolled pork and lime leaf bundles onto small skewers.

Heat a barbecue grill to medium and then grill the skewered rolls for 8–10 minutes.

Alternatively, working in batches if needed, heat a large pan with enough oil to fill a third of the pan to 170–180°C/340–350°F. If not using a thermometer, test the oil temperature by inserting wooden chopsticks into the oil – it should bubble vigorously around them. Fry the skewered rolls in the hot oil for 8–10 minutes, rotating them occasionally to ensure even cooking. Once cooked, remove the rolls from the oil, drain on paper towels and let them rest for a few minutes.

Serve the hot rolls as a starter (appetizer) or main dish, alongside rice and soup.

# GRILLED AUBERGINES WITH SPRING ONION OIL

## Cà Tím Nướng Mỡ Hành

Despite its name, most homes 'grill' the aubergines (eggplants) directly on their gas stove, just enough to char and peel the skin. In Vietnam, we use Chinese aubergines, which are thinner and meatier than the Italian variety due to having a lower water content. The perfect texture has been achieved when the aubergines hold their shape when stir-fried but still melt in your mouth.

Serves 3–4, to share
Preparation time: 30 minutes
Cooking time: 20–25 minutes

| V | VE | DF |

- 2 long aubergines (eggplants) (about 400 g/14 oz)
- 1 teaspoon sugar
- 2 teaspoons light soy sauce
- ¼ teaspoon black pepper
- 50 g/1¾ oz spring onions (scallions), chopped
- ¼ teaspoon salt
- 4 tablespoons neutral oil
- 10 g/¼ oz shallot, finely chopped

Preheat the oven to 210°C/410°F/Gas Mark 6.

Allow the oven to preheat for 15 minutes, then place the aubergines (eggplants) on a tray on the top rack and cook for 10–15 minutes.

Alternatively, you can carefully char the aubergines directly over a hob ring (stove burner) or barbecue grill until the skin is blackened (see steps 1–2, page 164), 6–10 minutes.

After grilling or roasting, allow the aubergines to cool. If using the oven method, you may need to let the aubergines sit in a covered bowl for 5 minutes before they can be peeled. When cool enough to handle, peel and trim the aubergines. You should have about 250 g/5½ oz of flesh. You can either cut the aubergines lengthways into 4 slices or leave them whole.

In a small bowl, mix together the sugar, soy sauce and pepper.

In a shallow dish, add the aubergine pieces and pour over the soy sauce mixture. Let marinate for at least 10 minutes to absorb the flavours.

In a small, non-reactive bowl, combine the spring onions (scallions) and salt.

In a small saucepan, heat the oil until it reaches around 180°C/356°F. If not using a thermometer, test the oil temperature by inserting wooden chopsticks into the oil – it should bubble vigorously around them.

Carefully pour the hot oil over the spring onion mixture. This will create a fragrant spring onion oil.

In a 20-cm/8-inch pan, heat 1 tablespoon of the hot spring onion oil over a medium-low heat. Add the shallot and fry until they start to turn golden. Add the marinated aubergine pieces to the pan and cook them until they are golden and caramelized on the outside, no more than 5 minutes.

Serve the grilled aubergines immediately, drizzled with the remaining spring onion oil.

## GRILLED FISH IN BANANA LEAVES

### Cá Đồng Nướng Lá Chuối

This traditional Mường recipe comes from bác Đinh Thị Như Thoa, who lives in Buôn Ma Thuột, the capital of Đắk Lắk province in the central highlands of Vietnam. While most Mường people (Vietnam's fourth-largest community after the Kinh, Tay and Thai) live in Hòa Bình, around 2,000 people migrated to the Central Highlands in the 1950s for new projects, including the Đinh family, who settled in Buôn Ma Thuột in 1956. Arriving at their home, I noticed that their garden was filled with edible plants. Miss Đinh Thị Thanh Đan, their daughter, told me that in their community they use the banana plant entirely: its leaves wrap and flavour the grilled fish, while its young stalk appears in Pork Bone Soup with Young Banana Stalk (page 378).

Serves 4
Preparation time: 15 minutes
Cooking time: 30 minutes

| DF |

- 15 g/½ oz piece young fresh ginger, thinly sliced
- 15 g/½ oz lemongrass
- 280 g/10 oz small river fish (cá đồng) such as baby carp or cat fish
- ½ teaspoon MSG (or soup powder/bột canh)
- ½ teaspoon all-purpose seasoning (hạt nêm)
- ¼ teaspoon salt
- ¼ teaspoon sugar
- 4–6 banana leaves, blanched (see step 3, page 390), cut into 40 × 30 cm/16 × 12 inch pieces, for wrapping

Put the ginger and lemongrass in a mortar and pound with a pestle until you achieve a fine paste.

In a mixing bowl, combine the small river fish with the ginger-lemongrass paste. Add the MSG (or soup powder), all-purpose seasoning, salt and sugar. Mix everything together well and let the fish briefly marinate.

Arrange the blanched banana leaves on a clean work surface in a cross shape. Place the marinated fish in the centre of the leaves. Wrap the banana leaves upwards around the fish, then wrap with string and tie a knot to hold everything in place. The bottom of the parcel should be flat.

Prepare a charcoal grill or wood fire. Wait for the coals to burn down to red embers, or the wood to burn completely down to embers.

Place the wrapped banana leaf parcels over indirect heat and cook for 25 minutes. Once ashes have formed on the coals, carefully move the parcels directly onto the grill grates and cook for an additional 5 minutes, watching closely to prevent burning.

Remove the leaves from the heat and serve immediately.

## SMOKED PORK BELLY

### Heo Gác Bếp

Translating as 'pork hung in the kitchen', *heo gác bếp* is a traditional preservation method still found in Vietnamese homes using traditional hearths. The pork is grilled, smoked and stored above the kitchen fire, where it slowly develops its distinct smoky flavour. While each region has its own approach, this method of preserving pork belly (side) comes from the Mạ community. Serve it with rice alongside Rattan Shoot Soup with Pork Ribs (page 383) or Simmered Gnetum Gnemon Leaves (page 338).

Serves 6–8
Preparation time: 20 minutes, plus smoking time (variable)
Cooking time: 14 minutes initially, then 20 minutes when smoked and ready to eat

| DF | GF | ≤5 |

- 1.25 kg/2 lb 12 oz pork belly (side), cut into 1.5–2-cm/⅝–¾-inch thick, 15–20-cm/6–8-inch long strips
- 1 teaspoon salt
- oil, for cooking

Preheat a charcoal grill to very low heat.

Season the pork with the salt and let sit for 10 minutes.

Grill the pork strips for 7 minutes on each side.

To smoke, hang the grilled pork strips in the kitchen above a stove or hearth. Allow the pork to smoke and dry for as long as possible; the longer it hangs, the more flavour it will develop.

When ready to eat, slice the desired amount of smoked pork and leave the remainder hanging.

To cook a portion of smoked pork, heat a barbecue grill to medium or heat 1 tablespoon of oil in a pan over medium and grill or fry the smoked pork for about 20 minutes before serving.

*Caution:* This recipe should only be made if you have a live fire constantly burning in your kitchen at home; the smoke is essential for correctly preserving the meat so that it is fully smoked.

# ROASTED PORK BELLY

## Thịt Heo Quay

While its origins might be Chinese, this roasted pork belly (side) has become a staple in Vietnamese cuisine. From appearing in Vietnamese Baguette with Roasted Pork Belly (page 69) to being served alongside *bánh hỏi* (fine rice vermicelli sheets) with spring onion (scallion) oil and herbs. Leftovers also find new life in Braised Roasted Pork Belly with Pickled Mustard Greens (page 300).

Serves 4–6
Preparation time: 20 minutes, plus 2 hours curing and overnight marinating times
Cooking time: 35 minutes

| DF |

850 g/1 lb 14 oz pork belly
20 g/¾ oz shallots, crushed
20 g/¾ oz piece fresh ginger, crushed
3 tablespoons coarse (kosher) salt
1 teaspoon vinegar

*For the marinade*
1 teaspoon all-purpose seasoning (hạt nêm)
½ teaspoon garlic powder
½ teaspoon black pepper
1 teaspoon Chinese rose cooking wine (I like Mei Kuei Lu Chiew)
1 teaspoon fish sauce
¼ teaspoon Vietnamese five-spice powder (ngũ vị hương)
1 teaspoon MSG
½ teaspoon chilli flakes

In a large shallow pan, add enough water to cover only the skin part of the pork belly (side) when it is placed skin-side down in the pan. Remove the pork belly and set aside.

Add the shallots and ginger to the water and bring to the boil. Place the pork belly skin-side down in the pan, ensuring the meat portion stays above the water. Blanch for 1 minute, then carefully remove the pork belly and thoroughly pat the skin dry with paper towels. Using a fork, cocktail stick or toothpick, or sharp knife, thoroughly prick the entire skin surface. On the meat side, make 2–3 shallow diagonal cuts across the surface.

Combine all the marinade ingredients in a small bowl and mix well.

Using a brush, apply the marinade mixture evenly on the meat side only, being careful to avoid the skin.

To salt cure the skin, spread the coarse (kosher) salt evenly on a tray to form a thin layer. Place the pork belly skin-side down onto the salt layer. Let it cure for 2 hours in the refrigerator.

Remove the pork from the salt tray, then brush the vinegar evenly over the skin.

Place the pork belly skin-side up on a rack over a tray and refrigerate, uncovered, overnight to allow the marinade to penetrate and the skin to dry.

The next day, preheat the oven to 200°C/400°F/Gas Mark 6.

Remove the pork from the refrigerator, place on a baking tray and roast on the middle rack of the oven for 30 minutes. Check the internal temperature: it should be 60°C/140°F. If not, continue roasting until it reaches 60°C/140°F (the cooking time may vary depending on the size of your pork belly). Remove the pork from the oven and allow to cool completely in the tray.

Using a sharp knife, slice into serving portions, then serve immediately or use in other recipes.

# GRILLED SNAKEHEAD FISH WITH SPRING ONION OIL

Cá Lóc Nướng Mỡ Hành

This is a great dish to share with friends, as everyone can wrap and roll their own fish rolls. The spring onion (scallion) oil gives an extra fattiness to the lean fish meat.

Serves 4–6
Preparation time: 30 minutes
Grilling time: 20 minutes

| DF |

- 20 g/¾ oz piece fresh ginger
- 1 × 1.3 kg/3 lb whole snakehead fish, cleaned (1 kg/2 lb 4 oz cleaned weight)
- 120 g/4¼ oz Spring Onion Oil (page 458)
- 50 g/1¾ oz (⅓ cup) Toasted Peanuts (page 459), coarsely crushed

*For the marinade*

- 20 g/¾ oz shallots, minced
- 20 g/¾ oz spring onion (scallion) whites, minced
- 2 tablespoons fish sauce
- ¼ teaspoon ground black pepper
- ½ teaspoon sugar
- 1 teaspoon Annatto Oil (page 457)

*To serve*

- aromatic mixed herbs (rau thơm – fish mint, perilla, peppermint, Thai basil, coriander/cilantro, Vietnamese balm, watermint)
- 1 young banana, sliced
- 1 cucumber, thinly sliced
- 150 g/5½ oz pineapple, sliced
- 2 star fruit, sliced
- rice paper and/or lettuce leaves
- 400 g/14 oz fresh rice noodles (bún)
- Seasoned Fermented Thick Fish Sauce (page 476)

In a large bowl or pot, crush the ginger and mix it with 1–2 litres/1¾–3½ pints (4¼–8½ cups) of water to make a ginger water solution.

Using your hands, rub this ginger water over the outside and inside the cavity of the fish. Make a cut along the bone to remove the middle bone (spine), while keeping the fish whole. Reserve the bones.

In a mixing bowl, combine all the marinade ingredients. Evenly coat the cleaned fish with the marinade mixture, then let the fish marinate for 15–20 minutes in the bowl.

Preheat a charcoal barbecue grill or oven grill (broiler) to 190°C/375°F/Gas Mark 5.

Place the marinated fish on a baking tray on the upper rack of the grill or oven and cook for 10 minutes. Then, move the fish to the lower rack and grill for another 10 minutes, until it is golden brown and cooked through.

In a small bowl, mix the spring onion oil with the peanuts. Pour this mixture over the grilled fish just before serving.

Arrange the mixed herbs on a serving platter. On a separate plate, place the sliced banana, cucumber, pineapple and star fruit. Provide a plate of rice paper wrappers and the fresh rice noodles. Serve the fish sauce on the side as a dipping sauce.

To eat, take a rice paper wrapper and/or a lettuce leaf, add some mixed herbs, rice noodles and grilled fish. Top with some fruit slices, then roll everything tightly. Dip the wrapped roll in the dipping sauce and enjoy immediately.

GRILLED SNAKEHEAD FISH WITH SPRING ONION OIL

# GRILLED BITTER AUBERGINES WITH CHILLI AND FIELD CRAB

Cà Nướng Giã Ớt Với Cua Đồng

Called *Trong̊ buh peh pơhăng̊ păng̊ kơ tam*, in the Bahnar dialect, this is a traditional Bahnar dish from Kontum province, in the Central Highlands, highlighting local ingredients like river crabs and bitter aubergine (egg-plant), a predecessor to the modern aubergine varieties. These aubergines are green and firm, eaten either raw and thinly sliced or grilled as in this recipe. Around the region, and notably in Buôn Ma Thuột, the Đắk Lắk province capital, the Ede make similar dishes but are known to use golden ants instead of lime for acidity.

Serves 4
Preparation time: 15 minutes
Cooking time: 30 minutes

| DF |

670 g/1 lb 8 oz bitter aubergines (eggplants) (about 12)
70 g/2½ oz field crabs (about 11)
10 g/¼ oz bird's eye chillies (about 4 chillies)
10 g/¼ oz lemongrass
5 g/⅛ oz lemon basil (lá é) leaves
5 g/⅛ oz sawtooth coriander (culantro)
1–2 tablespoons lime juice
1 teaspoon MSG
½ teaspoon all-purpose seasoning (hạt nêm)
½ teaspoon fish sauce
¼ teaspoon salt

Light a charcoal barbecue grill or wood fire. Wait for the coals to turn grey with a light ash coating and move the coals or wood to create hot and cool zones under the grill.

Place the aubergines (eggplants) on the cooler edge of the grill and cook for 20 minutes, turning every 10 minutes using tongs, until the aubergine skins blacken.

Alternatively, you can steam the aubergines. Bring water to the boil in a steamer, place the aubergines in the steaming basket, then steam for 15–20 minutes until tender.

When the aubergines are cooked, set aside to cool, then peel when cool enough to handle. You should have about 370 g/13 oz aubergines after peeling. Set aside.

To prepare the crabs, thread the crabs onto metal skewers, then place directly over the hot coals. Grill for 9–10 minutes, rotating frequently. Remove from the grill and let cool slightly, then remove the claws and legs and reserve the crab centre part.

Put the chillies and lemongrass in a mortar and pound with a pestle until you have a fine paste. Add the herbs to the mortar, then pound until incorporated. Add the lime juice and crab belly and pound until well combined. Add the peeled aubergine chunks and pound again. Mix in the MSG, all-purpose seasoning, fish sauce and salt, then gently pound and mix until well combined.

Serve immediately.

***Note:*** When grilling, these crabs will emit a very specific smell that is reminiscent of Rice Field Crab Noodle Soup, page 220.

# SUGAR CANE GRILLED BEEF

## Bò Nướng Mía

To keep the beef mixture from falling apart, let it rest in the refrigerator before grilling. While traditionally grilled on sugar cane, these can also be pan-fried. They can be served either as a starter (appetizer) or as a main course with herbs and noodles. If you can't find sugar cane, lemongrass stalks are totally acceptable.

Serves 4–6 ; makes 12 skewers
Preparation time: 45 minutes
Grilling time: 20–30 minutes

| DF |

- 50 g/1¾ oz pork fat
- 100 g/3½ oz Pork Paste (page 461)
- 20 g/¾ oz peeled shallots
- 10 g/¼ oz peeled garlic
- 500 g/1 lb 2 oz minced (ground) beef
- 2 teaspoons oyster sauce
- 2 teaspoons fish sauce
- 1 teaspoon honey
- 1 teaspoon Chilli and Lemongrass Oil (page 457)
- ½ teaspoon black pepper
- 50 g/1¾ oz egg (about 1 medium/US large egg)
- 3 sugar cane sticks

*To serve*

- fine rice vermicelli sheets (*bánh hỏi*)
- Spring Onion Oil (page 458)
- Toasted Peanuts (page 459), crushed
- aromatic mixed herbs (rau thơm – perilla, coriander/cilantro, basil, peppermint), optional
- Seasoned Fermented Thick Fish Sauce (page 476)

Put the pork fat, pork paste, shallots and garlic in a food processor. Blitz until well combined and paste-like.

In a large bowl, combine this mixture with the minced (ground) beef. Add the oyster sauce, fish sauce, honey, chilli and lemongrass oil, pepper and egg and mix thoroughly. Cover and refrigerate for 30 minutes to marinate and firm up.

Wash the sugar cane sticks in clean water to remove any impurities and peel the outer layer. Cut lengthways into 4 smaller sticks per big stick. You will need 12 sticks for this recipe.

Divide the meat mixture into 12 equal portions (about 60 g/2¼ oz each). Mould the meat mixture around each sugar cane stick. Ensure they are evenly thick for consistent cooking. Put the sticks on a tray and refrigerate for another 30 minutes to firm up again.

Preheat a charcoal barbecue grill or oven grill (broiler) to medium-high heat.

Grill the skewers on the barbecue for 20–30 minutes or under the oven grill for 10 minutes, turning regularly for even cooking. Brush with any of the remaining marinade while grilling.

Arrange the fine rice vermicelli sheets on a serving plate. Place the grilled beef skewers on top and garnish with the spring onion oil and toasted peanuts.

Serve immediately with the mixed herbs, if using, and fermented thick fish sauce on the side.

# HOTPOTS

## Món lẩu

---

As soon as the temperature drops below 20°C/68°F, the streets of Hanoi fill with tables of hotpots. With our tropical weather, 20°C is considered cold and provides the perfect excuse for a hotpot.

A base broth is placed in the centre of the table, with plates of vegetables, meat, mushrooms and tofu arranged around it. While the recipes in this chapter have a standard list of ingredients, I encourage you to be playful with the sides, as the dishes are very much open to interpretation. Each broth gradually develops more complex flavours as you add different ingredients. In Vietnam, it is common to finish the hotpot with a bowl of rice noodles, wheat noodles, rice or even bread. Hotpot is perfect for gatherings as it involves minimal cooking and creates a communal dining experience.

You can also turn some of the broths in the Accompanying Soups chapter (pages 353–385) into bases for hotpots. I would recommend Chicken Soup with River Leaf (page 374) or Pickled Bamboo Shoot Soup (page 376); usually a broth with a touch of acidity makes a great hotpot base.

---

# BEEF IN VINEGAR HOTPOT

## Bò Nhúng Dấm

Despite its name suggesting sourness, this hotpot balances vinegar with sweet coconut water broth, while the accompanying sauce's pungency is contrasted with the fresh pineapple's natural sweetness. Thin slices of beef are briefly cooked in the simmering broth, then wrapped in rice paper with noodles, fresh herbs, green banana and pineapple before dipping in anchovy sauce. The broth, growing richer with flavours throughout the process, can be enjoyed on its own or with the remaining noodles at the end.

Serves 4
Preparation time: 30–45 minutes, plus 1 hour chilling time
Cooking time: 15–20 minutes

| DF |

*For the marinated beef*
500 g/1 lb 2 oz beef, sliced
½ teaspoon black pepper
1 tablespoon fish sauce
1 teaspoon sugar
¼ teaspoon sesame oil

*For the seasoned thick fish sauce*
280 g/10 oz pineapple, cleaned
20 g/¾ oz peeled garlic
5 g/⅛ oz long red chilli
100 g/3½ oz fermented anchovy sauce (mắm nêm)
1 tablespoon calamansi juice
4 teaspoons brown sugar

*For the broth*
2 tablespoons neutral oil
20 g/¾ oz garlic, coarsely chopped
20 g/¾ oz shallots, coarsely chopped
480 ml/16 fl oz (2 cups) Homemade Vinegar (page 456)
480 ml/16 fl oz (2 cups) coconut water
2 teaspoons sugar
½ teaspoon salt
150 g/5½ oz onion, sliced
20 g/¾ oz spring onion (scallion) whites

*To serve*
300 g/10½ oz fresh rice noodles (bún)
1 green banana, sliced
1 sour star fruit, sliced
200 g/7 oz pineapple, peeled and sliced
140 g/5 oz aromatic mixed herbs (rau thơm – fish mint, mint, spearmint, perilla and basil)
1 cucumber, zebra peeled (see step 5 in top recipe, page 130), halved lengthways and then sliced on an angle
rice paper, for wrapping

To marinate the beef, in a large bowl, combine the beef with the pepper, fish sauce, sugar and sesame oil. Mix well to ensure even coating. Cover with clingfilm (plastic wrap) and marinate in the refrigerator for 1 hour.

To prepare the seasoned thick fish sauce, place the pineapple, garlic and chilli in a food processor and blend until smooth, about 30 seconds. Add the fermented anchovy sauce, calamansi juice and brown sugar and blend for 10 seconds, or until well combined. Transfer to a serving bowl and set aside.

To make the broth, heat the neutral oil in a large pot or electric hotpot over a medium heat, then add the garlic and shallots and fry for 1 minute, or until golden and fragrant. Add the vinegar, coconut water, sugar and salt and stir to combine. Add the onion and spring onion (scallion) whites. Bring to the boil, then reduce the heat and simmer for 10 minutes, or until the flavours meld.

Arrange the marinated beef, noodles, sliced fruits, mixed herbs and sliced cucumber on a large platter with the rice paper and seasoned thick fish sauce on the side.

Place the hotpot in the centre of the table over a portable burner, keeping the broth at a gentle simmer.

Let diners cook the beef slices in the simmering broth for 30–60 seconds until cooked to their desired doneness. Then they should wrap the cooked beef, as well as some rice noodles, mixed herbs, fruit and cucumber in rice paper and dip the wrapped rolls in the seasoned thick fish sauce.

Any remaining broth can be used to dip any remaining vegetables and served with any leftover noodles at the end of the meal.

# FERMENTED SHRIMP PASTE HOTPOT

## Lẩu Mắm Ruốc

A speciality from Central Vietnam, this hotpot is distinguished by its deep, savoury broth made from fermented shrimp paste, *mắm ruốc*. This paste differs from *mắm tôm*, another fermented shrimp paste more commonly used in the north. While *mắm tôm* has a strong shrimp aroma due to its shorter fermentation time of 1–3 months, *mắm ruốc* is darker in colour and sweeter to the nose with less fishiness, having been fermented for 6 months or longer. In addition to that, the salt concentration in *mắm ruốc* is much higher than that in *mắm tôm*.

While this recipe uses only beef as the protein, the vegetables can easily be substituted – from sliced aubergines (eggplants) to mushrooms and bitter gourds – depending on the season or market availability.

Serves 4–6
Preparation time: 45 minutes
Cooking time: 60 minutes

| DF | GF |

*For the broth*

- 100 g/3½ oz Huế-style fermented shrimp paste (mắm ruốc)
- 1 tablespoon neutral oil
- 1 tablespoon Annatto Oil (page 457)
- 2 bird's eye chillies, thinly sliced
- 25 g/1 oz lemongrass, cut into 10-cm/4-inch chunks
- 15 g/½ oz lemongrass, finely sliced
- 1 teaspoon Chilli and Lemongrass Oil (page 457)
- 10 g/¼ oz piece fresh ginger, sliced
- 20 g/¾ oz rock sugar
- ½ teaspoon caster (superfine) sugar
- 1.8 litres/3¼ pints (7½ cups) coconut water

*For the sauce*

- 1 tablespoon neutral oil
- 5 g/⅛ oz piece fresh ginger, cut into very thin matchsticks (julienned)
- 5 g/⅛ oz chilli (about ¼ chilli), deseeded, thinly sliced
- 10 g/¼ oz lemongrass root/stalk, thinly sliced
- 40 g/1½ oz Huế-style fermented shrimp paste (mắm ruốc)
- 1 tablespoon water
- 1 teaspoon Chilli and Lemongrass Oil (page 457)
- 1½ teaspoons caster (superfine) sugar
- 2 teaspoons lime juice

*For the beef*

- 360 g/12½ oz tender beef (such as tenderloin or sirloin/porterhouse), thinly sliced
- 60 g/2¼ oz onion, thinly sliced
- 10 g/¼ oz lemongrass stalks, thinly sliced on an angle

*To serve*

- 250 g/5½ oz courgette (zucchini) flowers, with a bit of courgette if you want
- 145 g/5 oz yellow velvet leaf (kèo nèo)
- 150 g/5½ oz morning glory (rau muống)
- 200 g/7 oz crown daisy
- 400 g/14 oz fresh rice noodles (bún)

To make the broth, in a small bowl, whisk the fermented shrimp paste with 80 ml/2½ fl oz (⅓ cup) of water until well combined.

Heat both the oils in a large (at least 4-litre/4-quart) pot over a medium heat. Add the bird's eye chillies, lemongrass, chilli and lemongrass oil, and ginger and fry, stirring frequently, for 2 minutes, or until fragrant. Add the shrimp paste mixture, rock sugar and caster sugar and reduce the heat to low. Cook for 6 minutes, stirring occasionally. Pour in the coconut water, bring to the boil, then reduce the heat and simmer for 40 minutes to develop the flavours.

Meanwhile, to make the sauce: heat the neutral oil in a small saucepan over a medium-low heat. Add the ginger, chilli and lemongrass, then fry for 1–2 minutes until aromatic.

In a small bowl, combine the fermented shrimp paste with 1 tablespoon of water and the chilli and lemongrass oil.

Add the fermented shrimp paste mixture and 1 teaspoon of the caster (superfine) sugar to the small pan with the ginger, chilli and lemongrass mixture. Cook for 2–3 minutes, stirring occasionally, until glossy. Reserve 1 tablespoon of the sauce for the beef marinade. To the remaining sauce, stir in the lime juice and add the remaining caster sugar.

To prepare the beef, in a bowl, combine the beef with the reserved sauce. Add the onion and lemongrass and mix well. Cover with clingfilm (plastic wrap) and refrigerate until ready to serve.

Cut the courgette (zucchini) flowers, yellow velvet leaf, morning glory and crown daisy into bite-size pieces.

Arrange the vegetables on a platter with the marinated beef. Place the pot of broth in the centre of the table over a portable burner, keeping the broth at a gentle simmer.

Let diners cook the beef and vegetables in the simmering broth to their preferred doneness (30–60 seconds for the beef, 2–3 minutes for the vegetables).

Serve with the fresh rice noodles, with the sauce on the side for dipping.

# CHICKEN HOTPOT WITH LEMON BASIL

## Lẩu Gà Lá É

While *lá é* (lemon basil) has long been used by Central Highland communities like the Bahnar and Ê Đê in their traditional dishes and seasonings, like in Grilled Snakehead Fish with Pounded Chilli and Herbs (page 156), this hotpot style is said to originate from Phú Yên, where the herb also grows abundantly. The dish later found popularity in Đà Lạt, where the cool weather makes this spicy hotpot especially appealing.

Serves 4–6
Preparation time: 30 minutes
Cooking time: 1 hour 20 minutes

| DF |

*For the broth*
300 g/10½ oz whole bamboo shoots
3 tablespoons neutral oil
25 g/1 oz shallots, coarsely chopped
800 ml/27 fl oz (3½ cups) coconut water
40 g/1½ oz lemongrass
40 g/1½ oz lemon basil (lá é) stalks
30 small green chillies
1 tablespoon plus 1 teaspoon fish sauce
4 tablespoons lime juice
1 teaspoon salt
300 g/10½ oz mini king oyster mushrooms
40 g/1½ oz garlic, minced

*For the marinated chicken*
1 tablespoon sugar
15 g/½ oz shallot, crushed
2 small green bird's eye chillies
12 g/½ oz garlic, crushed
15 g/½ oz lemon basil (lá é)
2 tablespoons fish sauce
all-purpose seasoning (hạt nêm) or MSG, optional
1 kg/2 lb 4 oz free-range chicken, cut into 5–10 cm/2–4-inch pieces

*For the lemon basil dipping sauce*
40 g/1½ oz lemon basil paste (see page 260)
1 teaspoon light brown sugar
½ teaspoon black pepper
1 teaspoon salt
lime juice, optional

*To serve*
100 g/3½ oz lemon basil (lá é) leaves
400 g/14 oz rice noodles (bún)
Lemon Basil Salt (page 479), optional

Slice the bamboo vertically in half, then slice each half lengthways into 5-mm-/¼-inch-thick slices. Bring a pan of water to the boil, add the bamboo slices and boil for 3 minutes. Drain and set aside.

To marinate the chicken, put the sugar, shallot, green bird's eye chillies and garlic in a mortar and pound with a pestle until it forms a paste. Add the lemon basil leaves and pound until crushed. Add the fish sauce and seasoning powder or MSG and continue pounding to create a pesto-like texture. Mix this marinade with the chicken pieces in a bowl and set aside to marinate while you prepare the broth.

To prepare the broth, in a large pot, heat 1 tablespoon of the oil over a medium–low heat, add the shallots and fry for 1 minute until they start to change colour. Add the marinated chicken and fry over a medium heat for 5 minutes. Pour in 1.3 litres/2¼ pints (5½ cups) of water and the coconut water. Tie the lemongrass and lemon basil stalks together and add to the pot, then simmer for 25 minutes. Add the small green chillies and continue cooking for another 25 minutes.

Add the 1 tablespoon of fish sauce, the lime juice and ½ teaspoon of the salt to taste. Add the bamboo shoots and king oyster mushrooms.

In a small pan, heat the remaining oil over a medium heat. Add the garlic and fry for 5–6 minutes until golden.

Add the fried garlic, the remaining salt and the remaining fish sauce to the hotpot and simmer for an additional 5 minutes.

To prepare the lemon basil dipping sauce, mix the lemon basil paste, light brown sugar, pepper and salt in a small bowl. Add the lime juice, if desired.

Place the hotpot in the centre of the table over a portable burner, keeping the broth at a gentle simmer. Place the lemon basil leaves on the side to put in the hotpot as you eat.

Serve with the noodles and lemon basil dipping sauce on the side. You can also serve with the lemon basil salt, if using, to dip the meat in.

# CHICKEN HOTPOT WITH CHILLI

※

## Lẩu Gà Ớt Hiểm

This fiery hotpot is not for the faint-hearted. The green chilies not only bring heat, they are also much crunchier than the red ones.

Serves 3–4
Preparation time: 30 minutes, plus 15–30 minutes marinating time
Cooking time: 40 minutes

| DF |

*For the chicken*
½ chicken (about 500 g/1 lb 2 oz), cut into 5-cm/2-inch chunks
½ teaspoon salt
1 teaspoon fish sauce
1 teaspoon sugar

*For the broth*
2 tablespoons neutral oil
35 g/1¼ oz shallots, roughly smashed
5 g/⅛ oz (about 8 medium) lime leaves
25 g/1 oz lemongrass, cut into 10-cm/4-inch pieces and pounded
1½ teaspoons salt
½ teaspoon sugar
1 tablespoon fish sauce
1 tablespoon lime juice
200 g/7 oz king oyster mushroom
50 g/1¾ oz green chillies (about 4)
2–5 red bird's eye chillies

*To serve*
100 g/3½ oz banana blossom (bắp chuối)
100 g/3½ oz morning glory (rau muống)
20 g/¾ oz peppermint (húng cây)
20 g/¾ oz Vietnamese balm (kinh giới)
20 g/¾ oz Thai basil (húng quế)

To prepare the chicken, in a bowl, combine the chicken pieces with the salt, fish sauce and sugar. Cover and marinate for 15–30 minutes at room temperature.

To make the broth, heat the oil in a pot or wok over a medium heat, then add the shallots, lime leaves and lemongrass and stir-fry for 3 minutes, stirring frequently, until fragrant. Add the marinated chicken and stir-fry for 5 minutes.

In a large pot, add 1.5 litres/2½ pints (6¼ cups) of water and the salt, then bring to a simmer. Add the chicken mixture, sugar, fish sauce and lime juice. Simmer for 20 minutes, or until the chicken is nearly tender. Add the mushrooms and cook for 4 minutes. Add both types of chilli and simmer for 5–6 minutes until the chicken is fully cooked and everything is fragrant.

Arrange the herbs and vegetables on a serving platter. Place the pot of broth in the centre of the table over a portable burner, keeping the broth at a gentle simmer.

Let diners cook the herbs and vegetables in the simmering broth to their preferred tenderness (2–3 minutes) and help themselves to the broth and chicken as desired.

# BARRAMUNDI AND TARO HOTPOT

## Lẩu Cá Chẽm Khoai Môn

Unlike other hotpots in this chapter, with their bold flavours from fermented paste, sourness or chillies, this hotpot has much subtler flavours. The contrast comes from its dipping sauce, Fermented Tofu Sauce (page 477). It can be enjoyed with either rice noodles or egg noodles.

Serves 4–6
Preparation time: 30 minutes, plus 20 minutes soaking and 15 minutes marinating times
Cooking time: 60 minutes

| DF | GF |

- 500 g/1 lb 2 oz taro, peeled (about 450 g/1 lb peeled)
- 80 ml/2½ fl oz (⅓ cup) neutral oil
- 700 g/1 lb 9 oz barramundi (cá chẽm), tail part, filleted and bones reserved (140 g/5 oz bones – ask your fish supplier)
- ½ teaspoon salt
- 70 g/2½ oz Chinese celery, cut into 4–5-cm/1½–2-inch long pieces
- 80 g/2¾ oz onion, thickly cut into 8 slices
- 15 g/½ oz long red chilli, deseeded and cut on an angle
- 400 20 g/¾ oz piece fresh ginger, peeled and sliced
- g/14 oz Chinese leaf (napa cabbage), cut into 5-cm/2-inch-thick pieces
- 200 g/7 oz (1 cup) mustard greens, cut into 5-cm/2-inch lengths
- 140 g/5 oz tofu skin (tàu hũ ky)
- Fermented Tofu Sauce (page 477), to serve

*For the broth*

- 1.1 litres/2 pints (4½ cups) coconut water
- 70 g/2½ oz onion (about ½ onion)
- 15 g/½ oz piece fresh ginger, cut into thin matchsticks (julienned)
- 300 g/10½ oz straw mushrooms, trimmed and soaked in salt water for 20 minutes
- 1 teaspoon salt
- 1 teaspoon sugar

Cut the taro into triangles, about 2 cm/¾ inch thick.

Heat the oil in a frying pan or skillet over a medium heat, add the taro pieces and fry for 10 minutes per side. Remove and set aside, reserving the oil in the pan.

Cut the barramundi fillets into 8 × 5-cm/3 × 2-inch pieces. Season with the salt and set aside to marinate for 15 minutes.

Heat the taro pan, add the fish and fry in the taro-infused oil over a medium heat for 5 minutes per side.

To make the broth, in a large pot, combine the coconut water and 900 ml/30 fl oz (3¾ cups) of water. Add the onion, ginger and fish bones, bring to the boil, then simmer for 30 minutes. Add half the mushrooms and season with the salt and sugar. Cook for 1 more minute, then remove from the heat.

Arrange the fried fish and taro, the remaining mushrooms for the broth and the celery, onion, chilli and ginger on a platter. On a second platter, arrange the cabbage and mustard greens. On a third platter, arrange the tofu skin.

Heat the broth to a simmer before serving, then place the pot in the centre of the table over a portable burner, keeping the broth at a gentle simmer

Let diners cook the vegetables and tofu skin in the simmering broth for 2–3 minutes.

Serve with the fermented tofu sauce.

# FIELD CRAB HOTPOT

## Lẩu Riêu Cua

This hotpot recipe comes from cô Vũ Hằng Nga, one of Hanoi's finest seafood vendors, known for her impeccable selection of ingredients. Despite running her full-time business, she makes everything herself and never eats out. During our short afternoon together, she taught us this dish. Her broth gets its red colour from gấc fruit, while *tai chua* (dried Garcinia cowa/cowa mangosteen) provides sourness, though tamarind or lime juice can work as substitutes.

Serves 4
Preparation time: 45 minutes
Cooking time: 30 minutes

| DF |

*For the broth*
200 g/7 oz whole field crabs, cleaned
1 teaspoon fish sauce
120 ml/4 fl oz (½ cup) fermented rice vinegar (giấm bỗng) or 60 ml/2 fl oz (¼ cup) tamarind paste, or to taste
1½ teaspoons soup powder (bột canh)
2 teaspoons MSG
4½ teaspoons light brown sugar
5 g/⅛ oz dried Garcinia cowa/cowa mangosteen (tai chua)

*For the aromatics*
2 tablespoons vegetable oil
60 g/2¼ oz shallots, sliced
gấc fruit, for colour, optional
20 g/¾ oz field crab roe (gạch cua đồng)
250 g/5½ oz tomatoes, quartered

*To serve*
350 g/12 oz fresh rice noodles (bún)
150 g/5½ oz herb salad (rau sống – lettuce, perilla, mint)
200 g/7 oz firm tofu, fried and cut into ¾-inch cubes
200 g/7 oz beef, thinly sliced
6–8 Vietnamese sausages (such as chả quế or giò tai)
20 g/¾ oz (4 teaspoons) Fried Shallots (page 458)

Place the crabs in a food processor, add 1.1 litres/2 pints (4½ cups) of water and blend until finely ground, 1–2 minutes. Strain through a fine-mesh sieve into a large pot, then repeat. You should have approximately 1.2 litres/2 pints (5 cups) of liquid.

To extract the crab mixture, or riêu, place the pot over a medium heat, then bring the liquid to a gentle simmer, stirring occasionally. As the mixture simmers, the crab mixture will float to the surface. (This is similar to making a consommé in French cuisine.) Using a slotted spoon, carefully collect the floating riêu and transfer to a bowl. Remove from the heat immediately after collecting the riêu.

Return the broth pot to low heat, then add the fish sauce, fermented rice vinegar or tamarind paste, soup powder, MSG and sugar. Stir until the sugar dissolves, then set aside.

To cook the aromatics, heat the oil in a large frying pan or skillet over a medium heat. Add the shallots, then fry for 2 minutes, or until softened. Add a scoop of the gấc fruit flesh, if using, and the crab roe and stir-fry for 1 minute. Add the tomatoes, cook for 1 minute more, then remove from the heat.

Bring the broth back to a simmer. Add the Garcinia cowa, then gently return the reserved riêu. Add the cooked tomato and aromatics mixture, then simmer for 5 minutes to combine the flavours.

Arrange the rice noodles, mixed herbs, fried tofu, sliced beef and Vietnamese sausages on platters.

Place the pot of broth in the centre of the table over a portable burner, keeping the broth at a gentle simmer.

Top with the fried shallots, then let everybody cook the ingredients in the simmering broth to their preferred tenderness.

# GOBY FISH HOTPOT

## Lẩu Cá Kèo

This small fresh water fish, found in ponds and rivers across the Mekong Delta, is often either caramelized as in *cá kèo kho tộ* (Braised Goby Fish and Pork Belly, page 274) or served in a hotpot. While this recipe lists essential vegetables and herbs, a traditional Mekong Delta hotpot feast features far more, thanks to the south's year-round abundance of fresh produce.

Servings: 4–6
Preparation time: 30 minutes
Cooking time: 1 hour 40 minutes

| DF |

- 500 g/1 lb 2 oz goby fish (cá kèo), cleaned
- 20 g/¾ oz sawtooth coriander (culantro)
- 15 g/½ oz rice paddy herbs
- 20 g/¾ oz (4 teaspoons) Fried Garlic (page 458)
- 10 g/¼ oz long red chilli, thinly sliced
- 220 g/7¾ oz pineapple, peeled and sliced
- 120 g/4¼ oz okra, sliced diagonally
- 80 g/2¾ oz river leaf vine (lá giang)
- 135 g/4½ oz Indian taro (bạc hà), sliced diagonally
- 100 g/3½ oz yellow sesbania flowers (bông điên điển, also known as Egyptian riverhemp)
- 220 g/7¾ oz tomatoes, thinly sliced
- fish sauce, for dipping
- sliced bird's eye chillies, to taste

*For the broth*

- 1 kg/2 lb 4 oz pork rib bones
- 1 tablespoon neutral oil
- ½ teaspoon salt

To prepare the broth, bring a pot of water to the boil, add the bones, then boil for 7 minutes. Drain, then rinse the bones in cold running water.

Add the oil to the pot and wipe with a paper towel to clean it. Return the bones to the pot with 2 litres/3½ pints (8½ cups) of fresh water and the salt, then bring to the boil. Reduce the heat and simmer for 1 hour 25 minutes, regularly skimming the surface. Strain the broth into a clean bowl or jug; it should yield about 1.1 litres/2 pints (4½ cups) of broth.

Arrange the fish, herbs and vegetables on platters. Provide individual bowls of fish sauce mixed with chilli slices.

Place the pot of broth in the centre of the table over a portable burner. Bring the hotpot to the boil, then add all the fish. Maintaining a gentle simmer throughout the meal, add the other ingredients from the platter gradually as you serve.

To eat, dip the cooked fish, herbs and vegetables in the chilli fish sauce on the side.

# FERMENTED TOFU HOTPOT

## Lẩu Chao

This vegetarian hotpot uses fermented tofu (*chao*) as its base, giving the broth depth without meat. The addition of coconut water brings extra sweetness. Like any hotpot, feel free to customize with your choice of greens and mushrooms.

Serves 5–6
Preparation time: 30 minutes
Cooking time: 40 minutes

**| V | VE | DF | GF |**

*For the broth*
65 g/2¼ oz fermented tofu (chao)
60 g/2¼ oz liquid from fermented tofu (chao)
55 g/2 oz lemongrass
1 tablespoon Annatto Oil (page 457)
1 tablespoon neutral oil
35 g/1¼ oz shallots, minced
600 ml/1 pint (2½ cups) coconut water
1 teaspoon salt
2 teaspoons sugar

*For the hotpot*
oil, for deep-frying
300 g/10½ oz firm tofu, cut into 4 × 2 × 2-cm/1½ × ¾ × ¾-inch cubes, plus 170 g/5¾ oz cut into square cubes
300 g/10½ oz taro (250 g/5½ oz after peeling), cut into chunks
80 g/2¾ oz carrots, cut into heart shapes about 4-cm/1½-inch long
70 g/2½ oz baby king oyster mushrooms, washed in salt water
70 g/2½ oz straw mushrooms, washed in salt water

*To serve*
100 g/3½ oz onion, cut into wedges
150 g/5½ oz morning glory (rau muống), stalks or with leaves, cut into 4–5-cm/1½–2-inch pieces
150 g/5½ oz (¾ cup) mustard greens (or other leafy greens like chrysanthemum or spinach)
400 g/14 oz of rice noodles or egg noodles
Fermented Tofu Sauce (page 477)

To prepare the broth, in a small bowl, mash the tofu with its liquid until smooth.

Put 40 g/1½ oz of the lemongrass in a mortar and pound with a pestle. Mince the remaining lemongrass.

In a 3-litre/102-oz (3-quart) pot, heat the annatto oil and neutral oil over a medium heat. Add the shallots and the pounded and minced lemongrass and stir-fry for 3–4 minutes until fragrant. Add the mashed fermented tofu and stir-fry for 1 minute.

Pour in the coconut water and 1 litre/1¾ pints (4¼ cups) of water, then add the salt and sugar. Bring to a simmer and cook for 15 minutes.

Meanwhile, prepare the hotpot. Half-fill a small, deep pot with the frying oil and heat to 160–170°C/325–340°F. If not using a thermometer, test the oil temperature by inserting wooden chopsticks into the oil – small bubbles should form rapidly around them. Working in batches if needed, add the 300 g/10½ oz of cubed tofu and fry for 6 minutes. Remove with a skimmer, drain on paper towels and set aside.

Using the same oil at the same temperature, add the taro chunks and fry for 8–9 minutes until golden. Remove with the skimmer, drain on paper towels and set aside.

To complete the hotpot, after 15 minutes of simmering the broth, add the carrots and fried taro and simmer for 5 more minutes. Add the mushrooms and the remaining unfried tofu cubes. This will give the sweet taste for the broth. Simmer for another 15 minutes.

Place the hotpot in the centre of the table over a portable burner, keeping the broth at a gentle simmer. Arrange the fried tofu, fresh vegetables and noodles on platters around the hotpot.

Provide individual bowls of the dipping sauce for each diner.

Add the ingredients gradually to the hotpot to avoid overcooking and let the diners cook their vegetables and noodles to their preferred doneness.

*Note:* This hotpot can also be made with duck. All you need to do is sear duck pieces with the fermented tofu and then add your liquid to make a savoury stock.

# PHAN THIẾT-STYLE 'YIN AND YANG' HOTPOT

## Lẩu Thả Phan Thiết

A speciality from Phan Thiết, this hotpot centres around local white sardines and takes its name '*lẩu thả*' (dropped hotpot) from fishermen's practice of cooking their fresh catch in seawater. Traditionally served on red banana flowers, this hotpot combines a variety of colours and flavours from the different components. Different restaurants would have their own variations on toppings, so you can easily substitute with what you have on hand.

Serves 3–4
Preparation time: 1 hour
Cooking time: 2 hours

| DF |

*For the broth*
550 g/1 lb 4 oz beef bones
250 g/5½ oz pork belly (side)
315 g/11 oz (about 6) large prawns (shrimp)
1 tablespoon neutral oil
30 g/1 oz shallots, sliced
1 tomato (about 235 g/8¼ oz), cut into 8 pieces
1 tablespoon Annatto Oil (page 457)
2 teaspoons Shrimp, Chilli and Lemongrass Oil (page 457)
4 teaspoons fish sauce
¾ teaspoon salt
1 teaspoon sugar

*For the hotpot*
1 teaspoon lime juice
2 tomatoes (315 g/11 oz), each cut into 8 pieces
30 g/1 oz spring onion (scallion) whites, halved

*For the garnishes*
90 g/3¼ oz green mango
90 g/3¼ oz cucumber
90 g/3¼ oz star fruit
90 g/3¼ oz young banana
1 banana blossom (bắp chuối) or 90 g/3½ oz shredded banana blossom
salt or lime juice, to prevent discolouring
2 eggs
1 teaspoon oil

*To serve*
Basic Dressing for Salad (page 478)
Toasted Peanuts (page 459), finely pounded
1 quantity White Sardine Salad (page 134)

Bring a large pot with enough water to cover the bones to a rolling boil. Add the bones and blanch for 5 minutes, then remove with a skimmer and rinse under cold running water. Set aside.

Fill the pan with fresh water and bring to the boil. Add the pork belly (side) and blanch for 2 minutes, then remove with a skimmer and rinse under cold running water. Set aside.

Fill the pan with fresh water once more and bring to the boil. Add the prawns (shrimp) and blanch for 1 minute, then remove with a skimmer and rinse under cold running water. Set aside. Discard the blanching water.

In a large stockpot, bring 2.5 litres/4½ pints (10½ cups) of water to a simmer.

Using a sharp knife, peel the prawns, reserving the shells. Add the peeled prawns to the simmering water and cook for 2–3 minutes, then remove with a skimmer and set aside.

Add the beef bones and pork belly to the pot, then simmer for 30 minutes.

In a heavy frying pan or skillet, heat the neutral oil, then add the shallots and fry for 1 minute. Add the prawn shells, tomato, annatto oil and shrimp, chilli and lemongrass oil to the pan. Fry for 5 minutes. Add 1 tablespoon of the fish sauce to the pan, then transfer everything to the simmering broth.

Add the salt, the remaining fish sauce and the sugar to the broth and simmer for 45 minutes. Remove the pork belly with a skimmer and cut into thin matchsticks (julienne). Continue simmering for another 45 minutes, then strain the broth into a clean pot.

To make the hotpot, just before serving, add the lime juice, tomatoes and spring onion (scallion) whites to the broth.

To prepare the garnishes, using a julienne peeler or sharp knife, cut all the vegetables and fruits into thin matchsticks (julienne).

If using a whole banana blossom, remove 6–8 outer leaves from the banana blossom to be your 'boats'. Shred the heart of the blossom.

In separate bowls, soak the julienned young banana and shredded banana blossom in salted water or lime water to prevent them from darkening.

In a bowl, whisk the eggs. Place a small pan over a medium heat and add the oil. Pour in the beaten eggs and cook for a few minutes, drawing the edges in, until the egg is set, to make an omelette. Remove from the pan, roll up and cut it into thin slices (julienne) with a sharp knife.

In a serving bowl, mix the basic dressing with the finely pounded toasted peanuts.

Place the hotpot in the centre of the table over a portable burner, keeping the broth at a gentle simmer. Arrange your banana blossom 'boats' around the pot, or use nice serving bowls.

Fill the boats with the garnishes (the julienned vegetables, fruits, omelette) as well as the cooked pork belly and prawns.

Let diners cook the raw ingredients in the hot broth and enjoy it with the dipping sauce. Serve with the white sardine salad as a side dish.

# NOODLES

## Món bún, mì, phở

---

Noodle dishes are central to Vietnamese cuisine, appearing in countless variations across the country. The foundation is always the broth, made from chicken, pork, beef, fish or vegetables, which is paired with different types of noodles. Beyond the common *bún* (rice noodles), each region has its specialties like *bánh canh bột lọc*, square thick tapioca noodles, a speciality unique to Huế.

This chapter focuses on core recipes that can be recreated in home kitchens. Some regional specialities like *cao lầu* from Hội An have been omitted as they require specific local ingredients. While fresh noodles are common in Vietnam, dry noodles also work well for these recipes. The key is the proper cooking technique: cool the noodles immediately after boiling to prevent overcooking, then quickly blanch them again before serving to warm them. Strain thoroughly, too, as excess water can dilute your broth. My personal touch, which might spark debate, is adding a little salt to the blanching water.

Noodle dishes are typically served with a plate of mixed herbs and an array of condiments, allowing everybody to season their own serving to their taste. These might include fresh chillies, chilli sauce, lime, pickled garlic, fermented bamboo shoots, fish sauce, MSG or black pepper. The recipes here serve as a base, but taste will always remain subjective.

---

# NORTHERN-STYLE PHỞ

## Phở Miền Bắc (Hà Nội)

While phở's origins remain debated, its northern roots are clear, a dish born from multiple influences in Vietnam's history. Chinese noodle soups had long been present through trade with southern China, influencing the development of *bánh phở* and *bánh ướt*. The French brought beef, importing cows from India for their colonial needs, perhaps explaining phở's popularity in Nam Định, where French textile factories and their workers concentrated, though some historians argue that phở, then known as *ngầu dục phấu*, was already established in Hanoi.

From these origins, phở has become Vietnam's national dish, sparking endless discussions about its heritage. Through my research, Northern-style phở is defined by its clear broth that focuses on beef flavour, using a specific combination of five spices: star anise, cardamom, cinnamon, ginger and pepper (the southern style adds cloves). Following historian Trịnh Bách's Northern recipe, we use sugar cane not primarily for sweetness but as a traditional ingredient to reduce the natural bone odour. The bowl comes topped simply with spring onions (scallions) and is served with homemade Hanoi-style Chilli Sauce (page 477) and Pickled Garlic in Vinegar (page 468); if you don't have pickled garlic, you can replace it with lime wedges instead.

Serves 6–8
Preparation time: 1 hour, plus 2–3 hours soaking time
Cooking time: 5–6 hours

| DF |

2 kg/4 lb 8 oz beef bones (ribs and knee, no marrow)
500–600 g/1 lb 2 oz–1 lb 5 oz beef brisket
400–500 g/14 oz–1 lb 2 oz tender beef (such as tenderloin or sirloin/porterhouse), partially frozen (for easier slicing)

*For the broth*
50 g/1¾ oz peeled shallots
55 g/2 oz piece fresh ginger (about 11 cm/4¼ inches)
1 star anise
1 black cardamom pod (thảo quả)
5 g/⅛ oz cinnamon stick
½ teaspoon black pepper
½ teaspoon coriander seeds
2 teaspoons salt
100 g/3½ oz onion, roasted (see note)
40 g/1½ oz fresh sugar cane, cut into chunks (or 1–2 teaspoons sugar)
2 tablespoons fish sauce
2½ teaspoons MSG

*To serve*
800 g/1 lb 12 oz fresh phở noodles (bánh phở)
160 g/5½ oz spring onion (scallion) greens, diagonally chopped
80 g/2¾ oz spring onion (scallion) whites, split
40 g/1½ oz coriander (cilantro), chopped
Hanoi-style Chilli Sauce (page 477)
Pickled Garlic in Vinegar (page 468)

To prepare the bones, in a large mixing bowl, soak the beef bones in cold water for 2–3 hours.

Fill an 8-litre/270-oz (8½-quart) stockpot with water, then bring to a rolling boil over a high heat. Using tongs, carefully add the soaked bones and brisket to the boiling water. Blanch for 3 minutes, or until foam rises, then remove the brisket with a skimmer and place in a colander. Continue to blanch the bones for a further 2 minutes, then remove with the skimmer, and place in the colander. Rinse thoroughly under cold running water, scrubbing with a clean brush to remove impurities. Set aside while you make the broth.

Place a grill (broiler) rack (see note) over a medium-high flame on the hob (stove) or preheat the oven grill (broiler) to 190°C/375°F/Gas Mark 5.

Using tongs, add the shallots and ginger to the grill rack. Grill for 5–7 minutes, turning with the tongs, until the shallots are charred and ginger fragrant and lightly blackened. Remove from the grill rack with the tongs and carefully remove any black spots with a knife. Set aside.

In a dry pan over a medium heat, toast the star anise, cardamom and cinnamon. After 1–2 minutes, add the pepper and coriander seeds. Toast for another 30 seconds. Place all the toasted spices in a spice cage or tea bag.

In the stockpot, combine the blanched bones, 4 litres/7 pints (17 cups) of fresh water, the grilled shallots and ginger, the salt and the spice cage or tea bag. Add the roasted onion and sugar cane. Place the pot over a high heat and bring to the boil. Reduce the heat to medium–low to maintain a gentle simmer. Partially cover the pot with a lid, then simmer for 1 hour.

Add the blanched brisket, and continue simmering for another hour. Remove the brisket using tongs and set aside. Add another 500 ml/18 fl oz (2 cups) water, 1 tablespoon of the fish sauce and 2 teaspoons of the MSG. Continue simmering for 2 more hours.

Using a fine-mesh sieve, strain the broth into a clean pot (it should yield about 3 litres/5¼ pints/12½ cups). Keep the spice cage or tea bag in the strained broth. Add the remaining MSG and the remaining fish sauce to the strained broth. Taste and adjust the seasoning if needed. Maintain the broth at a gentle simmer while you prepare to serve.

Slice the cooled brisket thinly against the grain.

Slice the partially frozen beef fillet (tenderloin) very thinly.

Arrange the sliced meats on a serving platter.

When you are ready to serve, fill a pot with water, then bring to the boil. Add a pinch of salt to the boiling water. Using the skimmer, working in batches per portion, add 100 g/3½ oz of the fresh phở noodles and blanch for about 10 seconds, then place the blanched noodles in individual bowls.

Arrange 3–4 slices of the cooked brisket and 3–4 slices of beef fillet on top of each bowl of noodles. Using a ladle, pour about 400 ml/14 fl oz (1⅔ cups) of the hot broth into each bowl to cook the beef. Garnish with the spring onion (scallion) greens and whites and the chopped coriander (cilantro).

Serve hot with the Hanoi-style chilli sauce and pickled garlic in vinegar on the side.

***Note:*** To roast the onion, char it over an open flame (see step 1, page 195) or roast in the oven at 180°C/350°F/Gas Mark 4 for 6–7 minutes.

# PHỞ WITH QUICKLY STIR-FRIED BEEF

## Phở Bò Tái Lăn

A modern take on Northern-style phở, and one of my favourites, where thin slices of rare (*tái*) beef are quickly stir-fried (*lăn*) in a wok with plenty of garlic and shallots. This high-heat cooking creates that distinctive '*wok hei*', a smoky aroma that adds another layer of richness to the clear broth.

Serves 4
Preparation time: 1 hour, plus 2–3 hours soaking time
Cooking time: 5–6 hours

| DF |

2.5–3 kg/5 lb 8 oz–6 lb 8 oz beef bones (ribs and knee, no marrow)

*For the broth*
50 g/1¾ oz shallots, grilled
55 g/2 oz piece fresh ginger (about 11 cm/ 4¼ inches), grilled
7 g/¼ oz peanut worms (sá sùng) (about 6), soaked for 15 minutes
5 g/⅛ oz cinnamon stick
1 star anise
1 black cardamom pod (thảo quả)
½ teaspoon coriander seeds
2 teaspoons salt
100 g/3½ oz onion, roasted (see note, page 183)
45 g/1½ oz fresh sugar cane, cut into chunks (or 1–2 teaspoons sugar)
2 tablespoons fish sauce
2½ teaspoons MSG

*For the quickly stir-fried beef*
1 teaspoon oyster sauce
1 teaspoon soy sauce
½ teaspoon black pepper
2 tablespoons neutral oil
40 g/1½ oz garlic, coarsely chopped
320 g/11¼ oz beef, thinly sliced

*To serve*
pinch of salt
400 g/14 oz phở noodles (bánh phở)
40 g/1½ oz spring onion (scallion) whites, split
80 g/2¾ oz spring onion (scallion) greens, diagonally sliced
12 g/½ oz coriander (cilantro), chopped
4 pinches black pepper
Hanoi-style Chilli Sauce (page 477), optional
Pickled Garlic in Vinegar (page 468), optional

To prepare the bones, in a large mixing bowl, soak the beef bones in cold water for 2–3 hours.

Fill a stockpot with water, then bring to a rolling boil over a high heat. Using tongs, carefully add the soaked bones to the boiling water. Blanch for 5 minutes, then remove with a skimmer, and place in a colander. Rinse thoroughly under cold running water, scrubbing the bones thoroughly with a clean brush to remove impurities. Set aside while you make the broth.

Place a grill (broiler) rack over a medium-high flame on the hob (stove) or preheat the oven grill (broiler) to 190°C/375°F/Gas Mark 5.

Using tongs, add the shallots, ginger to the grill rack. Grill for 5–7 minutes, turning with the tongs, until the shallots are charred and ginger fragrant and lightly blackened. Remove from the grill rack with the tongs and carefully remove any black spots with a knife. Set aside.

Reduce the flame to medium (or the oven grill to 180°C/350°F), then grill the peanut worms for 5 minutes, turning with tongs. Set aside and reserve.

In a dry pan over a medium heat, toast the cinnamon, star anise and cardamom for 1–2 minutes, then add the coriander seeds and toast for 30 seconds. Place all the toasted spices in a spice cage or tea bag.

Fill a 5-litre pot with 4 litres/7 pints (17 cups) of water, then add the blanched bones, grilled shallots and ginger, the salt and the spice cage or tea bag. Add the grilled peanut worms, roasted onion and sugar cane. Half-cover with the lid and simmer for 1 hour.

After 1 hour, if the broth has reduced drastically, add 500 ml/ 18 fl oz (2 cups) water. Add, 1 tablespoon of the fish sauce and 2 teaspoons of the MSG to the broth and continue simmering for another 2 hours.

Using a fine-mesh sieve, strain the broth into a clean pot (it should yield about 3 litres/5¼ pints/12½ cups of broth). Keep the spice cage or tea bag in the strained broth. Add the remaining MSG and the remaining fish sauce to the strained broth.

As soon as the broth is ready, prepare the quickly stir-fried beef. Mix the oyster sauce, soy sauce and pepper in a small bowl. Set aside.

Heat the oil in a pan over a medium heat, add the garlic and fry for 10 seconds. Add the beef, then quickly stir-fry for 1 minute to release some of its juices. You want to keep it a little juicy for serving. Add the sauce mixture, then stir-fry until smoky (about 1 minute 15 seconds–1 minute 30 seconds in total). Remove from the heat.

When you are ready to serve, fill a pot with water, then bring to the boil. Add a pinch of salt to the boiling water. Using the skimmer, working in batches per portion, add 100 g/3½ oz of the fresh phở noodles and blanch for about 10 seconds, then place the blanched noodles in individual bowls.

Top each bowl with about 30 g/ 1 oz of the quickly stir-fried beef. Ladle over the hot broth to cover all the ingredients. Add the spring onion (scallion) whites and greens and chopped coriander (cilantro). Finish with a pinch of pepper on top.

Serve hot, with the Hanoi-style chilli sauce and pickled garlic in vinegar on the side, if desired.

# SOUTHERN-STYLE PHỞ

Phở Miền Nam

Phở became more prevalent in Saigon after 1954, when the Geneva Accords led to a significant northern exodus. The southern version features a sweeter broth, often with the option of extra fatty broth (*nước béo*). While in the north the bowl comes as it is, with just spring onions (scallions) on top, the south would always serve it with a plate of herbs. Another signature of Southern-style phở is the accompaniment of hoisin sauce and a chilli sauce more similar to sriracha than *tương ớt Hà Nội* (Hanoi-style chilli sauce).

Serves 8
Preparation time: 1 hour
Cooking time: 4–5 hours

| DF |

- 2.3 kg/5 lb marrow bones
- 1 kg/2 lb 4 oz meaty bones
- 450 g/1 lb beef brisket
- 200 g/7 oz beef tendon
- 160–240 g/5½–8½ oz tender beef (such as tenderloin or sirloin/porterhouse), partially frozen (for easier slicing)
- 40 g/1½ oz onion, thinly sliced

*For the aromatics*

- 2 whole star anise
- 10 g/¼ oz cinnamon stick
- 1½ teaspoons coriander seeds
- 1 teaspoon fennel seeds
- 50 g/1¾ oz piece fresh ginger (about 10 cm/4 inches)
- 40 g/1½ oz peeled shallots

*For the broth*

- 2½ tablespoons salt
- 65 g/2¼ oz rock sugar
- 100 g/3½ oz onion
- 5 cloves
- 10 g/¼ oz coriander (cilantro) root
- 1 teaspoon MSG, optional
- 2 tablespoons fish sauce, plus 1 teaspoon, to taste

*To serve*

- 16 beef meatballs (bò viên) (about 240 g/8½ oz)
- 1 tablespoon salt
- 800 g/1 lb 12 oz Southern-style phở noodles
- 40 g/1½ oz spring onions (scallions), finely chopped
- 30 g/1 oz coriander (cilantro) leaves
- freshly ground black pepper
- aromatic mixed herbs (rau thơm – sawtooth coriander/culantro, Thai basil, rice paddy herbs, spearmint, bean sprouts)
- Vietnamese black bean sauce (tương đen)
- Vietnamese chilli sauce (tương ớt)
- lime slices
- sliced chillies, optional

In a large pot, bring 3 litres/5¼ pints (12½ cups) of water to the boil. Add all the bones, brisket and tendon, then return to the boil and cook for 5 minutes. Drain and rinse thoroughly under cold running water, scrubbing the bones clean of any residue. Set aside

To prepare the aromatics, heat a dry pan over a low heat, add the star anise, cinnamon, coriander seeds and fennel seeds and toast for 2–3 minutes, or until fragrant. Transfer the spices to a spice cage or tea bag.

Place a grill (broiler) rack over a medium-high flame on the hob (stove) or preheat the oven grill (broiler) to 190°C/375°F/Gas Mark 5.

Using tongs, add the ginger and shallots to the grill rack. Grill until charred and fragrant, 5–7 minutes. Remove from the grill rack with the tongs and set aside.

To make the broth, in a large stockpot, combine 7 litres/12 pints (29 cups) water with the blanched bones and tendon, salt and rock sugar.

Stud the onion with the cloves, then add it to the stockpot, along with the grilled aromatics, spice bag and coriander (cilantro) root. Bring to the boil, then reduce to gentle simmer. Simmer for 1 hour. Add the blanched brisket and simmer for 1 more hour until the brisket is tender. Remove the brisket, cover and set aside.

Add the MSG, if using, 2 tablespoons of the fish sauce and another 500 ml/18 fl oz (2 cups) water to the broth, then continue simmering for 1–2 more hours.

Using a fine-mesh sieve, strain the broth into a large pan (it should yield about 4–4.5 litres/ 7–8 pints/17–19 cups of broth. Keep the spice cage or tea bag in the strained broth. Add the remaining fish sauce, or to taste. Set aside.

When you are almost ready to serve, cut the brisket into 2–3 mm/⅛ inch thin slices. Cut the partially frozen beef into paper-thin slices. Soak the onion in iced water for at least 10 minutes.

To serve, heat the broth to 95–98°C/203–208°F, then add the meatballs and cook for 2 minutes, or until heated through.

Meanwhile, bring a large pot of water to a rolling boil. Add the 1 tablespoon of salt to the water and, working in batches for each serving (see note), place 100–120 g/4¼ oz of the phở noodles in a noodle strainer/basket, then dip into the boiling water for 10–15 seconds, for fresh noodles, or 30–45 seconds, for dried noodles. Remove and drain well, then place directly into individual bowls.

In each bowl of noodles arrange 3–4 brisket slices, 20–30 g/1 oz of the tender beef slices, 2 of the meatballs and 2 pieces of the beef tendon. Add 5 g/⅛ oz of the sliced onion and 1 teaspoon of the chopped spring onions (scallions) to each bowl. Finally, ladle approximately 500 ml/18 fl oz (2 cups) boiling broth over each bowl, then garnish with coriander (cilantro) and pepper.

Serve immediately with aromatic mixed herbs, small dishes of black bean sauce and chilli sauce, lime slices and sliced chillies, if desired, on the side.

***Notes:*** Don't be temped to blanch all the noodles at once – do them bowl by bowl for the best texture.

My recipe here serves as a base for you to season to taste, but there is one rule of thumb: make the broth a little saltier than you might think – once mixed with rice noodles, it'll balance out perfectly to avoid a bland bowl.

# DEEP-FRIED PHỞ NEST WITH EGG

## Phở Chiên Trứng

Beyond the familiar soup version, phở is served by Hanoi's street vendors in several crispy forms: stir-fried (*áp chảo*), puffed fried (*chiên phồng*), and these deep-fried nests with egg. Each is served with stir-fried beef and young mustard greens in a meat gravy. While fresh phở noodles are traditional, dried noodles work, too – just cook them first according to the packet instructions.

Serves 2
Preparation time: 30 minutes
Cooking time: 20 minutes

| DF |

*For the marinated beef*
120 g/4¼ oz beef, thinly sliced
5 g/⅛ oz garlic, minced
¾ teaspoon fish sauce
¼ teaspoon sesame oil
1 teaspoon oyster sauce
¼ teaspoon black pepper

*For the noodle nest*
1 egg (50 g)
neutral oil, for deep-frying
200 g/7 oz fresh phở noodles (bánh phở)

*For the sauce*
1 teaspoon cornflour (cornstarch)
1 teaspoon oyster sauce
1 teaspoon MSG
1 teaspoon fish sauce

*For the toppings*
1 teaspoon oyster sauce
150 g/5½ oz (¾ cup) young mustard greens (cải bẹ) or pak choi (bok choy), thinly sliced
60 g/2¼ oz onion, thinly sliced
30 g/1 oz tomato, quartered
1 teaspoon fish sauce
5 g coriander (cilantro), leaves picked

*To serve*
Northern-style Fish Sauce (page 471)
Hanoi-style Chilli Sauce (page 477)
Pickled Kohlrabi and Carrots (page 469)

To marinate the beef, in a small bowl, combine the beef with the garlic, fish sauce, sesame oil, oyster sauce and black pepper. Mix well and let marinate for 15–20 minutes at room temperature.

To prepare the noodle nest: beat 1 egg in a small bowl until the yolk and white are fully combined.

Fill a large non-stick pan halfway with neutral oil, then heat the oil to 190°C/375°F. If not using a thermometer, test the oil temperature by inserting wooden chopsticks into the oil – it should bubble vigorously around them. Carefully add the noodles to the hot oil. Fry, undisturbed, for 5 minutes, or until they turn golden. Using a slotted spoon, carefully lift the noodles slightly above the oil level.

Pour the beaten egg evenly over the noodles, then reduce the heat to medium and continue frying for 1–2 minutes until the egg sets. Remove with a skimmer or tongs and drain on a wire rack lined with paper towels. Reserve the frying oil.

To prepare the sauce, in a small bowl, combine 120 ml/4 fl oz (½ cup) of water with the cornflour (cornstarch). Add the oyster sauce, MSG and fish sauce and mix well until the cornflour completely dissolves. Set aside.

For the toppings, heat 1 tablespoon of the reserved frying oil in a wok over a high heat, then add the marinated beef to the pan and cook until browned, 2–3 minutes. Add the oyster sauce and stir to combine. Add the young mustard greens or pak choi (bok choy), onion and tomato, then stir-fry for 1 minute until the vegetables start to wilt. Add the fish sauce, then pour in the prepared sauce mixture. Stir continuously until the sauce thickens, about 1 minute. Garnish with coriander (cilantro).

Place the crispy noodle nest on a serving plate, top with the beef and vegetable mixture and serve immediately with the northern-style fish sauce, Hanoi-style chilli sauce and pickled vegetables.

*Variation: Puffed Phở Noodles (Phở Chiên Phồng):*
Layer 8 sheets (200 g/7 oz) of fresh phở noodles on a clean work surface, then firmly press with your palm to adhere the layers together. Using a sharp knife, cut into 5 × 5-cm/2 × 2-inch squares. Half-fill a large pan with neutral oil. Heat the oil to 180°C/350°F. Working in batches, and maintaining the oil temperature at 175–185°C/345–365°F, add the noodle squares to the hot oil, then fry, flipping continuously using a skimmer, until puffed and golden, 6–8 minutes. (This is like making pomme soufflé, as the steam inside the noodle squares will make each square puff up like a pillow.) Drain on a wire rack lined with paper towels. Top with the beef and vegetable mixture as above.

# STIR-FRIED PHỞ NOODLES WITH BEEF

## Phở Xào Bò

This dish is not only a quick meal option but also a practical way to use leftover phở noodles when you're out of broth.

Serves 2
Preparation time: 15 minutes
Cooking time: 10 minutes

| DF | ≤30 |

*For the noodles*
200 g/7 oz fresh phở noodles (bánh phở)
1 teaspoon light soy sauce
1 tablespoon pork fat or oil
½ teaspoon MSG

*For the tomato sauce*
1 tablespoon pork fat or oil
50 g/1¾ oz tomato, coarsely cut
1 teaspoon all-purpose seasoning (hạt nêm)
1 teaspoon MSG
1 teaspoon tapioca flour (starch)

*For the beef*
2 tablespoons pork fat or oil
20 g/¾ oz garlic, minced
100 g/3½ oz beef, thinly sliced
½ teaspoon MSG
½ teaspoon all-purpose seasoning (hạt nêm)

*For the vegetables*
½ teaspoon pork fat
40 g/1½ oz onion, sliced
100 g/3½ oz Chinese flowering cabbage (cải ngọt)
½ teaspoon all-purpose seasoning (hạt nêm)

In a mixing bowl, combine the noodles with the soy sauce. Mix well to evenly coat.

Heat the pork fat or oil in a non-stick pan over a medium heat, add the seasoned noodles and fry for 2 minutes, stirring occasionally. Add the MSG, stir until well combined, then remove the noodles and set aside.

To prepare the tomato sauce, heat the pork fat or oil in the same pan over a medium heat, add the tomato, all-purpose seasoning, MSG and 2 tablespoons of water, then fry for 2 minutes.

In a small bowl mix 120 ml/4 fl oz (½ cup) of water with the tapioca flour (starch). Add the mixture to the pan, then continue stirring for 2 minutes until thickened. Remove and set aside in a bowl.

To cook the beef, clean the pan and heat the pork fat or oil over a medium heat, add the garlic and fry for 1 minute, or until golden. Add the beef, MSG and all-purpose seasoning, then stir-fry for 30 seconds–1 minute until just cooked. Remove and set aside in a bowl.

To cook the vegetables, in the same pan, heat the pork fat over a medium heat, then add the onion and fry for 30 seconds. Add the Chinese flowering cabbage and all-purpose seasoning, then fry for another 1 minute.

The cooked beef in the bowl should have released some juices; pour these into the vegetables pan and fry for 30 seconds until the vegetables start wilting. Add the cooked beef back to the pan and cook for 1 minute.

To serve, arrange the stir-fried noodles on a plate, top with the beef and vegetable mixture, then pour the tomato sauce over the top or serve on the side.

Serve immediately, and mix well.

# SOUR PHỞ

## Phở Chua

Found in the mountain regions of Cao Bằng and Hà Giang provinces, this dry version of phở resembles a salad, distinctive by its sauce – a broth and vinegar mixture thickened with cornflour (cornstarch) to a syrupy consistency. While herbs and toppings may vary between vendors, the sauce remains the star. The dish also plays with texture, combining crispy fried phở noodles and peanuts for a satisfying crunch.

Serves 8
Preparation time: 30 minutes
Cooking time: 1 hour 30 minutes

| DF |

- 500 g/1 lb 2 oz pork (thịt đầu rồng heo – the part connecting the ham and the loin), with skin, cut 2–3 cm/1 inch thick
- 10 g/¼ oz spring onion (scallion) whites
- 15 g/½ oz peeled shallots
- ½ teaspoon salt

*For the fried phở noodles*

- oil, for deep-frying
- 100 g/3½ oz fresh phở noodles (bánh phở), broken into 5–10-cm/2–4-inch pieces

*For cooking the meat*

- 2 teaspoons light soy sauce
- 1 teaspoon oyster sauce
- ½ teaspoon black pepper
- ¼ teaspoon Vietnamese five-spice powder (ngũ vị hương)
- ½ teaspoon sugar

*For the sauce broth*

- 4 teaspoons light soy sauce
- 2 tablespoons rice vinegar
- 1 teaspoon MSG
- 1 tablespoon oyster sauce
- ¼ teaspoon black pepper
- 1 teaspoon sugar
- ¼ teaspoon salt
- 4 teaspoons cornflour (cornstarch)

*For garnish and assembly*

- 8 eggs
- oil, for deep-frying
- 320 g/11¼ oz cucumber, shredded
- 640 g/1 lb 7 oz phở noodles (bánh phở)
- 40 g/1½ oz coriander (cilantro) leaves, chopped
- 40 g/1½ oz mint leaves, chopped
- 80 g/2¾ oz (½ cup) Toasted Peanuts (page 459), coarsely pounded
- chilli oil, to serve

Fill a large stockpot with water, then bring to a rolling boil over a high heat. Using tongs, add the pork and blanch for 3 minutes. Remove the pork with a skimmer, then rinse under cold running water until the water runs clear.

In the same stockpot, combine 1 litre/1¾ pints (4¼ cups) of fresh water with the blanched pork, spring onion (scallion) whites, shallots and salt. Bring to the boil, then reduce the heat to medium-low and simmer for 30 minutes until the pork is tender. Remove the pork using the tongs, then let cool on a chopping (cutting) board. Reserve the broth.

To prepare the fried phở noodles, heat the oil in a deep frying pan or skillet to 190–200°C/375–390°F. If not using a thermometer, test the oil temperature by inserting wooden chopsticks into the oil – it should vigorously sizzle around them. Working in batches, carefully add the broken noodles and fry for 50–60 seconds until crispy. Carefully remove with the skimmer, then drain on paper towels. Set aside for the garnish.

To cook the meat, in a mixing bowl, combine 150 ml/5 fl oz (⅔ cup) of the reserved broth with 1 teaspoon of the soy sauce and the oyster sauce, pepper, five-spice powder and sugar. Set aside.

In a large frying pan or skillet over a medium-high heat, add the cooled pork and fry for 2 minutes 40 seconds. Glaze with the remaining soy sauce, then add the meat sauce, cover and cook for 10 minutes. Flip the meat, re-cover, then cook for 7 more minutes. Uncover, then cook for 1 more minute to reduce the sauce. Reserve 2 tablespoons of the sauce for the sauce broth.

To prepare the sauce broth, in a saucepan, combine all the ingredients, except the cornflour (cornstarch) with 480 ml/16 fl oz (2 cups) of the reserved broth and the reserved sauce, then bring to a simmer over a medium heat.

In a small bowl, mix the cornflour (cornstarch) with 4 tablespoons of water. Stir this mixture until smooth, then add to the simmering sauce broth. Cook for 2–3 minutes, stirring constantly, until thickened to a gravy consistency.

To prepare the garnish, bring a pan of water to the boil, add the eggs and boil for 15 minutes.

Meanwhile, prepare a bowl of iced water. When the eggs are cooked, cool in the iced water for 10 minutes, then peel.

Heat a pan of oil to 170°C/340°F: If not using a thermometer, test the oil temperature by inserting wooden chopsticks into the oil – small bubbles should form rapidly around them. Carefully add the peeled eggs, then deep-fry for 1 minute 50 seconds–2 minutes until golden. Set aside until cool enough to handle, then quarter.

To assemble, in each deep serving plate, arrange the shredded cucumber, fresh phở noodles, cooked pork in the centre of the plate and 4 fried egg quarters around the edges. Pour 4 tablespoons of the sauce broth over the noodles. Garnish with the chopped coriander (cilantro) and mint, fried phở noodles and pounded toasted peanuts, then serve immediately with chilli oil on the side.

# CHICKEN PHỞ

Phở Gà

According to 'Ẩm thực Thăng Long Hà Nội' by the Association of Vietnamese Folklorists, *phở gà* emerged in the late 1930s when beef was banned in Hanoi on Mondays and Fridays, though its origins remain debated. Today, vendors who sell *phở gà* typically offer a range of chicken dishes, from *phở gà trộn* (mixed chicken phở) to Chicken Congee (page 254) and Chicken, Meatball and Bamboo Shoot Soup with Rice Noodles (page 195). If you prefer, you can substitute *phở* noodles with vermicelli.

Serves 4
Preparation time: 15–20 minutes
Cooking time: 20 minutes

| DF |

*For the broth*
15 g/½ oz piece fresh ginger
1 g (½ teaspoon) coriander seeds
0.5 g (about 2.5 cm/1 inch) cinnamon stick
½ quantity Basic Chicken Stock (page 464)
10 g/¼ oz brown rock sugar
2.5 g (½ teaspoon) caster (superfine) sugar
½ teaspoon salt
1 tablespoons fish sauce

*To serve*
120 g/4¼ oz spring onion (scallion) whites
2 lime leaves, sliced very thinly
340 g/12 oz warm cooked chicken (from Basic Chicken Stock, page 464)
520 g/1 lb 2 oz phở noodles (bánh phở), cooked

In a dry frying pan or skillet over a medium heat, add the ginger and toast for 1 minute. Add the coriander seeds and toast for 30 seconds–1 minute 30 seconds, then add the cinnamon and toast for 30 seconds, stirring constantly until fragrant. Remove all the aromatics and place them in a spice cage or tea bag. Set aside.

Pour the chicken stock (broth) into a large pot over a medium–low heat. Add the sugars, salt and fish sauce. Stir gently to combine. Add the spice cage or tea bag and simmer for 15 minutes. Taste and adjust the seasoning if needed. Remove the spice cage or tea bag.

Meanwhile, shred the spring onion (scallion) whites, then soak in a bowl of iced water for 10–15 minutes until crisp. Drain when ready to serve.

Shred or slice the cooked chicken meat.

To assemble, divide the cooked noodles among 4 bowls, then top with the shredded chicken, spring onion whites and julienned lime leaves. Ladle 500 ml/18 fl oz (2 cups) hot broth over each bowl, and serve immediately, with extra spring onions on the side. You can also add additional herbs if desired, and serve with chilli sauce or other condiments, if desired.

# MIXED CHICKEN PHỞ

Phở Gà Trộn

While most people are familiar with the broth version of phở, this dry version can be a great option, especially during hot weather. I like to eat this with extra poached giblets and liver. Unlaid eggs are also a popular addition.

Serves 2
Preparation time: 5 minutes
Cooking time: 10 minutes

| DF | ≤30 |

*For the fried garlic*
1 tablespoon neutral oil
15 g/½ oz garlic, minced

*For the sauce*
2 tablespoons soy sauce
2 teaspoons oyster sauce
½ teaspoon sugar
½ teaspoon black pepper

*To serve*
200 g/7 oz phở noodles (bánh phở), freshly cooked and drained
300 g/10½ oz sliced chicken meat (from Basic Chicken Stock, page 464)
10 g/¼ oz picked coriander (cilantro) leaves
10 g/¼ oz spearmint (húng lủi)
10 g/¼ oz (1 tablespoon) Toasted Peanuts (page 459), coarsely pounded
10 g/¼ oz (2 teaspoons) Fried Shallots (page 458)
small bowls of Basic Chicken Stock (page 464), to taste

To prepare the fried garlic, heat the oil in a small saucepan over a low heat. Add the garlic to the pan and fry for 4–5 minutes, stirring occasionally, until golden. Watch carefully to prevent burning. Remove the garlic from the oil using a fine-mesh sieve; reserve both the garlic and the garlic-flavoured oil.

To make the sauce, in a small bowl, combine the soy sauce, oyster sauce and 1 tablespoon of water. Add the reserved fried garlic and 1½ teaspoons of the reserved garlic-flavoured oil. Stir in the sugar and pepper, mixing well until the sugar dissolves.

In each serving bowl, place 100 g/3½ oz of the cooked and drained noodles and top with 150 g/5½ oz of the sliced chicken meat. Drizzle over 2 tablespoons of the prepared sauce, then toss everything together using chopsticks until well combined. Garnish with the coriander (cilantro), spearmint, pounded toasted peanuts and fried shallots.

Mix everything together, and serve this alongside a bowl of basic chicken stock (broth).

# CHICKEN, MEATBALL AND BAMBOO SHOOT SOUP WITH RICE NOODLES

Bún Gà Măng Mọc

Named after Mọc village in Hanoi where its signature pork meatballs originated, *bún mọc* comes in two distinct Hanoi variations. The classic version features a pork rib broth and can include *dọc mùng* (taro stem), sometimes seasoned with turmeric. This chicken-based version (*gà* is chicken and *măng* is bamboo), on the other hand, combines the meatballs with bamboo shoots and mushrooms in a light chicken broth.

Serves 4–6
Preparation time: 45 minutes
Cooking time: 2 hours

| DF |

*For the chicken broth*
1 onion (75 g/2¾ oz), unpeeled
1 × 1.2 kg/2 lb 12 oz chicken, cut in half lengthways (ask your butcher or prepare yourself)
55 g/2 oz piece fresh ginger (about 11 cm/4¼ inches), crushed
25 g/1 oz spring onion (scallion) (about 1)
2 tablespoons fish sauce
1 teaspoon sugar
¾ teaspoon salt
1 teaspoon all-purpose seasoning (hạt nêm)
oil, for brushing, optional

*For the bamboo and mushrooms*
2 tablespoons neutral oil
40 g/1½ oz shallots, thinly sliced
10 shiitake mushrooms (30 g/1 cup before soaking), soaked
40 g/1½ oz dried bamboo, soaked in hot water for 30 minutes, then rinsed twice in cold running water
2 tablespoons fish sauce
½ tablespoon sugar
½ teaspoon salt

*For the meatballs (mọc) (makes 20 balls)*
130 g/4½ oz pork, minced
200 g/7 oz Pork Paste (page 461)
20 g/¾ oz peeled garlic
20 g/¾ oz peeled shallots
¼ teaspoon black pepper
½ teaspoon sugar
1 teaspoon all-purpose seasoning (hạt nêm)
½ teaspoon salt
1 teaspoon fish sauce

*To serve*
500–600 g/1 lb 5 oz cooked rice noodles
35 g/1¼ oz spring onions (scallions), thinly sliced

To prepare the chicken broth, using tongs, place the unpeeled onion directly over a medium-high gas flame and char for 5–7 minutes, rotating the onion every 1–2 minutes until the skin is charred black on all sides. Let cool, then peel off the charred skin. Set aside.

In a large stockpot, bring 3 litres/5¼ pints (12½ cups) of water to the boil over a high heat, then add the chicken, peeled onion, ginger and spring onion (scallion). Season with the fish sauce, sugar, salt and all-purpose seasoning. Reduce the heat to medium-low and poach the chicken until cooked through, about 30 minutes.

Prepare a bowl of iced water. Carefully remove the chicken from the broth and submerge it in the iced water, then pat dry, remove the meat from the bones and shred. Brush with oil, if desired. Cover and set aside.

Return the bones to the broth and simmer for 1 more hour.

Meanwhile, prepare the bamboo and mushrooms. Heat the neutral oil in a saucepan over a medium heat, add the shallots, then stir-fry for 3–4 minutes until golden. Add the mushrooms and bamboo shoots. Season with the fish sauce, sugar and salt, then stir-fry for 2–3 minutes until fragrant.

To prepare the meatballs, in a mixing bowl, combine all the meatball ingredients. Mix thoroughly until well combined. Form into 20 equal-size balls, about 15–20 g/¾ oz each.

Strain the broth through a fine-mesh sieve into a large pot, then bring the broth back to a gentle simmer. Add the meatballs, and poach for 5–7 minutes until cooked through.

To serve, place 100 g/3½ oz of the cooked noodles in each bowl. Add some shredded chicken meat, 3–4 meatballs and a portion of the bamboo-mushroom mixture to each bowl. Sprinkle with the sliced spring onions, then ladle 350 ml/12 fl oz (1½ cups) hot broth over each bowl.

Serve immediately.

# PRAWN CRACKER SOUP

## Bánh Canh Phồng Tôm

A recent addition to Vietnamese cuisine, this interesting dish uses unfried prawn crackers as 'noodles'. The crackers, already seasoned, impart additional flavour to the soup as they soften. It's a popular choice for any meal, from breakfast to dinner.

Serves 4–6
Preparation time: 30–40 minutes
Cooking time: 50–60 minutes

| DF |

500 g/1 lb 2 oz pig's trotters (feet)
350 g/12 oz pork ribs
1¾ teaspoons salt
180 ml/6 fl oz (¾ cup) fish sauce
1 tablespoon light brown sugar
1 teaspoon caster (superfine) sugar
90 g/3¼ oz jicama, peeled
380 g/13 oz carrots, peeled
200 g/7 oz daikon, peeled
350 g/12 oz uncooked medium prawns (shrimp), or 18 boiled and peeled prawns

*For the meatballs*
5 g/⅛ oz dry wood ear mushrooms, soaked and finely chopped
200 g/7 oz Pork Paste (page 461)
10 g/¼ oz shallot, minced
½ teaspoon fish sauce
½ teaspoon Annatto Oil (page 457)
¼ teaspoon black pepper

*For the fried shallots and garlic*
2 tablespoons neutral oil
50 g/1¾ oz shallots, sliced
25 g/1 oz garlic, coarsely chopped

*For the prawn crackers*
200 g/7 oz prawn crackers
800 ml–1 litre/1½–1¾ pints (3½–4¼ cups) warm water, for soaking

*To garnish*
15 g/½ oz long red chilli, deseeded and sliced
20 g/¾ oz spring onions (scallions), chopped

In a pot, bring 2 litres/3½ pints (8½ cups) of water to the boil. Add the pig's trotters (feet) and pork ribs, ensuring they are fully covered by the water, and boil for 2 minutes. Remove with a skimmer, then rinse under cold running water. Set aside.

In another large pot, bring 3.5 litres/6 pints (14¾ cups) of water to a simmer. Add the salt, fish sauce, light brown sugar and caster (superfine) sugar. Add the blanched pig's trotters and pork ribs and the jicama and continue to simmer for 25 minutes.

Meanwhile, using a sharp knife, cut the carrots and daikon into 4.5 × 1.5-cm/1¾ × ¾-inch chunks. Optionally, carve the vegetables into flower shapes.

If using uncooked prawns (shrimp), bring a pan of water to the boil, add the prawns and blanch them in the boiling water for 2–3 minutes until pink. Drain and let cool slightly. Once cooled enough to handle, peel the prawns. Set aside.

To make the meatball mixture, combine all the ingredients in a mixing bowl. Let marinate until the broth has been simmering for the 25 minutes.

Add the daikon and carrots to the broth, loosely cover and continue to simmer for another 15 minutes while you prepare the fried shallots and garlic.

In a small frying pan or skillet, heat the oil over a low heat. Add the shallots and fry for about 4 minutes, then add the garlic and fry for another 5 minutes, or until golden. Set aside half the fried shallots and garlic, then add the remainder to the broth and simmer for another 5 minutes.

Using a spoon, scoop out small portions of the marinated meatball mixture and add them directly to the simmering broth. Cook for 10–15 minutes until they float, then remove from the pan with a slotted spoon.

Place the prawn crackers in a bowl and pour in the measured warm water – you need enough water to cover the crackers by double their height. Let soak for 15 minutes, then drain well.

In a shallow pan, add the strained prawn crackers and scoop out 250 ml/8 fl oz (1 cup) of the broth into the pan. Cook the prawn crackers over a medium heat for 8 minutes to infuse them with more flavour.

Add the prepared prawns to the broth and let everything cook together for a few more minutes.

To serve, divide the prawn crackers among serving bowls. Ladle the hot broth, vegetables, prawns and meatballs over the crackers. Top with the reserved fried shallots and garlic and the sliced chillies and spring onions (scallions). Serve immediately.

***Note:*** You can substitute the pork paste with minced (ground) pork, semi-blitzing it in a food processor for a finer consistency, if liked.

# CRAB AND THICK NOODLE SOUP

## Bánh Canh Cua

Unlike other Vietnamese noodle soups with their clear broths, *bánh canh cua's* broth is thickened with cornflour (cornstarch). The noodles themselves, made from rice and tapioca flour (starch), are notably thicker and more slippery. I prefer using crabs from Ca Mau for this dish, as they lend a particular sweetness to the broth, especially when combined with sweetcorn. The dish can be topped with pork knuckles and coagulated blood.

Serves 6
Preparation time: 45–60 minutes
Cooking time: 2 hours–2 hours 30 minutes

| DF |

*For the broth*
1 teaspoon salt
25 g/1 oz peeled shallots
1 sweetcorn cob (335 g/11½ oz)
1 tablespoon fish sauce, plus extra to serve
800 g/1 lb 12 oz pork ribs, cut small and blanched (see step 1, page 121)

*For the seafood*
2 crabs (about 565 g/1 lb 4 oz in total)
260 g/9 oz (about 12) prawns (shrimp)

*For the quail eggs*
12 quail eggs

*For the fried shallots*
60 ml/2 fl oz (¼ cup) neutral oil
1 tablespoon Annatto Oil (page 457)
80 g/2¾ oz peeled shallots

*To finish the broth*
300 g/10½ oz straw mushrooms
2 tablespoons Annatto Oil (page 457)
15 g/½ oz peeled garlic
35 g/1¼ oz peeled shallots
1 teaspoon salt
2 tablespoons fish sauce
1 teaspoon sugar
5 teaspoons cornflour (cornstarch)

*For the noodles*
2 tablespoons Annatto Oil (page 457)
600–700 g/1 lb 5 oz–1 lb 9 oz thick tapioca noodles (bánh canh bột lọc)
2 tablespoons fish sauce

*To serve*
250 g/5¼ oz fried Tuna Fish Cake (page 463) or any other fish cake
25 g/1 oz coriander (cilantro), chopped
30 g/1 oz spring onion (scallion) greens, sliced
freshly ground black pepper
lime wedges

In a large stockpot, bring 3.75 litres/6½ pints (16 cups) of water to a rolling boil over a high heat. Add the salt, whole shallots, sweetcorn cob, fish sauce and the blanched pork ribs to the boiling water. Reduce the heat to medium–low and maintain a gentle simmer, occasionally skimming any foam that rises to the surface, for 1 hour 30 minutes, or until the meat is tender and the broth is fragrant.

Meanwhile, prepare the seafood. Put the crabs and the prawns (shrimp) in the simmering broth and poach for about 15 minutes.

Meanwhile, prepare a large bowl of iced water. As soon as the seafood is cooked, transfer it to the iced water. Let the seafood cool in the ice bath for 10 minutes. Remove the crabs and shrimp or prawns from the ice bath and pat dry. Peel the prawns and set aside for serving.

For the crabs, first detach all claws and legs from the body. Carefully separate the top shell from the body using your thumbs. Using a spoon, gently take the white meat and any roe from the body cavity. Cut the body section in half and remove the remaining meat using a spoon. Using a crab cracker or mallet, crack the claws and legs. Carefully remove the meat from the claws and legs using a small spoon or pick. Separate and reserve all the white meat for serving. Put the top shells from the crabs and the roe into the broth while it continues to simmer.

Meanwhile, prepare a bowl of iced water. In a small saucepan, add the quail eggs and enough water to cover the eggs. Bring it to the boil over a high heat, then cook for about 5–7 minutes for hard-boiled eggs. Immediately transfer the eggs to the ice bath using a slotted spoon. Let cool for 5 minutes. Peel the eggs. Set aside.

To prepare the fried shallots, in a frying pan or skillet, heat the oils over a medium heat until shimmering. Add the shallots and fry, stirring constantly, for 5–7 minutes until golden brown and crispy. Remove with a slotted spoon and drain on paper towels. Set aside.

After the broth has been simmering for 1 hour 30 minutes, remove the pork ribs and set aside. Strain the broth through a fine-mesh sieve into a clean pot. Discard the crab shells and aromatics. You should have about 2.5–3 litres/4½–5¼ pints (10½–12½ cups) of broth.

To finish the broth, add the mushrooms and cook over a low heat for 10 minutes, or until the mushrooms are tender.

In a small pan, heat the annatto oil over a medium heat. Add the whole garlic and shallots. Fry until golden and fragrant, 2–3 minutes, then add to the broth. Season the broth with the salt, fish sauce and sugar.

In a small bowl, mix the cornflour (cornstarch) with 60 ml/2 fl oz (¼ cup) of cold water until smooth. Slowly stir this cornflour mixture into the simmering broth until thickened.

To prepare the noodles, in a large pot, heat the annatto oil over a medium heat, add the noodles and fish sauce, then stir gently for 30 seconds to colour the noodles evenly. Remove from the heat.

To assemble, place 100–115 g/3½–4 oz of the noodles in each serving bowl and top with some white crab meat, 2 whole prawns, 2 quail eggs, some sliced fish cake and 1 piece of pork rib. Garnish with the fried shallots, chopped coriander (cilantro), sliced spring onion (scallion) greens and pepper. Ladle 580 ml/19 fl oz (2½ cups) hot broth into each bowl. Serve with lime wedges and extra fish sauce.

# HUẾ-STYLE SNAKEHEAD FISH AND THICK NOODLE SOUP

## Bánh Canh Cá Lóc Huế

On the streets of Huế, vendors demonstrate their skill by making fresh noodles for this dish. The rice and tapioca dough is wrapped around a cylinder, and vendors slice the noodle threads directly into boiling water. These handmade noodles are bouncy, chewy and slightly thicker than their machine-made counterparts, and are paired with a rich fish broth seasoned with *mắm ruốc* (Huế-style fermented shrimp paste). On the table, you will often see *chả cây Huế* (Huế-style pork rolls wrapped in banana leaves), quail eggs and pork scratchings that you can add as extra toppings. Unlike many Vietnamese noodle soups, this Huế speciality comes without herbs, and its small portions make it an ideal snack-size dish. You can find the *chả cây Huế*, frozen in Asian supermarkets, or just substitute it with Pork Roll (page 462).

Serves 3–4
Preparation time: 30 minutes
Cooking time: 1 hour 30 minutes

| DF |

*For the broth*

- 300 g/10½ oz pork bones
- 10 g/¼ oz piece fresh ginger, sliced
- 15 g/½ oz shallot, sliced
- 10 g/¼ oz spring onion (scallion) whites, cut into 5-cm/2-inch lengths and split lengthways if thick
- 1½ teaspoons salt
- 5 teaspoons fish sauce
- 3 teaspoons sugar
- 450 g/1 lb snakehead fish, cut into 5–7-mm-/¼–⅜-inch-thick slices
- 3 tablespoons Annatto Oil (page 457)
- ¼ teaspoon black pepper

*For the broth seasoning*

- 2 tablespoons Annatto Oil (page 457)
- 30 g/1 oz shallots, thinly sliced
- 1 teaspoon Chilli and Lemongrass Oil (page 457)
- 25 g/1 oz Huế-style fermented shrimp paste (mắm ruốc)
- 1½ teaspoons sugar

*To serve*

- 400 g/14 oz Homemade Thick Noodles (page 456), cooked
- 6–8 boiled and peeled quail eggs
- 6–8- Huế-style pork rolls wrapped in banana leaf (chả cây huế)
- 25 g/1 oz spring onion (scallion) whites, shredded
- 25 g/1 oz spring onion (scallion) greens, chopped
- 40 g/1½ oz crispy pork scratchings (crackling)
- lime wedges, optional
- blitzed chilli, to taste (see note)
- fish sauce, for dipping, optional

Fill a large stockpot with enough water to cover the bones and bring to a rolling boil over a high heat, add the pork bones and blanch for 3–5 minutes until foam rises to the surface. Remove the bones with a skimmer and rinse thoroughly under cold running water.

In a clean stockpot, combine 2 litres/3½ pints (8½ cups) of water with the blanched pork bones, ginger, shallot and spring onion (scallion) whites. Add the salt, 1 tablespoon of the fish sauce and 1½ teaspoons of the sugar. Bring the mixture to the boil, then reduce the heat to maintain a gentle simmer. Add the fish slices and simmer for 20 minutes. Remove the fish from the broth using the skimmer and let cool slightly. Continue simmering the broth for another 1 hour 10 minutes.

Meanwhile, carefully fillet the fish to obtain about 250 g/5½ oz of meat, keeping the pieces as large as possible. Return all the bones and head to the simmering broth.

Marinate the fish fillets in a bowl with 1 teaspoon of the fish sauce for 15–30 minutes.

Heat the annatto oil in a frying pan or skillet over a medium-high heat, then add the marinated fish pieces and remaining 1½ teaspoons of sugar to caramelize. Sprinkle with the pepper and the remaining fish sauce. Fry for 8 minutes, turning occasionally, until the fish is crispy and well-coloured on all sides. Remove from the pan and set aside.

Using a fine-mesh sieve, strain the broth into a clean pot and discard the bones.

To prepare the broth seasoning, in a pan, heat the annatto oil over a medium heat, then add the shallots and fry until crispy, about 5 minutes. Add the chilli and lemongrass oil and stir to combine.

In a separate bowl, mix the fermented shrimp paste with 60 ml/2 fl oz (¼ cup) of the hot broth until smooth.

Add the shrimp paste mixture to the shallot mixture, then bring to a simmer while stirring constantly.

Add the broth seasoning, including the sugar, to the main broth.

To serve, place 100 g/3½ oz of the cooked noodles to each serving bowl. Add portions of fried fish, 2 quail eggs and 2 pork rolls in each bowl. Garnish with the shredded spring onion whites, chopped spring onion greens and crispy pork scratchings (crackling). Ladle the hot broth over the noodles.

Serve immediately with lime wedges, if using, blitzed chillies and fish sauce, if using, on the side.

***Note:*** Put a few trimmed chillies in a food processor and blitz to a fine paste, then store in the refrigerator to add to dishes as needed.

# COCONUT AND THICK NOODLE SOUP

## Bánh Canh Nước Cốt Dừa

This speciality from Vietnam's southwestern provinces stands out for its unique preparation: the noodles are first cooked in water, then simmered in coconut milk stock (broth), giving them a distinctive sweetness and richness. Spring onions (scallions) and fried shallots help balance the coconut's sweetness, which is more commonly associated with desserts. In Cà Mau, known for its crab, a popular variation is *bánh canh cua nước cốt dừa* (coconut, crab and thick noodle soup).

Serves 4–5
Preparation time: 20–25 minutes
Cooking time: 35–40 minutes

| **DF** |

*For the meatballs*
300 g/10½ oz prawns (shrimp)
150 g/5½ oz pork, minced
25 g/1 oz shallots, coarsely chopped
1 tablespoon neutral oil
1 tablespoon fish sauce
1 teaspoon sugar
½ teaspoon black pepper

*For the broth*
1 litre/1¾ pints (4¼ cups) coconut water
20 g/¾ oz rock sugar
¾ teaspoon salt
2 tablespoons fish sauce
500–600 g/1 lb 2–5 oz fresh thick noodles (bánh canh), pre-made or homemade (Homemade Thick Noodles, page 456)
200 g/7 oz (scant 1 cup) coconut milk
25 g/¾ oz Fried Shallots (page 458), plus optional extra to serve
½ teaspoon black pepper

*To serve*
25 g/1 oz spring onion (scallion) greens, chopped
25 g/1 oz coriander (cilantro), leaves picked and chopped

To make the meatballs, set up a steamer and bring the water to the boil over a medium-high heat. Place the prawns (shrimp) in the steamer basket, set over the boiling water and steam for 6–8 minutes until they turn pink and are just cooked through. Alternatively, blanch in boiling water for 6–8 minutes. Let cool slightly, then peel. You should have approximately 130 g/4½ oz (4½ oz) peeled prawns. Set the peeled prawns aside and reserve the heads and any liquid from the heads for the broth.

Put the pork, shallots, oil, fish sauce, sugar and pepper in a food processor. Blend for 30 seconds, or until well combined and slightly sticky.

Using wet hands, form the pork mixture into small balls about 2.5 cm/1 inch in diameter; you should get 12–15 meatballs.

To prepare the broth, in a large stockpot, combine the coconut water, 500 ml/18 fl oz (2 cups) of water, the rock sugar, salt and fish sauce. Bring to a simmer over a medium heat, then add the reserved prawn heads and simmer for 5 minutes. Remove the prawn heads using a slotted spoon, then continue simmering for 5 more minutes.

Add the meatballs to the simmering broth and cook for 5 minutes, or until they float to the surface. Add the noodles and cook for 3 minutes, or until they are tender but still chewy. Stir in the coconut milk and peeled prawns, then simmer for 5 more minutes. Add the fried shallots and pepper, then taste and adjust the seasoning if needed.

To serve, portion the hot soup evenly among 4–5 bowls. You can use a slotted spoon along with the ladle to ensure even distribution of the noodles and prawns and meatballs. Garnish each bowl with 1 tablespoon of the chopped spring onion (scallion) greens, 1 tablespoon of the coriander (cilantro) and additional fried shallots, if desired. Serve immediately.

# TRẢNG BÀNG-STYLE THICK NOODLE SOUP

## Bánh Canh Trảng Bàng

Unlike the tapioca-based *bánh canh* noodles for *bánh canh cua* (Crab and Thick Noodle Soup, page 197), these pristine white rice noodles come from Khmer rice varieties, a reflection of Trảng Bàng's proximity to the Cambodian border. The noodles, typically handmade by each vendor, have a distinctive bouncy texture characteristic of these slightly sticky grains. The broth, enriched with coconut water, offers a natural sweetness. In Trảng Bàng, locals start their day with these noodles served with paper-thin slices of pork, often accompanied by *bánh mì* (Vietnamese Baguette, page 66) for dipping into the broth and sauce.

Serves 6–8
Preparation time: 25–30 minutes
Cooking time: 1 hour 10 minutes

| DF |

*For the broth*
- 1.7 kg/3 lb 12 oz pork shin (shank), deboned but keep the bone (about 1.2 kg/2 lb 12 oz meat and 500 g/1 lb 2 oz bones)
- 2 litres/3½ pints (8½ cups) coconut water
- 3 teaspoons salt
- 70 g/2½ oz shallots, peeled
- 4 tablespoons fish sauce
- 30 g/1 oz rock sugar
- 600 g/1 lb 5 oz pork leg, hoof split in two and the rest cut into rounds
- 1 white onion (about 110 g/3¾ oz), peeled

*For the fried shallots*
- 4 tablespoons vegetable oil
- 100 g/3½ oz shallots, sliced

*For the dipping sauce*
- 1½ teaspoons fish sauce, or to taste
- ¼ teaspoon sugar, or to taste
- ½ teaspoon salt, or to taste
- ½ teaspoon black pepper, or to taste
- 1 teaspoon lime juice, or to taste
- 5 g/⅛ oz fresh chillies, chopped, optional

*To serve*
- 500–600 g/1 lb 2–5 oz thick rice noodles (bánh canh bột gạo)
- 30 g/1 oz spring onion (scallion) greens, chopped

Tightly roll the deboned pork shin (shank) meat into a cylinder (approximately 10 cm/4 inches in diameter) and tie with kitchen string at 5-cm/2-inch intervals.

In a large stockpot, combine 3 litres/5¼ pints (12½ cups) of water with the coconut water. Add the salt, whole shallots, fish sauce and rock sugar. Bring to a simmer over a medium-high heat, then add the rolled pork meat, pork leg pieces and whole onion. Maintain a gentle simmer (small bubbles breaking the surface) for 50 minutes.

Meanwhile, make the fried shallots. Heat the oil in a small frying pan or skillet over a medium heat, add the shallots and fry for 5–7 minutes, stirring frequently, until golden brown and crispy. Remove with a slotted spoon and drain on paper towels.

To finish the broth, remove the pork leg rounds and halved hoof with a slotted spoon. Cut the hoof into pieces. Set the pork leg rounds and hoof pieces aside.

Continue simmering the broth for 10 more minutes, then remove the rolled pork shin with a slotted spoon and let cool slightly before slicing.

To prepare the dipping sauce, in a small bowl, combine all the dipping sauce ingredients to your preferred taste, stirring until the sugar dissolves. Adjust the seasonings to taste.

To serve, place 75–100 g/3½ oz of the thick rice noodles in each bowl, then add 100–150 g/3½–5½ oz of sliced rolled pork shin, 2–3 pieces of the pork leg rounds and 1 piece of the hoof, if desired, to each bowl. Ladle approximately 600 ml/1 pint (2½ cups) hot broth over the ingredients in each bowl. Garnish with 1 tablespoon of the chopped spring onion (scallion) greens and 2 tablespoons of the crispy fried shallots.

Serve immediately with individual bowls of the prepared dipping sauce on the side.

# PHÚ YÊN FISH NOODLE SOUP

## Bánh Canh Phú Yên

This Phú Yên speciality highlights the region's unique Chinese chives (lá hẹ), which are smaller and more fragrant than their regular counterparts. The broth, made from pork and local mackerel, reflects both the flavours and the terroir of this central coast province.

Serves 5
Preparation time: 15–20 minutes
Cooking time: 1 hour 30 minutes

| DF |

*For the broth*
500 g/1 lb 2 oz pork bones
2 teaspoons salt
1 tablespoon sugar
2 teaspoons fish sauce
45 g/1½ oz onion, peeled and halved
25 g/1 oz shallots, peeled
300 g/10½ oz tuna steak

*To serve*
10 quail eggs
500 g/1 lb 2 oz Homemade Thick Noodles (page 456) or store-bought thick noodles
450 g/1 lb Tuna Fish Cake (page 463), fried and cut into 5-cm/2-inch chunks
120 g/4¼ oz Chinese chives (from Phu Yen) (lá hẹ Phú Yên), cut into 5-cm/2-inch lengths
lime wedges, optional
blitzed chilli, to taste (see note, page 198)
fish sauce, for dipping, optional

Bring 3 litres/5¼ pints (12½ cups) of water to a rolling boil in a large stockpot over a high heat. Add the pork bones, salt, sugar, fish sauce, onion and whole shallots to the boiling water. Reduce the heat to medium-low and simmer for 7 minutes.

Carefully add the tuna steak to the simmering broth and cook the tuna for exactly 15 minutes. Remove the tuna using a skimmer, flake or slice the meat into large chunks, then cover to keep warm.

Continue to simmer the broth for 1 hour, maintaining a gentle bubble, then strain the broth through a fine-mesh sieve into a clean pot.

Meanwhile, cook the quail eggs. Prepare a bowl of iced water. Bring a small saucepan of water to a rolling boil over a high heat. Gently lower the quail eggs into the boiling water. Cook for 5 minutes until the quail eggs are hard-boiled. Immediately transfer the eggs to an ice bath using a slotted spoon. Once cooled, carefully peel each egg. Set aside.

To prepare the noodles: bring a large pot of water to a vigorous boil over a high heat. Add the thick noodles and cook for a few minutes until they float and are just tender (or according to the packet instructions if using pre-prepared noodles). Drain immediately in a colander. Rinse thoroughly with cold running water to stop them cooking any further and prevent sticking.

To serve, place 100 g/3½ oz of the cooked noodles in each serving bowl. Top each bowl with chunks of the cooked tuna, 4 pieces of the fried fish cake, 2 quail eggs and the Chinese chives. Ladle 600 ml/1 pint (2½ cups) of the hot broth over the ingredients in each bowl.

Serve with lime wedges, if using, blitzed chillies and fish sauce, if using, or additional condiments in separate dishes.

# HUẾ BEEF NOODLE SOUP

## Bún Bò Huế

In the past, this soup was sold in Huế from shoulder-pole vendors, with a distinctive rounded aluminium pot of broth simmering over charcoal at one end, balanced by baskets of noodles and condiments at the other. As the dish spread across Vietnam, each region and family developed their own version – my family's Southern recipe includes Vietnamese coriander/cilantro, which you won't find in Huế, and pineapple for sweetness.

Serves 6
Preparation time: 30 minutes, plus 15–30 minutes marinating time
Cooking time: 2 hours 30 minutes

| DF |

*For the broth*
- 3½ teaspoons salt
- 3 tablespoons fish sauce
- 30 g/1 oz rock sugar
- 415 g/14½ oz pork neck bone, blanched (see step 1, page 121)
- 500 g/1 lb 2 oz pork leg bones, chopped and blanched (see step 1, page 121)
- 1 pig's trotter (foot), split into 3 rounds and halved (about 375 g/13 oz), blanched (see step 1, page 121)

*For the aromatics*
- 4 stalks lemongrass (130 g/4½ oz), bottoms smashed
- 1 × 595 g/1 lb 5 oz pineapple, peeled (495 g/1 lb 1 oz peeled weight)
- half an onion (about 70 g/2½ oz)
- 20 g/¾ oz shallots, peeled

*For the beef and pork shins*
- 800 g/1 lb 12 oz beef shin (shank)
- 1.125 kg/2 lb 8 oz pork shin (shank), deboned and blanched (see step 1, page 121)
- 20 g/¾ oz lemongrass, minced
- 1 tablespoon fish sauce
- 10 g/¼ oz (2 teaspoons) Chilli and Lemongrass Oil (page 457)
- 70 g/2½ oz Huế-style fermented shrimp paste (mắm ruốc)
- 1 tablespoon neutral oil
- 20 g/¾ oz shallots, minced
- 10 g/¼ oz garlic, minced
- 1 tablespoon Annatto Oil (page 457)
- 1 teaspoon sugar
- 1 litre/1¾ pints (4¼ cups) boiling water

*To finish the broth*
- 3 tablespoons Annatto Oil (page 457)
- 35 g/1¼ oz shallots, finely sliced
- 60 g/2¼ oz Huế-style fermented shrimp paste (mắm ruốc)

*To serve*
- 800 g/1 lb 12 oz round, thick Huế noodles
- crab cakes, optional
- Pork Roll (page 462), optional
- 30 g/1 oz onion, sliced and soaked in iced water, then drained
- 20 g/¾ oz spring onions (scallions), finely chopped
- 20 g/¾ oz Vietnamese coriander/cilantro (rau răm)
- 2 tablespoons Chilli and Lemongrass Oil (page 457)
- lime wedges
- fish sauce with a few slices of chilli, to taste
- big plate of herb salad (rau sống – banana blossom (bắp chuối), shredded morning glory stalks, Vietnamese coriander/cilantro, bean sprouts, peppermint)

In a large stockpot, combine 3 litres/5¼ pints (12½ cups) of water with the salt, fish sauce and rock sugar. Bring the liquid to a full boil over a high heat. Add the blanched pork neck bones and leg bones to the boiling broth. Reduce the heat to medium-low and simmer for 60 minutes, occasionally skimming any foam that rises.

Meanwhile, prepare the aromatics. Place a grill (broiler) rack over a medium-high flame on the hob (stove). Using tongs, add the lemongrass stalks, half the pineapple, the half onion and shallots and grill until lightly charred, 3–4 minutes. Remove from the grill with the tongs and carefully remove any black spots with a knife. Add these grilled aromatics to the simmering broth.

In a blender, combine the remaining half of the pineapple with 120 ml/4 fl oz (½ cup) water and blend until smooth. Strain through a fine-mesh sieve to obtain 320 g/11¼ oz (1½ cups) of pineapple juice.

To marinate the beef and pork shins (shanks), in a large mixing bowl, combine the beef shin and blanched pork shin with the minced lemongrass, fish sauce, chilli and lemongrass oil, and half the fermented shrimp paste. Mix to evenly coat all the meat.

Heat the neutral oil in a saucepan over a medium heat, then add the shallots and garlic and fry for 2–3 minutes until fragrant. Add the annatto oil and continue stir-frying for 4 minutes over a low heat. Add the remaining fermented shrimp paste and cook for 1 minute, stirring constantly, until well combined. Remove from the heat and stir in the sugar.

Add this paste to the marinated meat and combine thoroughly. Allow the beef and pork shins to marinate for a further 15–30 minutes.

When the broth has simmered for the 60 minutes, using a skimmer, carefully remove all the aromatics, except the lemongrass, from the broth and set aside. Leave the broth simmering while you finish cooking the marinated meat.

To cook the marinated beef and pork shins. Heat a large pan over a medium-low heat and sear the marinated meat on all sides until lightly browned. Return the seared meat to the marinade bowl.

Pour the pineapple juice into the same pan, then cook over a medium heat for 2 minutes. Add the meat back to the pan.

Pour the measured boiling water into the marinade bowl to collect the remaining flavours, then add this liquid to the pan with the seared meat and pig's trotter (foot) pieces and bring to a simmer to deglaze. Simmer for 1 hour or until the meat is tender. Using a slotted spoon, remove the meat, except the pig's trotter, cover and allow to cool to room temperature. Slice, then cover until ready to serve.

To finish the broth, in a separate pan, heat the annatto oil over a medium heat, then add the shallots and fry for 5–6 minutes until golden. Add the fried shallots and oil to the broth. Add the fermented shrimp paste to the broth and cook for a final 15 minutes. Cover and let the meat rest in the hot broth.

To serve, divide the noodles among bowls, add the sliced meat, pig's trotter, crab cake and pork roll, if using. Top with the sliced onion, spring onions (scallions) and Vietnamese coriander/cilantro. Add a teaspoon of chilli and lemongrass oil to each bowl and pour some hot broth over the top.

Serve with lime wedges, a small bowl of fish sauce with chillies and a plate of herb salad on the side.

# VEGAN BEEF NOODLE SOUP

## Bún Bò Chay

In Vietnam, Buddhist practitioners observe vegan days twice a month during the full moon, and many Quan eateries adapt their menus accordingly. Noodle shops create vegan versions of their offerings, like this spicy 'beef' noodle soup, where salted soybeans and *sa tế* (Chilli and Lemongrass Oil, page 457) replace the traditional *mắm ruốc* (Huế-style fermented shrimp paste). While vegan meat alternatives made from seitan are common in Vietnam, you can simply add more daikon and carrots if these aren't available.

Serves 4
Preparation time: 30 minutes, plus 15–20 minutes soaking time
Cooking time: 2 hours

| V | VE | DF |

- 30 g/1 oz dry vegan beef slices (thịt bò chay), or any vegan beef substitute or just vegetables
- 95 g/3½ oz vegan pork roll (chả chay)
- 40 g/1½ oz dried tofu skin (tàu hũ ky), or 200 g/7 oz fried tofu
- ½ teaspoon salt
- 60 ml/2 fl oz (¼ cup) neutral oil

*For the broth*

- 1.1 litres/2 pints (4½ cups) coconut water
- 1 teaspoon salt
- 40 g/1½ oz lemongrass
- 300 g/10½ oz jicama (củ sắn)
- 65 g/2¼ oz onion
- 1 pineapple (560 g/1 lb 4 oz), peeled
- 200 g/7 oz straw mushrooms
- 50 g/1¾ oz salted soybeans (tương hột)
- ½ teaspoon sugar
- ½ teaspoon Chilli and Lemongrass Oil (page 457)

*For the fried chilli and lemongrass oil*

- 60 ml/2 fl oz (¼ cup) neutral oil
- 100 g/3½ oz shallots, sliced
- 55 g/2 oz lemongrass, sliced
- 2 tablespoons Annatto Oil (page 457)
- 130 g/4½ oz salted soybeans (tương hột)
- 1 teaspoon sugar
- ½ teaspoon Chilli and Lemongrass Oil (page 457)
- 30 g/1 oz (3 tablespoons) Toasted Peanuts (page 459)

*To serve*

- 500 g/1 lb 2 oz of thick rice noodles
- 70 g/2½ oz onion, sliced
- 20 g/¾ oz Vietnamese coriander/cilantro (rau răm)
- 40 g/1½ oz spring onions (scallions), sliced
- 100 g/3½ oz morning glory (rau muống), shredded
- 100 g/3½ oz banana blossom (bắp chuối), thinly sliced
- 50 g/1¾ oz bean sprouts
- herb salad (rau sống – Vietnamese balm, Thai basil, sawtooth coriander/culantro, Vietnamese coriander/cilantro)

Soak the dry vegan beef slices and vegan pork rolls in a bowl of water for 10 minutes to rehydrate.

Bring a pan of water to the boil, add the vegan pork rolls and boil for a few minutes, then drain and set aside.

Soak the dried tofu skin in a bowl of warm water for 15–20 minutes until soft and pliable. Drain and gently squeeze out the excess water. Cut into bite-size pieces, then set aside. If using fried firm tofu instead, cut it into squares, then set aside.

To prepare the broth, in a large pot, combine the coconut water and 1 litre/1¾ pints (4¼ cups) of water. Add the salt, lemongrass, jicama, onion, and half the pineapple (about 215 g/7½ oz flesh). Simmer for 1 hour 20 minutes. Using a slotted spoon, remove everything except the pineapple from the broth. Add the straw mushrooms and cook for a further 8 minutes. Add the salted soybeans, sugar and chilli and lemongrass oil.

Meanwhile, make the fried chilli and lemongrass oil. Heat the neutral oil in a pan over a medium heat, then add the shallots and lemongrass and fry them in for 10 minutes. Add the annatto oil and continue frying for another 5 minutes, then strain. Set the fried shallots and lemongrass aside and reserve the oil.

Return 2 tablespoons of the reserved oil to the pan. Add the salted soybeans and sugar and fry for 3 minutes. Add the chilli and lemongrass oil and fry for another minute. Transfer three-quarters of the soybean mixture to a bowl and set aside for the broth. Add the toasted peanuts to the pan and mix well, then set aside for serving.

Add the reserved soybean mixture to the broth, along with a third of the reserved fried lemongrass and shallots.

Meanwhile, in a blender, blitz the remaining half of the pineapple (about 215 g/7½ oz flesh). Strain through a fine-mesh sieve to obtain about 110 g/3¾ oz of pineapple juice. Add the pineapple juice to the broth.

Season the rehydrated vegan beef slices with the salt. Heat the neutral oil in a small pan and fry the vegan beef for about 7 minutes.

Add half the fried vegan beef to the broth and cook for 10 minutes.

Add the remaining fried vegan beef, the boiled vegan pork rolls and tofu skin (or fried tofu) to the broth about 10 minutes before serving.

Cook the thick noodles according to the packet instructions.

To serve, divide the cooked noodles among 4 bowls, then ladle the hot broth over the noodles, making sure to include the vegan proteins and mushrooms. Top each bowl with the sliced onion, Vietnamese coriander/cilantro, sliced spring onions (scallions), shredded morning glory, sliced banana blossom and bean sprouts. Finish by adding 1 teaspoon (or more to taste) of the reserved fried chilli and lemongrass oil and the remaining reserved fried lemongrass and shallots on top of each bowl.

Serve with the herb salad on the side.

# RICE NOODLES WITH FRIED TOFU AND SHRIMP PASTE

## Bún Đậu Mắm Tôm

This dish began as a simple combination of fresh rice noodle nests (*bún lá*), hot fried tofu straight from local makers and *mắm tôm* (Hanoi-style fermented shrimp paste). Today's version has expanded into a complete platter with *chả cốm* (young green rice and sausage patty), *dồi huyết* (blood sausage), *dồi sụn* (pork cartilage sausage) and *nem rán* (spring rolls). This recipe uses shin (shank), though pork belly (side) works well, too, and the meat portion can be adjusted to your preference.

Serves 4–6
Preparation time: 45 minutes, plus 30 minutes drying time
Cooking time: 2 hours

| DF |

*For the pork*
- 1 kg/2 lb 4 oz pork shin (shank), deboned
- ½ teaspoon salt
- 1 tablespoon fish sauce
- 20 g/¾ oz onion, smashed
- 10 g/¼ oz shallot, smashed

*For the young green rice and sausage patties (chả cốm)*
- 250 g/5½ oz Pork Paste (page 461)
- 200 g/7 oz minced (ground) pork
- 60 g/2¼ oz pork fat, diced and blanched for 3–4 minutes until translucent
- 150 g/5½ oz young green rice (cốm), roughly crushed by hand
- ½ teaspoon black pepper
- 1 teaspoon sugar
- 1 teaspoon all-purpose seasoning (hạt nêm) or ½ teaspoon MSG, optional
- ½ teaspoon salt
- ½ tablespoon fish sauce

*For the tofu and deep-frying*
- 400 g/14 oz firm tofu
- neutral oil, for deep-frying

*To serve*
- 600 g/1 lb 5 oz fresh rice noodle nests (bún lá), cooked
- Pork Blood Sausages (page 32), cooked, optional
- Pork Cartilage Sausages (page 148), cooked, optional
- 200 g/7 oz cucumber, sliced
- 100 g/3½ oz perilla leaves, leaves picked
- 100 g/3½ oz Vietnamese balm (kinh giới), leaves picked
- Seasoned Fermented Shrimp Paste Dipping Sauce (page 476)

For the pork, tightly roll the deboned pork shin (shank) into a long, round shape, then securely tie using kitchen string, to maintain the shape during cooking.

In a large pot, combine 2 litres/3½ pints (8½ cups) of water with the salt, fish sauce, onion and shallot. Bring the mixture to a simmer. Carefully add the rolled pork shin to the simmering liquid, cover the pot and simmer for 1 hour 20 minutes, or until the pork is tender. Let cool at room temperature. Slice, then keep covered until ready to serve.

Set up a steamer and bring the water to the boil.

To make the young green rice and sausage patties, in a large mixing bowl, combine the pork paste, minced (ground) meat, blanched pork fat and green rice. Mix thoroughly. Add the pepper, sugar, all-purpose seasoning or MSG, if using, salt and fish sauce. Mix until well combined. Shape the mixture into 1.5-cm/⅝-inch-thick patties (80–85 g/3 oz each).

Place the patties into the steamer basket, set over the boiling water and steam for 30 minutes.

Cut the tofu into uniform 3 × 5 × 3-cm/1¼ × 2 × 1¼-inch cubes (size consistency is important for even cooking). Leave the tofu on paper towels or on a grill (broiler) rack to dry for 30 minutes.

To deep-fry, fill a pan with oil and heat to 180°C/350°F. Carefully add the steamed patties and fry for 3–4 minutes until golden. Carefully remove with a slotted spoon, drain on paper towels and set aside. Slice if you like.

Carefully add the tofu to the oil in batches and fry for 7–8 minutes until the edges are crispy and golden. Carefully remove with a slotted spoon and drain on paper towels.

To serve, on each plate arrange some of the noodles, 3–4 pieces of the fried tofu, 2–3 slices of the pork, 2 of the young green rice and sausage patties (or a few slices), some blood sausage and pork cartilage sausages, if using, 4–5 cucumber slices and a small handful each of the herbs.

Alternatively, to serve in a traditional way, present on a large bamboo platter (*mẹt*): the noodles in one section; the fried tofu, sliced pork and young green rice and sausage patties in separate sections; the blood sausage and pork cartilage sausage, if using, in a separate sections; and the herbs and sliced cucumber in another section.

Serve with individual small bowls of the seasoned fermented shrimp paste dipping sauce with the remaining herbs on the side.

# TUNA NOODLE SOUP

## Bún Cá Ngừ

Along Vietnam's 3,444-km/2,140-mile coastline, each region has its own fish noodle soup, varying from sea to freshwater to brackish water fish. This version features a sweet broth enriched with pineapple and tomatoes, unlike some of the clear broths found elsewhere. In Hải Phòng, for example, they deep-fry the fish slices and add dọc mùng (taro stem) slices instead of Chinese celery. Fried fish cake can also be added to the dish.

Serves 6–8
To preparation time: 30 minutes
Cooking time: 1 hour 40 minutes

| DF |

*For the aromatics*
40 g/1½ oz piece fresh ginger, halved
15 g/½ oz shallot, peeled
30 g/1 oz lemongrass (about 1 stalk)
150 g/5½ oz pineapple, peeled and cut into 50-g/2-oz chunks

*For the broth*
800 g/1 lb 12 oz pork bones
1 teaspoon salt
1 small tuna (about 925 g/2 lb) cut into 6 tuna steaks and 1 head
3 tablespoons fish sauce
4 teaspoons sugar
½ teaspoon salt

*For the fried shallots and garlic*
3 tablespoons neutral oil
40 g/1½ oz shallots, thinly sliced
40 g/1½ oz garlic, thinly sliced

*To serve*
600–800 g/1 lb 5–12 oz thin fresh rice noodles (bún tươi), cooked (see step 12, page 184)
250 g/5½ oz pineapple, halved, cored and thinly sliced
310 g/11 oz tomato, thinly sliced
6 long red chilli, sliced, plus extra to serve
120 g/4¼ oz Chinese celery, cut into 2–3-cm/1-inch lengths, optional
60 g/2¼ oz spring onions (scallions), chopped
Shrimp, Chilli and Lemongrass Oil (page 457)
200 g/7 oz lettuce or morning glory (rau muống), shredded
200 g/7 oz banana blossom (bắp chuối), shredded
65 g/2¼ oz peppermint (húng cây), leaves picked
200 g/7 oz bean sprouts

To grill the aromatics, place a grill (broiler) rack directly over a medium-high flame on the hob (stove).

Using tongs, add the ginger to the grill rack. Grill for 3–5 minutes, turning with the tongs, until the ginger is charred, fragrant and lightly blackened. Remove from the grill rack with the tongs.

Continue grilling the aromatics in this way. Grill the whole shallot for 2–3 minutes, until fragrant. Grill the lemongrass stalk for 3–4 minutes until fragrant. Finally, grill the pineapple pieces for 3–4 minutes until lightly charred, then carefully remove any black spots with a knife.

To make the broth, In a large stockpot, bring water to a rolling boil over a high heat, then add the pork bones and blanch for 3 minutes. Drain and rinse the bones under cold running water.

In a clean stockpot, combine 3 litres/5¼ pints (12½ cups) of water with the salt, blanched bones and all the grilled aromatics. Bring to the boil, then reduce the heat and simmer for 30 minutes. Add the tuna pieces and 1 tablespoon of the fish sauce to the broth and cook for 20 minutes over a medium-low heat. Carefully remove the tuna pieces from the broth using a skimmer. Set aside to cool slightly, then remove the meat from the bones and break into large chunks.

Continue to simmer the broth for another 30 minutes over a medium-low heat. Season the broth with the sugar, salt and remaining fish sauce. Stir well to combine all the seasonings, then strain into a clean pot (or just scoop out the aromatics with a straining spoon).

Meanwhile, prepare the fried shallots and garlic. Heat the oil in a frying pan or skillet over a medium heat. Add the shallots and garlic and fry for 10 minutes, stirring frequently, until golden brown and crispy. Remove with a slotted spoon and drain on paper towels.

To serve, in each large serving bowl, arrange the noodles, tuna chunks, sliced pineapple, sliced tomato, sliced red chilli, sliced Chinese celery, if using, and chopped spring onions (scallions). Ladle 375–400 ml/13–14 fl oz (1⅔ cups) of hot broth into each bowl. Top each bowl with a portion of the fried shallots and garlic and add 1–2 teaspoons of the shrimp, chilli and lemongrass oil on top.

Serve hot, with some shredded lettuce or morning glory, shredded banana blossom, peppermint leaves and bean sprouts on the side for diners to add as desired. Provide small dishes of additional shrimp, chilli and lemongrass oil and sliced chillies on the side for those who prefer extra heat and flavour.

# PHÚ QUỐC-STYLE COCONUT, FISH AND NOODLE SOUP

## Bún Kèn Phú Quốc

A dish with Khmer origins (*'kèn'* meaning 'coconut milk'), this soup is most associated with Phú Quốc, where it features local *cá ngân* (yellow tail scad) or *cá nhồng* minced into a thick broth. The An Giang version uses freshwater fish in a thinner, golden broth spiced with turmeric and cloves. This dish can be served with either thin rice noodles or bread.

Serves 5–6
Preparation time: 30 minutes
Cooking time: 1 hour 45 minutes

| DF |

*For the broth*
- 1 kg/2 lb 4 oz yellow tail scad (cá ngân) or mackerel, cleaned and gutted
- 20 g/¾ oz lemongrass, cut into chunks
- 15 g/½ oz shallot, peeled
- 15 g/½ oz piece fresh ginger
- 15 g/½ oz peeled garlic
- 1 teaspoon salt
- 2 teaspoons fish sauce
- 2 teaspoons sugar
- 210 g/7¼ oz (scant 1 cup) coconut milk

*For the stir-fried fish*
- 2 tablespoons Annatto Oil (page 457)
- 30 g/1 oz garlic, minced
- 30 g/1 oz shallots, minced
- 20 g/¾ oz lemongrass, minced
- 1 teaspoon sugar
- ½ teaspoon Vietnamese curry powder
- 200 g/7 oz (scant 1 cup) coconut milk
- ½ teaspoon salt

*For the dipping sauce*
- 10 g/¼ oz garlic, finely chopped
- 10 g/¼ oz long red chillies, deseeded and finely chopped
- 1 tablespoon lime juice
- 2 teaspoons sugar
- 1 tablespoon fish sauce

*To serve*
- 180 g/6 oz bean sprouts
- 500 g/1 lb 2 oz rice noodles
- 225 g/8 oz cucumber, shredded
- 200 g/7 oz green papaya (starting to turn orange), shredded (see note)
- 125 g/4¼ oz carrots, shredded
- 20 g/¾ oz Vietnamese coriander/cilantro (rau răm)
- 50 g/1¾ oz (⅓ cup) peanuts, toasted and coarsely crushed
- 5 teaspoons Chilli and Lemongrass Oil (page 457)

Fillet the fish, reserving the bones and head for the broth.

In a large pot, bring 2 litres/3½ pints (8½ cups) of water to the boil with the lemongrass, whole shallot, piece of ginger, whole garlic, salt, fish sauce, and fish bones and head. Simmer for 20 minutes, then strain the broth and return to the pot. Bring the strained broth to the boil, add the fish fillets and poach for 8 minutes, or until cooked. Remove the fillets using a slotted spoon, let cool slightly, then flake into pieces.

To prepare the stir-fried fish, heat 1 tablespoon of the oil in a pan over a medium heat, add the garlic, shallots and lemongrass and fry for 3–4 minutes until golden. Add the flaked fish, the remaining oil, the sugar and curry powder and stir-fry for 13 minutes. Remove half the stir-fried fish and set aside. Add the coconut milk and salt to the remaining fish and stir-fry for 7–8 minutes.

To finish the broth, add the remaining stir-fried fish and coconut mixture to the stock, then simmer for 8 minutes. Add the coconut milk, then simmer for 40 minutes over a low heat. You should have about 1.8 litres/3¼ pints (7½ cups) of stock that is thicker than a usual noodle broth.

To prepare the dipping sauce, combine all the ingredients and 2 tablespoons of water in a bowl and mix well.

To serve, divide the bean sprouts, noodles, shredded cucumber, shredded papaya and shredded carrots evenly among 5 bowls. Top with the Vietnamese coriander/cilantro and reserved stir-fried fish. Ladle the hot broth over the noodles and garnish with the crushed toasted peanuts and chilli and lemongrass oil.

Serve immediately, with the prepared dipping sauce on the side.

***Note:*** You may not need a whole papaya to yield the 200 g/7 oz needed for this recipe; if you have leftover papaya, you can use it to make Papaya Soup with Baby Shrimp (page 372).

# KHMER NOODLE SOUP

## Bún Num Bờ Chóc – Num Banh Chok

In Vietnam's southwestern provinces, where you can see Khmer cultural influences on local cuisine, *bún num bờ chóc* is characterized by its use of *mắm bò hóc* (prahok paste). This fermented fish paste, common in regions bordering Cambodia, combines with *củ ngải bún* (fingerroot) to create a distinctly southwestern Vietnamese flavour profile. Unlike other Vietnamese fish noodle soups that feature chunks of fish, here the fish is fully cooked and flaked back into the broth, a technique also seen in *bún kèn* from Phú Quốc, another dish with Khmer origins. Prahok paste can be found in other dishes like Khmer-style Mixed Vegetable and Pork Stew (page 384) or Snakehead Fish and Crispy Pork Belly Noodle Soup (page 213).

Serves 6–8
Preparation time: 45 minutes
Cooking time: 1 hour 30 minutes

| DF |

*For the broth*
100 g/3½ oz prahok paste (mắm bò hóc – Cambodian fermented fish paste)
700 g/1 lb 9 oz snakehead fish (cá lóc), cleaned and cut into 10–15-cm/4–6-inch steaks
25 g/1 oz piece fresh turmeric, peeled
30 g/1 oz peeled garlic
30 g/1 oz lemongrass leaves, thinly sliced
15 g/½ oz fingerroot (củ ngải bún)
30 g/1 oz dried shrimp, rinsed
2 tablespoons sugar
1 teaspoon salt

*To serve*
600–800 g/1 lb 5 oz–1 lb 12 oz fresh rice noodles (bún)
fish sauce
chilli slices
lime wedges
black pepper
50 g/1¾ oz morning glory (rau muống), shredded
50 g/1¾ oz bean sprouts
40 g/1½ oz cabbage, shredded
45 g/1½ oz Chinese chives (lá hẹ), from Phú Yên
50 g/1¾ oz banana blossom (bắp chuối)
60 g/2¼ oz water lily (bông súng)
60 g/2¼ oz yellow velvet leaf (kèo nèo)
60 g/2¼ oz water celery (rau cần nước)
40 g/1½ oz peppermint (húng cây), leaves picked
20 g/¾ oz Vietnamese coriander/cilantro (rau răm), leaves picked
100 g/3½ oz long beans (đậu đũa)

In a large pot, bring 3 litres/5¼ pints (12½ cups) of water to a simmer over a medium heat.

To make the broth, in a small bowl, combine one ladle (about 120 ml/4 fl oz/½ cup) of the simmering water with the prahok paste. Strain the liquid through a fine-mesh sieve into the large pot of simmering water. Discard the solids.

Add the snakehead fish to the broth and simmer for 20 minutes, or until just cooked through. Remove the fish using a slotted spoon and set aside. Continue to simmer for another 20 minutes.

Meanwhile, put the turmeric, garlic, lemongrass, and fingerroot in a mortar and pound with a pestle until you achieve a fine paste, 5–7 minutes. (Do not be tempted to use a food processor instead of a mortar and pestle.)

Add 200 g/7 oz of the cooked fish and the dried shrimp to the spice paste in the mortar and pound with the pestle until you have a smooth, curry-like paste, approximately 5 minutes.

Once the broth has simmered for 40 minutes in total, season with the sugar and salt. Stir the fish and spice paste into the broth until well combined, then simmer for an additional 5 minutes.

To serve, place 100 g/3½ oz noodles in each bowl and ladle the broth on top. Provide small individual dishes containing fish sauce, sliced chillies, lime wedges and pepper on the side.

Allow diners to customize their bowls by adding their preferred combination of herbs and vegetables, then seasoning with the fish sauce, chillies, lime juice, and pepper to taste.

# SNAKEHEAD FISH AND CRISPY PORK BELLY NOODLE SOUP

## Bún Nước Lèo

This noodle soup, with Khmer roots, gets its distinct flavour from *ngải bún* (a ginger-like root specific to the Mekong Delta) and *mắm bò hóc* (Khmer fermented fish paste). The dish varies by region – in Tra Vinh, the broth is less sweet than this version from Soc Trang, and comes with crispy pork belly (side) wrapped in paper and *chả giò* (spring rolls) on the side. This recipe doesn't include the latter but you can add Crab/Prawn Spring Rolls (page 116) if you want.

Serves: 4–6
Preparation time: 30 minutes
Cooking time: 2 hours 30 minutes

| DF | GF |

*For the broth*
500 g/1 lb 2 oz uncooked prawns (shrimp), or 12–18 cooked and peeled prawns
1 teaspoon salt
1 kg/2 lb 4 oz pork bones, blanched (see step 1, page 121)
700 g/1 lb 9 oz snakehead fish (cá lóc), cleaned, including bones and head
30 g/1 oz lemongrass, cut into 15-cm/6-inch chunks
50 g/1¾ oz fingerroot (củ ngải bún), washed
13 g/½ oz piece fresh ginger (about 2.5 cm/1 inch), sliced with skin on
2 tablespoons sugar, plus extra if needed

*For the seasoned fish paste (mắm)*
20 g/¾ oz lemongrass
300 g/10½ oz prahok paste (mắm bò hóc – Cambodian fermented fish paste)

*To serve*
400–600 g/1 lb 5 oz fresh rice noodles (bún)
300 g/10½ oz roasted pork belly (side), sliced
50 g/1¾ oz bitter herbs (rau đắng)
40 g/1½ oz peppermint (húng cay)
100 g/3½ oz banana blossom (bắp chuối), shaved
100 g/3½ oz morning glory (rau muống), shredded
100 g/3½ oz yellow velvet leaf (kèo nèo), cut into 5-cm/2-inch chunks
50 g/1¾ oz bean sprouts

If using uncooked prawns (shrimp), bring a pan of water to the boil, add the prawns and cook them for 10 minutes, or until fully cooked. Set aside.

In a large pot, bring 4 litres/7 pints (17 cups) of water to a simmer. Add the salt and blanched pork bones and cook for 20 minutes. Add the fish (including the bones and head) and cook for 15 minutes. Remove the fish with a slotted spoon. Let cool, then slice and set aside.

Meanwhile, preheat the oven grill (broiler) to 200°C/400°F. Place the lemongrass, fingerroot and ginger slices on a baking tray and grill (broil) on the top rack until fragrant, 5–10 minutes. Scrape off any charred parts.

Add the roasted aromatics to the stockpot along with the sugar and continue simmering for another 1 hour 25 minutes. Strain the broth twice into a clean pot to remove any residue.

To prepare the seasoned fish paste, in a small pot, combine 300 g/10½ oz water with the lemongrass and prahok paste. Bring to a simmer, stirring with chopsticks. Cook for about 10 minutes, then strain into the main broth.

Taste the broth and add an extra tablespoon of sugar if needed, depending on the mắm's flavour.

To serve, place about 100 g/3½ oz of the noodles in each bowl. Arrange on top of the noodles: 2–3 cooked prawns, a few slices of fish fillet, sliced roasted pork belly (side) and a mix of the prepared herbs and vegetables: bitter herbs, peppermint, banana blossom, morning glory, yellow velvet leaf and bean sprouts. Ladle the hot broth over the noodles and toppings, ensuring each bowl gets an equal amount of liquid. Serve immediately.

# FERMENTED FISH NOODLE SOUP

## Bún Mắm

This noodle soup showcases the complexity of southwestern Vietnamese cuisine. The broth develops layers of sweetness from bones, coconut water and pineapple, while its savoury foundation comes from *mắm cá linh* (fermented Siamese mud carp sauce). The dish's herb selection represents the rich diversity of edible plants found in the Mekong Delta region. Best suited for large gatherings rather than everyday cooking due to its time-intensive preparation, this soup can be adapted using more commonly available ingredients. While the fermented fish paste can be found in Asian supermarkets, the traditional herbs may be harder to source. Shaved morning glory or banana blossom make good substitutes – the key is maintaining a varied mix of fresh herbs, with different textures and flavour profiles.

Serves 6
Preparation time: 1 hour, plus 30 minutes marinating time
Cooking time: 2 hours 15 minutes

| DF |

*For the seasoned fermented fish sauce*
500 g/1 lb 2 oz jarred fermented Siamese mud carp sauce (mắm cá linh)
30 g/1 oz lemongrass, roughly cut

*For the broth*
500 ml/18 fl oz (2 cups) coconut water
425 g/15 oz pineapple, peeled and halved vertically
55 g/2 oz lemongrass (2 stalks), smashed
700 g/1 lb 9 oz pork bones (preferably leg bones)
50 g/1¾ oz rock sugar
1 teaspoon salt
3 tablespoons fish sauce

*For the fish-stuffed chillies*
200 g/7 oz uncooked mixture from Fried Strabismus Fish Cake (page 463)
1 teaspoon fish sauce
8 large long red chillies, deseeded
4 tablespoons neutral oil

*For the aromatics*
65 g/2¼ oz lemongrass, chopped
45 g/1½ oz garlic, chopped
55 g/2 oz shallots, chopped
1 tablespoon Annatto Oil (page 457)

*For the seafood*
450 g/1 lb prawns (shrimp) (14 medium), head part slightly cut and feet trimmed
8 small cuttlefish or squid (410 g/14½ oz), cleaned and sliced

*To serve*
600–800 g/1 lb 5–12 oz fresh rice noodles (bún tươi)
640 g/1 lb 7 oz Roasted Pork Belly (page 161), sliced
300 g/10½ oz aubergine (eggplant), quartered lengthways into 6-cm/2½-inch chunks and soaked in a bowl of water
180 g/6 oz courgette (zucchini) flowers (12–18 flowers)
165 g/5¾ oz Egyptian riverhemp (bông điên điển)
35 g/1¼ oz peppermint (húng cây)
80 g/2¾ oz Chinese chive flowers (bông hẹ)
130 g/4½ oz morning glory (rau muống) stalks
60 g/2¼ oz water hyssop (rau đắng biển)
190 g/6¾ oz water lily (bông súng)
50 g/1¾ oz water mimosa (rau nhút)
135 g/4½ oz yellow velvet leaf (kèo nèo)

To prepare the seasoned fermented fish sauce, in a pot, combine the fermented Siamese mud carp sauce with the lemongrass and 500 ml/18 fl oz (2 cups) water. Bring the mixture to the boil over a high heat. Once boiling, reduce the heat to medium and cook for 10 minutes. Remove from the heat and let the mixture marinate for 30 minutes.

Using a fine-mesh sieve over a clean bowl, strain the mixture, pressing gently on the solids. Pour 500 ml/18 fl oz (2 cups) water over the strained solids and strain again. Discard the solids and set aside the strained seasoned fermented fish sauce.

To make the broth, in a large stockpot, combine 2.5 litres/4½ pints (10½ cups) water with the coconut water, pineapple and lemongrass. Bring the liquid to a rolling boil over a high heat.

Meanwhile, clean the pork bones. Bring a separate pot of water to the boil, add the pork bones and blanch for 3 minutes to remove impurities, then rinse under cold running water until clean.

Add the cleaned bones to the boiling broth. Once the liquid returns to the boil, reduce the heat to low, cover the pot, and simmer for 1 hour. Add the rock sugar and continue to simmer for 15 minutes, or until fully dissolved. Gently pour in the strained seasoned fermented fish sauce mixture and stir carefully to combine.

To prepare the fish-stuffed chillies, in a mixing bowl, stir the uncooked mixture from the fried strabismus fish cake with the fish sauce until well combined.

Carefully cut a slit lengthways in each deseeded chilli, being careful not to cut all the way through.

Using a small spoon or piping (pastry) bag, stuff each chilli with some of the fish paste mixture, ensuring even distribution.

Heat the neutral oil in a large frying pan or skillet over a medium heat. Working in batches if necessary to avoid overcrowding, carefully place the stuffed chillies in the hot oil and fry for 2–3 minutes per side until golden brown and the filling is cooked through. Remove the chillies with a slotted spoon and place on paper towels to drain the excess oil. Keep warm. Reserve the oil in the pan.

To prepare the aromatics, using the same frying pan or skillet with the reserved oil, place over medium-low heat, then add the lemongrass, garlic and shallots and stir-fry for 3–4 minutes until the shallots become translucent and the mixture becomes very fragrant. Be careful not to burn the garlic. Add the annatto oil and continue cooking for another 1 minute. Remove from heat and set aside while you prepare the rest of the ingredients.

To cook the seafood, bring the prepared broth back to a gentle simmer over a medium heat. Add the prawns (shrimp) and cook for 3 minutes, or until they turn bright orange-red and curl into a loose 'C' shape. Do not overcook. Remove the prawns with a skimmer or slotted spoon and set aside.

Add the cuttlefish or squid to the broth. Cook for 2 minutes or until just opaque and slightly curled.

Remove the cuttlefish or squid with the skimmer or slotted spoon and set aside.

Season the broth with the salt and fish sauce and let simmer for 5 minutes. Add the prepared aromatic mixture to the broth and continue to simmer for 10 minutes, allowing the flavours to meld together.

To serve, place 100 g/3½ oz of the noodles in each of 6 large bowls. Arrange on top of noodles in this order: the sliced roasted pork, prawns, cuttlefish or squid, 1 fish-stuffed chilli, aubergine (eggplant) chunks, 2–3 courgette (zucchini) flowers, Egyptian river-hemp, peppermint, Chinese chive flowers, morning glory stalks, water hyssop, water lily, water mimosa and yellow velvet leaf. Ladle 250 ml/8 fl oz (1 cup) of the hot broth over all ingredients in each bowl. Serve immediately.

*Note:* If you don't have time to make the Roasted Pork Belly (page 161), you can purchase it pre-made.

# RICE NOODLES WITH PORK AND FERMENTED THICK FISH SAUCE

## Bún Mắm Nêm

Originally from the Cham people, Huế's *mắm nêm* is a thick fermented fish sauce traditionally best made from anchovies. Usually the sauce is balanced with pineapple juice's natural sweetness and brightened with fresh red chillies and garlic. Because of the sauce's complexity, the proteins – here the pork belly (side) and ear – don't need heavy marinades; they can simply be poached. It is therefore very important to use good quality meat to really appreciate this dish. I've always been told that the pork in Huế and its region tastes better than in big cities like Ho Chi Minh and Hanoi, as it is less industrial.

Serves 4
Preparation time: 20–25 minutes
Cooking time: 15–20 minutes

| DF |

*For the pork*
400 g/14 oz pork belly (side), cut 3–4-cm/1¼–1½-inch thick
1 pig's ear (about 300 g/10½ oz)
20 g/¾ oz lemongrass stick, cut into 10-cm/4-inch pieces
1 teaspoon fish sauce

*For the fried garlic and lemongrass*
1 tablespoon neutral oil
10 g/¼ oz garlic, finely minced
15 g/½ oz lemongrass, finely minced

*To serve*
400 g/14 oz fresh or dried rice noodles (bún)
100 g/3½ oz herb salad (rau sống – perilla, lettuce, Vietnamese balm, Thai basil, fish mint)
120 g/4¼ oz cucumber, thinly sliced (2–3 mm/⅛ inch thick)
100 g/3½ oz bean sprouts
40 g/1½ oz (¼ cup) Toasted Peanuts (page 459)
200 g/7 oz Seasoned Fermented Thick Fish Sauce (page 476)

In a pot, bring 500 ml/18 fl oz (2 cups) of water to a simmer over a medium heat. Add the pork belly (side), pig's ear, lemongrass and fish sauce and cook over a medium heat for 10 minutes. Remove from the heat and let the meat continue cooking in the residual heat for another 5–10 minutes. Using a slotted spoon, remove the meat from the cooking liquid and let it cool slightly.

Slice the pork belly and pig's ear thinly (2–3 mm/⅛ inch thick), aiming for about 20 slices in total. You will need about 120 g/4¼ oz of the pig's ear for this dish; reserve the remaining slices for another use.

To make the fried garlic and lemongrass, in a small frying pan or skillet, heat the oil over a medium-low heat, add the garlic and lemongrass and sauté for 4–5 minutes, stirring frequently, until golden brown and fragrant. Remove from the heat and transfer to a small bowl.

If using dried noodles, cook according to the packet instructions. If using fresh noodles, briefly rinse in cold water and drain well.

To serve, place 100 g/3½ oz of the prepared noodles in each serving bowl. Arrange 5 slices of pork belly and 30 g/1 oz of the pig's ear on top. Add some of the herb salad, sliced cucumber and bean sprouts. Sprinkle 1 tablespoon of the toasted peanuts over each serving, then top with the fried garlic and lemongrass mixture. Drizzle 3 tablespoons of the seasoned fermented thick fish sauce into each bowl.

Serve with extra herbs, cucumber slices and bean sprouts on a shared plate, and the remaining seasoned fermented thick fish sauce in a small bowl. Instruct diners to mix all the ingredients thoroughly before serving.

# SNAIL NOODLE SOUP

Bún Ốc

I grew up with the southern version of *bún ốc* for breakfast, where tamarind gives the broth its tang. In the north, where this dish originates, the signature sourness comes from *giấm bỗng*, a gentler fermented rice vinegar derived from Fermented Sticky Rice (page 442). This dish can be served lukewarm, known as *bún ốc nguội*, where individual portions of fresh rice noodle nests (*bún lá*) are eaten dipped into a cooled snail broth. This version is now much rarer to find. In Hanoi, locals still consider late July through September the prime season for enjoying this dish.

Serves 6–8
Preparation time: 45 minutes
Cooking time: 2 hours 15 minutes

| DF |

*For the fried shallots*
2 tablespoons vegetable oil
1 tablespoon Annatto Oil (page 457)
125 g/4¼ oz shallots, sliced

*For the broth*
1.2 kg/2 lb 12 oz pork bones (shoulder blade and leg)
20 g/¾ oz lemongrass, smashed
40 g/1½ oz whole shallots, peeled
1 teaspoon salt
1 tablespoon fish sauce

*For the snails*
1.1 kg/2 lb 7 oz apple snails (ốc bươu), soaked and cleaned
1 lemongrass stalk, cut into 5-cm/2-inch chunks
½ long red chilli, sliced

*To finish the broth*
1 teaspoon salt
1 teaspoon light brown sugar
3 tablespoons fermented rice vinegar (giấm bỗng)
2 tablespoons plus 2 teaspoons fish sauce
275 g/9¾ oz fried tofu, cubed
3 tomatoes (350 g/12 oz), quartered

*To serve*
600–800 g/1 lb 5–12 oz fresh rice noodles (bún tươi)
herb salad (rau sống – perilla, lettuce, Vietnamese balm)
Seasoned Fermented Shrimp Paste Dipping Sauce (page 476)
Vietnamese chilli in oil (ớt chưng), optional

To make the fried shallots, heat the vegetable oil and annatto oil in a small frying pan or skillet over a medium heat. Add the shallots and fry for 5–7 minutes, stirring frequently, until golden brown and crispy. Transfer to a paper towel-lined plate to drain while you make the broth.

In a large pot, bring 2 litres/3½ pints (8½ cups) of water to the boil over a high heat. Add the pork bones to the boiling water, return to the boil and cook for 5 minutes, skimming off any foam or impurities that rise to the surface, which is normal. Drain the bones in a colander and rinse thoroughly under cold running water, scrubbing gently with a clean brush to remove any remaining impurities.

In a large stockpot, combine 4.5 litres/8 pints (19 cups) of water with the lemongrass, whole shallots, salt and fish sauce. Bring to the boil over a high heat. Add the blanched pig bones, reduce the heat to low and simmer, partially covered, for 1 hour 30 minutes. Add 1 tablespoon of the fried shallots and simmer for another 30 minutes.

Meanwhile cook the snails. Place the apple snails, lemongrass and chilli in a saucepan, cover with water and cook over a medium heat for 10–12 minutes until the snails are just cooked through; they should be tender but not rubbery. Strain and let cool slightly. Using a small fork or pick, remove the snails from their shells (you should end up with about 290 g/10 oz of meat). Remove and discard the dark stomach sac from each snail. Set the cleaned meat aside.

To finish the broth, after 2 hours of total simmering, add the salt, sugar, vinegar, fish sauce, fried tofu and tomatoes to the broth. Simmer for 10 minutes, or until the tomatoes are softened but still hold their shape. Add the cooked snail meat to the broth and simmer for 5 minutes more. Taste and adjust the seasoning if needed.

To serve, place about 100 g/3½ oz of the noodles in each serving bowl. Arrange the snail meat, fried tofu and tomato quarters over the noodles. Ladle approximately 500 ml/18 fl oz (2 cups) of hot broth into each bowl. Top with the fried shallots.

Serve immediately with the herb salad and small bowls of seasoned fermented shrimp paste dipping sauce and Vietnamese chilli in oil, if desired, on the side for diners to add to taste.

# RICE FIELD CRAB NOODLE SOUP

Bún Riêu

*Bún riêu* began in Northern Vietnam as *Canh riêu cua* (crab soup) served over rice before developing into a noodle dish at local markets. This Hanoi dish combines thin rice noodles with rice field crabs, tomatoes and *giấm bỗng* (fermented rice vinegar), traditionally served with *rau diếp* (shredded lettuce) and Vietnamese balm. This recipe comes from our family kitchen with chị Thu Ba and it's prepared Southern style, by adding meatballs to it and using this specific herb selection. While *riêu* (river field crab) is a key ingredient, you can omit it and the dish would still be good.

Serves 6–8
Preparation time: 45 minutes
Cooking time: 2 hours

| DF |

*For the fried tofu and fried shallots*
240 ml/8 fl oz (1 cup) neutral oil, for frying
300 g/10½ oz firm tofu, cut into 12 cubes
130 g/4½ oz peeled shallots

*For the broth*
1 kg/2 lb 4 oz pork bones
2 tablespoons Annatto Oil (page 457)
570 g/1 lb 4 oz tomatoes (5 medium), each sliced into 8
500 g/1 lb 2 oz whole river field crabs, cleaned
55 g/2 oz Hanoi-style fermented shrimp paste (mắm tôm)
2½ teaspoons salt
20 g/¾ oz rock sugar
350 g/12 oz pig's blood curd (huyết)
2 tablespoons fish sauce
1 tablespoon caster (superfine) sugar
4 tablespoons fermented rice vinegar (giấm bỗng)

*For the meatballs*
220 g/7¾ oz Pork Paste (page 461)
60 g/2¼ oz brown crab meat (or you can replace it with chopped prawn/shrimp meat)
10 g/¼ oz spring onion (scallion) greens, thinly sliced
½ teaspoon fish sauce
1 teaspoon tempura flour
3 tablespoons neutral oil

*For the tamarind shrimp sauce*
1 teaspoon neutral oil
40 g/1½ oz Hanoi-style fermented shrimp paste (mắm tôm)
60 g/2¼ oz tamarind paste
1 teaspoon sugar
5 g/⅛ oz garlic, minced
1 chilli, minced

*To serve*
200 g/7 oz morning glory (rau muống) shredded
140 g/5 oz banana blossom (bắp chuối)
600–800 g/1 lb 5–12 oz fresh rice noodles (bún)
115 g/4 oz peppermint (húng cây)
100 g/3½ oz Vietnamese balm (kinh giới), leaves picked (50 g/1¾ oz leaves)
60 g/2¼ oz sawtooth coriander (culantro)
200 g/7 oz bean sprouts
35 g/1¼ oz spring onions (scallions), sliced
2 long red chillies, finely minced

Heat the oil in a 21-cm/8-inch-deep pan until hot. In batches, carefully add the tofu and fry until golden, about 4 minutes per batch. Carefully remove with a slotted spoon and drain on paper towels. Set aside.

In the same oil, fry the sliced shallots until golden. Strain, set aside the fried shallots and reserve the oil.

Fill a large pot with enough water to cover the bones completely. Bring the water to a rolling boil over a high heat. Add the pork bones and blanch for 5 minutes. Remove the bones using a skimmer, then rinse thoroughly under cold running water.

Heat 1 tablespoon of the reserved oil and the annatto oil in a shallow pan. Add the tomatoes and fry for 6 minutes 30 seconds, or until they have a paste-like consistency.

In a large stockpot, bring 3 litres/5¼ pints (12½ cups) of water to the boil. Add the blanched pork bones and simmer for 1 hour 30 minutes.

Meanwhile, place the crabs in a food processor, add 1.1 litres/2 pints (4½ cups) of water and blend until finely ground, 1–2 minutes. Strain through a fine-mesh sieve into a large pot, then repeat. You should have approximately 1.2 litres/2 pints (5 cups) of liquid.

Mix the field crab paste with 700 ml/24 fl oz (scant 3 cups) water, then strain several times into a pot to remove the shells. To extract the crab mixture (riêu), place the pot over a low heat and simmer until the crab mixture floats to the surface. Use the skimmer to remove the crab mixture and carefully transfer to a plate, then add the remaining liquid to the broth along with the fried tomatoes and shrimp paste.

While the broth is simmering, prepare the meatballs. In a mixing bowl, combine the pork paste, brown crab meat, spring onion (scallion) greens, fish sauce, tempura flour and 2 tablespoons of the oil. Marinate the mixture for 15 minutes. Form into equal-size balls.

Heat the remaining oil in a pan over a medium heat and, in batches, fry the meatballs until golden, about 7 minutes.

When the broth has been simmering for the 1 hour 30 minutes, add the salt and rock sugar and simmer for another 10 minutes. Add the pig's blood and cook for another 10 minutes. Add the fried tofu, fish sauce, sugar and vinegar and continue simmering while you prepare the sauce and garnishes.

To prepare the tamarind shrimp sauce, heat the oil in a pan over a medium–low heat, add the shrimp paste and 2 tablespoons of water and fry for 2–3 minutes.

In a bowl, mix the fried shrimp paste with the tamarind paste, sugar, garlic and chilli.

To prepare the garnishes, bring a pan of water to the boil, add the morning glory stalks and blanch for 30 seconds, then rinse in cold water.

Thinly slice the banana blossom, then soak in lemon water to prevent it from browning.

To serve, place 100 g/3½ oz of the noodles in each bowl. Add a few fried tofu pieces, some crab and pork balls, some blanched morning glory stalks and a portion of crab mixture. Then add the peppermint, Vietnamese balm, sawtooth coriander (culantro), banana blossom and bean sprouts. Ladle the hot broth with the tomatoes over the contents of each bowl. Garnish with the fried shallots, sliced spring onions, minced red chilli and tamarind shrimp sauce.

# RICE NOODLE SOUP

## Canh Bún

While most Vietnamese rice vermicelli dishes lead with '*bún*' (like *bún riêu*, *bún chả*, *bún ốc*), this soup uniquely starts with '*canh*' (soup), giving it a deceptively simple name. The dish shares similarities with Rice Field Crab Noodle Soup (page 220) in its broth and toppings, but uses thicker noodles like those found in Huế Beef Noodle Soup (page 204). What sets it apart is the addition of boiled water spinach/morning glory, which adds a nice crunch from the stalks to the soup.

Serves 6
Preparation time: 45 minutes
Cooking time: 2 hours 20 minutes

| DF |

*For the broth*
- 1.5 kg/3¼ lb bones (neck bones are good)
- 2 teaspoons salt
- 2 tablespoons Annatto Oil (page 457)
- 310 g/11 oz ripe tomatoes (about 4 medium), chopped
- 50 g/1¾ oz Hanoi-style fermented shrimp paste (mắm tôm)
- 15 g/½ oz rock sugar
- 2 teaspoons light brown sugar
- 1 tablespoon fish sauce
- 1 teaspoon all-purpose seasoning (hạt nêm)
- 30 g/1 oz (2 tablespoons) Fried Shallots (page 458)
- 25 g/1 oz spring onion (scallion) whites, cut into 2-cm/3/4-inch lengths
- 650 g/1 lb 7 oz morning glory (rau muống), leaves trimmed into 10-cm/4-inch stalk lengths, then first stalks removed (400 g/14 oz after trimming)
- 300 g/10½ oz pig's blood curd (huyết)
- 300 g/10½ oz fried tofu, cut into 4-cm/1½-inch cubes
- 200 g/7 oz tomatoes, cut into 8 wedges

*For the fake crab balls*
- 50 g/1¾ oz dried shrimp
- 150 g/5½ oz minced (ground) meat
- 10 g/¼ oz shallot, peeled
- 1 tablespoon fish sauce
- ¼ teaspoon black pepper
- ½ teaspoon sugar
- ½ teaspoon Annatto Oil (page 457)

*To serve*
- 500 g/1 lb 2 oz thick rice noodles (bún sợi to)
- 2 teaspoons Annatto Oil (page 457)
- 1 teaspoon fish sauce
- 10 g/¼ oz Fried Shallots (page 458)
- 10 g/¼ oz Chinese chives (lá hẹ)
- 20 g/¾ oz spring onion (scallion) greens
- lime, cut into wedges
- shrimp paste or tamarind sauce

In a large pot, bring 3 litres/5¼ pints (12½ cups) of water to the boil over a high heat. Add the bones to the boiling water, return to the boil and cook for 5 minutes. Drain the bones and rinse thoroughly under cold running water to clean off any remaining impurities.

In a large stockpot, bring 4 litres/7 pints (17 cups) of water to a simmer over a medium heat. Add the blanched bones and the salt and maintain a gentle simmer for 1 hour, skimming any foam that rises.

Meanwhile, in a saucepan, heat the annatto oil over a medium heat, then add the chopped tomatoes and fry for 15 minutes, stirring occasionally, until softened. Remove the tomatoes and set aside.

To make the fake crab balls, in a food processor, blend together the dried shrimp, minced (ground) meat and shallot until it forms a smooth paste. Transfer the paste to a mixing bowl and add the fish sauce, pepper, sugar and annatto oil. Mix thoroughly by hand. Form into 18 equal-size balls (approximately 12 g/½ oz each).

After the broth has simmered for the 1 hour, add the fake crab balls and fried tomatoes.

In a small bowl, mix the shrimp paste with 4 tablespoons of the hot broth until smooth.

Add the shrimp paste mixture to the broth, along with the rock sugar, light brown sugar, fish sauce and all purpose seasoning. Simmer for 16 minutes. Remove the fake crab balls using a skimmer and set aside.

Add half the fried shallots and the spring onion (scallion) whites to the broth and simmer for another 24 minutes.

Meanwhile, prepare a bowl of iced water. Bring a separate pot of water to the boil, add the morning glory and blanch for 4–5 minutes until tender but still crisp. Immediately transfer the blanched morning glory to the ice bath to maintain the colour, then drain well and set aside.

To finish the broth, after 1 hour and 40 minutes of total simmering time, add the pig's blood, fried tofu and tomato wedges to the broth and simmer for another 20 minutes.

To prepare the noodles, bring a pot of water to the boil, add the noodles and quickly blanch until just tender, then drain well.

In a large bowl, season the noodles with the oil, fish sauce and fried shallots. Toss gently to combine and evenly coat.

To finish the broth (it should have had 2 hours total cooking time), add the remaining fried shallots, then taste and adjust the seasoning if needed.

To serve, place 85 g/3 oz of the seasoned noodles in each bowl. Add 3 fake crab balls and some fried tofu cubes, blanched morning glory, tomato wedges and 50 g/1¾ oz of the pig's blood curd to each bowl. Ladle 600 ml/1 pint (2½ cups) of the hot broth over the ingredients in each bowl. Garnish with the Chinese chives and spring onion greens.

Serve immediately with 2 lime wedges and a small dish of shrimp paste or tamarind sauce on the side.

# COMBO NOODLE SOUP

## Bún Thang

A Northern dish served after *Tết* (Lunar New Year) celebrations, typically on the fourth day, using leftover festival ingredients like poached chicken, *giò lụa*, and *ruốc sỏi* (tiny meatballs). The name '*thang*' likely refers to either the layered arrangement of ingredients like a ladder, or to the careful combination of multiple components, similar to Chinese medicine. The soup was traditionally flavoured with *cà cuống* essence, a seasoning so distinctive it was mentioned in *ca dao* folk poetry.

Serves 4–6
Preparation time: 1 hour
Cooking time: 2–3 hours

| DF |

35 g/1¼ oz dried squid or peanut worms (sá sùng)
35 g/1¼ oz (1 cup) dried shiitake mushrooms
45 g/1½ oz dried shrimp
1 tablespoon fish sauce
1½ teaspoons salt
1 teaspoon soup powder (bột canh)
1.1 kg/2 lb 7 oz free-range yellow (e.g. corn-fed) chicken, halved
350 g/12 oz pork bones
95 g/3½ oz onion
40 g/1½ oz shallots, peeled

*For the egg ribbons*
3 eggs
1 tablespoons neutral oil

*For the shallots and salted radish*
2 tablespoons neutral oil
20 g/¾ oz shallots, sliced
150 g/5½ oz salted radish (ca la thầu)
½ teaspoon all-purpose seasoning (hạt nêm)

*To serve*
400–600 g/14 oz–1 lb 5 oz fresh rice noodles (bún tươi)
125 g/4¼ oz Pork Roll (page 462), cut into matchsticks
50 g/1¾ oz spring onions (scallions), thinly sliced
30 g/1 oz Vietnamese coriander/cilantro (rau răm)

Soak the dried squid or peanut worms in a bowl of warm water for 15 minutes, or until soft. Drain and set aside.

Meanwhile, in separate bowl, soak the shiitake mushrooms in warm water for 15 minutes. Drain, reserving the mushroom soaking liquid, and set aside.

Also meanwhile, in a third bowl, soak the dried shrimp in warm water for 15 minutes. Drain and set aside.

Bring 3.5 litres/6 pints (14¾ cups) of water to a simmer in large stockpot over a medium heat. Add the fish sauce, salt and soup powder, then gently lower the chicken and pork bones into the simmering water. Maintain a gentle simmer, skimming any foam that rises, for 30 minutes.

Meanwhile, grill the whole onion and shallots directly over a gas flame (see step 1, page 195) or in a dry pan until charred and fragrant.

Add the grilled onion and shallots to the broth, along with the soaked shiitake mushrooms and soaked squid or peanut worms.

Using tongs, remove the chicken from the broth and let cool for 10 minutes. Carefully remove the meat from the bones while still warm, then return the bones to the simmering stock.

Once the chicken meat is completely cool, shred finely by hand, then set aside.

Using a fine-mesh sieve, dip the soaked shrimp into the simmering stock 3–4 times, then transfer to a mortar and pound with a pestle until the texture becomes light and flaky.

Heat a small, dry pan over a medium heat, add the shrimp flakes and fry for 2 minutes, stirring constantly. Set aside for a garnish.

To make the egg ribbons, beat the eggs thoroughly in a mixing bowl until completely combined.

Heat 1 tablespoon of the oil in a small non-stick pan over a medium-low heat, pour a thin layer of egg to cover the bottom of the pan, then cook until just set but not browned. Roll up the egg sheet, then transfer to a plate and slice into thin ribbons.

To prepare the shallots and salted radish, heat the oil in a frying pan or skillet over a medium heat, then add the sliced shallots and salted radish. Season with the all-purpose seasoning, then fry for 10 minutes, stirring occasionally. Divide the mixture in half. Add one portion to the simmering stock. Reserve the other portion for a garnish.

To finish the broth, continue simmering on a very low heat until the cooking time has been 2–3 hours. Strain through a fine-mesh sieve and adjust the seasoning if needed.

To serve, place about 100 g/3½ oz of noodles in each bowl. Arrange in alternating sections around the bowl the shredded chicken, egg ribbons, matchsticks of pork roll, fried shrimp flakes, reserved shallots and salted radish mixture, sliced spring onions (scallions), 1–2 shiitake mushroom, halved, and Vietnamese coriander/cilantro leaves. Focus on creating contrasting colours and textures through careful arrangement of the ingredients; each should be visible and balanced in proportion

Just before serving, pour the hot broth around the edges, then serve immediately while the broth is piping hot.

# HẢI PHÒNG PRAWN NOODLE SOUP

## Bún Tôm Hải Phòng

This dish is a speciality from northern Vietnam's port city Hải Phòng. It utilizes every part of the prawn (shrimp), from the deep-flavoured broth to its garnish.

Serves 4–5
Preparation time: 45 minutes
Cooking time: 25 minutes

| DF |

500 g/1 lb 2 oz large prawns (shrimp)
2 tablespoons salt
juice of 1 lime (or rice wine)
200 g/7 oz water celery (rau cần nước)
15 g/½ oz dried wood ear mushrooms
1 tablespoon cooking oil
15 g/½ oz shallot, finely chopped
¼ teaspoon black pepper
1 teaspoon all-purpose seasoning (hạt nêm)
1 teaspoon salt
½ teaspoon sugar

*For the broth*
1 tablespoon Annatto Oil (page 457)
15 g/½ oz shallot, finely chopped
500 g/1 lb 2 oz tomatoes, cut into wedges
1 teaspoon MSG
1 teaspoon salt
1 teaspoon all-purpose seasoning (hạt nêm)
1 teaspoon sugar

*To serve*
500 g/1 lb 2 oz fresh rice noodles (bún tươi)
30 g/1 oz dill

Soak the prawns (shrimp) in a large bowl of water with 1 tablespoon of the salt and the lime juice (or rice wine) for 2–3 minutes. Rinse the prawns 2–3 times in a colander with fresh water.

Bring a pot of water to the boil, add the prawns and boil for 2–5 minutes until just cooked.

Meanwhile, prepare a bowl of iced water. When cooked, transfer the prawns immediately to the iced water. Peel and devein the prawns, reserving the shells.

In a blender, process the prawn shells with 1.5 litres/2½ pints (6¼ cups) of water until finely ground. Strain the mixture through a fine-mesh sieve 2–3 times until clear; reserve the prawn broth.

Soak the water celery in a large bowl of water with the remaining salt for 10–20 minutes, then drain. Cut the water celery into 5–7-cm/2–3-inch lengths, then rinse in a colander.

Prepare another bowl of iced water.

Bring a pot of water to the boil, then add the water celery and blanch for 20–45 seconds. Transfer immediately to the iced water bath, then drain well in a colander. Set aside.

Soak the wood ear mushrooms in a small bowl of warm water for 20 minutes, then drain. Remove the stalks of the wood ear mushrooms, then rinse, drain and slice the mushrooms thinly.

Heat the oil in a wok over a medium heat, then fry the shallot until golden. Add the peeled prawns and sauté for 2–3 minutes. Add the sliced mushrooms and cook for 1–2 minutes. Season with the pepper, all-purpose seasoning, salt and sugar. Stir-fry for 2 minutes, or until well-seasoned.

To make the broth, in a large pot over a medium heat, heat the annatto oil, then add the shallot and fry for 4–5 minutes until golden. Add the tomatoes, then cook 1–2 minutes until soft. Add the reserved prawn broth, then bring to the boil. Season with the MSG, salt, all-purpose seasoning and sugar. Simmer for 1–2 minutes.

To serve, place 100–125 g/3½–4¼ oz of the noodles in each bowl. Add a portion of the water celery and some dill, then top with 4–5 prawns and mushrooms, then ladle the hot broth over the top.

Serve immediately.

# QUẢNG-STYLE NOODLES

## Mì Quảng (Quảng Nam)

Despite its name suggesting wheat noodles (*mì*), *mì Quảng* is made with rice noodles – specifically from '13/2' rice, prized for its high starch content that creates chewy noodles that stay firm when cool. Originating from Quảng Nam province, this dish has spread to different regions like Đà Lạt, where local variations exist, particularly in the choice of meat and accompanying herbs. Originally made with affordable seafood ingredients like prawns (shrimp) and crab roe for the broth, this recipe presents a modern version of Mì Quảng, with more toppings, including quail egg.

Serves 6
Preparation time: 1 hour
Cooking time: 2 hours 30 minutes

| DF |

565 g/1 lb 4 oz chicken carcasses
550 g/1 lb 4 oz pork bones (ideally leg bones)
310 g/11 oz chicken breast with skin
600 g/1 lb 5 oz baby back ribs, cut into 6-cm/2½-inch-long pieces

*For the broth*
1 litre/1¾ pints (4¼ cups) coconut water
2 tablespoons fish sauce
1 teaspoon salt
1 whole onion (95 g/3½ oz), peeled
1 teaspoon sugar

*For the protein mixture*
45 g/1½ oz chive bulbs (củ nén)
40 g/1½ oz shallots, finely chopped
20 g/¾ oz garlic, finely chopped
4 teaspoons fish sauce
4 tablespoons neutral oil
30 g/1 oz piece fresh turmeric, peeled and finely sliced on an angle
½ teaspoon salt
275 g/9¾ oz uncooked prawns (shrimp), or 12 prawns, cooked and peeled
12 quail eggs, cooked and peeled
1 teaspoon tapioca flour (starch)

*To serve*
50 g/1¾ oz banana blossom (bắp chuối), thinly sliced
100 g/3½ oz watermint (húng lủi), leaves picked
90 g/3¼ oz (scant ½ cup) baby mustard greens (rau cải con)
1 head of lettuce, leaves separated
50 g/1¾ oz bean sprouts
600 g/1 lb 5 oz Mì Quảng noodles
50 g/1¾ oz (⅓ cup) Toasted Peanuts (page 459)
3 crispy sesame rice crackers

In a large pot, bring 2 litres/3½ pints (8½ cups) of water to the boil Add the chicken carcasses, pork bones, chicken breast and baby back ribs, return to the boil and cook for 5 minutes. Drain and rinse all the meats and bones thoroughly under cold running water. When cool enough to handle, cut the blanched chicken breast into 2 × 6-cm/¾ × 2½-inch pieces.

To make the broth, in a large pot, combine 1.5 litres/2½ pints (6¼ cups) of water with the coconut water. Add the blanched chicken carcasses and pork bones, 1 tablespoon of the fish sauce and ½ teaspoon of the salt. Bring to the boil, then reduce to a gentle simmer for 30 minutes. Add the blanched baby back ribs, then simmer 20 more minutes. Using tongs, remove the ribs and set aside.

Place a grill (broiler) rack over a medium-high flame on the hob (stove) or preheat the oven grill (broiler) to 190°C/375°F/Gas Mark 5.

Using tongs, add the whole peeled onion on the grill rack. Grill for 5–7 minutes, turning with the tongs, until charred, fragrant and lightly blackened. Remove from the grill with the tongs and carefully remove any black spots with a knife.

Add the grilled onion to the broth and continue simmering for an additional 1 hour–1 hour 10 minutes – the longer, the better. Season with remaining salt, the sugar and the remaining fish sauce.

To prepare the protein mixture, pour hot water over the chive bulbs to help remove the skin more easily, then peel and finely chop. Combine in a bowl with the shallots and garlic. Set aside.

Season the chicken breast pieces and reserved ribs with 1 tablespoon of the fish sauce.

Heat the oil in a large, deep pan over a medium heat. Add the turmeric and the chive bulb, shallot and garlic mixture and stir-fry for 2 minutes. Reduce the heat, then stir-fry for 6 more minutes. Remove half the turmeric mixture and set aside.

Add the seasoned chicken and ribs to the pan. Increase the heat, then fry until browned on all sides, 6–10 minutes. Return the reserved turmeric mixture to the pan, then fry for 3 more minutes. Add 5 ladles of the broth to the pan (about 400 ml/14 fl oz/1⅔ cups) and the salt. Cover, then simmer for 20 minutes. Add the prawns (shrimp), quail eggs and the remaining fish sauce.

In a small bowl, mix the tapioca flour (starch) with 1 tablespoon of the broth; add this to the pan, then simmer for 1–2 minutes until the sauce thickens slightly.

To serve, arrange the herbs and vegetables on serving platters. Place 100 g/3½ oz of the noodles in each bowl. Top each bowl with 2 prawns, 2 quail eggs, 50 g/1¾ oz of the chicken breast pieces, 100 g/3½ oz of the ribs and the sauce from the protein mixture. Ladle 80–100 ml/2½–3½ fl oz (⅓ cup) hot broth over each bowl and garnish with 2 tablespoons of the toasted peanuts.

Serve immediately with the platter of fresh herbs and vegetables, sesame rice crackers, and the remaining toasted peanuts on the side, with extra broth in small bowls if desired.

# 'KNOCKING' NOODLE SOUP

Hủ Tiếu Gõ

Growing up in Vietnam, I still remember the distinct knocking sounds made by ambulant street vendors selling *hủ tiếu gõ*. Each noodle cart would station somewhere while sending out 'knockers', typically family members, who would announce their presence with their own signature rhythm or voice. This was before the era of apps and delivery services, when each vendor needed their own way to stand out. While this particular sound is disappearing for *hủ tiếu gõ*, you can still hear other vendors, especially those selling *bánh giò*, broadcasting recorded announcements as they cycle through the streets. Unlike Phnom Penh-style Noodle Soup (page 227), this version is known for being one of the most affordable meals you can get, as it is very simple. For a quicker version, you can even use frozen Basic Chicken Stock (page 464).

Serves 6
Preparation time: 30 minutes
Cooking time: 2 hours 40 minutes

| DF |

1 kg/2 lb 4 oz pork bones
1 tablespoon fish sauce
1½ teaspoons salt
½ teaspoon sugar
170 g/5¾ oz small daikon, cut into chunks
20 g/¾ oz shallots, peeled
2 tablespoons shallot oil (from Fried Shallots, page 458), optional

*For the pork shoulder*
600 g/1 lb 5 oz pork shoulder
1 tablespoon fish sauce
½ teaspoon sugar

*To serve*
500 g/1 lb 2 oz Hủ Tiếu noodles
60 g/2¼ oz Crispy Fried Pork Fat (page 459)
60 g/2¼ oz (4 tablespoons) Fried Shallots (page 458)
50 g/1¾ oz Chinese chives (lá hẹ)
30 g/1 oz spring onions (scallions), finely chopped
6 tablespoons rice vinegar
6 tablespoons soy sauce
sliced red chillies

Fill a large pot with enough water to fully cover the bones (about 2 litres/3½ pints/8½ cups). Bring the water to a rolling boil over a high heat. Add the pork bones and blanch for 3–5 minutes until foam rises. Drain and rinse the bones thoroughly under cold running water, brushing each piece to remove any impurities.

In a clean large stockpot, combine 3 litres/5¼ pints (12¾ cups) of water with the blanched pork bones. Add the fish sauce, salt, sugar, daikon and whole shallots. Place the pot over a high heat and bring to a vigorous boil. Reduce the heat to medium-low, then maintain a gentle simmer for 20 minutes, using a fine-mesh skimmer to remove any impurities that rise to the surface.

To prepare the pork shoulder, in a mixing bowl, combine the pork shoulder with the fish sauce and sugar. Using your hands or tongs, mix well to ensure even coating. Let marinate at room temperature for 10 minutes.

After the broth has simmered for the 20 minutes, carefully add the marinated pork shoulder to the pot. Continue to simmer for 40 minutes, or until the meat is tender when pierced with a fork. Using tongs, remove the cooked pork shoulder from the broth. Place on a clean chopping (cutting) board and let cool slightly. Once cooled enough to handle, cover with aluminium foil and set aside for later slicing.

Continue simmering the broth for 1 additional hour to develop deeper flavours, maintaining the heat at medium-low, ensuring a gentle simmer, and occasionally skimming any impurities that rise to the surface. If using the shallot oil, add it to the broth just before serving.

When you are almost ready to serve, fill a pot with water and bring to the boil over a high heat. Cook the noodles according to the packet instructions until just tender, then drain in a colander.

Using a sharp knife, slice the cooled pork shoulder thinly against the grain.

Prepare small condiment dishes for each diner containing 1 tablespoon rice vinegar, 1 tablespoon light soy sauce and 2–3 sliced red chillies.

To serve, divide the cooked noodles among 6 large soup bowls. Arrange the sliced pork shoulder, crispy fried pork fat, fried shallots, Chinese chives and finely chopped spring onions (scallions) on top of the noodles. Using a ladle, pour approximately 500 ml/18 fl oz (2 cups) hot broth over the contents of each bowl.

Serve immediately, with the condiment dishes on the side.

## PHNOM PENH-STYLE NOODLE SOUP

Hủ Tiếu Nam Vang

Nam Vang is the Sino-Vietnamese name for Phnom Penh. Originally known as *kuy teav* in Cambodia, this noodle dish made its way to Vietnam through various communities emigrating from Cambodia from the 1960s. It can be served two ways: noodle soup (with bone and vegetable broth being poured over) or 'dry' (with aromatic garlic oil and a thick soy sauce-based dressing), with a separate bowl of broth.

Serves 6–8
Preparation time: 1 hour 30 minutes
Cooking time: 3 hours 30 minutes

| DF |

*For the broth*
20 g/½ oz piece fresh ginger, smashed
20 g/¾ oz shallots, peeled
30 g/1 oz dried shrimp
25 g/1 oz dried squid
1.1 kg/2 lb 7 oz pork bones (mix between rib bone and leg bone), blanched (see step 1, page 121)
115 g/4 oz daikon, cut into chunks
95 g/3½ oz salted daikon (xá bấu), soaked in water for 5 minutes
1 teaspoon salt
25 g/1 oz rock sugar
60 ml/2 fl oz (¼ cup) neutral oil
25 g/1 oz garlic, peeled and halved or quartered
2 tablespoons fish sauce
20 g/¾ oz (4 teaspoons) Fried Shallots (page 458)
500 g/1 lb 2 oz pork shoulder (without skin), blanched (see step 1, page 121)

*For the garnish*
1 pork liver (about 300 g/10½ oz, soaked in beer or milk for an hour)
1 pig's heart (about 370 g/13 oz)
10 g/¼ oz piece fresh ginger, sliced
15 g/½ oz shallot, peeled
10 g/¼ oz lemongrass, sliced
½ teaspoon salt
1 tablespoon fish sauce
300 g/10½ oz kidney (about 2 kidneys), soaked in iced water for an hour, optional
12–14 prawns (shrimp) (about 250 g/5½ oz)
12 quail eggs, boiled and peeled
50 g/1¾ oz garlic, minced

*For the minced meat*
300 g/10½ oz minced (ground) pork
1 tablespoon fish sauce
½ teaspoon sugar
¼ teaspoon black pepper
½ teaspoon all-purpose seasoning (hạt nêm)

*For the sauce*
2 tablespoons oyster sauce
4 tablespoons light soy sauce
½ teaspoon black pepper
3 teaspoons sugar
1 teaspoon vinegar
2 teaspoons rice vinegar
20 g/¾ oz (4 teaspoons) Fried Shallots (page 458)
4 tablespoons Fried Garlic (page 458)

*To serve*
800 g/1 lb 12 oz flat rice-tapioca noodles (sợi hủ tiếu dai), cooked
300 g/10½ oz Crispy Fried Pork Fat (page 459)
250 g/5½ oz crown daisy (rau tần ô)
45 g/1½ oz Chinese chives (lá hẹ), cut into 5-cm/2-inch lengths
80 g/2¾ oz Chinese celery, coarsely chopped, plus 80 g/2¾ oz picked leaves

Using a grill (griddle) pan over a low heat, grill the smashed ginger, whole shallots, dried shrimp and dried squid for 5–10 minutes until they start to colour. Carefully rub off any black spots.

In a large pot, bring 4 litres/7 pints (17 cups) of water to a simmer. Add the blanched pork bones, the grilled ginger, shallots, shrimp and squid to the pot. Add the daikon, salted daikon, salt and rock sugar and simmer for 30 minutes.

In a small pan, heat the oil over a low heat, add the garlic and fry for about 5 minutes until golden. Strain the garlic and add it to the broth, reserving the garlic oil.

Simmer the broth for another 30 minutes. Add the fish sauce and fried shallots and simmer for 30 minutes. Add the blanched pork shoulder and simmer for a final 30 minutes, or until it is fully cooked. Using tongs, carefully remove the pork shoulder from the stockpot. Let cool slightly and slice into 2-mm/⅛-inch-thick pieces.

Pour boiling water over the liver and heart in a bowl, then rinse well under running water.

In a 4-litre/135-oz (4-quart) pot, bring 2 litres/3½ pints (8½ cups) of water to a simmer. Add the sliced ginger, whole shallots, lemongrass, salt and fish sauce. Add the liver and heart and cook for 20 minutes.

Meanwhile, prepare an large bowl of iced water. After the liver has been cooking for 20 minutes, remove it from the broth with a slotted spoon and transfer to the iced water.

Continue cooking the heart for 4 minutes. If using the kidney, add it to the pot and cook for 6 minutes. Using a slotted spoon, transfer the, heart and kidney, if using, to the iced water. When cool, drain, then slice the cooled offal (variety meats) into 2-mm/⅛-inch-thick pieces.

Bring a pan of lightly salted water to the boil, add the prawns (shrimp) and boil for 2–3 minutes until pink. Drain and allow to cool. Peel the prawns and set aside.

Heat 60 ml/2 fl oz (¼ cup) of the reserved garlic oil over a medium-low heat. Add the garlic and fry for 5–6 minutes until golden brown. Strain and set aside for garnish. Reserve the oil.

Place the minced (ground) meat in a bowl with the fish sauce, sugar, pepper and all-purpose seasoning, mix well and marinate for 5–10 minutes.

Heat 2 teaspoons of the reserved garlic oil in a pan over a medium heat and stir-fry the marinated minced meat for about 6 minutes.

To prepare the sauce, in a bowl, combine 120 ml/4 fl oz (½ cup) of the hot broth, the oyster sauce and soy sauce. Add the pepper, sugar, vinegar, rice vinegar and fried shallots and fried garlic. Mix well and set aside.

Just before you are ready to serve, heat a pan of water to 90°C/195°F, and blanch the noodles for 30 seconds using a sieve.

To serve, divide the blanched noodles among 8 serving bowls. To each bowl, add 1 teaspoon of the crispy fried pork fat and 1½ tablespoons of the sauce. Use chopsticks or tongs to mix thoroughly until the noodles are well-coated. Arrange on top of the noodles: 2–3 slices each of pork shoulder, heart, liver and kidney, if using, 2 whole prawns; 2 whole quail eggs; 1 tablespoon of the minced (ground) pork; 2 teaspoons of the fried pork fat; 1 tablespoon of the fried garlic and a small amount of crown daisy.

In separate small bowls, pour in the hot broth, then add the Chinese chives and Chinese celery.

Serve with a plate of the remaining crown daisy leaves.

# PRAWN AND PORK NOODLE SOUP

## Bún Suông

From Trà Vinh province, this noodle soup's name, *suông* (or *đuông*), refers to its shrimp paste rolls shaped like coconut worms (*đuông dừa*). To make the paste, some people would add *giò sống* (Pork Paste, page 461), but here we kept it like in Trà Vinh, and use only a prawn (shrimp) mixture. If you put it in a piping (pastry) bag, you can pipe it directly into the broth.

Serves 5
Preparation time: 30 minutes, plus 30 minutes chilling time
Cooking time: 1 hour 30 minutes

| DF |

*For the broth*
350 g/12 oz pork bones
400 g/14 oz baby back ribs
10 prawns (shrimp)
95 g/3½ oz onion
2 teaspoons salt
1 tablespoon Annatto Oil (page 457)
50 g/1¾ oz shallots, peeled
320 g/11¼ oz daikon, peeled
1 tablespoon sugar
1 tablespoon fish sauce
355 ml/12 fl oz (1½ cups) coconut water

*For the prawn mixture (suông)*
280 g/10 oz prawns (shrimp), peeled
1 tablespoon Annatto Oil (page 457)
1 teaspoon fish sauce
15 g/½ oz (1½ tablespoons) tapioca flour (starch)
¼ teaspoon black pepper
¼ teaspoon all-purpose seasoning (hạt nêm)
¼ teaspoon sugar
1 ice cube (20–25 g/¾–1 oz)
10 g/¼ oz shallot, chopped

*For the tamarind sauce*
20 g/¾ oz tamarind paste
3 tablespoons hot water
1 teaspoon sugar
1½ teaspoons fish sauce
½ teaspoon Chilli and Lemongrass Oil (page 457)
5 g/⅛ oz long red chillies, chopped

*To serve*
500 g/1 lb 2 oz fresh rice noodles (bún tươi)
300 g/10½ oz Turkish cabbage, shredded, plus extra to serve
100 g/3½ oz bean sprouts, plus extra to serve
20 g/¾ oz peppermint (húng cây)
40 g/1½ oz Vietnamese balm (kinh giới)
10 g/¼ oz coriander (cilantro), chopped
40 g/1½ oz spring onions (scallions), chopped
salt

To make the broth, bring a stock pot of water to a simmer. Add the pork bones, baby back ribs, prawns (shrimp), onion and salt and cook for 10 minutes. Using a slotted spoon, remove the prawns and set aside, then continue simmering while you cook the shallots.

Heat the oil in a pan over a medium-low heat, add the whole shallots and fry for about 7 minutes. Add to the broth and continue to simmer for 35 minutes. Add the daikon, sugar and fish sauce to the broth, then simmer for another 30 minutes. Carefully remove the baby back ribs with a slotted spoon. Strain the broth into a large bowl or jug (large measuring cup) and then return the broth to the pot. Add the coconut water and return the baby back ribs to the pot. Maintain the broth at a gentle simmer while you prepare the prawn mixture.

Place all the ingredients in a food processor or blender. Blitz until the mixture becomes a smooth paste.

Transfer the mixture to a piping (pastry) bag. Seal the piping bag and remove any air pockets, then place the piping bag in the refrigerator and chill for at least 30 minutes before use.

Pipe the chilled prawn mixture into the simmering broth and poach for 3–4 minutes.

Meanwhile, to prepare the tamarind sauce, mix the tamarind with the measured hot water. Sieve out the seeds to get about 2 tablespoons of tamarind paste. Add the sugar, fish sauce, chilli and lemongrass oil and chillies.

To serve, bring a pan of salted water to the boil, then add the noodles and quickly blanch for 1 minute.

Place 100 g/3½ oz of the noodles in each bowl and top with some poached prawn mixture, a portion of cooked baby back ribs, 2 whole cooked prawns, the shredded Turkish cabbage, bean sprouts, peppermint, Vietnamese balm, coriander (cilantro) and spring onions (scallions). Ladle 600 ml/1 pint (2½ cups) of the hot broth over each bowl and serve immediately. Serve with individual small bowls of the tamarind sauce and extra shredded cabbage and beansprouts on the side.

***Note:*** The prawns (shrimp) can be replaced with meat or squid in the prawn mixture.

# HANOI-STYLE FISH WITH TURMERIC AND DILL

## Chả Cá Hà Nội

Growing up, I knew this as *chả cá Lã Vọng*, after the famous Hanoi restaurant that created it, before learning that '*chả cá Hà Nội*' better reflects its roots as a capital speciality. Where most Vietnamese *chả* dishes use minced (ground) fish or meat, here chunks of Bagridae (*cá lăng*) are chosen for their firm meat. The cooking method is what makes it special: the fish is first grilled over charcoal, then refried at the table with onion and dill, like you would for hotpot, in the middle of the table. Usually at the restaurant you can order extra plates of dill and onion if you run out.

Serves 4–6
Preparation time: 45 minutes, plus 30 minutes–1 hour marinating time
Cooking time: 15 minutes

| DF |

*For the marinated fish*
- 40 g/1½ oz galangal, peeled (25 g/1 oz after peeling), thinly sliced
- 35 g/1¼ oz shallots, sliced
- 4 g piece fresh turmeric
- 520 g/1 lb 2 oz bagridae (cá lăng) fillet (cut into about 10 pieces, 3 cm/1¼ inches thick, 8 cm/3½ inches long)
- 30 g/1 oz (2 tablespoons) pork lard, optional (helps prevent dryness)
- 100 g/3½ oz fermented rice (cơm mẻ)
- ¼ teaspoon ground turmeric
- 1 teaspoon fish sauce
- ¼ teaspoon salt

*For the fermented shrimp sauce*
- 40 g/1½ oz Hanoi-style fermented shrimp paste (mắm tôm)
- 20 g/¾ oz lime juice
- 2 teaspoons light brown sugar
- 10 g/¼ oz chilli (about ½ chilli), chopped

*To serve*
- 30 g/1 oz (2 tablespoons) pork lard, optional
- 100 g/3½ oz dill, cut into rough 5-cm/2-inch pieces
- 100 g/3½ oz spring onions (scallions), cut into rough 5-cm/2-inch pieces
- 450 g/1 lb fresh rice noodles (bún tươi)
- 15 g/½ oz coriander (cilantro)
- 5 g/⅛ oz mint
- 20 g/¾ oz Toasted Peanuts, crushed if desired
- lime wedges

Put the galangal, shallots and fresh turmeric in a mortar and pound with a pestle until they form a fine paste.

In a large bowl, combine the bagridae with the pounded aromatic paste, pork lard, if using, fermented rice, ground turmeric, fish sauce and salt. (The addition of pork lard helps prevent the fish from becoming dry during cooking.) Allow to marinate for 30 minutes–1 hour for the best flavour absorption.

Preheat the oven grill (broiler) to 180°C/350°F.

Place the marinated fish pieces on a grill (broiler) rack, reserving the marinade, and grill (broil) for 10 minutes, or until the edges turn light brown, then remove and set aside.

To prepare the fermented shrimp sauce, in a bowl, combine the shrimp paste, lime juice and sugar. Using a spoon, stir the mixture vigorously until it becomes foamy and starts to thicken. Add the chilli, mix well and then set aside.

To serve following the traditional method, set up a portable burner at the dining table. Heat a large non-stick pan over a medium heat, then add 2 tablespoons of pork lard, if using, to the hot pan. Carefully add the grilled fish pieces and fry for 2 minutes, or until golden. Add 1 tablespoon of the reserved marinade and the dill and spring onions (scallions), then gently stir-fry for 1 minute, or until the herbs just begin to wilt.

Alternatively, cook this in the kitchen and set the pan on the table to serve.

Divide the noodles equally among serving plates, placing them beside each diner. Provide each person with a small bowl for their individual portions and let them assemble their bowls by taking some noodles, adding pieces of the hot fish and wilted herbs, garnishing with coriander (cilantro), mint and crushed toasted peanuts, and seasoning with the fermented shrimp sauce. Serve with lime wedges on the side for adjusting the flavours as desired.

# VENISON NOODLES WITH CHILLI AND LEMONGRASS OIL

Hủ Tiếu Sa Tế Nai

Originating from the Chaozhou community in Saigon's Chinatown, this dish has evolved to include coconut milk and is served with Vietnamese herbs. As there are two parts to this dish, it can take a while. I would recommend making the stock (broth) for the first 2–3 hours, as the longer it simmers the better it will taste, before continuing with the rest of the recipe. If you can, It's best prepared in advance, allowing flavours to meld overnight. If liked, serve with sliced tomatoes and shredded cucumber for freshness and Pickled Garlic in Vinegar (page 468) for acidity.

Serves 6–8
Preparation time: 40 minutes
Cooking time: 3–4 hours

| DF |

*For the broth*

- 500 g/1 lb 2 oz pork bones, blanched (see step 1, page 121)
- 500 g/1 lb 2 oz beef or venison bones, blanched (see step 1, page 121)
- 1 tablespoon sugar
- 2 tablespoons fish sauce
- 1 tablespoon light soy sauce
- 1 teaspoon salt
- 1 onion (130 g/4½ oz), peeled
- 25 g/1 oz shallots, peeled
- 30 g/1 oz piece fresh ginger (6 cm/2½ inches)
- 60 g/2¼ oz galangal
- 50 g/1¾ oz lemongrass
- 3 peanut worms (sá sùng), optional
- 1 star anise
- 2 cloves
- 1 g dried orange peel, optional
- 1 black cardamom pod (thảo quả)
- 2 slices liquorice root, optional
- 5 g/⅛ oz cinnamon stick
- 5 g/⅛ oz coriander seeds

*For the chilli and lemongrass oil broth*

- 20 g/¾ oz lemongrass, thinly sliced
- 80 g/2¾ oz shallots, minced
- 20 g/¾ oz garlic, peeled
- 30 g/1 oz dried shrimp
- 6 tablespoons Annatto Oil (page 457)
- 65 g/2¼ oz peanut butter
- 2 tablespoons oyster sauce
- 1 teaspoon Vietnamese curry powder
- 1 teaspoon chilli powder
- 2 tablespoons Shrimp, Chilli and Lemongrass Oil (page 457), plus extra to serve
- 2 teaspoons rice wine or cooking wine
- 2 tablespoons neutral oil
- 70 g/2½ oz (½ cup) Toasted Peanuts (page 459), blitzed
- 80 g/2¾ fl oz (⅓ cup) coconut milk
- 1 teaspoon sugar
- 1 tablespoon fish sauce
- 1 teaspoon MSG, optional

*For the marinated meat*

- 300 g/10½ oz lean venison or beef fillet (tenderloin), thinly sliced
- 1 teaspoon oyster sauce
- 1 teaspoon fish sauce
- ¼ teaspoon black pepper
- 1 teaspoon sugar
- 1 teaspoon cornflour (cornstarch)
- 1 teaspoon light soy sauce

*To serve*

- 600 g/1 lb 5 oz fresh phở noodles (bánh phở), cooked (see step 12, page 184)
- 50 g/1¾ oz sawtooth coriander (culantro), stalks removed and thinly sliced
- 50 g/1¾ oz basil, leaves picked
- 60 g/2¼ oz (4 tablespoons) Fried Shallots and Garlic (page 459)
- 10–16 beef meatballs (bò viên), optional

In a large pot, combine the blanched bones, 3.5 litres/6 pints (14¾ cups) of water and the sugar, fish sauce, soy sauce and salt. Bring to the boil, then reduce the heat and simmer.

Place a grill (broiler) rack over a medium-high flame on the hob (stove) or preheat the oven grill (broiler) to 190°C/375°F.

Using tongs, add the whole onion, whole shallots, pieces of ginger, galangal and lemongrass to the grill rack. Grill for 4–6 minutes, turning with the tongs, until fragrant. Remove from the grill with the tongs and carefully remove any black spots with a knife. Grill the peanut worms, if using, for 1 minute.

Toast the star anise, cloves, dried orange peel, if using, cardamom, liquorice root, if using, and cinnamon stick in a dry pan for 2 minutes, adding the coriander seeds for the last 30 seconds.

Add the grilled and toasted aromatics and peanut worms to the simmering broth and continue to simmer for at least 2 hours over a low heat. Strain and reserve 2.8–3 litres/5–5¼ pints (12–13 cups) of the broth.

To prepare the chilli and lemongrass oil broth, first make a paste.Put the lemongrass, shallots, garlic, dried shrimp and 2 tablespoons of the annatto oil together in a food processor and blitz.

In a separate bowl, mix together the peanut butter, oyster sauce, curry powder, chilli powder, shrimp, chilli and lemongrass oil, and rice wine.

In a large pot, heat the remaining annatto oil and the neutral oil. Add the blitzed paste and fry over a medium heat for 3 minutes. Add the blitzed toasted peanuts and fry over a lower heat for 2 minutes. Add 80 ml/2½ fl oz (⅓ cup) of the hot broth to the paste and continue frying for 2 minutes. Add the peanut butter mixture and cook for 3 minutes, or until the oil starts to separate. Add another 160 ml/5½ fl oz (⅔ cup) of the hot broth, the coconut milk and sugar, then simmer for another 1 hour. If serving with the beef meatballs, add these 10 minutes before the end of the cooking time.

Meanwhile, marinate the meat. Mix the venison or beef with the oyster sauce, fish sauce, pepper, sugar, cornflour (cornstarch) and soy sauce. Set aside to marinate while preparing the other components.

To finish the chilli and lemongrass oil broth, add the fish sauce and MSG, if using. Taste and adjust seasoning if necessary.

To serve, in each serving bowl, place 85 g/3 oz of the cooked noodles at the bottom. Layer 40 g/1½ oz of the marinated meat on top. Pour 430 ml/14½ fl oz (1¾ cups) of the hot chilli and lemongrass oil broth over the top to cook the meat. Garnish with the sawtooth coriander (culantro), basil and fried shallots and garlic.

Serve hot with the beef meatballs, if using, and extra shrimp, chilli and lemongrass oil.

# SILKWORM CAKE WITH COCONUT CREAM

## Bánh Tằm Bì

These long, thin rice noodles earned their name '*tằm*' from their resemblance to silkworms. While this version comes with shredded pork skin (*bì*) and coconut sauce, other regional variations include *bánh tằm cay*, with spicy curry sauce, and *bánh tằm khoai mì* (Cassava Silkworm Cake, page 425).

Serves 6
Preparation time: 45 minutes
Cooking time: 30 minutes

| DF |

200 g/7 oz pork skin
50 g/1¾ oz Toasted Rice Powder (page 459)
1 tablespoon neutral oil
15 g/½ oz shallot, chopped
15 g/½ oz garlic, chopped
1 teaspoon fish sauce
½ teaspoon sugar
¼ teaspoon salt

*For the meat*
¼ teaspoon salt
200 g/7 oz pork shoulder blade

*For the noodle dough*
100 g/3½ oz (⅔ cup) sticky (glutinous) rice flour, plus extra for dusting
100 g/3½ oz (⅔ cup) rice flour
30 g/1 oz (¼ cup) tapioca flour (starch)
½ teaspoon salt
4 tablespoons coconut milk
120 ml/4 fl oz (½ cup) boiling water
1 teaspoon neutral oil

*For the coconut sauce*
315 g/11 fl oz (1¼ cups) fresh or canned coconut milk
½ teaspoon salt
2 teaspoons tapioca flour (starch)
5 g/⅛ oz spring onion (scallion) greens, chopped

*To garnish*
60 g/2¼ oz (4 tablespoons) Fried Shallots (page 458)
35 g/1¼ oz (¼ cup) Toasted Peanuts (page 459), crushed
15 g/½ oz mint leaves
15 g/½ oz peppermint (húng cây)
80 g/3 oz Spring Onion Oil (page 458)
Sweet and Sour Fish Sauce (page 471)

Put the pork skin in a bowl and add the toasted rice powder.

In a small pan, heat the oil, add the shallot and garlic and stir-fry 6–8 minutes until golden.

Add the shallot and garlic mixture to the pork skin, along with the fish sauce, sugar, and salt. Mix well.

In a small pot, bring 400 ml/14 fl oz (1⅔ cups) of water and the salt to the boil. Add the pork shoulder blade, cover and cook for about 20 minutes or until fully cooked. Using tongs, carefully remove the cooked pork shoulder blade and set aside to cool slightly. When cool enough to handle, cut into thin matchsticks (julienne) and add them to the pork skin mixture. Set aside.

To make the noodle dough, in a heatproof bowl, mix together both rice flours, the tapioca flour (starch), salt and coconut milk. Gradually add the measured boiling water while stirring with a spoon, then knead until smooth and no longer sticky. Add the neutral oil to the dough and continue kneading until it becomes white and smooth.

To shape the noodles, divide the dough into small portions. Roll each portion between your palms or on a clean surface to form medium-thick noodles. Lay out on the surface and dust with flour to prevent them sticking.

To cook the noodles, bring a pan of water to the boil, add the noodles and cook for a minute until they float. Drain and rinse with cold water. Set aside.

For the coconut sauce, combine the coconut milk, salt and tapioca flour (starch) in a pan. Add the spring onions (scallions) and place over a medium-low heat while stirring until slightly thickened.

To serve, place the cooked noodles in bowls, top with the pork skin and pork shoulder mixture, add the fried shallots and crushed toasted peanuts, then garnish with the mint and peppermint. Pour the warm coconut sauce over the top, then add the spring onion oil.

Serve with sweet and sour fish sauce on the side.

# RICE NOODLES WITH STIR-FRIED PORK

## Bún Thịt Xào

The marinated pork in this recipe can either be stir-fried or cooked on a charcoal barbecue grill. You can be playful with the amount of fresh herbs, sauces and toasted peanut you want to serve with this dish.

Serves 4–5
Preparation time: 30 minutes
Cooking time: 35 minutes

| DF |

- 180 g/6 oz pork back fat, cut into 1.5-cm/⅝-inch matchsticks (julienned)
- 100 g/3½ oz shallots, sliced
- 100 g/3½ oz spring onions (scallions), chopped
- 40 g/1½ oz garlic, chopped
- 225 g/8 oz onion, peeled and sliced

*For the marinated pork*

- 30 g/1 oz shallots, finely minced
- 15 g/½ oz spring onion (scallion) whites, finely minced
- 10 g/¼ oz garlic, finely minced
- 25 g/1 oz lemongrass, finely minced
- 700 g/1 lb 9 oz pork shoulder blade, thinly sliced
- 1 teaspoon oyster sauce
- 1 tablespoon fish sauce
- 1 teaspoon sugar
- ¼ teaspoon salt
- ½ teaspoon black pepper

*To serve*

- 500 g/1 lb 2 oz fresh rice noodles (bún tươi)
- 100 g/3½ oz cucumber, cut into thin matchsticks (julienned)
- 50 g/1¾ oz bean sprouts
- 50 g/1¾ oz aromatic mixed herbs (rau thơm – perilla, Thai basil, peppermint, coriander/cilantro), plus extra to taste
- 75 g/2¾ oz (½ cup) Toasted Peanuts (page 459)

Heat a saucepan over a medium-low heat, add the pork back fat and fry for about 15 minutes, stirring occasionally until golden and crispy. Using a slotted spoon, remove the crispy pork fat pieces and drain on paper towels. Reserve the rendered pork lard in the pan.

Return the pan with the pork lard to medium heat, then fry the shallots for 6–7 minutes until golden brown. Remove with a slotted spoon and drain on paper towels. Reserve the lard.

To prepare the marinated pork, in a large mixing bowl, combine all the ingredients with the rendered pork fat pieces. Mix thoroughly and let marinate for 15–20 minutes.

Heat 75 ml/2 ½ fl oz (⅓ cup) of the reserved rendered pork lard in a large wok over a high heat, then add the spring onions (scallions) and stir-fry for 1 minute. Add the garlic and stir-fry for 30 seconds, or until fragrant. Add the marinated pork and spread in a single layer, then cook for 7–8 minutes, stirring occasionally, until the pork is fully cooked. Add the onion and cook for another 1 minute, or until just wilted.

To serve, divide the noodles among 4–5 serving bowls, then top with the cooked pork, julienned cucumber, fresh bean sprouts, mixed herbs and crushed toasted peanuts. Garnish with the crispy pork fat pieces, fried shallots and additional herbs, if desired.

Serve immediately, while the meat is still hot, and allow diners to mix all the ingredients before eating.

# SOUTHERN VIETNAMESE BEEF NOODLE SALAD

## Bún Thịt Xào Bò – Bún Bò Nam Bộ

Known in France as '*bò bún*' (though this reversal of words would puzzle Vietnamese speakers, as noodle names always precede the protein), this dish has become a favourite among the Vietnamese diaspora in France, alongside *bánh mì thịt khìa* (Caramelized Pork Sandwich, page 68). It's a dish that can be eaten straight away or later on, as the only cooking needed is to stir-fry the beef. The key is to not overcook the meat, as it will become chewy.

Serves 3
Preparation time: 30 minutes
Cooking time: 15 minutes

| DF |

*For the marinated beef*
300 g/10½ oz beef, ideally ribeye or flank, thinly sliced (maximum 5-mm/¼-in thick)
½ teaspoon sesame oil
¼ teaspoon black pepper
1 teaspoon sugar
1 tablespoon light soy sauce

*For the fish sauce*
4 teaspoons sugar
1 tablespoon vinegar
2 tablespoons plus 1 teaspoon fish sauce
15 g/½ oz garlic, minced
20 g/¾ oz chillies (1–2 chillies), deseeded and minced
juice of 2 calamansi (equivalent to 2 teaspoons)
2 tablespoons grated carrot, optional

*For the fried aromatics*
4 tablespoons neutral oil
20 g/¾ oz garlic, finely chopped
35 g/1¼ oz shallots, thinly sliced
15 g/½ oz lemongrass, finely chopped
2 teaspoons fish sauce
180 g/6 oz onion, thinly sliced

*To serve*
150 g/5½ oz cucumber
300 g/10½ oz fresh rice noodles (bún), cooked
80 g/2¾ oz aromatic mixed herbs (rau thơm – perilla leaves, basil, mint, coriander), thinly sliced
50 g/1¾ oz Pickled Daikon and Carrots (page 468)
70 g/2½ oz bean sprouts
20 g/¾ oz (2 tablespoons) Toasted Peanuts (page 459)
30 g/1 oz Spring Onion Oil (page 458)

To marinate the beef, in a small bowl, mix the beef with the sesame oil, pepper, sugar and soy sauce, the let marinate for 15 minutes.

To prepare the fish sauce, in a small saucepan, add the sugar, 120 ml/4 fl oz (½ cup) of water and the vinegar. Bring it to a simmer. When the sugar has dissolved, add the fish sauce and remove from the heat. Add the garlic and chillies to the sauce, together with the calamansi juice and grated carrot, if using. Set aside.

To prepare the fried aromatics, in a small pan, add 2 tablespoons of the neutral oil, add the garlic, shallots and lemongrass and fry over a medium heat for about 5 minutes until they just turn golden. Remove with a skimmer, then set aside.

Meanwhile, using a sharp knife, for the Vietnamese way of slicing cucumber, cut the cucumber in half horizontally, then with a small knife, make cutting movements into the flesh, then slice across it.

In a pan (about 25 cm/10 inches), heat up the remaining neutral oil over a medium heat. When the oil is hot, add the marinated beef and the fried aromatics. Stir-fry over a medium-high heat for 1 minute 30 seconds. Add 1 teaspoon of the fish sauce and continue stirring for another 1 minute 30 seconds. Add the onion and stir-fry for 1 more minute. Finish with the remaining fish sauce.

To serve, arrange the noodles in individual bowls. Top with the beef mixture, sliced cucumber, mixed herbs, pickled vegetables and bean sprouts, then garnish with toasted peanuts and finish with spring onion oil.

Serve with the remaining fish sauce mixture in small sauce bowls on the side.

# VEGETARIAN STIR-FRIED RICE NOODLES

## Bún Xào Chay

Always use dried noodles for stir-frying as fresh ones can stick to the pan. Direct frying after soaking the noodles prevents breakage and mushiness. Rice vermicelli could also be used for this dish.

Serves 3–4
Preparation time: 45 minutes
Cooking time: 25 minutes

| V | VE | DF |

*For the noodles*
- 250 g/5½ oz dried rice noodles (bún gạo khô)
- 2 tablespoons plus 1 teaspoon light soy sauce, plus extra to serve
- 235 g/8¼ oz bean sprouts
- ¼ teaspoon black pepper
- 100 g/3½ oz fried tofu, sliced horizontally 5-mm/¼-inch thick
- 25 g/1 oz (2½ tablespoons) Toasted Peanuts (page 459), crushed, to serve

*For the vegetables*
- 340 g/12 oz leaf mustard (about 435 g/15 oz before preparation), trimmed
- 200 g/7 oz carrots, peeled (180 g/6 oz after peeling)
- 150 g/5½ oz green beans, trimmed and halved
- 1¼ teaspoon salt
- 1 teaspoon sugar
- 1 tablespoon neutral oil
- 180 g/6 oz straw mushrooms, quartered if large, halved if small
- 1 teaspoon soy sauce
- 30 g/1 oz spring onions (scallions), sliced

*For the aromatics*
- 60 ml/2 fl oz (¼ cup) neutral oil
- 45 g/1½ oz garlic, coarsely chopped
- 25 g/1 oz shallots, coarsely chopped

Soak the noodles in warm water until soft, 8–10 minutes depending on the size of the dried noodles, then strain.

Next, prepare the vegetables. Split the leaf mustard stalk in half, then cut into 5-cm/2-inch long pieces.

Shred the carrots using a mandoline or make very thin strips with a peeler.

Prepare a bowl of iced water bath.

Bring a large pot of water to the boil, then add the green beans and blanch for 1 minute. Add the leaf mustard and blanch for 20 seconds. Using a slotted spoon, transfer to the iced water.

Add the carrots to the leaf mustard, then blanch for an additional 30 seconds. Using a slotted spoon, transfer to the iced water.

Season the blanched vegetables with 1 teaspoon of the salt and the sugar and mix well. Set aside.

To prepare the aromatics, heat the oil in a wok over a medium heat, then add the garlic and fry for 5–7 minutes until golden brown, stirring constantly. Remove the garlic with a slotted spoon and set aside.

Add the shallots to the wok with the same oil and fry for 5–7 minutes until golden. Remove the shallots and set aside, reserving the oil.

Add one third of the fried garlic to the blanched vegetables.

To cook the noodles, add 1 tablespoon of the light soy sauce to the strained noodles. Heat the reserved oi in a pan over a medium heat, add the bean sprouts, then stir-fry for 20 seconds. Add the noodles, season with 1 tablespoon of the soy sauce, then stir-fry over a medium heat for 2–3 minutes until the noodles are cooked. Strain and transfer to a large bowl. Add half the fried shallots and another third of fried garlic to the noodle bowl.

To cook the vegetables, heat the oil in a wok over a medium heat, add the mushrooms, increase the heat to high, add the soy sauce and stir-fry for 1 minute. Add the seasoned blanched vegetables and the remaining salt. Stir-fry for 4 minutes 30 seconds or until cooked but still crisp, then add the spring onions (scallions) and fry for a further 30 seconds. Strain the vegetables to remove any excess liquid, then add the strained vegetables to the noodles.

To finish the noodles, add the pepper, fried tofu, remaining fried shallots and fried garlic and the remaining soy sauce. Top with crushed toasted peanuts and mix thoroughly.

Serve hot and provide extra light soy sauce on the side, if desired.

# STIR-FRIED GLASS NOODLES WITH CRAB

## Miến Xào Cua

This versatile dish is usually served at family gatherings or as the finale at seafood eateries. With pre-picked crab meat, this stir-fry comes together quickly.

Serves 2
Preparation time: 30 minutes
Cooking time: 30 minutes

| DF |

- 100 g/3½ oz dried Northern-style vermicelli (mung bean glass noodles)
- 20 g/¾ oz (⅔ cup) shiitake mushrooms
- 70 g/2½ oz carrots, cut into thin matchsticks (julienned)
- 30 g/1 oz spring onions (scallions), cut into 5-cm/2-inch lengths
- 2 tablespoons Annatto Oil (page 457)
- 20 g/¾ oz garlic, finely chopped
- 20 g/¾ oz piece fresh ginger, finely chopped
- 70 g/2½ oz cooked crab meat
- 1 teaspoon all-purpose seasoning (hạt nêm)
- 1 tablespoon brown sugar
- 1 tablespoon pork lard
- 10 g/¼ oz coriander (cilantro), cut into 5-cm/2-inch lengths
- 1 teaspoon oyster sauce
- 2 teaspoons light soy sauce
- ½ teaspoon black pepper
- 100 g/3½ oz (scant ½ cup) of the liquid from cooking the crab or chicken stock (broth)
- 1 teaspoon sesame oil

*To serve*

- 15 g/½ oz coriander (cilantro) leaves, or to taste
- light soy sauce
- chilli slices

In a bowl, soak the vermicelli in warm water for 15 minutes, or until softened. Drain in a colander and set aside.

In another bowl, soak the shiitake mushrooms in warm water for 15 minutes. Once softened, drain and slice thinly.

Bring a pot of water to the boil over a high heat, then add the carrots and blanch for 1 minute. Remove the carrots with a slotted spoon and place in a colander to drain. Set aside.

In the same water, blanch the spring onions (scallions) for 30 seconds. Remove and drain well. Set aside.

Heat 1 tablespoon of the annatto oil in a wok over a medium heat, then add a third of the garlic and ginger and fry for 6–7 minutes until golden brown. Add the crab meat, all-purpose seasoning and 1½ teaspoons of the sugar, then stir-fry for 30 seconds, being careful not to break up the meat too much. Transfer the entire mixture to a small bowl and set aside.

In the same wok, heat the pork lard and the remaining annatto oil over a medium heat, then add the remaining garlic and ginger, and fry for 6–7 minutes until golden and fragrant. Add the sliced mushrooms and stir-fry for 1 minute. Add all the blanched vegetables and season the mushroom-vegetable mixture with the oyster sauce, soy sauce, the remaining sugar and half the pepper. Stir-fry for another 1 minute. Add the drained vermicelli, tossing well to combine. Pour in the crab cooking liquid or chicken stock (broth) and stir fry for 2–3 minutes until the noodles are soft.

To finish the dish, return the reserved crab mixture to the wok. Add the sesame oil and gently toss everything together. Sprinkle the remaining pepper over the mixture.

Divide between 2 serving plates and garnish with coriander (cilantro). Serve immediately with light soy sauce and chilli slices on the side.

# RICE

## Món cơm và xôi

This chapter includes essential rice preparations like basic white rice and sticky (glutinous) rice, alongside rice dishes that fall outside the traditional meal. Rice is a versatile ingredient used in myriad ways across Vietnam, from seasoning to a complete meal.

Sticky rice dishes (*món xôi*) are frequently eaten for breakfast or lunch or as snacks, and are often presented as offerings on an ancestral altar. I've included several base recipes for congee (*cháo*), another breakfast favourite that can be enjoyed on its own or served alongside dishes like Chicken and Banana Blossom Salad (page 128) at family gatherings.

The remaining rice dishes represent either interesting regional cooking methods or one-plate rice dishes, which have come about as a result of urbanization, where limited time demands efficient meals for workers during their lunch breaks. These recipes work equally well for family gatherings, like Broken Rice (page 270), or as simple weekday meals, like Garlicky Fish Sauce Chicken with Rice (page 265).

## WHITE RICE

Cơm Trắng

To a lot of Vietnamese people, rice is the most important component of a meal, as it is the basis to sustenance. Each grain should be distinct and glossy, never mushy; the individual grains should be clear in every bite. If you increase the amount of rice in this recipe, you might have to increase the cooking time, too; if cooking on the hob (stove), add an additional 5 minutes of cooking time per extra 50–100 g/1¾–3½ oz of rice.

Serves 3–4
Preparation time: 5 minutes
Cooking time: 20–25 minutes

| V | VE | DF | GF | ≤5 | ≤30 |

250 g/9 oz (1¼ cups) Thai fragrant (jasmine) rice

Gently wash the rice with clean running water about 3 times, using light stirring motions, then drain in a colander.

If using a rice cooker, place the washed rice into a rice cooker pot, then add 250 ml/8 fl oz (1 cup) water until it covers the rice by 5 mm–1 cm/¼–½ inch (the amount will vary by the rice type). Select 'cook rice' or 'white rice' setting and let it cook until the cycle completes. Open the lid when the cooking cycle finishes and gently fluff the rice with chopsticks, then transfer to a serving bowl.

If cooking on the hob (stove), transfer the washed rice to an appropriately sized pot (not too large or small, 1–1.5 litres/34–50 oz/1–1.5 quarts), then add 255–260 ml/8¾ fl oz (1 cup plus 1 tablespoon) of water (more water than the rice cooker method as the evaporation is higher in a pot). Bring to the boil over a medium-high heat and stir. Cover the pot, reduce the heat to low and cook for 15 minutes. Fluff the rice with chopsticks and remove from the heat, then keep covered and let rest for 10 minutes.

Serve hot with other dishes.

## RICE IN BAMBOO TUBES

Cơm Lam

This traditional method of cooking rice in bamboo tubes, practiced by the Tay, Thai, Êđê, Bahnar and other ethnic groups across Southeast Asia, developed from hunting-gathering communities. Sticky (glutinous) rice, which predates the white rice common today, can keep longer in these tubes. We learned this traditional preparation from chị Y Thoang in Kon Tum. Sticky rice can be naturally coloured using butterfly pea flowers.

Makes 10 bamboo tubes
Preparation time: 5 hours soaking time
Cooking time: 1 hour

| V | VE | DF | GF | ≤5 |

20 g/¾ oz fresh butterfly pea flowers (hoa đậu biếc), optional
1 kg/2 lb 4 oz (8 cups) sticky (glutinous) rice
1 teaspoon salt
1 tablespoon neutral oil
Sesame and Peanut Salt (page 479), to serve

*For wrapping*
10 bamboo tubes (30–60 cm/12–24 inches long, 3–4 cm/1¼–1½ inches in diameter), cleaned
banana leaves
old nứa tree branches (3–4 cm/1¼–1½ inches in diameter)

If using the butterfly pea flowers for colouring, in a pot, combine the flowers with 1 litre/1¾ pints (4¼ cups) of water. Bring to a simmer and cook for 10 minutes, or until the water becomes a dark blue colour. Strain the flowers and let the water cool completely.

Thoroughly wash the rice twice. Place in a bowl and cover with water (or the cooled butterfly pea water, if using) about 2 cm/¾ inch above the rice level and soak for at least 5 hours. Drain the rice well in a colander and then mix with the salt and oil.

Preheat a charcoal grill.

Fill the bamboo tubes with the prepared rice until it reaches up to the length of your middle finger from the end when pushed. Add 1 tablespoon of water to each tube. Create 'corks' from the banana leaves and use them to close the top of the bamboo tube.

Wait for the charcoal to turn bright red before cooking. Use the tree branches as supports to elevate the bamboo tubes: *do not* place the bamboo tubes directly on the charcoal or bury them in the charcoal. Position the tubes at an angle with the 'cork' side up. Grill until the rice is fully cooked but not dry, approximately 45 minutes–1 hour.

Remove from the heat and let cool away from the direct heat (keep the grill lit) for about 15 minutes.

Peel off one half of each bamboo tube, then grill the exposed rice surface until lightly charred, 4–5 minutes.

Serve with the sesame and peanut salt.

## COCONUT STICKY RICE

Xôi Nước Cốt Dừa

While you can make this basic sticky (glutinous) rice with just water, coconut milk adds a rich creaminess. Make sure to keep it covered when not serving immediately, as it dries quickly, though it can be steamed again. Serve hot with savoury dishes such as traditional accompaniment to Huế-style braised pork belly (see page 249).

Serves 2–3
Preparation time: 10 minutes, plus 5–6 hours or overnight soaking time
Cooking time: 20 minutes

| V | VE | DF | GF | ≤5 |

200 g/7 oz (generous 1 cup) sticky (glutinous) rice
¼ teaspoon salt
3 tablespoons coconut milk

Soak the rice in 500 ml/18 fl oz (2 cups) of water overnight or for 5–6 hours.

Rinse the soaked rice with 500 ml/18 fl oz (2 cups) of water, then drain well in a colander. Mix the drained rice with the salt.

Bring water to the boil in a steamer, then place the salted rice in the steamer basket and steam for 10 minutes.

Open the lid and fluff the rice with chopsticks, then add 2 tablespoons of the coconut milk and mix well. Cover and steam for 5 more minutes, then open the lid, add the remaining coconut milk and mix well.

Cover and steam for the final 5 minutes, then fluff the rice and transfer to a serving bowl.

## STEAMED MOMORDICA STICKY RICE

Xôi Gấc

Red symbolizes luck and happiness in Vietnam, making this vibrant sticky rice a popular choice for ancestral offerings, weddings and Lunar New Year celebrations. There's a saying that when offered to the kitchen god, its sticky texture prevents him from speaking ill of the family to the other gods. The dish gets its striking colour from gấc fruit, known for its high beta-carotene content. While fresh gấc is rarely found outside Vietnam, frozen versions are now available in Asian supermarkets.

Serves 4–6
Preparation time: 10 minutes, plus 8 hours or overnight soaking time
Cooking time: 50 minutes

| V | VE | DF | GF |

300 g/10½ oz (⅔ cup) sticky (glutinous) rice, soaked for a minimum of 8 hours
200 g/7 oz gấc flesh
1 tablespoon rice wine
30 g/1 oz (2 tablespoons) coconut milk
1 bunch pandan leaves, optional
banana leaf, optional

*To finish*
70 g/2½ oz (scant ⅓ cup) coconut milk
¼ teaspoon salt
40 g/1½ oz (3 tablespoons) sugar

Drain the soaked rice.

In a large bowl, thoroughly mix the drained rice, gấc flesh, rice wine and the 30 g/1 oz (2 tablespoons) coconut milk.

Set up a steamer and bring the water to the boil. If using pandan leaves, add them to the steaming water.

Line the steamer basket with muslin (cheesecloth) or a banana leaf. Spread the rice mixture evenly in the lined steamer basket, set over the boiling water and steam for 45 minutes, or until the rice is tender.

Drizzle the 70 g/2½ oz (scant ⅓ cup) of coconut milk over the hot rice in the steamer basket, then evenly sprinkle with the salt and sugar. Gently fold the ingredients together until well combined, then cover immediately to prevent it from drying out.

Serve hot or at room temperature, keeping the rice covered until serving.

# STICKY RICE WITH SWEETCORN

## Xôi Bắp

This sticky rice dish can often be found in the morning outside of schools, universities and office buildings as it provides a hearty breakfast, and can either be eaten sweet or savoury. If you are having this as a savoury dish, you can pair it with either Steamed Chicken with Lime Leaves (page 283) or Roasted Chicken Leg (page 284).

Serves 4
Preparation time: 15 minutes, plus overnight soaking time
Cooking time: 30 minutes

| V | VE | DF | GF |

- 335 g/11½ oz sweetcorn cob
- 130 g/4½ oz (¾ cup) sticky (glutinous) rice, soaked overnight
- ½ teaspoon salt
- 120 g/4¼ oz (½ cup) coconut milk

*To serve*

- 2 teaspoons sugar, or more to taste, optional
- 50 g/1¾ oz (3 tablespoons) Seasoned Coconut Milk (page 465), optional
- 20 g/¾ oz (4 teaspoons) Fried Shallots (page 458), optional
- Spring Onion Oil (page 458), to serve, optional
- 1 tablespoon Sesame and Peanut Salt (page 479)

Shave the corn kernels off the cob using a peeler or sharp knife. You should have around 190 g/6¾ oz (1¼ cups) of corn kernels.

Drain the soaked rice, then mix in a bowl together with the corn kernels and ¼ teaspoon of the salt.

In a separate bowl, season the coconut milk with the remaining salt, then set aside.

Set up a steamer and bring the water to the boil.

If the basket holes are too big to prevent the rice falling through, place a piece of banana leaf or a damp muslin (cheesecloth) in the basket first. Arrange the rice mixture in the steamer basket in a doughnut shape, creating a hole in the middle for more even cooking.

Set the basket over the boiling water and steam for approximately 30 minutes; while steaming, every 5 minutes gradually pour 1–2 tablespoons of the seasoned coconut milk onto the rice to infuse it with flavour.

Once the rice is cooked, fluff it up with chopsticks by stirring well, and transfer to a serving plate.

To serve sweet for breakfast, sprinkle the sugar on top, pour over the seasoned coconut milk and garnish with the fried shallots. Alternatively, for a savoury dish, omit the sugar and seasoned coconut milk and serve with the fried shallots and spring onion oil. Sprinkle the sesame and peanut salt on top or serve small bowls of the salt for dipping.

# STICKY RICE WITH SPLIT MUNG BEANS

## Xôi Đậu Xanh

*Xôi đậu xanh*, sticky rice with split mung beans, serves multiple purposes in Vietnamese culture, from ceremonial offerings during death anniversaries and lunar calendar celebrations to family gatherings and everyday breakfasts. The dish can be topped according to preference with Pork Floss (page 461), Sesame and Peanut Salt (page 479), char siu pork, roasted pork, Pork Rolls (page 462) or omelette.

Serves 6–8
Preparation time: 10 minutes, plus 4 hours soaking time
Cooking time: 20 minutes

| V | VE | DF | GF | ≤5 |

- 500 g/1 lb 2 oz (2¾ cups) sticky (glutinous) rice, soaked for 4 hours
- 100 g/3½ oz (½ cup) yellow split mung beans (đậu xanh không vỏ)
- ¼ teaspoon ground turmeric
- ¼ teaspoon salt
- 120 g/4¼ oz (½ cup) coconut milk
- 2 tablespoons sugar, to serve

Set up a steamer and bring the water to the boil.

Drain the soaked rice, then mix in a bowl together with the split mung beans, ground turmeric and salt. Add the mixture to the steamer basket, set over the boiling water and steam for 20 minutes.

Sprinkle the coconut milk over the mixture and toss the rice with chopsticks. Finish by adding the sugar and thoroughly mixing. Serve warm.

# CASSAVA STICKY RICE WITH SPRING ONION OIL

Xôi Khoai Mì Mỡ Hành

In Vietnam, especially in the south, people love combining sweet and salty flavours, and this simple breakfast staple is a perfect example. The sticky (glutinous) rice and cassava are sweetened with coconut milk and sugar, while toppings like Fried Shallots (page 458) and spring onion (scallion) oil lean towards savouriness. For many, including myself, this is a very nostalgic breakfast.

Serves 4–5
Preparation time: 30 minutes, plus overnight soaking time
Cooking time: 1 hour

| V | VE | DF | GF |

200 g/7 oz (generous 1 cup) sticky (glutinous) rice, soaked overnight
300 g/10½ oz cassava, peeled, diced and washed
½ teaspoon salt, or more to taste
75 g/2½ oz (⅓ cup) coconut milk
1 tablespoon sugar, or more to taste

*For the spring onion oil (mỡ hành)*
1 tablespoon neutral oil
20 g/¾ oz spring onions (scallions), finely chopped

*To serve*
approx. 20 g/¾ oz (⅓ cup) fresh shredded (grated) coconut
20 g/¾ oz (4 teaspoons) Fried Shallots (page 458)

Set up a steamer and bring the water to the boil.

Drain the soaked rice, then combine with the cassava in the steamer basket. Sprinkle the salt evenly over the mixture.

Set the basket over the boiling water and steam for 20 minutes. Drizzle 4 tablespoons of the coconut milk over the mixture, then continue steaming for an additional 40 minutes.

Meanwhile make the spring onion oil. In a small pan, heat the neutral oil over a medium heat. Add the spring onions (scallions) and stir-fry for 5 seconds, then remove from the heat. Set aside.

Sprinkle the sugar over the rice and cassava mixture, then drizzle the remaining coconut milk over the rice.

Transfer the rice and cassava to a serving plate. Top with the shredded (grated) coconut, fried shallots and spring onion oil. Adjust the seasoning with additional salt or sugar to taste.

# YOUNG GREEN RICE WITH COCONUT

Cốm Xào Dừa

Autumn in Hanoi brings *cốm* (young green rice), a delicacy made from young rice kernels that have to be processed by specific craftspeople. Both Làng Cốm Mễ Trì and Làng Vọng are artisanal villages still processing this grain. The fresh *cốm* can be enjoyed simply wrapped in lotus leaves, or transformed into various dishes like this snack or cakes, or used as an ingredient in young green rice and sausage patties (*chả cốm*, page 207). Once presented to kings and traditionally wrapped in lotus leaves, it remains a cherished ceremonial gift, particularly at weddings.

Serves 4
Preparation time: 15 minutes (plus 4 hours soaking time if using dry rice)
Cooking time: 20–25 minutes

| V | VE | DF | GF |

250 g/5½ oz (generous 1 cup) fresh or dried Vietnamese young green rice (cốm)
40 g/1½ oz (3 tablespoons) sugar
¼ teaspoon salt
110 g/3¾ oz (½ cup) coconut milk
¼ teaspoon vanilla extract, optional

*For the sweetened fresh grated coconut*
1 tablespoon sugar
50 g/1¾ oz (⅔ cup) fresh grated coconut

If using dried green rice, soak it in a bowl of cold water for 4 hours, then drain thoroughly in a fine-mesh sieve. If using fresh green rice, skip to the next step.

In a saucepan, combine 240 ml/8 fl oz (1 cup) of water with the sugar and salt. Bring to a gentle simmer over a medium heat. Add the green rice and stir well, then simmer for 5 minutes, stirring occasionally. Pour in the coconut milk and add the vanilla extract, if using. Continue cooking for 15–20 minutes until the rice has a loose porridge-like consistency, stirring frequently to prevent sticking. If using dried green rice, you may need to add an extra 60 ml/2 fl oz (¼ cup) water; if needed, add 2 tablespoons at a time.

To prepare the sweetened fresh grated coconut, heat a heavy pan over a medium heat, then add the sugar and stir constantly until it has melted. Add the coconut and stir until it becomes translucent. Remove from the heat immediately.

Divide the green rice among serving bowls and top with the sweetened coconut. Serve warm or at room temperature.

# SAVOURY STICKY RICE

## Xôi Mặn

While its exact origins are unclear, *xôi mặn* (savoury sticky rice) shows its Chinese roots through ingredients like Chinese sausage (*lạp xưởng*), salted daikon (*xá bấu*) and soy sauce. Today's versions incorporate additional elements such as *thịt nguội* (Vietnamese-style Cold Cuts, page 80), quail eggs, grilled meat, *siu mai*, pâté and *đồ chua* (Pickled Daikon and Carrots, page 468). Soaked overnight and finished with coconut milk, the rice should maintain a soft, chewy texture. Keep your sticky (glutinous) rice covered until serving, as it can dry out really fast. In the streets of Ho Chi Minh, vendors will wrap each portion in banana leaf for taking away, which is a very sustainable way to wrap food.

Serves 4
Preparation time: 10 minutes, plus 8 hours or overnight soaking time, as well as 30 minutes soaking time
Cooking time: 1 hour

| DF |

- 16 quail eggs
- 150 ml/5 fl oz (⅔ cup) neutral oil, plus extra for shallow-frying
- 50 g/1¾ oz Pork Liver and Minced Pâté (page 81)
- 70 g/2½ oz Spring Onion Oil (page 458)
- 400 g/14 oz (generous 2 cups) sticky (glutinous) rice, soaked overnight
- ½ teaspoon salt
- 150 g/5½ oz salted daikon (xá bấu), shredded, rinsed and soaked for 30 minutes, then drained
- 1 Chinese sausage (lạp xưởng) (about 45 g/1½ oz)
- 100 g/3½ oz (scant ½ cup) coconut milk
- 2 teaspoons soy sauce

*To serve*

- 170 g/5¾ oz Pork Roll (page 462), sliced
- 50 g/1¾ oz Chicken Floss or Pork Floss (pages 460 or 461, or pre-prepared)
- 30 g/1 oz (3 tablespoons) Toasted Peanuts (page 459), crushed
- chilli sauce, to taste

Prepare a bowl of iced water.

Bring a pan of water to the boil, add 8 of the quail eggs and boil for 2–3 minutes. Transfer to the iced water to cool, then peel and set aside.

Heat a little neutral oil in a pan over a medium heat, break in the 8 remaining quail eggs and fry for a minute, then flip and fry on the other side for a minute to cook over easy. Set aside.

Set up a steamer and bring the water to the boil.

In a bowl, mix together the pâté with the spring onion oil and set aside.

Drain the soaked rice, then mix the drained rice with the salt. Add to the steamer basket, set over the boiling water and steam for 20 minutes.

Heat the neutral oil in a small pot over a medium-low heat. Carefully add the salted daikon and fry for about 20 minutes until crispy. Remove and drain on paper towels.

In the pot with the same oil, add the Chinese sausage and fry for 4–5 minutes until crispy. Remove and drain on paper towels, then slice when cool.

When the rice is finished steaming, drizzle half the coconut milk over the rice, then cover and steam for another 10 minutes. Add the remaining coconut milk, then steam for a final 10 minutes. Remove from the heat and let rest for 10 minutes.

To serve, place 140 g/5 oz of the sticky rice in each bowl, then add ½ teaspoon of the soy sauce to each portion. Top each bowl of rice with 2 boiled quail eggs, 2 fried quail eggs, sliced pork roll, chicken or pork floss, sliced Chinese sausage, fried salted daikon, crushed toasted peanuts and the spring onion oil and pâté mixture. Serve with chilli sauce to taste.

# HUẾ-STYLE STICKY RICE WITH BRAISED PORK BELLY

Xôi Thịt Hon Huế

While this recipe calls for 30 minutes of boiling the peanuts, you need to make sure they're completely soft before moving to the next steps – depending on your peanuts, this might take longer. Often served as breakfast in Huế, this dish works well with either sticky (glutinous) rice or regular rice.

Serves 4–6
Preparation time: 10 minutes, plus 5 minutes soaking time
Cooking time: 2 hours 35 minutes

| DF |

- 60 g/2¼ oz raw peanuts
- 450 g/1 lb pork belly (side), quickly blanched (see step 1, page 121)
- 30 g/1 oz lemongrass, finely chopped
- 10 g/¼ oz shallot, minced
- ¼ teaspoon ground turmeric
- 1 tablespoon neutral oil
- 1 teaspoon sugar
- ¼ teaspoon black pepper
- 400 ml/14 fl oz (1⅔ cups) coconut water
- 1 tablespoon fish sauce
- 1 teaspoon Huế-style fermented shrimp paste (mắm ruốc)
- steamed sticky (glutinous) rice, to serve

Soak the peanuts in a bowl of water for 5 minutes (or longer if not fresh).

Bring a pan of water to the boil, then add the peanuts and boil for 30 minutes. Drain and let cool slightly, then peel and crush some of them by hand.

Cut the blanched pork belly (side) into 10-cm/4-inch-thick pieces, then combine in a bowl with the lemongrass, shallot and turmeric.

Heat the oil in a pan. Add the pork mixture and stir-fry for 4 minutes. Add the sugar and pepper. Stir-fry over a low heat for about 5 minutes until the liquid evaporates. Add the coconut water, fish sauce and 300 ml/10 fl oz (1¼ cups) water, then cook for 15 minutes. Add the peeled peanuts and shrimp paste, then continue cooking for another 1 hour 30 minutes, or until the pork is tender.

Serve hot with steamed sticky (glutinous) rice.

# SPRING ONION CONGEE

Cháo Hành

This congee, commonly known as 'cháo giải cảm' (fever relief congee), is often eaten when sick. In Vietnamese culture, spring onions (scallions) and ginger are believed to help fight flu and colds as their spiciness is thought to open up the pores, allowing us to sweat out sickness, which helps with recovery.

Serves 2–3
Preparation time: 10 minutes
Cooking time: 1 hour

| DF |

- 60 g/2¼ oz (⅓ cup) Thai fragrant (jasmine) rice
- 1.3 litres/2¼ pints (5½ cups) Basic Chicken Stock or Basic Pork Broth (page 464)
- 10 g/¼ oz piece fresh ginger, peeled and sliced
- 15 g/½ oz lemongrass, cut into 10-cm/4-inch sticks
- ½ teaspoon sugar
- 1 teaspoon fish sauce
- ¼ teaspoon salt

*To serve*

- 35 g/1¼ oz spring onions (scallions), finely chopped
- ¼ teaspoon black pepper

Put the rice, chicken or pork broth, ginger and lemongrass together in a pot, bring to a simmer and cook at a simmer for 45 minutes. Season with the sugar, fish sauce and salt and continue simmering for another 15 minutes.

To finish, add the spring onions (scallions) and pepper. Serve hot.

# PRAWN AND MEAT CONGEE

## Cháo Tôm Thịt

This is a comforting dish for cold nights. While the recipe calls for uncooked rice, you could also use leftover rice to make this dish.

Serves 3–4
Preparation time: 25 minutes
Cooking time: 45 minutes

| DF |

*For the congee*
- 70 g/2½ oz (⅓ cup) Thai fragrant (jasmine) rice
- 20 g/¾ oz shallots, coarsely chopped
- 4 teaspoons fish sauce
- 1 teaspoon salt
- 1 teaspoon sugar
- ¼ teaspoon black pepper

*For the meat and prawn mixture*
- 10 uncooked prawns (shrimp) (about 300 g/10½ oz)
- 200 g/7 oz minced (ground) pork
- 1 tablespoon neutral oil
- 20 g/¾ oz shallots, coarsely chopped
- 1 tablespoon fish sauce
- 1 teaspoon sugar
- ½ teaspoon black pepper

*For the fried shallots*
- 2 tablespoons neutral oil
- 45 g/1½ oz shallots, thinly sliced

*To serve*
- 1 tablespoon neutral oil from the fried shallots
- 20 g/¾ oz spring onions (scallions), chopped
- 20 g/¾ oz coriander (cilantro), chopped

Heat a dry pan, add the rice and toast over a medium heat for 4 minutes, or until the rice turns opaque. Set aside.

To make the meat and prawn mixture, bring a pot of water to the boil. Add the prawns (shrimp) and blanch for 5 minutes, or until just cooked. Remove the prawns and set aside until cool enough to handle. Peel the prawns, reserving their heads, to get about 170 g/5¾ oz peeled meat.

In a food processor, add the minced (ground) pork, peeled prawns, oil and shallots and blitz until well blended, about 1 minute. Add the fish sauce, sugar and pepper and blitz again for 30 seconds to incorporate.

Form the mixture into 15–16 meatballs (about 20 g/¾ oz each). Set aside in the refrigerator while you prepare the congee.

In a large pot, combine 1.5 litres/2½ pints (6¼ cups) water with the shallots and toasted rice. Bring to a simmer and cook for 10 minutes over a medium-low heat. Add the reserved prawn heads and cook for another 13 minutes. Using a slotted spoon, remove and discard the prawn heads, then add the fish sauce, salt and sugar. Add the chilled meatballs to the broth and continue simmering for another 13 minutes.

Meanwhile, make the fried shallots. In a small pan over a low heat, heat the oil, then add the shallots and fry for about 10 minutes until golden. Remove the shallots and set aside, reserving the oil.

Add 1 tablespoon of the reserved hot shallot oil to the congee. Season with the pepper, then remove from the heat.

Serve hot, garnished with the fried shallots, chopped spring onions (scallions) and chopped coriander (cilantro).

# SNAKEHEAD CONGEE

## Cháo Cá Lóc

Snakehead congee, a speciality of the western region of Vietnam, is particular for two things: the rice grains here are first lightly toasted, giving a layer of nutty aroma to the broth; and the congee is always paired with a plate of *rau đắng biển* (water hyssop) and *rau đắng đất* (slender carpetweed). The bitterness of these two plants is said to be medicinal, and in Vietnamese food philosophy, it has cooling properties. Conveniently, it grows quite easily in people's gardens and all year long in those regions. While it is bitter, it also has a crunch to it, adding a different texture to the dish.

Serves 4
Preparation time: 45 minutes
Cooking time: 1 hour and 15 minutes

| DF |

*For the marinated fish*
1 × 950/2 lb 2 oz whole snakehead fish (cá lóc), cleaned, with stomach intact and offal (variety meats) removed
2 tablespoons fish sauce

*For the congee*
70 g/2½ oz (generous ⅓ cup) Thai fragrant (jasmine) rice
1 teaspoon salt
250 g/5½ oz straw mushrooms
1 luffa gourd (about 340 g/12 oz)
20 g/¾ oz lemongrass, sliced
10 g/¼ oz piece fresh ginger, sliced
400 g/14 oz white fish bones (ask your fish supplier)
20 g/¾ oz shallots, peeled
1 tablespoon fish sauce

*For the fried shallots*
2 tablespoons neutral oil
45 g/1½ oz shallots, peeled

*To serve*
40 g/1½ oz spring onions (scallions), white parts cut into 2-cm/¾-inch pieces, green parts sliced into 5-mm/¼-inch pieces
15 g/½ oz coriander (cilantro), finely chopped
black pepper, optional
100 g/3½ oz water hyssop (rau đắng biển)
100 g/3½ oz slender carpetweed (rau đắng đất)
160 g/5½ oz bean sprouts
10 g/¼ oz piece fresh ginger, finely minced
2 bird's eye chillies, thinly sliced
fish sauce, for dipping
Tamarind Dipping Sauce (page 476)

Cut the snakehead into 4 pieces horizontally (head plus three body sections), then combine in a bowl with the fish sauce. Let marinate for 30 minutes at room temperature while you prepare the congee.

To make the congee, heat a dry pan, add the rice and toast over a medium heat for 4 minutes, or until the rice turns opaque. Set aside.

In a bowl, mix 600 ml/1 pint (2½ cups) water with ½ teaspoon of the salt, then add the mushrooms and soak for 10 minutes to whiten them. Drain and set aside.

Peel the gourd and cut it into 1.5-cm/⅝-inch rounds, then slice each round into 3 pieces, creating 1.5-cm/⅝-inch-thick chips (fries).

Place all the lemongrass and ginger in a spice cage or tea bag.

Bring 2 litres/3½ pints (8½ cups) of water to the boil, then add the toasted rice, shallots and the tea bag and simmer for 20 minutes. Add the fish bones and marinated fish head to the congee. Add the fish sauce and remaining salt, then continue simmering for 20 minutes.

Using a slotted spoon, carefully remove the fish head, then add the remaining three pieces of marinated fish and continue simmering for 10 minutes.

Using a slotted spoon, remove all the fish pieces and set aside. Remove and discard the fish bones and the spice cage. Continue cooking the congee for an additional 20 minutes, then remove from the heat.

Meanwhile, make the fried shallots. In a small pan over a low heat, heat the oil, then add the whole shallots and fry for about 10 minutes until golden. Remove the shallots and set aside, reserving the oil.

Add 1 tablespoon of the reserved hot shallot oil to the congee.

When ready to serve, bring the congee back to the boil. Add the gourd and the drained mushrooms, then simmer for 5 minutes, or until tender.

Meanwhile, arrange the fish pieces on a plate, top with the fried shallots, the prepared spring onion (scallion) whites and greens and the chopped coriander (cilantro) and season with black pepper, if desired.

Ladle the congee into individual bowls and serve with the fish and the water hyssop, slender carpetweed, bean sprouts and minced ginger on the side. Mix the chillies with fish sauce in small bowls and serve along with small bowls of the tamarind dipping sauce.

## MINCED MEAT CONGEE

Cháo Thịt Bằm

This simple congee combines rice porridge with minced (ground) meat and ginger, valued for its flu-healing properties. It also serves as the foundation for *cháo dinh dưỡng* (nutritious congee), which can be enriched with diced root vegetables or blended greens. Either minced pork or beef works well in this recipe. The key to congee lies in the ratio, typically one part rice to nine parts liquid, with the cooking time determining whether the result is thick like oat porridge or has a more soup-like in consistency.

Serves 2
Preparation time: 10 minutes
Cooking time: 45 minutes

| DF |

100 g/3½ oz minced (ground) meat
¾ teaspoon sugar
¼ teaspoon salt
1½ teaspoons fish sauce
15 g/½ oz shallot, chopped (divided into two equal portions)
½ teaspoon ground black pepper, plus extra to serve
10 g/¼ oz spring onion (scallion) whites, chopped
¼ teaspoon neutral oil
50 g/1¾ oz (¼ cup) Thai fragrant (jasmine) rice
25 g/1 oz (2 tablespoons) sticky (glutinous) rice
800–900 g/1 lb 12 oz–2 lb (3⅓–3¾ cups) hot water
20 g/¾ oz piece fresh ginger, sliced, plus 5 g/⅛ oz (about 1 cm/½ inch), sliced, to serve

*To serve*
spring onion (scallion) greens, chopped
coriander (cilantro) leaves

In a bowl, mix the minced (ground) meat with the sugar, salt, 1 teaspoon of the fish sauce, half the shallot, the pepper and the spring onion (scallion) whites. Set aside to marinate while preparing the rice.

Heat the oil in a pot, add both types of rice and toast over a medium-low heat for 4–5 minutes. Add 800 g/1 lb 12 oz (3⅓ cups) of the measured hot water to the toasted rice and bring to the boil. Add the marinated minced meat mixture and stir well. Bring to the boil again, then reduce the heat to low. Add the ginger. Cover and cook for 35–40 minutes until it reaches a porridge consistency, stirring every 15 minutes. Add the remaining fish sauce. If needed, add more hot water to achieve your preferred consistency; this congee is usually served a little looser than risotto. Add the remaining shallot and stir.

Serve hot, garnished with extra sliced ginger, chopped spring onion greens, coriander (cilantro) leaves and pepper.

## BLACK BEAN RICE CONGEE

Cháo Đậu Cà

In Hanoi's summer heat, this black bean congee is a popular choice, as black beans are traditionally considered 'cooling' for the body. The tapioca flour (starch) helps bind the rice and beans together while giving the congee a clearer appearance. While *cà pháo muối* (pickled aubergines/eggplants) is a classic topping, you can use any fermented vegetables you have at home.

Serves 4–5
Preparation time: 10 minutes, plus 8 hours or overnight soaking time
Cooking time: 1 hour 15 minutes

| DF | GF |

120 g/4¼ oz (⅔ cup) black beans
20 g/¾ oz (4 teaspoons) white rice
½ teaspoon salt
½ teaspoon MSG
20 g/¾ oz (2 tablespoons plus 2 teaspoons) tapioca flour (starch)

*To serve*
8–10 pieces of Fried Tofu with Spring Onion Sauce (page 48)
4–5 cooked salted duck eggs, halved
8–10 Salted Small White Aubergines (page 466)

Soak the black beans in cold water for 6–8 hours, or overnight.

Drain and rinse the beans. Rinse the rice twice under cold running water. Drain thoroughly.

In a pot, combine the soaked beans, rinsed rice and 1 litre/1¾ pints (4¼ cups) of water. Bring to the boil over a high heat, skimming any foam that rises to the surface. Reduce to medium heat, then add the salt and MSG. Cover and cook for 1 hour, stirring occasionally, until beans and rice are tender.

To thicken the congee, in a small bowl, mix the tapioca flour (starch) with 4 teaspoons of water and stir until the tapioca flour has dissolved. Slowly stir the starch mixture into the congee and cook for 1 more minute, or until thickened.

To serve, ladle 250 ml/8 fl oz (1 cup) of the hot congee into each bowl. Top with 2 pieces of fried tofu, 1 halved salted duck egg and 2 salted white aubergines (eggplants). Serve immediately.

# CHICKEN CONGEE

Cháo Gà

You can have this chicken congee plainly with shredded chicken from the Basic Chicken Stock on page 464, or you can use that chicken to make Chicken and Banana Blossom Salad (page 128) or even just the chicken salad from Hội An Chicken Rice (page 263).

Serves 4
Preparation time: 15 minutes
Cooking time: 50 minutes

| DF |

- 100 g/3½ oz (½ cup) Thai fragrant (jasmine) rice
- 35 g/1¼ oz green mung beans
- 1.5 litres/2½ pints (6¼ cups) Basic Chicken Stock (page 464)
- 1 teaspoon salt
- 1 teaspoon sugar
- 2 teaspoons fish sauce

*To serve*

- 320 g/11¼ oz cooked chicken (from Basic Chicken Stock, page 464), shredded
- 15 g/½ oz picked coriander (cilantro) leaves
- 15 g/½ oz spring onion (scallion) greens, chopped
- 20 g/¾ oz (4 teaspoons) Fried Shallots (page 458)

Rinse the rice and mung beans separately until the water runs clear.

In a pan over a low heat, add the rinsed rice and dry toast for 10 minutes, stirring occasionally. The rice should just begin to change colour, becoming slightly golden.

Add the toasted rice and rinsed mung beans to a large pot. Pour in 1 litre/1¾ pints (4¼ cups) of the chicken stock (broth) and the salt. Bring the mixture to the boil over a high heat, then reduce to low. Cover the pot with a lid, leaving it slightly ajar to allow the steam to escape. Simmer for 20 minutes, stirring occasionally to prevent sticking.

Add the remaining 500 ml/18 fl oz (2 cups) of the chicken broth and continue to simmer for another 20 minutes, stirring occasionally. The congee should be thick and creamy, with the grains of rice and mung beans soft and broken down. Add the sugar and fish sauce, stir well and let simmer for an additional 5 minutes to incorporate the flavours. Taste and adjust seasoning if necessary.

To serve, ladle the hot congee into bowls and serve with your choice of toppings, such as shredded chicken, coriander (cilantro), chopped spring onion (scallion) or fried shallots.

# DUCK CONGEE

## Cháo Vịt

In Vietnamese markets, when you order a freshly slaughtered duck, nothing goes to waste. The blood is often taken to make *tiết canh* (raw blood soup), while the meat can be prepared in various ways, including for this duck congee and for Poached Duck and Cabbage Salad (page 129). Duck dishes in Vietnamese cuisine typically include ginger to reduce gamey flavours, whether used for cleaning or cooking the duck, or in dipping sauces. In this congee, the meat remains firm and 'crunchy', unlike the tender style of Herbal Stewed Duck (page 311).

Serves 6–8
Preparation time: 30 minutes
Cooking time: 1 hour 50 mins

| DF |

100 g/3½ oz (½ cup) Thai fragrant (jasmine) rice

*For the stock*
1 litre/1¾ pints (4¼ cups) coconut water
1 tablespoon fish sauce
½ teaspoon salt
15 g/½ oz lemongrass, cut into 15-cm/6-inch chunks
20 g/¾ oz peeled shallots
20 g/¾ oz piece fresh ginger
1.4 kg/3 lb 2 oz duck meat chunks (legs, whole breast, neck and wings)
1 duck head and 2 feet, optional
20 g/¾ oz of raw duck fat

*To serve*
15 g/½ oz coriander (cilantro), finely chopped
35 g/1¼ oz spring onions (scallions), finely chopped
white or black pepper
Ginger Dipping Fish Sauce (page 474)

To prepare the stock (broth), in a large pot, combine 1 litre/1¾ pints (4¼ cups) of water, the coconut water, fish sauce, salt, lemongrass, whole shallots and ginger and bring to a simmer. Add the duck meat chunks, head and feet, if using, and duck fat to the pot. Simmer for 20 minutes.

While the stock is simmering, heat a dry pan over a medium-low heat, add the rice and toast for about 3 minutes until lightly browned.

Using a slotted spoon, remove the duck meat chunks from the broth, but keep the head and feet in the pot for more flavour. Reserve half the duck meat chunks for another recipe. For the other half, either use a cleaver to chop it into bite-size pieces with bones, or shred the duck to eat without bones.

Add the toasted rice to the stock. Skim off any excess fat if needed (discard or reserve for other uses), then simmer over a low heat for about 1 hour 30 minutes until the mixture becomes a thick congee. Using a slotted spoon, remove and discard the duck head and feet before serving.

To serve, ladle the hot congee into individual bowls, add the bite-size pieces of duck meat, either on top or mixed in, then garnish with the finely chopped coriander (cilantro), finely chopped spring onions (scallions) and a sprinkle of pepper. Serve with individual small bowls of the ginger dipping fish sauce for dipping the duck meat.

# PORK ORGAN CONGEE

## Cháo Lòng

A dish born from nose-to-tail cooking, this congee varies across Vietnam, from the north's mixture of sticky (glutinous) and regular rice to Central and Southern versions with blood sausage and seasoned offal (variety meats). Regional adaptations include Binh Dinh's addition of *bánh hỏi* (fine rice vermicelli sheets) and the Mekong Delta's inclusion of rice noodles. I prefer having this in the afternoon when the broth has developed deeper flavours from simmering all day. This recipe uses only regular rice that is toasted, but you can make it a mix if you like.

Serves 4–5
Preparation time: 30 minutes
Cooking time: 2 hours 15 minutes

| DF |

- 100 g/3½ oz small pig's stomach
- 100 g/3½ oz pig's small intestine
- 370 g/13 oz pork femur bone
- 500 g/1 lb 2 oz pig's oesophagus (throat)
- 150 g/5½ oz pig's blood curd (huyết heo)
- 200 g/7 oz (1 cup) Thai fragrant (jasmine) rice
- 40 g/1½ oz lemongrass stalks
- 1½ teaspoon salt
- plate of Pork Cartilage Sausages (page 148) or Pork Blood Sausages (page 32), optional
- 2 tablespoons fish sauce
- 2 teaspoons sugar
- 5 g/⅛ oz (1 teaspoon) Fried Shallots and Garlic (page 459)
- ½ teaspoon black pepper

*For the fried shallots*
- 2 tablespoons neutral oil
- 35 g/1¼ oz peeled shallots

*To serve*
- chilli slices, to taste
- lime wedges
- 150 g/5½ oz bean sprouts
- 25 g/1 oz spearmint (húng lủi)
- 25 g/1 oz spring onions (scallions), thinly sliced
- 15 g/½ oz coriander (cilantro) leaves

Bring a pan of water to the boil, add the pig's stomach, pig's intestine, pig's femur bone, and pig's oesophagus and blanch for 10 minutes, then remove with a slotted spoon. Add the pig's blood curd and blanch for 5 minutes. Clean the bone thoroughly with a brush under running water.

Heat a 5-litre/175-oz (5-quart) pot over a high heat, add the rice and toast for 4 minutes, or until the rice becomes opaque and starts to change colour to light brown. Remove and set aside.

Add 2.5 litres/4½ pints (10½ cups) of water to the pot and bring to the boil. Add the lemongrass and 1 teaspoon of the salt to flavour. Add the blanched stomach, femur bone and oesophagus (throat). Cover with a lid and simmer for 20 minutes. Add the toasted rice and cook for a further 30 minutes. Add the blanched small intestine and 500 ml/18 fl oz (2 cups) of water if the liquid has reduced. Cook for another 50 minutes. If using the sausages, add then 10 minutes before the end of the cooking time.

Using a slotted spoon, remove all the meats from the pot. Slice the intestine into 4–5-cm/1½–2-inch rounds. Slice the stomach into 1-cm/½-inch slices. Thinly slice the oesophagus. Cut the sausages, if using, into 3-cm/1¼-inch chunks. Remove the meat from the bones thoroughly.

Return the bones to the pot to continue flavouring the broth. Add the blanched pig's blood curd, fish sauce, sugar and fried shallots and garlic to the pot. Season with the remaining salt. Cook for another 10 minutes, then remove from the heat until ready to serve.

Meanwhile, make the fried shallots. Heat the oil in a pan over a medium heat, add the whole shallots and fry for 5–6 minutes until golden.

Add the pepper and the fried shallots to the congee.

When ready to serve, add the various sliced meats to the congee and bring the congee to a simmer.

To serve, ladle the hot congee into bowls and garnish with chilli slices, lime wedges, bean sprouts, spearmint, thinly sliced spring onions (scallions), and coriander (cilantro), with a plate of sausages on the side.

# BAHNAR-STYLE THICK RICE PORRIDGE WITH PORK

## Tơpung Păng Kơting Xem

This Bahnar dish is thicker than typical congee, closer to polenta in consistency, so it can be served on banana leaves without spilling. While traditionally finished with fresh pig's blood during celebrations where a pig would be slaughtered, this modern version, taught to us by bác A Wơr and his family, omits the blood. Some people use banana trunk ash and pea flower water to replace the colour that the blood otherwise gives to the dish.

Serves 4–6
Preparation time: 30 minutes
Cooking time: 40 minutes

| DF |

500 g/1 lb 2 oz (2¾ cups) Thai fragrant (jasmine) rice

*For the stock*
1 tablespoon neutral oil
5 g/⅛ oz garlic, crushed
¼ teaspoon black pepper
350 g/12 oz pork ribs, cut into 2 × 3-cm/¾ × 1¼-inch chunks
2 teaspoons fish sauce
1½ teaspoons MSG
1 teaspoon all-purpose seasoning (hạt nêm)
½ teaspoon sugar
1½ teaspoons salt

Soak the rice in cold water for 5 minutes, then drain well and spread on a drying rack. Sun-dry until semi-dry (it should weigh 520 g/1 lb 2 oz at this point.)

Put the rice in a mortar and pound with a pestle until its texture resembles coarse (kosher) salt. (Traditionally, without modern milling machines, people would pound rice to dehusk it from the grain before cooking.) Set aside.

To make a stock (broth), heat the oil in a 26-cm/10½-inch pot over a medium heat, then add the garlic and pepper and stir for 30 seconds, or until fragrant. Add the pork rib pieces and 1 teaspoon of the fish sauce, then continue frying for 1 minute, stirring constantly. Pour 2 litres/3½ pints (8½ cups) of water into the pot with the pork. Bring to a simmer over a medium heat. Add the MSG, all-purpose seasoning, sugar, salt and the remaining fish sauce, then simmer for 20 minutes, skimming any foam.

In a large bowl, mix the pounded rice with 300 ml/10 fl oz (1¼ cups) of water until well combined.

The next part requires two people (see note): one person slowly pours the rice mixture into the simmering broth, while the second person constantly stirs it to prevent lumps. Continue stirring vigorously for 2 minutes.

Reduce the heat to low, then cover and cook for 1 minute. Uncover and stir well, then repeat the cover-and-stir process for a total of 10 minutes. Remove from the heat, then let rest, covered, for a minimum of 10 minutes before serving.

***Notes:*** To achieve the right consistency for this dish, there is a step where two people are required, so grab a friend or family member to help pour the rice mixture into the simmering stock, while you constantly stir the pot. This will help prevent lumps.

You can also make this on your own if you cook a smaller quantity, so you can pour one-handed while you stir with your dominant hand.

## SWEET POTATO RICE

Cơm Độn Khoai Lang

*Cơm độn khoai lang* is a dish that stands as a reminder of the difficult times in Vietnam's history, when rice was scarce, and people had to bulk up their meals with roots like cassava and sweet potatoes. This dish is a nostalgic favourite among the older generation who remember these challenging times. Nowadays, it might have disappeared from the usual meal, but I do think it is important to include this recipe, as a reminder for us younger generation of Vietnam's tumultuous history, and the resilience in its people.

Serves 1–2
Preparation time: 15 minutes
Cooking time: 30–35 minutes

| V | VE | DF | GF | ≤5 |

1 sweet potato (about 205 g/7¼ oz), preferably with purple skin and yellow flesh, peeled and cut into 2 × 4-cm/ ¾ × 1½-inch chunks
100 g/3½ oz (½ cup) Thai fragrant (jasmine) rice

Wash the sweet potato chunks and rice together until the water runs clear. Soak them in a bowl of fresh cold water for 10 minutes. Drain well.

To cook in a rice cooker, place the drained sweet potato and rice in the rice cooker. Add water according to the rice cooker's instructions (usually a 1:1.5 ratio). Select the normal rice cooking setting and cook. Do not stir during cooking.

To cook on the hob (stove), place the drained sweet potato and rice in a heavy pot. Add 150 ml/15 fl oz (⅔ cup) of water, then bring to the boil over a high heat. Reduce the heat to the lowest setting, cover tightly, then simmer for 18–20 minutes without stirring. Remove from the heat, then keep covered for 10 minutes.

Once cooked, by either method, gently fluff with a fork, being careful not to mash the sweet potato. Serve hot.

## COCONUT RICE FROM BẾN TRE PROVINCE

Cơm Dừa Bến Tre

Ben Tre, Vietnam's coconut capital, is known for coconut-based specialties including this rice cooked directly in a coconut shell. It is best enjoyed hot before the rice absorbs too much coconut oil and turns yellow. It is often paired with *tép rang dừa* (Caramelized Shrimp in Coconut Milk, page 310).

Serves 1
Preparation time: 15–20 minutes
Cooking time: 35 minutes

| V | VE | DF | GF | ≤5 |

1 small coconut (about 475 g/1 lb)
⅛ teaspoon salt
150 g/5½ oz (¾ cup) Thai fragrant (jasmine) rice
Caramelized Shrimp in Coconut Milk (page 310), to serve, optional

Carefully cut the top part off the coconut to create a lid. Pour out all the coconut water and measure it. You should have about 220 g/7¾ oz (scant 1 cup) of liquid. Mix 150 g/5½ oz (⅔ cup) of the coconut water with the salt. (Save any remaining coconut water for another use. It will keep in the refrigerator for up to 2 days.)

Wash the rice several times under running water until the water runs clear. Place the washed rice into the coconut shell, then pour the salted coconut water over the rice. Cover the coconut with its lid.

Set up a steamer and bring the water to the boil.

Place the filled coconut (with its lid) in the steamer basket, set over the boiling water and steam for 35 minutes. (If you use more rice, the steaming time can be longer.) Remove from the heat and carefully remove the coconut from the steamer. Let it rest for 5 minutes before serving.

Serve the rice directly in the coconut shell. The coconut flesh can be scraped and eaten along with the rice. Accompany the rice with the caramelized shrimp in coconut milk, if desired.

# LEMON BASIL FRIED RICE

Cơm Chiên Lá É

Good fried rice starts with day-old rice from the refrigerator – the dried grains are less likely to stick when frying. When cooking the rice, choose a rice variety that isn't too sticky when cooked (not to be confused with sticky/glutinous rice). If you don't have old rice, you can cook your rice as per the package instructions but reduce the water quantity by 10 per cent, and make sure it cools down completely before frying. You can make this rice vegan if you omit the eggs.

Serves 4
Preparation time: 10 minutes
Cooking time: 8–10 minutes

| V | DF | ≤30 |

500 g/1 lb 2 oz (4 cups) cooked rice, cooled
2 eggs
2 tablespoons neutral oil
30 g/1 oz garlic, minced

*For the lemon basil paste (makes 100 g/ 3½ oz)*
300 g/10½ oz lemon basil (lá é), leaves picked (about 80 g/2¾ oz leaves), chopped
3 teaspoons salt
16 small green chillies
4 teaspoons all-purpose seasoning (hạt nêm)

Put the cold cooked rice into a bowl. Break the eggs into the rice and mix well. Set aside.

To make the lemon basil paste, put all the ingredients in a food processor, then blend until a smooth paste forms. Alternatively, you can prepare the paste using a hand blender or a mortar and pestle. Reserve 50 g/1¾ oz of the paste for the rice; store the remainder for another recipe (see note).

In a large frying pan or skillet, heat the oil over a medium heat, then add the garlic and fry for 30 seconds, or until it starts to become golden. Add the rice and egg mixture to the pan and fry for another 2–3 minutes, stirring constantly. Add the reserved lemon basil paste to the pan. Continue to fry for another 2–3 minutes while stirring, ensuring the rice turns a nice bright green.

Serve immediately.

***Note:*** The remaining lemon basil paste can be used in Vietnamese Chicken Hotpot with Lemon Basil (page 170) or any other stir-fry recipes. Store in an airtight container in the refrigerator for up to 3 days.

# SALTED FISH FRIED RICE

Cơm Chiên Cá Mặn

In Vietnam's wet markets, you'll always find vendors specializing in dried fish – a preservation method that predates even the salt farms of South Central Vietnam established in the nineteenth century. For this dish, you need to pick a meaty dried fish, like threadfin, boesemania or striped catfish. And for the rice, I recommend using old, cooked rice, as it won't make your fried rice soggy or sticky.

Serves 3–4
Preparation time: 15 minutes
Cooking time: 30 minutes

| DF |

230 g/8 oz dried fish
3 tablespoons neutral oil
2 eggs
650 g/1 lb 7 oz (3¼ cups) rice, cooked and cooled
1 tablespoon Annatto Oil (page 457)
¼ teaspoon fish sauce
70 g/2½ oz garlic, coarsely chopped
25 g/1 oz spring onion (scallion) greens
13 g/½ oz coriander (cilantro), roughly picked
½ teaspoon black pepper

Pour boiling water over the dried fish to clean it, then pat dry and cut into roughly 6 × 4-cm/ 2½ × 1½-inch squares.

In a 20-cm/8-inch pan, add 1 tablespoon of the neutral oil and fry the fish pieces over a low heat until they become really crispy, about 15 minutes.

Meanwhile, separate the eggs. Set the egg whites aside. Mix the yolks with the cooked rice. Add the annatto oil and fish sauce to the rice mixture.

Once the fish is fried, remove it from the pan. Carefully shred the fish and set aside. You should have 150 g/5½ oz of shredded fish.

In a large pan, heat the remaining neutral oil. Add the garlic and fry until it starts to change colour, then remove half of it and add it to the rice mixture. Leave the remaining fried garlic in the pan. Add the shredded fish to the pan with the fried garlic and fry for 1 minute.

Using a pair of chopsticks, mix the rice mixture well, then add the rice mixture to the pan. Thoroughly mix the rice and the fish, then fry until it becomes dry, about 8 minutes, stirring occasionally. Add the egg whites and continue to fry for about 3 minutes, tossing so the egg whites evenly cook. Finally, add the spring onion (scallion) greens, coriander (cilantro) and pepper. Mix well.

Serve immediately.

# FRIED RICE WITH PICKLED MUSTARD GREENS AND BEEF

## Cơm Rang Dưa Bò

You can serve this dish with a Simple Omelette (page 347) or you can directly add an egg into the cooked rice before frying.

Serves 2–3
Preparation time: 40 minutes
Cooking time: 15 minutes

| DF |

- 150 g/5½ oz Pickled Mustard Greens (page 467)
- 2 tablespoons neutral oil
- 20 g/¾ oz garlic, minced
- 15 g/½ oz shallot, minced
- 350 g/12 oz (1¾ cups) cooked rice, cooled
- 1 teaspoon all-purpose seasoning (hạt nêm)
- spring onion (scallion) greens, to taste, or 2–3 fried eggs, to serve

*For the marinated beef*

- 200 g/7 oz beef, thinly sliced
- 1 teaspoon all-purpose seasoning (hạt nêm)
- 1 teaspoon sugar
- ¼ teaspoon salt
- ⅛ teaspoon black pepper
- 1 tablespoon soy sauce
- 1 tablespoon oyster sauce

To marinate the beef, combine all the ingredients in a bowl, mix well and marinate for 30 minutes.

Wash the pickled mustard greens and drain well, then cut into 5-mm/¼-inch pieces and set aside.

Heat 1 tablespoon of the oil in a wok over a medium heat, add half of the garlic and shallot and fry for 1–2 minutes until fragrant. Add the marinated beef and the prepared pickled mustard greens, then stir-fry for 2 minutes, or until the beef is cooked. Remove the beef and pickled mustard green mixture from the wok and set aside.

In the same wok, heat the remaining oil over a medium-high heat, add the remaining garlic and fry for 1 minute, or until fragrant. Add the cooked rice and all-purpose seasoning, then stir-fry for 5 minutes. Return the beef and pickled mustard green mixture to the wok, then stir-fry everything together for 3 minutes, or until well combined. Taste and adjust seasoning if needed.

To serve, divide among serving plates and garnish each portion with some spring onion (scallion) greens or a fried egg, if using.

# HỘI AN CHICKEN RICE

## Cơm Gà Hội An

In Hội An, in Quảng Nam, Central Vietnam, this chicken rice dish starts with rice cooked in chicken and turmeric broth, then is topped with shredded meat, pickled onion, Vietnamese coriander/cilantro and papaya. What makes it unique is *nước mạ*, a dipping sauce made from giblets and offal (variety meats). The dish shares some elements with Hainanese chicken rice, which isn't surprising – the Hainanese were one of the five major Chinese communities who settled in Hội An's flourishing trading port over 200 years ago. Yet this dish has grown into something distinctly its own. Even within Vietnam, you'll find different takes on it.

Serves 2–3
Preparation time: 30 minutes
Cooking time: 1 hour 30 minutes

| DF | GF |

*For the chicken*
25 g/1 oz piece fresh ginger, sliced
1 peeled shallot
1 lemongrass stalk
5 lime leaves
1 teaspoon salt
½ chicken (450 g/1 lb)

*For the broth*
1 teaspoon salt
30 g/1 oz chicken fat
½ teaspoon ground turmeric
1 small onion (150 g/5½ oz)
1 shallot (15 g/½ oz)

*For the papaya salad*
435 g/15 oz green papaya

*For the pickled onion*
115 g/4 oz onion, peeled and thinly sliced
1 tablespoon sugar
60 ml/2 fl oz (¼ cup) vinegar
70 g/2½ oz ice

*For the yellow rice*
1 tablespoon neutral oil
20 g/¾ oz garlic, minced
200 g/7 oz (generous 1 cup) Thai fragrant (jasmine) rice

*For the giblets and the serving sauce (nước mạ)*
50 g/1¾ oz chicken giblets
¼ teaspoon sugar
¼ teaspoon MSG
¼ teaspoon salt
⅛ teaspoon black pepper
⅛ teaspoon Vietnamese five-spice powder (ngũ vị hương)
1 teaspoon Annatto Oil (page 457)
5 g/⅛ oz shallot, minced
5 g/⅛ oz garlic, minced

*To serve*
Vietnamese coriander/cilantro (rau răm)
Hoi An chilli sauce

Bring 2 litres/3½ pints (8½ cups) of water to the boil in a large pot over a high heat, then add the piece of ginger, whole shallot, lemongrass, lime leaves and salt, then allow the mixture to boil for 10 minutes to infuse the flavours. Carefully add the chicken to the pot, then blanch for 5 minutes. Using tongs, carefully remove the chicken and rinse it thoroughly under cold running water. Set the chicken aside. Discard the blanching water.

To make the broth, bring 2 litres/3½ pints (8½ cups) of fresh water to the boil in a clean large pot over a high heat. Once boiling, add the salt, chicken fat and ground turmeric, whole onion and whole shallot. Using tongs, gently lower the blanched chicken into the pot, then reduce the heat to maintain a gentle simmer and cook for 20 minutes.

Meanwhile, prepare a large bowl of iced water.

When the chicken is cooked, carefully remove the chicken from the broth using tongs, then immediately submerge it in the bowl of iced water for 15–20 minutes. Keep the broth simmering for an additional 25 minutes, then strain through a fine-mesh sieve into a clean container; it should yield 1 litre/1¾ pints (4¼ cups) of broth.

Prepare another bowl of iced water.

To prepare the papaya salad, using a mandoline or sharp knife, finely cut the papaya into thin matchsticks (julienne). Immediately submerge the julienned papaya in the iced water to maintain its crispness. Set aside both bowls until ready to serve.

To make the pickled onion, combine onion, sugar, vinegar and ice in a bowl and mix well. Set aside until ready to serve.

To cook the yellow rice, heat the neutral oil in a small pan over a medium heat, add the garlic and fry for 2 minutes, or until fragrant but not browned. Transfer the fried garlic and its oil to a rice cooker bowl. Add the rice and 200 ml/7 fl oz (scant 1 cup) of water to the bowl and mix well. Cook in the rice cooker until done.

In a small mixing bowl, combine the giblets with the sugar, MSG, salt, pepper and five-spice powder. Mix thoroughly to coat the giblets and then let marinate for about 5 minutes.

Heat the annatto oil in pan over a medium heat, add the shallot and garlic and fry until fragrant, about 1 minute. Add the seasoned giblets, then stir-fry for 2 minutes. Pour in 60 ml/2 fl oz (¼ cup) of water and cook for 5 minutes, or until the giblets are tender. Remove the giblets with a slotted spoon and set aside; reserve the cooking sauce (this is called '*nước mạ*').

Remove the cooked chicken from the iced water. Using your hands, shred the meat into fine, even pieces. With a sharp knife, slice the chicken skin into thin strips (not too thin). Set both aside.

To serve, place a portion of the hot yellow rice in the centre of each plate. Arrange the shredded chicken meat and sliced skin over the rice, then add the stir-fried giblets alongside. Drain the papaya well, then place a portion on the side of each plate. Add a portion of pickled onions, then garnish with fresh Vietnamese coriander/cilantro leaves. Serve with a small bowl of the reserved giblet sauce on the side. Add chilli sauce as desired.

# CRISPY FRIED CHICKEN WITH FRIED RICE

Cơm Gà Xối Mỡ

This is a very popular worker's lunch. Double-cooking the chicken ensures crispy skin while maintaining juicy meat.

Serves 2
Preparation time: 15 minutes, plus 30 minutes marinating time
Cooking time: 30 minutes

| DF |

700 g/1 lb 9 oz chicken legs (2 pieces)
1 tablespoon fish sauce
20 g/¾ oz peeled garlic
6 g/⅛ oz spring onion (scallion) whites
½ teaspoon Chinese rose cooking wine (I like Mei Kuei Lu Chiew)
¼ teaspoon black pepper
¼ teaspoon salt

*For cooking the chicken*
10 g/¼ oz piece fresh ginger
1 peeled onion (about 50 g/1¾ oz)
¼ teaspoon salt
1 tablespoon soy sauce (for brushing chicken)
750 ml/25 fl oz (3 cups) rendered chicken fat or neutral oil (for frying the chicken)

*For the fried rice*
420 g/15 oz (2½ cups) cooked rice, cooled
1 egg
1 teaspoon Annatto Oil (page 457)
1 teaspoon fish sauce
1 tablespoon chicken fat or oil

*For the sauce*
½ teaspoon oyster sauce
½ teaspoon sugar
1 tablespoon soy sauce
10 g/¼ oz garlic, finely chopped
1 teaspoon neutral oil

*To serve*
tomato slices
cucumber slices

Pierce the chicken legs with a knife and drizzle with the fish sauce.

Put the garlic and spring onion (scallion) whites in a mortar and pound with a pestle until a paste forms. Spread this paste on the chicken legs.

Put the chicken legs in a bowl along with cooking wine, pepper and salt. Marinate for 30 minutes.

To cook the chicken, fill a pot with water, add the piece of ginger and whole onion and bring to the boil. Add the marinated chicken legs, cover and cook for 15 minutes. Using tongs, remove the chicken, then add the salt to the broth. Let the chicken cool, then brush with the soy sauce.

To prepare the rice, in a large bowl, mix together the cooled cooked rice with the egg, annatto oil and fish sauce.

Heat the 1 tablespoon of the chicken fat or oil in a pan over a medium-high heat. Add the rice and fry for 3–4 minutes until golden. Set aside.

To fry the chicken, put the rendered chicken fat or neutral oil in another pan and heat to 170°C/340°F. If not using a thermometer, test the oil temperature by inserting wooden chopsticks into the oil – small bubbles should form rapidly around them. Carefully add the chicken and fry for about 8 minutes. Carefully remove with a slotted spoon and drain on paper towels.

For the sauce, combine the oyster sauce, sugar, soy sauce and 1 tablespoon water in a bowl and mix well.

Heat a small pan over a medium heat, add the garlic and fry for 1–2 minutes until golden, then add the oyster sauce and soy sauce mixture. Stir for 10 seconds, or until slightly thickened, then remove from the heat.

Serve the crispy fried chicken over the fried rice, drizzled with the prepared sauce and serve with tomato slices and cucumber slices on the side.

# GARLICKY FISH SAUCE CHICKEN WITH RICE

## Cơm Gà Chiên Mắm Tỏi

This dish is typically served with white rice or fried rice, similar to *gà xối mỡ* (see opposite). The twice-cooked method ensures you have a crispy exterior while the flesh still stays juicy and moist. The leg is then basted in a fish sauce and fried garlic sauce. You can serve this alongside slices of cucumber and tomatoes.

Serves 2
Preparation time: 45 minutes
Cooking time: 30 minutes

| DF |

- ½ teaspoon salt
- ⅛ teaspoon ground turmeric
- 700 g/1 lb 9 oz chicken legs (2 legs, thigh and drumstick together)
- 10 g/¼ oz piece fresh ginger, crushed (unpeeled)
- 20 g/¾ oz peeled garlic
- 1 teaspoon fish sauce
- ½ teaspoon black pepper
- neutral oil, for deep-frying
- 20 g/¾ oz (2 tablespoons) cornflour (cornstarch)

*For the sauce*

- 1 tablespoon fish sauce
- 2 teaspoons sugar
- ¼ teaspoon black pepper
- ¼ teaspoon dried chilli flakes
- 1 tablespoon boiling water

*For the fried garlic*

- 3 tablespoons neutral oil
- 100 g/3½ oz garlic, finely chopped

*To serve*

- 1 quantity Crispy Fried Chicken with Fried Rice (page 264), or 2 portions of cooked white rice
- slices of cucumber
- slices of tomatoes

Bring 500 ml/18 fl oz (2 cups) of water to the boil with the salt and turmeric. Add the chicken legs and blanch for about 2 minutes, then remove. When cool enough to handle, make small incisions on the inside of each leg for better marination.

Put the ginger and garlic in a mortar and pound with a pestle, then finely chop.

Put the chicken legs in a bowl along with the chopped ginger and garlic, the fish sauce and pepper, then rub the mixture over the chicken legs. Marinate for 30 minutes.

To make the sauce, mix the sauce ingredients in a small bowl and set aside.

Heat the oil for deep frying in a pot to 170–185°C/340–365°F. If not using a thermometer, test the oil temperature by inserting wooden chopsticks into the oil – small bubbles should form rapidly around them. Coat each marinated chicken leg in cornflour (cornstarch), then carefully add each leg to the oil and fry for 10 minutes until golden. Carefully remove and then set aside.

To prepare the fried garlic, in a pan, heat the oil, then add the garlic and fry over a medium-low heat for 8–9 minutes until golden, stirring constantly. Strain and reserve the garlic and oil separately.

In the same pan with the reserved oil, add the sauce mixture over a low heat, then add half of the fried garlic and the fried chicken legs to the pan. Stir and baste for 5–6 minutes, allowing the sauce to evenly glaze the chicken. Continue cooking until the sauce seeps into the chicken and the fat separates, re-crisping the exterior, 2–4 minutes.

Divide between plates and serve hot, garnished with the remaining fried garlic, alongside the fried rice and sliced cucumber and sliced tomatoes.

# CHĂM-STYLE MIXED RICE

## Cơm Trộn – Lithei jrau

At chú Kiều Anh and cô Đạo Thị Tuyết's home in Phan Rang, we learned this traditional Chăm dish (*Lithei jrau* is the name of this dish in the Chăm dialect) that showcases their seafood-centric cuisine. The rice is mixed with *muthin ngưik* (tamarind anchovy sauce) and fresh herbs picked from their garden, characteristic of how Chăm cooking relies on fresh herbs, vegetables and seafood-based seasonings. Their dishes, particularly as Chăm Bà-ni practises Islam, emphasize fresh ingredients prepared simply – a culinary approach well-suited to their coastal environment and the region's heat.

Serves 3–4
Preparation time: 20 minutes
Cooking time: 15 minutes

| DF | GF |

*For the rice*
150 g/5½ oz herb salad (rau sống – basil, perilla, spearmint, coriander/cilantro, lemon basil, Vietnamese balm)
30 g/1 oz tamarind leaves
80 g/2¾ oz acacia leaves (lá dẹp/lá keo)
30 g/1 oz young mango leaves
30 g/1 oz young Burmese grape leaves (trái da đá )
70 g/2½ oz piper lolot leaves
100 g/3½ oz banana root, shaved
mint basil, to taste
720 g/1 lb 9 oz (5¾ cups) cooked rice, cooled
4 tablespoons tamarind anchovy sauce (see below)

*For the fried mackerel scad (makes 350 g/12 oz)*
350 g/12 oz mackerel scad (2 fish), cleaned
½ teaspoon salt
½ teaspoon MSG
1 tablespoon neutral oil

*For the tamarind anchovy sauce (mắm nêm me – muthin ngưik), makes 250 g/9 oz (1 cup)*
20 g/¾ oz peeled shallots
15 g/½ oz peeled white onion
6 g/⅛ oz green chilli, stemmed
50 g/1¾ oz green tamarind, cleaned
1 tablespoon MSG
3 tablespoons brown sugar
150 g/5½ oz fermented anchovy sauce (mắm nêm)

Chop or tear all the herbs into bite-size pieces.

Place the cooled cooked rice in a large bowl, then add all the prepared herbs. Set aside.

To prepare the fried mackerel scad, combine the fish, salt and MSG in a bowl.

Heat the oil in a pan until hot, then add the fish and fry for 15 minutes, turning occasionally for even cooking, until completely dry and crispy. You will need 4 tablespoons for this recipe; store the leftovers in a jar in the refrigerator for up to 1 week (it is good for dipping poached meats).

To prepare the tamarind anchovy sauce, put the whole shallots, whole onion and chilli in a mortar or food processor and pound or blitz until a fine paste forms. Add the green tamarind and continue grinding or blitzing. Add the MSG and sugar and pound or blitz again. Add the anchovy sauce and thoroughly mix. Strain, if desired, for a smoother texture. Adjust the seasoning to taste.

To serve, add 90 g/3¼ oz of the fried mackerel scad pieces to the rice bowl. Add 4 tablespoons of the tamarind anchovy sauce, then gently toss all the ingredients, ensuring even distribution of the herbs and fish.

Serve immediately.

*Note:* Any leftover sauce will keep in a jar in the refrigerator for up to 1 week.

# BABY BASKET CLAM RICE

Cơm Hến

One of Huế's many specialties using baby basket clams, this mixed rice dish has humble origins – traditionally made with leftover rice and simple, accessible ingredients. While originally a poor person's meal, it's being made from scratch here, using the rice-washing water to clean the clams of impurities. If baby clams aren't available, jarred vongole can work as a substitute, though you'll need to use chicken or pork stock (broth) to replace the missing clam broth.

Serves 4–5
Preparation time: 30 minutes, plus 1 hour 30 minutes soaking time
Cooking time: 45 minutes

| DF |

- 380 g/13 oz (2 cups) Thai fragrant (jasmine) rice
- 1.3 kg/3 lb baby basket clams (hến) in shells
- 2 tablespoons Annatto Oil (page 457)
- 20 g/¾ oz shallots, chopped
- 20 g/¾ oz garlic, chopped
- 1 tablespoon fish sauce
- 20 g/¾ oz spring onions (scallions), chopped
- 1 teaspoon Chilli and Lemongrass Oil (page 457)
- ½ teaspoon lime juice

*For the fried pork skin*
- 15 g/½ oz dried pork skin
- 240 ml/8 fl oz (1 cup) neutral oil

*For the broth*
- 1 teaspoon all-purpose seasoning (hạt nêm)
- ¼ teaspoon salt
- 15 g/½ oz piece fresh ginger, sliced
- 5 g/⅛ oz Vietnamese coriander/cilantro (rau răm), chopped

*For the Vietnamese fermented shrimp paste sauce*
- 1 tablespoon Vietnamese fermented shrimp paste
- 4½ teaspoons sugar
- 10 g/¼ oz green chilli (about ½ chilli), thinly sliced
- 2 tablespoons lime juice
- 2 teaspoons Shrimp, Chilli and Lemongrass Oil (page 457)

*To garnish*
- 50 g/1¾ oz (⅓ cup) Toasted Peanuts (page 459)
- 12 g/½ oz holy basil (húng cây), leaves picked
- 90 g/3¼ oz banana blossom (bắp chuối)
- 70 g/2½ oz Indian taro (bạc hà), peeled
- 60 g/2¼ oz star fruit
- 90 g/3¼ oz bean sprouts
- 12 g/½ oz Vietnamese coriander/cilantro (rau răm), leaves picked

*To serve*
- 5 lime wedges
- crispy sesame rice crackers

Wash the rice and reserve the cleaning water to soak the clams. (This will help clean the baby basket clams as well.)

Soak the clams in the rice washing water for 1 hour and 30 minutes.

Cook the rice according to the packet instructions. Set aside.

To prepare the fried pork skin, fill or half-fill a small pot with the oil and heat to about 180°C/350°F. If not using a thermometer, test the oil temperature by inserting wooden chopsticks into the oil – it should bubble vigorously around them. Carefully add the pork skin and fry until it puffs up, 1–2 minutes. Remove with a slotted spoon and set aside.

To cook the clams, in a pot, bring 800 ml/27 fl oz/3½ cups of water to a simmer over a medium heat, then add the soaked clams and boil until they separate from the shells, 4–5 minutes. Turn off the heat and let the clams and liquid cool slightly. Swirl the water to make a vortex so the clam meat rises up; sieve it out. You should have about 260 g/9 oz of clam meat. Reserve the cooking liquid.

In a pan, heat the annatto oil over a medium heat. Add the shallots and garlic and fry for 2 minutes, or until fragrant. Increase the heat, then add the clam meat and fish sauce and stir-fry for 1 minute. Add the spring onions (scallions), chilli and lemongrass oil and lime juice. Set aside.

To prepare the broth, in a pot, combine 600 ml/1 pint (2½ cups) of the reserved cooking liquid with the all-purpose seasoning, salt and ginger. Bring to a simmer. (When serving, garnish each bowl of broth with the Vietnamese coriander/cilantro.)

To prepare the Vietnamese fermented shrimp paste sauce, in a small bowl, combine the shrimp paste with 3 tablespoons of the hot broth, the sugar, chilli, lime juice, and shrimp, chilli, and lemongrass oil. Add 2 tablespoons of water and mix well.

To serve: divide the rice among 4 plates. Divide the clams on top of the rice. Garnish each bowl as you wish with the toasted peanuts, the fried pork skin and herbs, fruit and vegetables. Add 1 tablespoon of the Vietnamese fermented shrimp paste sauce to each portion, then serve with the broth, a lime wedge and a sesame rice cracker on the side.

To eat this, add two spoons of the hot broth to the rice, mix everything together and eat with a spoon, adding more sauce if needed. Crumble the sesame rice cracker on top of the dish to add another level of crunchiness.

***Note:*** You can substitute dried pork skin with premade chicharrones or pork rinds.

# BROKEN RICE

## Cơm Tấm

*Gạo tấm* refers to broken rice grain leftovers from harvest, which Mekong Delta farmers would eat out of necessity so they could sell their whole grains. Today, *cơm tấm* has evolved into a worker's lunch staple, where everything comes on one plate – a departure from the traditional *mâm cơm gia đình* where multiple dishes are shared. Even the way it's eaten sets it apart: just a spoon, no chopsticks needed. At vendors, each person orders their own combination: *cơm bì sườn* (rice, shredded pork skin, grilled pork chop) or *cơm sườn chả* (rice, grilled pork, egg meatloaf), with sides of cucumber, tomato and pickles. While this recipe includes all three toppings, you can swap in Sautéed Pork Belly (page 299) or try it Long Xuyên-style with the shredded meat from Caramelized Pork Sandwich (page 68).

Serves 4
Preparation time: 45 minutes, plus 30 minutes soaking and overnight and 30 minutes marinating times
Cooking time: 1 hour 15 minutes

| DF |

*For the marinated grilled pork (sườn cốt lết nướng)*
4 pork cutlets (125–150 g/4¼–5½ oz each)
25 g/1 oz peeled garlic
15 g/½ oz peeled shallot
1 teaspoon oyster sauce
1 teaspoon condensed milk
2 teaspoons fish sauce
1 teaspoon light brown sugar
¼ teaspoon Vietnamese five-spice powder (ngũ vị hương)
¼ teaspoon black pepper
1 teaspoon Annatto Oil (page 457) or normal oil
½ teaspoon honey

*For the egg meatloaf (chả trứng)*
10 g/¼ oz dried wood ear mushroom
10 g/¼ oz dried rice vermicelli noodles (bún tàu)
60 g/2¼ oz onion
45 g/1½ oz jicama
40 g/1½ oz peeled shallots
200 g/7 oz minced (ground) pork
1 teaspoon brown sugar
1 tablespoon fish sauce
¼ teaspoon salt
½ teaspoon black pepper
4 eggs, 2 separated
1 tablespoon melted pork lard
½ teaspoon Annatto Oil (page 457)

*For the broken rice*
400 g/14 oz (2 cups) broken rice (gạo tấm)
400 ml/14 fl oz (1⅔ cups) coconut water

*To serve*
250 g/5½ oz Shredded Pork Skin Seasoned with Toasted Rice (page 460)
60 g/2¼ oz Pickled Daikon and Carrots (page 468)
slices of cucumber
slices of tomato
4 eggs, fried
50 g/1¾ oz Spring Onion Oil with Fried Pork Fat (page 458)
240 ml/8 fl oz (1 cup) Sweet and Sour Fish Sauce (page 471)

The day before, prepare the pork. Bash the pork cutlets with a meat mallet to thin them out, then make small cuts on the surface to prevent them from curling when cooked.

Put the garlic and shallot in a mortar and pound with a pestle to form a paste, then mix with all the other marinade ingredients and mix with the pork. Cover and marinate overnight in the refrigerator.

To prepare the egg meatloaf, in separate bowls, soak the mushrooms and noodles in warm water for 30 minutes until soft.

Meanwhile, in a food processor or with a knife, finely mince the onion, jicama and shallots.

Drain and slice the soaked mushrooms. Drain and cut the soaked vermicelli into shorter pieces.

In a large bowl, add the mushrooms, noodles, minced vegetables and minced (ground) pork, then mix together for 5 minutes until everything is well incorporated. Mix in the seasonings, 2 whole eggs and 2 egg whites (reserve the yolks). Add the melted lard, then mix well. Let marinate 30 minutes.

Set up a steamer and bring the water to the boil.

Line a 15-cm/6-inch mould with baking (parchment) paper and pour the meatloaf mixture into the mould. Add to the steamer basket, place over the boiling water and steam for 30 minutes.

Mix the annatto oil with the reserved egg yolks, and brush on top of the steamed meat mixture. Steam for an additional 15 minutes. Set aside.

To cook the rice, thoroughly wash the broken rice, then add to a rice cooker. Add the coconut water, then cook in the rice cooker. Alternatively, cook in a pan (see page 240). When done, keep warm in a steaming basket in a steamer set over a low heat.

Preheat the oven grill (broiler) to 200°C/400°F (or preheat a charcoal grill).

Grill the marinated pork for 7 minutes on each side. Set aside.

To serve, place 100 g/3½ oz of the warm broken rice in the centre of each plate. To each portion of rice, add 1 slice of the egg meatloaf (about 100 g/3½ oz), 1 portion of the grilled pork and about 50 g/1¾ oz of the shredded pork skin seasoned with toasted rice. Arrange the pickled vegetables, sliced cucumber and sliced tomato on the side of the plate, along with a fried egg, then drizzle 1 tablespoon of the spring onion oil with fried pork fat.

Serve with a small bowl of sweet and sour fish sauce on the side.

# MAIN DISHES

## Món chính

In Vietnamese meals, though rice takes centre stage, fish and meat dishes play important supporting roles. As proteins have traditionally been expensive ingredients, Vietnamese cooking developed its own techniques and pairings to make whatever protein that was available more flavourful and stretch further. Even simply poached meats are paired with aromatic herbs or pungent dipping sauces to create satisfying dishes.

The use of ovens has never been common in Vietnamese home kitchens. Instead, dishes are typically simmered, braised, steamed, poached or stir-fried. Even Roasted Chicken Leg (page 284) is prepared in a pan. The recipes range from simple preparations like Poached Pork Belly with Shrimp Paste (page 300) to complex, long-simmered dishes like Beef Stew (page 316), with options for every time frame you have for cooking. This collection focuses on core Vietnamese cooking techniques that you can adapt to different proteins available to you.

When hosting guests, rather than increasing portions, consider preparing two dishes from this chapter, like Lemongrass Fried Tofu (page 282) alongside Braised Pork Belly with Pickled Bamboo Shoots (page 304), or Braised Tuna with Pineapple (page 276) paired with Caramelized Pork Spare Ribs (page 298).

## BRAISED CARP WITH PICKLED BAMBOO SHOOTS

Cá Chép Kho Măng Chua

This northern mountain speciality combines two household staples: rice field carp and preserved bamboo shoots. Black cardamom lifts up the whole dish. If you don't have carp, other freshwater fish or chicken would work equally well.

Serves 3–4
Preparation time: 15 minutes
Cooking time: 50 minutes

| DF | ≤5 |

- neutral oil, for frying
- 415 g/14½ oz carp (whole small fish or large fish cut into portions)
- 430 g/15 oz pickled bamboo shoots
- 1 teaspoon salt
- 1½ teaspoons ground black cardamom (thảo quả)
- 1 tablespoon all-purpose seasoning (hạt nêm)
- 1 tablespoon fish sauce

Fill a large pan a quarter full with oil and place over a medium heat. Carefully add the carp and fry for 8 minutes until seared on all sides. Remove the fish and set aside.

In a pan, combine 920 ml/31 fl oz (scant 4 cups) of water with the pickled bamboo shoots and salt.

Add the fried fish to the pan, then bring to a simmer and cook for 35 minutes. Add the cardamom, all-purpose seasoning, fish sauce and 1 tablespoon of water to the pan, then continue simmering for 5 more minutes.

Serve hot.

## BRAISED GOBY FISH AND PORK BELLY

Cá Kèo Kho Tộ

Goby fishes are small freshwater fish mainly found in the Mekong Delta of Southern Vietnam. They can be enjoyed in a Goby Fish Hotpot (page 176), or simply caramelized and braised as in this recipe. Due to their small size and lean meat, they are paired here with pork belly (side) and crispy pork fat to bulk up the dish. They might be small and bony, but there's great satisfaction in eating them.

Serves 4, as a part of meal
Preparation time: 30 minutes, plus 20 minutes marinating time
Cooking time: 1 hour 30 minutes

| DF |

- 1 tablespoon neutral oil
- 100 g/3½ oz pork back fat, cubed
- 300 g/10½ oz pork belly (side), cut 4 × 1-cm/1½ × ½-inch strips
- 25 g/1 oz garlic, minced
- 1 teaspoon sugar
- 2 tablespoons fish sauce
- 25 g/1 oz spring onion (scallion) whites
- 1 teaspoon Caramel Braising Sauce (page 456)
- 400 ml/14 fl oz (1⅔ cups) coconut water
- 6 bird's eye chillies

*For the marinated fish*

- 1 kg/2 lb 4 oz goby fish (cá kèo), cleaned
- 1 tablespoon fish sauce
- 1 tablespoon sugar
- 15 g/½ oz shallot, minced
- ½ teaspoon salt

*To serve*

- ½ teaspoon black pepper
- 15 g/½ oz spring onion (scallion) greens, finely chopped, to garnish
- 15 g/½ oz long red chillies, sliced on an angle

To marinate the fish, in a bowl, mix the goby fish with the fish sauce, sugar, shallot and salt; let marinate for 20 minutes.

Heat the oil in a shallow pan over a medium-low heat, add the pork back fat and fry for 20 minutes, or until rendered, crispy and golden. Remove the crispy fried lard and set aside.

Add the pork belly (side) to the same pan and fry until coloured, about 5 minutes. Strain away the excess rendered lard but keep the pork belly in the pan. Return 1 teaspoon of the rendered lard to the pan, add the garlic and fry for 5 minutes, or until golden. Add the sugar and fry for 2 more minutes. Add 1 tablespoon of the fish sauce and remove from the heat.

Transfer everything to a large pan with a lid in a single layer with the marinated fish. Spread the fish and pork belly evenly. Mix in the spring onion (scallion) whites and caramel braising sauce. Cover and simmer on low heat for 20 minutes. Remove the lid and let the sauce caramelize for 5 minutes.

Add the coconut water, bird's eye chillies and remaining fish sauce. Continue cooking for another 1 hour until caramelized and dark brown.

Garnish with the pepper, crispy fried lard, spring onion greens and sliced chilli before serving.

***Note:*** You can substitute the goby fish and pork belly with a bigger type of fish. In Vietnam, howling fish (*Pangasius conchophilus*) or catfish is often used for this dish.

## STEAMED RICE FIELD CARP WITH LEMONGRASS AND SAWTOOTH CORIANDER

Cá Chép Hấp Sả Và Ngò Gai

During our time in Hà Giang province, Anh Triệu Tà Phấu showed us how small rice field carps, when steamed for over 1 hour 30 minutes, become tender enough to eat whole as their bones break down. While this dish traditionally uses these local carps, the marinade works well with any type of fish.

Serves 4
Preparation time: 30 minutes
Steaming time: 1 hour–1 hour 30 minutes

| **DF** |

- 600 g/1 lb 5 oz rice field carp (approximately 8 small fish), cleaned
- 70 g/2½ oz lemongrass, finely minced
- 30 g/1 oz sawtooth coriander (culantro), finely minced
- 1 teaspoon Indian prickly ash (mắc khén)
- 1½ teaspoons salt
- 1 teaspoon ground black cardamom (thảo quả)
- 2 teaspoons all-purpose seasoning (hạt nêm)
- 1 tablespoon neutral oil

Pat the fish dry with paper towels, then make 2–3 diagonal slits on each side of the fish.

Combine the lemongrass and sawtooth coriander (culantro) in a mixing bowl. Add the Indian prickly ash, salt, cardamom, all-purpose seasoning and oil and mix thoroughly until well combined.

Stuff the belly of each fish with the aromatic mixture. Place the remaining mixture in the slits made on the sides.

Set up a steamer and bring the water to the boil.

Arrange the fish on a steaming plate and add to the steamer basket. Set over the boiling water and steam for 1 hour–1 hour 30 minutes. The fish is done when the skin can be easily peeled off.

Serve immediately.

## BRAISED TUNA WITH PINEAPPLE

Cá Kho Thơm

This central- and southern-style braised fish would go really well with any sour soups in this book (see pages 368–371).

Serves 3–4
Preparation time: 20 minutes, plus 15 minutes marinating time
Cooking time: 1 hour

| **DF** |

- 610 g/1 lb 6 oz tuna steak (1 whole Vietnamese tuna) (about 3-cm/1¼-inch thick steak)
- ½ teaspoon salt
- 60 ml/2 fl oz (¼ cup) neutral oil
- 25 g/1 oz shallots, sliced
- 25 g/1 oz spring onions (scallions), whites and greens separated, greens cut into 2–3-cm/1-inch lengths
- 3 tablespoons fish sauce
- 2 teaspoons sugar
- 300 ml/10 fl oz (1¼ cups) coconut water
- 1 red tomato (140 g/5 oz), halved and sliced 5 mm/¼ inch thick
- 400 g/14 oz peeled pineapple (½ pineapple), halved lengthways, core removed and sliced into 1-cm/½-inch-thick triangles
- 25 g/1 oz Crispy Fried Pork Fat (page 459), optional
- 10 g/¼ oz long green chilli, or ½ chilli, sliced
- 11 g/¼ oz long red chillies, sliced
- ¼ teaspoon black pepper

Put the tuna in a bowl with the salt and leave to marinate for 15 minutes.

In a large 30-cm/12-inch pan, heat the oil over a medium heat, add the tuna steaks and sear for 18 minutes until golden.

Add the shallots and spring onion (scallion) whites and cook for another 4 minutes. Add 2 tablespoons of the fish sauce and the sugar and continue to cook for another 3 minutes, or until the fish sauce glazes the fish. Add the coconut water and tomato. Bring to a simmer over a medium heat and cook for 10 minutes. Add the pineapple, sprinkle in the remaining fish sauce, then cook for a further 15 minutes. Add the fried pork fat, if using, and continue cooking for another 10 minutes until the sauce has become a nice glaze and when you pull the meat apart, it's all opaque. Remove from the heat.

Add the sliced chillies and the spring onion greens on top. Finish with the pepper.

# STEAMED SNAKEHEAD FISH IN BOTTLE GOURD

## Cá Lóc Hấp Bầu

This dish requires a bottle gourd large enough to contain the whole fish, allowing the cooking juices to steep into the gourd flesh. While traditionally made with snakehead fish, any freshwater fish, including trout, can be used in this steaming method. Make sure everything can fit in your steamer as well.

Serves 2–3
Preparation time: 25 minutes, plus 10 minutes marinating time
Cooking time: 35 minutes

| DF |

- 1 calabash (bottle gourd) (about 700 g/ 1 lb 9 oz)
- 1¾ teaspoon fish sauce
- 1 × 400 g/14 oz snakehead fish (cá lóc), cleaned and kept whole with head on
- ¼ teaspoon salt
- ½ teaspoon black pepper
- ½ teaspoon sugar
- 1 tablespoon neutral oil
- 12 g/½ oz shallot, cut into 1-cm/½-inch chunks
- 5 g/⅛ oz spring onion (scallion) white, smashed
- 10 g/¼ oz lemongrass stalk
- 30 g/1 oz coriander (cilantro), stalks trimmed (but leaves still attached), to garnish

Cut the calabash (bottle gourd) lengthways so the bottom part is large enough to hold the fish, with the top part being thinner to serve as a lid. (Use a small knife to draw the cutting line before cutting to ensure evenness.)

Use a small paring knife to cut and a spoon to carve out the middle of the bottom part. For the top lid, make small incisions into the skin so steam can escape, but no carving is needed. Wash thoroughly and scrape a bit of the skin off, but don't use a peeler to avoid removing too much green colour. Brush the inside of the bottle gourd with ¾ teaspoon of the fish sauce.

In a bowl, season the fish with the salt, ¼ teaspoon of the pepper, the remaining fish sauce and the sugar. Let it marinate for 10 minutes.

Heat the oil in a small pan, add the shallot and spring onion (scallion) white. Fry for about 3 minutes.

Smash the lemongrass and cut it into 4-cm/1½-inch chunks. Put the lemongrass into the mouth of the fish and pour any leftover marinade into it.

Place the fish inside the bottle gourd and close it with 4 cocktail sticks or toothpicks, securing each side like a box.

Pour a little water into the bottom of a large wok with a lid and place a circular grill rack inside the wok (the water should sit below the grill). Bring the water to the boil. Carefully fit the gourd on the grill, cover and steam for 30 minutes, or until fully cooked.

Just before serving, garnish with the coriander (cilantro) and sprinkle the remaining black pepper on top.

## SIMMERED TUNA STEAK WITH CHILLI AND GARLIC

Cá Ngừ Rim Tỏi Ớt

This dish showcases the abundance of bonito tuna found along the central east coast of Vietnam. The tuna steaks are simmered in a caramelized relish of garlic, chilli, fish sauce and pork fat, creating a sweet and spicy flavour. If tuna is unavailable, it can be substituted with any firm fish, like turbot (halibut) or swordfish.

Serves 2–4 to share
Preparation time: 15 minutes
Cooking time: 30 minutes

| DF |

- 350 g/12 oz bonito tuna steak, skin on (2–3 slices)
- ½ teaspoon salt
- 2 tablespoons neutral oil
- 70 g/2½ oz garlic, finely chopped
- 35 g/1¼ oz red chillies (about 3), deseeded and finely chopped
- 1 tablespoon lard (or neutral oil)
- 1 tablespoon sugar
- 2 tablespoons fish sauce
- 15 g/½ oz spring onion (scallion) greens, finely chopped

Wipe clean the tuna steaks and marinate in a bowl with the salt for 15 minutes to remove any fishy smell.

In a pan large enough to fit the fish in a single layer, heat the oil over a medium-low heat, add the garlic and chillies and fry over low heat until golden, about 8 minutes. Add the fish steaks and sear on each side for 1 minute on each side. Then add the lard (or oil), sugar and 1 tablespoon of the fish sauce. Cook until the liquid has fully evaporated, resulting in a caramelized relish, about 8 minutes. Add 60 ml/2 fl oz (¼ cup) of water and braise the fish for 5 minutes. Add the remaining fish sauce and braise for another 5 minutes.

Finish the dish with the finely chopped spring onion (scallion) greens and serve hot.

## BRAISED MACKEREL IN COCONUT WATER

Cá Nục Kho

This dish can simply be eaten with rice, but it also goes well in a *bánh mì* (Vietnamese Baguette, page 66), served with fresh cucumbers and coriander (cilantro).

Serves 2–3
Preparation time: 20 minutes
Cooking time: 25 minutes

| DF |

- 30 g/1 oz shallots, sliced
- 400 g/14 oz mackerel scad (about 3 fish), cleaned and halved widthways

*For the sauce*

- 1 tablespoon Annatto Oil (page 457)
- 1 tablespoon neutral oil
- 10 g/¼ oz shallot, minced
- 20 g/¾ oz long red chilli, minced
- ½ teaspoon salt
- 2 tablespoons plus 2 teaspoons fish sauce
- 1 tablespoon light brown sugar
- 570 ml/19 fl oz (2½ cups) coconut water

In a bowl, spread the sliced shallots over the fish and set aside to marinate until ready to cook.

To make the sauce, heat the annatto oil and neutral oil in a pan over a medium-low heat, add the minced shallot and fry for 2 minutes until fragrant. Add the chilli and cook for 2 minutes, or until aromatic.

Place the fish in the pan. Add the salt, 2 tablespoons of the fish sauce and the sugar. Cook for 3 minutes. Add the coconut water, 500 ml/18 fl oz (2 cups) of water and the remaining fish sauce. Bring to a gentle simmer, then cook until the sauce reduces and the fish is tender, 10–15 minutes.

Serve hot.

BRAISED MACKEREL IN COCONUT WATER

## FRIED FISH WITH LEMONGRASS

### Cá Chiên Sả

This recipe works with any small to medium fish similar to red or black mullet or red snapper. The secret is to fry the seasoned marinade ingredients until crispy, but not burned, then scatter them over the finished fish. Serve with simple fish sauce, or try it with Ginger Dipping Fish Sauce (page 474) or Sweet and Sour Fish Sauce (page 471). You can replace the fish with firm tofu if you want to make this dish vegetarian.

Serves 2
Preparation time: 15 minutes, plus 10 minutes marinating time
Cooking time: 15 minutes

| DF | GF |

480 g/1 lb 1 oz kissing gourami (cá hường) (about 2 fish), cleaned and scaled
120 ml/4 fl oz (½ cup) cooking oil
30 g/1 oz lemongrass, roughly chopped

*For the marinade*
50 g/1¾ oz garlic, minced
90 g/3¼ oz lemongrass, finely chopped
3 g red bird's eye chilli, minced
½ teaspoon black pepper
¼ teaspoon salt

To make the marinade, in a bowl, combine the garlic, lemongrass, chilli, pepper and salt.

Score 3 diagonal incisions on each side of the cleaned fish. Rub the marinade all over the fish, making sure to coat it evenly. Let it marinate for 10 minutes.

Heat the oil in a large frying pan or skillet over a medium heat. The oil should be about 5 mm/¼ inch deep in the pan. Once the oil is hot, add the lemongrass and fry for about 1 minute, or until fragrant. Remove the fried lemongrass and set aside.

Carefully add the marinated fish to the pan of oil. Fry for 7–8 minutes on each side, or until the fish is golden brown and cooked through. Remove the fish from the pan and place on a paper towel-lined plate to drain the excess oil.

Serve hot, garnished with the fried lemongrass pieces.

## CHICKEN CURRY

### Cà Ri Gà

Like many foreign dishes that found their way into Vietnamese kitchens, this curry evolved to include local touches – our curry powder blend uses ground annatto seeds for colour and lemongrass for fragrance. Typically served with bread or noodles, *cà ri gà* has a soupier consistency than its Indian counterparts.

Serves 4–6
Preparation time: 1 hour
Cooking time: 55 minutes

| DF |

120 ml/4 fl oz (½ cup) neutral oil
400 g/14 oz potatoes, peeled and cut into 4 × 5-cm/1½ × 2-inch chunks
450 g/1 lb sweet potatoes, peeled and cut into 4 × 5-cm/1½ × 2-inch chunks
30 g/1 oz garlic, minced
50 g/1¾ oz shallots, minced
3 bird's eye chillies, minced
40 g/1½ oz lemongrass stalks, minced
3 tablespoons Annatto Oil (page 457)
40 g/1½ oz green lemongrass tops, cut into 6-cm/2½-inch lengths, smashed
1 teaspoon Vietnamese curry powder
28 fresh curry leaves
1 kg/2 lb 4 oz chicken, chopped into 5-cm/2-inch chunks with bones and skin on
1 teaspoon salt
10 g/¼ oz (2 teaspoons) Chilli and Lemongrass Oil (page 457)
2 tablespoons sugar
3 tablespoons fish sauce
400 ml/14 oz (1⅔ cups) canned coconut milk
300 ml/10 fl oz (1¼ cups) coconut water
140 g/5 oz onion, peeled and cut into wedges

*To serve*
lime wedges
20 g/¾ oz of picked coriander (cilantro) leaves
cooked rice or rice noodles or Vietnamese Baguette (page 66)

Heat the neutral oil in a pan over a medium heat, add the potato and sweet potatoes in batches and fry for about 6 minutes each until the edges are sealed and brown. Remove the fried potatoes and sweet potatoes and set aside, and reserve 2 tablespoons of the oil.

In a 5-litre/175-oz (5-quart) casserole (or Dutch oven), heat the reserved oil over low heat. Add the garlic, shallots, chillies and minced lemongrass and stir-fry for 2 minutes. Add the annatto oil, smashed lemongrass tops and curry powder and sauté for 4 minutes. Add half the curry leaves and fry for another 1 minute.

Add the chicken and salt. Stir-fry for 5 minutes over medium-low heat, rotating the chicken occasionally. Add the chilli and lemongrass oil, sugar and 2 tablespoons of the fish sauce and cook for 10 more minutes.

Add three-quarters of the coconut milk, along with the fried potatoes and sweet potatoes. Pour in the coconut water and 200 ml/7 fl oz (scant 1 cup) of water. Cook for 20 minutes. Add the onion wedges and remaining fish sauce, then cook for a further 3 minutes. Add the remaining coconut milk and curry leaves.

Serve the curry with lime wedges and coriander (cilantro) as a garnish, alongside rice, noodles or baguettes.

# SNAILS WITH YOUNG BANANA AND TOFU STEW

Ốc Om Chuối Đậu

We learned this recipe from cô Lê Thị Hải Yến during one of her home gatherings, which is why this recipe serves about 15 people. While this northern dish traditionally uses *cơm mẻ* (fermented rice) for seasoning, some families, like cô Yến's, prefer to make it without.

Serves 15
Preparation time: 1 hour
Cooking time: 1 hour 30 minutes

| DF |

3 kg/6 lb 8 oz young bananas
135 ml/4½ fl oz (½ cup plus 1 tablespoon) neutral oil
300 g/10½ oz pork belly (side), thinly sliced
700 g/1 lb 9 oz firm tofu, cut into 4 × 2 × 2-cm/ 1½ × ¾ × ¾-inch cubes
55 g/2 oz chive bulbs (củ nén), crushed
10 g/¼ oz piece fresh turmeric, sliced and crushed
550 g/1 lb 4 oz cooked snail meat (see note)
2 tablespoons fish sauce
540 g/1 lb 3 oz red tomatoes, cut into eighths
2.1 litres/3¾ pints/8¾ cups snail broth (see note)
500 g/1 lb 2 oz pork stock (broth)
40 g/1½ oz Hanoi-style fermented shrimp paste (mắm tôm)
2 teaspoons soup powder (bột canh)
1 teaspoon MSG
200 g/7 oz mixed perilla and piper lolot leaves, thinly sliced

To prepare the young bananas, carefully peel the young bananas, removing all outer skin, then cut into uniform batons about 5 cm/ 2 inches long, similar to large French fries. Immediately submerge the cut pieces in a bowl of cold water. Change the water 3–4 times until the water is clear to remove excess starch, then drain well and set aside.

Heat 1 tablespoon of the oil in a large frying pan or skillet over a medium-high heat. Carefully lay the pork belly (side) slices in the hot oil without overlapping, then fry until crispy on both sides, 7–10 minutes. Remove and drain on paper towels. Set aside.

In the same pan, add the tofu pieces and fry until golden and crispy on all sides, 10–15 minutes. Remove and drain on paper towels. Set aside.

Heat the remaining oil in a large wok or deep pan over a medium heat, add the chive bulbs and turmeric and fry for exactly 2 minutes, stirring constantly until fragrant, being careful not to burn.

Add the snail meat, then pour in 1 tablespoon of the fish sauce. Stir constantly for 30 seconds to evenly coat the snails.

Add the tomato pieces, distributing them evenly, then add the remaining 1 tablespoon of fish sauce and continue stirring for another 30 seconds.

Add the crispy pork belly, mixing gently to combine. Add the prepared banana pieces to the pot, then cook, stirring continuously, for 6 minutes, being vigilant as the bananas tend to stick to the bottom of the pan. Continue cooking for a further 10 minutes, stirring every 2–3 minutes during this time, monitoring the heat to maintain a gentle simmer.

Add the fried tofu pieces, being careful to avoid breaking them, then gently stir everything together to combine. Cook for 5 minutes until the tofu absorbs the flavours.

Pour in the snail broth and pork stock (broth), add the fermented shrimp paste, soup powder and MSG, then stir gently to incorporate all the ingredients. Reduce the heat to low, cover with the lid and simmer for 30 minutes; check occasionally and stir gently to prevent sticking. Remove from the heat, add the perilla and piper lolot leaves, then stir once more to wilt the herbs.

Serve hot.

***Notes:*** To yield the desired quantity of snail meat and broth, boil 3 kg/6 lb 8 oz apple snails with lemongrass and chilli, following the method in Snail Noodle Soup (page 218), then pick the meat and reserve the clear and flavourful broth.

You can add fermented rice to this dish: if using, blend it with the turmeric in a small food processor or mortar until smooth. Add this mixture at the same time as the fermented shrimp paste for traditional Northern-style flavour.

## BRAISED RICE FIELD RAT WITH GINGER

Chuột Nấu Gừng

Found in Vietnamese cuisine from the Mekong Delta to Hà Giang's rice fields, these rats feed on field crops, vegetables, fruits and small insects – distinctly different from their urban counterparts. In Hà Giang, they are simply braised with ginger to balance the meat's gamey flavour, while southern preparations include clay pot roasting and curry.

Serves 2–3
Preparation time: 15 minutes, plus 10–15 minutes marinating time
Cooking time: 15 minutes

| DF | GF | ≤5 |

600 g/1 lb 5 oz field rat meat (about 2 rats), cleaned
1 tablespoon salt
½ teaspoon MSG
2 tablespoons rice wine
3 tablespoons pork fat
110 g/3¾ oz piece fresh ginger (about 22 cm/8½ inches), smashed

Cut the field rats into chunks, similar to portioning a chicken (cut off the legs and backbone and cut the chest if needed).

In a bowl, mix the rat meat with the salt, MSG and rice wine. Marinate for 10–15 minutes.

Heat the pork fat in a large wok over a high heat, add the marinated rat meat and stir-fry for 3 minutes until the liquid evaporates. Add the ginger and stir-fry for 4 minutes. Pour in 240 ml/8 fl oz (1 cup) of water and continue simmering for another 4–6 minutes until the water reduces and the liquid slightly thickens.

Transfer to a serving dish. Serve hot.

## LEMONGRASS FRIED TOFU

Đậu Hũ Chiên Sả

Pair this fried tofu with Stir-fried Aubergine with Fermented Soybean Paste (page 325) for a vegetarian meal, or with rice noodles, herbs and soy sauce for a one-plate dish.

Serves 2
Preparation time: 25 minutes
Cooking time: 20 minutes

| V | VE | DF | GF | ≤5 |

190 g/6¾ oz fresh firm white tofu, cut into 3 pieces
¼ teaspoon salt
80 ml/2½ fl oz (⅓ cup) neutral oil, for frying

*For the marinade*
30 g/1 oz lemongrass
12 g/½ oz peeled garlic
10 g/¼ oz long red chilli (or bird's eye chilli for extra heat), trimmed
¼ teaspoon salt

Rinse the tofu and pat dry. Cut diagonal slits into the tofu pieces to absorb the filling. Sprinkle the salt over the tofu.

To prepare the marinade, finely chop the lemongrass, garlic and chilli together. Add the salt to the chopped mixture and continue chopping until very fine.

Stuff half of the marinade mixture into the slits of the tofu and set aside to marinate for 10 minutes. Reserve the rest of the marinade.

Heat the oil in a small pan over a medium-low heat, then carefully add the marinated tofu pieces; leave the excess marinade on the plate to avoid burning. Fry the tofu for 10 minutes over low heat. Flip the tofu and fry for another 4 minutes, or until golden. Add the reserved marinade to the pan and continue frying for an additional 2–3 minutes until the marinade is cooked and fragrant.

Serve hot.

## STIR-FRIED FROGS' LEGS

Ếch Xào Lăn

Particularly prized during the rainy season when their meat is fattest, frogs' legs have earnt the nickname 'countryside chicken' or 'field chicken' for their plump, white meat. An old Vietnamese saying, *'Nồi đồng nấu ốc, nồi đất nấu ếch'* (Copper pot for snails, clay pot for frogs), hints at their traditional preparation. Here, they're stir-fried with onions and turmeric for a bright yellow colour, though chicken pieces can be substituted if frogs' legs aren't available.

Serves 2–3
Preparation time: 15 minutes, plus 30 minutes marinating time
Cooking time: 10 minutes

| DF |

*For the marinated frog's legs*
1 tablespoon salt
500 g/1 lb 2 oz frog legs (6 pairs of legs)
1 tablespoon fish sauce
1 teaspoon sugar
¼ teaspoon ground turmeric

*For stir-frying*
3 tablespoons pork lard or neutral oil
20 g/¾ oz garlic, coarsely chopped
35 g/1¼ oz red shallots, coarsely chopped
1 teaspoon fish sauce
½ teaspoon sugar
110 g/3¾ oz onion, sliced
12 g/½ oz long red chilli, sliced
5 g/⅛ oz small red chilli, sliced

Fill a bowl with 500 ml/18 fl oz (2 cups) water and add the salt. Add the frogs' legs and marinate for 30 minutes.

Drain the frogs' legs and transfer to a clean bowl. Add the fish sauce, sugar and turmeric and marinate for 15–30 minutes.

In a large frying pan or skillet, heat 2 tablespoons of the pork lard or oil over a medium-high heat, add the garlic and shallots and stir-fry until golden, 2–3 minutes. Add the marinated frog legs and keep stirring to avoid burning the garlic and shallots. Stir-fry for a 1 minute. Add the fish sauce, the remaining pork lard or oil and the sugar. Keep stir-frying over low heat until the frog legs are cooked, 3–4 minutes. Finally, add the onion and both chillies to the pan and cook for another 1 minute.

Serve immediately.

## STEAMED CHICKEN WITH LIME LEAVES

Gà Hấp Lá Chanh

In some areas like Binh Hoa, known for its pomelo orchards, this dish is made with pomelo leaves rather than lime leaves. The subtle fragrance of either leaf complements steamed or boiled chicken without overwhelming it, unlike the stronger flavour of lemongrass which pairs better with grilled chicken. Old Vietnamese cookbooks note that lime leaves were believed to have antiseptic properties which, combined with salt, could help prevent tooth decay. You can eat this dish alongside dishes like Bát Tràng-style Stir-fried Kohlrabi with Squid (page 345), and the leftovers can be used to make Combo Noodle Soup (page 222).

Serves 2–3
Preparation time: 15 minutes
Cooking time: 20 minutes

| DF |

70 g/2½ oz lemongrass, cut into 10-cm/4-inch pieces
4 g lime leaves (about 8 leaves), 3 thinly sliced, to serve
1 teaspoon fish sauce
900 g/2 lb (½ large) yellow chicken, half cut into pieces, half in one piece
100 g/3½ oz chicken offal (variety meats: liver, giblets, hearts), cut into pieces

*For the dipping sauce*
½ teaspoon salt
1 teaspoon black pepper
½ teaspoon sugar
1 lime leaf
1 wedge of lime
2 chillies, sliced

In a large pot, add the lemongrass, whole lime leaves, fish sauce and 200 ml/7 fl oz (scant 1 cup) of water, then place the chicken pieces and chicken offal (variety meats) on top. Place over a medium heat and steam the chicken for 20 minutes, then remove from the heat and let rest, covered, to finish cooking.

To make the dipping sauce, in a small bowl, mix together the salt, pepper, sugar and lime leaf. Add the wedge of lime and sliced chillies to the bowl. Pour 2 tablespoons of the chicken stock (broth) from the steaming pot into the bowl and stir well to create the dipping sauce.

Carefully remove the chicken from the pot and transfer to a chopping (cutting) board. Remove the whole leg, then chop it into 4 pieces. Remove the breast bones, then slice the chicken into 2–3-cm/¾–1¼-inch chunks (or chop with a cleaver), and plate it on a serving plate. Sprinkle the thinly sliced lime leaves over the steamed chicken.

Serve the steamed chicken with the prepared dipping sauce.

# ROASTED CHICKEN LEG

Gà Rô Ti Nước Dừa

Despite its name suggesting 'roasted' chicken (*'rô ti'* from the French *'rôti'*), this dish is traditionally braised until the sauce reduces to a syrup, as Vietnamese households rarely had/have ovens. The term *'rô ti'* is one of many French words absorbed into Vietnamese cooking vocabulary during the colonial period, like *'phô mai'* from *'fromage'* (cheese) or *'xà lách'* from 'salade' (salad).

Serves 1
Preparation time: 10 minutes, plus 30 minutes–1 hour marinating time
Cooking time: 45 minutes

**| DF |**

20 g/¾ oz piece fresh ginger, unpeeled
1 lemongrass stalk (28 g/1 oz)
1¼ teaspoons salt
1 chicken leg (450 g/1 lb)
25 g/1 oz shallots, finely chopped
40 g/1½ oz garlic, finely chopped
1 teaspoon oyster sauce
½ teaspoon sugar
1 teaspoon fish sauce
¼ teaspoon black pepper
240 ml/8 fl oz (1 cup) neutral oil
240 ml/8 fl oz (1 cup) coconut water
1 tablespoon light soy sauce

***To finish***
¼ teaspoon black pepper
5 g/⅛ oz coriander (cilantro)
4 long red chillies, sliced

Bring 700 ml/24 fl oz (scant 3 cups) of water to the boil. Add the ginger, lemongrass and 1 teaspoon of the salt and simmer for 10 minutes.

Meanwhile, use a paring knife to make incisions all over the chicken leg. Place it in a large bowl. Pour the boiling blanching water over the chicken and leave it in the water for 5 minutes. Drain and pat the chicken dry.

In a bowl, mix the chicken with the shallots, garlic, oyster sauce, remaining salt, the sugar, fish sauce and pepper. Let it marinate for 30 minutes–1 hour.

In a 26-cm/10½-inch shallow pan, heat the oil over a medium heat. Add the marinated chicken leg and fry for 3 minutes while basting it. Reserve the empty marinade bowl on the side.

Use a sieve to remove the garlic and shallot bits from the pan, and put them back in the marinade bowl to prevent them from burning. Cook the chicken leg for another 9 minutes, continuing to baste it.

Remove the majority of the oil from the pan, leaving about 1 tablespoon of it in the pan. Return the garlic and shallots and any leftover marinade to the pan, and fry for 1 minute 30 seconds. Add the coconut water and cook for 5 minutes. Add the soy sauce and braise for 17 minutes, continuing to baste the chicken leg, until the sauce has reduced into a beautiful glaze. You should have about 80 ml/2½ fl oz (⅓ cup) of sauce left.

To finish, add the pepper, coriander (cilantro) and sliced chillies.

# CHICKEN RAGOUT

## Lagu Gà

While French in origin, *lagu gà* has become distinctly Vietnamese through the use of annatto oil and coconut water. Some households add milk for creaminess, similar to Italian ragù, and serve it with rice or *bánh mì* (Vietnamese Baguette, page 66).

Serves 6–8
Preparation time: 15 minutes, plus 30 minutes marinating time
Cooking time: 1 hour 45 minutes

| DF |

*For the potatoes*
60 ml/2 fl oz (¼ cup) neutral oil, for frying
3 medium potatoes (485 g/1 lb 1 oz), peeled and cut into 4 pieces

*For the tomato sauce*
3 tablespoons Annatto Oil (page 457)
15 g/½ oz garlic, coarsely chopped
15 g/½ oz shallot, coarsely chopped
400 g/14 oz ripe tomatoes (or 2 tomatoes), blanched and peeled

*For the marinated chicken*
1.4 kg/3 lb 2 oz chicken, bone-in (chicken thighs work well), cut into 10 × 5-cm/4 × 2-inch chunks
1 teaspoon salt
1 tablespoon sugar
2 teaspoons fish sauce
2 teaspoons oyster sauce

*For the ragout*
1 tablespoon neutral oil
1 tablespoon Annatto Oil (page 457)
25–30 g/1 oz shallots, chopped
25 g/1 oz garlic, chopped
500 g/1 lb 2 oz (2 cups) coconut water
240 g/8½ oz (1½ cups) cooked and drained white beans (or fresh white beans)
3 medium carrots (about 630 g/1 lb 6 oz), peeled, cut into 2.5-cm/1-inch rounds and carved into flower shapes (see step 2, page 102)
½ teaspoon salt
1 tablespoon brown sugar
85 g/3 oz onion (about ½ onion), sliced into 4
12 g/½ oz coriander (cilantro), chopped, to garnish

Heat the oil for frying in a pan over a medium heat, add the potatoes and fry for about 5 minutes to seal the edges. Remove from the pan and set aside.

To prepare the tomato sauce, heat the annatto oil in a pan over a medium-low heat, add the garlic and shallot and cook for 1 minute 30 seconds. Add the tomatoes and cook for 8 minutes. Set aside.

To marinate the chicken, combine the chicken with the salt, sugar, fish sauce and oyster sauce. Add the tomato sauce and coat evenly. Marinate for 30 minutes.

To cook the ragout, in a casserole (or Dutch oven), heat the neutral oil and annatto oil, add the shallots and garlic and fry for 2 minutes, or until they turn golden. Add the marinated chicken and stir-fry for 10 minutes. Add the coconut water and 300 ml/10 fl oz (1¼ cups) of water, lower the heat and simmer, covered, for 5 minutes. Add the white beans and carrot flowers, stir gently to incorporate, then simmer for 40 minutes. Add the fried potatoes, salt and brown sugar. Stir well and simmer for another 30 minutes. Add the onion slices on top, simmer for another 1 minute, then remove from the heat.

Garnish with the chopped coriander (cilantro) and serve.

# CHICKEN STEW WITH LOTUS SEEDS

## Gà Hầm Hạt Sen

This nutritious dish begins with the choice of chicken; older hens are preferred as their meat produces a deeper, richer broth. The ingredients that accompany it are valued in traditional Vietnamese food philosophy and TCM (Traditional Chinese Medicine): Chinese apples and jujubes are known for their antioxidant properties, while lotus seeds are believed to strengthen the spleen and kidneys.

Serves 4–5
Preparation time: 15 minutes, plus 15–30 minutes marinating time
Cooking time: 40 minutes

| **DF** |

- 1 tablespoon neutral oil
- 30 g/1 oz shallots, coarsely chopped
- 180 g/6 oz fresh lotus seeds, soaked
- 1 small carrot, peeled and cut into 7 rounds, then carved to make flowers (see step 2, page 102)
- 55 g/2 oz dried Chinese apples (jujubes), soaked
- 1 teaspoon Annatto Oil (page 457), optional
- 500 ml/18 fl oz (2 cups) coconut water, optional
- 20 g/¾ oz (⅔ cup) dried shiitake mushrooms, soaked in water
- ½ teaspoon salt
- 1 teaspoon fish sauce
- coriander (cilantro) leaves, to garnish

*For the marinated chicken*

- 750 g/1 lb 10 oz chicken, cut into 5-cm/2-inch chunks
- 1 tablespoon fish sauce
- 1 teaspoon oyster sauce
- 1 teaspoon light brown sugar
- ½ teaspoon salt

To marinate the chicken, put the chicken in a bowl, then add with the fish sauce, oyster sauce, light brown sugar and salt and let marinate for 15–30 minutes.

In a pot, heat the neutral oil over medium-low heat. Add the shallots and stir-fry for 30 seconds. Add the marinated chicken pieces and stir-fry for 1 minute, then cover with a lid and cook for 2 minutes.

Drain the soaked lotus seeds, then add to the pot with the carved carrot flowers and Chinese apples (jujubes). Stir, cover with the lid and continue cooking for 8 minutes over a medium-low heat to concentrate the meat juices.

Add the annatto oil, then cook for another 8 minutes. (Skip this step if using corn-fed yellow chicken.)

Add 1 litre/1¾ pints (4¼ cups) of water (or a 50:50 mixture of water or coconut water) and simmer for 20 minutes.

Rinse the shiitake mushrooms, squeeze out the water and add the mushrooms to the pot. Continue simmering for another 10 minutes. Season with the salt and fish sauce.

Garnish the stew with some coriander (cilantro).

CHICKEN STEW WITH LOTUS SEEDS

## BRAISED GINGER CHICKEN

### Gà Kho Gừng

Pair this chicken dish with a simple mustard green soup, such as Young Mustard Green Soup (page 366). Boiled gourd slices make excellent dippers for the gingery sauce.

Serves 3–4
Preparation time: 15 minutes
Cooking time: 35 minutes

| DF |

- 2 tablespoons neutral oil
- 30 g/1 oz piece fresh ginger (about 6 cm/2½ inches), cut into 3–5 mm-/⅛–¼-inch-thick matchsticks (julienned)
- 20 g/¾ oz garlic, cut into thin matchsticks (julienned)
- 500 g/1 lb 2 oz chicken, chopped into 4 × 5-cm/1½ × 2-inch chunks
- ¼ teaspoon salt
- 1 tablespoon fish sauce
- 1 tablespoon sugar

*To finish*

- 25 g/1 oz piece fresh ginger, peeled and cut into thin matchsticks (julienned)
- 10 g/¼ oz long red chillies, sliced into rounds
- 30 g/1 oz onion, sliced into wedges

In a wok or shallow pan about 24–25 cm/10 inches in diameter, heat the oil over a medium-low heat, then add the ginger to the pan and stir-fry for 1 minute 30 seconds. Add the garlic and continue to fry until golden, about another 1 minute 30 seconds.

Add the chicken pieces to the pan and sprinkle with the salt. Stir-fry for about 5 minutes. Add the fish sauce and sugar to the pan. Increase the heat to high and cook for another 2 minutes to incorporate the flavours into the chicken. Reduce the heat to low, add 2 tablespoons of water, cover the pan with a lid and let it braise for 20 minutes. You may need to add an extra 1– 2 tablespoons of water if it becomes too dry.

Remove the lid and increase the heat to high to let the sauce reduce and glaze the chicken. Cook until the chicken starts to look golden and caramelized, stirring continuously, about 3 minutes 30 seconds, until the fat separates from the sauce. Remove 4–5 tablespoons of fat from the pan.

To finish the dish, add the ginger and 60 ml/2 fl oz (¼ cup) of water to deglaze the pan. Let it reduce over a medium-low heat for another 1 minute. Add the sliced chillies and stir for another 1 minute. Add the onion wedges.

Serve immediately.

## CHICKEN WITH PICKLED BAMBOO AND MAGNOLIA SEEDS

### Gà Nấu Măng Chua Hạt Dổi

Originally from the Mường communities of Hòa Bình and Phú Thọ provinces, where magnolia seeds grow wild, this dish travelled south with migrating families, including bác Đinh Thị Như Thoa's family. Even today in the Central Highlands, you can find this northern influence through ingredients like these seeds. They are often paired, like here, with poultry.

For this recipe, the weight of the magnolia seeds needs to be 3 g precisely, as they have a very strong flavour.

Serves 4–5
Preparation time: 15 minutes
Cooking time: 40 minutes

| DF |

- 3 g Michelia tonkinensi (also called magnolia seeds; hạt dổi) (8–9 seeds; see note)
- 1 tablespoon neutral oil
- 5 g/⅛ oz shallot, thinly sliced
- 750 g/1 lb 10 oz chicken (about ½ chicken), cut into 5-cm/2-inch chunks
- 1½ teaspoons MSG or soup powder (bột canh)
- 1 teaspoon all-purpose seasoning (hạt nêm)
- 315 g/11 oz pickled bamboo shoots (măng chua)

Heat a small dry pan over a medium heat, add the magnolia seeds and toast for 1 minute, stirring constantly, until fragrant. Remove from the heat immediately and grind to a fine powder using a spice grinder or mortar and pestle. Set aside.

Heat the oil in a large frying pan or skillet over a medium-high heat, add the shallot and stir for 2–3 minutes until fragrant. Add the chicken pieces, ½ teaspoon of the MSG (or soup powder), and all the all-purpose seasoning. Fry for 8 minutes, or until the chicken is just cooked through but not browned. Set aside.

In a large pot, combine the pickled bamboo shoots with 1.2 litres/2 pints (5 cups) of water. Bring to the boil over a high heat, then reduce to simmer for 5 minutes. Add the remaining MSG (or soup powder) and stir well. Add the cooked chicken to the simmering bamboo shoots, cover the pot and simmer over low heat for 20 minutes. Add the ground magnolia seeds, then stir well to combine. Simmer for an additional 2–3 minutes to integrate the flavours.

Serve hot.

CHICKEN WITH PICKLED BAMBOO AND MAGNOLIA SEEDS

## STIR-FRIED CHICKEN WITH LEMONGRASS AND CHILLI

Gà Xào Sả Ớt

You can serve this dish with herb salad (*rau sống*), baby mustard greens and a leafy green soup for a complete meal.

Serves 3–4
Preparation time: 10 minutes, plus 30 minutes marinating time
Cooking time: 25 minutes

| DF |

*For the marinated chicken*
500 g/1 lb 2 oz chicken
1 tablespoon fish sauce
1 teaspoon sugar
¼ teaspoon salt
10 g/¼ oz lemongrass, thinly sliced

*For cooking the chicken*
4 tablespoons neutral oil
45 g/1½ oz garlic, chopped
20 g/¾ oz shallots, chopped
50 g/1¾ oz lemongrass, thinly sliced
1 bird's eye chilli, finely chopped
¼ teaspoon ground turmeric
10 g/¼ oz long red chillies, finely chopped
1 tablespoon light brown sugar
1 tablespoon fish sauce
¼ teaspoon salt

Using a sharp knife, cut the chicken into 5 × 5-cm (2 × 2-inch) chunks.

In a bowl, mix together the chicken with the fish sauce, sugar, salt and lemongrass. Let it marinate for 30 minutes.

Heat the oil in a large wok over a medium heat, add the garlic and shallots and fry for 2 minutes until fragrant. Add the lemongrass and chillies and cook for another 3 minutes. Add the marinated chicken pieces and the turmeric to the wok. Fry for 3 minutes, coating the chicken evenly. Add the sugar, fish sauce and salt. Continue cooking for 5 minutes. Pour in 60 ml/2 fl oz (¼ cup) of water. Let it simmer until the water has reduced, approximately 10 minutes.

If the dish appears too greasy, skim off about three-quarters of the fat from the wok, depending on how fatty your chicken is.

Serve immediately.

## CHICKEN STEW WITH BEANS

Gà Nấu Đậu

A hearty stew that pairs well with noodles, bread or rice. Using coconut water for stewing adds natural sweetness to proteins.

Serves 6–8
Preparation time: 30 minutes, plus 20 minutes marinating time
Cooking time: 1 hour 15 minutes (plus 45 minutes if cooking fresh beans)

| DF |

100 g/3½ oz (1 cup) fresh or (⅔ cup) canned white beans, drained
100 g/3½ oz (1 cup) fresh butter (lima) beans
1 kg/2 lb 4 oz chicken, chopped into pieces
1 tablespoon Annatto Oil (page 457)
1 tablespoon sugar
1 tablespoon fish sauce
½ tablespoon oyster sauce
1 tablespoon neutral oil
40 g/1½ oz shallots, coarsely chopped
270 g/9½ oz jicama, cut into chunks
500 ml/18 fl oz (2 cups) coconut water
200 g/7 oz carrots, peeled and cut into 1.5-cm/2-inch thick flower rounds
200 g/7 oz (1⅓ cups) petit pois (small garden peas)
1 teaspoon salt
17 g/½ oz coriander (cilantro)

If using fresh beans, bring a pan of water to the boil, add the beans and cook them in the water for about 45 minutes until tender. Drain and set aside.

In a bowl, mix the chicken with the annatto oil, sugar, fish sauce and oyster sauce. Let it marinate for at least 20 minutes.

In a large shallow pan, heat the neutral oil over a medium heat, add the shallots and fry for 2–3 minutes until they start to get some colour. Add the marinated chicken and stir-fry for 7 minutes. Add the jicama chunks, coconut water and 900 ml/30 fl oz (3¾ cups) of water to the pan. Bring to a simmer and cook for 15 minutes. Add the carrots, petit pois (small garden peas) and cooked beans (or canned beans, if using) to the pan. Add the salt and continue to simmer for another 45 minutes.

Using a slotted spoon, remove the jicama from the pan and discard. Garnish with coriander (cilantro) before serving.

***Note:*** You can substitute the fresh white and butter (lima) beans with 100 g/3½ oz (½ cup) each of dried beans. The dried beans will need to be soaked in a bowl of water overnight before making this recipe.

## CHICKEN MEATBALLS

### Hò Mọọc Gà

This traditional Black Thai recipe, taught to us by chị Sầm Thảo Trang, appears at every important celebration – from engagements to weddings, and especially as an ancestral offering on Lunar New Year's morning (*sáng mùng 1 Tết*). The meatballs are made entirely by hand, using chicken and its cartilage, and the binder for all of it is pounded sticky (glutinous) rice.

Makes 6; each meatball serves 3–4
Preparation time: 1 hour
Cooking time: 40 minutes

| DF |

- 500 g/1 lb 2 oz banana blossom (bắp chuối)
- 300–320 g/11¼ oz free-range chicken
- 300 g/10½ oz (1⅔ cups) sticky (glutinous) rice
- 85 g/3 oz lemongrass, thinly sliced
- 5 g/⅛ oz bird's eye chilli (about 2 chillies), or to taste, sliced
- 2 teaspoons all-purpose seasoning (hạt nêm)
- 1 teaspoon MSG
- 1 teaspoon soup powder (bột canh)
- ½ teaspoon salt
- 20 g/¾ oz dill

*For wrapping*

- 6 banana leaves, dong leaves or fig leaves (traditional, edible)
- lemongrass stalks, for tying

In salted water, trim the banana blossom and finely shred; you should have 350 g/12 oz. Transfer to a chopping (cutting) board and chop further by hand to ensure it has a fine texture. Set aside.

Carefully debone the chicken, reserving the meat and cartilage. Use a sharp knife to mince the chicken meat and cartilage very fine (it should yield about 220 g/ 7¾ oz chicken flesh). Set aside.

Soak the rice in a bowl of cold water for 40 minutes. Drain well. (The soaked weight of the rice should increase to 355 g/12 oz).

In a large mortar, combine the lemongrass and chillies and drained rice. Pound with a pestle until well combined and paste-like.

In a large bowl, combine the minced chicken with the all-purpose seasoning, MSG, soup powder and salt. Mix vigorously by hand for about 5 minutes until the mixture holds together well.

Lay the banana, dong or fig leaves on a clean work surface. Place one-sixth of the chicken mixture in the centre of a leaf, then wrap loosely and secure with lemongrass ties. Repeat to create 6 equal-size pouches.

Set up a steamer and bring the water to the boil.

Place the wrapped pouches in the steamer basket, set over the boiling water and steam at medium-high heat for 40 minutes. Let cool slightly before serving as a part of a meal.

## STEAMED EGG MEATLOAF WITH SALTED FISH

### Mắm Chưng

Made with the same fermented fish used in Fermented Fish Noodle Soup (page 214), this intensely flavoured loose meatloaf pairs well with plain rice or can be served as a 'dip' with fresh vegetables like cucumber slices and raw winged beans.

Serves 4–6
Preparation time: 20 minutes
Cooking time: 25 minutes

| DF |

- 7 g/¼ oz bird's eye chillies (about 3 chillies), minced
- 20 g/¾ oz garlic, minced
- 15 g/½ oz spring onion (scallion), minced
- 15 g/½ oz shallot, minced
- 200 g/7 oz minced (ground) pork
- 140 g/5 oz fermented Siamese mud carp sauce (*mắm cá linh*)
- 2 teaspoons neutral oil, plus extra for greasing
- ¼ teaspoon black pepper
- 1 teaspoon sugar
- ½ teaspoon fish sauce
- 3 duck eggs
- lemongrass trimmings, chopped, optional

Finely chop the chillies, garlic, spring onion and shallot with the minced (ground) pork and fermented Siamese mud carp sauce until it forms a paste. (You want to chop everything together, so that fermented fish sauce is finely minced and everything is thoroughly mixed together.) Add the oil, pepper, sugar, fish sauce and 1 tablespoon of water to the mixture. Mix thoroughly.

Keeping one egg yolk aside to brush on top, and add the rest of the eggs to the mixture and thoroughly mix.

Set up a steamer and bring the water to the boil. If desired, you can add chopped lemongrass trimmings into the water for a better aroma.

Brush oil into an 18-cm/7-inch mould to prevent sticking. Add the pork and carp mixture to the mould, then place the mould in the steamer basket. Set over the boiling water and steam for 18 minutes.

Brush the reserved egg yolk on top of the steamed mixture. Continue steaming for an additional 5–7 minutes until the egg yolk is set and the dish is fully cooked.

Serve hot.

# NORTHERN-STYLE BRAISED PIG'S TROTTER

Giò Heo Giả Cầy

This dish of pig's trotters (feet) is prepared in a style that traditionally mimicked the taste of dog meat (*cầy*). The term '*giả cầy*' has evolved to represent a specific combination of seasonings – galangal, fermented rice and *mắm tôm* (Hanoi-style fermented shrimp paste) – originally used to reduce gamey flavours. Today, this seasoning style extends beyond pork to other proteins like goose. It is often served in a northern family meal, and we were lucky to learn it from cô Nguyễn Thị Ngọc Bích, whose family also hold one of the oldest moon-cake artisanal bakeries in Hanoi, Bảo Phương. She told us if we didn't have fermented rice, we could replace it with Northern-style rice vinegar (*dấm bỗng*).

Serves 4–6
Preparation time: 30 minutes, plus 30 minutes marinating time
Cooking time: 50 minutes

| DF |

1.1 kg/2 lb 7 oz whole pig's trotters (feet)
30 g/1 oz Vietnamese coriander/cilantro (rau răm), leaves picked
15 g/½ oz spring onion (scallion), finely chopped

*For the marinade*
100 g/3½ oz galangal, minced
35 g/1¼ oz Hanoi-style fermented shrimp paste (mắm tôm)
60 g/2¼ oz fermented rice (cơm mẻ) or fermented rice vinegar (giấm bỗng)
2 teaspoons MSG
2 teaspoons soup powder (bột canh)
1½ tablespoons honey
1 teaspoon ground turmeric

To prepare the pig's trotters (feet), using a blow torch, torch the pig's trotters until the skin is lightly charred and any remaining hair is burned off. Using a heavy cleaver on a sturdy chopping (cutting) board, cut the trotters into 5-cm/2-inch chunks.

To prepare the marinade, in a pot, combine the galangal, shrimp paste, fermented rice or fermented rice vinegar, MSG, soup powder, honey, ground turmeric and 6 tablespoons of water. Mix well until the shrimp paste has dissolved and all the seasonings are combined.

Add the prepared pig's trotters to the marinade, then mix thoroughly using a wooden spoon, ensuring all the pieces are well-coated. Let the mixture marinate at room temperature for 30 minutes.

Place the pot with the marinated meat over a medium-high heat and allow the mixture to come to a bubble (about 2 minutes), stirring well to ensure nothing sticks to the bottom of the pot and making sure all ingredients are evenly distributed. Add 620 ml/22 fl oz (2½ cups) of water to the pot and stir to combine, then return to the boil. Reduce the heat to maintain a gentle simmer, cover the pot with a lid, then let cook for approximately 45 minutes, stirring occasionally, until the meat is tender enough to easily fall off the bone. Remove the lid and check the seasoning: the sauce should be rich and flavourful. Add the Vietnamese coriander/cilantro leaves and spring onion (scallion) and give a final gentle stir.

Transfer to a deep serving bowl and serve hot.

# BRAISED SQUID STUFFED WITH PORK

## Mực Nhồi Thịt Rim Nước Mắm

This dish is a classic Vietnamese meal. Squid tubes are stuffed with mushroom, minced (ground) pork and vermicelli, then fried and quickly braised in a fish sauce glaze. The squid tubes are first quickly blanched to make it easier to stuff them, and they are pierced with a knife to make sure they don't explode during cooking.

Serves 2
Preparation time: 45 minutes
Cooking time: 25 minutes

| DF |

*For the squid*
- 10 g/¼ oz piece fresh ginger
- 10 g/¼ oz lemongrass tops
- 2 squid (total weight 320–350 g/11¼–12 oz), cleaned, tubes and tentacles separated but kept whole
- 60 ml/2 fl oz (¼ cup) lard, chicken fat or oil, for frying

*For the stuffing*
- 15 g/½ oz dried vermicelli rice noodles, soaked in water until soft, then drained and finely chopped
- 5 g/⅛ oz dried wood ear mushroom, soaked in water until soft, then drained
- 10 g/¼ oz shallot, chopped
- 12 g/½ oz spring onion (scallion) whites, chopped
- 4 g garlic, chopped
- 100 g/3½ oz minced (ground) pork
- 1 tablespoon fish sauce
- ½ teaspoon sugar
- ¼ teaspoon ground black pepper

*For the sauce*
- 5 g/⅛ oz spring onion (scallion) whites, chopped
- 10 g/¼ oz garlic, chopped
- 15 g/½ oz Crispy Fried Pork Fat (page 459), optional
- 1 teaspoon sugar
- 1 tablespoon fish sauce
- ½ teaspoon black pepper
- 25 g/1 oz spring onion (scallion) greens, cut into 5-cm/2-inch lengths

In a pot (about 20–25 cm/8–10 inches in diameter), add 300 ml/10 fl oz (1¼ cups) of water, along with the ginger and lemongrass tops. Bring to a rapid boil. Add the squid tentacles and blanch for 15 seconds, then remove. Add the tubes and blanch for 30–40 seconds to firm them up, then remove.

To make the stuffing, in a large bowl, mix together the noodles, mushroom, shallot, spring onion (scallion) whites and garlic with the minced (ground) pork. Add the fish sauce, sugar and pepper.

Make two incisions at the end of a squid so it won't explode, and then stuff with the meat mixture. Cover with a tentacle on top like a lid and use a cocktail stick or toothpick to secure it closed. Repeat with the other squid. If you have any leftover filling, set it aside.

In a 24-cm/9½-inch pan with a lid, heat the lard, chicken fat or oil over a medium heat. When hot, add the two stuffed squids. Sear all the surfaces of the squid; this will take about 10 minutes. Remove half of the oil from the pan and discard.

To make the sauce, in the same pan over a medium heat, add the spring onion whites, garlic and crispy fried pork fat. If you had any leftover filling, you can make it into a meatball and add it to the pan.

In a bowl, mix 2 tablespoons of water with the sugar, fish sauce and pepper.

Remove the aromatics from the pan and reserve. Reduce the heat to low, then add the fish sauce mixture. Cook for another 2 minutes, basting the squid.

Return the aromatics to the pan, cover and cook over a low heat for another 5 minutes. Finish with the spring onion greens.

Serve hot, sliced on a platter if desired.

## BRAISED PORK RIBS WITH PINEAPPLE

### Sườn Kho Thơm

This dish needs a pineapple that's ripe but still firm, balancing sweetness with acidity to create the sauce's sweet and sour profile. In Vietnam, back ribs are cut into smaller, chopstick-friendly pieces that can be eaten easily from bone to bowl.

Serves 3–4
Preparation time: 20 minutes
Cooking time: 55 minutes

| DF |

290 g/10 oz pineapple (½ pineapple), peeled
1 tablespoon neutral oil
25 g/1 oz shallots, chopped
20 g/¾ oz garlic, chopped
500 g/1 lb 2 oz baby back ribs, cut into 4-cm/1½-inch chunks
1 tablespoon fish sauce
10 g/¼ oz (2 teaspoons) Chilli and Lemongrass Oil (page 457)
1 tablespoon sugar
½ teaspoon salt
60 g/2¼ oz onion, sliced

*To finish*
½ long buffalo chilli, deseeded
20 g/¾ oz spring onions (scallions), cut into 4-cm/1½-inch lengths
½ teaspoon black pepper to garnish

Halve the pineapple vertically, remove the core, and slice it into triangles.

In a pan, heat the oil over a medium heat, then add the shallots and garlic and stir-fry for about 3 minutes until they start turning golden. Add the baby back ribs and stir-fry for 2 minutes. Add the fish sauce, chilli and lemongrass oil, sugar and salt, stirring everything together. Pour in 80 ml/2½ fl oz (⅓ cup) of water, cover the pan and let it simmer for 30 minutes.

Add the pineapple slices to the pan and continue cooking for an additional 20 minutes. Add the onion and cook for another 30 seconds–1 minute, then remove from the heat.

Add the deseeded chilli and the spring onions (scallions), sprinkle with the black pepper and serve.

## CRISPY FRIED PORK BABY BACK RIBS

### Sườn Non Chiên Giòn

These crispy ribs can be served as is or coated in various sauces, from sweet and sour to salted egg sauce (see page 92).

Serves 3–4
Preparation time: 30 minutes
Cooking time: 20 minutes

| DF |

500 g/1 lb 2 oz pork spare ribs, cut into 4-cm/1½-inch chunks
¼ teaspoon black pepper
2 teaspoons fish sauce
15 g/½ oz garlic, finely chopped
20 g/¾ oz shallots, finely chopped
10 g/¼ oz spring onion (scallion), finely chopped
50 g/1¾ oz tempura flour or bột chiên giòn (see note)
240 ml/8 fl oz (1 cup) neutral oil, or more if needed

In a bowl, mix the ribs with the pepper, fish sauce, garlic, shallots and spring onion (scallion). Let it marinate for 20 minutes.

Add the tempura flour to the marinated ribs and coat everything evenly.

In a small pan, heat the oil over a medium heat. Make sure the pan is half-filled with oil. Heat to 180°C/350°F. If not using a thermometer, test the oil temperature by inserting wooden chopsticks into the oil – it should bubble vigorously around them. Carefully add the pieces of ribs to the pan. Fry the ribs for about 20 minutes over low heat, until they are golden and crispy. Carefully remove the ribs from the oil and let them drain on paper towels before serving.

***Note:*** You can find bột chiên giòn at Vietnamese markets; or you can use a homemade mix of equal parts cornflour (cornstarch), rice flour and plain (all-purpose) flour, with ¼ teaspoon of salt.

# CARAMELIZED PORK SPARE RIBS

Sườn Ram Mặn

Unlike Braised Pork Ribs With Pineapple (page 296), the flavour profile here is more towards caramel, sweet and salty. The ribs are braised slowly in the coconut water, which thanks to its sugar content reduces and helps to caramelize the meat. I recommend to pair this with Morning Glory Boiled Water (Northern-style) (page 354).

Serves 3–4, to share
Preparation time: 5 minutes, plus 20–30 minutes marinating time
Cooking time: 40 minutes

| DF |

500 g/1 lb 2 oz baby back ribs, cut into bite-size 3-cm/1¼-inch pieces
2 tablespoons neutral oil
30 g/1 oz garlic, finely chopped
50 g/1¾ oz shallots, finely chopped
1 tablespoon sugar
4 teaspoons fish sauce
200 ml/7 fl oz (scant 1 cup) coconut water
20 g/3/4 oz chilli slices
100 g/3½ oz onion, sliced
1 teaspoon black pepper

*For the rib marinade*
1 tablespoon fish sauce
¼ teaspoon salt
1 teaspoon sugar

In a bowl, mix the baby back ribs with the marinade ingredients. Let it sit for 20–30 minutes.

In a large frying pan or skillet, heat the oil over a medium-low heat, add the garlic and shallots to the pan and fry until golden, 4–5 minutes. When three-quarters of the garlic and shallots are golden, add the marinated ribs to the pan. Add the sugar and 3 teaspoons of the fish sauce. Cook for an additional 12 minutes, until the sugar caramelizes and the meat looks coated in caramel.

Add the coconut water and simmer over low heat until it reduces, about 10 minutes. Add half of the chillies and continue to cook for another 10 minutes. Add the onion and the remaining fish sauce and cook for an additional 2 minutes.

Sprinkle with the black pepper and garnish with the remaining chilli slices. Serve immediately.

# TAMARIND GLAZED PORK RIBS

Sườn Xào Sốt Me

Vinegar can be used as a substitute for tamarind paste in this sweet and sour sauce.

Serves 2–3
Preparation time: 15 minutes
Cooking time: 45 minutes

| DF |

400 g/14 oz baby back ribs, washed and cut into 3–4-cm/1¼–1½-inch pieces
¼ teaspoon salt
80 ml/2½ fl oz (⅓ cup) neutral oil, or more if needed, for frying
240 ml/8 fl oz (1 cup) coconut water
1 tablespoon calamansi juice
1 teaspoon sugar
1 tablespoon fish sauce
fresh herbs, to garnish, optional

*For the tamarind sauce*
40 g/1½ oz garlic, chopped
25 g/1 oz shallots, chopped
2 tablespoons neutral oil
35 g/1¼ oz tamarind paste
120 ml/4 fl oz (½ cup) coconut water
1 teaspoon sugar
1 teaspoon fish sauce
¼ teaspoon salt

Sprinkle the baby back rib with the salt.

In a wok or large pan, heat the oil over a medium-high heat (make sure a third of the pan is filled with oil). Carefully add the ribs and fry for about 10 minutes until just cooked. Remove and set aside. Strain and reserve the oil.

To braise the ribs, add the coconut water to the same pan and cook for a few minutes to deglaze the pan. Add the calamansi juice, sugar and fish sauce. Bring to a simmer.

Return the fried ribs to the pan, then cover and simmer for 10 minutes. Add 1 teaspoon each of the chopped garlic and shallots from the tamarind sauce ingredients. Uncover and simmer for another 15 minutes, or until the liquid has completely reduced and the oil becomes clear. Remove from the heat.

To prepare the tamarind sauce, in a small pan, heat the oil over a medium heat, add the remaining chopped garlic and shallots and fry for 1–2 minutes until golden. Add the tamarind paste, coconut water, sugar, fish sauce and salt. Simmer for 1 minute.

To finish the dish, add the tamarind sauce to the wok with the ribs. Return the wok to high heat and fry for another 4 minutes, or until the ribs are golden.

Serve hot, garnished with fresh herbs, if desired.

# SAUTÉED PORK BELLY

## Thịt Ba Rọi Áp Chảo

This pork belly (side) can be eaten as a part of a family meal alongside a vegetable and a broth, or it can be served with Broken Rice (page 270).

Serves 4–6
Preparation time: 15–20 minutes, plus 1 day marinating time
Cooking time: 8–10 minutes

| DF |

- 11 g/¼ oz peeled garlic
- 20 g/¾ oz peeled shallots
- 400 g/14 oz pork belly (side), cut into 4-cm/1½-inch wide strips
- ¼ teaspoon Vietnamese five-spice powder (ngũ vị hương)
- ¼ teaspoon black pepper
- ½ teaspoon salt
- 2 teaspoons light soy sauce
- ½ teaspoon honey
- ½ tablespoon light brown sugar
- 240 ml/8 fl oz (1 cup) neutral oil, for frying

Put the garlic and shallots in a mortar and pound with a pestle to create a liquid marinade.

Add the liquid marinade to the pork belly (side) strips and ensure they are coated evenly. Add the rest of the ingredients, except the oil, and marinate for at least 1 day,

In a wok or pan, heat the oil, or enough oil to half-fill the pan, to about 160°C/320°F. If not using a thermometer, test the oil temperature by inserting wooden chopsticks into the oil – it should gently bubble around them.

Carefully add the marinated pork belly to the heated oil. (Use an oil splatter screen as the pork belly may cause the oil to splatter due to its fat and water content.) Fry for about 6 minutes until the pork is fully cooked.

If desired, fry the pork belly for 2 minutes longer to make it crispy. Alternatively, remove it from the heat and let it rest while you get the rest of your meal ready, then fry the pork belly again for 2 minutes on each side just before serving.

# PAN-SEARED PORK BELLY WITH CHILLI AND LEMONGRASS OIL

## Thịt Ba Rọi Áp Chảo Sa Tế

The key to this dish is slowly frying the pork belly until the edges caramelize while keeping the meat tender inside, being careful not to burn the aromatics. This dish pairs perfectly with Broken Rice (page 270) or it can be served on its own alongside stir-fried vegetables, like Stir-fried Winged Beans with Garlic (page 328) or Pickled Mustard Greens (page 467).

Serves 4–5
Preparation time: 15 minutes, plus 15–30 minutes marinating time
Cooking time: 30–35 minutes

| DF |

- 750 g/1 lb 10 oz pork belly (side), cut into 5-cm/2-inch-thick slices
- 15 g/½ oz garlic, finely chopped
- 25 g/1 oz shallots, finely chopped
- 2 tablespoons fish sauce
- ¼ teaspoon black pepper
- ¼ teaspoon salt
- 2 teaspoons Chilli and Lemongrass Oil (page 457)
- 240 ml/8 fl oz (1 cup) neutral oil, for frying
- pickles, to serve

In a bowl, mix the pork belly (side) with the garlic, shallots, fish sauce, pepper, salt and chilli and lemongrass oil and let marinate for 15–30 minutes.

In a wok, heat the neutral oil over a medium heat. Carefully add the marinated pork belly pieces to the wok. (Use an oil splatter screen as the pork belly may cause the oil to splatter due to its fat and water content.) Lower the heat immediately.

Fry the pork belly for 30–35 minutes over a low heat, turning occasionally until the exterior is crispy and golden brown. To check if the pork is cooked, pierce the meat with a chopstick, the juices should run clear.

Once the pork belly is cooked, remove it from the wok and let it rest on paper towels to drain excess oil.

Slice the pork belly and serve with the pickles.

# POACHED PORK BELLY WITH SHRIMP PASTE

## Thịt Heo Luộc và Mắm Tôm

The success of this simple dish depends on choosing good pork belly (side). In the north, it's paired with *mắm tôm* (Hanoi-style fermented shrimp paste), while in Huế you might find it with *tôm chua* (fermented/pickled whole shrimp), but all follow the same principle of pairing subtle meat with strong fermented flavours. It's an easy dish to prepare since most Vietnamese households keep fermented shrimp paste on hand. It's usually served with Salted Small White Aubergine (page 466), but you can serve it with any pickles or ferments available.

Serves 2
Preparation time: 5 minutes
Cooking time: 30 minutes

| DF | ≤5 |

300 ml/10 fl oz (1¼ cups) coconut water (this is more southern style)
1 teaspoon fish sauce
300 g/10½ oz pork belly (side)

*To serve*
Hanoi-style fermented shrimp paste (mắm tôm)
50 g/1¾ oz Salted Small White Aubergines (page 466)
basil and perilla leaves, optional

In a small pot, bring the coconut water and fish sauce to a simmer. Add the pork belly (side), cover and let steam to cook for 30 minutes, or until the meat is fully cooked but not mushy. Remove the pork belly from the pot and let it cool slightly. Slice the pork belly into thin pieces.

Serve with Hanoi-style fermented shrimp paste and salted small white aubergines (eggplants) on the side. Add some basil and perilla for extra flavour, if desired.

# BRAISED ROASTED PORK BELLY WITH PICKLED MUSTARD GREENS

## Thịt Heo Quay Kho Dưa Cải

A great way to use leftover Roasted Pork Belly (page 161) is by braising it with Pickled Mustard Greens (page 467), an ingredient always present in Vietnamese households. Some families make their own pickles and preserves, especially during celebratory periods, but you can also find large jars of pickled mustard greens at vendor stalls in wet markets, which every district has.

Serves 4
Preparation time: 15 minutes
Cooking time: 20 minutes

| DF |

2 tablespoons plus 1 teaspoon neutral oil
40 g/1½ oz garlic, coarsely chopped
15 g/½ oz shallot, coarsely chopped
500 g/1 lb 2 oz Roasted Pork Belly (page 161), cut into 8 × 2 × 2-cm/3¼ × ¾ × ¾-inch cubes
1 tablespoon plus 1 teaspoon light soy sauce
2 teaspoons light brown sugar
430 g/15 oz Pickled Mustard Greens (page 467), rinsed and sliced 1.5 cm/⅝ inch thick
¼ teaspoon salt
1 teaspoon pork lard
45 g/1½ oz spring onions (scallions), cut into 3-cm/1¼-inch lengths
½ teaspoon black pepper

In a large pan that can accommodate everything, heat the oil over a medium heat, add the garlic and shallot and stir-fry together for 5 minutes, or until they start to get golden. Add the pork belly (side), 1 tablespoon of the soy sauce and 1 teaspoon of the sugar. Fry for 2 minutes, then remove from the heat and transfer to a bowl. Set aside.

In the same pan, over a high heat, stir-fry the pickled mustard greens for 2–4 minutes. Add the remaining sugar, the salt and the pork lard. Fry for 1 minute on high heat. Return the pork belly to the pan and continue stir-frying for 5 minutes. Finish with the remaining soy sauce, stir, then remove from the heat.

Sprinkle the spring onions (scallions) on top of the meat, then sprinkle with the pepper and serve.

## BRAISED PORK BELLY WITH COCONUT

Thịt Kho Dừa

While braised pork belly is a Vietnamese staple, this version incorporates coconut flesh and coconut water in the braising liquid. Other regional variations might use daikon or *quả trám đen* (black canarium) or *trái sung* (cluster fig).

Serves 4
Preparation time: 30 minutes
Cooking time: 1 hour 5 minutes

| DF |

- 2 old coconuts
- 500 g/1 lb 2 oz pork belly (side), cut into 1.5 × 1.5 × 6 cm/⅝ × ⅝ × 2½-inch pieces
- 2 tablespoons fish sauce
- ¾ teaspoon salt
- 2 teaspoons sugar
- 15 g/½ oz garlic, finely chopped
- 17 g/½ oz shallots, finely chopped
- 10 g/¼ oz red chilli (about ½ chilli), deseeded and finely chopped

Carefully cut open the coconuts to extract the water (you will need 620 ml/21 fl oz/2½ cups), then split them in half and scoop out the meat. The older the coconut, the sweeter the juice and the thicker the coconut meat will be. Slice 240 g/8½ oz of the coconut meat into 1-cm/½-inch-thick pieces.

Put the pork belly pieces in a pan with the fish sauce, ¼ teaspoon of the salt and 1 teaspoon of the sugar. Simmer over a low heat for about 15 minutes until the colour starts becoming amber. Add 500 ml/18 fl oz (2 cups) of the coconut water and continue simmering for another 15 minutes. Add the sliced coconut meat and the garlic, shallots and chilli to the pan. Continue simmering for another 25 minutes until the mixture is glazed and the pork is fully coated.

Add the remaining sugar and the remaining salt, stir well. Add another 120 ml/4 fl oz (½ cup) of coconut water and continue to simmer for an additional 8 minutes; the finished dish should still be saucy. You can cook further if you prefer a thicker consistency.

## BRAISED PORK BELLY IN FERMENTED SHRIMP PASTE

Thịt Kho Mắm Ruốc

Although this traditional Huế dish is considered a 'poor person's' dish, it is an extremely comforting and popular Vietnamese meal. Because of its strong flavour, you need only very little to accompany your rice. During times of hardship, where meat was expensive, a little bowl of this could go a long way. This dish should be served alongside fresh cucumber slices, blanched cabbage leaves or raw winged beans. While I use pork belly (side), it can also be made with minced pork instead.

Serve 4–6
Preparation time: 45 minutes
Cooking time: 40 minutes

| DF |

- 440 g/15½ oz pork belly (side)
- 1 tablespoon fish sauce
- 30 g/1 oz garlic, finely minced
- 25 g/1 oz shallots, finely minced
- 35 g/1¼ oz lemongrass, finely minced
- 1 bird's eye chilli, or more depending on your preference, finely minced
- 10 g/¼ oz long red chillies, finely minced
- 120 ml/4 fl oz (½ cup) neutral oil
- 100 g/3½ oz Hue-style fermented shrimp paste (mắm ruốc)
- ½ teaspoon Chilli and Lemongrass Oil (page 457)
- 35 g/1¼ oz (2½ tablespoons packed) light brown sugar

Clean the pork belly (side) by pouring boiling water on it. Dice the pork belly into 1-cm/½-inch matchsticks (julienne).

In a bowl, mix the pork belly with the fish sauce, then set aside to marinate.

In another bowl, mix together the garlic, shallots, lemongrass and chillies. Reserve 2 tablespoons of this mixture to finish the dish.

Heat the neutral oil in a large pan over a medium–low heat. Add the rest of the aromatic mixture and fry for 4–5 minutes, until the lemongrass and garlic start changing colour. Add the marinated pork and continue frying for 10 minutes, or until the fat renders.

Meanwhile, mix the shrimp paste with 100 ml/3½ fl oz (scant ⅓ cup) of water, the chilli and lemongrass oil and brown sugar.

Turn down the heat under the pork to low, then add the shrimp paste mixture and continue to cook for about 20 minutes until the meat starts to caramelize and look sticky and has a nice, glazed feel to it. Add the reserved 2 tablespoons of the aromatic mixture to the pan and cook for another 5 minutes.

Serve hot.

# BRAISED PORK BELLY WITH EGGS

## Thịt Kho Trứng

This dish is essential during Lunar New Year, when cooking traditionally stops for several days. It can be reheated multiple times, becoming more tender with each warming – leading to its nickname '*thịt heo kho rệu*' (over-tender braised pork) in southwestern Vietnam. Traditionally, especially in countryside neighbourhoods, families would fatten a pig for the holidays and share it among themselves for various dishes including this one. As pigs symbolize fertility and prosperity, this dish often appears among offerings to ancestors and gods. The recipe here uses a homemade caramel to lend its dark colour; in other regions, some would omit it, and some would add pounded long red chillies to the marinade to give it a red-hued colour.

Serves 4–5
Preparation time: 15 minutes, plus 15–30 minutes marinating time
Cooking time: 2 hours 10 minutes

| DF |

- 400 g/14 oz pork belly (side), cut into 3 × 3 × 4-cm/1¼ × 1¼ × 1½-inch pieces, blanched (see step 1, page 192)
- 25 g/1 oz garlic, coarsely chopped
- 30 g/1 oz shallots, coarsely chopped
- 2 tablespoons fish sauce
- 1 teaspoon salt
- 1 teaspoon Caramel Braising Sauce (page 456) or 1 tablespoon sugar plus 1 tablespoon neutral oil
- 500 ml/18 fl oz (2 cups) coconut water
- 120 ml/4 fl oz (½ cup) neutral oil, optional
- 6 duck eggs (or chicken eggs), boiled and peeled
- 1 teaspoon sugar

*For the seasoned pickled mustard greens*

- 100 g/3½ oz Pickled Mustard Greens (page 467)
- 28 g/1 oz garlic, finely chopped
- 10 g/¼ oz long red chillies, deseeded and finely chopped
- 2 teaspoons fish sauce
- 1 teaspoon lime juice
- 1 teaspoon brown sugar

*To serve*

- 12 g/½ oz spring onion (scallion), chopped
- 13 g/½ oz chilli (about 1), sliced
- ¼ teaspoon black pepper
- 100 g/3½ oz Pickled Daikon and Carrots (page 468) or Pickled Bean Sprouts (page 468)

In a bowl, combine the blanched pork belly (side) with the garlic, shallots, 1 tablespoon of the fish sauce and salt and caramel braising sauce, if using (see the next step if using the sugar and oil). Mix well. Marinate the pork belly for 15–30 minutes.

If not using the caramel braising sauce in the marinade, in a pot that will fit everything, melt the 1 tablespoon of sugar in the 1 tablespoon of oil over a medium heat, without stirring but swirling the pan every now and then, until it is past the amber-coloured caramel stage but just before it burns: you want it to be a very dark brown colour.

Add the marinated pork belly to the pot and stir until each piece is coated with the caramel. Cook for 3 minutes.

Fill the bowl used for marinating the pork belly with the coconut water, swirl it around to rinse, then add it to the pot. Add 350 ml/12 fl oz (1½ cups) of water to the pot and cover with a lid. Cook over a low heat for 1 hour, allowing the pork belly to slowly braise.

Meanwhile, if desired, heat the 120 ml/4 fl oz (½ cup) of oil in a small pan, add the boiled duck eggs and fry for 5 minutes, or until they turn golden. (You can skip this step, but frying the boiled eggs before adding them to the braising pork belly will make them hold their shape for longer.)

Use a chopstick or skewer to pierce a small hole in the middle of each egg. (This will allow the eggs to absorb the braising liquid better.) Add the fried or boiled eggs to the pot of braised pork belly. Add the remaining 1 tablespoon of the fish sauce and the 1 teaspoon of sugar to the pot, and continue cooking with the lid on for an additional 1 hour.

While the pork is cooking, season the preserved mustard greens by combining them in a bowl with the garlic, long red chillies, fish sauce, lime juice and brown sugar. Mix well and set aside.

Once the pork is thoroughly cooked and tender, garnish with the chopped spring onion (scallion), chilli slices and pepper.

Serve hot with the seasoned preserved mustard greens and pickled daikon and carrots or pickled bean sprouts on the side.

## BRAISED PORK BELLY WITH PICKLED BAMBOO SHOOTS

Thịt Kho Măng Chua

Pickled Dragon Bamboo Shoots (page 470) are a staple fermented dish. However, if they aren't available, Pickled Mustard Greens (page 467) make an excellent substitute.

Serves 3–4
Preparation time: 10 minutes, plus 20–30 minutes marinating time1
Cooking time: 1 hour 25 minutes

| DF |

- 350 g/12 oz pork belly (side)
- 3 tablespoons fish sauce
- 2 teaspoons sugar
- 8 g/¼ oz (½ tablespoon) Chilli and Lemongrass Oil (page 457)
- 1 tablespoon neutral oil
- 10 g/¼ oz spring onion whites, cut into 3-cm/1¼-inch lengths
- 10 g/¼ oz peeled garlic
- 10 g/¼ oz peeled shallot
- 10 g/¼ oz long red chilli, coarsely chopped, plus extra, sliced on an angle, to serve
- ¼ teaspoon salt
- 280 g/10 oz Pickled Dragon Bamboo Shoots (page 470)
- 12 g/½ oz palm sugar
- ¼ teaspoon black pepper
- 30 g/1 oz spring onions (scallions), coarsely chopped into about 1-cm/½-inch pieces

Clean the pork belly (side) by pouring boiling water on it. Slice the pork belly into 1.5-cm/¾-inch-thick pieces.

In a bowl, mix the pork belly with 1 tablespoon of the fish sauce, 1 teaspoon of the sugar and the chilli and lemongrass oil, then leave to marinate, covered, for 20–30 minutes.

In a shallow pot, heat the neutral oil over a medium–low heat, add the spring onion (scallion) whites, garlic, shallot and chopped chillies and fry for about 1 minute 30 seconds–2 minutes until they start to brown. Add the marinated pork belly, increase the heat, keep stirring and add the salt. Continue cooking until the meat firms up and starts to colour, about 2 minutes. Lower the heat and continue cooking for another 20 minutes, or until the meat becomes sticky and has a nice red colour. Add 300 ml/10 fl oz (1¼ cups) of water to the pot and cook for a further 50 minutes.

Add the pickled bamboo shoots, the remaining fish sauce and the remaining sugar, the palm sugar and pepper. Cook for another 10 minutes, then add half of the chopped spring onions (scallions) and mix. Remove from the heat.

Garnish with the remaining spring onion and chilli slices before serving.

## BRAISED PORK BELLY WITH BLACK PEPPER

Thịt Kho Tiêu

For this braised pork belly (side), I start by poaching the meat – the leftover stock (broth) makes an excellent base for *canh* (broth) with whatever vegetables are on hand. This initial poaching also ensures the meat becomes melt-in-your-mouth tender during braising. Since the dish keeps well, I often make large batches for the freezer. I recommend using Vietnamese black pepper from Phú Quốc or Buôn Ma Thuột for its fragrance.

Serves 6–8
Preparation time: 15 minutes, plus 15 minutes marinating time
Cooking time: 45 minutes

| DF |

- 5 tablespoons fish sauce
- 15 g/½ oz peeled shallot
- 1.175 kg/2 lb 9 oz pork belly (side)
- 2 tablespoons sugar

*For braising the pork*

- 1 tablespoon neutral oil
- 3 tablespoons Caramel Braising Sauce (page 456)
- 3 tablespoons fish sauce
- 3 tablespoons ground black pepper (or more if desired)
- 40 g/1½ oz spring onions (scallions), finely chopped, to garnish

Mix 1.2 litres/2 pints (5 cups) of water with 1 tablespoon of the fish sauce and the whole shallot in a pan. Bring to the boil, then add the pork and simmer for 20 minutes. Drain, reserving 3 tablespoons of the cooking liquid, and set aside to slightly cool. When cool enough to handle, cut the pork belly into pieces measuring approximately 2 × 4 × 1 cm/¾ × 1½ × ½ inches.

In a large bowl, mix the pork with the remaining fish sauce and the sugar, then let marinate for 15 minutes.

To braise the pork, in a pot, heat the oil over a medium heat, add the marinated pork and stir-fry for 5–10 minutes. Add the caramel braising sauce and cook for 2–3 minutes. Add the reserved cooking liquid and fish sauce, then lower the heat, and cover the pot. Let it cook for 15 minutes.

Add the pepper. Adjust the seasoning with more fish sauce and black pepper as needed. Add the spring onions (scallions), then serve.

# PORK MEATBALLS WITH TOMATO SAUCE

## Xíu Mại

This is a very versatile dish: stuff it in *bánh mì* for breakfast, serve with rice noodles as a lunch or make it one of the mains for a family meal. In Đà Lạt these meatballs are served alongside *bánh căn*, a mini rice pancake cooked over charcoals.

Makes 30 meatballs
Preparation time: 30 minutes
Cooking time: 25 minutes

| **DF** |

*For the meatballs*
600 g/1 lb 5 oz pork, minced
200 g/7 oz Pork Paste (page 461) (for extra bounce, you can substitute with regular minced/ground meat)
60 g/2¼ oz onion, coarsely chopped
40 g/1½ oz shallots, chopped
40 g/1½ oz breadcrumbs
4 teaspoons Annatto Oil (page 457)
4 teaspoons fish sauce
1 teaspoon sugar
½ teaspoon black pepper

*For the tomato sauce*
390 g/13¾ oz tomatoes (about 4 medium), cut into coarse chunks
½ teaspoon salt
1½ teaspoons sugar
2 tablespoons neutral oil
1½ teaspoons Annatto Oil (page 457)
25 g/1 oz shallots, coarsely chopped
20 g/¾ oz garlic, coarsely chopped
70–90 ml/2½–3 fl oz (5–6 tablespoons) cooking liquid from the steamed meatballs (see above)
2 teaspoons tapioca flour (starch)
90 g/3¼ oz onion, sliced into rings
5 g/⅛ oz coriander (cilantro), to garnish

Set up a steamer and bring the water to the boil.

Mix all the meatball ingredients together in a large bowl. Form the mixture into 30 balls (6–8 g/¼ oz each).

Working in batches if needed, place the meatballs on a flameproof plate, then place in the steamer basket, setting it over the boiling water, and steam for 20 minutes.

Meanwhile, make the tomato sauce. Mix the tomatoes with the salt and sugar in a bowl.

Heat both oils in a large pan over a medium-low heat, add the shallots and garlic and fry for 3 minutes. Add the tomato mixture and stir over a medium heat for 10 minutes.

In a small bowl, mix the cooking liquid from the meatball plate with the tapioca flour (starch), then add to the tomato sauce.

Add the meatballs to the pan, then cook for 1–2 minutes until they absorb the sauce. Add the onion, cover and simmer for 1 minute.

Garnish with coriander (cilantro) before serving.

# FISH SAUCE GLAZED PORK BELLY

## Thịt Rang Cháy Cạnh

This Northern dish's name translates to 'meat with burned edges', referring to the golden crust that forms when frying the pork belly (side). The key lies in blanching the meat first and letting it cool – this removes excess moisture from the raw meat that would otherwise prevent proper browning during stir-frying.

Serves 3–4
Preparation time: 20 minutes
Cooking time: 15 minutes

**| DF | GF |**

- 1 teaspoon salt
- 2 slices of fresh ginger
- 400 g/14 oz pork belly (side), thinly sliced (3 cm/1¼ inches wide, 5 mm–1 cm/¼–½ inch thick)
- 2 tablespoons pork fat
- 1 tablespoon fish sauce
- ½ teaspoon MSG
- ¼ teaspoon Caramel Braising Sauce (page 456)
- 30 g/1 oz spring onions (scallions), cut into 2–3-cm/1-inch lengths

Bring 2 litres/3½ pints (8½ cups) of water to the boil in a large pot. Add the salt and ginger to the pot, then add the pork belly (side) and blanch for 2–3 minutes until its colour changes. Drain in a colander and rinse under cold water. Pat dry thoroughly with paper towels.

Heat a wok over a medium-high heat, add the pork fat and heat until hot but not smoking. Add the blanched pork slices in a single layer, then stir-fry continuously for 3 minutes, allowing the edges to burn a bit. Add the fish sauce, MSG and the caramel braising sauce, then continue stir-frying for 5 minutes until the edges of the pork are crispy. Add the spring onions (scallions) and stir-fry for 30 seconds until fragrant.

Transfer to serving plate and serve hot.

# FRIED STUFFED TOFU WITH TOMATO SAUCE

## Đậu Hũ Nhồi Thịt

This recipe stuffs meat into tofu, but the same filling can be used for *cà chua nhồi thịt* (stuffed tomatoes): simply cut off the tops of the tomatoes, hollow out the centres with a spoon, and trim the bottoms to help them stand. Fill with the same stuffing, pan-sear meat-side down first, then fry the tomatoes before braising them in the sauce as shown here.

Serves 3–4
Preparation time: 20 minutes, plus 15 minutes soaking time
Cooking time: 30 minutes

| DF |

450 g/1 lb tofu, or 2 medium blocks of tofu
120 ml/4 fl oz (½ cup) neutral oil, for frying
coriander (cilantro), leaves picked, to garnish

*For the stuffing*
20 g/¾ oz dried wood ear mushroom
35 g/1¼ oz shallots, minced
15 g/½ oz garlic, chopped
100 g/3½ oz minced (ground) pork
¼ teaspoon black pepper
1 teaspoon fish sauce
1 teaspoon sugar
¼ teaspoon salt

*For the sauce*
1 tablespoon Annatto Oil (page 457)
17 g/½ oz garlic, finely chopped
25 g/1 oz shallots, finely chopped
300 g/10½ oz tomatoes or 2 medium tomatoes, finely diced
2 teaspoons fish sauce
2 teaspoons sugar
2 tablespoons coconut water
20 g/¾ oz onion, sliced into rings
1 tablespoon soy sauce, or to taste

First, prepare the mushrooms for the stuffing. Soak the dried wood ear mushrooms in a bowl of warm water for 15 minutes, or until fully softened and expanded. Rinse thoroughly under cold running water, then mince finely using a sharp knife.

Meanwhile, cut each block of tofu horizontally into two even pieces (or if you have one large block, cut into 4 slices) and thoroughly pat dry with paper towels.

Heat the neutral oil in a large frying pan or skillet over a medium-high heat until shimmering (around 175°C/345°F). If not using a thermometer, test the oil temperature by inserting wooden chopsticks into the oil – it should bubble vigorously around them. Carefully slide the whole tofu pieces into the hot oil and fry until they turn light golden, 3–4 minutes per side. Carefully remove the tofu using a slotted spoon, then drain on paper towels and let cool until comfortable to handle. Set aside the tofu pan and the oil for reheating the tofu later on.

To make the stuffing, in a mixing bowl, thoroughly combine the shallots, garlic, minced (ground) pork, minced wood ear mushrooms, pepper, fish sauce, sugar and salt until everything is evenly distributed.

Carefully make a horizontal slit partway through the fried tofu pieces and stuff a portion of the meat mixture (2–3 tablespoons) into the slits.

Reheat the tofu pan over medium heat, then return the stuffed tofu pieces to the oil and fry for 15 minutes, turning once halfway through, until the outside is golden brown and crispy and the stuffing is cooked through.

To make the sauce, in a saucepan, heat the annatto oil over a medium heat until shimmering. Add the garlic and shallots, cooking until fragrant and softened but not browned, 1–2 minutes. Add the tomatoes, fish sauce, sugar and coconut water, stirring to combine. Carefully place the fried stuffed tofu into the sauce and simmer gently for 10 minutes, occasionally spooning the sauce over the tofu and adding the onion rings 2 minutes before the end of the cooking time. Taste and adjust the seasoning by adding the soy sauce if needed.

To serve, transfer the tofu pieces to serving plates, spoon generous amounts of the sauce over the top, garnish with coriander (cilantro) and serve immediately.

# CARAMELIZED SHRIMP IN COCONUT MILK

## Tép Rang Dừa

In Vietnam, this dish traditionally uses small shrimp, often cooked unpeeled as their shells are quite thin. The shells help prevent the meat from drying out during caramelization. If using peeled shrimp, reduce the cooking time by 5 minutes to avoid the meat becoming too chewy.

Serves 2–3
Preparation time: 10 minutes
Cooking time: 25–30 minutes

| DF |

- 160 g/5½ oz fresh greasyback shrimp, trimmed (or any shrimp you have to hand: the smaller the better)
- ¼ teaspoon salt
- ½ teaspoon sugar
- 1 tablespoon neutral oil
- 6 g/⅛ oz shallot or spring onion (scallion) whites, finely chopped
- 12 g/½ oz garlic, minced
- 1 teaspoon fish sauce
- 1 teaspoon Annatto Oil (page 457)
- 80 g/2¾ oz (1/3 cup) coconut milk
- Coconut Rice from Bến Tre Province (page 258), to serve, optional

In a bowl, mix the shrimp with the salt and sugar. Set aside.

Heat the neutral oil in a pan over a medium heat, add the shallot (or spring onion/scallion whites) and garlic. Stir-fry for about 1 minute until fragrant. Add the seasoned shrimp to the pan and stir-fry for 1–2 minutes.

Drizzle the fish sauce and annatto oil over the shrimp, stirring to coat evenly. Pour in the coconut milk and reduce the heat to medium-low. Simmer, while continuously stirring, for about 20–25 minutes, until the coconut milk has reduced to coat the shrimp, then starts to split and caramelize around the shrimp.

Serve hot, preferably with coconut rice.

# CARAMELIZED PRAWNS

## Tôm Rim

This quickly simmered prawns (shrimp) is different from braised prawns in that this is quicker to prepare and does not involve marinating the prawns beforehand. You can also make *tôm kho*, which is prepared similarly to Braised Pork Belly with Black Pepper (page 304), where it is braised it for longer and black pepper is added.

Serves 2–3
Preparation time: 15 minutes
Cooking time: 5–6 minutes

| DF | ≤30 |

- 14 whole prawns (shrimp) (260 g/9 oz)
- 2 tablespoons neutral oil
- 20 g/¾ oz garlic, crushed and minced
- 10 g/¼ oz shallot, crushed and minced
- 1½ tablespoons fish sauce
- ¾ tablespoon sugar
- ¼ teaspoon Caramel Braising Sauce (page 456)
- 10 g/¼ oz spring onion (scallion), sliced
- ¼ teaspoon black pepper

Bring a pan of water to the boil, add the prawns (shrimp) and blanch for about 1 minute. Drain, let cool a little, then peel them, leaving the tails intact. (You should have 130 g/4½ oz peeled prawns.) Set aside.

Heat the oil in a frying pan or skillet over a medium heat, add the garlic and shallot to the pan and fry until fragrant, about 30 seconds, making sure not to let them brown. Add the fish sauce and sugar to the pan. Mix until the mixture develops a nice colour. Add the caramel braising sauce and the sliced spring onion (scallion) to the pan. Stir well. Add the peeled prawns to the pan and sprinkle with the black pepper. Cook for about 3 minutes, stirring occasionally, until the prawns are cooked through and well-coated with the sauce.

# HERBAL STEWED DUCK

## Vịt Tiềm

You'll often find this dish in District 5, Ho Chi Minh's own Chinatown, and it bears resemblance to *Guaydtiaao Bpet Dtoon* (Thai duck noodles), as the duck leg is braised in a herbal soy sauce-based broth. All the spices used here are part of Chinese herbal medicine – *bắc đỗ trọng* (eucommia bark), *thục địa* (dried *Rehmannia glutinosa*) and goji berries are for improving kidney energy, while *hoài sơn* (Chinese yam), *phòng đảng sâm* (*Codonopsis pilosula* root) and jujubes help with the digestive system, balancing out the rich fried and braised duck leg.

Serves 4–6
Preparation time: 10 minutes, plus 30 minutes marinating time
Cooking time: 2 hours 30 minutes

| DF |

13 g/½ oz garlic, coarsely chopped
10 g/¼ oz shallot, coarsely chopped
8 g/¼ oz ginger, peeled and coarsely chopped
1 kg/2 lb 4 oz duck, either legs or meaty pieces (big chunks with bones)
½ teaspoon salt
½ teaspoon Annatto Oil (page 457)
1 tablespoon light soy sauce
60 ml/2 fl oz (¼ cup) neutral oil, for frying
20 g/¾ oz (⅔ cup) dried shiitake, soaked and drained
100 g/3½ oz fresh lotus seeds
1 tablespoon fish sauce
1¼ teaspoon salt

*For the broth*
1.5 litres/2½ pints (6¼ cups) coconut water
3 g eucommia bark (bắc đỗ trọng)
35 g/1¼ oz Chinese yam (hoài sơn)
4 g Codonopsis pilosula root (dangshen/ phòng đảng sâm)
1.5 g dried Rehmannia glutinosa root ( Chinese foxglove/thục địa)
5 g/⅛ oz Polygonatum odoratum (ngọc trúc)
2 g Ligusticum striatum (xuyên khung)
10 jujubes (Chinese apples)
5 g/⅛ oz goji berries

*To serve*
500 g/1 lb 2 oz pak choi (bok choy), blanched
200 g/7 oz (1 cup) baby mustard greens (cải bẹ xanh)
500 g/1 lb 2 oz Hong Kong-style noodles, optional

Put the garlic, shallot and ginger in a mortar and pound with a pestle until fully smashed and the juice is released; this will take 1–2 minutes.

In a bowl, combine the duck with the smashed aromatics, along with the salt, annatto oil and soy sauce. Let marinate for about 30 minutes.

To make the broth, mix 1 litre/1¾ pints (4¼ cups) of water with the coconut water in a large pot (about 5-litre/169-oz/5¼-quart capacity) and bring to the boil. Add all the remaining ingredients, except the goji berries, to the pot and simmer for 40 minutes.

Meanwhile, heat the oil in a pan over a medium heat, add the marinated duck and fry for about 10 minutes. Add the fried duck pieces to the simmering pot of broth.

Add the soaked shiitake mushrooms to the broth and simmer for another 10 minutes. Add the lotus seeds, fish sauce and 1 teaspoon of the salt to the pot and simmer for 1 hour 20 minutes. Add the goji berries and simmer for an additional 20 minutes. Adjust to taste with the remaining salt.

Serve with the blanched pak choi (bok choy), baby mustard leaves and Hong Kong-style noodles, if using.

# DUCK STEWED WITH RAMBUTAN

## Vịt Hầm Chôm Chôm

Utilizing fruit in savoury dishes is quite common in Vietnamese cuisine, from Pomelo Salad (page 124) to Braised Young Jackfruit (page 333). In the Southwest region of Vietnam where rambutans grow, they are paired with duck and other local produce. The rambutan and coconut water lend a delicate natural sweetness to this broth, perfectly balancing the savoury duck. This dish can be served with rice, noodles, or as a soup (*canh*).

Serves: 4
Preparation Time: 30 minutes
Cooking Time: 55 minutes

| DF |

- 25 g/1 oz piece fresh ginger, roughly smashed
- 1 kg/2 lb 4 oz Muscovy or Barbary duck, cut into 45–60 g/1½–2¼ oz chunks (4 × 7-cm/1½ × 2¾-inch pieces)
- 1 tablespoon neutral oil
- 30 g/1 oz shallots, minced
- 5 g/⅛ oz garlic, minced
- 3 tablespoons fish sauce
- ½ teaspoon salt
- 550 ml/19 fl oz (2¼ cups) coconut water
- 1 kg/2 lb 4 oz rambutans, peeled and rinsed
- 10 g/¼ oz coriander (cilantro), to garnish

In a pot, boil enough water to cover the duck. Add the ginger and boil for 2 minutes.

Place the duck pieces in a large bowl and pour over the boiling ginger water. Soak for 2 minutes, then strain and discard the ginger.

Heat the oil in a pot or 5.2-litre/176-oz (5½-quart) casserole (or Dutch oven) over a medium heat. Add the shallots and garlic and stir-fry for 3–5 minutes until they start to brown. Add the duck pieces and cook, stirring frequently, for 2 minutes over a high heat. Add 2 tablespoons of the fish sauce and the salt. Continue stirring the duck over a medium heat to release its liquid and concentrate the flavours, about 10 minutes. Pour in the coconut water and 450 ml/15 fl oz (scant 2 cups) of water. Bring to a simmer, then reduce the heat and cook for 10 minutes. Add the rambutans, cover with a lid and cook for 15 minutes. Skim off some of the fat layer that has risen to top, then cook for a further 15 minutes.

Finish the dish with the remaining fish sauce and garnish with the coriander (cilantro). Serve hot.

# 'SHAKEN' BEEF

## Bò Lúc Lắc

The name '*lúc lắc*' refers to the shaking motion used while cooking the beef in the wok. This dish cleverly adapts the French love for steak into bite-size pieces easily eaten with chopsticks, and a nod to the Chinese, through the use of the wok. *Bò lúc lắc* can be eaten with fried rice, plain white rice or chips (fries), or even on a bed of lettuce leaves, with sliced tomatoes and cucumbers on the side.

Serves 2
Preparation time: 15 minutes, plus 1 hour 30 minutes marinating time
Cooking time: 10 minutes

| DF |

- 250 g/5½ oz beef (fillet/tenderloin, ribeye, or any tender cut), diced into 1.5-cm/⅝-inch cubes
- ½ tablespoon oyster sauce
- 3/4 tablespoons soy sauce
- ¼ teaspoon black pepper
- 2 tablespoons cooking oil
- 20 g/¾ oz garlic, minced
- 180 g/6 oz onion (about 1 medium), roughly sliced
- 1 tablespoon sugar

In a bowl, combine the beef with the oyster sauce, soy sauce and black pepper. Marinate for 1 hour 30 minutes.

Heat 1 tablespoon of the oil in a pan large enough to fit all the meat in one layer over a medium-high heat. Add the garlic and fry until it starts to turn golden, about 30 seconds. Quickly add the marinated beef and stir-fry for 2–3 minutes, until just barely cooked. Remove from the pan and set aside.

In the same pan, dry-fry the onion for about 1 minute. Remove and set aside.

Add the remaining oil and the sugar to the pan. Lower the heat and allow the sugar to caramelize until it turns dark amber, 2–3 minutes. Immediately return the cooked beef to the pan and stir to coat with the caramel. Return the onions to the pan and stir to combine.

Serve immediately.

# BEEF STEW

## Bò Kho

This stew goes by two names – *bò sốt vang* in the north (from French *vin rouge*/red wine) and *bò kho* in the south. While its French colonial influence is often cited, my experience eating it for breakfast with noodles at Chinese-Vietnamese family restaurants hints at more complex origins. You can serve it with bread, rice noodles, egg noodles or rice. I've included a homemade spice blend you can make ahead and store: if you can't get the pre-seasoning mix at an Asian supermarket, make the homemade beef seasoning below.

Serves 6–8
Preparation time: 30 minutes, plus 30 minutes marinating time
Cooking time: 1 hour 50 minutes

| DF |

- 1 kg/2 lb 4 oz beef ribs, finger or brisket, cut into 3.5 × 3.5-cm/1½ × 1½-inch cubes
- 25 g/1 oz lemongrass
- 25 g/1 oz piece fresh ginger

*For the stew*

- 50 g/1¾ oz peeled shallots
- 20 g/¾ oz piece fresh ginger
- 3 lemongrass stalks (40–50 g/1½–1¾ oz)
- 4 teaspoons fish sauce
- 10 g/¼ oz tomato purée (paste)
- 1 teaspoon Vietnamese five-spice powder (ngũ vị hương)
- 1 teaspoon ground turmeric or annatto powder
- 2 tablespoons neutral oil
- 10 g/¼ oz garlic, finely chopped
- 1.5 litres/2½ pints (6¼ cups) coconut water
- 30 g/1 oz lemongrass, smashed
- 10 g/¼ oz rock sugar
- 2 teaspoons salt
- 570 g/1 lb 4 oz carrots (about 3 carrots), peeled, trimmed, halved, then cut into 4-cm/1½-inch-thick semi-circles

*For the beef seasoning mix (gia vị bò kho)*

- 5 g/⅛ oz (about 3–4) star anise
- 3 g cinnamon stick
- 5 g/⅛ oz black cardamom pods (thảo quả)
- 5 g/⅛ oz (2 teaspoons) black pepper
- 5 g/⅛ oz (1 teaspoon) cloves
- 2 g bay leaves (about 2)

*To finish*

- 35 g/1¼ oz sawtooth coriander (culantro), leaves picked
- 20 g/¾ oz basil, leaves picked
- 30 g/1 oz Vietnamese basil (húng quế), leaves picked
- 65 g/2¼ oz spring onion (scallion) greens, chopped

Preheat a gas barbecue.

In a large pot, combine 1 litre/1¾ pints (4¼ cups) of water with the beef ribs, lemongrass and ginger. Bring to a simmer, and simmer for 20 minutes to clean the beef pieces, then drain and set aside.

On the barbecue grill, carefully place the whole shallots, piece of ginger and lemongrass stalks and grill for 5–7 minutes until charred. Alternatively, grill (broil) them under the oven grill (broiler) at 200°C/400°F for 7–10 minutes. Remove from the grill and set aside.

To make the beef seasoning mix, heat a dry pan over a medium heat, add the star anise, cinnamon and cardamom, and dry-fry for 2 minutes. Add the pepper and cloves and toast for an additional 1 minute. You want to be able to smell the aroma, but the spices should not burn. Put the toasted seasoning mix into a spice cage or tea bag with the bay leaves and set aside.

Slice the grilled shallots, then place them in a bowl with the cleaned beef pieces. Add 1 tablespoon of the fish sauce and the tomato purée (paste), five-spice powder and ground turmeric or annatto powder. Marinate for at least 30 minutes.

In a 5-litre/175-oz (5¼-quart) casserole (or Dutch oven), heat the oil over a medium heat. Add the garlic and grilled lemongrass and stir-fry for 4–5 minutes until it starts to colour. Add the marinated beef with the marinade and continue to cook for 5 minutes until the meat is browned.

Add the coconut water, smashed lemongrass, rock sugar, salt, spice cage or tea bag, the remaining fish sauce and the grilled ginger to the pot. Bring to a simmer, skim and partially cover. Cook for 45 minutes. Add the carrots, then continue to cook for another 45 minutes, or until the beef and carrots are tender. Remove from the heat, cover with a lid and let it sit until ready to serve.

Serve with the sawtooth coriander (culantro), basil, Vietnamese basil and spring onions (scallion) greens.

# BUFFALO OFFAL STEW

## Thắng Cố

In Hà Giang's markets, you'll find this stew simmering for hours in large flat pans. While traditionally a H'mong dish made with horse meat, it's now prepared by various communities across Northern Vietnam's mountains. We learned this buffalo version from anh Triệu Văn Kính of the Red Dao, while staying with his family in Hoàng Su Phì, and it's a quicker version than the traditional one, which needs 12 hours simmering.

Serves 4–6
Preparation time: 15 minutes
Cooking time: 3–4 hours

| DF |

- 600 g/1 lb 5 oz mixed buffalo offal (variety meats: skin, liver, lungs)
- 50 g/1¾ oz piece fresh ginger (about 10 cm/4 inches), pounded
- 4.5 g (1 teaspoon) ground black cardamom (thảo quả)
- 2 tablespoons all-purpose seasoning (hạt nêm)
- 2 tablespoons neutral oil
- ½ teaspoon salt
- 15 g/½ oz Vietnamese coriander/cilantro (rau răm), leaves picked, to garnish

Bring a large pan of water to the boil, add the mixed buffalo offal (variety meats) and blanch for 1 hour. Drain, let cool slightly, then cut them into small pieces.

Mix the cut offal (variety meats) with the pounded ginger, cardamom and all-purpose seasoning.

Heat the oil in a pan. Add the seasoned offal and stir-fry for 1 minute. Add 1.26 litres/2¼ pints (5¼ cups) of water and the salt. Cover with a lid and simmer for 1 hour. Add 600 ml/1 pint (2½ cups) water. Simmer for 2–3 hours, until everything is soft, keeping the meat covered with water as it reduces and adding more water as needed throughout cooking. By the end, there should be enough water to just cover the meat.

Garnish with the Vietnamese coriander/cilantro leaves before serving.

# GOAT BROTH, POACHED GOAT AND CHĂM HERB SALAD

## Nước Lèo Thịt Dê, Rau Trộn – Ia Tanut Pè, Lo Pè Tuk, Najm Gem

Through chị Kiều Thị Hồng Vân (Kiều Maily), who has spent over ten years documenting and preserving Chăm food culture, we were able to visit her parents, chú Kiều Anh and cô Đạo Thị Tuyết, to learn this dish. Present at most Chăm celebrations, this dish was traditionally served only during worship ceremonies when goats were sacrificed to the god Yang. Among Vietnam's Chăm communities, the Balamon Chăm do not eat beef while the Bani Chăm do not eat pork, making goat meat a commonly shared protein. The broth features pounded rice for thickening and young tamarind leaves for acidity; it is served with large plates of shredded banana stalks and herbs.

Serves 8–10
Preparation time: 15 minutes, plus 15–30 minutes soaking time
Cooking time: 1 hour 20 minutes

| DF |

150 g/5½ oz rice
1.5 kg/3¼ lb goat leg with bones
6 g/⅛ oz green chilli (about ¼ chilli)
1¼ teaspoons salt, plus 1½ teaspoons salt if needed
105 g/7 oz peeled shallots
65 g/2¼ oz fermented anchovy sauce (mắm nêm)
205 g/7¼ oz tomatoes, thinly sliced
½ teaspoon sugar
3 tablespoons fish sauce
3 tablespoons MSG
100 g/3½ oz young tamarind leaves
60 g/2¼ oz spring onions (scallions), finely chopped
25 g/1 oz coriander (cilantro), chopped
40 g/1½ oz lemon basil (lá é), finely chopped

*To serve*
800 g/1 lb 12 oz banana root, shredded
100 g/3½ oz piper lolot leaves
100 g/3½ oz mint basil
tamarind anchovy sauce from Chăm-style Mixed Rice (page 266)

Heat a dry frying pan or skillet over low heat, add the rice and toast for 7–8 minutes until golden-brown. Let cool completely, then grind to fine powder in a food processor.

Soak the toasted rice powder in a bowl with 700 ml/24 fl oz (scant 3 cups) of water for 15–30 minutes.

In a large pot, combine the goat leg and 4.5 litres/8 pints (19 cups) of water. Bring to the boil and cook for 1 hour.

Using tongs, remove the goat, keeping the broth at a simmer, and let cool slightly, then thinly slice the meat off the bones. Cover the meat and set aside.

Return the bones to the simmering broth. Add the soaked toasted rice powder mixture to the broth, then bring the broth to the boil and cook for an additional 10 minutes.

Meanwhile, put the green chilli and salt in a mortar and pound with a pestle, then add the shallots and pound again.

Remove the broth from the heat and strain into a clean pot. Add the pounded chilli-shallot mixture and all the remaining ingredients.

To serve, ladle the broth into individual bowls and serve with a plate of the sliced meat and a plate of the shredded banana roots, piper lolot leaves and mint basil, with the tamarind anchovy sauce in a dipping bowl on the side.

GOAT BROTH, POACHED GOAT AND CHĂM HERB SALAD

# SIDE DISHES

## Món phụ

In Vietnamese meals, vegetables play a crucial role both as nourishment and medicine. The tropical climate favours leafy greens, which dominated the diet long before root vegetables like carrots and potatoes were introduced during French colonization.

This chapter covers vegetable stir-fries, omelettes and lighter protein dishes that complement the main course. The recipes include proteins like bamboo worms and crickets, ingredients that might be unfamiliar to some but are standard fare across Vietnam, valued for their nutrition and taste. These are ingredients that showcase the Vietnamese people's resourcefulness and ingenuity.

Most recipes serve as bases for experimentation – bitter gourd (bitter melon) in a stir-fry with eggs (page 330) can be replaced with chayote or pumpkin, while omelettes will welcome various herbs like piper lolot, Vietnamese coriander/cilantro or mugwort. These dishes tend to be lighter in flavour than mains and are often served with dipping sauces – fish sauce or soy sauce with chillies. Even simple boiled vegetables with fish sauce qualify as essential sides, reflecting the Vietnamese principle of balancing meals with fresh vegetables.

# BEEF AND CELERY STIR-FRY

## Bò Xào Rau Cần

This stir-fry is really easy to make, but the key here is not overcooking the meat, and allowing the tomato to release enough juice to give the sauce a nice gravy-like consistency. You can substitute Chinese celery with morning glory or any leafy greens.

Serves 2–3
Preparation time: 20 minutes, plus 15 minutes marinating time
Cooking time: 10 minutes

| DF | ≤30 |

*For the marinated beef*
300 g/10½ oz beef, thinly sliced
15 g/½ oz garlic, minced
1 tablespoon fish sauce
1 teaspoon oyster sauce
½ teaspoon black pepper
½ teaspoon sugar

*For the aromatics and vegetables*
4 tablespoons neutral oil
15 g/½ oz spring onion (scallion) whites, chopped
½ onion (about 80 g/2¾ oz), sliced
20 g/¾ oz garlic, minced
10 g/¼ oz shallot, minced
1 cucumber (265 g/9¼ oz), sliced lengthways and cut into 1-cm/½-inch slices on an angle
1 large tomato (180 g/6 oz), quartered and seeds removed
1 tablespoon fish sauce
90 g/3¼ oz Chinese celery, stalks and leaves separated

*To finish*
½ tablespoon fish sauce
1 long chilli (20 g), sliced
extra black pepper

In a bowl, marinate the beef with the garlic, fish sauce, oyster sauce, pepper and sugar for 15 minutes. Set aside.

In a wok, heat 2 tablespoons of the oil over a medium heat. Add the spring onion (scallion) whites and onion, and quickly stir-fry for 1–2 minutes. Add the marinated beef and stir-fry for 1 minute 30 seconds, or until it is barely cooked. Remove the beef and set it aside.

In the same wok, add the remaining oil. Once hot, add the garlic and shallot and stir-fry for 1–2 minutes until they start to turn golden. Add the cucumber and stir-fry for 30 seconds, keeping the mixture moving constantly. Add the tomato and fish sauce, then add the stalks of the Chinese celery.

Pour any remaining marinade from the bowl into the wok and cook until the vegetables are about three-quarters done, 2–3 minutes.

Return the beef to the wok and quickly stir everything together for an additional 30 seconds. Add the Chinese celery leaves and stir for another 30 seconds. Remove from the heat.

To finish the stir-fry, add the fish sauce and the sliced chilli, then sprinkle with the pepper.

Serve hot.

## STIR-FRIED PUMPKIN

Bí Đỏ Xào

To make this dish vegan, you can omit the fish sauce and replace it with ½ teaspoon of *bột canh* (soup powder) or *hạt nêm* (all-purpose seasoning). If you bought a whole pumpkin and need to use the rest, you can make Minced Pork and Pumpkin Soup (page 361) or the Squash and Peanut Soup (page 358).

Serves 2–3
Preparation time: 15 minutes
Cooking time: 15 minutes

| DF | ≤30 |

2 tablespoons neutral oil
15 g/½ oz shallots, coarsely chopped
25 g/1 oz garlic, coarsely chopped
400 g/14 oz pumpkin, peeled and cut into 5-mm × 3-cm × 4-cm / ¼ × 1¼ × 1½-inch pieces
120 ml/4 fl oz (½ cup) blanching water, stock (broth) broth or water
¼ teaspoon salt
1 teaspoon fish sauce
15 g/½ oz spring onions (scallions), cut into 1-cm/½-inch chunks

In a large frying pan or skillet, heat the oil over a medium heat. Once the oil is hot, add the shallot and garlic. Cook for 2 minutes until they start to turn golden.

Add the pumpkin pieces to the pan and stir-fry for a couple of minutes. Pour in the blanching water, stock (broth) or water, then add the salt and fish sauce. Put the lid on and simmer for 4 minutes. Remove the lid and cook for another 3 minutes to evaporate some of the liquid.

Finish by adding the spring onions (scallions), then stir-fry for an additional minute.

## FRIED CRICKETS WITH LIME LEAVES

Dế Rang

After a year spent travelling in Vietnam, I've grown to appreciate insects, especially crickets with their surprisingly crunchy texture.

Serves 4
Preparation time: 5 minutes
Cooking time: 13 minutes

| DF | GF | ≤5 | ≤30 |

200 g/7 oz fresh crickets
1½ tablespoons vegetables oil
5 lime leaves, very thinly sliced (julienned)
½ teaspoon salt
½ teaspoon MSG

Heat a pan over a medium heat, add the crickets and 1 tablespoon of water. Cook for 5 minutes 30 seconds, stirring occasionally to ensure even cooking.

Pour 1½ tablespoons of the oil around the edge of the pan, then continue cooking for 7 minutes, stirring frequently until the crickets become crispy.

Add the lime leaves and season with the salt and MSG. Stir well to combine all the ingredients.

Serve hot as a snack or side dish.

# BITTER AUBERGINE WITH DRIED FISH

## Cá Khô Xào Cà Đắng (Trong Tăng Pai Atum Ca Kro)

Before currency was common in the mountains, Bahnar communities, also called the montagnards, would trade rice for salted fish from Kinh/Việt merchants coming from Quy Nhơn. This doesn't use extra salt, as the fish gives it a natural saltiness; salt is now used for cleaning the aubergines (eggplants) but traditionally none would be used at all. Originally topped with only lemon basil, many cooks now add spring onions (scallions) and coriander (cilantro).

Serves 2–3
Preparation time: 20 minutes, plus 10 minutes soaking time
Cooking time: 10 minutes

| DF |

- 230 g/8 oz bitter aubergines (eggplants) (about 4)
- 30 g/1 oz dried fish, cut into 2-cm/¾-inch squares
- ½ teaspoon salt
- 2 tablespoons neutral oil
- 10 g/¼ oz shallot, thinly sliced
- 1 teaspoon all-purpose seasoning (hạt nêm)
- ½ teaspoon MSG
- ½ teaspoon sugar

*To garnish*

- 20 g/¾ oz spring onions (scallions), finely chopped
- 10 g/¼ oz coriander (cilantro) (or lemon basil/lá é for traditional version)

Peel the bitter aubergines (eggplants) and thinly slice into rounds. Soak in a bowl of salted water for 5–10 minutes . Set aside.

Meanwhile, soak the dried fish in another bowl with 240 ml/8 fl oz (1 cup) water and the salt for 5–10 minute. Set aside.

Heat the oil in a pan over a medium heat. Add the shallot and cook for 30 seconds.

Drain the fish and add to the pan, then fry over a medium-low heat for 30 seconds.

Drain the bitter aubergines and add to the pan.

Season with the all-purpose seasoning, MSG and sugar. Cook for 3½–4 minutes until the vegetables soften. Add 80 ml/2½ fl oz (⅓ cup) of water and simmer, uncovered, for 5 minutes until the water evaporates.

Transfer to a serving plate. Garnish with the spring onion (scallion) and coriander (cilantro) or lemon basil. Serve hot.

# STIR-FRIED AUBERGINE WITH FERMENTED SOYBEAN PASTE

## Cà Tím Xào Tương Hột

In Vietnamese vegetarian cooking, soybean paste often replaces fish sauce. Try it here or with fried tofu or mushrooms.

Serves 3–4
Preparation time: 20 minutes, plus 15–30 minutes soaking time
Cooking time: 35 minutes

| V | VE | DF |

- 1 teaspoon salt
- 2 long aubergines (eggplants) (about 500 g/1 lb 2 oz)
- 1 tablespoon neutral oil
- 10 g/¼ oz shallot, coarsely chopped
- 250 g/5½ oz fermented soybean paste (tương hột)
- ½ teaspoon sugar
- 120 ml/4 fl oz (½ cup) water or coconut water

*To finish*

- ½ teaspoon black pepper
- 20 g/¾ oz spring onions (scallions), cut into 1-cm/½-inch pieces

In a bowl, mix 600 ml/1 pint (2½ cups) of water with the salt. Cut the aubergines (eggplants) into 6-cm/2½-inch-thick rounds, then quarter each round. Add the aubergine pieces to the salted water bowl and soak for 15–30 minutes. Drain.

In a pan that can fit all the aubergines, heat the oil over a medium heat. Add the shallot and fry for 1 minute–1 minute 30 seconds. Add the soybean paste, then stir-fry for 15 seconds before adding the soaked aubergine pieces. Add the sugar, cover with a lid and let cook for 15 minutes. The goal is to let the water come out of the aubergines initially and then to add more water as it evaporates.

Add the water or coconut water, then continue cooking for about 15 minutes until the mixture is glazed.

Finish with a sprinkle of pepper and the chopped spring onions (scallions).

# HANOI SANDWORM PATTIES

## Chả Rươi

Every November, when the cool weather arrives, cô Vũ Hằng Nga begins selling live sandworms, a Hanoi delicacy. She sells them as they are or mixed in their batter, ready to be fried at home. These are traditionally paired with *quýt hôi* (smelly mandarin) peel – not just for flavour but also to balance the sandworms' 'cold' nature with the citrus peel's 'warming' properties, a principle important in traditional medicine. The patties should be fried only once and eaten immediately hot, which is why they're often cooked at the table in continuous batches as people eat.

Makes 8 patties; serves 2–3
Preparation time: 15 minutes
Cooking time: 20 minutes

| DF |

190 g/6¾ oz live sandworms
50 g/1¾ oz minced (ground) pork
1 teaspoon MSG
½ teaspoon soup powder (bột canh)
¾ teaspoon black pepper
1 tablespoon tempura flour
½ teaspoon brown sugar
30 g/1 oz dill, coarsely chopped
5 g/⅛ oz dried mandarin peel (from Lang Son or Cao Bang), thinly sliced, then chopped
2 extra-small (US small) egg yolks or 1 medium (US large) egg yolk
vegetable oil, for frying

*To serve*
200 g/7 oz fresh rice noodles (bún)
10 g/¼ oz coriander (cilantro)
Northern-style Fish Sauce (page 471)
Pickled Kohlrabi and Carrots (page 469)

Rinse the sandworms thoroughly 4 times under cold running water using a fine-mesh sieve.

In a large mixing bowl, combine the cleaned sandworms and minced (ground) pork. Add the MSG, soup powder, pepper, tempura flour, sugar, dill and mandarin peel. Mix thoroughly. Mix in the egg yolk(s) until well combined.

Pour oil into a pan to a 1-cm/½-inch depth. Heat the oil over a medium heat. Using a large spoon, portion approximately 2 tablespoons of mixture per patty, then gently place each patty in the hot oil, pressing down to form 6–7-cm/2½–2¾-inch-diameter patties. Fry for 1 minute on each side, or until golden brown. The patties should be crispy on the outside, soft on the inside. Remove and drain on paper towels.

Arrange the noodles in serving bowls, place 2–3 hot patties on top and garnish with coriander (cilantro).

Serve hot with the northern-style fish sauce and pickled vegetables.

## MOUNTAIN-STYLE SOY CURD

Cháo Lảo / Tẩu Chúa

This northern mountain dish, known as *cháo lảo* by the Tay and Red Dao or *tẩu chúa* among the Hmong communities, is essentially a ricotta made from coarse soy milk and flavoured with *cải bẹ* (mustard greens). For the best results, homemade soy milk is essential – it provides the fresh taste and texture that makes this dish special.

Serves approx. 4–6
Preparation time: 30 minutes, plus overnight soaking time
Cooking time: 25–30 minutes

| DF | ≤5 |

- 1 kg/2 lb 4 oz dried soybeans, soaked overnight, then drained (about 1.6 kg/3 lb 8 oz after soaking)
- 3 tablespoons lard or cooking oil
- 500 g/1 lb 2 oz (2½ cups) mountain mustard greens (cải bẹ mào gà), washed and thinly sliced
- 1 tablespoon all-purpose seasoning (hạt nêm)
- 1 tablespoon salt
- 1 tablespoon lime juice

Put the soaked soybeans in a wet grinder or food processor with 1.8 litres/3¼ pints (7½ cups) of water and grind into a coarse mixture. Strain through a fine-mesh sieve into a fresh bowl to obtain a coarse soy milk.

In a pot, heat the lard or oil over a medium heat, then add 900 ml/30 fl oz (3¾ cups) water and bring to a simmer. Add the mustard greens and simmer, stirring, for 1–2 minutes. Add the all-purpose seasoning and salt. Pour in the coarse soy milk and simmer over a medium-low heat, stirring constantly in a clockwise direction to prevent burning, for 3 minutes 30 seconds.

Start drizzling in the lime juice, little by little, while stirring constantly. Cook for another 17 minutes (about 20 minutes total), stirring continuously, until the mixture thickens and resembles ricotta.

Serve warm as a protein component in a meal.

## STIR-FRIED WINGED BEANS WITH GARLIC

Đậu Rồng Xào Tỏi

Winged beans maintain the best texture when lightly cooked to retain their crunchiness. Frying them in a wok or large pan that can comfortably accommodate all the pieces is recommended, as if you over crowd it, there is a risk that they might become soggy.

Serves 4, as part of a meal
Preparation time: 10 minutes
Cooking time: 5–6 minutes

| DF | ≤5 | ≤30 |

- 300 g/10½ oz winged beans (cigarillas)
- 1 tablespoon cooking oil
- 30 g/1 oz garlic, coarsely chopped
- 2 tablespoons fish sauce
- ¼ teaspoon salt

Trim off the top and bottom of each winged bean, then slice on an angle into 1-cm/½-inch-thick pieces.

Heat the oil in a pan over a medium heat. Once hot, add the garlic and stir-fry until it turns golden, 1–2 minutes. Quickly add the winged beans, stirring continuously. Increase the heat to high, then add the fish sauce and salt. Continue stirring to prevent the garlic from burning, and cook for 3–4 minutes.

Serve immediately.

STIR-FRIED WINGED BEANS WITH GARLIC

## STIR-FRIED BEAN SPROUTS AND CHINESE CHIVES

Giá Xào Hẹ

Though the base of this dish is simply bean sprouts and Chinese chives, Vietnamese families often add sliced liver, coagulated blood (*huyết*) or pork belly (side) to the mix.

Serves 4 to share
Preparation time: 5 minutes
Cooking time : 5 minutes

| DF | ≤30 |

- 85 g/3 oz Chinese chives (lá hẹ), cut into 4.5-cm/1¾-inch pieces
- 240 g/8½ oz bean sprouts
- 1 tablespoon plus 1 teaspoon neutral oil or lard
- 17 g/½ oz shallot, coarsely chopped
- 17 g/½ oz garlic, coarsely chopped
- 2 teaspoons fish sauce
- ¼ teaspoon black pepper
- ¼ teaspoon salt

In a bowl, mix together the Chinese chives and bean sprouts. Set aside.

Heat 1 tablespoon of the oil or lard in a wok or frying pan over a high heat, then add the shallot and garlic and fry until they turn half golden, about 3 minutes.

Add the Chinese chive and bean sprout mixture and stir-fry over a high heat for 1 minute–1 minute 30 seconds, depending on how well-cooked you prefer it.

Drizzle in the fish sauce, then remove from the heat and continue stirring for 30–45 seconds. The dish will finish cooking with the residual heat.

Sprinkle the pepper and salt over the top, give the mixture a final toss and serve while it's hot.

## STIR-FRIED BITTER GOURD WITH EGGS

Khổ Qua Xào Trứng

This recipe is a great introduction to bitter gourd (bitter melon). The eggs help temper the bitter gourd's bitterness, and it tastes even better dipped in light soy sauce.

Serves 1–2
Preparation time: 15 minutes
Cooking time: 10 minutes

| DF | ≤30 |

- 2 tablespoons neutral oil
- 30 g/1 oz garlic, coarsely chopped
- 3 small bitter gourd/bitter melon (khổ qua) (about 300 g/10½ oz), seeds removed, halved lengthways and sliced into 5-mm-/¼-inch-thick pieces
- 2 teaspoons fish sauce
- 2 eggs

*To serve*

- 10 g/¼ oz spring onion (scallion) greens, coarsely chopped
- 10 g/¼ oz coriander (cilantro), coarsely chopped
- ¼ teaspoon black pepper

In a large frying pan or skillet, heat the oil over a medium heat. Once the oil is hot, add the garlic. Fry until for 1–2 minutes until it turns golden. Add the bitter melon and cook for 1 minute. Add the fish sauce and continue to cook for another 2–3 minutes.

Crack the 2 eggs into the pan on the side and allow them to slightly cook. When the bitter gourd (bitter melon) pieces can be easily pierced with a chopstick, mix in the eggs.

Transfer to serving plates and serve with the chopped spring onion (scallion) greens and coriander (cilantro) on top. Sprinkle the black pepper over the dish and serve.

STIR-FRIED BITTER GOURD WITH EGGS

# KING OYSTER MUSHROOMS STIR-FRIED WITH LEMONGRASS AND CHILLI

Nấm Đùi Gà Xào Sả Ớt

While traditionally prepared with chicken or frog, this lemongrass and chilli stir-fry uses king oyster mushrooms, making it suitable for *ngày rằm* (full moon days) when many Vietnamese Buddhists eat vegetarian food.

Serves 2
Preparation time: 15 minutes
Cooking time: 10 minutes

| V | VE | DF | ≤30 |

- 210 g/7¼ oz king oyster mushrooms
- 2 tablespoons neutral oil
- 30 g/1 oz lemongrass, minced
- 30 g/1 oz shallots, minced
- 10 g/¼ oz garlic, minced
- 5 g/⅛ oz bird's eye chilli, minced
- ¼ teaspoon curry powder
- ½ teaspoon salt
- 1 teaspoon soy sauce
- 1 teaspoon sugar
- 1 teaspoon Annatto Oil (page 457)
- 90 g/3¼ oz onion, sliced 5 mm/¼ inch thick
- 1 teaspoon light soy sauce

Cut the king oyster mushrooms in half, then slice on an angle into chunks 1–1.5-cm/½–⅝-inch thick. Put the mushrooms in a bowl, then pour boiling water over them to clean. Drain.

In a pan, heat the neutral oil over a medium heat. Add the lemongrass, shallots, garlic and chilli. Stir-fry for 2 minutes. Add the curry powder and stir-fry for another 2 minutes. Add the mushrooms to the pan, then season with the salt, soy sauce, sugar and annatto oil. Stir-fry for an additional 3 minutes, or until the mushrooms release their moisture and are fully cooked. Finally, add the onion and light soy sauce. Stir well, then remove from the heat and serve hot.

# STIR-FRIED CASSAVA LEAVES WITH STEAMED MACKEREL

Lá Mì Xào, Cá Nục Hấp

Across Vietnam's Central Highlands, including Kontum and Buôn Ma Thuột, cassava leaves feature prominently in local cooking, from stir-fries to soups, and are even fermented with bamboo shoots. The Ede, Bahnar and Jarai communities each prepare this dish in their own way – some use *hla dao* herbs instead of MSG, others add bitter berries, *cà quẻng*. Only the tender, bright green young leaves of the cassava should be used, as older ones become stringy. They can be prepared by hand-squeezing (*vò*) or pounding; but never cover the dish after cooking, or the leaves will turn yellow. Here, I use steamed mackerel, but sliced pork belly (side) or dried fish can also be cooked with the cassava leaves.

Serves 3–4
Preparation time: 30 minutes
Cooking time: 15 minutes

| DF |

- 160 g/5½ oz cassava leaves (lá mì)
- 20 g/¾ oz (scant ¼ cup) green bird's eye chillies, trimmed
- 25 g/1 oz chive bulbs, trimmed
- 1¼ teaspoon MSG (or Hla Dao herbs as a traditional substitute)
- 3 tablespoons chicken fat or pork fat
- 60 g/2¼ oz steamed mackerel meat (no bones)
- 15 g/½ oz garlic, chopped
- 45 g/1½ oz papaya flower buds
- ¼ teaspoon salt
- 1 teaspoon all-purpose seasoning (hạt nêm)

Put the cassava leaves in a mortar and pound with a pestle until they form a thick paste. Set aside.
In a clean mortar, combine the chillies, chive bulbs and ½ teaspoon of the MSG. Pound with a pestle until well combined, Set aside.

Heat the chicken or pork fat in a large wok over a high heat, add the steamed mackerel and fry for 1 minute. Add the garlic and cook for 30 seconds, then add the pounded cassava leaves and the papaya flower buds and stir-fry quickly for 1 minute to seal in the flavours.

Add 350 ml/12 fl oz (1½ cups) of water, the salt, the remaining MSG and the all-purpose seasoning. Simmer on high heat for 3–5 minutes.

Add the pounded chilli-chive mixture, then continue cooking for 6 minutes, or until the aromatics are fragrant and everything is well-cooked.

Serve hot.

## BRAISED YOUNG JACKFRUIT

### Mít Non Kho

In Vietnam, young jackfruit is either fermented like in Fermented Young Jackfruit (Central Vietnamese Style) (page 470) or used in vegetarian dishes for its meat-like texture. Processing requires an hour of boiling to remove the tannins and sap before cooking. To save time, many Vietnamese wet markets offer preboiled young jackfruit if ordered a day in advance.

Serves 2–3
Preparation time: 20 minutes
Cooking time: 15 minutes, plus 1 hour boiling time

| V | VE | DF |

- 485 g/1 lb 1 oz young jackfruit, boiled for 1 hour
- 120 ml/4 fl oz (½ cup) plus 1 tablespoon neutral oil
- 10 g/¼ oz shallot, coarsely chopped
- 10 g/¼ oz garlic, coarsely chopped
- 16 g/½ oz spring onion (scallion) whites, thinly sliced into 5-mm/¼-inch rounds

*For the sauce*

- 3 tablespoons Vietnamese soy sauce (xì dầu)
- 2 tablespoons water
- 1 teaspoon light brown sugar
- ½ teaspoon salt
- 1 tablespoon coconut milk
- ½ teaspoon black pepper

Slice the jackfruit into half-moons, 1.5–2 cm/⅝–¾ inch thick.

In a pan, heat the 120 ml/4 fl oz (½ cup) oil over a medium–low heat. Add the jackfruit slices and fry, turning halfway through, for 7 minutes, or until the edges are nicely golden. Set aside.

Cut the fried jackfruit into small chunks of about 6 g/⅛ oz each, approximately 10 triangles from each half-moon of the jackfruit.

In a pan (about 25 cm/10 inches) over a medium–low heat, add the remaining oil. Add the shallot and garlic and stir-fry until golden brown, about 4 minutes. Add all the sauce ingredients with 2 tablespoons of water, then add the fried jackfruit chunks and continue frying for 3–4 minutes until the jackfruit has absorbed the sauce. Add the spring onion (scallion) whites and mix.

Serve hot.

***Note:*** Jackfruit contains a white substance that numbs the hands, so some Asian stores sell already cleaned and cut jackfruit. If you buy a whole fruit you might like to wear gloves when handling it.

## STIR-FRIED FERMENTED YOUNG JACKFRUIT

### Nhút Thanh Chương Xào

This is great alongside steamed dishes like Steamed Chicken with Lime Leaves (page 283), as it has a strong, tangy flavour from the fermented jackfruit and pairs well with steamed meats.

Serves 2
Preparation time: 5 minutes
Cooking time: 5 minutes

| V | VE | DF | GF | ≤30 |

- 1½ tablespoons vegetable oil
- 5 g/⅛ oz chive bulb (củ nén) or shallot, thinly sliced
- 95 g/3½ oz Fermented Young Jackfruit (Central Vietnamese Style) (page 470), squeezed
- ½ teaspoon MSG
- 1 teaspoon sugar
- ¼ teaspoon black pepper
- 3 g lime leaves (about 5 leaves), very thinly sliced (julienned)
- cooked rice, to serve

Heat the oil in a wok over a medium–high heat, add the chive bulbs or shallot and fry for 1–2 minutes until golden. Add the fermented young jackfruit and stir-fry for 2 minutes 30 seconds, then remove from the heat.

Add the MSG, sugar, pepper and lime leaves and mix well.

Serve immediately with cooked rice.

# SQUID STIR-FRIED WITH PINEAPPLE AND TOMATO

Mực Xào Thơm Cà

The key to this dish lies in not overcooking the squid. After a quick initial cook, set it aside while stir-frying the other ingredients, only returning it at the end to prevent it from becoming chewy. Since tomatoes release liquid during cooking, achieving the right consistency is crucial before adding the squid back. Here, we finish it with extra virgin olive oil, as this recipe has been adapted to my mother's love for EVO – though you can use neutral oil or sesame oil if you prefer.

Serves 2–3
Preparation time: 30 minutes, plus 15 minutes marinating time
Cooking time: 15 minutes

| **DF** |

1 × 180 g/6 oz squid
1½ teaspoons sugar
2 teaspoons all-purpose seasoning (hạt nêm)
½ teaspoon black pepper, plus extra to taste
1 tablespoon oyster sauce
2 tablespoons neutral oil
25 g/1 oz garlic, minced
15 g/½ oz shallot, minced
210 g/7¼ oz tomatoes (about 2 tomatoes), cut into eighths
190 g/6¾ oz cucumber, sliced
160 g/5½ oz pineapple (about 1 quarter), trimmed, peeled and sliced
50 g/1¾ oz fresh shiitake mushrooms (about 4 mushrooms), quartered
130 g/4½ oz onion (about ½ onion), sliced
30 g/1 oz spring onion (scallion) whites, chopped
1 tablespoon extra virgin olive oil, optional
50 g/1¾ oz Chinese celery tops or celery, chopped
20 g/¾ oz spring onion (scallion) greens, chopped

Place the squid in a bowl and mix with 1 teaspoon of the sugar, 1 teaspoon of the all-purpose seasoning, the pepper and 1½ teaspoons of the oyster sauce. Let it marinate for 15 minutes.

In a pan, heat 1 tablespoon of the neutral oil over a medium-high heat. Add 20 g/¾ oz of the garlic and 10 g/¼ oz of the shallot and fry for 30 seconds–1 minute. Add the marinated squid and fry for 1 minute 30 seconds, or until the squid changes colour from translucent to opaque. Remove the pan from the heat.

In another pan or wok, heat the remaining neutral oil over a high heat. Add the remaining garlic and shallot and fry for 10 seconds. Add the tomatoes and stir-fry for 1 minute. Lower the heat to medium, add the cucumber and stir-fry for 1 minute 30 seconds. Add the pineapple and mushrooms. Season with the remaining all-purpose seasoning, the remaining sugar and the remaining oyster sauce. Stir-fry for 3 minutes and 30 seconds. Add the onion and spring onion (scallion) whites and increase the heat. Continue stir-frying for 4 minutes and 30 seconds, or until the tomatoes have reduced to a nice sauce, not too liquid.

Add the marinated squid to the pan, then add the extra virgin olive oil, if using, and cook for 1–2 minutes. Add the Chinese celery, spring onion greens and the remaining pepper to taste and stir everything together.

Serve hot.

## FRIED WILD FROGS

Nhái Chiên

In Hoa Tiến village (Quỳ Châu, Nghệ An province), Cô Sầm Thị Bích, from the Black Thai Community showed us how they traditionally catch these frogs – placing baskets in the fields and collecting them in the evening after rainfall when they're most active. These wild frogs are also known as *Vũ nữ chân dài* (long-legged dancers).

Serves 4
Preparation time: 10 minutes
Cooking time: 15 minutes

| DF | GF | ≤30 |

- vegetable oil, for frying
- 400 g/14 oz whole wild frogs (nhái)
- 25 g/1 oz chive bulbs (củ nén), crushed
- 15 g/½ oz piece fresh ginger, peeled and coarsely chopped into small chunks
- 5 g/⅛ oz fresh chilli, sliced into thin rings
- ½ teaspoon salt
- ½ teaspoon MSG
- ¼ teaspoon black pepper
- 5 g/⅛ oz lime leaves (about 12 medium), very thinly sliced (julienned), to garnish
- chilli sauce, to serve

Fill a large, non-stick pan with the oil to 2 cm/¾ inch deep and place over a medium heat until hot (around 180°C/350°F – if not using a thermometer, test the oil temperature by inserting wooden chopsticks into the oil – it should bubble vigorously around them).

Once the oil is hot, carefully lower the whole frogs into the oil using a skimmer. Fry over a medium heat, maintaining the temperature for about 13 minutes, turning the frogs every 3–4 minutes, until they turn golden brown and crispy.

Meanwhile, put the chive bulbs in a mortar and crush with a pestle to release their flavour.

Add the ginger, crushed chive bulbs and chilli to the pan with the frogs. Stir gently to evenly distribute the aromatics. Continue cooking for 1 minute to release the flavours. Season evenly with the salt, MSG and pepper.

Using the skimmer, carefully remove the frogs and aromatics from the oil, then drain well on paper towels to remove the excess oil.

Transfer to a serving plate. Garnish with julienned lime leaves. Serve immediately with a small bowl of chilli sauce on the side.

## STIR-FRIED BEE LARVAE WITH PICKLED BAMBOO SHOOTS

Nhộng Ong Xào Măng Chua

During my research in Hà Giang, anh Triệu Tà Phẩu from the Red Dao community shared that while pigs and buffalo were reserved for celebrations due to their size and cost, mountain communities historically relied on foraged proteins like bee larvae as part of their regular diet alongside chicken. This dish pairs fatty and rich larvae with pickled bamboo shoots, which can be kept for a long time and bring more of a sharp acidity to the dish.

Serves 2–3
Preparation time: 5 minutes
Cooking time: 5 minutes

| DF | GF | ≤5 | ≤30 |

- 130 g/4½ oz pickled bamboo shoots (măng chua)
- 2 tablespoons pork fat
- ½ teaspoon salt
- ½ teaspoon MSG
- 250 g/8¾ oz bee larvae (nhộng ong)

Slice the bamboo shoots into thin matchsticks (julienne).

In a wok or large frying pan, heat the pork fat over a high heat, add the bamboo shoots to the hot fat. Stir-fry for 30 seconds. Add the salt, MSG and bee larvae, then stir-fry over a high heat for 4 minutes. Be careful not to crush the ingredients while stirring.

Transfer to a serving plate. Serve hot as a main dish or side dish.

## SILKWORM LARVAE STIR-FRY WITH LIME LEAVES

Nhộng Xào Lá Chanh

This side dish demonstrates Vietnamese resourcefulness in using what would otherwise be discarded from silk-making, one of Vietnam's traditional handicrafts. When silkworms create their cocoons by spinning silk fibres, locals carefully cut through to retrieve these protein and calcium-rich larvae rather than boiling them. The key is not to over-fry, keeping them plump rather than hard and chewy.

Serves 2
Preparation time: 10 minutes
Cooking time: 15 minutes

| DF | ≤30 |

- 2 tablespoons pork lard
- 28 g/1 oz garlic, finely chopped
- 200 g/7 oz silkworm larvae (nhộng)
- 2 teaspoons light brown sugar
- ½ teaspoon black pepper
- 1 tablespoon fish sauce
- ½ teaspoon lime juice
- 1 teaspoon coconut water
- 5 g/⅛ oz lime leaves (about 12 medium), finely sliced

In a small pan, melt 1 tablespoon of the pork lard over a low heat. Add the garlic and fry for about 5 minutes until the garlic is golden. Strain the garlic and set aside; keep the fat in the pan.

Melt the remaining pork lard in the same pan over a medium-low heat. Test the heat by dropping one of the larvae into the pan; if it sizzles, the oil is ready. Fry the larvae for 4–5 minutes. Add the sugar, pepper, fish sauce, lime juice and coconut water. Continue to braise for another 2–3 minutes until the sauce glazes around the larvae.

Remove from the heat and add the sliced lime leaves and fried garlic.

Serve hot.

## STEAMED PIG'S BRAIN

Óc Heo Chưng

As a child, I remember being served this dish now and then – there was a belief that eating pig's brain would make children smarter. Though it wasn't my cup of tea, it did help me become more comfortable with eating offal (variety meats) in general. Today, pig's brain is still popular and can be prepared either steamed with ginger as shown here, or fried. You can also add it to Crab Soup (page 121) for extra nutrients. This dish works well in a meal alongside others like Fried Stuffed Tofu with Tomato Sauce (page 308) as a part of a family meal.

Serves 2–3
Preparation time: 10 minutes
Cooking time: 13 minutes

| DF | ≤5 | ≤30 |

- 1 pig's brain
- 10 g/¼ oz piece fresh ginger, peeled and cut into thin matchsticks (julienned)
- ½ teaspoon fish sauce
- ¼ teaspoon black pepper
- ¼ teaspoon sugar
- 20 g/¾ oz spring onion (scallion) whites, chopped

Place the pig's brain in a flameproof bowl. Cover the brain with the ginger. Sprinkle the brain with the fish sauce, pepper and sugar.

Set up a steamer and bring the water to the boil. Put the bowl with the brain in the steamer basket, setting it over the boiling water, and steam for 13 minutes. Add the spring onion (scallion) whites to the bowl.

Carefully remove from the steamer and serve immediately.

## SIMMERED GNETUM GNEMON LEAVES

Rau Lá Bép Kho

This traditional dish from the Mạ community features young Gnetum Gnemon leaves simmered with a special spice mix. While in Bảo Lộc, I discovered many leaves unfamiliar to the Kinh people, opening my eyes to Vietnam's diverse edible plants. Not every community uses fish sauce for seasoning, particularly those in mountainous regions far from the coast. Here, I use *ro nhau* – a seasoning made of toasted rice and dried local herbs, including the mature leaves of gnetum gnemon (also known as melinjo).

Serves 4–6
Preparation time: 15 minutes
Cooking time: 1 hour 40 minutes

| V | VE | DF | GF | ≤5 |

- 60 g/2¼ oz cored cây prũ (a type of root in the ginger family), or you could use young ginger or young galangal
- 480 g/1 lb 1 oz young gnetum gnemon (rau lá bép non), leaves picked
- ¼ teaspoon MSG
- 1 tablespoon toasted rice seasoning with herbs (ro nhau)
- ¾ teaspoon salt

Bring 1 litre/1¾ pints (4¼ cups) of water to a simmer in a pot. Add the prepared cây prũ and half the gnetum gnemon leaves to the simmering water. Push down and cook until they have wilted. Add the remaining gnetum gnemon leaves and push down. Cover with a lid and simmer for 1 hour, stirring well every 20 minutes.

Add the MSG, toasted rice seasoning and ½ teaspoon of the salt. Stir well to combine. Cook for another 15–20 minutes, keeping the pot covered, to allow the rice seasoning to infuse. Add the remaining salt, then stir well to combine.

Serve hot as a vegetable side dish.

## RICE AND GNETUM GNEMON LEAF SOUP

Lá Bép Nấu Với Gạo

This traditional dish from the Mạ community uses *rau lá bép* (gnetum gnemon leaves), with mature green leaves particularly valued for helping new mothers' milk production. Despite containing rice, it serves as a side dish in Mạ family meals. While in Bảo Lộc, we learned that instead of fish sauce, their community creates distinctive flavours using local spices mix like lá ro nhau and techniques – like the rattan ash in this recipe, which adds a unique layer to the dish.

Serves 2–3
Preparation time: 45 minutes, plus 30 minutes soaking time
Cooking time: 25–30 minutes

| V | VE | DF | GF | ≤5 |

- 40 g/1½ oz (3 tablespoons) rice
- 15 g/½ oz old gnetum gnemon leaves (rau lá bép già)
- 50 g/1 ¾ oz rattan sticks
- 1 tablespoon toasted rice seasoning with local herbs (lá ro nhau), optional
- ¼ teaspoon salt
- ¼ teaspoon MSG
- cooked rice, to serve

Preheat a charcoal grill or wood fire.

In a bowl, soak the rice in 2 tablespoons of water for 30 minutes.

Roll the old gnetum gnemon leaves and finely dice them.

Carefully place half of each rattan stick on the coals or in the fire (using the other half as a handle) and burn until they are completely charred; then remove them from the fire and collect the ash from the burned section on a plate or in a bowl.

Put the diced gnetum gnemon leaves, soaked rice and the rattan ash in a mortar and pound with a pestle until very fine. This is a long process but crucial for the dish; it takes 15–30 minutes.

In a pot, bring 630 ml/21 fl oz (2⅔ cups) of water to a simmer. Slowly add the leaf and rice mixture, stirring constantly, for 1 minute. Add the toasted rice seasoning. Cook, uncovered, over a very low heat, stirring constantly, for 20 minutes.

Add the salt and MSG, then cook for an additional 4–5 minutes, still stirring; at this point, thanks to the rice, the soup should be thick like a velouté.

Serve hot on top of cooked rice.

## STIR-FRIED FIDDLEHEAD FERNS WITH PAPAYA FLOWERS

Rau Dớn Xào Hoa Đu Đủ

While most people know papaya as a fruit or in salads, in Vietnam, we also cook its flowers, stir-frying them with green vegetables or eggs as part of a meal. You'll usually find this dish in homes with papaya trees in their gardens, where the flowers can be picked and cooked right away. Since the flowers taste quite bitter, they're often paired with other ingredients to balance the flavour, like the fiddlehead ferns in this recipe.

Serves 3–4
Preparation time: 10 minutes
Cooking time: 6–7 minutes

| DF | ≤5 | ≤30 |

- 2 tablespoons pork fat
- 330 g/11½ oz fiddlehead ferns (rau dớn)
- 230 g/8 oz papaya flowers
- 1 tablespoon all-purpose seasoning (hạt nêm)
- 1 teaspoon salt

Heat the pork fat in a large pan over a medium-high heat. When the fat is hot, add the fiddlehead ferns and papaya flowers to the pan. Stir-fry for 1 minute.

Add the all-purpose seasoning and salt. Stir well to combine, then cook, stirring occasionally, for about 5 minutes, until the water released from the vegetables evaporates.

Transfer to a serving dish and serve hot.

## STIR-FRIED SWEET POTATO LEAVES WITH GARLIC

Rau Lang Xào Tỏi

While this recipe uses sweet potato leaves, you can replace them with any green leaves you have on hand, from morning glory and malabar spinach to pak choi (bok choy) and even kale. As it's quite simple, it can go with any main dish, or can even be paired with Minced Pork Omelette (page 348) to make a quick meal.

Another alternative, my personal favourite, is to fry the sweet potato leaves in pork fat, adding Crispy Fried Pork Fat (page 459) while stir-frying. This gives the dish another layer of flavour and texture.

Serves 3–4
Preparation time: 10 minutes
Cooking time: 15 minutes

| DF | ≤5 | ≤30 |

- 500 g/1 lb 2 oz bunch of sweet potato leaves (rau lang)
- 1½ tablespoons neutral oil
- 40 g/1½ oz garlic, coarsely chopped
- 2 teaspoons fish sauce
- ¼ teaspoon salt

Bring a pan of water to the boil, add the sweet potato leaves and blanch them for 3 minutes 30 seconds–4 minutes. Once blanched, drain and set aside.

In a large frying pan or skillet, heat the oil over a medium heat, then add the garlic and fry until golden, 2–4 minutes. Add the blanched sweet leaves and stir-fry for a few minutes. Season with the fish sauce and salt, stir well to combine all the ingredients and cook for another 2–3 minutes.

Serve immediately.

# STIR-FRIED MORNING GLORY IN FERMENTED TOFU

## Rau Muống Xào Chao

The hollow morning glory (*rau muống*) stalks stay crispy in this vegan stir-fry, while soaking up the deep and savoury flavour of the fermented tofu (*chao*) sauce. For extra heat, add some Chilli and Lemongrass Oil (page 457).

Serves 3–4
Preparation time: 15 minutes
Cooking time: 10 minutes

**| V | VE | DF | GF | ≤5 | ≤30 |**

- 600 g/1 lb 5 oz morning glory (rau muống)
- 2 tablespoons neutral oil
- 30 g/1 oz peeled garlic
- 30 g/1 oz (2 tablespoons) fermented tofu (chao)
- 3 tablespoons liquid from fermented tofu (chao)

Prepare the morning glory by picking the leaves and tender stalks, then cut them into 10-cm/4-inch pieces lengthways. There should be 460 g/1 lb after picking.

In a large frying pan or skillet, heat the oil over a medium heat. Once the oil is hot, add the whole garlic and stir-fry for about 1 minute until it becomes fragrant and starts to turn golden. Add the morning glory to the pan and stir-fry for 3–4 minutes until it starts to wilt. Add the fermented tofu and its liquid to the pan, mixing well to evenly coat the morning glory. Continue to stir-fry for another 2–3 minutes until the morning glory is tender but still vibrant green.

Serve immediately.

# MƯỜNG-STYLE MIXED VEGETABLE STIR-FRY

## Rau Xào Thập Cẩm Người Mường

At bác Đinh Thị Như Thoa's home in Buôn Ma Thuột, Đắk Lắk province, we gathered ingredients for this stir-fry from her garden. She shared how papaya flowers were once easy to get from Kinh neighbours who didn't cook with them, though nowadays they're sold pre-blanched at markets and have become much more popular. The dish's unique feature is its use of both papaya leaves and flowers – ingredients I hadn't encountered before in Vietnamese cooking.

Serves 3–4
Preparation time: 30 minutes
Cooking time: 45 minutes

| DF |

*For the vegetables*
55 g/2 oz papaya leaves, hand-shredded
120 g/4¼ oz young cassava leaves (lá mì non)
15 g/½ oz piper lolot leaves
60 g/2¼ oz sawtooth coriander (culantro), cut into 5-cm/2-inch lengths
50 g/1¾ oz small round green bitter aubergines (eggplants) (cà quẹng)
100 g/3½ oz papaya flowers

*For the seasoning*
15 g/½ oz garlic, thinly sliced
2 tablespoons cooking oil
1 teaspoon MSG
½ teaspoon all-purpose seasoning (hạt nêm)
20 g/¾ oz sawtooth coriander (culantro) for finishing, coarsely chopped
1 teaspoon fish sauce

Set up a steamer and bring the water to the boil.

Combine all the vegetables except the papaya flowers in a bowl. Add to the steamer basket, setting it over the boiling water, and steam for 13–15 minutes until wilted but still bright green. Remove from steamer and let cool, then squeeze out the excess water and set aside.

Add the papaya flowers to the steamer basket, set over the boiling water, and steam for 25 minutes. Set aside the steamed papaya flowers.

Place the garlic in a mortar and lightly crush with a pestle.

Heat the oil in a large wok over a medium heat, add the crushed garlic and fry for 1 minute, or until fragrant. Add the steamed papaya flowers, then briefly stir-fry for 1 minute. Add the remaining steamed vegetables, then season with the MSG and all-purpose seasoning and stir-fry for 3 minutes 30 seconds. Add the sawtooth coriander (culantro) and fish sauce. Continue stir-frying for 1 minute 30 seconds until the vegetables absorb the fish sauce.

Transfer to a serving plate and serve hot as a side dish.

## STEAMED MACKEREL SCAD WITH WILD VEGETABLES

Cá Nục Hấp Rau Rừng – Hla Hiong Xao Ka Xin

Chú A Wơr shared how seawater fish entered Bahnar cuisine through trade with Kinh people who followed French missionaries to the coastal city of Quy Nhơn in Bình Định province. In earlier times, before modern borders, they would trade for salt blocks from Laos, dipping them into dishes during cooking, while herbs served as natural seasonings. Today, although MSG and all-purpose seasoning are common, local ingredients remain essential – as in this dish where steamed mackerel is stir-fried with wild mountain leaves that chú A Wơr foraged during our visit.

Serves 2–3
Preparation time: 15 minutes
Cooking time: 5–6 minutes

| DF | ≤30 |

- 475 g/1 lb mixture of wild vegetables, such as mimosa pudica (shrinking leaf; hla hiong) and hla po le (similar to baby bamboo leaf), or use fiddlehead fern or another wild green leaf
- 1 × 270 g/9½ oz steamed mackerel scad
- 3 tablespoons neutral oil
- 5 g/⅛ oz garlic, coarsely chopped
- 5 g/⅛ oz shallot, coarsely chopped
- ½ teaspoon black pepper
- 5 g/⅛ oz sawtooth coriander (culantro), chopped
- ½ teaspoon salt
- 1 teaspoon MSG
- 1 teaspoon all-purpose seasoning (hạt nêm)

Place the wild vegetables in a big pot with 240 ml/8 fl oz (1 cup) of water, cover, bring to a simmer and steam for 1 minute. Alternatively, bring a pan of water to the boil, add the wild vegetables and blanch for 2 minutes, then rinse and squeeze out the excess water. Cut the steamed or blanched wild vegetables coarsely.

Pick the meat from the steamed mackerel scad; you need about 200 g/7 oz of clean fish meat.

Heat a wok over a medium heat, add the oil, garlic and shallot and cook for 1 minute. (Do not cover the wok during cooking.)

Add the pepper, then add the picked fish meat with 300 ml/10 fl oz (1¼ cups) of water. Bring it to a simmer. Add the prepared wild vegetables, sawtooth coriander (culantro), salt, MSG and all-purpose seasoning. Stir-fry for 3 minutes.

Remove from the heat and serve warm.

## BAMBOO WORMS FRIED WITH LIME LEAVES

Sâu Măng Rang Lá Chanh

During our research in Hà Giang, anh Triệu Tà Phẩu introduced us to these bamboo worms, which appear in autumn and winter when they nest in clusters within the lower joints of bamboo trees. They typically inhabit already damaged bamboo, making their harvest less impactful to healthy trees. The cooking method is specific – the worms need three rounds of dry-frying before being finished with pork fat for crispiness.

Serves 2–3
Preparation time: 10 minutes
Cooking time: 10–12 minutes

| DF | GF | ≤5 | ≤30 |

- 190 g/6¾ oz bamboo worms (sâu măng)
- ¾ teaspoon MSG
- 6 g/⅛ oz lime leaves (about 14 leaves)
- 2 tablespoons pork fat

Wash the bamboo worms thoroughly in water several times. Drain well.

Heat a dry pan over a medium heat. Add the washed and drained worms. Sprinkle the MSG over the worms. Cook for 5 minutes, stirring continuously, allowing water to evaporate. The worms will wilt and puff up about 3 times during cooking.

Add the lime leaves to the pan and continue cooking for 1 minute, still stirring.

Add 1 tablespoon of the pork fat to the pan. Cook, stirring constantly, for 3 minutes, being careful to keep stirring and watching the heat to prevent the worms from exploding.

Add the remaining pork fat, then continue frying, stirring constantly, for another 2 minutes, or until the worms are crispy.

Transfer to a serving dish and enjoy while hot.

# BÁT TRÀNG-STYLE STIR-FRIED KOHLRABI WITH SQUID

Su Hào Xào Mực (Bát Tràng)

About 14 km/8¾ miles from Hanoi lies Bát Tràng, one of Vietnam's oldest pottery villages. While famous for its ceramics, the village maintains an even more traditional and formal dining culture than Hanoi itself. Among its signature dishes are this stir-fried kohlrabi with squid and Bát Tràng Bamboo Shoot and Squid Soup (page 379). Though none of the ingredients in these dishes are native to the area, they've become local specialities. The daughter-in-law of Bà Nguyễn Thị Lâm, a renowned Bát Tràng chef, taught us that both dishes require female dried squid from Thanh Hóa for their sweeter flesh.

Serves 4, as part of a meal
Preparation time: 20 minutes, plus 30 minutes soaking time
Cooking time: 10 minutes

| DF |

- 35 g/1¼ oz dried female squid (preferably from Thanh Hoa province, Vietnam)
- rice wine or water, for soaking dried squid, enough for covering the squid
- 20 g/¾ oz piece fresh ginger, sliced
- 1 tablespoon neutral oil or pork lard
- 12 g/½ oz peeled shallot
- ¼ teaspoon sugar
- 1 teaspoon fish sauce
- ¼ teaspoon black pepper
- 5 g/⅛ oz coriander (cilantro), to garnish

*For the vegetables*

- 300 g/10½ oz kohlrabi, peeled and shredded (240 g/8½ oz after shredding)
- 45 g/1½ oz carrots, shredded
- 1 teaspoon salt

Remove all the tentacles and outer skin from the dried squid. Keep only the opaque white flesh inside.

Soak the dried squid in a bowl of rice wine or water with the ginger for about 30 minutes. Once softened, shred into very fine strips.

Meanwhile, for the vegetables, combine the kohlrabi and carrots in a bowl with the salt and 500 ml/18 fl oz (2 cups) of water. Soak for 5–10 minutes. Squeeze out all the liquid thoroughly.

Heat the oil or lard in a pan over a low heat, add the shallot and fry for 2 minutes. Add the shredded squid and fry for 30 seconds. Add the sugar, ½ teaspoon of the fish sauce and the pepper. Fry until the squid turns golden, about 2 minutes. Add the squeezed kohlrabi and carrots. Stir-fry for 2–3 minutes until the vegetables wilt. Add the remaining fish sauce.

Garnish with coriander (cilantro). Serve immediately.

## STIR-FRIED CHAYOTE WITH EGGS

### Su Su Xào Trứng

Any firm gourd or squash can replace chayote, even kohlrabi works well in this recipe.

Serves 4 to share
Preparation time: 15 minutes
Cooking time: 15 minutes

| V | DF | GF | ≤30 |

- 2 chayote (440 g/15½ oz)
- 2 tablespoons neutral oil
- 25 g/1 oz garlic, minced
- 4 g shallot, minced
- 1½ teaspoons salt
- ½ teaspoon sugar
- 2 eggs
- 20 g/¾ oz spring onions (scallions), chopped
- 10 g/¼ oz coriander (cilantro), chopped, to garnish

Peel the chayote and cut them into long strips.

Heat the oil in a large frying pan or skillet over a medium heat, add the garlic and shallot to the pan and stir-fry for 2 minutes until fragrant. Add the chayote strips to the pan and stir-fry for 2 minutes. Season with the salt, then add 2 tablespoons of water to the pan to help the chayote cook faster. Continue cooking until the chayote is fully cooked, another 2–3 minutes. Pierce with a chopstick to see if it's cooked; it should easily go through the chayote. Stir in the sugar and mix well.

In a small bowl, beat the eggs. Pour them into the pan, stirring quickly to combine with the chayote. Add the spring onions (scallions) and continue to stir-fry until the eggs are fully cooked, about 1 minute.

Garnish with the chopped coriander (cilantro) before serving.

## STIR-FRIED BABY SHRIMP WITH STARFRUIT

### Tép Khô Xào Khế

In Vietnam, we're lucky to have many types of shrimp, including tiny tép eaten whole. Find them dried in Asian stores for this recipe.

Serves 2–3
Preparation time: 10 minutes, plus 15 minutes soaking time
Cooking time: 6 minutes

| DF | ≤30 |

- 1 starfruit (carambola) (about 170 g/5¾ oz)
- salt, for soaking water
- 70 g/2½ oz dried baby shrimp (tép khô)
- 2 tablespoons pork lard
- 15 g/½ oz garlic, coarsely chopped
- ½ bird's eye chilli, chopped
- 8 g/¼ oz spring onion (scallion) whites, chopped
- 1 teaspoon fish sauce
- 1 teaspoon brown sugar
- 10 g/¼ oz spring onion (scallion) greens, cut into 1-cm/½-in pieces, to garnish

Peel the edges of the starfruit, cut it vertically into two halves, then slice each half. Soak the slices in salted water for 15 minutes.

Meanwhile, quickly rinse the dried baby shrimp under running water.

In a large pan or wok, melt 1 tablespoon of the lard over a medium heat and stir-fry the garlic, chilli and spring onion (scallion) whites for 30 seconds, or until they change colour. Add the shrimp to the pan and keep stir-frying for 3 minutes 30 seconds. Lower the heat and add the fish sauce, sugar and the remaining lard. Stir well.

Drain the sliced starfruit and add to the pan. Stir-fry for another 2 minutes.

Garnish with the spring onion greens and serve immediately.

## SIMPLE OMELETTE

### Trứng Chiên

This omelette was taught to me by cô Chán Mùi in Tồ Thầu, Hoàng Su Phì. What makes it special is her unique seasoning method – when the omelette turns golden, she drizzles fish sauce into the pan, flips the omelette and turns off the heat, letting the residual heat caramelize the fish sauce around the edges.

Serves 1
Preparation time: 2 minutes
Cooking time: 2–2¼ minutes

| DF | ≤5 | ≤30 |

2 eggs
1–1½ teaspoons neutral oil
1 teaspoon fish sauce

In a bowl, whisk the eggs until well combined.

Heat the oil in an 18-cm/7-inch pan over a medium heat, then pour the beaten eggs into the pan and cook for about 1 minute 30 seconds.

While the omelette is still cooking, pour the fish sauce evenly over the surface.

Carefully flip the omelette. Remove from the heat immediately after flipping.

Let the residual heat cook the other side for 30–45 seconds. The total cooking time should be about 2 minutes–2 minutes 15 seconds.

Slide the omelette onto a plate and serve immediately.

## PIPER LOLOT LEAF OMELETTE

### Trứng Chiên Lá Lốt

This simple yet flavourful Vietnamese dish combines eggs with aromatic *lá lốt* (piper lolot). You can also use other herbs like *lá mơ*, skunkvine/Chinese fever vine or *ngải cứu* (common mugwort), which is believed to help with headaches and menstrual discomfort.

Serves 1
Preparation time: 5 minutes
Cooking time: 3 minutes

| V | DF | GF | ≤5 | ≤30 |

2 medium eggs
20 g/¾ oz piper lolot leaves (lá lốt), finely sliced
¼ teaspoon MSG
¼ teaspoon salt
¼ teaspoon black pepper
1 tablespoon neutral oil

In a bowl, whisk the eggs until well combined.

Add the piper lolot leaves, MSG, salt and black pepper to the egg mixture. Mix all the ingredients thoroughly.

Heat the oil in a pan over a medium heat, pour the egg mixture into the pan, spreading it evenly, then cook for 2 minutes 30 seconds–3 minutes, or until the bottom is golden and the top is set.

Slide the omelette onto a plate. Serve hot as a side dish or light meal.

## MINCED PORK OMELETTE

Trứng Chiên Thịt Bằm

My go-to Vietnamese dish as a broke student overseas, this omelette is really easy to make. The key is stir-frying the shallots in oil first – this imparts their flavour into the cooking oil, making the omelette much more flavourful. By the time your omelette is done, the shallots should be golden brown. You can replace the minced (ground) pork with *hến*, baby basket clams, and turn it into a Baby Basket Clam Omelette (below).

Makes a 20-cm/8-in omelette; serves 4 as a side or 1–2 as a main
Preparation time: 15 minutes
Cooking time: 10–15 minutes

| DF | ≤30 |

3 eggs
½ tablespoon fish sauce
½ teaspoon ground black pepper
½ teaspoon sugar
20 g/¾ oz spring onions (scallions), thinly sliced into rounds
30 g/1 oz red shallots, peeled and minced
200 g/7 oz minced (ground) pork (20 per cent fat)

*For frying*
2 tablespoons cooking oil
20 g/¾ oz red shallots, peeled and thinly sliced

*To serve, optional*
soy sauce
fresh chilli slices

In a bowl, whisk the eggs until well combined.

Add the fish sauce, pepper and sugar to the eggs and mix well. Stir in the spring onions (scallions), minced shallots and minced (ground) pork. Mix thoroughly.

Heat the oil in a 20-cm/8-inch pan with a lid over a medium heat, add the sliced shallots and stir-fry until they start to turn golden, 2–3 minutes.

Pour the egg mixture into the pan, ensuring it's evenly distributed. Cover the pan with the lid and lower the heat. After 5 minutes, check the omelette: the edges should be fully cooked.

Carefully slide the omelette onto a plate, then flip it back into the pan to cook the other side. Continue cooking until the omelette is fully done, 3–5 more minutes.

Transfer to a serving plate and cut into wedges.

Serve the omelette hot, accompanied by soy sauce and fresh chilli slices for dipping, if desired.

## BABY BASKET CLAM OMELETTE

Trứng Chiên Hến

While I use baby basket clams in this recipe, any clam meat will work, just keep the same ratio.

Serves 2–3
Preparation time: 15 minutes
Cooking time: 10 minutes

| DF | ≤30 |

275 g/9¾ oz eggs (about 5 eggs)
220 g/7¾ oz baby basket clam meat
1 teaspoon sugar
1 teaspoon black pepper
1 teaspoon fish sauce
¼ teaspoon salt
3 tablespoons neutral oil
50 g/1¾ oz shallots, chopped
35 g/1¼ oz spring onions (scallions), finely sliced

In a small bowl, whisk the eggs until well combined.

Add the clam meat, sugar, pepper, fish sauce and salt to the eggs and mix well.

Heat 2 tablespoons of the oil in a pan over a medium heat, add the shallots and fry for 2–4 minutes until golden brown.

Add the fried shallots and their oil and the spring onions (scallions) to the egg mixture, stirring to combine.

Heat the remaining oil to the same pan over a medium heat. Pour the egg mixture into the pan and evenly spread it over the pan. Cook until the bottom is set and golden brown, 2–3 minutes, then flip and cook the other side for another 2–3 minutes until done.

Transfer to a serving plate and cut into wedges.

Serve hot.

# FRIED STUFFED PUMPKIN FLOWERS

## Bông Bí Nhồi Thịt Chiên Giòn

Found in local markets bundled with their green stalks attached, pumpkin flowers feature in many Vietnamese dishes, from Pumpkin Flower Soup with Strabismus Fish Paste (page 364) to simple preparations like boiling, then dipping in fish sauce or stir-frying. This stuffed version is often prepared for death anniversaries and family gatherings, with multiple family members joining in with the preparation.

Serves 4–6
Preparation: 30 minutes
Cooking: 20–25 minutes

| DF |

100 g/3½ oz pumpkin flowers or 24 pumpkin flowers, cleaned
600 ml/1 pint (2½ cups) neutral oil, for frying

*For the meat filling*
115 g/4 oz Pork Paste (page 461)
7 g/¼ oz wood ear mushroom, fried
140 g/5 oz minced (ground) pork
15 g/½ oz peeled shallot
15 g/½ oz peeled garlic
5 g/⅛ oz spring onion (scallion) greens, finely chopped
¼ teaspoon black pepper
½ teaspoon sugar
1 teaspoon fish sauce

*For the batter*
2 egg yolks
145 g/5¼ oz (1 cup minus 2 teaspoons) tempura flour
80 ml/2½ fl oz (⅓ cup) sparkling water, plus 1 tablespoon, if needed
½ teaspoon salt

To make the meat filling, place all the ingredients in a mixing bowl and mix well until all the ingredients are thoroughly combined.

Carefully fill each pumpkin flower with about 15 g/½ oz (1 tablespoon) of the meat filling. There should be enough filling for all the flowers.

To prepare the batter, in a bowl, mix the egg yolks, 70 g/2½ oz (⅓ cup plus 2 tablespoons) of the tempura flour and the sparkling water. Stir until smooth. This is a wet batter.

In another bowl, combine the remaining tempura flour and the salt. Mix well. This is a dry batter.

Pour the oil into a shallow pan with a diameter of about 25 cm/10 inches. If using a smaller or larger pan, make sure the oil fills at least a third of the pan. Heat the oil to 175°C/345°F. If not using a thermometer, test the oil temperature by inserting wooden chopsticks into the oil – it should bubble vigorously around them.

First, coat each stuffed pumpkin flower in the dry batter. Then, dip it into the wet batter, ensuring it is fully covered. You may need to add an extra tablespoon of sparkling water to the wet batter if it becomes too thick.

Working in batches to avoid overcrowding the pan, carefully place the batter-coated pumpkin flowers in the hot oil and fry for 4–5 minutes, or until they are fully cooked and golden brown. Remove the fried pumpkin flowers from the oil and place them on a paper towel-lined plate to drain the excess oil.

Serve immediately.

# STIR-FRIED BEEF WITH FRENCH FRIES

## Thịt Bò Xào Khoai Tây

In Vietnamese, the names for both potato (*khoai tây*) and white onion (*hành tây*) carry the word '*tây*' meaning 'Western', reflecting their introduction during French colonization, along with beef – previously rare in Vietnamese cooking. In this popular chopstick-friendly dish, which can be found in homes, traditional restaurants and *quán nhậu* (beer halls), beef tenderloin is sliced thinly to stretch the (still considered) premium ingredient, then stir-fried with French fries.

I grew up eating this dish in 1990s Ho Chi Minh City. At home we would eat it with white rice, alongside a plate of Vinegar-Dressed Lettuce Salad (page 135) and a broth.

Serves 2–3
Preparation time: 30 minutes, plus 10 minutes soaking and 15 minutes marinating times
Cooking time: 25 minutes

*For the French fries*
315 g/11 oz potatoes
Neutral oil, for deep-frying

*For the marinated beef*
150 g/5½ oz beef tenderloin, thinly sliced
¼ teaspoon sugar
½ teaspoon fish sauce
¼ teaspoon oyster sauce
½ teaspoon soy sauce
¼ teaspoon sesame oil
⅛ teaspoon black pepper
5 g/⅛ oz shallot, coarsely chopped
5 g/⅛ oz garlic, coarsely chopped

*For stir-frying*
2 teaspoons neutral oil
20 g/¾ oz garlic, coarsely chopped
20 g/¾ oz unsalted butter
4 teaspoons oyster sauce
60 g/2¼ oz onion, sliced
⅛ teaspoon black pepper

Peel the potatoes and cut them into French fries, then soak in a bowl of water for 5–10 minutes. Drain and pat thoroughly dry.

Heat a pan of oil to 130°C/265°F. If not using a thermometer, test the oil temperature by inserting wooden chopsticks into the oil – it should very gently bubble around them. Carefully add the potatoes and fry for 12 minutes, or until a skin forms. Carefully remove with a slotted spoon and drain on paper towels.

Combine all the marinade ingredients in a bowl. Marinate for 15 minutes.

In a pan, heat 1 teaspoon of the oil, add the marinated beef and stir-fry over a high heat for 1 minute 30 seconds–2 minutes until just done. Transfer to a bowl.

Increase the temperature of the oil to 175–180°C/345–350°F. If not using a thermometer, test the oil temperature by inserting wooden chopsticks into the oil – it should bubble vigorously around them. Carefully return the fried potatoes to the pan and fry for the second time for 3–4 minutes until golden. Carefully remove with the slotted spoon and drain on paper towels.

In another pan, heat the remaining oil. Add the garlic and fry until golden, 45–60 seconds. Add the fried potatoes and the butter, then shake the pan. Add the oyster sauce, reduce the heat, then cook until the sauce is bubbling. Add the stir-fried beef, then the onion and stir-fry for 10 seconds.

Remove from the heat, finish with the black pepper and serve immediately.

# ACCOMPANYING SOUPS

## Món canh

*Canh* (soup) is fundamental to Vietnamese meals, particularly in family meals. When meals are simplified due to necessity, soup often becomes the main accompaniment to rice, providing a complete dish of protein, vegetables and liquid in one bowl. This broth element was essential, since traditionally, Vietnamese people did not drink during meals, saving tea for after, though since 1974 drinks like beer and soda have become more common at the table. At its simplest, broth can be made from the cooking water of boiled greens, seasoned with fish sauce, salt or MSG. More elaborate versions begin with a stock of beef, pork, chicken, fish, prawns (shrimp) or clams, enriched with vegetables and finished with complementary herbs, such as dill to brighten fish and tomato broths, or coriander (cilantro) and spring onion (scallion)to soften pork-based ones. Across Vietnam, sour broths (*canh chua*) vary by region: tamarind is predominantly used in the south, dracontomelon in the north, while some versions use fermented mustard greens or simply lime juice for sourness.

*Canh* remains a constant at Vietnamese meals through all seasons; there's even a common belief that hot broth can help cool the body during summer months, cementing its year-round appearance.

## MORNING GLORY BOILED WATER (NORTHERN STYLE)

Nước Rau Muống Luộc

This really simple soup is often eaten during the hot summer days in the north. As it is usually humid and hot, people tend to eat more boiled vegetables. In the north, you would use the blanching water from either morning glory or cabbage and mix it with *quả sấu*, dracontomelon fruit, to give acidity and another layer of flavour to the soup; meanwhile in the south, we would normally use quartered tomatoes for that extra acidity. Cô Nguyễn Thị Ngọc Bích taught us how to make this simple yet so refreshing soup, amongst other northern style dishes, including Fish Sauce Glazed Pork Belly (page 306), which would go great with this.

Serves 4–6
Preparation time: 10 minutes
Cooking time: 10 minutes

| V | VE | DF | ≤5 | ≤30 |

- 200 g/7 oz morning glory (rau muống)
- 75 g/2¾ oz dracontomelon fruit (quả sấu) or 2 medium tomatoes
- 2 teaspoons soup powder (bột canh)
- 2 tablespoons lime juice, optional
- Dracontomelon Fish Sauce Dip (page 472), to serve

Bring 1.4 litres/2½ pints (6 cups) of water to the boil over a high heat. Add the morning glory, using chopsticks to submerge it. Keeping the heat high during cooking so the morning glory keeps its bright colour, continue stirring up and down for 4 minutes. Remove the morning glory, then set aside for another recipe or serve it as a side dish.

Add the dracontomelon fruit to the boiling water. Cover, then simmer for 5–6 minutes until the fruit is soft. Remove one of the fruit and reserve for another use, for example in Dracontomelon Fish Sauce Dip (page 472). Mash the remaining fruit into the soup.

Season with the soup powder and the lime juice, if desired, and serve with a small bowl of dracontomelon fish sauce dip on the side.

*Notes:* You can substitute the soup powder with ½ teaspoon MSG, ½ teaspoon salt or 2 teaspoons fish sauce.

Any spare broth can be stored in the refrigerator for 2–3 days.

## COWSLIP CREEPER SOUP WITH PORK BALLS

Canh Thiên Lý Nấu Mọc

*Thiên lý* (cowslip creeper, also known as *Telosma cordata*) is often cultivated in gardens for both shade and eating. The young leaves and umbels can be used in soups like this one or stir-fried with prawns (shrimp) or garlic. The plant itself has medicinal properties, helping to reduce fatigue and relieve pain. If you don't have fresh pork paste, you can make meatballs or use baby back ribs to make the soup.

Serves 4 to share
Preparation time: 15 minutes
Cooking time: 15 minutes

| DF | ≤30 |

- 200 g/7 oz cowslip creeper cymes/umbels (flower clusters)
- 200 g/7 oz pre-prepared or homemade Pork Paste (page 461)
- 5 g/⅛ oz spring onion (scallion) greens, finely chopped
- ½ tablespoon vegetable oil
- 10 g/¼ oz shallot, minced
- 20 g/¾ oz garlic, minced
- 900 ml/30 fl oz (3¾ cups) boiling water
- 20 ml/¾ fl oz (4 teaspoons) fish sauce, or more to taste
- ¼ teaspoon salt

Thoroughly rinse the cowslip creeper flowers and set aside to drain.

In a large bowl, thoroughly mix the pork paste with the spring onion (scallion) greens.

Heat the oil in a pot over a medium heat, add the shallot and garlic and stir-fry for about 3 minutes until they turn golden brown and fragrant. Pour the measured boiling water into the pot, then add the fish sauce and salt. Stir well to combine all the ingredients.

Gently add the drained cowslip creeper flowers to the pot. Simmer for 5 minutes, or until the flowers become tender.

Shape the pork paste mixture into small quenelles (see note) or meatballs.

Carefully drop the pork quenelles/meatballs into the simmering soup. Cook for an additional 3–5 minutes until they float to the surface.

Taste the soup and adjust the seasoning by adding more fish sauce if desired.

*Note:* As the pork paste is quite sticky, use two spoons to form quenelles: scoop the paste with one spoon, then use the other to shape it before dropping it into the soup.

# STUFFED BITTER GOURD SOUP

## Canh Khổ Qua Nhồi Thịt

In Vietnamese traditional medicine, bitter gourd (bitter melon) is considered a *mát* (cooling) ingredient that helps expel heat, making this soup particularly refreshing in summer. The meat filling enriches the soup with its natural sweetness, while the addition of the single chilli (chị Nguyen Thi Thu Ba's tip) helps balance the gourd's bitterness.

Serves 4 to share
Preparation Time: 20 minutes
Cooking Time: 45 minutes

| DF |

40 g/1½ oz dried wood ear mushrooms
4 small bitter gourds (bitter melons) (khổ qua) (410 g/14½ oz)
10 unpeeled prawns (shrimp) (110 g/3¾ oz), cleaned (55 g/2 oz cleaned weight)
55 g/2 oz shallots, sliced
150 g/5½ oz lean minced (ground) pork
135 g/4½ oz onion, finely chopped
100 g/3½ oz Pork Paste (page 461)
1 teaspoon black pepper
½ tablespoon sugar
½ teaspoon fish sauce

*For the soup*
½ tablespoon neutral oil
30 g/1 oz shallots, chopped
15 g/½ oz garlic, chopped
½ teaspoon fish sauce
1 bird's eye chilli
1.3 litres/2¼ pints (5½ cups) boiling water
55 g/2 oz onion (1 small)
¾ tablespoon all-purpose seasoning (hạt nêm)
6 spring onions (scallions), blanched, for wrapping

Soak the mushrooms in a bowl of water until they expand to 100 g/3½ oz. Set aside.

Wash the bitter gourds (bitter melons), make a vertical slit across them, open them up slightly and core out the middles with a spoon.

Chop the prawns (shrimp) and shallots together. In a bowl, mix the chopped prawns and shallot with the minced (ground) pork and onion. Add the pork paste to the meat mixture and mix well. Season the mixture with the pepper, sugar and fish sauce.

Chop the 40 g/1½ oz of soaked mushrooms and add them to the meat mixture.

To make the soup, in a separate pot that can fit everything, heat the oil, add the shallots and garlic and fry until fragrant and slightly browned, about 1 minute 30 seconds. Add the fish sauce, chilli and the measured boiling water to the pot. Add the onion to the pot.

Stuff the prepared bitter gourds with the seasoned meat mixture.

To secure the stuffed bitter gourds, thread a cocktail stick or toothpick through both sides of the slit. Wrap the blanched spring onions (scallions) around the bitter gourds and tie together.

Place the stuffed bitter gourds in the pot with the soup. Bring the soup to a simmer over a low heat and cook for 15 minutes. Add the remaining soaked mushrooms and the all-purpose seasoning and cook for a further 15 minutes.

Remove the cocktail sticks before serving.

***Notes:*** You can substitute the pork paste with sausage meat or minced (ground) meat if it's unavailable.

For larger bitter gourds (bitter melons), halve, carve out the seeds and stuff the meat mixture inside the empty cores.

# SQUASH AND PEANUT SOUP

## Canh Bí Đỏ Đậu Phộng

In Vietnam, fresh peanuts are readily available – either in shells or just with their skins – and they're much more tender than those found in Asian supermarkets abroad. This makes a difference for this soup, as cooking times can vary significantly. While my recipe suggests 10 minutes, you'll need to test for doneness – the peanuts should be soft. If using peanuts from outside of Vietnam or Southeast Asia, soak them for at least 6 hours, like you would beans, and adjust the cooking time based on their texture.

Serves 3–4
Preparation time: 20 minutes
Cooking time: 35 minutes

| V | VE | DF |

- 100 g/3½ oz raw peanuts with skin
- 1 × 1.17-kg/2-lb 9-oz whole squash (ideally butternut squash but pumpkin is also fine), trimmed, peeled and deseeded (600 g/1 lb 5 oz prepared weight)
- 1 tablespoon neutral oil
- 25 g/1 oz shallots, coarsely chopped
- 10 g/¼ oz garlic, coarsely chopped
- 1½ teaspoon salt
- 1 teaspoon mushroom seasoning powder
- 10 g/¼ oz sawtooth coriander (culantro), plus extra to serve, optional
- 10 g/¼ oz rice paddy herb, plus extra to serve, optional
- ¼ teaspoon black pepper, or more to taste

Bring a pan of water to the boil, add the peanuts and simmer for about 10 minutes. Using a skimmer or slotted spoon, remove the peanuts. Transfer half to a mortar and pound with a pestle, discarding some of the skins.

Cut the pumpkin into 2-cm/¾-inch-thick circles. Halve to make a semi-circle, and then cut into 2 × 2 × 4-cm/¾ × ¾ × 1½-inch chunks. Wash the pumpkin thoroughly.

In a pot, heat the oil over a medium heat. Add the shallots and garlic and stir-fry for 1–2 minutes, then add all the peanuts and fry for a few minutes.

Add the pumpkin chunks, 700 ml/24 fl oz (scant 3 cups) of water and the salt and seasoning powder. Bring the mixture to the boil, then reduce to a simmer and cook over a low heat for 20 minutes. Add the sawtooth coriander (culantro) and rice paddy herb to the pot. Sprinkle with the pepper, or more to taste.

Serve hot, with extra herbs on the side, if desired.

## STUFFED CABBAGE ROLL SOUP

### Canh Bắp Cải Nhồi Thịt

While stuffed cabbage rolls appear in many cuisines, this version transforms them into a light soup, letting their filling season the soup as they simmer. While the pork paste helps bind the filling, you can easily substitute sausage meat or finely minced pork. Serve with fish sauce on the side for dipping the rolls.

Serves 6
Preparation time: 30 minutes
Cooking time: 50 minutes

**| DF |**

390 g/13¾ oz pig bones
1 tablespoon fish sauce
¼ teaspoon salt
1 × 850-g/1-lb 14-oz cabbage head
120 g/4¼ oz spring onions (scallions), white and green parts separated
30 g/1 oz coriander (cilantro)
fish sauce with a few slices of bird's eye chillies, to taste, to serve

*For the meat filling*
500 g/1 lb 2 oz minced (ground) pork
220 g/7¾ oz Pork Paste (page 461)
25 g/1 oz shallots, minced
1 tablespoon fish sauce
½ teaspoon black pepper
¼ teaspoon salt
125 g/4¼ oz carrots, cut into small, even cubes (brunoised)

In a large pot, add 1.2 litres/2 pints (5 cups) of water, the pig bones, fish sauce and salt. Bring to the boil, then reduce to a simmer and cook for 30 minutes to make a stock (broth).

Meanwhile, bring a large pot of water to the boil. Add the cabbage head. Remove from the heat after 15 seconds and drain. Carefully roll the cabbage to wilt it. Set aside to cool.

To make the meat filling, combine all the ingredients in a mixing bowl and mix well.

Carefully peel off the cabbage leaves. Slice the larger leaves in half, about 12 × 17 cm/4½ × 6½ inches each.

Place a small amount (about 30 g/1 oz) of the meat filling in the centre of a cabbage leaf and roll it up. Use the spring onion (scallion) greens to tie the rolls to keep them rolled up. Continue until all the meat mixture is used up, making smaller rolls with the smaller cabbage leaves, if necessary.

Mince 20–30 g/¾–1 oz of the spring onion whites and set aside. Add the cabbage rolls and whole spring onion whites to the pot of stock and simmer for 15–20 minutes.

Just before serving, add the reserved minced spring onion whites and the coriander (cilantro) to the pot.

Serve hot, with a small bowls of fish sauce with a few slices of bird's eye chillies, to taste, on the side.

## BEE LARVAE SOUP WITH GINGER

### Canh Nhộng Ong Nấu Gừng

In Hà Giang, anh Triệu Tà Phẩu introduced us to bee larvae, considered a delicacy and rich in protein, and the young ginger is known to add warmth and aid digestion. While traditionally this soup depends on the luck of finding wild bee nests in the trees, nowadays some will freeze their catch to enjoy later.

Serves 4–6
Preparation time: 10 minutes
Cooking time: 5 minutes

**| DF | GF | ≤5 | ≤30 |**

66 g/2¼ oz young ginger
1 tablespoon pork lard
1½ teaspoons salt
½ teaspoon MSG
280 g/10 oz bee larvae (nhộng ong)

Smash the young ginger with the back of a knife or pound it with a pestle in a mortar until finely mashed.

In a pan, heat the pork lard over a medium heat, then add 1.2 litres/2 pints (5 cups) of water. Add the salt and MSG and bring to a simmer. Add the bee larvae and mashed ginger. Simmer for 5 minutes.

Serve immediately.

## MINCED PORK AND PUMPKIN SOUP

Canh Bí Đỏ Thịt Bằm

Thanks to the natural sweetness of the pumpkin, this soup requires minimal simmering to extract the meat's flavour. This soup is perfect for everyday meals, pairing well with dishes like *thịt kho* – braised meat dishes (pages 302, 303 and 304) or *cá chiên* – fried fish dishes (pages 280). If you can't find pre-portioned pumpkins at the store, don't worry – any leftover pumpkin can be used in dishes such as Squash and Peanut Soup (page 358) or Stir-fried Pumpkin (page 324).

Serves 2–3
Preparation time: 20 minutes
Cooking time: 20 minutes

| DF |

265 g/9¼ oz pumpkin
100 g/3½ oz minced (ground) pork
10 g/¼ oz shallot, finely chopped
8 g/¼ oz garlic, finely chopped
¼ teaspoon black pepper
1 tablespoon fish sauce
2 teaspoons neutral oil
½ teaspoon salt

*To garnish*
5 g/⅛ oz rice paddy herb, chopped
3 g sawtooth coriander (culantro), chopped
3 g spring onion (scallion), chopped

Peel and cut the pumpkin into 15 g/½ oz chunks (approximately 3 × 2 cm/1¼ × ¾ inches).

To prepare the garnish, in a bowl mix together the rice paddy herb, sawtooth coriander (culantro) and spring onion (scallion). Set aside.

In a bowl, combine the minced (ground) pork with half the shallot, half the garlic and the pepper and fish sauce.

Heat the oil in a pot over a medium heat, add the remaining shallot and garlic and stir-fry until fragrant and lightly golden, about 2 minutes. Add the seasoned minced pork and cook until it starts to brown, about 3 minutes. Add the pumpkin chunks and 500 ml/18 fl oz (2 cups) of water to the pot. Bring to a simmer and cook for about 15 minutes or until the pumpkin is soft. Season with the salt.

Serve the soup garnished with the prepared herb mixture.

## BEEF AND PIPER LOLOT LEAF SOUP

Canh Bò Lá Lốt

While many are familiar with *bò nướng lá lốt* (Grilled Beef in Piper Lolot Leaves, page 144), the combination of beef and piper lolot leaves can also be applied in a soup for an everyday meal. For this recipe, you don't need a lot of meat, but good fillet will go a long way. Hand chopping the beef is encouraged as it will give it more texture.

Serves 4
Preparation time: 25 minutes, plus 15 minutes marinating time
Cooking time: 20 minutes

| DF |

*For the marinated beef*
160 g/5½ oz beef filet or any tender cut
30 g/1 oz shallots, sliced
½ teaspoon black pepper
2 tablespoons fish sauce
½ teaspoon sugar

*For the soup*
2 teaspoons neutral oil
1 teaspoon salt
300 g/10½ oz bunch piper lolot leaves, picked and sliced (approx. 140 g/5 oz prepared weight)
½ teaspoon black pepper

Hand chop the beef until it reaches a coarsely ground consistency. Add the shallots and continue chopping until well combined. Transfer the mixture to a bowl, then add the pepper, fish sauce and sugar. Leave to marinate for 15 minutes.

To make the soup, heat the oil in a pot (20–25 cm/8–10 inches in diameter) over a medium-low heat, add the marinated beef and stir-fry for 2–3 minutes until the meat juices have evaporated.

Add 1 litre/1¾ pints (4¼ cups) of water and the salt to the pot. Bring to a simmer and skim off any scum. Cook for 10 minutes to allow the soup to absorb the flavours. Add the piper lolot leaves and continue to simmer for an additional 3–4 minutes.

Remove from the heat and sprinkle the pepper on top. Serve hot.

*Note:* Piper lolot is also known as wild betel leaf or *lá lốt* in Vietnamese.

# TARO LEAF WITH BEEF SKIN SOUP

Môn Nấu Da Bò

We learned this Mường recipe from cô Đinh Thị Như Thoa in Buôn Ma Thuột, the capital of Đắk Lắk province. It is traditionally made with dried beef skin stored above wood-burning kitchen stoves, then grilled and pounded before cooking. Today, preboiled beef skin is used as the dried variety is rarely found. A Black Thái version, shared by cô Sầm Thị Lương in Nghệ An, adds *mắc khén* (Indian prickly ash), red chilli and *hạt dổi* (*Michelia tonkinensi*, also called magnolia seeds) to the soup.

Serves 3–4
Preparation time: 30 minutes, plus 15 minutes marinating time
Cooking time: 1 hour 20 minutes

| DF |

- 200 g/7 oz beef tendon, thinly sliced
- 1½ teaspoons MSG or soup powder (bột canh)
- 1½ teaspoons all-purpose seasoning (hạt nêm)
- 10 g/¼ oz shallot, minced
- 1 teaspoon neutral oil
- 165 g/5¾ oz beef skin, cut into 1 × 1 × 3-cm/ ½ × ½ × 1¼-inch strips
- 270 g/9½ oz purple bitter aubergines (eggplants)
- 320 g/11¼ oz sweet taro leaves (môn), cut into 8-cm/3¼-inch lengths
- 10 g/¼ oz piper lolot leaves (lá lốt)
- salt

In a bowl, combine the beef tendon with ½ teaspoon each of the MSG or soup powder and all-purpose seasoning and the shallot. Marinate for 15 minutes.

Heat ½ teaspoon of the oil in a pan over a medium heat, add the marinated beef tendon and stir-fry for about 3 minutes to remove its moisture.

Bring 900 ml/30 fl oz (3¾ cups) of water to a simmer in a large pot. Add the stir-fried beef tendon and the beef skin, reduce the heat to low and simmer for 40 minutes.

Prepare a bowl of salted water. Trim the aubergines (eggplants) and halve each lengthways, placing them in the salted water as you go to prevent discolouration.

Heat the remaining oil in a pan over a medium-low heat. Drain the aubergines and add them to the pan, then season with ½ teaspoon each of the all-purpose seasoning and MSG or soup powder. Fry for 3 minutes.

When the beef tendon has simmered for 40 minutes, add the taro leaves, then cover and cook until the leaves and stalks are completely soft, about 10 minutes. Add the fried aubergines, then simmer, covered, over a medium-low heat for 20 minutes. Add the remaining MSG or soup powder and all-purpose seasoning.

Slice the piper lolot leaves thinly (5 mm/¼ inch), then lightly crush the leaves between your hands and add to the soup. Cook for a final 10 minutes.

Serve hot.

# WILD VEGETABLE AND PRAWN SOUP

Canh Rau Rừng Tôm

This dish exemplifies foraged cuisine, utilizing wild vegetables and freshly caught river prawns (shrimp). As I have learned in Bảo Lộc in Lâm Đồng province, where we followed the stream upstream to catch prawns for this dish, the amount of prawns varies with the season – rainy days yield less, while the best catching period is after December. Foragers would follow the river's course, gathering ingredients along their route.

Serves 2–3
Preparation time: 10 minutes
Cooking time: 10 minutes

| DF | GF | ≤5 | ≤30 |

- 50 g/1¾ oz freshly caught river prawns (shrimp) or fish
- 100 g/3½ oz wild herbs (rau rừng – wild malabar spinach and gnetum gnemon leaves)
- ½ teaspoon salt
- ½ teaspoon MSG

In a pot, bring 700 ml/24 fl oz (scant 3 cups) of water to the boil. Add the river prawns (shrimp) or fish to the pot and cook for 5 minutes. Add the wild herbs, cover and cook for 7 minutes over a medium heat. Add the salt and MSG, then continue simmering for another 3 minutes.

Serve hot as a light, nourishing soup.

WILD VEGETABLE AND PRAWN SOUP

# PUMPKIN FLOWER SOUP WITH STRABISMUS FISH PASTE

Canh Bông Bí
Cá Thác Lác

While I use fish paste to stuff the pumpkin flowers, you can substitute it with the same filling from Stuffed Cabbage Roll Soup (page 360).

Serves 4
Preparation time: 30 minutes
Cooking time: 15 minutes

| DF |

200 g/7 oz barely bloomed pumpkin flowers (about 35 flowers)
200 g/7 oz fish paste from Fried Strabismus Fish Cake (page 463)
4 g/⅛ oz spring onion (scallion), finely chopped
14 g/½ oz red shallot, finely chopped
1 teaspoon plus 1 tablespoon fish sauce
2 teaspoons plus 1 tablespoon neutral oil
¼ teaspoon black pepper
15 g/½ oz garlic, finely chopped
10 g/¼ oz white shallot, finely chopped
10 g/¼ oz spring onion (scallion) whites, finely chopped
½ teaspoon salt

*To garnish*
spring onion (scallion) greens, thinly sliced
coriander (cilantro) leaves
black pepper

To clean each pumpkin flower, bend the stalk until it cracks, and peel the outer layer of the leftover stalk. Remove the calyx (the green outer 'cup' of the flower), then slit open one of the petals and remove the stigma (the long tip that collects the pollen). This slit will also be where you will stuff your mixture. Each flower should weigh 4–5 g/⅛ oz after cleaning.

Mix the fish paste with the finely chopped spring onion (scallion), red shallot, 1 teaspoon of the fish sauce, 2 teaspoons of the oil and the pepper.

Fill the cleaned flowers, dividing the fish paste mixture evenly among them, using 8 g/¼ oz (about 1 teaspoon) per flower.

In a large pot, heat the remaining oil over a medium-low heat. Add the garlic and white shallot and fry until fragrant and starting to turn golden, 2–3 minutes. Add the spring onion whites to the pot and fry for another 1 minute.

Pour in 500 ml/18 fl oz (2 cups) of water and bring to the boil. Add the salt and remaining fish sauce to the boiling water.

Carefully add the stuffed flowers to the pot and bring back to the boil. Reduce the heat and simmer for a few minutes until the flowers are cooked through.

Remove from the heat, garnish with sliced spring onion greens, coriander (cilantro) leaves and pepper. Serve hot.

# FISH SOUP WITH DILL

Canh Cá Thì Là

Common in Northern Vietnamese cooking, dill appears almost exclusively in fish dishes like Hanoi-style Fish with Turmeric and Dill (page 230) and Hanoi Sandworm Patties (page 326). While this soup traditionally uses mackerel, any fatty fish will work, and you can adjust the sourness with quả sấu (dracontomelon), rice vinegar or lime juice. This simple soup pairs well with braised dishes like Braised Tuna with Pineapple (page 276).

Serves 2–3
Preparation time: 15 minutes
Cooking time: 15 minutes

| DF | ≤30 |

260 g/9 oz mackerel, cut into steaks
¾ teaspoon salt
1 tablespoon neutral oil
15 g/½ oz shallot, coarsely chopped
1 tablespoon fish sauce
1 teaspoon sugar
325 g/11½ oz tomatoes, quartered
60 g/2¼ oz dill, cut into 5-cm/2-inchs lengths
25 g/1 oz spring onions (scallions), finely chopped
steamed rice, to serve, optional

Pat dry the mackerel steaks with paper towels. Season with ¼ teaspoon of the salt. Let marinate for 5–10 minutes to remove any blood residue, then place in a bowl of water to clean before cooking.

Heat the oil in a pot over a medium-low heat, add the shallot and stir-fry for 1–2 minutes until golden.

As soon as the shallot is golden, add 750 ml/25 fl oz (3 cups) of water, then add the fish sauce, sugar and the remaining salt. Bring to a gentle simmer. Add the fish steaks and tomatoes. Cook for 10 minutes.

Remove from the heat. Add the dill and spring onions (scallions), cover and let stand for 1–2 minutes.

Serve hot with steamed rice, if desired, for the best flavour.

PUMPKIN FLOWER SOUP WITH STRABISMUS FISH PASTE

## SOUR FISH SOUP WITH ELEPHANT APPLE

Canh Cá Chua Quả Sổ

During our stay in Hồ Thầu, a village in Hoàng Su Phì, in Hà Giang province, local cook and homestay owner chị Triệu Mùi Chiều taught us how to make this dish using ingredients from her garden. Coming from a Red Dao background and married into a Nùng family, she shared her knowledge of both communities' cooking traditions and mountain herbs used for medicine. Like many families there, she grows her own rice and raises Lung Pu black pigs (indigenous to northern Vietnam) and chickens, including the one we prepared for Grilled Chicken with Indian Prickly Ash (page 149). This soup gets its distinctive sourness from elephant apple, a fruit local to the region, where the leaves are used in the red dao herbal baths, as they are known to help against itchiness and scabies.

Serves 4–6
Preparation time: 15 minutes
Cooking time: 35 minutes

| DF | GF | ≤5 |

60 ml/2 fl oz (¼ cup) neutral oil
525 g/1 lb 3 oz small river fish
215 g/7½ oz elephant apple (quả sổ), sliced
2 teaspoons salt
30 g/1 oz water mimosa (rau rút)

In a large pan, heat the oil over a medium heat. Fry the river fish in the oil for 15 minutes, turning, until golden brown, then remove from the oil and set aside.

Arrange half the elephant apple on the bottom of a small pot. Arrange the fried fish on top of the elephant apple. Add 1 litre/1¾ pints (4¼ cups) of water and the salt, then cover the fish with the remaining elephant apple and the water mimosa.

Bring the pot to a simmer, then cook for 20 minutes over a low heat.

Serve hot as a soup course in a traditional Vietnamese meal.

## YOUNG MUSTARD GREEN SOUP

Canh Cải Ngọt

While traditionally mustard greens are used here, I think the base stock (broth) is versatile enough for you to substitute with any green mustardy leaves you have in hand, like mizuna, but even pak choi (bok choy) would do the job. If you don't have fresh straw mushrooms, oyster mushrooms can also be a good substitute.

Serves 4
Preparation time: 15 minutes
Cooking time: 15 minutes

| DF | ≤30 |

2 teaspoons neutral oil
32 g/1 oz shallots, roughly chopped
12.5 g/½ oz garlic, coarsely chopped
90 g/3¼ oz straw mushrooms, halved
2 teaspoons fish sauce
1.2 litres/2 pints (5 cups) pork stock (broth)
380 g/13 oz mustard greens, trimmed and cut into 4–10-cm/1½–4-inch lengths
½ teaspoon salt
½ teaspoon sugar

*To garnish*
13 g/½ oz coriander (cilantro), chopped
13 g/½ oz spring onions (scallions), chopped

Heat 1 teaspoon of the oil in a pot over a medium heat. Add half of the shallots and garlic and fry until fragrant, 2–3 minutes. Add the mushrooms and stir-fry for 1 minute. Then add 1 teaspoon of the fish sauce and stir to combine. Remove the mushrooms from the pot and set aside.

In the same pot, add the remaining oil, the remaining shallots and the remaining garlic. Fry until fragrant, 2–3 minutes. Add the pork stock (broth) and bring to a simmer. Add the mustard greens, bring to the boil, then reduce the heat and cook for 5 minutes.

Season the soup with the salt, the remaining fish sauce and the sugar.

Serve, garnished with the chopped coriander (cilantro) and chopped spring onions (scallions).

## TARO AND PORK RIB SOUP

Canh Sườn Khoai Sọ

This is a very hearty soup. Serve it alongside a Simple Omelette (page 347) to make a full meal.

Serves 4–6
Preparation time: 20 minutes
Cooking time: 1 hour

| DF | ≤5 |

- 500 g/1 lb 2 oz baby back ribs, cut into 5-cm/2-inch chunks
- 1 tablespoon fish sauce
- ½ teaspoon salt
- 400 g/14 oz taro (about 2), peeled and cut into 4-cm/1½-inch chunks

*To garnish*

- 10 g/¼ oz sawtooth coriander (culantro), roughly chopped
- 10 g/¼ oz paddy herbs, roughly chopped
- ¼ teaspoon black pepper

Bring a large pot of water to the boil over a high heat. Add the baby back ribs and blanch for 2–3 minutes. Drain in a colander, then rinse under cold running water until clean. Set aside.

In a large pot, bring 1.5 litres/2½ pints (6¼ cups) of water to the boil over a high heat. Add the fish sauce and salt, then stir to combine. Add the blanched ribs and simmer for 30 minutes.

Add the taro to the pot and continue simmering for another 25 minutes, until the taro is soft; you can test by inserting a fork into a taro chunk – it should go through easily.

Serve immediately, garnished with the chopped herbs and sprinkled with the pepper.

## VEGETABLE AND RIB SOUP

Canh Súp

This is the Vietnamese adaption of the traditional French vegetable soup, a bone soup with leeks, potatoes and carrots, ingredients brought over during the French Period (1858–1954). The difference lies in the seasoning, as well as the garnish made of coriander (cilantro) and spring onion (scallion). This version uses pork ribs, but could be substitute with beef short ribs. If you can't find the chayote, you can easily replace it with a kohlrabi.

Serves 4–6
Preparation time: 20 minutes
Cooking time: 35 minutes

| DF |

- 1 tablespoon neutral oil
- 20 g/¾ oz shallots, minced
- 8 g/¼ oz garlic, minced
- 60 g/2¼ oz leek whites, sliced
- 300 g/10½ oz pork ribs, cut into 10-cm/4-inch pieces
- 1 litre/1¾ pints (4¼ cups) hot water
- 140 g/5 oz carrots, peeled and cut into chunks (100 g/3½ oz prepared weight)
- 145 g/5 ¼ oz daikon, cut into 5-cm/2-inch lengths and quartered (115 g/4 oz prepared weight)
- 230 g/8 oz chayote, peeled (170 g/5¾ oz peeled weight), quartered and core removed
- 180 g/6 oz potato, peeled and cut into chunks (150 g/5½ oz prepared weight)
- ½ teaspoon all-purpose seasoning (hạt nêm)
- ½ teaspoon sugar
- 340 g/12 oz cauliflower (about ½ head), cut into florets (280 g/10 oz prepared weight) and washed in salt water

*To garnish*

- 10 g/¼ oz coriander (cilantro), leaves picked
- 10 g/¼ oz spring onion (scallion) greens, chopped
- ¼ teaspoon black pepper

Heat the oil in a pot over a medium heat, add the shallots, garlic and leeks. Fry briefly, 1–2 minutes. Add the pork ribs and measured hot water, then bring to the boil.

Add the carrots to the pot, then reduce the heat and simmer for 15 minutes. Add the daikon and chayote and simmer for a 8 minutes. Add the potato and simmer for 4 minutes. Add the all-purpose seasoning and sugar, then simmer for a further 3 minutes.

Add the cauliflower florets, bring to the boil, then remove from the heat and let stand for 4 minutes.

Serve hot, garnished with the coriander (cilantro) and spring onion (scallion) and sprinkled with the pepper.

# SWEET AND SOUR SOUP (MEKONG DELTA STYLE)

Canh Chua Miền Tây

In the Mekong Delta, this hot-weather favourite comes in endless variations, each celebrating local ingredients – snakehead fish, grass carp with water lily, baby mudfish with yellow velvetleaf flowers, even frog. What defines the region's style is its gentle balance: tamarind provides sourness, vegetables add depth, and a touch of sugar brings everything together and balances the acidity. While the south typically uses tamarind, lime juice, rice vinegar or *lá giang* (river leaf vine) for sourness, northern versions might feature *quả sấu* (dracontomelon), *tai chua khô* (dried Garcinia cowa/cowa mangosteen) or *giấm bỗng*, vinegar from making Fermented Sticky Rice (page 442).

Serves 3–4, as part of a meal
Preparation time: 20 minutes
Cooking time: 15 minutes

| DF |

4 teaspoons sugar
¾ teaspoon salt
1 tablespoon fish sauce
100 g/3½ oz tamarind paste
180 g/6 oz peeled small prawns (shrimp)
1 large tomato (205 g/7¼ oz), cut into eighths
265 g/9¼ oz cabbage, cut into 2-cm/¾-inch squares
90 g/3¼ oz okra, stalks removed, then cut on an angle into 3 pieces
50 g/1¾ oz Chinese celery (top part), cut into 2-cm/¾-inch pieces
½ long red chilli, thinly sliced

*For the garlic oil*
1 tablespoon neutral oil
20 g/¾ oz garlic, chopped

*To serve*
steamed rice
fish sauce with a few slices chilli, to taste

To prepare the garlic oil, heat the oil in a small pan over a medium heat, add the garlic and fry until golden brown, 3–4 minutes. Immediately remove from the heat. Transfer the garlic and oil mixture to a small bowl. Set aside.

To make the soup, in a large pot, bring 1 litre/1¾ pints (4¼ cups) of water to the boil. Add the sugar, salt, fish sauce and tamarind paste, stir to combine, then return to the boil. Add the prawns (shrimp), then return to the boil. Add the tomato, cabbage and okra. Let the soup return to the boil one more time, then remove from the heat.

Add the Chinese celery, chilli and reserved garlic oil mixture, then stir well.

Serve immediately, with steamed rice and small bowls of fish sauce with a few slices of chillies, to taste, on the side. The vegetables can be dipped in the fish sauce while eating.

SWEET AND SOUR SOUP (MEKONG DELTA STYLE)

## VEGAN SWEET AND SOUR SOUP

Canh Chua Chay

One way to impart more flavour to vegan broth in Vietnam is the use of either coconut water, as in this case, or sometimes even sugar cane juice. Here, I use calamansi juice for the acidity, but you can use tamarind paste.

Serves 6–8
Preparation time: 30 minutes
Cooking time: 15 minutes

| V | VE | DF | GF |

195 g/6¾ oz tomato, quartered
1 × 775-g/1-lb 11-oz pineapple, peeled and core removed (255 g/9 oz cored weight), then cut into small pieces or sliced 1 cm/½ inch thick on an angle
3 teaspoons sugar
1½ teaspoons salt
750 ml/25 fl oz (3 cups) coconut water
130 g/4½ oz pickled bamboo shoots
100 g/3½ oz fried tofu
165 g/5¾ oz okra (approx. 13), trimmed (150 g/5½ oz trimmed weight), then cut on an angle into 3 pieces
45 ml/1½ fl oz (3 tablespoons) calamansi juice
150 g/5½ oz straw mushrooms
120 g/4¼ oz bean sprouts
95 g/3½ oz Indian taro (bạc hà), peeled
16 g/½ oz long red chilli

***For the chilli salt, optional***
10 g/¼ oz long green chilli, deseeded
10 g/¼ oz (2 teaspoons) salt

***To serve***
30 g/1 oz Chinese celery leaves
5 g/⅛ oz sawtooth coriander (culantro)
10 g/¼ oz basil
Lemon Basil Salt (page 479), optional

In a 4.7-litre/160-oz (5-quart) pot over a low heat, add the tomato and pineapple and dry-fry for 3 minutes. Add 1 teaspoon of the sugar, ½ teaspoon of the salt, the coconut water and bamboo shoots. Bring it to the boil.

Add the fried tofu, okra, calamansi juice, the remaining sugar and the remaining salt. Let it simmer for 5 minutes. Remove from the heat.

If you wish to make the chilli salt, put the chilli and salt in a mortar and mash together with a pestle. Set aside.

When you are ready to serve, bring the soup back to the boil. Add the mushrooms, bean sprouts, Indian taro and chilli. Boil for 1 minute, then remove from the heat.

Serve with the all the herbs and the chilli salt, if using. Alternatively, you can serve this with lemon basil salt.

## SOUR SOUP WITH GOLDEN ANTS

Canh Chua Kiến Vàng – Dhăm sieo tôk hong can

In Buôn Ma Thuột, chị H Duyên Êban shared this traditional Ê Đê recipe (*dhăm sieo tôk hong can* is the name of this dish in the Ede dialect) that showcases how her community used forest ingredients before modern seasonings became available. Unlike other Vietnamese sour soups that use tamarind or river leaf, this dish gets its sourness from the golden ants. The preparation of ants involves carefully breaking ant nests in water to collect both ants and eggs, followed by multiple washings. Some people make a seasoning salt by stir-frying the ants with lemongrass, salt and MSG.

Serves 2–3
Preparation time: 15 minutes
Cooking time: 20 minutes

| DF | GF | ≤30 |

350 g/12 oz snakehead fish (cá lóc)
30 g/1 oz chive bulbs (củ nén)
20 g/¾ oz bird's eye chilli, plus extra to serve
1½ teaspoons MSG
30 g/1 oz golden ants (kiến vàng)
¾ teaspoon salt
100 g/3½ oz Indian taro (bạc hà), sliced

Cut the snakehead fish into steaks (including fish head). Clean thoroughly and set aside.

Put the chive bulbs, chilli and ½ teaspoon of the MSG in a mortar and pound with a pestle until you have a smooth paste. Set aside.

In a large pot, bring 750 ml/25 fl oz (3 cups) of water to the boil, then add the snakehead fish and cook for 10 minutes. Add the golden ants, salt and the remaining MSG. Simmer for 5 minutes Add the sliced Indian taro. Cook for another 1 minute 30 seconds.

Remove from the heat and add the chilli-chive paste, stirring to combine well.

Serve immediately, with extra chillies on the side.

SOUR SOUP WITH GOLDEN ANTS

## SALTED RADISH SOUP

Canh Củ Cải Muối

Also known as '*canh xá bấu*,' this soup features salted and dried daikon radish, readily available in Chinese supermarkets. Besides this soup, the same radish appears in Combo Noodle Soup (page 222), braised with pork belly (side) or fried in omelettes. In traditional medicine, these salted radishes are believed to help release toxins from the body.

Serves 4
Preparation time: 20 minutes, plus 45 minutes soaking time
Cooking time: 50 minutes

| DF | ≤5 |

150 g/5½ oz salted radish
300 g/10½ oz pork rib bones
¼ teaspoon salt
½ teaspoon sugar
1 teaspoon fish sauce

***To garnish***
20 g/¾ oz spring onions (scallions), finely chopped
¼ teaspoon black pepper

Soak the salted radish in a large bowl of water for 30 minutes. Drain in a colander and rinse the radish thoroughly under running water.

On a chopping (cutting) board, thinly slice the rinsed radish. Soak the sliced radish again in a bowl of fresh water for 15 minutes. Drain well in the colander and set aside.

Bring a large pot of water to the boil over a high heat. Add the pork rib bones and blanch for 2–3 minutes. Drain in a colander, then rinse under cold running water and scrub with a clean brush until clean. Set the blanched bones aside.

In a large pot, bring 1 litre/1¾ pints (4¼ cups) of water to a simmer over a medium heat. Add the salt, sugar and fish sauce, then stir until well combined. Add the blanched pork bones and simmer for 15 minutes.

Add the prepared radish slices to the pot, cover and simmer for another 30 minutes, or until the radish is tender and the pork fully cooked.

Serve, garnished with the chopped spring onions and black pepper and serve immediately.

## PAPAYA SOUP WITH BABY SHRIMP

Canh Đu Đủ Tép

This soup should be made with papaya that's not fully ripe but still firm to the touch with a green rim and orange flesh, with just enough sweetness before it turns soft and orange, and with black seeds not white. You can use half the papaya for this soup and save the rest for Green Papaya Salad with Prawn and Pork (page 138). While traditionally made with baby shrimp (*tép*), any shrimp or prawns will work well.

Serves 4–6
Preparation time: 30 minutes, plus 15 minutes soaking time
Cooking time: 25 minutes

| DF |

½ unripe papaya (see recipe introduction; about 725 g/1 lb 9 oz)
1 tablespoon neutral oil
15 g/½ oz garlic, chopped
15 g/½ oz spring onion (scallion) whites, chopped
140 g/5 oz baby shrimp (tép), head and tail trimmed (105 g/3¾ oz trimmed weight), or prawns (shrimp), cut into smaller pieces
1 teaspoon salt
1 teaspoon fish sauce
¼ teaspoon black pepper

***To garnish***
10 g/¼ oz coriander (cilantro)
5 g/⅛ oz Vietnamese coriander/cilantro (rau răm)

Peel the papaya and remove the seeds. You should have about 530 g/1 lb 3 oz of papaya flesh. Cut it into 1.5-cm/⅝-inch chunks, then quarter lengthways. Soak the chunks in a bowl of water for at least 15 minutes to remove any sap.

In a pot (22–25 cm/8½–10 inches in diameter), heat the oil over a medium heat, then add the chopped garlic and spring onion (scallion) whites. Stir-fry until the garlic starts to turn golden, 2–3 minutes.

Add the baby shrimp to the pot and stir-fry for 1 minute. Add the papaya and stir for a few more minutes.

Pour in 700 ml/24 fl oz (scant 3 cups) of water. Bring the mixture to the boil over a low heat. Skim off any foam that forms on the surface. Let it cook for 20 minutes.

Add the salt to the pot. Stir in the fish sauce and black pepper.

Garnish the soup with the chopped coriander (cilantro) and Vietnamese coriander/cilantro before serving.

## PICKLED MUSTARD GREENS AND PORK RIB SOUP

Canh Dưa Chua Sườn Heo

A staple in Vietnamese households, fermented mustard greens are typically kept in jars for side dishes like Braised Pork Belly with Eggs (page 303) or stir-fried in lard with Crispy Fried Pork Fat (page 459). Here, they add sourness to the soup, one of many ways Vietnamese cooks create sour soups; others include Pickled Bamboo Shoot Soup (page 376), Clam Soup with Star Fruit (page 382), and Chicken Soup with River Leaf (page 374).

Serves 4–6
Preparation time: 15 minutes
Cooking time: 1 hour

| DF |

900 g/2 lb Pickled Mustard Greens (page 467), rinsed and cut
70 g/2½ oz shallots, 55 g/2 oz thinly sliced, 15 g/½ oz crushed and roughly chopped
1 teaspoon black pepper
1½ tablespoons sugar
1 tablespoon fish sauce
200 g/7 oz tomatoes, cut into wedges
1¾ tablespoons neutral oil
15 g/½ oz garlic, crushed and roughly chopped
a little pork fat, minced, for added flavour
390 g/13¾ oz pork ribs, cut into pieces
1.8 litres/3 pints (7½ cups) boiling water
1 teaspoon all-purpose seasoning (hạt nêm)
1 tablespoon Annatto Oil (page 457)

In a bowl, mix together the pickled mustard greens, sliced shallots, pepper, 1 tablespoon of the sugar, the fish sauce and tomatoes.

Heat the neutral oil in a pot over a medium heat, add the garlic and chopped shallot and stir-fry for 1–2 minutes until it starts to become golden. Add the pork fat, then add the pork ribs and stir. Add the prepared mustard green mixture and stir-fry for 2–3 minutes to combine the flavours.

Pour over 300 ml/10 fl oz (1¼ cups) of the measured boiling water, then cover and simmer for 3 minutes. Add the remaining measured boiling water and simmer for a further 40 minutes.

Add the all-purpose seasoning, the remaining sugar and annatto oil. Continue cooking for a further 10 minutes, then remove from the heat.

Serve hot.

## DRACONTOMELON FRUIT SOUP WITH PORK RIBS

Canh Sườn Chua Quả Sấu

A staple of Northern Vietnamese cooking, dracontomelon fruit brings its characteristic sourness to many dishes, including Morning Glory Boiled Water (Northern Style) (page 354) and Dracontomelon Fish Sauce Dip (page 472). It is eaten fresh during summer and often used in drinks, and many families freeze packets of the fruit to use year-round. Serve this as a *canh* (soup) alongside Fried Tofu with Spring Onion Sauce (page 48) or Roasted Chicken Leg (page 284), or turn it into *bún sườn chua* with fresh rice noodles.

Serves 3
Preparation time: 15 minutes
Cooking time: 1 hour 5 minutes

| DF |

450 g/1 lb baby back ribs, cut into 5-cm/2-inch chunks
1 teaspoon soup powder (bột canh)
3 teaspoons all-purpose seasoning (hạt nêm)
½ teaspoon sugar
170 g/5¾ oz tomatoes, cut into rounds
50 g/1¾ oz dracontomelon fruit (quả sấu)
1 teaspoon fish sauce
steamed rice or rice noodles, to serve, optional

*To garnish*
10 g/¼ oz Vietnamese basil (húng quế), coarsely chopped
10 g/¼ oz coriander (cilantro), coarsely chopped
15 g/½ oz spring onions (scallions), cut into 2-cm/¾-inch lengths

Fill a pot with enough water to fully submerge the baby back ribs. Bring the water to a rolling boil over a high heat. Add the baby back ribs to the boiling water and blanch for 3–5 minutes until foam rises to the surface. Drain, then rinse the ribs thoroughly under cold running water.

In a stockpot, bring 1 litre/1¾ pints (4¼ cups) of water to a rolling boil over a high heat. Add the blanched rib pieces to the boiling water, reduce the heat to medium–low and simmer for 45 minutes, occasionally skimming any foam.

Add the soup powder, all-purpose seasoning, sugar, tomatoes and dracontomelon fruit. Continue to simmer for another 15 minutes. Season with the fish sauce and garnish with the herbs.

Serve hot, with steamed rice or rice noodles if you like.

## CHICKEN SOUP WITH RIVER LEAF

### Canh Gà Lá Giang

This Southern Vietnamese sour soup gets its distinct tartness and acidity from river leaf (*lá giang*), a herb similar in taste to sorrel, which can be used as a substitute. The recipe can be adapted into *lẩu gà lá giang*, a hotpot version, by adding more chicken stock (broth) and the same vegetables used in Chicken Hotpot with Lemon Basil (page 170). You can eat this either with rice as a part of a sharing meal or with noodles as a one-pot dish.

Serves 4
Preparation time: 15 minutes
Cooking time: 25 minutes

| DF |

- 500 g/1 lb 2 oz chicken, cut into 4-cm/1½-inch pieces
- 4 teaspoons fish sauce
- ½ teaspoon salt
- 100 g/3½ oz river leaf vine (lá giang), or sorrel
- 1 teaspoon lime juice
- ½ teaspoon sugar
- 5 g/⅛ oz basil leaves, to garnish

*For the aromatics*

- 1 tablespoon cooking oil
- 28 g/1 oz garlic, minced
- 10 g/¼ oz shallot, minced

Clean the chicken by pouring boiling water over the pieces, then strain and set aside.

In a pot, combine 950 ml/32 fl oz (4 cups) of water with the cleaned chicken, fish sauce and salt. Bring to a simmer over a medium heat. Once simmering, reduce the heat to low and cook for 20 minutes. Add the river leaf vine or sorrel, lime juice and sugar and cook for an additional 5 minutes.

Meanwhile cook the aromatics. In a small pan, heat the oil over a medium heat, add the garlic and shallot and stir-fry until golden.

Add the fried aromatics chicken soup and stir.

Serve immediately, garnished with the basil leaves.

## CHIVE SOUP WITH TOFU AND MINCED PORK

### Canh Hẹ Đậu Hũ Thịt Bằm

You can replace the minced (ground) pork for minced prawns (shrimp) or chicken for this soup.

Serves 4
Preparation time: 15 minutes
Cooking time: 15 minutes

| DF | ≤30 |

*For the marinated pork*

- 175 g/6 oz minced (ground) pork
- 1 teaspoon fish sauce
- 1 teaspoon sugar
- 1 teaspoon all-purpose seasoning (hạt nêm)
- ½ teaspoon black pepper

*For the soup*

- ½ tablespoon neutral oil
- 35 g/1¼ oz shallots, minced
- 20 g/¾ oz garlic, minced
- ¼ teaspoon MSG, optional
- 220 g/7¾ oz soft tofu, cut into bite-size chunks
- 140 g/5 oz Chinese chives (lá hẹ), cut into 2–3-cm/3/4–1¼-inch lengths
- ½ teaspoon fish sauce
- ⅛ teaspoon salt

To marinate the pork, in a mixing bowl, combine the minced (ground) pork with the fish sauce, sugar, all-purpose seasoning and pepper. Mix well and set aside to marinate while you start the soup.

Heat the oil in a large pot over a medium heat, add the shallots and garlic, then fry for a few minutes until fragrant. Add 1 litre/1¾ pints (4¼ cups) water, then bring to the boil. Add the marinated pork mixture to the boiling water, reduce to a simmer, add the MSG, if using, then simmer for 2 minutes. Add the tofu and simmer for 7 minutes. Add the Chinese chives and season with the fish sauce and salt.

Serve immediately.

## PURPLE YAM SOUP

Canh Khoai Mỡ

Unlike other light soups, this soup has a heartier texture thanks to the purple yam, which creates a rich, gooey consistency similar to okra. You can make it with basic pork stock (broth), or for a lighter version, use a stock made from prawn (shrimp) shells.

Serves 4–6
Preparation time: 15 minutes
Cooking time: 15 minutes

| DF |

- 500 g/1 lb 2 oz purple yam, trimmed (400 g/14 oz trimmed weight)
- 1.5 litres/2½ pints (6¼ cups) Basic Pork Stock (page 464)
- 155 g/5½ oz deshelled baby shrimp or minced prawns (ground shrimp)
- ⅛ teaspoon black pepper
- 2 tablespoons pork lard or neutral oil
- 17 g/½ oz shallots, coarsely chopped
- 10 g/¼ oz garlic, coarsely chopped

*To garnish*

- 13 g/½ oz paddy herb, chopped
- 13 g/½ oz sawtooth coriander (culantro), chopped

Halve the yam, then using a spoon, scrape out the purple flesh. Alternatively, you can peel the yam, then scrape the flesh until it becomes mushy.

In a pan, bring the pork stock (broth) to the boil. Add the scraped purple yam and the baby shrimp or minced prawns (ground shrimp) and bring it to the boil again. Skim off any impurities that rise to the surface. Add the pepper and stir, then simmer for 10 minutes.

In a separate pan, heat the pork lard or oil over a medium heat, then add the shallots and garlic and fry until they turn golden, 4–5 minutes. Strain the fried shallots and garlic and set aside, reserving the aromatic oil.

Add half of the fried shallots and garlic and half the reserved aromatic oil to the pot with the pork stock for flavour. (The leftover aromatic oil can be used to stir-fry other dishes.)

Just before serving, garnish the soup with the remaining fried shallots and garlic, the chopped paddy herb and the chopped sawtooth coriander (culantro).

## COCONUT VEGETABLE SOUP

Canh kiểm

Unlike most Vietnamese vegetarian dishes that mimic meat dishes in name, *kiểm* stands on its own, and it's commonly served during full moon days and death anniversaries in homes and temples. The dish evolved from the Teochew's '*tàu thưng*' (bean soup) dessert, transforming it into a savoury-sweet (*mặn ngọt*) main course, appreciated especially by the southerners. It is versatile in ingredients: you can add green beans, swap in taro or regular potatoes, include shiitake mushrooms, and enjoy it with rice, noodles or Vietnamese baguettes.

Serves 6–8
Preparation time: 30 minutes
Cooking time: 55 minutes

| V | VE | DF | GF |

- 70 g/2½ oz (½ cup) peanuts with skin, soaked in boiling water
- 790 g/1 lb 12 oz (3¼ cups) coconut milk
- 345 g/12 oz pumpkin, peeled and cut into 4–5-cm/2-inch chunks
- 245 g/9 oz sweet potatoes, peeled and cut into 3-cm/1¼-inch chunks
- 25 g/1 oz dried wood ear mushroom, soaked for 10 minutes (85 g/3 oz soaked weight)
- dried tapioca strips, soaked overnight, optional
- 7 Siamese bananas (about 800 g/1 lb 12 oz), peeled (480 g/1 lb 1 oz peeled weight), cut on an angle into 3 chunks
- 2 tablespoons sugar
- 2 teaspoons salt

In a large pot, combine the peanuts with 720 ml/24 fl oz (3 cups) of water, then bring to a simmer over a medium heat. Add 570 g/1 lb 4 oz (2⅓ cups) of the coconut milk and cook, maintaining a gentle simmer over a low heat for 10 minutes. Add the pumpkin and sweet potatoes, then cook for a further 20 minutes.

Drain the soaked mushrooms and tapioca strips, if using, then add them to the pot and cook for a further 5 minutes. Add the bananas and sugar, then cook for 10 more minutes. Add 1½ teaspoons of the salt, then cook for another 5 minutes. Add the remaining salt, then cook for a final 5 minutes. Stir in the remaining coconut milk, then remove from the heat.

Serve hot.

## MALABAR SPINACH SOUP WITH RICE FIELD CRAB

Canh Mồng Tơi Cua Đồng

This soup takes its flavour from the rice field crab paste, which must be freshly made. You can also use other vegetables like *rau dền* (amaranth leaves) or *rau ngót* (katuk leaves) with this crab stock (broth).

Serves 4–5 to share
Preparation time: 15 minutes
Cooking time: 15 minutes

| DF | ≤30 |

465 g/1 lb malabar spinach
300 g/10½ oz rice field crab (cua đồng), soaked to remove impurities and sand
1 tablespoon neutral oil
25 g/1 oz shallots, thinly sliced
1 teaspoon fish sauce
½ teaspoon all-purpose seasoning (hạt nêm)
½ teaspoon sugar
200 g/7 oz squash (mướp), peeled and cut into 1-cm/½-inch-thick half-moons

Pick through the malabar spinach, trim if needed and thoroughly wash: you should have 300 g/10½ oz after preparing. Set aside.

To make a crab stock (broth), in a blender, combine the rice field crab and 630 ml/21 fl oz (2⅔ cups) of water. Blend on high speed for 1–2 minutes. Strain the mixture through a fine-mesh sieve 2–3 times to remove all the shell pieces.

Pour the strained crab mixture into a pot and slowly bring to a simmer until the crab mixture rises and floats, 5–7 minutes. Remove from the heat. Using a perforated ladle, remove the floating crab meat. Set the crab meat aside in a bowl. Reserve the crab stock.

To make the soup, heat the oil in a pan over a medium heat, add the shallots and fry until crispy, about 3 minutes. Pour the reserved crab stock into the pot. Season with the fish sauce, all-purpose seasoning and sugar. Add the squash, then simmer for 5 minutes. Add the prepared malabar spinach, then cook for 1 minute. Add the crab meat, then remove from the heat immediately.

To serve, ladle the soup into a large serving bowl. Serve immediately while hot, to be shared among the diners.

## PICKLED BAMBOO SHOOT SOUP

Canh Măng Chua

While we use fish in this version, the soup works well with any protein you prefer. For a vegetarian take, straw mushrooms or oyster mushrooms make perfect substitutes, and you can swap the fish sauce for salt, MSG and all-purpose seasoning; using coconut water instead of plain water adds extra depth.

Serves 6
Preparation time: 15 minutes
Cooking time: 30 minutes

| DF |

1¼ teaspoons salt
600 g/1 lb 5 oz Pangasius conchophilus (cá hú) fillet or steak, cut 5 cm/2 inches thick
14 g/½ oz paddy herbs
10 g/¼ oz sawtooth coriander (culantro), chopped
12 g/½ oz long red chillies, sliced
220 g/7¾ oz tomatoes, half left whole, half sliced
2 tablespoons sugar
720 g/1 lb 9 oz Pickled Dragon Bamboo Shoots (page 470)
35 g/1¼ oz kumquat juice
1 tablespoon fish sauce
1 tablespoon neutral oil
25 g/1 oz garlic, mashed

In a large pot, combine 1 litre/1¾ pints (4¼ cups) of water with 1 teaspoon of the salt and bring to the boil. Add the fish to the boiling water and poach for 10 minutes, then remove from the heat and let it soak in the pot for 5 minutes. Using a slotted spoon, remove the fish, transfer to a plate and garnish with the paddy herbs, sawtooth coriander (culantro) and chillies, then set aside. You should have 700 ml/24 fl oz (scant 3 cups) of liquid left.

Add the whole tomatoes to the pot with the broth. Top up with 300 ml/10 fl oz (1¼ cups) of water, then add the sugar, cover and cook until the tomato is soft. Mash the tomatoes into the soup.

Add the pickled dragon bamboo shoots, sliced tomatoes, kumquat juice, the remaining salt and the fish sauce.

Heat the oil in a small pan, add the garlic and fry until golden, 4–5 minutes. Reserve three-quarters of the fried garlic for garnish.

Add one-quarter of the fried garlic to the soup for additional flavour.

Serve hot, garnished with the reserved garlic.

MALABAR SPINACH SOUP WITH RICE FIELD CRAB

# PORK BONE SOUP WITH YOUNG BANANA STALK

## Canh Loóng

This Mường soup is served at both daily meals and ceremonial occasions, including weddings, *Tết* (Lunar New Year), and ancestral offerings. Chu Đinh Công Đông told us that traditionally, people would add dried porcupine stomach to the soup for a touch of bitterness, a flavour particularly appreciated in Mường cuisine. The Bahnar people make their own version called *Nhăm Nhung pai atum krodret bri*, using less water and adding cassava leaves and wild herbs along with the banana stalks. The young banana shoots must be harvested carefully to allow the plant to regrow.

Serves 3–4
Preparation time: 15 minutes, plus 15 minutes marinating time
Cooking time: 1 hour 45 minutes (or 45 minutes with a pressure cooker)

| DF |

*For the pork stock (broth)*
- 325 g/11½ oz pork tail bones, cut into 2-cm/¾-inch chunks
- ½ teaspoon all-purpose seasoning (hạt nêm)
- ½ teaspoon MSG or soup powder (bột canh)
- 10 g/¼ oz shallot, minced

*For the soup*
- lime juice, for soaking
- 260 g/9 oz young banana stalk
- 1 teaspoon all-purpose seasoning (hạt nêm)
- ½ teaspoon soup powder (bột canh) or MSG
- 15 g/½ oz piper lolot leaves (lá lốt), sliced and crushed
- 65 g/2¼ oz spring onions (scallions), thinly sliced

To make the pork stock (broth), in a bowl, add the pork bones with the all-purpose seasoning, MSG or soup powder and shallot. Mix well and let marinate for 15 minutes.

Heat a dry pan over a medium heat, add the marinated bones and stir-fry for 3 minutes.

Pour 1 litre/1¾ pints (4¼ cups) of water over the stir-fried bones, bring to a simmer and cook, covered, for 1 hour 30 minutes. Alternatively, transfer to a pressure cooker and cook for 30 minutes. Ensure about 1 litre/1¾ pints (4¼ cups) of liquid remains, topping up if needed.

Meanwhile, prepare the banana stalk. Prepare a large bowl of salted water with the lime juice.

Using a knife, remove the outer skin of the young banana stalk, then using a mandoline, thinly slice the stalk. Immediately place the sliced banana stalk in the prepared water (the water should cover the banana stalk). Set aside until ready to use.

To complete the soup, drain the banana stalk in a colander.

Heat the pork stock (broth) over a medium-low heat (or transfer the stock from the pressure cooker into a large pot), then add the drained banana stalk. Add the all-purpose seasoning and soup powder or MSG. Increase the heat to high until the soup is hot, then reduce to a simmer for 12 minutes. Add the piper lolot leaves, then immediately remove from the heat and add the spring onions (scallions).

Serve immediately while hot.

# BÁT TRÀNG BAMBOO SHOOT AND SQUID SOUP

## Canh Măng Mực Bát Tràng

Along with Bát Tràng-style Stir-fried Kohlrabi with Squid (page 345), this soup is a speciality of Bát Tràng village in Hanoi. At the home of bà Nguyễn Thị Lâm, one of Vietnam's culinary artists, we experienced this more traditional style of Northern family dining. Each of their dishes is more elaborate than most modern family meals, and in the case of this soup, each step is precise – from grilling and finely shredding the squid and bamboo shoots to creating a clear yet rich chicken stock (broth).

Serves 4–6
Preparation time: 20 minutes, plus 2 days and 1 hour soaking times
Cooking time: 2 hours

| DF |

50 g/1¾ oz dried bamboo shoots (150 g/5½ oz after preparation)
fresh herbs, to garnish, optional

*For the squid*
110 g/3¾ oz dried squid (about 4 squid, preferably from Thanh Hóa province)
12 g/½ oz ginger, crushed

*For the chicken stock (broth)*
½ yellow chicken (about 720 g/1 lb 9 oz)
1 tablespoon fish sauce
1 teaspoon sugar
½ teaspoon salt
20 g/¾ oz peeled shallots
140 g/5 oz onion, quartered

*For the soup*
1 tablespoon neutral oil
1.5 litres/2½ pints (6¼ cups) chicken stock (broth) (from above)
¼ teaspoon salt (or to taste)

Soak the dried bamboo shoots in a bowl of water for 2 days, changing the soaking water daily, then drain.

Bring a pan of water to the boil, add the drained bamboo shoots and boil, covered, for 20 minutes. Drain, set aside to cool slightly, then shred the boiled bamboo shoots; you will have about 150 g/5½ oz shredded bamboo shoots.

To prepare the squid, soak the dried squid in a bowl of warm water with the ginger for 1 hour to remove some of its odour. Drain.

Preheat the oven grill (broiler) to 190°C/375°F.

Grill (broil) the soaked and drained squid for 5 minutes, or until you can start smelling it, then remove and shred it.

To make the chicken stock (broth), bring a pot of water to the boil, add the chicken and blanch for 3 minutes in the boiling water. Drain, then rinse the chicken in running cold water until the water runs clear.

In a large pot, bring 3 litres/5¼ pints (12¾ cups) of water to the boil. Add the blanched chicken, fish sauce, sugar, salt, whole shallots and onion. Simmer over a low heat for 1 hour 20 minutes.

To prepare the soup, heat the oil in a pan over a medium-low heat, add the shredded squid and fry for 2 minutes. Add the shredded bamboo shoots and fry for 3–4 minutes. Remove from the heat and wait 30 seconds.

Add the measured chicken stock and slowly bring to a gentle simmer. Season with the salt, or more to taste.

Serve hot, garnished with fresh herbs if desired.

# KATUK LEAF SOUP

## Canh Rau Ngót

While this recipe is made with minced (ground) pork, this soup works equally well with prawns (shrimp) or oyster mushrooms. If using mushrooms, replace the fish sauce with soup powder (*bột canh*) or all-purpose seasoning (*hạt nêm*).

Serves 2–3
Preparation time: 10 minutes
Cooking time: 15 minutes

| DF | ≤30 |

1 teaspoon neutral oil
5 g/⅛ oz garlic, chopped
10 g/¼ oz spring onion (scallion) whites, chopped
65 g/2¼ oz minced (ground) pork
1 teaspoon fish sauce
½ teaspoon salt
200 g/7 oz katuk (rau ngót), leaves picked (115 g/4 oz leaves)

In a 21-cm/8¼-inch pot, heat the oil over a medium heat, then add the garlic and spring onion (scallion) whites and stir-fry for 1 minute, or until fragrant. Add the minced (ground) meat and stir-fry over a medium heat until it is browned, 3–5 minutes. Season the meat with the fish sauce and continue to fry for another 2 minutes.

Pour in 500 ml/18 fl oz (2 cups) of water and add the salt to the pot. Bring the mixture to a simmer and let it cook for 5 minutes. Add the katuk leaves, bring the soup to a rolling boil, then remove from the heat.

Serve hot.

# CLAM AND GOURD SOUP

## Canh Nghêu Bầu

This soup is perfect for summer, as both main ingredients, clams and gourd, are recognized for their cooling property in traditional Vietnamese medicine. Prior to cooking, soaking the clams in salt water with chillies ensures they get rid of any remaining sand.

Serves 4 to share
Preparation time: 20 minutes, plus 15 minutes soaking time
Cooking time: 15–20 minutes

| DF |

1 tablespoon salt
sliced chillies, for soaking
450 g/1 lb Venus clams
500 g/1 lb 2 oz gourd, peeled
1½ tablespoons neutral oil
20 g/¾ oz shallots, minced
18 g/½ oz garlic, minced
900 ml/30 fl oz (3¾ cups) hot water

*For the seasoning*
¼ teaspoon black pepper
1 teaspoon fish sauce
1 teaspoon sugar
1 teaspoon all-purpose seasoning (hạt nêm) or MSG, optional

*To garnish*
25 g/1 oz spring onion (scallion) greens, finely chopped
10 g/¼ oz coriander (cilantro) leaves
black pepper

In a bowl, mix 1 litre/1¾ pints (4¼ cups) of water with the salt and some sliced chillies. Add the clams and soak for 15 minutes to cleanse them of any impurities. Drain and thoroughly rinse the clams.

Cut the gourd into rounds about 1.5 cm/⅝ inch thick, then cut each round into halves.

Heat the oil In a stockpot, add the garlic and shallots and sauté over a medium-low heat until they become translucent, 2–3 minutes. Add the measured hot water to the pot. Once it reaches the boil, add the gourd and cook for 3–4 minutes until slightly tender. Stir in all the seasoning ingredients, followed by the clams. Return to the boil and cook for 2 minutes, or until most of the clams have opened.

Remove from the heat, cover and let stand for 2–3 minutes to allow the residual heat to open the rest of the clams.

Just before serving, uncover and reheat the soup briefly if needed. Adjust the seasoning to taste, then garnish with the chopped spring onion (scallion) greens, coriander (cilantro) leaves and a sprinkling of pepper.

CLAM AND GOURD SOUP

# CLAM SOUP WITH STAR FRUIT

## Canh Nghêu Nấu Khế

In Vietnamese traditional medicine, both clams and star fruit are considered cooling ingredients, rich in yin, making this light, sour soup especially welcome during hot summers, where people prefer light and sour soup to counteract the heat.

Serves 4–6
Preparation time: 20 minutes, plus 15 minutes soaking and 10 minutes standing times
Cooking time: 15 minutes

| DF |

¼ teaspoon salt, plus extra for soaking
sliced chillies, for soaking
1.2 kg/2 lb 12 oz Venus clams, cleaned
175 g/6 oz star fruit
1 teaspoon neutral oil
10 g/¼ oz shallots, coarsely chopped
10 g/¼ oz spring onion (scallion) whites, cut into 7-cm/2¾-inch-long pieces, plus 10 g/¼ oz spring onion (scallion), coarsely chopped
2 tomatoes (about 265 g/9¼ oz), cut into wedges
1 tablespoon plus 2 teaspoons fish sauce
30 g/1 oz dill, coarsely chopped
1 tablespoon lime juice
steamed rice, to serve

In a bowl, mix 1 litre/1¾ pints (4¼ cups) of water with ½–1 tablespoon salt and some sliced chillies. Add the clams and soak for 15 minutes to cleanse them of any impurities. Drain and thoroughly rinse the clams.

Clean and slice the star fruit, then soak in a bowl of water. Set aside.

To cook the clams and make the stock (broth), in a large pot, bring 850 ml/29 fl oz (3½ cups) of water to the boil. Add the clams to the boiling water and cook until three-quarters of the clams have opened, 3–4 minutes. Remove from the heat immediately. Using a sieve, remove the opened clams and set aside.

Let the remaining clams finish cooking in the residual heat of the water. Using a sieve, remove the remaining clams from the pot, then let the cooking water sit for 10 minutes to allow any sand to settle at the bottom. Carefully pour the cooking liquid into a large bowl, stopping just before reaching the sandy sediment at the bottom. Reserve the cooking liquid.

Using chopsticks or picks, remove the meat from the clam shells. Discard the empty shells and set the clam meat aside.

To make the soup, heat the oil in a pan over a medium heat, add the shallots, spring onion (scallion) whites and tomatoes, then stir-fry for about 2 minutes. Add 1 tablespoon of the fish sauce, then cook for 30 seconds. Add the reserved cooking liquid, then bring to the boil.

Drain the sliced star fruit, then add to the soup and cook for 5 minutes.

Add the clam meat, dill and chopped spring onion. Season with the salt, the remaining fish sauce and the lime juice. Cook for 2–3 minutes until well combined and heated through.

Serve immediately, with steamed rice.

## CHAYOTE AND SHRIMP SOUP

### Canh Su Su Nấu Tôm

This soup uses dried shrimp, though you can follow the same ratios as Papaya Soup with Baby Shrimp (page 372) if using fresh shrimp. In this case I feel that dried shrimp tends to have a more concentrated, savoury flavour compared to the sweeter taste of fresh shrimp. In France, my aunt and uncle would make their own dried shrimp by dehydrating boiled, peeled supermarket shrimp – often cheaper than buying the imported dried shrimp.

Serves 4–6
Preparation time: 15 minutes, plus 15–20 minutes soaking time
Cooking time: 20 minutes

| DF |

25 g/1 oz dried shrimp
250 g/9 oz chayotes (about 2)
½ tablespoon neutral oil
15 g/½ oz shallot, coarsely chopped
1.2–1.5 litres/2½ pints (5–6¼ cups) Basic Chicken Stock or Basic Pork Stock (page 464)
1 teaspoon sugar
1 teaspoon salt

Soak the dried shrimp in a bowl of warm water for 15–20 minutes, then drain and set aside.

Peel the chayotes, then cut them into quarters lengthways. Remove the seeds from each quarter and cut into 1-cm/½-inch-thick chunks. Set aside.

Heat the oil in a frying pan or skillet over a medium heat, add the shallot and soaked dried shrimp, then fry for a few minutes until fragrant. Set aside.

In a large pot, bring the stock (broth) to the boil. Add the fried shallot and shrimp mixture and the chayote chunks. Season with the sugar and salt, reduce the heat to medium-low, then simmer for about 15 minutes, until the chayote is tender.

Serve immediately.

## RATTAN SHOOT SOUP WITH PORK RIBS

### Đọt Mây Nấu Xương Heo

In Bảo Lộc, we were showed this traditional Mạ recipe using wild rattan shoots foraged from the forest – a dish that, like many from this community, uses no fish sauce. While the thorny rattan plant is known for its durable stalks used in furniture making, its tender shoots are a local delicacy that can be grilled, stir-fried or, as here, made into soup. The savoury pork stock (broth) balances the shoots' natural bitterness, creating a soup that several communities, from the Mạ to the Ê Đê, believe aids digestion and helps detoxify alcohol.

Serves 4–6
Preparation time: 15 minutes
Cooking time: 1 hour

| DF | GF | ≤5 |

520 g/1 lb 1 oz pork ribs, blanched (see step 1, page 121)
780 g/1 lb 12 oz whole rattan shoots (đọt mây)
4 rattan sticks, peeled (330 g/11½ oz after peeling)
½ teaspoon MSG
1 tablespoon salt, or less to taste
steamed rice, to serve

In a large pot, bring 1.15 litres/2 pints (4¾ cups) of water to the boil. Add the blanched pork ribs. Cover and simmer for 30 minutes. Add the whole rattan shoots and peeled rattan sticks and continue simmering for another 30 minutes. Add the MSG and salt and stir well to combine. Remove from the heat.

Serve hot, with steamed rice.

# KHMER-STYLE MIXED VEGETABLE AND PORK STEW

## Canh Xiêm Lo (Simlo)

In Trà Vinh, home to Vietnam's largest Khmer community, chị Sa Quan taught us this complex stew alongside *tép bạc muối me non* (Young Tamarind and Shrimp Sauce, page 478). The stew gets its distinctive flavour from *mắm bò hóc* (prahok, a fermented fish paste), a Khmer staple ingredient that has since influenced Vietnamese cuisine. This dish is often made as a communal dish – neighbours bringing their vegetables to chi Sa Quan, and she cooks for everyone. Sometimes locals call it the 'hundred vegetable soup', as you can add any vegetables you have on hand, as long as there are plenty. While I use pork belly (side) here, fish works too, and though vegetable-rich, you can adjust the quantities based on availability. What matters most is the toasted rice and *mắm bò hóc* seasoning, with the optional lime for acidity.

Serves 8–10
Preparation time: 45 minutes
Cooking time: 55 minutes

| DF | GF |

*For the base*
6 tablespoons neutral oil
100 g/3½ oz lemongrass, minced
4 bird's eye chillies, minced
15 g/½ oz garlic, chopped
300 g/10½ oz pork belly (side), sliced

*For the first addition*
400 g/14 oz daikon, peeled and chunked
300 g/10½ oz green beans
225 g/8 oz young bitter gourd (bitter melon), deseeded and sliced, optional
420 g/15 oz aubergines (eggplants), peeled cut into chunks
740 g/1 lb 10 oz green papaya, peeled and sliced

*For the seasoning*
65 g/2¼ oz Toasted Rice Powder (page 459)
40 g/1½ oz (3 tablespoons) sugar
5 teaspoons MSG
310 g/11 oz prahok paste (mắm bò hóc – Cambodian fermented fish paste)

*For the second addition*
345 g/12 oz stalks from katuk (rau ngót) or morning glory (rau muống)
235 g/8¼ oz Limnophila aromatica leaves (rau ngổ trâu – see notes)
190 g/6¾ oz morning glory (rau muống), leaves picked
300 g/10½ oz prawns (shrimp), trimmed
200 g/7 oz straw mushrooms, soaked in salt water, then drained and halved

*To finish*
150 g/5½ oz vegetable hummingbird (Sesbania grandiflora; bông so đũa)
80 g/2¾ oz picked katuk leaves

In a large pot (about 30 cm/12 inches wide and 20 cm/8 inches deep), heat the oil over a medium heat. Add the lemongrass, chillies and garlic. Stir-fry for 30 seconds. Add the pork belly (side) and stir-fry for another 1 minute.

Add the first addition ingredients: the daikon, green beans, bitter gourd (bitter melon), aubergines (eggplants) and green papaya. Stir-fry for 5 minutes.

Add the toasted rice powder, sugar, MSG and 20 g/¾ oz of the prahok paste. Continue frying for 2 minutes. Pour in 3 litres/5¼ pints (12¾ cups) of water and bring to the boil. Cook for 10 minutes.

Strain the remaining prahok paste through a sieve into the soup. Cook for another 10 minutes.

Add the second addition ingredients: the katuk or morning glory stalks, Limnophila aromatica, morning glory leaves, prawns (shrimp) and straw mushrooms. Simmer for 10 more minutes.

To finish, add the vegetable hummingbird and katuk leaves. Cook for a final 5 minutes.

Serve hot, accompanied by other dishes as desired.

***Notes:*** This recipe is flexible. You can substitute pork with fish, or adjust the vegetables based on availability and preference. Lime juice can be added for extra acidity if desired.

*Limnophila aromatica* is similar to rice paddy herbs (it is in the same family), but it is bigger; while we use the young ones for Sweet and Sour Soup (Mekong Delta Style) (page 368), here we use the bigger leaves.

# YOUNG JACKFRUIT SOUP

## Canh Mít Non

While ripe jackfruit is often eaten as a snack or fruit, young jackfruit also appears in many Vietnamese dishes, from Braised Young Jackfruit (page 333) to Fermented Young Jackfruit (Central Vietnamese Style) (page 470) and here in a prawn (shrimp)-flavoured soup. Found in Asian markets' frozen sections, the jackfruit should be fully thawed and patted dry before use. The soup can be made vegetarian by using vegetable stock (broth) instead of prawn stock, and some versions include *lá lốt* (piper lolot leaves) for added flavour.

Serves 2–3
Preparation time: 15 minutes
Cooking time: 25 minutes

| DF |

- 200 g/7 oz prawns (shrimp) with shells (about 8 medium prawns)
- 300 g/10½ oz young jackfruit (see note, page 333)
- 1 teaspoon vegetable oil
- 10 g/¼ oz shallot, finely chopped
- 1 teaspoon fish sauce
- ¼ teaspoon salt

*To garnish*

- 5 g/⅛ oz coriander (cilantro), chopped
- 5 g/⅛ oz spring onion (scallion), chopped

Peel and devein the prawns (shrimp), reserving the heads and shells. Chop the prawn meat coarsely and set aside.

Peel the young jackfruit, remove any threads and then cut into 1–2-cm/½–¾-in-thick chunks or slice it. Set aside.

Heat the oil in a small pot over a medium heat, add the shallot and sauté for about 1 minute until fragrant. Add the reserved prawn heads, a couple of prawn tails and a small portion of the chopped prawn meat. Stir-fry for 1 minute. Add the fish sauce and fry for another 1 minute. Using a slotted spoon, remove the prawn heads and set aside. Add 300 ml/10 fl oz (1¼ cups) of water to the pot and bring to the boil. Add the salt.

Place the prawn heads in a mortar and pound with the pestle to extract their juices. Place the pounded prawn heads in a fine-mesh sieve and dip it into the boiling soup to release the juices without letting any solids through. Remove.

Add the young jackfruit chunks to the soup. Simmer for about 20 minutes until the jackfruit is tender. Add the remaining chopped prawn meat and cook for an additional 2–3 minutes until the prawns are pink and cooked through. Taste and adjust the seasoning if needed.

Garnish with the chopped coriander (cilantro) and chopped spring onion (scallion).

# SAVOURY AND SWEET CAKES

## Bánh ngọt, bánh mặn

---

Cakes in Vietnam encompass diverse textures and flavours that showcase remarkable creativity. Unlike Western baking traditions, Vietnamese cakes are traditionally steamed, boiled or fried. When 'baking' was done, it often involved filling a mould with batter, covering it with a lid and cooking it between layers of hot coals. Modern ovens arrived much later with French colonial influences, though they remained primarily in commercial bakeries rather than home kitchens.

The distinctive textures of Vietnamese cakes come from using starches (rice, sticky/glutinous rice and tapioca) rather than ground grain flours, creating their characteristic elasticity and chewiness. I've assembled a collection ranging from everyday snacks to ceremonial Huế-style cakes and celebration dishes.

Since these doughs lack gluten, their texture and behaviour may be unfamiliar to those used to wheat-based baking. Don't expect the same reactions you'd get with wheat flour. I recommend steaming a small portion first to test if your cake has achieved the right elasticity, as environment and starch age will affect your results. Another tip for steamed or boiled cakes in this chapter: always keep your dough covered, as dry environments will crack the surface and create unwelcome skin.

---

# SQUARE STICKY RICE CAKES

## Bánh Chưng

Legend tells of how the sixth Hùng king chose his successor through a contest, which was to create the most meaningful and delicious offering for the ancestral altar. While his wealthy sons offered rare and exotic delicacies from far and wide, Lang Liêu, the eighteenth and poorest son, was visited in a dream that inspired him to create two simple but profound rice cakes: the square *bánh chưng* representing Earth, and the round *bánh dày* symbolizing Heaven. These humble offerings, made from the most fundamental ingredients of Vietnamese life, so moved the king that he chose Lang Lieu as his heir.

At chị Nguyễn Thị Thu Ba's home, we experienced how this tradition brings whole families together – from the early preparations of soaking rice and cleaning leaves, to the careful wrapping of each cake. The night-long cooking over wood fire needs constant attention, but it's a time of stories and sharing. Even after 10 hours of cooking, we're not done – the cakes need to be pressed and dried on grill racks, a step that gives them their firm texture and longer shelf life.

In the south, we would eat a cylindrical version, *bánh tét*, which would be rolled similarly to Pork Roll (page 462). Both versions are great, but I do Iove *bánh tét*, as it can be sliced into rounds rather than wedges, with leftovers fried until crispy for breakfast. The traditional way to serve it is with Pickled Chinese Onions (page 466) and Braised Pork Belly with Eggs (page 303).

Makes 3 cakes
Preparation time: 2 hours, plus 4 hours soaking, 30 minutes marinating and overnight pressing times
Cooking time: 8–10 hours per batch

| DF |

*For the rice*
1.2 kg/2 lb 12 oz (6½ cups) sticky (glutinous) rice, soaked for at least 4 hours or overnight
1 teaspoon salt

*For the mung beans*
1 kg/2 lb 4 oz (4½ cups) yellow split mung beans, washed and rinsed, then soaked for 4 hours
½ teaspoon salt

*For the marinated pork*
1 kg/2 lb 4 oz pork belly (side), cut into 2-cm/¾-inch-thick slices
1 tablespoon fish sauce
1 teaspoon black pepper
20 g/¾ oz shallots, minced

*For assembly and wrapping*
30 banana leaves (18 large pieces, 12 smaller pieces), sun-dried or blanched (see step 3, page 390)
1 cardboard frame/box without a bottom (15 × 15 × 4.5 cm/6 × 6 × 1¾ inches)
nylon string, 2.5–3 m/8–10 feet, cut into 4

To prepare the rice, drain the soaked rice and mix with the salt. Set aside.

To prepare the mung beans, in a pot, combine the soaked and rinsed mung beans, 500 ml/18 fl oz (2 cups) of water and the salt. Bring to the boil, then reduce the heat and simmer, covered, for 20 minutes, or until fully cooked and the water has evaporated. Set aside to cool.

In a bowl, mix the pork belly (side) with the fish sauce, pepper and shallots. Let marinate for 30 minutes.

To prepare the wrapping materials, cut the 18 large banana leaves into rectangles that are 15 cm/6 inches wide and 54 cm/21 inches long (you will need 6 of these large leaf pieces per cake). Then cut the 12 smaller banana leaves into rectangles that are 4.5 cm/1¾ inches wide (the same width as the height of the cardboard frame/box) and 12 cm/4½ inches long (you will need 4 of these smaller leaf pieces per cake).

To assemble each cake, fold one of the large leaf pieces in half to find the centre, then unfold. Thread it through the inside of the frame, then place the leaf against one side of the frame so the fold is halfway up the side of the frame, then fold it over the top and bottom edges so you have an equal overhang on the top and bottom. Repeat this with 3 more of the large leaf pieces, so each inside edge of the frame has a leaf folded over it.

Arrange 2 large leaf pieces in a cross, one leaf placed lengthways and the other widthways, with the darker sides facing upwards. Place the crossed leaves on top of the frame, with the centre of the crossed leaves over the centre of the frame, then gently push the crossed leaves down into the frame to line both the base and the sides of the frame.

Fold 4 of the smaller leaf pieces in half and then unfold so they are bent at a right angle (like an L shape); place them in the four corners of the frame, tucked behind the two layers of leaves lining the sides of the frame.

Spread a layer of rice (about 200 g/7 oz/1 cup) in the leaf-lined frame. Add a layer of mung beans (140–175 g/5–6 oz/¾ cup) in the centre. Place a slice of marinated pork (330 g/11½ oz) on top of the mung beans. Cover with another layer of mung beans (140–175 g/5–6 oz/¾ cup). Top with another layer of rice (200 g/7 oz/1 cup).

To wrap each cake, press firmly to compact the ingredients. Fold the overhanging edges of the leaves over the filling, one at a time working anti-clockwise. Continue folding the remaining leaves on the bottom to shape the cake. Adjust the corners of the parcel to ensure a square shape and even filling. Gently lift out of the frame.

Tie the string around the wrapped cake in in a chequered pattern, but not too tightly: thread a quarter of the string's length under the cake, slightly to the right. Bring around to the front and twist the two ends slightly to the front, then thread under the cake again and bring to the front. Twist, this time slightly to the back, then thread under the cake again to create a parallel line with the previously tied string. Repeat this process, this time slightly to the left, creating 4 criss-crossed lines on the cake in a chequered pattern. Wrap the remaining length of string around the side of the cake and tie it to secure.

Repeat the assembly and wrapping process until you have 3 cakes.

To cook the cakes, place the wrapped cakes in a large pot of water. You may need to cook in batches depending on your pot size. Bring the water to the boil, then reduce the heat to a gentle simmer. Cook for 8–10 hours, ensuring the cakes remain submerged; top up with hot water as needed during cooking.

To serve, carefully remove the cakes from the water and put the cakes flat on a grill rack, then add a flat, heavy weight on top and leave overnight; it will help compress the cakes, and remove extra moisture and air.

Unwrap the cakes and cut into wedges to serve: you can use the nylon string to slice the wedges, as it won't stick as much as if using a knife blade.

# RICE PYRAMID DUMPLINGS

## Bánh Giò

A popular breakfast or midday snack, especially for children, these pyramid-shaped dumplings are traditionally wrapped in banana leaves, which impart a distinctive aroma when steamed. If there are no banana leaves available, you could also steam them in bowls, but the leaves' flavour won't be present. Serve these dumpling hot with chilli sauce or fish sauce – all you need is a spoon. Thanks to the banana leaf parcel, they can also be kept for later eating.

Makes 8 dumplings
Preparation time: 30 minutes, plus 1 hour resting time
Cooking time: 40–45 minutes

| DF |

*For the dough*
- 185 g/6½ oz (1¼ cups) rice flour
- 25 g/1 oz (3 tablespoons plus 1 teaspoon) tapioca flour (starch)
- 1 tablespoon all-purpose seasoning (hạt nêm)
- 600 ml/1 pint (2½ cups) Basic Chicken Stock (page 464), hot
- 600 ml/1 pint (2½ cups) boiling water
- 2 tablespoons neutral oil

*For the filling*
- 1 tablespoon neutral oil
- 1 shallot, finely minced
- 400 g/14 oz minced (ground) pork
- 1 tablespoon all-purpose seasoning (hạt nêm)
- 20 g/¾ oz dried wood ear mushrooms, soaked and finely chopped
- ¼ teaspoon ground black pepper

*For wrapping*
- 8 banana leaf pieces (40 × 40 cm/16 × 16 inches)

*To serve, optional*
chilli sauce, Pork Roll (page 462) or roasted pork

To prepare the dough, in a large bowl, combine the rice flour, tapioca flour (starch) and all-purpose seasoning. Mix well. Gradually add the chicken stock (broth) and the measured boiling water while stirring. Mix until it forms a smooth batter. Let it rest for 1 hour.

To make the filling, heat the oil in a frying pan or skillet over a medium heat, add the shallot and fry for 2–3 minutes until fragrant. Add the minced (ground) pork and all-purpose seasoning. Cook for 2–3 minutes or until the pork is just done, keeping some moisture. Add the mushrooms and pepper. Stir-fry for another minute and set aside.

To prepare the wrappings, bring a pot of water to a gentle boil. Blanch the banana leaves for 1 minute, then remove and let cool. Wipe the leaves dry.

Transfer the rested dough batter to a pan and add the oil. Place over a medium-low heat, then cook, stirring constantly, for 5–7 minutes until the mixture becomes translucent and thickens. Remove from the heat.

To assemble and wrap the dumplings, fold a banana leaf into a triangle, then fold the triangle in half. Open the cut edge and hold in your hand to form a cone, ensuring there are no holes.

Add 2–3 tablespoons (about 45 g/1½ oz) of the cooked dough to the cone; add about 25 g/1 oz of the filling; then top with another 2–3 tablespoons (about 45 g/1½ oz) of the cooked dough.

Fold one of the corners of the cone down over the filling. Fold in one edge to the centre, fold in the opposite edge and then fold in the final corner to form a pyramid shape; tuck any excess leaf into the folds.

Repeat the assembly and wrapping process until you have 8 dumplings.

To steam the dumplings, set up a steamer and bring the water to the boil.

Add the dumplings to the steamer basket, set over the boiling water and steam for 25–30 minutes.

Let cool slightly before serving warm with chilli sauce, pork roll or roasted pork, if desired.

# PYRAMIDAL STICKY RICE CAKES

## Bánh Ú

These cakes are traditionally made for the fifth day of the fifth lunar month, also known as Mid-autumn Festival. Chị Nguyen Thi Thu Ba invited me to help prepare them, as it takes several people working together over a wood fire in the garden to complete the process. A traditional variation uses ash-soaked (lye-soaked) rice, which turns the grains transparent and imparts a distinctive 'lye water' taste. These cakes can either be steamed or boiled, depending on their size; the timing might varied, but it has to be cooked to the point where the grains of rice merge together into one.

Makes 35–50 cakes
Preparation time: 30 minutes, plus 4–6 hours soaking and overnight hanging times
Cooking time: 2–3 hours

| DF |

- 150 g/5½ oz dried shrimp
- ½ tablespoon Annatto Oil (page 457)
- 1 tablespoon neutral oil
- 150 g/5½ oz dry shiitake mushrooms
- 1½ teaspoons fish sauce
- 15 salted egg yolks
- 350 g/12 oz pork char siu (you can buy this at any Chinese restaurant) or caramelized pork (see page 68)

*For the marinated pork belly*

- 1.35 kg/3 lb pork belly (side), cut into 2-cm/¾-inch cubes
- 35 ml/1 fl oz (2 tablespoons plus 1 teaspoon) fish sauce
- 1 tablespoon black pepper
- 100 g/3 ½ oz shallots, pounded

*For the sticky rice*

- 3 kg/6 lb 8 oz (16 cups) sticky (glutinous) rice from the North of Vietnam, soaked for 2 hours
- 1½ tablespoons salt

*For the salted mung beans*

- 1 kg/2 lb 4 oz (4½ cups) yellow split mung beans, soaked for 4–6 hours
- 2 teaspoons salt

*For wrapping*

- 1.5 kg/3 lb 5 oz dong leaves or 1 kg/2 lb 4 oz banana leaves, blanched (see step 3, page 390) and cut into 30 × 40-cm/12 × 16-inch pieces
- roll of nylon or other food-safe string

Wash the dried shrimp in hot water, then drain and pat dry with paper towels. Put the shrimp in a mortar and pound with a pestle.

Heat the annatto oil in a pan over a medium-low heat, add the pounded shrimp and stir-fry for 5–6 minutes until dry. Set aside.

Heat the neutral oil in a pan over a medium-low heat, add the mushrooms and stir-fry for 3–4 minutes. Add the fish sauce, then remove from the heat and set aside.

To prepare the marinated pork belly (side), cut the pork belly into 2-cm/¾-inch cubes. Mix with the fish sauce, pepper and shallots. Marinate for 15–30 minutes. Remove the shallots after marinating.

To prepare the sticky rice, drain the soaked rice and mix with the salt. Set aside.

To prepare the salted mung beans, season the mung beans with the salt. Set aside.

Wash the salted egg yolks with hot water, very gently rubbing if needed, to remove the egg whites.

To assemble and wrap each cake, fold a dong and/or banana leaf into a triangle, then fold the triangle in half. Open the cut edge and hold in your hand to form a cone, ensuring there are no holes.

Add the fillings to the cone in the following order: 50 g/1¾ oz of the sticky rice, 25 g/1 oz of the salted mung beans, 40 g/1½ oz of the marinated pork belly, 25 g/1 oz of the char siu, 10 g/¼ oz of the fried mushrooms, 5 g/⅛ oz of the fried shrimp, 1 salted egg yolk, 25 g/1 oz of the salted mung beans and finish with 50 g/1¾ oz of the sticky rice on top.

Fold one of the corners of the cone down over the filling. Fold in one edge to the centre, fold in the opposite edge and then fold in the final corner to form a pyramid shape; tuck any excess leaf into the folds, ensuring it is well closed. Tie securely with string.

Repeat the assembly and wrapping process to make the rest of the cakes.

Set up a steamer and bring the water to the boil.

Place the cakes in the basket, set over the boiling water and steam for 2–3 hours, topping up the water as needed, until fully cooked. Alternatively you can boil them, ensuring they remain submerged, for 2–3 hours.

Carefully remove from the steamer or pan and hang the cakes from a hook set over a bowl or a rack set over a tray overnight, either at room temperature or in the refrigerator as preferred, to drain all the excess liquid inside. The cakes will keep for 1 day.

# SAVOURY STEAMED COCONUT RICE CAKE

Bánh Đúc Mặn

Usually eaten as a snack, this rice cake has countless variations across Vietnam, with different ratios of rice to tapioca flour (starch), varied toppings, regional sauces and distinct texture. In the north, it's sometimes made with rice flour and peanuts, served with fermented soybean sauce or plain and sliced into Rice Field Crab Noodle Soup (page 220), but minus the noodles. Central Vietnam pairs it with shrimp paste, molasses or braised meat. The southern version, as in this recipe, incorporates coconut milk, reflecting the region's abundance of coconuts. There's also *bánh đúc nóng*, a thinner version served in hot stock (broth) with minced (ground) meat, that's perfect for winter.

Serves 4–5 to share
Preparation time: 15 minutes, plus 30 minutes resting time
Cooking time: 35 minutes

| DF |

*For the batter*
140 g/5 oz (scant 1 cup) rice flour
30 g/1 oz (¼ cup) tapioca flour (starch)
¼ teaspoon salt
oil, for greasing
165 g/5¾ oz (⅔ cup) coconut milk

*For the topping*
2 tablespoons Annatto Oil (page 457)
10 g/¼ oz garlic, finely chopped
20 g/¾ oz shallots, finely chopped
70 g/2½ oz prawns (shrimp), cooked and peeled (60 g/2¼ oz peeled weight)
60 g/2¼ oz minced (ground) pork
40 g/1½ oz carrot, finely diced
60 g/2¼ oz jicama, finely diced
½ teaspoon sugar
1 tablespoon fish sauce

*For the coconut cream*
300 g/10½ oz (1¼ cups) coconut milk
1 teaspoon sugar
½ teaspoon salt
5 g/⅛ oz of spring onion (scallion), chopped

*To serve*
15 g/½ oz spring onions (scallions), chopped
coriander (cilantro) sprig, optional

To prepare the batter, in a bowl, mix together the rice flour, tapioca flour (starch), 300 ml/10 fl oz (1¼ cups) of water and the salt. Let it rest for 30 minutes.

Line a round mould, 15–20 cm/6–8 inches in diameter, with baking (parchment) paper and grease with oil. Set up a steamer and bring the water to the boil.

Mix the coconut milk into the batter, then transfer to a pan and cook over a medium-low heat, whisking continuously, for 6–7 minutes until thickened.

Pour the batter into the prepared mould. Place in the steamer basket, place a cloth between the lid and the basket, then set over the boiling water and steam for 15 minutes.

Meanwhile, prepare the topping. Heat 1 tablespoon of the annatto oil in a pan, add the garlic and shallots and stir-fry for 2–3 minutes. Add the prawns (shrimp), minced (ground) pork, carrot, jicama, the remaining annatto oil, the sugar and fish sauce. Stir-fry for another 5 minutes, or until cooked.

When the batter has steamed for 15 minutes, remove from the steamer, add the topping mixture, then continue steaming for another 10 minutes, or until completely set; it should have a bouncy feel to it and shouldn't look wet.

Meanwhile, prepare the coconut cream. In a pan, bring the coconut milk, sugar and salt to a simmer, then add the spring onion, remove from the heat and set aside until ready to serve.

Serve the coconut rice cake warm with the coconut cream poured over the top, garnished with the chopped spring onion (scallion) and coriander (cilantro) sprig, if using. Alternatively, scoop the topping off the top of the cake and serve thick slices of the cake with the coconut cream poured over the top and some of the topping on the side.

# POUNDED STICKY RICE CAKES

## Bánh Dày

These cakes hold deep symbolic meaning in Vietnamese culture through the legend of Lang Liêu, who created *bánh dày* and *bánh chưng* (Square Sticky Rice Cakes, page 388) as offerings to the Hung King, representing Heaven and Earth. The plain version, served with *giò chả* (meat rolls), is used for *Tết* (Lunar New Year), engagement ceremonies and the Hùng kings' death anniversary celebrations. The cakes are arranged in pairs between banana leaves, placed face-to-face like yin and yang, which also prevents them from sticking together. Other variations come with sweet or savoury fillings and are coated in bean powder. While modern versions use sticky (glutinous) rice flour and are steamed, our version uses more of a traditional method, which involves hand-pounding cooked sticky rice, similar to Japanese mochi.

Makes 6–8 cakes
Preparation time: 30 minutes
Cooking time: 30 minutes

| DF | GF | ≤5 |

300 g/10½ oz (1½ cups) sticky (glutinous) rice
¼ teaspoon salt
cornflour (cornstarch) or potato starch, for dusting

*To serve, optional*
Pork Roll (page 462)
Salt and Pepper Seasoning Mix (page 480)

Wash the rice until the water runs clear.

Combine the rice, 350 ml/12 fl oz (1½ cups) of water and the salt in a rice cooker or pot. For the rice cooker, choose the rice cooking mode. Cook until the rice is tender. Let the rice rest, covered, for 5 minutes after cooking. The final weight should be approximately 610 g/1 lb 6 oz (3 cups) of cooked rice.

Transfer the hot rice to mortar, then pound the rice vigorously with a pestle. Continue pounding until the rice becomes smooth and very sticky. The rice should be completely uniform with no visible grains. This process typically takes 15–20 minutes.

Dust a clean work surface with cornflour (cornstarch) or potato starch. Transfer the pounded rice mixture to the dusted surface, then pat or roll it into about 1 cm/½ inch thick, and cut it into 5–8-cm/2–3-inch rounds using a biscuit (cookie) cutter. Dust each cake lightly with starch to prevent them from sticking to each other.

Serve warm or at room temperature. Traditionally, these cakes are served with pork rolls sandwiched in the middle of two cakes, with a layer of salt and pepper seasoning mix on the surface.

***Note:*** Once made, the cakes can be wrapped individually in clingfilm/plastic wrap for storage. They will keep in the refrigerator for 1–2 days; you may need to steam them to freshen them up.)

# STEAMED CHIVE DUMPLINGS

## Bánh Lá Hẹ

These steamed chive dumplings originate from the Teochew (Chaozhou) community in Vietnam. Once made for only special occasions like Lunar New Year, death anniversaries and first birthdays, they're now commonly found at stalls selling Fried Rice Flour Cake with Eggs (page 62), served either steamed or steamed and fried, always with a sweet and sour dipping sauce.

Makes 3 dumplings
Preparation time: 30 minutes
Cooking time: 20 minutes

| DF |

*For the filling*
100 g/3½ oz Chinese chives (lá hẹ), cut into 5-mm/¼-inch lengths
½ teaspoon oyster sauce
¼ teaspoon salt
¼ teaspoon black pepper
½ teaspoon sugar

*For the dough*
200 g/7 oz (1⅓ cups) rice flour
2 tablespoons sticky (glutinous) rice flour
¼ teaspoon salt
205 ml/7 fl oz (¾ cup plus 2 tablespoons) boiling water
1 tablespoon Annatto Oil (page 457)
banana leaves, cut into 10-12-cm/4-4½-inch rounds or squares, for steaming

*For the sauce*
60 ml/2 fl oz (¼ cup) coconut water
120 ml/4 fl oz (½ cup) soy sauce
1½ teaspoons sugar
5 g/⅛ oz minced chilli
2 tablespoons vinegar

To prepare the filling, in a bowl, mix the Chinese chives with the oyster sauce, salt, pepper and sugar. Set aside.

To prepare the dough, in another bowl, combine the rice flour, sticky (glutinous) rice flour and salt. Slowly add the measured boiling water to the flour mixture. Bring the flours and water together with a wooden spatula at the start, then when it is cool enough to handle, use your hand to knead until smooth.

To make the dumplings, divide the dough into three portions, approximately 130 g/4½ oz each. Flatten each portion with the palm of your hand into a large circle 15 cm/6 inches in diameter.

Add a third of the filling to the centre of each circle, then wrap the outer edge into the centre to form a ball. Flatten each ball into an 11-cm/4¼-inch disc about 1.5 cm/⅝ inch thick. Brush the oil onto each disc, then place each disc on a piece of banana leaf.

Set up a steamer and bring the water to the boil.

Place the dumplings on their banana leaves in the steamer basket, set over the boiling water and steam for 20 minutes.

Meanwhile make the sauce. In a small bowl, mix together the coconut water, soy sauce, sugar, chilli and vinegar. Stir well until the sugar has dissolved.

Serve the dumplings with the prepared sauce.

***Note:*** You can eat the dumplings as soon as they have finished steaming or wait until they have cooled completely, then heat a little oil in a pan over a medium heat and fry on each side until golden. It is important to let them cool completely before frying, or they will be too sticky.

# HUẾ-STYLE WATER FERN CAKES

## Bánh Bèo Huế

A cornerstone of Huế snack culture alongside *bánh nậm* and *bánh bột lọc*, these delicate steamed rice cakes get their name from the process of '*đổ bánh bèo*' – pouring batter into small cups arranged in a steamer. By Huế standards, each cake should have a circular depression in the centre, maintaining their traditional round shape, which ancient Huế people believed symbolized Heaven. The dish takes different forms across Vietnam, from Hải Phòng's rectangular leaf-wrapped version with pork and wood ear mushrooms to Quảng Bình's plates topped with dried prawn (shrimp) floss and crispy pork rinds, and to Bình Dương's distinctive *bánh bèo bì* with shredded pork skin. This Huế version is traditionally enjoyed hot as a snack between meals.

Makes approx. 28 small cakes
Preparation time: 1 hour 15 minutes, plus 1 hour resting time
Cooking time: 1 hour

| DF | GF |

*For the batter*
200 g/7 oz (1⅓ cups) rice flour
15 g/½ oz (2 tablespoons) tapioca flour (starch)
½ teaspoon salt

*For the fried pork skin*
neutral oil, for deep-frying
20 g/¾ oz dried pork skin, cut into 1-cm/½-inch squares (or 30 g/1 oz Thai chicharrones)

*To serve*
30 g/1 oz Prawn Floss (page 460)
30 g/1 oz Crispy Fried Pork Fat (page 459)
100 g/3½ oz Spring Onion Oil (page 458)
Huế-style Dipping Sauce for Savoury Cakes (page 473), to serve

To make the batter, mix together the rice flour, tapioca flour (starch), 500 ml/18 fl oz (2 cups plus 1 tablespoon) of water and the salt in a bowl. Sieve the mixture to remove any lumps. Let it rest for at least 1 hour before use.

Heat a pan of neutral oil to 180°C/350°F. If not using a thermometer, test the oil temperature by inserting wooden chopsticks into the oil – it should bubble vigorously around them. Carefully add the dried pork skin or chicharrones to the oil and fry for 1 minute 30 seconds–2 minutes until golden brown. Carefully remove and drain on paper towels, then set aside.

Set up a steamer and bring the water to the boil.

Pour 25 g/1 oz of the batter into 6–9-cm/2½–3½-inch bowls or moulds, then put the bowls or moulds in the steamer basket. Place a cloth between the lid and the steamer basket to prevent excess moisture loss. Set over the boiling water and steam for approximately 15 minutes.

Top each serving with ½ teaspoon of the prawn floss, 1 piece of crispy fried pork fat, 1 piece of fried pork skin or chicharrones and ½ teaspoon of the spring onion oil.

Serve with the dipping sauce on the side.

***Note:*** For a Southern serving variation, substitute the toppings with 1 teaspoon of mashed cooked mung beans and sprinkle with chopped spring onions (scallions). You can also drizzle over Seasoned Coconut Milk (page 465).

# CLEAR MUNG BEAN DUMPLINGS

## Bánh Bột Lọc Đậu Xanh

In Huế, *bánh bột lọc* comes in two forms: one version wrapped in banana leaves and steamed, and a 'naked' (*trần*) version boiled in water. The boiled version can also be called *bánh quai vạc*, and is served with spring onion (scallion) oil on top, like here. These half-moon-shaped dumplings, unlike their longer, leaf-wrapped cousins, are cooked until they float to the surface. Boiled 'naked' dumplings, *bánh bột lọc trần,* come with two filling options: prawns (shrimp) and pork or this vegetarian version with mung bean (*đậu xanh*).

Makes about 10–11 dumplings; serves 2–3
Preparation time: 30 minutes, plus 1 hour soaking time
Cooking time: 40 minutes

| V | VE | DF |

*For the filling*
100 g/3½ oz (½ cup) yellow split mung beans
200 ml/7 fl oz (¾ cup plus 1 tablespoon) tepid water, for soaking
2 teaspoons neutral oil
30 g/1 oz shallots, minced
1 teaspoon all-purpose seasoning (hạt nêm)
¼ teaspoon salt
½ teaspoon sugar

*For the dough*
220 g/8 oz (1¾ cups) tapioca flour (starch)
200 ml/7 fl oz (¾ cup plus 1 tablespoons) boiling water

*To serve*
40–50 g/1½–1¾ oz Spring Onion Oil (page 458)
Seasoned Vegetarian Fish Sauce (page 472), Huế-style Dipping Sauce for Savoury Cakes (page 473) or Basic Dipping Fish Sauce (page 470)

To prepare the filling, in a large bowl, soak the mung beans in the measured tepid water for 1 hour. Rinse 2–3 times under running water until the water runs clear.

In a small pot, add the soaked mung beans and 150 ml/5 fl oz (⅔ cup) of water. Place over a medium heat and cook for 15 minutes. Add 50 ml/2 fl oz (3½ tablespoons) of water and cook for an additional 10 minutes until the beans are soft and water evaporated.

Transfer the beans to a food processor and process until smooth.

To cook the filling, heat the neutral oil in a frying pan or skillet over a medium heat, add the shallot and fry for 3–4 minutes until they become a nice light brown colour and fragrance the oil. Add the processed mung bean paste. Season with the all-purpose seasoning, salt and sugar. Mix well until combined, then cook for a further 1 minute. Remove from the heat and let cool completely.

Form the filling into 7-g/¼-oz balls, making about 20 filling balls. (You will need 10–11 balls for this recipe; use the leftover filling for other dishes; they will keep in the refrigerator for 4–5 days.)

To make the dough, place 150 g/5½ oz (1¼ cups) of the tapioca flour (starch) in a large bowl. Add 100 ml/3½ fl oz (⅓ cup plus 1 tablespoon) of the measured boiling water, then mix well. Add the remaining tapioca flour, then the remaining measured boiling water. Knead until smooth and pliable.

To shape the dumplings, form the dough into 20 g/¾ oz balls, making 10–11 balls. Flatten each ball into a thin circle, then place one mung bean filling ball in the centre. Fold the wrapper in half to form a half-moon shape, pressing the edges to seal. Optionally, use a fork to create decorative ridges along the sealed edge.

To cook the dumplings, prepare a bowl of iced water. Bring 1 litre/1¾ pints (4¼ cups) of water to the boil in a large pot. Add the dumplings and cook for 8 minutes, or until the wrappers become translucent. Remove with a slotted spoon and place in the iced water for 10 minutes for better clarity.

Remove from the water and place all the dumplings on a plate, then drizzle the spring onion oil on top.

Serve with your chosen dipping sauce.

# FLAT STEAMED RICE DUMPLINGS

## Bánh Nậm Huế

Also known as *bánh lá chả tôm* in Huế, these soft flat dumplings are often served alongside *bánh bèo* (water fern cakes) and *bánh bột lọc* (clear tapioca dumplings) in a combination known as '*bèo nậm lọc*'. Being the softest of these cakes, they're traditionally given to children as an afternoon snack or to those recovering from illness. While *lá dong* leaves are preferred for their aroma, banana leaves make a practical substitute, especially outside Vietnam.

Makes 10 dumplings
Preparation time: 45 minutes
Cooking time: 45 minutes

| DF |

*For the batter*
250 g/9 oz (1⅔ cups) rice flour
50 g/1¾ oz (⅓ cup plus 2 teaspoons) tapioca flour (starch)
½ teaspoon salt
650 ml/22 fl oz (2¾ cups) warm water
1 tablespoon neutral oil

*For the filling*
200 g/7 oz minced (ground) pork
½ teaspoon fish sauce
¾ teaspoon sugar
10 g/¼ oz shallot, minced, plus 15 g/½ oz shallot, chopped
300 g/10½ oz prawns (shrimp) (about 10 prawns)
15 g/½ oz dried shrimp, rinsed and soaked for 5 minutes if hard
¼ teaspoon salt
¼ teaspoon black pepper
1 tablespoon plus 1 teaspoon Annatto Oil (page 457)
15 g/½ oz garlic, chopped
1 tablespoon neutral oil

*For wrapping*
1 tablespoon neutral oil, for brushing
10–15 pieces of dong (lá dong) or banana leaves, blanched (see step 3, page 390), or aluminium foil, cut to 20 × 15 cm/8 × 6 inches
10 g/¼ oz spring onion (scallion), chopped

*To serve*
Huế-style Dipping Sauce for Savoury Cakes (page 473) or fish sauce mixed with chilli slices

To prepare the batter, in a bowl, mix together the rice flour, tapioca flour (starch), salt, measured warm water and neutral oil until smooth. Set aside.

To prepare the filling, in a bowl, combine the minced (ground) pork with the fish sauce, ¼ teaspoon of the sugar and the minced shallot. Let marinate for 10–15 minutes. Set aside.

Meanwhile, bring a pan of water to the boil, add the prawns (shrimp) and blanch for 10 minutes. Drain and set aside until cool enough to handle, then peel, reserving the head juices in a small bowl. You should have 130 g/4½ oz of peeled prawns.

Place the peeled prawns and dried shrimp in a food processor, then blitz. Add the salt, pepper and 1 tablespoon of annatto oil and mix well.

Heat the 1 teaspoon of annatto oil in a pan over medium-low heat, add the chopped shallot and the garlic and stir-fry for 1 minute. Add the marinated pork and the reserved prawn head juice, stir-fry for another 3 minutes 30 seconds. Add the prawn and dried shrimp mixture. Cook for another 2 minutes. Add the remaining sugar and neutral oil. Mix well.

To cook the batter, pour the batter into a pan over a low heat and cook, stirring continuously to avoid lumps, for 6–8 minutes until it forms a paste.

To wrap the dumplings, brush a thin layer of neutral oil onto the middle of a dong leaf, banana leaf or piece of aluminium foil. Spread 50 g/1¾ oz of the cooked batter on the leaf or foil. Add 15 g/½ oz of the filling on top. Add a few pieces of spring onion (scallion) on top.

With the longer edge of the leaf or foil facing you, fold the bottom third of the leaf or foil over the filling, then fold the top third over the filling, too. Flatten the creases, then fold shorter edges at either end underneath to form a rectangular parcel. Press down on the parcel to evenly spread the filling.

Repeat with the remaining batter and filling.

To steam the dumplings, set up a steamer and bring the water to the boil.

Place the parcels in the steamer basket, set over the boiling water and steam for about 20 minutes until cooked through.

To serve, unwrap the dumplings and serve with your chosen dipping sauce.

To eat this the traditional way, roll the dumplings from top to bottom and pour a bit of the sauce on top.

# CRISPY RICE CAKE WITH STEAMED RICE DUMPLINGS

## Bánh Ram Ít

This is one of my favourite Huế cakes for its playful contrasts – a tender, meat-filled sticky (glutinous) rice dumpling sitting on a crispy fried base. At Quán ăn An Tâm, a small restaurant in Huế, cô Công Huyền Tôn Nữ Bích Hà, whose name marks her connection to Vietnam's royal family (as indicated by her name Công Huyền), taught us her recipe, sharing her secret for the perfect crispy fried base; she also shared with us her Huế-style Dipping Sauce for Savoury Cakes (page 473).

Serves 30
Preparation time: 1 hour
Cooking time: 1 hour

| DF |

*For the dough*
800 g/1 lb 12 oz (5⅓ cups) sticky (glutinous) rice flour, plus 4 teaspoons, if needed
2 teaspoons salt
2 teaspoons sugar
600 ml/1 pint (2½ cups) hot water
4 tablespoons neutral oil

*For the prawn and pork belly filling*
160 g/5½ oz small prawns (shrimp) (if you can't find these, use medium size prawns cut into 2–3 pieces)
200 g/7 oz fatty pork belly (side) (with skin)
2 tablespoons Annatto Oil (page 457)
10 g/¼ oz shallot, finely chopped
10 g/¼ oz garlic, finely chopped
2 teaspoons light brown sugar
¼ teaspoon annatto powder, optional
1 teaspoon fish sauce
¼ teaspoon salt
¼ teaspoon black pepper

*For the crispy rice cake base*
200 g/7 oz (1⅓ cups) sticky (glutinous) rice flour
35 g/1¼ oz (¼ cup) rice flour
35 g/1¼ oz (¼ cup) tapioca flour (starch)
½ teaspoon salt
½ teaspoon sugar
55 g/2 oz steamed orange sweet potato, mashed
1 tablespoon neutral oil, plus extra for deep-frying

*To serve*
Prawn Floss (page 460)
Huế-style Dipping Sauce for Savoury Cakes (page 473)

To make the dough, in a bowl mix together sticky (glutinous) rice flour, salt and sugar, then gradually add the measured hot water, mixing with a spatula. Allow to cool enough to touch, then knead the dough until it's malleable. Add the neutral oil and knead until smooth. Wrap in clingfilm (plastic wrap) and let cool. If it is sticky, sprinkle with the extra sticky rice flour.

To prepare the prawn (shrimp) and pork belly filling, bring a pan of water to the boil (or you can use the water for Huế-Style Dipping Sauce for Savoury Cakes, page 473), add the prawns and boil for 11 minutes. Drain and let cool, then peel; it should yield about 85 g/3 oz peeled prawns. Set aside.

Remove the pork belly (side) skin and discard, then dice the belly into 1-cm/½-inch cubes.

Heat the annatto oil in a pan over a medium heat, add the shallot and garlic and fry for 1 minute. Add the diced pork, then fry for 2 minutes. Add the sugar, then fry for a further 1 minute. Add the prawns, annatto powder, if using, the fish sauce, salt and pepper, then stir-fry for 17 minutes until glossy.

Set up a steamer and bring the water to the boil.

To make each dumpling, take 20 g/¾ oz of the dough and form it into a small ball, then press down the middle with your thumb, so the sides are a bit thicker than the centre. Fill the centre with one prawn and one piece of stir-fried pork belly from the filling mixture and then wrap the edges of the dough around it to form a ball. Repeat until you have used all the dough, prawns and pork belly; you should have about 30 dumpling balls. Make sure your dumplings are covered with a clingfilm (plastic wrap), while you do this.

Add a batch of dumplings to the steamer basket, keeping the uncooked dumplings covered so they do not dry out and crack. Place a cloth between the lid and basket to prevent excess moisture loss, then set over the boiling water and steam for 10 minutes.

To make the crispy rice cake base, mix all the dry ingredients together in a bowl. Add the sweet potato and oil and knead until smooth. Divide the dough into 30 portions (about 8 g/¼ oz each). Shape each portion into a ball and flatten with your hand (or use a rolling pin if you prefer) into patties 5 cm/2 inches in diameter, 5 mm/¼ inch thick.

Heat a pan of neutral oil to 180°C/350°F. If not using a thermometer, test the oil temperature by inserting wooden chopsticks into the oil – it should bubble vigorously around them. Carefully add the patties to the hot oil and fry for 10–14 minutes until golden brown, then carefully remove from the oil and drain well on paper towels.

Serve the steamed rice dumplings on top of the crispy rice cake bases. Sprinkle the prawn floss on top and serve with a dipping bowl of the Huế-style dipping sauce for savoury cakes on the side.

To eat this the traditional way, we were taught to dip the full crispy base into the sauce, and eat everything in one bite.

# SAVOURY STICKY RICE AND MUNG BEAN DUMPLINGS

Bánh Ít Trần

In Huế, cô Nguyễn Thị Thủy shared this savoury white *bánh ít*, a sticky (glutinous) rice dumpling filled with mung beans, different from the black, sweeter version that uses ramie leaf known as *bánh ít lá gai* (Ramie Leaf Sticky Rice Cakes, page 426). The white variety comes in two forms: *bánh ít lá* wrapped in banana leaves, and this 'naked' version (*trần*) steamed on banana leaf-lined racks. It can eaten when slightly cooled to reduce its stickiness, and can be combined with *bánh ram*, fried crispy dough, to create a vegan version of Crispy Rice Cake with Steamed Rice Dumplings (page 400).

Makes approx. 15–20 dumplings
Preparation time: 1 hour, plus 6–8 hours or overnight soaking time
Cooking time: 50 minutes

| V | VE | DF |

*For the filling*
- 350 g/12 oz (1½ cups) yellow split mung beans
- 70 ml/2½ fl oz (scant ⅓ cup) neutral oil
- 95 g/3½ oz peeled shallots
- 1 tablespoon MSG
- 1 tablespoon all-purpose seasoning (hạt nêm)
- ¼ teaspoon salt
- ½ teaspoon black pepper

*For the dough*
- 400 g/14 oz (2⅔ cups) sticky (glutinous) rice flour
- 300 ml/10 fl oz (1¼ cups) boiling water
- 240 ml/8 fl oz (1 cup) neutral oil, for shaping

*For wrapping*
- 15–20 banana leaf pieces, cut into 10-cm/4-inch squares

*To serve*
- 70 g/2½ oz Spring Onion Oil (page 458)
- Huế-style Dipping Sauce for Savoury Cakes (page 473), Basic Dipping Fish Sauce (page 470) or Seasoned Vegetarian Fish Sauce (page 472)

To prepare the filling, soak the mung beans in water for 6–8 hours or overnight.

Set up a steamer and bring the water to the boil.

Drain the soaked beans and place in the steamer basket. Set over the boiling water and steam for 20–30 minutes until soft and easily mashed. You should have about 700 g/1 lb 9 oz of cooked mung beans.

Meanwhile, heat the neutral oil in a pan over a medium heat, add the shallots and fry for about 4 minutes 30 seconds until golden.

Transfer the cooked mung beans to a bowl and mash with a large spoon. Season the mashed beans with the MSG, all-purpose seasoning, salt, pepper and the fried shallots with their oil. Mix well.

To prepare the dough, in a large bowl, mix the rice flour with the measured boiling water. Knead until a smooth dough forms.

Pour the neutral oil into a bowl and have ready on the side for shaping the dumplings.

To make the dumplings, form the dough into 15–20 small balls and flatten them. Place a portion of the filling in the centre of each piece of dough and wrap the dough around it, using the oil to prevent sticking while shaping. Roll each piece of dough into a ball and place it on a banana leaf square.

To cook the dumplings, set up a steamer and bring the water to the boil.

Place the dumplings on their banana leaves in the steamer basket, set over the boiling water and steam for 20 minutes over a high heat.

Before eating, add a little bit of spring onion oil on top of each dumpling. Serve hot, with your chosen dipping sauce.

# HUẾ-STYLE CLEAR PRAWN DUMPLINGS

## Bánh Bột Lọc Huế

These chewy dumplings from Huế are traditionally filled with small river prawns (*tôm đất*) with edible shells. When *tôm đất* isn't available, regular prawns are used, and some stalls add a piece of caramelized pork fat. Wrapped in banana leaves and steamed, they can also be made in a vegan version using stir-fried mushrooms. The dumplings should be served slightly cooled, dipped in pure fish sauce and green chillies, unlike the other cakes that are usually dipped in seasoned fish sauce.

Makes 20 dumplings; serves 4–5
Preparation time: 45 minutes
Cooking time: 40 minutes

| DF |

*For the filling*
1 tablespoon neutral oil
½ tablespoon Annatto Oil (page 457)
10 g/¼ oz garlic, minced
20 g/¾ oz shallots, minced
300 g/10½ oz prawns (shrimp) (about 10 large or 30 small river prawns/ tôm đất)
1 teaspoon fish sauce
1 teaspoon sugar
¼ teaspoon salt
¼ teaspoon black pepper

*For the coating*
50 g/1¾ oz (⅓ cup plus 2 teaspoons) tapioca flour (starch)
1 teaspoon neutral oil

*For the dough*
300 g/10½ oz (2½ cups) tapioca flour (starch)
¼ teaspoon salt
350 ml/12 fl oz (1½ cups) boiling water

*For wrapping*
20 banana leaf squares (20 cm/8 inches)
20 banana leaf strips (20 × 1 cm/8 × ½ inch), for tying

To prepare the filling, heat both oils in a frying pan or skillet over a medium heat, add the garlic and shallots, then fry for 1 minute. Add the prawns (shrimp), then stir until they turn light orange, 5–7 minutes. Add the fish sauce, sugar, salt and pepper, then cook for 2 more minutes until the prawns are glazed and sweet.

To prepare the coating, in a small bowl, combine the tapioca flour (starch) with 50 ml/2 fl oz (3½ tablespoons) of water and the neutral oil. Mix well and set aside.

To make the dough, in a pot, combine the tapioca flour and salt. Add the measured boiling water and stir vigorously with chopsticks or a wooden spoon. Place over a high heat, stirring continuously for about 5 minutes until the dough starts clumping onto your spoon or chopsticks and starts sticking to the bottom of the pan; as soon as this starts to happen, reduce the heat to medium. Continue stirring until the dough is two-thirds cooked: it should look like very thick yogurt. Remove from the heat, then immediately add the prepared coating mixture. Mix until well combined. If not using the dough immediately, transfer to a bowl so it does not continue cooking in the hot pan.

Bring a pot of water to the boil, add the banana leaves to the boiling water and blanch for 2–3 minutes. Dry the leaves with a clean dish towel.

To wrap the dumplings, place 20–25 g/3/4–1 oz (about 1½ tablespoons) of the dough in the centre of each leaf square. Spread the dough to 6–7 cm/2½–2¾ inches long, then place 2 prawns, lengthways, on the dough. Fold the leaf in half lengthways twice, then pinch the edge in the middle, twist slightly and fold the side down underneath; repeat on the other side. This folding style is called 'frog fold' due to its appearance. Wrap with a banana leaf strip and tie to secure.

To steam the dumplings, set up a steamer and bring the water to the boil.

Arrange the wrapped dumplings in the steamer basket, set over the boiling water and steam until translucent, 15–20 minutes, so the banana leaf imparts its flavour.

Serve hot.

# STEAMED RICE ROLLS

## Bánh Ướt

These steamed rice rolls can be enjoyed simply with Prawn Floss (page 460) or Pork Rolls (page 462), featured in dishes like Nghệ An Eel Soup with Steamed Rice Rolls (page 408), or used as the base for various rice rolls. One of my favourite ways to eat these rolls is to serve them with grilled pork (page 145).

A Hanoi vendor shared her secret to achieving the perfect soft yet chewy texture: let the batter rest overnight so the flour fully hydrates.

Makes approx. 20–25 sheets (24 cm/ 9½ inches in diameter)
Preparation time: 30 minutes, plus overnight soaking and overnight resting times
Cooking time: 1 minute per sheet

**| V | VE | DF | GF | ≤5 | ≤30 |**

400 g/14 oz (2 cups plus 2 tablespoons) Thai fragrant (jasmine) rice, soaked overnight
30 g/1 oz (¼ cup) tapioca flour (starch)
½ teaspoon salt

To make the batter, drain the soaked rice; you should have about 560 g/1 lb 4 oz (2¾ cups) of hydrated rice. Place the rice in a blender, along with the tapioca flour (starch), salt and 490 ml/17 fl oz (2 cups) water. Blend on high speed for 1–3 minutes until smooth. Strain the mixture through a fine-mesh sieve into a bowl. You should have about 1 kg/2 lb 3 oz or so of batter and the batter should have the consistency of light cream or coconut milk. If necessary, add another 1½–2 tablespoons of water to achieve the right consistency. A thicker batter is easier to handle, but a thinner batter produces a more closed texture. Cover and chill it in the refrigerator overnight before using.

To steam the rice rolls, fill a 24-cm/9½-inch diameter pot with a rounded lid (not a flat lid) two-thirds full with water. Stretch a cotton cloth (not too thick and not stretchy) over the pot, and use a metal tightening strap to tighten and flatten the cloth. If you do not have a tightening strap, you could use an elastic (rubber) band or string, but the cloth must be perfectly flat. Pierce a hole on the side of the cloth to prevent inflation during cooking. Bring the water to a simmer.

Using a ladle, pour 40–50 g/1½–1¾ oz of batter onto the cloth, then steam for 1 minute with the pot covered. Carefully remove the rice sheet with a thin chopstick or spatula. Repeat with the remaining batter. Be cautious when handling the sheets, as they can be very hot and delicate.

# SOUTHERN VIETNAMESE STEAMED RICE ROLLS

## Bánh Cuốn Miền Nam

I grew up with this southern version, where rice rolls come generously garnished with fresh herbs and vegetables – a contrast to the minimalist northern style. We serve ours with a spread of sides: fried shallots, *nem chua* (fermented pork rolls) or Pork Rolls (page 462), Fried Prawn and Mung Bean Cakes (page 409), blanched bean sprouts, cucumber, and herbs. Unlike the northern style, where sauce is for dipping, here we pour diluted fish sauce (or you can use Northern-style Fish Sauce, page 471, if you prefer) directly over the steamed rice rolls.

Serves 3
Preparation time: 30 minutes
Cooking time: 20 minutes

| DF |

80 g/2¾ oz bean sprouts
oil, for brushing
1 quantity batter from Steamed Rice Rolls (page 403)
300 g/10½ oz Minced Pork and Jicama Filling (page 464)

*To serve*
10 g/¼ oz (2 teaspoons) Fried Shallots (page 458)
25 g/1 oz Pork Roll (page 462), sliced
2 Fried Prawn and Mung Bean Cakes (page 409), halved
90–120 g/3–4 oz cucumber, sliced into thin strips
15 g/½ oz peppermint (húng cây)
1 quantity Northern-style Fish Sauce (page 471)
minced chillies, to taste

Set up a steamer and bring the water to the boil.

Add the bean sprouts to the steamer basket, set over the boiling water and steam lightly, for 1–2 minutes, then set aside.

Lightly brush a plate with oil and have ready on the side.

Heat a non-stick pan over very low heat or set up a specialized steamer for steaming rice rolls and bring the water to the boil. Alternatively, you can use a cotton cloth tightly stretched over a pan (see page 403).

Pour a thin layer of batter (about 50 g/1¾ oz) onto the pan or steamer basket, swirling to evenly coat. Fry or steam for about 1 minute until the batter is set but still slightly moist. Remove from the pan or steamer and place on the prepared plate.

Spread 25 g/1 oz of the minced pork and jicama filling in a strip across one side of the rice sheet. Carefully roll the rice sheet around the filling. Set aside, covered, while you make the rest of the rolls.

Repeat until you have made 12 rolls. If desired, you can steam them again for about 30 seconds before serving.

To prepare the serving plates, arrange 4 rolls on each plate. On each plate, sprinkle 5–10 g/⅛–¼ oz (2 teaspoons) of the fried shallots over the rolls. Add 25 g/1 oz of the sliced pork roll. Place half a fried prawn and mung bean cake on each plate. Add 30–40 g/½–1½ oz of the cucumber strips and 25 g/1 oz of the steamed bean sprouts to each plate. Garnish with the peppermint.

Serve immediately while still warm with small bowls of the northern-style fish sauce mixed with minced chillies on the side.

# LẠNG SƠN STEAMED EGG RICE ROLLS

## Bánh Cuốn Trứng Lạng Sơn

From Lạng Sơn province comes this distinctive take on steamed rice rolls, where an egg is cracked into the batter during cooking. Instead of the usual pork and wood ear mushroom filling, it's topped with caramelized minced (ground) pork. You can request your egg runny, fully cooked or scrambled into the batter. Like many Vietnamese dishes, it comes with an array of condiments – from black pepper and Hanoi-style Chilli Sauce (page 477) to fresh chillies, fish sauce and soy sauce, so feel free to customize your hot stock (broth) to taste.

Serves 4
Preparation time: 30 minutes
Cooking time: 20 minutes

| DF |

*For the braised pork mince*
1 tablespoon neutral oil
25 g/1 oz shallots, finely chopped
100 g/3½ oz minced (ground) pork
½ teaspoon sugar
1 teaspoon fish sauce
¼ teaspoon black pepper, plus extra to serve
650 ml/22 fl oz (2⅔ cups) pork stock (broth) (such as Basic Pork Stock, page 464, or stock from Hà Giang Steamed Rice Rolls recipe, page 406)

*For the rice rolls*
1 quantity batter from Steamed Rice Rolls (page 403)
4 eggs

*To serve*
20 g/¾ oz (4 teaspoons) Fried Shallots (page 458)
20 g/¾ oz spring onions (scallions), chopped
20 g/¾ oz coriander (cilantro), chopped
fish sauce, soy sauce, Pickled Garlic in Vinegar (page 468) or sliced chillies, optional

To prepare the braised pork mince, heat the oil in a small pan over a medium heat, add the shallots and stir-fry for 1 minute. Add the minced (ground) pork and stir-fry for 1 minute. Add the sugar and fish sauce and fry for 5 minutes, continuously breaking down the meat until it is nicely browned. Reduce the heat and cook for another 1–2 minutes. Add the pepper and 2 tablespoons of the pork stock (broth) to deglaze the pan, then remove from the heat immediately. Set aside.

To make the rice rolls, heat a non-stick pan over very low heat or set up a specialized steamer for steamed rice rolls and bring the water to the boil. Alternatively, you can use a cotton cloth tightly stretched over a pan (see page 403).

Pour a thin layer of the batter onto the pan or steamer and let it cook for 1 minute. Immediately crack an egg onto the batter and swirl to evenly spread. Fry or steam for 1–2 minutes until the batter and egg are set. Carefully roll the rice sheet. Repeat to make 4–8 rolls (1–2 per serving).

Pour the remaining pork stock into a pan and bring to a simmer.

To assemble each serving, place 1–2 egg rice rolls on a plate. Top each roll with 5 g/⅛ oz (1 tablespoon) of the braised pork mince and 5 g/⅛ oz (1 teaspoon) of the fried shallots.

In a small bowl, combine 25 g/1 oz (about ⅓ cup) of the braised pork mince with the chopped spring onions (scallions) and coriander (cilantro). Pour about 150 ml/5 fl oz (⅔ cup) of the hot pork stock over the pork and herbs.

You can add extra fish sauce, soy sauce, pickled garlic in vinegar or fresh cut chillies to your stock to taste. Sprinkle with black pepper.

To eat, use scissors to cut the rolls if needed, then dip into the stock.

# HÀ GIANG STEAMED RICE ROLLS

## Bánh Cuốn Hà Giang

I discovered this version in Hà Giang, though it's popular throughout Vietnam's northern mountains, where winter temperatures can drop to 0°C/32°F. Unlike the southern versions with their cold dipping sauces, these rice rolls come with a warming bone broth. Served whole rather than cut, the rolls are meant to be dipped in the light pork stock (broth). Often *chả cay*, thin pork rolls, would be cooked in that stock, absorbing the flavours and becoming plumper. Scissors are left on the tables, so you can cut the rice rolls and pork rolls yourself if needed.

Serves 4–5; makes 16–20 rolls
Preparation time: 30 minutes, plus 15–30 minutes soaking time
Cooking time: 1 hour 20 minutes

| DF |

4–5 pork rolls (chả quay or chả lụa/chả que)
1 quantity batter for Steamed Rice Rolls (page 403)

*For the filling*
16 g/½ oz dried wood ear mushrooms
1 tablespoon neutral oil
10 g/¼ oz shallot, coarsely chopped
10 g/¼ oz garlic, coarsely chopped
100 g/3½ oz minced (ground) pork
2 teaspoons fish sauce
1 teaspoon black pepper

*For the stock (broth)*
600 g/1 lb 5 oz pork leg bones, blanched (see step 1, page 121)
100 g/3½ oz jicama, peeled
1 tablespoon fish sauce
½ teaspoon salt
25 g/1 oz peeled shallots

*To garnish*
50 g/1¾ oz (2 tablespoons) Fried Shallots (page 458)
15 g/½ oz coriander (cilantro), leaves picked
15 g/½ oz spring onion (scallion) greens, thinly sliced

*To serve*
2 calamansi, halved
Pickled Kohlrabi and Carrots (page 469)
Northern-style Fish Sauce (page 471), optional (but highly recommended)
minced chilli, to taste, optional
black pepper, to taste

To prepare the filling, soak the dried wood ear mushrooms in a bowl of water for 15–30 minutes until soft, then finely chop.

In a small pan, heat the oil over a medium heat. Add the shallot and garlic and fry for 1 minute. Add the minced (ground) pork and 1 teaspoon of the fish sauce and fry until the pork is fully cooked and the liquid evaporates, 3–4 minutes. Add the chopped mushrooms. Season with the pepper and the remaining fish sauce. Stir fry for 4 minutes 20 seconds. Set aside.

To prepare the stock (broth), in a large pot, add the blanched pork bones and 1.5 litres/2½ pints (6¼ cups) of water. Bring to the boil and simmer for 10 minutes. Add the jicama, fish sauce, salt and whole shallots. Simmer for 1 hour. Strain the stock. You should have 800–900 ml/27–30 fl oz (3½–3¾ cups) of stock left.

Unwrap the banana leaves from the pork rolls and add the pork rolls to the stock. Keep the stock warm while you cook the rice rolls.

To steam the rice rolls, fill a 24-cm/9½-inch diameter pot with a rounded lid (not a flat lid) two-thirds full with water. Stretch a cotton cloth (not too thick and not stretchy) over the pot, and use a metal tightening strap to tighten and flatten the cloth. If you do not have a tightening strap, you could use an elastic (rubber) band or string, but the cloth must be perfectly flat. Pierce a hole on the side of the cloth to prevent inflation during cooking. Bring the water to a simmer.

Using a ladle, pour 12.5 g/½ oz of batter onto the cloth, then steam for 1 minute with the pot covered. Carefully remove the rice sheet with a thin chopstick or spatula. Be cautious when handling the sheets, as they can be very hot and delicate.

Place the rice sheet on a clean work surface or plate in front of you, then spread 30 g/1 oz of the filling in a line near the edge closest to you. Wrap the rice sheet over the filling and roll away from you so the filling is tucked well inside.

Repeat with the remaining batter and filling.

To serve, place 4 rice rolls on each plate and garnish with fried shallots and calamansi halves. In a small bowl, add 125 ml/4¼ fl oz of the hot stock. Carefully remove one the pork rolls from the stock pot, slice, then add to the to the stock in the bowl. Garnish the stock with the coriander (cilantro) and sliced spring onion (scallion) greens. Serve with a side of pickled vegetables and a small bowl of northern-style fish sauce mixed with minced chillies, if using. Add black pepper to taste.

# NGHỆ AN EEL SOUP WITH STEAMED RICE ROLLS

## Bánh Mướt Súp Lươn Nghệ An

Eels are a key ingredient in Nghệ An cuisine, brought alive from districts like Diễn Châu, Nam Đàn and even southern Thạnh Hoá. While cleaning them takes time, both the meat and blood are served in the dish – the latter is believed to have refreshing properties – and the bones are used for the stock (broth). This recipe, shared by chu Nguyễn Như Hồng and cô Lê Thị Hải Yến in Vinh City, can be served with *bánh mướt* (the local name for *bánh ướt* – Steamed Rice Rolls, page 403) or Vietnamese Baguette (page 66), or as a base for noodle dishes. Like many regional dishes, it features *củ nén*, a small but pungent onion bulb, which can be substituted with chive bulbs.

Serves 4–5
Preparation time: 45 minutes
Cooking time: 1 hour

| DF |

*For the eels*
- 2 kg/4 lb 8 oz fresh live freshwater eels (small field eels)
- salt, for cleaning
- 10 g/¼ oz turmeric root, or more (see method), for cleaning

*For the soup*
- 5 g/⅛ oz turmeric, peeled and sliced
- 55 g/2 oz chive bulbs (củ nén)
- 2 tablespoons Annatto Oil (page 457)
- 3 tablespoons neutral oil
- 1 teaspoon chilli flakes
- 2 tablespoons fish sauce
- 1 teaspoon MSG
- 3 teaspoons soup powder (bột canh)

*To serve*
- 2 litres/3½ pints (8½ cups) Basic Pork Stock (page 464)
- 30 g/1 oz spring onions (scallions), finely chopped
- 30 g/1 oz coriander (cilantro), finely chopped
- 30 g/1 oz sawtooth coriander (culantro), finely chopped
- 90 g/3¼ oz Vietnamese coriander/cilantro (rau răm), finely chopped
- 1 quantity Steamed Rice Rolls (page 403), or alternatively use Vietnamese Baguette (page 66), white congee or glass noodles (miến)

To clean the eels, fill a large pot a quarter full with water and measure the water. For each 1 litre/1¾ pints (4¼ cups) of water, add 1 tablespoon of salt and 10 g/¼ oz turmeric root. Bring the water to the boil. Wearing gloves to protect your hands from any eel blood (see caution), add the live eels and stir, then cook for 3–4 minutes. Strain and rinse the boiled eels under cold running water and set aside until cool enough to handle.

To debone the eels, run a finger along the bones to remove the fillet (it should easily remove as it is cooked). Find the blood line in the middle of the eel (it should have coagulated during blanching) and reserve. Discarding the guts. Set the cleaned eel meat aside for cooking. You should have 450–500 g/1 lb–1 lb 2 oz eel bones.

To make the eel bone stock (broth), place all the eel bones in a large pot, add 1.5 litres/2¾ pints (6¼ cups) of water to the pot and bring to the boil over a high heat. Reduce the heat to low, cover and simmer for 30 minutes. Strain the stock and set aside; you should have about 1.3 litres/2¼ pints (5½ cups) of eel bone stock.

To make the soup, put the turmeric and chive bulbs in a mortar and pound with a pestle.

Heat the annatto and neutral oils in a pan over a medium heat, add the pounded turmeric and chive mixture and fry for 3 minutes. Lower the heat and continue cooking for 8 minutes or until soft, then remove from the heat and add the chilli flakes. Add the cleaned eel meat to the aromatic mixture. Add the fish sauce and MSG, then gently stir in.

Pour in the eel bone stock and the reserved blood line and bring to a simmer over a medium heat. Add the soup powder and stir well, then simmer for 11 minutes, skimming off any impurities from the surface. Remove from the heat.

To serve, heat the pork stock in a pan until hot. Ladle a portion of the pork stock into each serving bowl, add a ladle of the cooked eel and its stock, then top with a generous amount of the chopped spring onions and chopped herbs.

Serve immediately, with the steamed rice rolls, baguette, congee or glass noodles.

*Caution:* Eel blood is toxic if consumed raw. It contains ichthyotoxin, a protein that can be harmful to humans if ingested or if it enters the bloodstream through cuts. To ensure safety, always cook eel thoroughly, as heat neutralizes the toxin, making it safe to eat. When handling raw eel, wear gloves and clean all surfaces and tools after preparation to prevent cross-contamination. Never consume raw eel unless it has been properly processed. Once cooked, eel is completely safe.

# FRIED PRAWN AND MUNG BEAN CAKES

## Bánh Cống

This Mekong Delta speciality gets its name from the *cống* – an old grocery store measuring cup that became the signature mould for these crispy cakes. Made with rice flour and mung beans, topped with a whole prawn (shrimp) and fried in this distinctive cylindrical mould, they stay remarkably light without absorbing excess oil. A variation called *bánh giá* uses bean sprouts and pork liver instead. It's perfect for rainy days with friends, served with fresh herbs, dipping sauce or alongside Southern Vietnamese Steamed Rice Rolls (page 403).

Makes 15
Preparation time: 1 hour 30 minutes, plus 2–4 hours soaking time
Cooking time: 1 hour 10 minutes, plus 12 minutes per batch

| DF |

125 g/4¼ oz (generous ½ cup) green mung beans
½ teaspoon salt
15 medium-size prawns (shrimp), peeled and deveined (heads and tails intact)
neutral oil, for deep frying

*For the batter*
550 g/1 lb 4 oz (3⅔ cups) rice flour
50 g/1¾ oz cornflour (cornstarch)
30 g/1 oz (3 tablespoons) plain (all-purpose) flour
1¼ teaspoon baking powder
1¼ teaspoon salt

*To serve*
100 g/3½ oz salad greens
50 g/1¾ oz aromatic mixed herbs (rau thơm – peppermint, Vietnamese basil, perilla, fish mint)
Basic Dipping Fish Sauce (page 470)

Soak the mung beans in a bowl of salted water for 2–4 hours.

Drain the mung beans, then fill a pan with 720 ml/24 fl oz (3 cups) of water and bring to the boil. Add the mung beans and simmer for 45 minutes–1 hour until soft. Drain and set aside.

Bring a pan of water to the boil, add the prawns (shrimp) and cook in the boiling water for 10 minutes. Drain and set aside.

To prepare the batter, in a large bowl, mix the rice flour, cornflour (cornstarch), plain (all-purpose) flour, baking powder and salt. Gradually add 610 ml/20 fl oz (2½ cups) of water to the flour mixture, stirring to create a smooth batter. Add the cooked mung beans to the batter. Let rest for 5 minutes.

Fill a pot with oil and heat to 170°C/340°F. If not using a thermometer, test the oil temperature by inserting wooden chopsticks into the oil – small bubbles should form rapidly around them.

Carefully submerge a bánh cống mould (see note) in the hot oil to heat it. Very carefully remove the hot mould (caution: the handle will be very hot).

Fill the hot mould with batter and top with a prawn.

Carefully lower the mould into the oil and fry at 170°C/340°F for about 2 minutes 30 seconds. Baste the top of the cake with the hot oil for 30 seconds to seal it, then continue frying for 1 minute. Baste again for 30 seconds, then fry for another 5 minutes 30 seconds, occasionally basting. Carefully remove the cake from the mould and fry for an additional 1 minute or until golden all over. Carefully remove from the hot oil and drain on paper towels.

Repeat the process with the remaining batter and prawns.

To serve, arrange the mung bean cakes on a plate with the salad greens and mixed herbs. Serve with the dipping sauce on the side.

***Note:*** You will need a *bánh cống* mould or paddle for this recipe. If you do not have a mould, you can use a ladle – it should be large enough to fit the whole prawn.

# PRAWN AND SWEET POTATO FRITTERS

※

## Bánh Tôm Khoai Lang

These light southern Vietnamese fritters need plenty of pickles and fresh herbs to balance the richness. Daikon and carrot pickles work perfectly.

Serves 4–6
Preparation time: 20 minutes
Cooking time: 30 minutes

| DF |

500 g/1 lb 2 oz prawns (shrimp)
190 g/6¾ oz sweet potato
750 ml/25 fl oz (3 cups) neutral oil, for deep-frying

*For the batter*
20 g/¾ oz (2 tablespoons) plain (all-purpose) flour
50 g/1¾ oz (⅓ cup) rice flour
50 g/1¾ oz (⅓ cup plus 1 tablespoon) cornflour (cornstarch)
1 teaspoon salt
20 g/¾ oz spring onion (scallion) greens, finely chopped
¼ teaspoon black pepper
120 ml/4 fl oz (½ cup) cold water
½ teaspoon baking powder

*To serve*
130 g/4½ oz head of lettuce, leaves separated
150 g/5½ oz cucumber, sliced
100 g/3½ oz aromatic mixed herbs (rau thơm – Vietnamese basil, spearmint, fishmint, Vietnamese coriander/cilantro, perilla, peppermint)
Basic Dipping Fish Sauce (page 470)

Peel and devein the prawns (shrimp), leaving the tails on. (They should yield 240 g/8½ oz after peeling.)

Peel the sweet potato and slice it into thin matchsticks (julienne). Soak in a bowl of water for 10 minutes to prevent it from darkening.

Meanwhile, to prepare the batter, in a large bowl, mix the plain (all-purpose) flour, rice flour, cornflour (cornstarch), salt, spring onion (scallion) greens and pepper. Gradually add the measured cold water, stirring to create a smooth batter. Add the baking powder and mix well. Let the batter rest for 5 minutes to allow the flour to absorb the liquid.

Drain the sweet potato strips, then add them to the batter. Mix well.

In a large, deep pan or wok, heat the oil over a medium-high heat to around 175°C/345°F. If not using a thermometer, test the oil temperature by inserting wooden chopsticks into the oil – it should bubble vigorously around them.

Place a metal ladle (12–15 cm/4½–6 inches in diameter, 60–80 ml/2–2¾ fl oz/¼–⅓ cup capacity) in the hot oil to heat up, then carefully remove the heated ladle (caution: the handle will be hot).

Fill the ladle with about 60 ml/2 fl oz (¼ cup) of batter, then place 2 prawns on top, belly-side down and back up.

Carefully lower the ladle back into the oil, and allow the fritter to slide off. Fry for 5 minutes, then gently flip and fry for another 5 minutes until golden and crispy. Remove and drain on paper towels.

Repeat with the remaining prawns and sweet potato batter.

To serve, arrange the lettuce leaves on a plate, place the hot fritters on the lettuce, then serve with the sliced cucumber, mixed herbs and dipping sauce on the side.

# HANOI-STYLE PRAWN FRITTERS

## Bánh Tôm Hồ Tây

This Hanoi version of prawn (shrimp) fritters, named after West Lake (Hồ Tây), is distinct for not including sweet potatoes, unlike its southern counterpart (Prawn and Sweet Potato Fritters, page 410), which uses a different batter and adds julienned sweet potatoes. Originally sold by mobile street vendors around West Lake, they are now found throughout Hanoi, often sold alongside Pillow-Shaped Cakes (page 414).

Makes 8 fritters; serves 4–6
Preparation time: 15 minutes, plus 30 minutes resting time
Cooking time: 30 minutes

| DF |

500 ml/18 fl oz (2 cups) vegetable oil, for deep-frying
16 medium-size prawns (shrimp) (300 g/10½ oz), peeled and deveined

*For the yeast activation*
3 tablespoons warm water
1 teaspoon fast-action (active) dried yeast
½ teaspoon sugar

*For the batter*
200 g/7 oz plain (all-purpose) flour
50 g/1¾ oz (⅓ cup) crispy fried powder mix (bột chiên giòn) (see note on page 415)
½ teaspoon salt
½ teaspoon ground turmeric

*To serve*
130 g/4½ oz head of lettuce, leaves separated
150 g/5½ oz cucumber, sliced
100 g/3½ oz aromatic mixed herbs (rau thơm – Vietnamese basil, coriander/cilantro, perilla, Vietnamese balm), leaves picked
Northern-style Fish Sauce (page 471)
Pickled Kohlrabi and Carrots (page 469)

To activate the yeast, in a small bowl, combine the measured warm water, yeast and sugar. Stir well and cover. Let rest for 10 minutes until foamy.

To make the batter, in a large mixing bowl, combine the flour, crispy fried powder mix, 350 ml/12 fl oz (1½ cups) of water, the salt and the ground turmeric. Mix until smooth. Add the activated yeast mixture, then mix thoroughly until well combined. Let rest for 30 minutes.

Heat the oil in a deep pan or wok over a medium-high heat to 175°C/345°F. If not using a thermometer, test the oil temperature by inserting wooden chopsticks into the oil – it should bubble vigorously around them.

Place a metal ladle (12–15 cm/4½–6 inches in diameter, 60–80 ml/2–2¾ fl oz/¼–⅓ cup capacity) in the hot oil to heat up, then carefully remove the heated ladle (caution: the handle will be hot).

Fill the ladle with about 60 ml/2 fl oz (¼ cup) of batter, place 2 prawns on top, belly-side down and back up.

Carefully lower the ladle back into the oil and allow the fritter to slide off. Fry for 5 minutes, then gently flip and fry for another 5 minutes until golden and crispy. Remove and drain on paper towels.

Repeat with remaining prawns and batter.

To serve, arrange the lettuce leaves on a plate, place the hot fritters on the lettuce, then serve with the sliced cucumber, mixed herbs and dipping sauce on the side.

# MOUNTAIN-STYLE FRIED RICE CAKES

Bánh Áp Chao

*Bánh áp chao* is a fried snack found in the mountainous regions of Vietnam, such as Cao Bằng, Lạng Sơn and Hà Giang. Traditionally, the batter uses a blend of freshly grounded soybean and sticky (glutinous) rice to make the batter, but in modern kitchens like ours, using premade flour is very acceptable. It features a crispy exterior with a piece of meat in the centre, typically pork belly (side) or duck breast. This recipe is based on the version from Hà Giang, which I ate during market days.

Makes 5 cakes
Preparation time: 10 minutes, plus 1 hour resting time
Cooking time: 10 minutes per cake

| DF |

vegetable oil, for deep-frying

*For the batter*
- 130 g/4½ oz (¾ cup) sticky (glutinous) rice flour
- 40 g/1½ oz (¼ cup) rice flour
- 3 teaspoons soybean flour
- ¼ teaspoon salt
- ¼ teaspoon sugar
- ½ teaspoon MSG
- ⅛ teaspoon fast-action (active) dried yeast
- 200 g/7 oz warm water

*For the marinated meat*
- 120 g/4¼ oz pork shoulder or duck breast, thinly sliced
- ½ teaspoon MSG
- ¼ teaspoon black pepper
- ¼ teaspoon fish sauce

*To serve*
- Northern-style Fish Sauce (page 471)
- Pickled Kohlrabi and Carrots (page 469)

To prepare the batter, in a bowl, mix together all the dry ingredients for the batter. Gradually add the measured warm water while stirring with a spoon until well combined. Let the batter rest, loosely covered, at room temperature for at least 1 hour.

To prepare the marinated meat, in another bowl, mix together the pork or duck breast with the MSG, pepper and fish sauce. Set aside to marinate for 10–15 minutes.

Have a traditional 7-pointed star mould (see note) ready.

Fill a deep pan with oil, about 1 cm/½ inch higher than the height of the mould, and heat the oil to 170°C/340°F. If not using a thermometer, test the oil temperature by inserting wooden chopsticks into the oil – small bubbles should form rapidly around them.

Carefully submerge the mould in the hot oil to heat it. (You can do a few at a time if you have several moulds.) When hot, carefully remove the mould from the oil.

Add a layer of batter to the mould, then a few slices of marinated meat, and cover with more batter.

Carefully lower the mould into the hot oil and fry for about 3 minutes, occasionally pouring hot oil over the cake with a ladle. When the cake easily comes off the mould, remove the mould and continue frying for an additional 6–7 minutes until golden brown. Carefully remove from the oil and drain on paper towels.

Cut the cakes in half and serve hot, with the northern-style fish sauce and pickled vegetables on the side.

***Notes:*** Ideally, you will need a traditional 7-pointed star mould for this recipe. If you do not have this mould, you can use any other metal mould.

For best results, ensure the oil temperature stays between 175–180°C/345–350°F.

You can add shredded taro (khoai môn) to the filling for extra flavour and texture.

# PILLOW-SHAPED CAKES

## Bánh Gối

According to writer Nguyễn Ngọc Tiến, these half-moon shaped pastries were brought to Hanoi by Guangdong immigrants before 1954, their pillow-like shape with crispy, ridged edges inspiring the name '*bánh gối*' (pillow cake). Particularly sought-after during Hanoi's windy, cold autumn days, you'll often find them at vendors selling various fried snacks, including Hanoi-style Prawn Fritters (page 411). The way to fold the ridged edges is very similar to Argentinian empanadas.

Makes 12 cakes
Preparation time: 1 hour, plus 1 hour resting time
Cooking time: 15–20 minutes

| DF |

12 quail eggs, boiled and peeled
1 litre/1¾ pints (4¼ cups) neutral oil, for deep-frying

*For the dough*
150 g/5½ oz (1 cup) rice flour
350 g/12 oz (2⅓ cups) plain (all-purpose) flour
1 tablespoon tempura flour
1½ teaspoons light brown sugar
½ teaspoon salt
¼ teaspoon ground turmeric
250 ml/8½ fl oz (1 cup plus 2 teaspoons) warm water, plus 1–2 tablespoons if needed
1 tablespoon pork lard

*For the filling*
2 tablespoons neutral oil, plus extra for greasing
12 g/½ oz shallot, minced
15 g/½ oz garlic, minced
5 g/⅛ oz spring onion (scallion), minced
280 g/10 oz minced (ground) meat
2 tablespoons fish sauce
200 g/7 oz jicama, peeled and diced into 6–8-mm/¼–⅜-inch chunks
15 g/½ oz dried wood ear mushrooms, soaked in warm water, then drained and chopped (60 g/2¼ oz prepared weight)
40 g/1½ oz dried vermicelli, soaked in warm water, drained then finely chopped
½ teaspoon black pepper

*To serve*
20 g/¾ oz Pickled Kohlrabi and Carrots (page 469)
Northern-style Fish Sauce (page 471)
Hanoi-style Chilli Sauce (page 477)

To make the dough, combine the rice flour, plain (all-purpose) flour and tempura flour in a large mixing bowl.

In another bowl, mix the sugar, salt and turmeric with the measured warm water until the sugar dissolves, then add the lard.

Slowly pour the liquid mixture into the dry flour mixture, combining well. Add more water if needed to form a well-hydrated dough (see note). Knead the dough until there are no dry spots and then let it rest for about 1 hour, covered.

To prepare the filling, heat the oil in a large frying pan or skillet over a low heat, add the shallots, garlic and spring onion (scallion) and fry for 1 minute 30 seconds. Increase the heat to medium and add the minced (ground) meat and 1 tablespoon of the fish sauce. Cook for 2 minutes. Add the jicama and cook for an additional 3 minutes, then add the mushrooms. Cook for another 1 minute.

Transfer the filling mixture to a bowl, add the vermicelli, and mix in the remaining fish sauce and the pepper.

Divide the dough into 12 equal-size portions. Brush a clean work surface with a little oil and roll out the dough on the surface into 13-cm/5-inch rounds.

Add a portion of the filling and a peeled quail egg to each round, then fold over the filling to form a semi-circle and firmly press the edges to seal.

To crimp the edges, fold over a corner of the sealed edge and press with your thumb, then work your way around the sealed edge, folding it over in small increments and pressing with your thumb to crimp. When you come to the final corner, fold and press firmly to seal.

Pour the oil for deep-frying into a pan and heat to 175°C/345°F. If not using a thermometer, test the oil temperature by inserting wooden chopsticks into the oil – it should bubble vigorously around them. Carefully add the pillow-shaped cakes and fry for 7–10 minutes until golden brown. Carefully remove from the oil and drain on paper towels.

Serve warm, with the pickled vegetables and bowls of northern-style fish sauce and Hanoi-style chilli sauce on the side.

***Note:*** The age of your flour can affect how much water it can absorb when making the dough, so older flours will need more liquid.

# 'SIZZLING' PANCAKES FROM MEKONG RIVER DELTA

## Bánh Xèo Miền Tây

In the rainy season, my mother recalls her grandmother making these pancakes one by one for the family, a memory shared by many southern households, including my father's. During those wet days when nobody could go out, the tradition of cooking these sizzling hot pancakes became a way to bond over warm food in cool weather. Named for the '*xèo*' sound of the batter hitting the hot pan, these large, thin pancakes feature coconut milk in the batter, distinguishing them from their central cousin Huế-style Savoury Pancakes (page 418). While traditionally filled with mung beans, bean sprouts, pork and prawns (shrimp), in some places like Cần Thơ coconut shoots are added for extra texture.

Makes 11–12 pancakes; serves 4–5
Preparation time: 40–45 minutes, plus 20 minutes resting time
Cooking time: 30–35 minutes

| DF |

- lard or neutral oil, for frying (1 teaspoon for each pancake)
- 11–12 cooked prawns (shrimp) (about 90 g/3¼ oz), halved lengthways and deveined
- 110 g/3¾ oz onion, thinly sliced into rounds
- 120 g/4¼ oz bean sprouts
- 255 g/9 oz jicama, peeled and cut into thin matchsticks (julienned) (230 g/8 oz prepared weight)
- 150 g/5½ oz carrots, peeled and cut into thin matchsticks (julienned) (125 g/4¼ oz prepared weight)

*For the batter*

- 100 g/3½ oz (⅔ cup) rice flour
- 30 g/1 oz crispy fried powder mix (bột chiên giòn) (see note)
- ½ teaspoon ground turmeric
- 220 g/7½ oz (scant 1 cup) coconut milk
- 40 g/1½ oz spring onion (scallion) greens, chopped

*For the pork filling*

- 1 tablespoon neutral oil
- 5 g/⅛ oz shallot, coarsely chopped
- 5 g/⅛ oz garlic, coarsely chopped
- 200 g/7 oz pork belly (side), in a 3–4-cm/1¼–1½-inch-thick slab, thinly sliced
- 1 tablespoon fish sauce

*To serve*

- 150 g/5½ oz aromatic mixed herbs (rau thơm – fish mint, perilla, Vietnamese basil, peppermint, spearmint; see notes)
- 120 g/4¼ oz mustard leaves
- 120 g/4¼ oz lettuce leaves
- young mango slices, to taste
- cucumber slices, to taste
- Pickled Daikon and Carrots (page 468)
- Basic Dipping Fish Sauce (page 470)

To prepare the batter, in a large mixing bowl, combine the rice flour, crispy fried powder mix, 220 ml/7½ fl oz (scant 1 cup) of water, the ground turmeric and the coconut milk. Whisk until the mixture is completely smooth. Let it rest for 20 minutes. Stir in the spring onion (scallion) greens.

Meanwhile, to prepare the filling, heat the neutral oil in a frying pan or skillet over a medium-low heat, add the shallot and garlic and cook for 1–3 minutes until fragrant. Add the pork belly (side) and cook for 1 minute. Add the fish sauce and continue cooking for 2 minutes, or until the meat is cooked through. Remove from heat and set aside.

To cook each pancake, heat a wok or 28–30-cm/11–12-inch flat-bottomed pan with a lid over a medium-high heat. Using paper towels, carefully grease the hot surface of the pan with 1 teaspoon of fat. Pour about 50 ml/1¾ fl oz (3½ tablespoons) of batter into the pan, cover with the lid and cook for about 1 minute until the batter is set.

Add a small handful of the pork filling, prawns (shrimp), onion, bean sprouts, jicama and carrots on one side of the pancake. Fold the empty half over to cover the filling (forming a half-moon shape), then cook until everything is heated through and the pancake is crispy, 1–2 minutes.

Repeat with the remaining batter and fillings; it should make 11–12 pancakes.

To serve, carefully transfer the pancakes to a serving plate and serve immediately with the mixed herbs, mango slices, cucumber slices, pickled vegetables and basic dipping fish sauce.

***Notes:*** If you don't have crispy fried powder mix (bột chiên giòn), you can replace it with a 50:50 mix of cornflour (cornstarch) and rice flour.

In some regions they would serve the mixed herbs with even more vegetables, including young mango leaves, ambarella leaves and wrinkled marshweed.

# MINI SAVOURY PANCAKES

## Bánh Khọt

The name '*khọt*' is said to come from the sound made when removing the cakes from their moulds. According to some *bánh khọt* artisans, the dish may have evolved from *bánh căn* of Bình Thuận, Ninh Thuận and Khánh Hòa provinces. While both use rice flour, *bánh khọt* is fried in oil using cast iron or aluminium moulds, whereas *bánh căn* is poured directly onto earthenware moulds over a charcoal fire without oil – a technique requiring considerable skill to prevent them from sticking. The two cakes also differ in their toppings depending on the region, with this version drawing inspiration from the southwest, adding turmeric to the batter and finishing with seasoned coconut milk for richness.

Makes 30 mini pancakes; serves 6
Preparation time: 45 minutes, plus 5 hours or overnight soaking and 20 minutes resting times
Cooking time: 25 minutes, plus 5 minutes per batch

| DF |

15 medium prawns (shrimp), boiled and peeled
50 g/1¾ oz (¼ cup) yellow split mung beans, soaked for at least 5 hours or overnight
neutral oil, for frying
Basic Dipping Fish Sauce (page 470), to serve

*For the batter*
100 g/3½ oz (⅔ cup) rice flour
30 g/1 oz crispy fried powder mix (bột chiên giòn) (see note on page 415)
½ teaspoon ground turmeric
220 g/7½ oz (scant 1 cup) coconut milk
40 g/1½ oz spring onion (scallion) greens, chopped

*For the pork filling*
1 tablespoon neutral oil
5 g/⅛ oz shallot, coarsely chopped
5 g/⅛ oz garlic, coarsely chopped
100 g/3½ oz pork belly (side), thinly sliced or minced
1 tablespoon fish sauce

*For the coconut cream*
140 g/5 oz (scant ⅔ cup) coconut milk
¼ teaspoon salt
1 teaspoon tapioca flour (starch)
1 teaspoon plain (all-purpose) flour

To prepare the batter, in a large mixing bowl, combine the rice flour, crispy fried powder mix, 220 ml/7½ fl oz (¾ cup plus 2½ tablespoons) water, the ground turmeric and the coconut milk. Whisk until the mixture is completely smooth, then let it rest for 20 minutes. Stir in the chopped spring onion (scallion) greens.

Meanwhile, to prepare the pork filling: heat the oil in a pan, add the shallot, garlic and pork belly (side) and cook for 1 minute. Add the fish sauce and continue frying for 2 minutes, or until the meat is fully cooked through.

Cut each boiled and peeled prawn (shrimp) in half and remove the prawn's digestive tract, if visible.

To make the coconut cream, in a small pot, combine the coconut milk, salt, tapioca flour (starch) and plain (all-purpose) flour and whisk well to combine. Cook over a low heat for 2 minutes, whisking constantly until thickened. Set aside.

To cook the mung beans, drain the soaked mung beans, then place in a saucepan with 500 ml/18 fl oz (2 cups) of water. Bring to the boil and cook for 20 minutes, or until tender. Drain well and set aside.

Preheat a bánh khọt pan (or you could use a Dutch mini pancake/poffertjes pan) over a medium heat.

To cook a pancake, add ½ teaspoon of oil to each mould. Fill each mould halfway with the batter, then add ½ teaspoon of the cooked mung beans, a small amount of the pork filling, then place one prawn half in the centre. Cover and cook for 4 minutes.Uncover and cook for an additional 1 minute–1 minute 30 seconds until golden. Remove the pancake from the mould and repeat with the remaining batter and fillings.

To serve, divide the pancakes among serving plates (5 pancakes per plate), then drizzle with coconut cream and serve immediately with small bowls of the basic dipping fish sauce on the side.

# HUẾ-STYLE SAVOURY PANCAKES

## Bánh Khoái

Unlike its southern cousin 'Sizzling' Pancakes from Mekong River Delta (page 415), this smaller, crispier pancake from the central region is made without coconut milk. The name evolved from '*bánh khói*' (smoke cake), referring to the heavy smoke from wood-fire cooking that would make people's eyes water, which over time became '*khoái*' in Huế dialect. Traditionally folded and sliced, they're wrapped in leaves with herbs and served with dipping sauce. In Huế, some vendors add *trái vả* (*Ficus auriculata lour*, a fig cousin) for tartness, or *cá kình* (pinspotted spinefoot fish) – its bitter offal (variety meats) supposedly aiding sleep. While I use fermented soybean sauce here, Basic Dipping Fish Sauce (page 470) works well, too.

Makes 8–10 pancakes
Preparation time: 10 minutes, plus 30 minutes resting time
Cooking time: 6–7 minutes per pancake

| **DF** |

neutral oil, for frying
8–10 prawns (shrimp)
200 g/7 oz Pork Paste (page 461) or minced (ground) pork
200 g/7 oz bean sprouts
8–10 quail eggs

***For the batter***
150 g/5½ oz (1 cup) rice flour
¼ teaspoon ground turmeric
½ teaspoon salt

***For the fermented soybean sauce (sốt tương bần)***
240 ml/8 fl oz (1 cup) pork stock (broth) or water
100 g/3½ oz fermented soybean paste (tương bần)
35 g/1¼ oz peanut butter
1 teaspoon fish sauce
4 teaspoons sugar
2 teaspoons rice flour
1 tablespoon roasted sesame seeds
20 g/¾ oz (2 tablespoons) Toasted Peanuts (page 459), crushed

***To serve***
green figs (trái vả), thinly sliced
herb salad (rau sống – sliced cucumber, lettuce, spearmint, peppermint, Vietnamese basil)

To prepare the batter, sift the rice flour through a fine-mesh sieve to ensure it's fine and free of clumps. Mix together the rice flour, ground turmeric and salt in a bowl. Gradually add 380 ml/13 fl oz (1½ cups plus 1 tablespoon) of water, stirring to achieve a milk-like consistency. Let the batter rest for 30 minutes.

To prepare the fermented soybean sauce, in a saucepan, combine the stock (broth) or water, fermented soybean paste, peanut butter, fish sauce and sugar.

In a small bowl, mix the rice flour with 2 tablespoons of water.

Bring the stock mixture to a simmer, then add the rice flour mixture. Stir in the roasted sesame seeds and toasted peanuts. Keep warm.

To cook the pancakes, heat 2 tablespoons of oil in a 20-cm/8-inch pan over a medium heat. Pour in 60 ml/2 fl oz (¼ cup) of the batter, spreading it thinly, then cover and cook for 2 minutes. Uncover and cook for 3–4 minutes until the moisture evaporates.

Add 1 prawn (shrimp), 20 g/¾ oz of the pork paste and 15–20 g/½–¾ oz of the bean sprouts on one side of the pancake, then crack 1 quail egg on top. Fold the empty half of the pancake over to cover the fillings (forming a half-moon shape) and cook for 10 seconds on each side. Transfer the pancake to a colander to drain any excess oil.

Repeat with the remaining batter and fillings; it should make 8–10 pancakes.

To serve, place each pancake on a serving plate and serve with the warm fermented soybean sauce, thinly sliced green figs and a plate of herb salad.

# PUFF PASTRY MEAT PIES

## Pa Tê Sô

A dish from the French colonial period (1858–1954), *pa tê sô* is the Vietnamese pronunciation of *pâté chaud* (hot pie). More commonly found in Southern Vietnam, these meat pies were traditionally made in bakeries since ovens were uncommon in Vietnamese homes.

Makes 20–25 pies
Preparation time: 30 minutes
Cooking time: 25 minutes

- 6 puff pastry sheets (enough to make 40–50 × 8-cm/3¼-in rounds)
- 1 egg yolk
- 1 teaspoon milk

*For the filling*

- 2 tablespoons neutral oil
- 90 g/3¼ oz onion, diced
- 20 g/¾ oz shallots, minced
- 10 g/¼ oz garlic, minced
- 115 g/4 oz jicama, diced
- 20 g/¾ oz dried wood ear mushrooms, soaked (80 g/2¾ oz after soaking), then finely chopped
- 250 g/9 oz minced (ground) pork
- 150 g/5½ oz Pork Liver and Minced Pâté (page 81) or pre-prepared pâté
- ½ teaspoon black pepper
- 1 teaspoon fish sauce
- 1 teaspoon oyster sauce

To prepare the filling, heat the oil in a pan, add the onion and shallots and fry for 1 minute 30 seconds. Add the garlic and fry for 2 more minutes. Add the jicama and fry for a further 2 minutes. Finally, add the mushrooms and fry for 30 seconds. Remove from the heat and stir for another 30 seconds. Let the mixture cool slightly.

Transfer the cooled mixture to a bowl, add the minced (ground) pork, pâté, pepper, fish sauce and oyster sauce and mix well.

Preheat the oven to 180°C/350°F/Gas Mark 4.

Cut the puff pastry into 8-cm/3¼-inch rounds. Place 25–35 g/1–1¼ oz of filling in the centre of a round, place another round on top, then use a fork to press down and seal the edges. Repeat with the remaining pastry and filling.

In a small bowl, mix together the egg yolk and the milk. Brush the pies with the egg wash.

Place the pies on a baking sheet, then bake for 20 minutes, or until golden brown.

Serve hot as a starter (appetizer) or snack.

## STEAMED RICE WINE HONEYCOMB CAKES

### Bánh Bò Hấp Cơm Rượu

These steamed cakes gets their distinctive honeycomb texture and slightly fermented flavour from *cơm rượu* (rice wine lees), which traditionally acts as the rising (leavening) agent. Though industrial fast-acting yeast is commonly used today for a quicker process, I prefer using rice wine lees because it gives the cakes a very distinct aroma when eaten. In Vietnam you have specific small moulds for these cakes, similar to cupcake or flan moulds, but you can also make it into a larger round cake; this might affect your steaming time.

Serves 10–15
Preparation time: 20–30 minutes, plus 10–11 hours proofing time
Cooking time: 15 minutes per batch

| V | VE | DF | GF |

- 200 g/7 oz (1⅓ cups) rice flour
- 100 g/3½ oz (¾ cup) cooked rice
- 40 ml/1¼ fl oz (2½ tablespoons) rice wine
- 100 ml/3 ½ fl oz (⅓ cup plus 1 tablespoon) coconut water or water
- 100 g/3½ oz (½ cup) sugar
- ½ teaspoon salt
- 150 ml/5 fl oz (⅔ cup) coconut water or pandan water
- 1 tablespoon neutral oil, plus extra for greasing

In a mixing bowl, combine the rice flour, cooked rice, rice wine and coconut water or water. Wearing gloves, mix thoroughly by hand. Let the mixture prove at room temperature for 8–9 hours.

In a small saucepan, combine the sugar, salt and coconut or pandan water (the pandan water will give the cakes a green colour). Heat over a medium-low heat until the sugar and salt are fully dissolved. Let the syrup cool completely.

After the initial proofing, add the cooled syrup to the batter. Mix well and let it prove for another 2 hours, or until bubbly. Strain the batter through a fine-mesh sieve into a jug (large measuring cup), then stir in the oil.

Set up a steamer and bring the water to the boil.

Brush bánh bò moulds (6–8 cm/2½–3 inches in diameter, 1.5–2 cm/¾ inch deep) with oil and place them in the steamer basket, then set over the boiling water to heat the moulds.

When the moulds are hot, remove the lid and pour in the batter to half-fill each mould. Cover and steam for 15 minutes.

Remove the cakes from the moulds and serve warm.

*Notes:* You can use the flan moulds from Crème Caramel (page 424) for this dish.

The proofing time is crucial for developing the characteristic honeycomb texture and flavour.

Ensure your steamer is sufficiently heated before adding the batter to achieve the best results.

## STEAMED BANANA CAKE

### Bánh Chuối Hấp

Steamed Vietnamese cakes are all about texture: you want something chewy yet firm. Always let this cake cool to room temperature before eating, and keep it covered to prevent it drying.

Serves 6–8
Preparation time: 15–20 minutes
Cooking time: 40 minutes

| V | VE | DF |

- 580 g/1 lb 4 oz ripe bananas (about 18 cm/7 inches long), peeled and sliced into rounds
- 100 g/3½ oz (½ cup) sugar
- ⅛ teaspoon salt
- 45 g/1½ oz (⅓ cup plus 2 teaspoons) tapioca flour (starch)
- 10 g/¼ oz (1 tablespoon) plain (all-purpose) flour
- 10 g/¼ oz (1 tablespoon) rice flour
- pandan leaves, for steaming
- Toasted Peanuts (page 459), crushed, to decorate
- 1 quantity Seasoned Coconut Milk (page 465), to serve

In a bowl, coat the bananas with the sugar and salt.

In a separate bowl, combine 300 ml/10 fl oz (1¼ cups) of water with the tapioca flour (starch), plain (all-purpose) flour and rice flour, stirring until smooth. Add the coated bananas and mix, ensuring they are evenly coated.

Set up a steamer, adding the pandan leaves to the water for extra fragrance, and bring to the boil.

Pour the banana mixture into an 18-cm/7-inch mould, place the mould in the steamer basket, set over the boiling water and steam the mixture for 40 minutes, or until fully cooked.

Let cool, then turn out and sprinkle with the toasted peanuts. Serve with the seasoned coconut milk.

## BAKED BANANA CAKE

### Bánh Chuối Nướng

Similar to a bread pudding, this cake transforms leftover Vietnamese Baguette (page 66) and *chuối sứ* (Siamese bananas) into a fantastic chewy cake, with the use of tapioca flour (starch) and rice flour. Soaking the bananas overnight in rum adds flavour and creates a purple-reddish hue when baked.

Serves 8–10
Preparation time: 30–40 minutes, plus 5 hours or overnight marinating time
Cooking time: 45 minutes

| V |

- 1 tablespoon salt
- 5 bananas (ideally Siamese) (about 700 g/1 lb 9 oz)
- 70 g/2½ oz (⅓ cup plus 2 teaspoons) sugar
- 2 tablespoons rum

***For the batter***

- 225 g/8 oz (scant 1 cup) coconut milk
- 125 g/4¼ oz old bread, torn into chunks
- ½ teaspoon salt
- 50 g/1¾ oz (2½ tablespoons) condensed milk
- 50 g/1¾ oz (3½ tablespoons) butter, melted
- ½ teaspoon vanilla extract
- 40 g/1½ oz (¼ cup) rice flour (see note)
- 10 g/¼ oz (1½ tablespoons) tapioca flour (starch)

In a bowl, mix 1 litre/1¾ pints (4¼ cups) of water with the salt. Peel the bananas (you should have about 395 g/14 oz peeled weight) and soak them in the salt water for 10 minutes to remove their bitterness. Drain.

In a bowl, coat the bananas with the sugar and rum. Allow them to marinate for at least 5 hours or, for a deeper red colour, overnight.

Preheat the oven to 175°C/345°F/Gas Mark 3¾. Line a loaf pan (12.5 × 20.5 cm/5 × 8 inches) with baking (parchment) paper.

To prepare the batter, mix the coconut milk with the bread, salt, condensed milk, melted butter and vanilla extract. Add the rice flour and tapioca flour (starch) and mix. Pour the liquid from the marinated bananas into the batter and mix well.

Slice each marinated banana into 3 pieces.

Layer the ingredients in the prepared loaf pan as follows: one layer of banana, one layer of batter, one layer of banana, one layer of batter and a final layer of banana. Bake for 30 minutes in the oven, increase the temperature to 180°C/355°F/Gas Mark 4 to achieve more caramelization on the bottom, then bake for a further 15 minutes.

Let the cake cool completely before turning it out and eating it.

***Note:*** If you don't have rice or tapioca flour (starch), you can use 50 g/1¾ oz (scant ⅓ cup) plain (all-purpose) flour, but the taste will be different.

## 'LIVER' CAKE

### Bánh Gan

This dessert from the Southwest gets its name from its appearance – dark brown with tiny holes resembling a pig's liver, though it contains no meat. The cake uses duck eggs rather than chicken eggs for its base and coconut milk as the liquid. While star anise was the traditional flavouring in my mother's time, modern versions often include instant coffee.

Serves 8
Preparation time: 30 minutes
Cooking time: 40 minutes

| V | DF | GF |

- 4 duck eggs (about 235 g/8¼ oz), plus 1 duck egg yolk (25 g/1 oz)
- 150 g/5½ oz (2/3 cup) coconut milk
- 50 g/1¾ oz condensed milk
- 5 g/⅛ oz (1 tablespoon) instant coffee
- ¼ teaspoon ground star anise
- 3 g whole star anise (2–3 pods)
- 150 g/5½ oz palm sugar
- ½ teaspoon bicarbonate of soda (baking soda)

***For the rice mix***

- 20 g/¾ oz (2 tablespoons) rice flour
- ¼ teaspoon salt
- 1 tablespoon coconut milk

In a bowl, mix together the duck eggs and yolk. Set aside.

In another bowl, combine the coconut milk, condensed milk and instant coffee. Add the ground star anise and stir well. Set aside.

Heat a pan over a low heat, add the whole star anise and toast for 1 minute. Remove from the pan and set aside.

Put the palm sugar in a mortar and pound with a pestle. Transfer to a pot and cook over a medium-low heat until it has completely melted, about 5 minutes. Add the toasted star anise, then the coconut milk mixture. Remove from the heat and let it cool for 5 minutes.

To make the rice mix, in a bowl, mix together the rice flour, salt, coconut milk and 1 tablespoon of water. Add the duck egg mixture to the bowl with mix well.

Sieve the rice and egg mixture into the cooled-down coconut mixture. Let stand for 5 minutes, then add the bicarbonate of soda (baking soda) to the batter and mix together.

Meanwhile, preheat the oven to 200°C/400°F/Gas Mark 6 and place an oval pan (roughly 21 × 10 cm/8¼ × 4 inches) inside for 5 minutes.

Remove the mould from the oven. Pass the batter through a sieve into the hot mould.

Reduce the oven temperature to 175°C/345°F/Gas Mark 3¾ and bake for 30 minutes.

## BAKED PALM SUGAR HONEYCOMB CAKE

Bánh Bò Nướng Đường Thốt Nốt

Named for its honeycomb interior, this chewy cake gets its brown colour from palm sugar, a Mekong Delta ingredient traditionally used by the Khmer community (*'thốt nốt'* comes from the Khmer word *'th'not'*) before becoming popular among Kinh people. The secret to achieving its signature texture lies in sieving the batter multiple times, adding rising (leavening) agents just before baking and using preheated moulds for the initial rise. Serve plain or with Seasoned Coconut Milk (page 465).

Serves 8–10
Preparation time: 30–40 minutes, plus 25 minutes resting time
Cooking time: 35 minutes

| V | GF |

140 g/5 oz palm sugar (ideally palmyra), broken into small pieces
180 g/6 oz (¾ cup) coconut milk
20 g/¾ oz butter, melted, plus extra for greasing
¼ teaspoon salt
115 g/4 oz (scant 1 cup) tapioca flour (starch)
15 g/½ oz (1½ tablespoons) rice flour
3 eggs
4 g (1 teaspoon) baking powder
5 g/⅛ oz (1 teaspoon) bicarbonate of soda (baking soda)

In a saucepan, cook the palm sugar over a medium heat until it turns a dark amber colour, about 5 minutes; do not stir the caramel, instead, gently swirl the pan to ensure even cooking. Remove the pan from the heat.

Very carefully add the coconut milk to the caramelized palm sugar (the pan might spit and sizzle). Let it cool and then add the melted butter, stirring to combine.

In a bowl, sift the salt, tapioca flour (starch), and rice flour together, then add to the caramel mixture and mix well.

In a separate bowl, whisk the eggs. Sieve the whisked eggs, then add them to the caramel mixture. Mix until well combined. Let the mixture rest for 25 minutes.

Meanwhile, preheat the oven to 170°C/340°F/Gas Mark 3½. Butter an oval pan (roughly 21 × 10 cm/ 8¼ × 4 inches) and place it in the oven for 10 minutes to heat.

Add the baking powder and bicarbonate of soda (baking soda) to the batter and then sieve the mixture into a clean bowl.

Remove the hot baking pan from the oven, pour the batter into the pan and bake in the oven for 15 minutes. Reduce the oven temperature to 155°C/310°F/Gas Mark 2½. Cover the baking pan with aluminium foil so it doesn't burn. Bake for an additional 15 minutes, or until a cocktail stick or toothpick inserted into the centre comes out clean. Remove from the oven and let the cake cool before serving.

## CRÈME CARAMEL

Bánh Flan

This adaptation of the French dessert was traditionally made with condensed milk and water when fresh milk was scarce or too expensive, and steamed rather than baked in a water bath, as ovens were not common in Vietnamese kitchens. Modern versions explore new flavours like tea, durian and coconut milk.

Serves 6
Preparation time: 20 minutes
Cooking time: 20 minutes

| V | GF |

4 eggs
1 pinch of salt
½ teaspoon vanilla extract or vanilla sugar
400 g/14 oz (1⅔ cups) hot milk
150 g/5½ oz (½ cup) condensed milk

*For the caramel*
70 g/2½ oz (⅓ cup plus 2 teaspoons) sugar
1 teaspoon lime juice

To make the caramel, add the sugar and 2 tablespoons of water to a pot. Heat over a medium heat, allowing the sugar to melt until it turns amber. Do not stir the caramel, instead, gently swirl the pot to ensure even cooking. Once the sugar is amber, remove it from heat. Add the lime juice and swirl the pot again to incorporate it into the caramel. Carefully pour the caramel into 6 ramekins or flameproof dishes.

In a bowl, whisk together the eggs, salt and vanilla extract.

In another bowl, mix together the hot milk and condensed milk. Then, while whisking, add the milk mixture to the egg mixture. Pass through a sieve into a jug (large measuring cup), then pour the mixture into the ramekins.

Set up a steamer half-full with water and bring to the boil.

Add the ramekins to the steamer basket, set over the boiling water and steam on low heat for 15 minutes. Alternatively use a bain-marie at 150°C/300°F/Gas Mark 2 for 15 minutes. Remove the ramekins from the steamer or bain-marie, and leave to cool for 5 minutes.

To serve, turn each ramekin upside down on a plate and gently shake so the crème caramel comes out.

# CASSAVA SILKWORM CAKE

## Bánh Tằm Khoai Mì

Another so-named silkworm-shaped noodle from the Mekong Delta, this sweet version uses cassava instead of rice flour like its savoury cousin Silkworm Cake with Coconut Cream (page 233). Here, I use turmeric for colour, though variations can be made using magenta plant or pandan extract. Serve with Seasoned Coconut Milk (page 465) if desired.

Serves 4–6
Preparation time: 20 minutes
Cooking time: 25 minutes

**| V | VE | DF | GF |**

370 g/13 oz cassava, grated
¼ teaspoon salt
½ teaspoon sugar
⅛ teaspoon ground turmeric
1 tablespoon coconut milk

*For the topping*
20 g/¾ oz (2 tablespoons) toasted sesame seeds
3 tablespoons sugar, or more to taste
50 g/1¾ oz (¾ cup) fresh coconut, shredded (or you can use 50 g/3/4 oz/½ cup desiccated/shredded dry coconut)

Place the cassava in a clean dish towel or muslin (cheesecloth) and squeeze out as much liquid as possible into a bowl. You should have about 230 g/8 oz of cassava pulp left. Let the liquid in the bowl settle, then carefully pour off the water, leaving about 60 g/2¼ oz of cassava starch at the bottom. Reserve the starch.

In a mixing bowl, combine the cassava pulp, salt, sugar and ground turmeric. Mix well. Add the reserved cassava starch and the coconut milk, then knead until it forms a smooth dough.

Spread a piece of clingfilm (plastic wrap) on a flat surface. Place the cassava dough on it and place another sheet of clingfilm on top, so it doesn't stick, then flatten the dough to about 1 cm/½ inch in thickness.

Set up a steamer and bring the water to the boil.

Place the flattened dough in the steamer basket, set over the boiling water and steam for 14 minutes. Carefully flip the cake and steam for an additional 7 minutes. Remove from the heat and let it cool slightly before slicing the cake into long, thin strips (like wide noodles).

To prepare the topping, in a bowl, mix together the sesame seeds, sugar and shredded coconut.

Serve the cake warm or at room temperature, generously sprinkled with the topping.

# RAMIE LEAF STICKY RICE CAKES

## Bánh Ít Lá Gai

Vietnamese traditional cakes often incorporate leaves into their dough for both colour and flavour, from apricot leaves in *bánh lá mơ* to ramie leaves in this recipe. While traditionally these leaves required lengthy pounding, dried ramie leaves are now readily available, making this version more accessible. This recipe was inspired by our time with cô Nguyễn Thị Thủy from Phước Tích, an ancient village in Huế.

Makes approx. 8–10 cakes
Preparation time: 40–45 minutes, plus 6 hours soaking and 30 minutes resting times
Cooking time: 1 hour

| V | VE | DF | GF |

*For the filling*
200 g/7 oz (1 cup) yellow split mung beans, soaked for 6 hours, then drained
10 g/¼ oz pandan leaves
60 g/2¼ oz (scant ⅓ cup) sugar
¼ teaspoon vanilla extract, optional
⅛ teaspoon salt

*For the dough*
400 g/14 oz (2⅔ cups) sticky (glutinous) rice flour, plus 15–20 g/½–¾ oz (1½–2 tablespoons) if needed
40 g/1½ oz (2 tablespoons) ramie leaf powder (bột lá gai)
90 g/3¼ oz (scant ½ cup) sugar
½ teaspoon salt
330 ml/11 fl oz (1⅓ cups plus 1 tablespoon) hot water

*For wrapping*
banana leaves, blanched (see step 3, page 390), cut into 10-cm/4-inch squares

To prepare the filling, place the soaked mung beans with 200 ml/7 fl oz (¾ cup plus 1 tablespoon) of water and the pandan leaves in a rice cooker and cook. Alternatively, set up a steamer, add the pandan leaves to the water and bring to the boil, then put the mung beans in the steamer basket, set over the boiling water and steam for 40 minutes.

In a bowl, mash the cooked mung beans with a spoon until thick like homemade mashed potatoes. Add the sugar, vanilla extract, if using, and salt. Mix well.

To prepare the dough, in a bowl, mix together the rice flour, ramie leaf powder, sugar and salt. Add the measured hot water, mixing and kneading well. If the dough is too wet, gradually add the additional rice flour while kneading. Cover the dough with clingfilm (plastic wrap) and let it rest for 30 minutes.

To assemble the cakes, divide the dough into 60-g/2¼-oz portions and form into balls; divide the filling into 35-g/1¼-oz portions and form into balls. Flatten a portion of dough into a 5–6-cm/2–2½-inch circle, place a portion of the filling in the centre and wrap the dough around it to completely enclose the filling.

Wrap each cake in a banana leaf, either in a square shape, by folding the top and bottom of the leaf over the filling, then folding both sides underneath, or in a traditional spheres (like Savoury Sticky Rice and Mung Bean Dumplings, page 401).

Set up a steamer and bring the water to the boil.

Place the wrapped cakes in the steamer basket, set over the boiling water and steam for 15–20 minutes or until cooked through.

# STEAMED PANDAN LAYER CAKE

## Bánh Da Lợn

Bánh Da Lợn, which literally translates as 'pig's skin cake', earns its name from its layered texture reminiscent of pork skin. Despite its association with Southern Vietnamese cuisine due to its main ingredients, the name curiously includes '*lợn*', the Northern Vietnamese word for 'pig', rather than the Southern '*heo*'. This steamed, chewy cake features alternating bright green layers coloured by pandan water and yellow layers of mung bean paste. Interestingly, similar layered cakes can be found in other Southeast Asian cuisines, such as *kuih lapis* in Indonesia and Malaysia, hinting at the complex connections between the region's diverse culinary landscape. You will need a large steamer basket and an 18-cm/7-inch round mould.

Makes an 18-cm/7-inch cake
Preparation time: 30–40 minutes
Cooking time: 30–35 minutes

| V | VE | DF | GF |

*For the yellow mung bean paste*
200 g/7 oz of mashed cooked Mung Bean Filling (page 465)
120 g/4¼ oz (½ cup) coconut milk
50 g/1¾ oz (⅓ cup plus 1 tablespoon) icing (confectioners') sugar
⅛ teaspoon salt
50 g/1¾ oz (⅓ cup plus 2 teaspoons) tapioca flour (starch)
⅛ teaspoon ground turmeric, optional

*For the pandan layer*
90 g/3¼ oz (¾ cup) tapioca flour (starch)
30 g/1 oz (scant ¼ cup) sticky (glutinous) rice flour
50 g/1¾ oz (⅓ cup plus 1 tablespoon) icing (confectioners') sugar
200 g/7 oz (scant 1 cup) Pandan Water (page 465)
50 g/1¾ oz (3½ tablespoons) coconut milk
⅛ teaspoon salt
½ teaspoon pandan extract
oil, for greasing

To make the mung bean paste, pass the cooked mung bean filling through a sieve into a bowl to get mashed mung bean filling. Put the mung bean filling in a blender with the coconut milk, icing (confectioners') sugar, salt, tapioca flour (starch) and 50 ml/1¾ fl oz (3½ tablespoons) of water. If desired, you can add the ground turmeric and hand blend it to make the colour nicer. Blend until smooth. Unlike for other cakes, this filling needs to be smooth and shouldn't have any bits in it.

For the pandan layer, in a bowl, mix together the tapioca flour, rice flour, icing sugar, pandan water, coconut milk, salt and pandan extract until smooth.

Set up a steamer one-third full of water and bring to the boil.

Fit an 18-cm/7-inch round mould inside the steaming basket on top. Brush the mould with oil and wrap the lid with a dish towel, then set over the boiling water to heat the mould.

When the steamer is hot, pour 60 ml/2 fl oz (¼ cup) of the pandan layer into the mould and steam for 5 minutes. Then carefully pour in 120 ml/4 fl oz (½ cup) of the yellow mung bean paste (you need to pour this gently so as not to make a dent into the previous layer) and steam for 6 minutes. Add another pandan layer and steam for 7 minutes.

Continue with alternating mung bean paste and pandan layers; for every new layer, adding 1 additional minute of steaming time. Repeat until all the mixtures are used.

To cut the steamed pandan layer cake, use dental floss instead of knife for a flawless cut.

# MEKONG DELTA-STYLE STICKY RICE DUMPLINGS

## Bánh Ít Miền Tây

*Bánh ít* is often prepared for death anniversary ceremonies, where hosts traditionally give these cakes to guests to take home to their children and grandchildren. This triangular sticky rice cake, found throughout Vietnam but particularly common in the Mekong Delta, shares its shape with *bánh ú* and *bánh giò*. While most Vietnamese sticky rice cakes use mung bean filling, this version distinctively features palm sugar and coconut.

Makes 15 dumplings; serves 4–5 as a snack
Preparation time: 30 minutes, plus 1 hour resting time
Cooking time: 1 hour 35 minutes

| V | VE | DF | GF |

*For the dough*
- 500 g/1 lb 2 oz (3⅓ cups) sticky (glutinous) rice flour
- 1 teaspoon salt
- 250 ml/8½ fl oz (1 cup plus 2 teaspoons) warm water
- 2 tablespoons palm or brown sugar

*For the filling*
- 150 g/5½ oz palm sugar
- 300 g/10½ oz fresh coconut, finely shredded
- 100 g/3½ oz Toasted Peanuts, coarsely crushed
- 1 tablespoon tapioca flour (starch)

*For wrapping*
- 3 tablespoons neutral oil
- 30 banana leaf pieces (25 × 15 cm/10 × 6 inches), blanched (step 3, page 390)

To make the dough, mix the rice flour and salt in a large mixing bowl.

In another bowl, mix the measured warm water with the sugar until the sugar dissolves.

Gradually add the warm sugar water to the flour mixture while kneading. Do not add the sugar water all at once because it will absorb more/less depending on your climate and the type of sticky (glutinous) rice flour you use. Add just enough until you have a pliable dough. Knead until the dough becomes smooth and no longer sticky. Cover the bowl tightly with clingfilm (plastic wrap), then let rest at room temperature for 1 hour for a smoother texture.

To prepare the filling, combine the palm sugar and 400 ml/14 fl oz (1⅔ cups) of water in a heavy-bottomed pan over a low heat. Stir with a wooden spoon until the sugar completely dissolves, about 10 minutes, and the water turns slightly yellow. Add the shredded coconut, then cook for 5 minutes until the coconut turns yellow. Add the toasted peanuts, then cook for 3 more minutes. Remove from the heat.

In a small bowl, mix the tapioca flour (starch) with 1 tablespoon of water, then add the tapioca mixture to the filling mixture while still hot. Stir until the mixture becomes sticky, then let cool for 15 minutes and set aside.

To shape the dumplings, divide the dough into 15 equal size balls and divide the cooled filling into 15 equal-size balls. Roll out the dough balls into 6–7-cm/2½–2¾-inch circles, place a portion of filling on each dough circle and wrap it around to form balls.

To wrap the dumplings, dip each dumpling in oil. Fold the shorter edge of a banana leaf to form a triangle with an extra rectangle of leaf at the top. A few centimetres (about an inch) below the rectangle (along the folded edge of the triangle), make a straight fold. Gather the folded corner in your hand and open up into a cone, adjusting the leaf so you have a smooth open edge.

Place one oiled dumpling ball inside the cone, then fold the edges of the cone into the middle over the dumpling and trim any overhang, if needed.

Place the cone at an angle in the middle of another banana leaf piece. Take the corner opposite the cone's point and fold it over the cone, tucking the corner over the base of the cone.

Press the folded leaf around the cone, rubbing your fingers along the sides to mould it around the cone.

Fold one of the top folded edges over itself into a narrow triangle, repeating a few times until you have folded it to the edge of the cone. Repeat on the other side.

Now fold the base. Fold one side of the banana leaf over the base of the cone, then fold over the other side. Finally, fold the other side over the base again, trimming a little of the overhang so you can tuck it in to secure. Repeat with remaining dumplings.

Set up a steamer with 2 litres/3½ pints (8½ cups) of water and bring to the boil.

Line the steamer basket with a cloth or baking (parchment) paper, then arrange the wrapped dumplings in the basket. Reduce the steamer to low heat, set the basket over the boiling water, then cover and steam for 1 hour.

Remove from the steamer and let cool completely before serving.

# DIPPED WAFERS

## Bánh Nhúng

This wafer gets its name '*bánh nhúng*' (dipped cake) from its cooking technique: dipping flower-shaped moulds, similar to those used for *buñuelos*, into batter before frying them in hot oil. The mould should not be completely submerged when dipping, as the batter needs to easily separate from the mould when fully cooked.

Makes 20–25 wafers
Preparation time: 20 minutes, plus 15 minutes resting time
Cooking time: 2 minutes per wafer

| V |

150 g/5½ oz (1 cup) plain (all-purpose) flour
100 g/3½ oz (⅔ cup) rice flour
60 g/2¼ oz (scant ⅓ cup) sugar
2 g baking powder (this needs to be exact)
3 eggs
400 g/14 oz (1⅔ cups) milk
1 teaspoon vanilla extract or vanilla sugar, optional
oil, for deep-frying

Sieve together the plain (all-purpose) flour, rice flour, sugar and baking powder.

In a separate bowl, whisk together the eggs, milk and vanilla, if using.

Combine the wet and dry ingredients and whisk until smooth with no lumps. Let the batter rest for 15 minutes.

Bring a pan of oil to 175°C/345°F. If not using a thermometer, test the oil temperature by inserting wooden chopsticks into the oil – it should bubble vigorously around them.

Carefully add a flower-shaped wafer mould to the hot oil to heat; the oil should cover the mould.

Once the mould is hot, carefully remove, then dip it in the batter bowl for 4–5 seconds: without covering it; it's very important that the upper surface of the mould is not covered with the batter.

Carefully put the mould with the batter back into the hot oil and fry for 1 minutes 30 seconds–2 minutes until golden brown and crispy; 50 seconds into cooking the batter should form a cake shape and separate from the mould. Carefully remove from the oil and place on wire rack to cool before serving.

Repeat with the remaining batter.

# ROYAL FLOWER-SHAPED CAKES

## Bánh Bông Cây Tiến Vua

*Bánh bông cây tiến vua* are traditional Vietnamese cakes originally made for royalty and festivals. This artisanal dish requires generations of skill to master. One of its most renowned artisans, Bà Hồ Thị Kiều, comes from Phước Tích village – a place historically known for crafting *nồi niêu đất* (rice clay pots) exclusively for the king, pottery so sacred they were broken after each royal meal to prevent others from using them. Bà Kiều began learning this craft from her maternal grandmother at just nine years old. As she told us, she had to make over 1,000 cakes before being allowed to play. The cakes traditionally used lotus seeds instead of mung beans in their royal version, as they were rarer, and both versions incorporate intricate designs of ginger, flowers and ginseng shapes.

Makes approx. 20–25 small cakes
Preparation time: 1 hour, plus 2–6 hours soaking time
Cooking time: 30 minutes
Drying time: 10–11 hours

| V | VE | DF | GF | ≤5 |

*For the dough*
100 g/3½ oz (½ cup) yellow split mung beans
hot water, for soaking, optional
50 g/1¾ oz (¼ cup) sugar
¼ teaspoon salt
35 g/1¼ oz (¼ cup) sticky (glutinous) rice flour, plus 5 g/⅛ oz (1½ teaspoons), if needed
25 g/1 oz (2½ tablespoons) bánh in flour (a type of toasted sticky/glutinous rice flour)
2 teaspoons tapioca flour (starch)

*For wrapping, optional*
tapioca flour (starch)
coloured foil

*For colouring, optional*
turmeric water
beetroot (beet) juice
artificial colouring

Soak the mung beans in hot water for 2 hours or cold water for 6 hours.

Drain the mung beans, then place in a rice cooker with enough water to cover the beans with an extra 5 mm/¼ inch of water, then cook. Alternatively cook in a pan (see page 388).

Pass the cooked beans through a fine sieve into a bowl or place in a food processor and blend until smooth. You should have about 180 g/6 oz of mashed beans.

In a pot, mix the mashed beans with the sugar and salt. Cook over a low heat (check the temperature is 80–100°C/176–212°F if you have a kitchen thermometer), stirring constantly for about 15 minutes until smooth.

Spread the bean mixture over a large tray to cool.

In a bowl, mix together the sticky (glutinous) rice flour, the bánh in flour and the tapioca flour (starch). Knead for 15–20 minutes until smooth. If sticky, add the additional sticky rice flour. Place the dough in a resealable plastic bag, seal and rest for 15 minutes to keep it moist.

Meanwhile, if you plan to use the coloured foil, prepare the tapioca glue: mix together equal parts tapioca flour and water in a pan, then cook over a low heat for 2–4 minutes until it becomes gooey like glue.

Divide the dough into 20–25 small equal-size portions. Shape and mould the dough into flowers or the shape of a ginger root with knobs and curves, if desired, using your fingers to shape or pinch it into shape. You can also colour some portions of dough with a few drops of the colouring. For uncoloured cakes, you can decorate with pieces of coloured foil: wrap them around small sections to decorate, then seal with tapioca flour glue.

Dry the cakes in the sun for 2–3 hours.

Preheat the oven to 70°C/160°F.

Place the sun-dried cakes on a baking sheet and dry in the oven for 8 hours, or until fully dry and crispy. (If your oven does not have this low temperature, adjust the drying time, for example you can dry at 100°C/210°F/Gas Mark ¼ for 4 hours.) Alternatively, to prepare using the traditional method: smoke the cakes over slow-burning charcoal for 4 hours instead of oven drying.

Store at room temperature for up to a week.

# GINGER-SHAPED RICE CAKES

## Bánh Gừng – Girong Riya

In Phan Rang, Bà Lượng Thị Dảnh, the grandmother of chị Kiều Thị Hồng Vân, taught us how to make these traditional cakes shaped like ginger roots. Each cake is moulded by hand, and it takes a few rounds of practice to get it right. During *Chăm* celebrations (*ģirong riya* is the Chăm name for this dish), including weddings and the Kate festival (the most important Chăm festival, often happening in October, which honours the dead and historic heroes), these cakes are skewered on bamboo sticks and arranged around decorated wooden or clay pillars with colourful paper patterns for ancestral offerings. The Khmer community make a similar version called *num khnhây*, which is used during wedding ceremonies as one of three essential cakes arranged in the shape of a Khmer tower. These are best eaten while still hot, as they can get soggy rapidly depending on the environment.

Serves 7–8 as a snack
Preparation time: 30 minutes
Cooking time: 7 minutes per batch

| V | DF | GF | ≤5 |

- 780 g/1 lb 12 oz (5¼ cups) sticky (glutinous) rice flour
- 3 eggs
- banana leaves, cut into 16 × 16 cm/6¼ × 6¼ inch pieces
- oil, for deep frying , plus extra for hands
- 50 g/1¾ oz (¼ cup) brown or caster (superfine) sugar, for sprinkling

Combine the rice flour and eggs with 150 ml/5½ fl oz (⅓ cup) of water in a large bowl. Mix thoroughly until a smooth dough forms. The dough should be firm but pliable. Rest, covered, for 5 minutes.

Lightly oil your hands to prevent the dough sticking. Take a handful of dough and place it on a piece of banana leaf. Shape the dough to resemble a ginger root with knobs and curves, using your fingers to shape or pinch it into shape. Carefully flip the dough over and reshape on the other side as needed to maintain the ginger form. Adjust the amount of dough as needed while shaping.

Repeat until you have used all the dough, covering the moulded 'ginger' shapes with clingfilm (plastic wrap) so they do not dry out and crack while you make the others.

Fill a pan 7.5 cm/3 inches deep with oil. Heat the oil to 160°C/325°F. If not using a thermometer, test the oil temperature by inserting wooden chopsticks into the oil – it should gently bubble around them. Carefully slide the shaped dough off the banana leaves into the hot oil, making sure not to break the dough, and fry for 7 minutes, in batches, turning occasionally for even cooking. Make sure to maintain consistent oil temperature when frying by not overcrowding the pan. Remove when golden brown and drain on paper towels.

To finish, sprinkle sugar on top of the ginger cakes. Eat warm while fresh and crispy. Leftovers will keep for a day or so but will quickly lose their crispness.

GINGER-SHAPED RICE CAKES

## STICKY RICE FLOUR SUGAR-COATED BALLS

Bánh Cà

A speciality of Hưng Tân commune in Nghệ An's Hưng Nguyên district, these cakes were traditionally prepared during *Tết* (Lunar New Year) for ancestral offerings and guests. Cô Nguyễn Thị Hằng, who taught us this recipe, now makes them in various flavours from sweet to spicy. While families once gathered to shape these treats by hand, nowadays some makers use machines to help with production throughout the year.

Serves 4–5 as a snack
Preparation time: 30 minutes
Cooking time: 20–25 minutes

| V | DF | GF | ≤5 |

500 g/1 lb 2 oz (3⅓ cups) sticky (glutinous) rice flour
5 eggs (250 g/9 oz total weight)
20 ml/¾ fl oz (1½ tablespoons) rice wine (rượu gạo)
1 tablespoon toasted sesame seeds, optional for sesame flavour
neutral oil, for deep-frying
185 g/6 oz (¾ cup plus 1 tablespoon) sugar

Place the rice flour in a bowl.

In a blender, combine the eggs, 35 g/1¼ oz (2 tablespoons plus 1 teaspoon) of water, the rice wine and the sesame seeds, if using, then blend until well combined.

Pour the egg mixture over the rice flour, then mix the wet ingredients into the flour with your hands. Knead until well combined.

Rinse the blender with 60 ml/2 fl oz (¼ cup) of water, then add the water to the dough. Continue kneading until the dough feels like clay.

Form the dough into small, uniform balls (about 1 cm/½ inch in diameter).

Fill a deep pan a third full with the oil, then add the dough balls to the cold oil (do not add them when the oil is hot or they will explode). Place the pan over a high heat and heat until the oil reaches 130–135°C/265–275°F, 4–5 minutes. If not using a thermometer, test the oil temperature by inserting wooden chopsticks into the oil – it should very gently bubble around them. When the dough balls start floating, stir gently, increase the heat to maintain 140–150°C/275–300°F (140°C/275°F is ideal).

Continuing to stir to keep the balls round, fry for 15–17 minutes until golden and crunchy. Carefully remove the balls with a strainer and drain on paper towels.

In a pot, combine the sugar with 240 ml/8 fl oz (1 cup) water, then bring to a simmer over a high heat. Cook until the syrup thickens but doesn't colour, 4–5 minutes; to check, place a spoon in the syrup and lift up, then look for heavy syrup drops to form.

Reduce the heat to maintain a gentle simmer, then add the fried balls to the syrup and stir over a low heat until the sugar crystallizes. Continue cooking for 1 minute–1 minute 30 seconds until the water evaporates; the balls should be evenly coated with a thin sugar layer.

Remove from the heat and let cool completely before serving.

## HOLLOW DOUGHNUTS

Bánh Tiêu

*Bánh tiêu* is a sweet, chewy fried bread that puffs up when cooked, creating a hollow centre under its sesame-coated surface. Traditionally, I grew up eating it as it is, but today, you might find modern versions stuffed with Steamed Rice Wine Honeycomb Cakes (page 420) or filled with sticky (glutinous) rice, toasted peanut sugar or just durian.

Makes 6 doughnuts
Preparation time: 10–25 minutes, plus 1 hour–1 hour 30 minutes proving time
Cooking time: 18 minutes

| V | VE | DF |

200 g/7 oz (1⅓ cups) plain (all-purpose) flour, plus extra if needed
½ teaspoon baking powder
3 g (1 teaspoon) fast-action (active) dried yeast
50 g/1¾ oz (¼ cup) brown sugar
100 ml/3 ½ fl oz (⅓ cup plus 1 tablespoon) warm/hot water (70°C/158°F)
1 tablespoon neutral oil, plus extra for frying
½ teaspoon salt
sesame seeds, for dipping

In a stand mixer, combine the flour, baking powder, yeast and sugar. Mix on low speed. Gradually add the measured warm/hot water and continue mixing until the mixture forms a dough. Add the 1 tablespoon of oil and mix until incorporated. Let the dough relax for 10 minutes.

Add 1 tablespoon of warm/hot water and the salt to the dough. Mix for another 3 minutes. If the dough is too sticky, add 1 teaspoon of flour and continue mixing. After 3 minutes, add another teaspoon of flour, if necessary, then form the dough into a ball in the mixer. Place the dough in a bowl and cover, then allow to prove for 1 hour–1 hour 30 minutes until it has doubled in size.

Divide the dough into 6 equal portions, roll them into balls and let them sit for 5 minutes.

Dip each portion of dough in sesame seeds and roll out on a clean work surface into 1-cm/½-inch thick circles.

Cover, then let the rolled dough prove on the work surface for another 10 minutes before frying.

Half-fill a large pan with oil and bring to 170°C/340°F. If not using a thermometer, test the oil temperature by inserting wooden chopsticks into the oil – small bubbles should form rapidly around them. Carefully add a dough disc and fry, flipping half way, for 3–5 minutes or until golden brown and all puffed up; you can use a skimmer to push down the dough. Carefully remove from the oil and drain on paper towels. Repeat for the remaining doughnuts.

Serve warm.

## SWALLOW'S NEST CAKES

Bánh Tai Yến

A traditional cake from the Mekong Delta, similar to the Cambodian *num jak jol*, this snack gets its name 'swallow's nest cake' from its distinctive shape, formed using a small wok to create a cone-like centre. Sometimes called *bánh nón* (cone cake), it's best enjoyed hot when the texture is at its crispiest.

Makes 10 cakes
Preparation time: 30 minutes
Cooking time: 25 minutes

| V | VE | DF | GF |

160 g/5½ oz (1 cup) rice flour
40 g/1½ oz (¼ cup) sticky (glutinous) rice flour
¼ teaspoon salt
25 g/1 oz palm sugar
160 ml/5½ fl oz (⅔ cup) warm water (50–60°C/120–140°F)
60 g/2¼ oz (¼ cup) coconut milk
30 g/1 oz (2 tablespoons) light brown sugar
30 g/1 oz (2 tablespoons) caster (superfine) sugar
120 ml/4 fl oz (½ cup) neutral oil, for frying

In a large mixing bowl, combine the rice flour, sticky (glutinous) rice flour and salt.

In a separate bowl, mix the palm sugar with the measured warm water. Once the sugar has melted, add the coconut milk to the mixture.

Pour the wet ingredients into the dry ingredients. Use your fingers and hands to mix thoroughly for about 10 minutes until the mixture reaches the consistency of double (heavy) cream.

Add the light brown sugar and caster (superfine) sugar to the batter. Continue mixing for another 10 minutes. Initially, the batter will become looser as the sugar dissolves, but it will start to thicken again. Let it rest for 5 minutes.

Heat the oil in a wok with a round bottom over a medium heat. (The round-bottomed shape of the wok is essential for making these swallow's nest cakes.)

Carefully pour less than 60 ml/2 fl oz (¼ cup) of the batter into the wok. Allow the batter to bubble up for about 20 seconds until it forms a ring. Then carefully flip it and cook for an additional 2 minutes 30 seconds until both sides are golden and cooked through. Carefully remove from the hot oil and drain on paper towels, then repeat for the remaining batter.

Serve hot.

# KHMER-STYLE COCONUT ROLLS

## Ọm Chiết - Bánh Rây Khmer

This traditional Khmer roll, known as *bánh rây* in Vietnamese (*rây* meaning sieve), uses a fascinating technique; slightly wet sticky (glutinous) rice flour is sieved onto a dry pan and dry-steamed until malleable, creating a texture that's both crispy and chewy. It takes several attempts to get the technique right, and the results can vary depending on the age of the flour. Once the pancake is cooked, it's filled and rolled. During our research we also found out that the Chăm have their own version of this, but the ones we ate were much smaller than here, and had a peanut filling rather than coconut like in this recipe.

Makes 6 rolls
Preparation time: 15 minutes, plus 30 minutes resting time
Cooking time: 15 minutes

| V | VE | DF | GF |

*For the filling*
15 g/½ oz Toasted Peanuts (page 459)
10 g/¼ oz (1 tablespoon) sesame seeds
120 g/4¼ oz (1⅓ cups) desiccated (shredded) coconut
½ teaspoon salt
55 g/2 oz (¼ cup) sugar

*For the wrap batter*
100 g/3½ oz (⅔ cup) sticky (glutinous) rice flour
2 teaspoons tapioca flour (starch)
2 teaspoons sugar
¼ teaspoon salt
5 tablespoons plus ½ teaspoon Pandan Water (page 465)

To prepare the filling, put the toasted peanuts in a mortar and coarsely pound with a pestle, leaving some larger pieces.

Heat a dry pan over a medium-low heat, add the sesame seeds and toast for 1–2 minutes.

Mix the peanuts and sesame seeds together and set aside.

In a bowl, combine the desiccated (shredded) coconut, salt and sugar. Let sit for 30 minutes.

Heat a pan over a medium heat, add the coconut mixture to the dry pan and stir-fry for 2 minutes 30 seconds. Add the peanut and sesame mixture, then stir-fry for 40 more seconds. Remove from the heat and set aside.

To prepare the wrap batter, mix the rice flour, tapioca flour (starch), sugar and salt in a bowl. Gradually add the pandan water, mixing with your hands until well combined. The dough should be neither too wet nor too dry; you are looking for a partly sand-like texture.

Fill a spray bottle with water and have ready on the side.

Heat a shallow 18-cm/7-inch pan with a domed lid over a medium heat. (You want the lid to be close to the wrap but not so close it sticks, when cooking.) When hot, put a sieve on top of the pan and add one-sixth of the wrap batter; sift (*rây qua rây*) the wrap batter into the pan, using your hand to mix the batter so it falls into the pan in an even layer: not too thin or thick.

Spray a couple of spritzes of water inside the pan before covering with the lid. Steam for about 2 minutes. Open the lid and add 1½ tablespoons of the filling in a line. Flip the edge of the wrap over the top to cover the filling, then flip again to form a loose roll, then immediately remove from the pan.

Repeat with the remaining batter to make 6 rolls.

Serve warm.

***Notes:*** The key to perfect *bánh rây* is achieving a balance between a crispy exterior and a chewy, glutinous interior. The '*rây qua rây*' technique of adding the batter ensures an even, thin layer.

If pandan water is not available, you can use regular water and add some drops of pandan extract.

# DESSERTS

## Món tráng miệng

In Vietnamese meals, fresh fruits traditionally mark the end of dining. However, desserts, enjoyed as afternoon treats, during tea with friends or purchased from street vendors, occupy their own special place in Vietnamese food culture. Sweet soups (*chè*) form the backbone of Vietnamese desserts, with dedicated shops offering dozens of variations, from simple red bean soup to elaborate combinations of fruit, beans, jellies and coconut milk. Regional specialities add their own character, as with Huế's tapioca dumplings with roasted pork filling, demonstrating how even Vietnamese desserts can bridge sweet and savoury.

For *Tết* (Lunar New Year), people prepare candied fruits and fermented sticky (glutinous) rice wine (*rượu nếp*) as both treats for guests and offerings to ancestors, reflecting how desserts in Vietnam often serve both social and spiritual purposes.

From simple everyday sweet soups to festival treats, this chapter covers a small collection of Vietnamese desserts that can be recreated in your home kitchen.

## FERMENTED STICKY RICE

### Cơm Rượu Nếp

Traditional to *Tết Đoan Ngọ* (Mid-Year Festival) on the fifth day of the fifth lunar month, this fermented rice connects to the legend of Đôi Truân. According to the story, when harvests were being destroyed by insects, an elder named Đôi Truân taught farmers to make offerings and exercise, which successfully rid their crops of pests. Because of this legend, people believed that consuming foods with strong flavours like this fermented rice during this hottest time of year would ward off harmful insects. While white sticky (glutinous) rice is most commonly available, northern versions might use *gạo nếp cẩm* (black sticky rice) or *gạo lứt nếp* (brown sticky rice). The black sticky rice version can also be combined with yogurt to make *sữa chua nếp cẩm* (black sticky rice and yogurt).

Serves 4–6
Preparation time: 30 minutes
Cooking time: 20 minutes, plus 3 days fermentation time

| V | VE | DF | GF | ≤5 |

- 300 g/10½ oz (1⅔ cups) sticky (glutinous) rice
- 2 teaspoons salt
- 5 banana leaves
- 10 g/¼ oz wine yeast (men rượu)

Rinse the rice in a sieve under running water. Transfer to a rice cooker with 300 ml/10 fl oz (1¼ cups) water and cook in the rice cooker until done. Alternatively, place the rice in a pot with the water and cook on the hob (stove) (see page 240). Once cooked, spread the rice on a plate to cool.

Prepare a salt water solution by mixing a small bowl of water with the salt to clean your hands.

On a banana leaf, spread the cooled rice and smooth the top to make it flat.

Wearing gloves, if you prefer, clean your fingers in the salt water solution to kill any bacteria, then break the yeast into a fine powder and sprinkle it on top of the rice. Mix the rice with the yeast thoroughly. As you mix, dip your fingers in the salt water solution to clean them and make the rice less sticky.

Dip your hands in the salt water again and layer a banana leaf or two in an airtight plastic container large enough to hold the rice (or in bowl in a cone shape).

Form small balls with the rice mixture and place them inside the container. Use banana leaves to separate the layers (you will probably have about two layers). Finally, cover the whole thing with banana leaves and put the lid on the container.

Let the rice balls ferment in a dark place (or wrapped in dish towel to block out the light) at room temperature for about 3 days, or an extra day or so longer if your climate is cool. It should have clear water coming out of it, a tiny fizz and should smell sweet and alcoholic, like a sweet rice wine smell.

## CANDIED SOUR-SOP

### Mứt Mãng Cầu

This southern *Tết* speciality is made from sour-sop, a fruit traditionally found on Lunar New Year fruit trays symbolizing good fortune and prosperity. To handle its sticky texture, it's wrapped in clear candy wrappers. Its sweet-sour taste pairs perfectly with hot tea.

Makes approx. 750–800 g/1 lb 10 oz–1 lb 12 oz
Preparation time: 20 minutes
Cooking time: 50 minutes

| V | VE | DF | GF | ≤5 |

- 1 kg/2 lb 4 oz sour-sop (mãng cầu), peeled (approx. 835 g/1 lb 13 oz flesh)
- 350 g/12 oz light brown rock sugar
- ½ teaspoon salt
- ½ teaspoon vanilla extract
- candy plastic wrappers (or baking/parchment paper)

In a large pot, combine the sour-sop flesh with the sugar, salt and vanilla extract. Place the pot over the lowest heat and bring to a simmer, then gently simmer, stirring as much as possible to prevent sticking and burning, for about 50 minutes; the mixture should reach a jam-like texture, becoming translucent and shiny. Remove from the heat and let it cool slightly until it is malleable and slightly less sticky.

Using two spoons or your hands (wear gloves if you like), drop small portions onto candy plastic wrappers or baking (parchment) paper and tightly wrap.

The candied sour-sop can be kept in an airtight container or resealable bag for up to 2 weeks.

## CANDIED COCONUT

### Mứt Dừa

Another *Tết* (Lunar New Year) dessert or snack found across Vietnam, this is served both as an ancestral offering and to visiting guests. While this traditional white version uses simply coconut, vanilla and sugar, modern variations incorporate natural colours and flavours from pandan and gấc fruit to cocoa or passion fruit, and can be shaped into decorative patterns. The leftover sugar is great to sprinkle on sticky rice or desserts, or can be re-used for the next batch.

Makes approx. 550–600 g/1 lb 4 oz–1 lb 5 oz
Preparation time: 15 minutes
Cooking time: 1 hour 30 minutes

| V | VE | DF | GF | ≤5 |

- 450 g/1 lb old coconut meat, sliced 4 mm/¼ inch thick
- ½ teaspoon salt
- ½ teaspoon vanilla extract
- 300 g/10½ oz (1⅓ cups) sugar

Put all the ingredients in a wok and stir together. Place over the lowest heat possible and bring to a simmer. Cook, stirring continuously, until the sugar has become syrup-like and glazes the coconut, about 1 hour.

Now the crucial part begins: using a pair of chopsticks in each hand, keep stirring the coconut shreds upwards. You want the sugar to dry slowly on the coconut, becoming like fine salt. Continue to stir until the coconut feels dry and the sugar has totally evaporated, about 5 minutes.

Pick the coconut out and reserve the remaining sugar for another batch.

The candied coconut can be kept in a dry container for about 2 weeks. Leftover sugar can also be kept in a jar indefinitely.

## CANDIED GINGER

### Mứt Gừng

A symbol of warmth and health for the Lunar New Year, this candied ginger is served to guests during *Tết* celebrations. It's traditionally presented on trays with an assortment of treats including watermelon seeds, dried apricots, Candied Sour-sop (page 442), and Candied Coconut (above).

Makes approx. 450–500 g/1 lb–1 lb 2 oz
Preparation time: 30 minutes
Cooking time: 1 hour

| V | VE | DF | GF | ≤5 |

- 570 g/1 lb 4 oz unpeeled ginger (buy big ones as you need to slice them)
- salt, for soaking water
- 400 g/14 oz brown rock sugar

Peel the ginger (you should have 500 g/1 lb 2 oz after peeling), then soak in a bowl of salted water for 2 minutes. Rinse in a sieve under running water.

Thinly slice the ginger, then soak it in a fresh bowl of water to remove all the spiciness, then drain.

In a big pan, mix the ginger and sugar, and place it over the lowest heat. Bring to a simmer, and cook, occasionally mixing for 40–45 minutes, until the sugar has reduced and coated the ginger. As soon as this happens, you need to stir it constantly to prevent burning, as the liquid will start to evaporate: with a pair of chopsticks in each hand, constantly stir the ginger until the sugar crystallizes, 10–12 minutes. Continue stirring until the sugar has become like fine sea salt and the ginger is semi-hard.

The candied ginger can be kept in a dry container for about 2 weeks.

## SWEET FLOATING RICE DUMPLINGS

### Chè Trôi

*Chè trôi* is a Vietnamese dessert traditionally prepared on the twenty-third day of the twelfth month of the Lunar Calendar to honour Ông Táo, the kitchen god. Similar to Chinese *tang yuan* and Japanese *mochi*, these dumplings consist of chewy sticky (glutinous) rice balls filled with mung bean paste and flavoured with pandan leaf. This dessert is served in a bowl of sugar syrup and is best enjoyed warm, as the dough becomes firmer when cool. In the north, people make a dry version of these balls, as a dessert known as *bánh trôi*, which are smaller and sometimes filled with a small piece of brown rock sugar.

Serves 10
Preparation time: 45 minutes
Cooking time: 25 minutes

| V | VE | DF | GF |

270 g/9½ oz Mung Bean Filling (page 465), rolled into 10 balls
1 quantity Seasoned Coconut Milk (page 465)
25 g/1 oz (3 tablespoons) toasted white sesame seeds, to serve

*For the sugar syrup*
80 g/2¾ oz ginger, thinly sliced
50 g/1¾ oz pandan leaves
460 g/1 lb palm sugar
400 g/14 oz rock sugar
1 teaspoon salt

*For the dough*
250 g/9 oz (1⅔ cups) sticky (glutinous) rice flour
¼ teaspoon salt
200 ml/7 fl oz (scant 1 cup) boiling water
2 tablespoons coconut milk

To prepare the sugar syrup, put all the ingredients in a pan with 1.4 litres/2½ pints (6 cups) of water and bring to a simmer. Cook at a simmer for 10–15 minutes until the sugar has dissolved and fragrant. Set aside.

To prepare the dough, in a bowl, mix the rice flour and salt. Slowly add the measured boiling water and coconut milk until a dough has formed.

Form 10 balls of dough, each 30 g/1 oz. Flatten each ball into a thin circle, then place one mung bean filling ball in the centre and wrap the dough around it to form a ball.

Use the remaining of the dough to form small balls 5–10 g/⅛–¼ oz each.

Bring a pot of water to the boil. Add the big balls and cook for 5 minutes, then add the small ones and cook for another 5 minutes.

Transfer the cooked balls to the sugar syrup and cook for an additional 10 minutes over a low heat, to infuse the flavour.

Serve the balls in a bowl with the sugar syrup and seasoned coconut milk. Sprinkle them with toasted sesame seeds.

## CORN SWEET SOUP

### Chè Bắp

While corn typically appears in savoury dishes, this soup celebrates its natural sweetness as a dessert. You can top it with white boba balls and toasted peanuts.

Serves 5–6
Preparation time: 30 minutes, plus overnight soaking time
Cooking time: 1 hour

| V | VE | DF | GF |

500 g/1 lb 2 oz sweet corn (about 1.5 cobs), kernels separated (about 260 g/9 oz/1⅔ cups kernels)
½ teaspoon salt
25 g/1 oz pandan leaves
100 g/3½ oz (½ cup) sticky (glutinous) rice, soaked overnight
¼ teaspoon vanilla extract
130 g/4½ oz (⅓ plus ¼ cup) coconut milk
1 teaspoon tapioca flour (starch)
50 g/1¾ oz (¼ cup) sugar
½ quantity Seasoned Coconut Milk (page 465)

In a large pot, combine the corn kernels, salt, 23 g/⅞ oz of the pandan leaves and 300 ml/10½ fl oz (1¼ cups) water. Bring the mixture to the boil, then reduce to a simmer for 15 minutes. Carefully remove the pandan leaves and discard.

Drain the soaked rice and add to the pot with the corn kernels. Add the vanilla extract and 75 g/2½ fl oz (⅓ cup) of the coconut milk, then cover and simmer for 15 minutes.

Meanwhile, in a separate bowl, mix 90 ml/3¼ fl oz (⅓ cup plus 2 teaspoons) of water with the remaining coconut milk, then cook over a low heat for 15 minutes. Add the tapioca flour (starch) and sugar. Stir for 1 minute and remove from the heat.

Add the mixture to the corn kernel and rice pot, and continue to cook for an additional 15 minutes.

Serve the corn sweet soup with the seasoned coconut milk drizzled on top.

## BANANA AND COCONUT SWEET SOUP

### Chè Chuối Chưng

I like to keep this sweet soup simple, but for extra texture, top with toasted peanuts or sesame seeds for crunchiness.

Serves 6–8
Preparation time: 20 minutes, plus overnight soaking time
Cooking time: 35 minutes

| V | VE | DF | GF |

- 300 g/10½ oz (1⅓ cups) coconut milk
- ½ teaspoon salt
- 300 g/10½ oz peeled sweet potatoes, cut into 5-cm/2-inch chunks
- 3 pandan leaves, tied in a knot
- 420 g/15 oz bananas, cut into 5-cm/2-inch chunks (ideally use Siamese bananas, halved on an angle)
- 60 g/2¼ oz dried tapioca sticks (bột khoai), soaked overnight and drained
- 25 g/1 oz (2½ tablespoons) tapioca pearls, soaked overnight and drained
- 45 g/1¾ oz (4 tablespoons) caster (superfine) sugar
- 17 g/½ oz rock sugar

In a large pot, combine the coconut milk, 800 ml/27 fl oz (3½ cups) water and the salt. Bring to a simmer. Add the sweet potatoes and pandan leaves. Continue to simmer for 10 minutes.

Bring the mixture to the boil, add the bananas and simmer for a further 15 minutes.

Add the drained dried tapioca sticks and the drained tapioca pearls, stir in 30 g/1½ oz (3 tablespoons) of the caster (superfine) sugar and the rock sugar and cook for another 10 minutes until everything is cooked through.

Finish by adding the remaining caster sugar and then remove from the heat.

This soup is best served hot or warm.

## BLACK BEAN SWEET SOUP

### Chè Đậu Đen

Black beans, representing the yin element, are known for their cooling effect during hot summer days. This versatile dessert can be enjoyed with crushed ice for a light, refreshing drink or with Seasoned Coconut Milk (page 465) as a snack or dessert. The generous amount of liquid in this dish is intentional, as black bean water is considered healthy to drink.

Serves 6
Preparation time: 15 minutes, plus 6 hours soaking time
Cooking time: 1 hour 10 minutes

| V | VE | DF | GF |

- 170 g/5¾ oz (generous ¾ cup) dried black beans, soaked in water for 6 hours and drained
- 13 g/½ oz pandan leaves
- 50 g/1¾ oz rock sugar
- 100 g/3½ oz caster (superfine) sugar
- ¼ teaspoon salt
- ¼ teaspoon vanilla extract, optional

*To serve*

- Seasoned Coconut Milk (page 465), for drizzling
- Toasted Peanuts (page 459) or freshly shaved coconut meat, optional
- crushed ice, optional

In a pot (about 25 cm/10 inches in diameter), combine the drained black beans with 1 litre/1¾ pints (4¼ cups) of water. Tie the pandan leaves into a knot and add to the pot. Bring the mixture to a simmer over a medium heat, which should take 5–7 minutes. Once simmering, reduce the heat to low, cover and cook for 45 minutes, stirring occasionally to prevent sticking, until they are soft enough to mash between two fingers.

Add the rock sugar, caster (superfine) sugar, salt and vanilla extract, if using, to the pot. Stir to combine, then cook for an additional 15 minutes until the soup has a light, soupy consistency. Carefully remove the pandan leaves and discard.

To serve, ladle the soup into small bowls, drizzle with the seasoned coconut milk and decorate with toasted peanuts or freshly shaved coconut meat, if desired.

Alternatively refrigerate overnight to allow the flavours to meld, then serve in tall glasses with crushed ice and seasoned coconut milk.

## MUNG BEAN SWEET SOUP

Chè Táo Xọn

A sweet soup from Northern and Central Vietnam, also known regionally as *chè táo soạn* or *chè hoa cau* (areca nut flower sweet soup), the latter name coming from its peeled mung beans' yellow colour resembling areca (betel) nut flowers.

Serves 4–5
Preparation time: 15 minutes, plus 5 hours soaking time
Cooking time: 25 minutes

| V | VE | DF | GF |

- 140 g/5 oz (⅔ cup) yellow split mung beans, soaked for 5 hours (about 300 g/10½ oz after soaking)
- ¼ teaspoon salt
- 3 pandan leaves (5 g/⅛ oz)
- tiny pinch ground turmeric
- 120 g/4¼ oz (⅔ cup) sugar
- 4 tablespoons tapioca flour (starch), mixed with 100 ml/3½ fl oz (scant ½ cup) water
- 1 quantity Seasoned Coconut Milk (page 465), to serve

In a pot, add the soaked mung beans and 300 ml/10 fl oz (1¼ cups) of water. Bring to the boil over a medium heat. Once boiling, reduce to a simmer and cook for 8 minutes until most of the water has evaporated. Drain, then soak the mung beans in cold water to stop the cooking process. The beans should be cooked but still retain their structure.

Strain the mung beans and add to a pot along with 500 ml/18 fl oz (2 cups) of fresh water, the salt, pandan leaves and ground turmeric. Bring to a simmer, then reduce the heat and cook for 6 minutes. Add the sugar and the tapioca flour (starch) mixture. Continue stirring for another 1–2 minutes until the sweet soup thickens to a loose porridge consistency with whole mung beans.

Serve the mung bean sweet soup with the seasoned coconut milk drizzled on top.

## COMBO BEAN SWEET SOUP

Chè Thưng

This southern Vietnamese sweet soup, also known as *chè bà ba*, combines various ingredients for different textures. The cooking time depends on the peanuts used, which need to become soft. While this version of the soup uses a basic combination of ingredients, variations can include cassava or sweet potatoes.

Serves 6–8
Preparation time: 15 minutes, plus overnight soaking time
Cooking time: 2 hours 15 minutes

| V | VE | DF | GF |

- 100 g/3½ oz (½ cup) yellow split mung beans, soaked overnight
- 100 g/3½ oz (⅔ cup) peanuts, soaked overnight
- 20 g/¾ oz seaweed, thinly sliced, soaked overnight
- 30 g/1 oz (3 tablespoons) dried tapioca pearls (bột báng), soaked overnight
- 50 g/1¾ oz dried tapioca sticks (bột khoai), soaked overnight

*For cooking*

- 1.5 litres/2½ pints (6¼ cups) coconut water
- 135 g/4½ fl oz (generous ½ cup) coconut milk
- ½ teaspoon salt
- 30 g/1 oz pandan leaves, tied together
- 120 g/4¼ oz (⅔ cup) sugar

Drain the mung beans, peanuts, seaweed, dried tapioca pearls and dried tapioca sticks and keep separate.

In a pot, bring 700 ml/24 fl oz (scant 3 cups) water to the boil. Add the drained peanuts, cover, and cook for about 1 hour 15 minutes or until soft. You can also use a pressure cooker for faster cooking. Drain.

Meanwhile, in a large pot, combine the coconut water, coconut milk, salt and pandan leaves. Add the drained mung beans and bring to a simmer over a low heat for 40 minutes.

Add the softened peanuts to the main soup. Lower the heat, cover and cook for another 20 minutes. Remove the lid and continue simmering for another 30 minutes.

Add the drained tapioca pearls and drained tapioca sticks and simmer for another 10 minutes. Add the sugar and drained seaweed and cook for 1 minute. Remove from the heat.

Serve warm or chilled as a dessert soup.

# CENDOL SWEET SOUP WITH RED BEANS

## Chè Đậu Đỏ Bánh Lọt

Also known as *chè ba màu* (three-colour dessert), this combines red beans, yellow mung beans and green *bánh lọt* (pandan tapioca noodles). The contrasting textures, from tender beans to chewy noodles, exemplify Vietnam's love for layered desserts and the play on texture.

Serves 4–5
Preparation time: 1 hour, plus overnight soaking time
Cooking time: 2 hours

| V | VE | DF | GF |

*For the red bean layer*
120 g/4¼ oz (⅔ cup) red beans, soaked overnight in 350 ml/12 fl oz (1½ cups) water and ¼ teaspoon bicarbonate of soda (baking soda)
50 g/1¾ oz palm sugar
¼ teaspoon salt

*For the mung bean layer*
100 g/3½ oz (½ cup) yellow split mung beans, soaked for 5 hours or overnight (200 g/7 oz after soaking)
2 tablespoons plus 1 teaspoon caster (superfine) sugar
⅛ teaspoon salt
4 tablespoons coconut milk

*For the pandan tapioca noodles (bánh lọt)*
50 g/1¾ oz (⅓ cup) rice flour
150 g/5½ oz (1¼ cups) tapioca flour (starch)
1 tablespoon caster (superfine) sugar
300 ml/10 fl oz (1¼ cups) Pandan Water (page 465)
a few drops pandan extract, optional
ice water, for chilling

*For the coconut sauce*
200 g/7 oz (scant 1 cup) coconut milk
9 g/¼ oz pandan leaves
⅛ teaspoon salt
½ teaspoon tapioca flour (starch)
2 teaspoons caster (superfine) sugar

*To serve*
shaved ice

To prepare the red bean layer, drain the soaked beans and place in a pot with 700 ml/24 fl oz (scant 3 cups) water. Bring to the boil, then simmer for 45 minutes until edible but still firm. Add the palm sugar and salt, then simmer for another 15 minutes.

To prepare the mung bean layer, drain the soaked mung beans, then place in a rice cooker with the caster (superfine) sugar, salt, 2 tablespoons of the coconut milk and 100 ml/3½ fl oz (scant ½ cup) of water. Cook on white rice mode. Alternatively cook in a pan on the hob (stove) (see page 388). After cooking, stir in the remaining coconut milk.

To prepare the pandan tapioca noodles, mix the rice flour, tapioca flour (starch), caster sugar and 260 ml/8¾ fl oz (1 cup plus 1 tablespoon) of water in a pot. Heat over a low heat, while stirring, for 3–4 minutes. Add the pandan water and pandan extract, if using, then cook until the mixture becomes translucent, 6–10 minutes. Let cool slightly, then transfer to a piping (pastry) bag.

Meanwhile, bring a pot of water to the boil. Prepare a bowl of iced water.

Cut a small hole in the piping bag. Carefully pipe the noodle mixture into the boiling water, cutting off every 5 cm/2 inches. Cook until all the noodles float to the surface, 1–2 minutes. Take them out and put them into the iced water to prevent sticking.

To make the coconut sauce, put all the ingredients in a pot, add 50 ml/1¾ fl oz (3½ tablespoons) water and mix to combine . Cook over a low heat until it boils, then remove from the heat and let cool.

To serve, in individual glasses or bowls, layer the cooked ingredients in the following order: 40 g/1½ oz red bean layer, 50 g/1¾ oz pandan tapioca noodles, 50 g/1¾ oz mung bean layer, 50 g/1¾ oz pandan tapioca noodles, 60 g/2¼ oz coconut sauce. Top with 40 g/1½ oz shaved ice just before serving. Mix when serving.

## MUNG BEAN AND LOTUS SEED SWEET SOUP

Chè Đậu Xanh Hạt Sen

You can use fresh or dried lotus seeds for this recipe, just soak dried ones first. I sometimes add longan or jujubes for variety.

Serves 3–4
Preparation time: 15 minutes, plus 2 hours soaking
Cooking time: 1 hour 15 minutes

| V | VE | DF | GF | ≤5 |

150 g/5½ oz (¾ cup) green mung beans, soaked for 2 hours
½ teaspoon salt
250 ml/8 fl oz (1 cup) coconut water
200 g/7 oz fresh lotus seeds
200 g/7 oz (1 cup) sugar
crushed ice or ice cubes, to serve

Drain the soaked mung beans and set them aside.

In a pot, combine 1 litre/34 fl oz (4¼ cups) water, the salt, coconut water and the soaked mung beans. Bring the mixture to the boil over a medium heat, then reduce the heat to low. Cook for 25 minutes until the mung beans are softened.

Add the lotus seeds to the pot and continue cooking for an additional 45 minutes.

Add another 1 litre/1¾ pints (4¼ cups) of water to the pot and bring it to the boil. Once it boils, remove from the heat.

Add the sugar to the pot and stir well until the sugar is completely dissolved. Allow the soup to cool down to room temperature. Chill in the refrigerator.

Serve the sweet soup in glasses with crushed ice or in bowls with ice cubes.

***Note:*** If you wish to use dry lotus seeds, soak them overnight.

## FRIED BANANA

Chuối Chiên

The key to achieving the crispy exterior and soft interior lies in choosing the right bananas – ideally the Siamese variety that are ripe but still firm. Double-dipping in batter creates an extra crispy layer.

Serves 6
Preparation time: 15 minutes
Cooking time: 20 minutes

| V | VE | DF | GF |

6 small Siamese bananas (230 g/8 oz)
120 ml/4 fl oz (½ cup) cold water
55 g/2 oz (¼ cup) coconut milk
70 g/2½ oz (scant ½ cup) rice flour
30 g/1 oz (scant ¼ cup) sticky (glutinous) rice flour
2 tablespoons tempura flour
3 tablespoons tapioca flour (starch)
20 g/¾ oz (1½ tablespoons) sugar
½ teaspoon salt
½ teaspoon bicarbonate of soda (baking soda)
1 tablespoon sesame seeds
neutral oil, for deep-frying

Peel the bananas and set them aside.

In a mixing bowl, combine the measured cold water, coconut milk, rice flour, sticky (glutinous) rice flour, tempura flour, tapioca flour (starch), sugar, salt, bicarbonate of soda (baking soda) and sesame seeds. Mix well until the batter is smooth and free of lumps.

Fill a frying pan with oil and heat to 170°C/340°F. If not using a thermometer, test the oil temperature by inserting wooden chopsticks into the oil – small bubbles should form rapidly around them.

Dip each banana piece into the batter, ensuring it is well-coated.

Carefully add the coated banana pieces to the hot oil. Flip over after 30 seconds, then fry the other side for 30 seconds. Remove the bananas from the oil and dip them in the batter again for a second coating. Fry the bananas a second time, on both sides, for 3 minutes, or until they are golden brown. Remove the fried bananas from the oil and drain on paper towels.

Serve hot.

# COCONUT PANDAN AGAR JELLY

Rau Câu Lá Dứa Cốt/Dừa

A basic recipe that invites creativity – in Vietnam, you'll find endless variations in flavours and shapes. The key to perfect layers of jelly (gelatin) is timing: pour the next layer just as the previous one sets, allowing them to stick properly, otherwise, the layers could easily split when served. It might take a couple of tries to perfect the technique, but this is a great recipe to experiment with.

Serves 8–10
Preparation time: 30 minutes, plus 2–3 hours setting time
Cooking time: 30–40 minutes

**| V | VE | DF | GF | ≤5 |**

***For the agar base***
25 g/1 oz (about 5 tablespoons) agar agar (bột rau câu giòn)
1.5 litres/2½ pints (6¼ cups) coconut water
200 g/7 oz (1 cup) sugar

***For the coconut layer***
150 g/5½ oz (⅔ cup) coconut milk
¼ teaspoon salt

***For the pandan layer***
200 ml/7 fl oz (scant 1 cup) Pandan Water (page 465)
⅛ teaspoon salt

To prepare the agar base, in a large pot, mix the agar agar with the coconut water and sugar. Set it aside to bloom for 20 minutes.

Place over a low heat and slowly heat the mixture to 90°C/195°F using a cooking thermometer, stirring constantly to prevent clumps (this may take up to 20 minutes depending on your hob/stove). Cook for 2 minutes at 90°C/195°F, continuing to stir.

To prepare the coconut layer, combine the coconut milk and salt in a pot.

To prepare the pandan layer, mix the pandan water with the salt in another pot.

Divide the agar base into 3 portions. Add one third of the agar base to the pandan mixture. Add one third of the agar base to the coconut milk mixture. Leave the remaining agar base in its pan.

Heat each of the three mixtures to 60–70°C/140–160°F, stirring to incorporate.

To layer the jelly (gelatin) (see notes), pour the first layer into a 350–500-ml/12–17-oz (1½–2-cup) mould or container. Allow it to set slightly before adding the next layer – do not let it set for too long because you need it to stick to the second layer. Continue layering as desired, ensuring each layer is slightly set before adding the next.

If the mixtures in the pots start to cool and set, gently reheat them to around 70°C/160°F and whisk before using.

Once all the layers are added, allow the jelly to set completely in the refrigerator for 2–3 hours.

Once set, cut the jelly into your desired shapes and serve chilled.

***Notes:*** You can layer the jelly in any order your prefer; thinner layers will give you more layers of each).The jelly layering step needs to be done really fast so all the layers can be set perfectly without splitting when serving.

You can use a fan on the side to cool the previous base quickly. When the liquid cools down, reheat it before adding another layer.

# PANTRY STAPLES

## Nguyên liệu, gia vị và nước chấm cơ bản

---

The Vietnamese pantry centres on prepared ingredients that are essential to cooking. Every home keeps pickles: fermented mustard greens for *Tết* (Lunar New Year) nationwide, pickled daikon and carrots in the south, pickled kohlrabi in the north. These add crunch and acidity to grilled meats, noodles and everyday meals.

Basic aromatics like fried shallots, spring onion oil and toasted peanuts appear across dishes, while different regions have distinct sauces and condiments reflecting local tastes. Seasoned salts serve multiple purposes; traditionally eaten with rice during hard times, they are now used as dips for seafood and poached meats.

Once you are familiar with these ingredients, feel free to experiment with these staples beyond Vietnamese recipes; they're versatile and adaptable for any style of cooking. Just as annatto oil appears in both Vietnamese and Mexican cuisines, many of these ingredients can cross kitchen borders.

---

## HOMEMADE THICK NOODLES

*Sợi Bánh Canh*

Unlike most Vietnamese noodles that require much more craftsmanship, these thick noodles are more manageable to make at home due to their size, cut and malleability. Traditionally used in Huế-style Snakehead Fish and Thick Noodle Soup (page 198), they work well in any *bánh canh* variation.

Serves 4
Preparation time: 10 minutes, plus 30 minutes resting time
Cooking time: 2 minutes–2 minutes 30 seconds

| V | VE | DF | GF | ≤5 |

340 g/12 oz (2½ cups) rice flour, plus extra for dusting
80 g/2¾ oz (½ cup plus 2 tablespoons) tapioca flour, plus extra for dusting
1 teaspoon salt
420 ml/14 fl oz (1¾ cups) boiling water

In a large bowl, mix the rice flour, tapioca flour (starch) and salt. Add the measured boiling water to the dry mixture and mix with a spatula or wooden spoon. Carefully (as the dough may still be hot – you can use gloves if needed), knead the dough briefly until it comes together. Cover the dough with clingfilm (plastic wrap). Let it rest at room temperature for 30 minutes. ❋ Sprinkle a work surface with and equal mix of tapioca and rice flour. Roll out the dough to about 2.5 mm/⅛ inches thick. ❋ Cut the rolled dough into strips 1 cm/½ inch wide. Dust the noodles generously with tapioca and rice flour to prevent them sticking together. ❋ Prepare a bowl of iced water. ❋ Bring a large pot of water to the boil. Add the noodles and cook for 2 minutes–2 minutes 30 seconds. Remove from the heat and immediately transfer the noodles to a bowl of iced water. Drain the cooled noodles. ❋ Use immediately or store in the refrigerator for up to 1 day for later use.

---

## CARAMEL BRAISING SAUCE

*Nước Màu*

Traditionally, this sauce is made with coconut water that's completely reduced. This version offers a quicker alternative while still providing the characteristic colour and flavour. This kitchen helper is perfect to give braised dishes a darker, more caramelized colour. I usually use a very little amount, as too much would impart bitterness to the dish. Be extremely careful when working with hot caramel, as it can cause severe burns.

Makes approx. 120 ml/4 fl oz (½ cup)
Preparation time: 1 minute
Cooking time: 3–4 minutes

| V | VE | DF | GF | ≤5 | ≤30 |

80 g/2¾ oz (generous ⅓ cup) sugar

In a small, heavy saucepan, combine the sugar with 2 tablespoons of water. Place the pan over a low heat. Do not stir; let the sugar dissolve and begin to caramelize. ❋ Allow the mixture to caramelize for 3–4 minutes, or until it turns a dark brown colour. Unlike with regular caramel, you want to push it one step further for that distinctive colour and flavour. ❋ Once the caramel reaches a deep brown colour (be careful not to burn it), remove the pan from the heat. Immediately add 2 tablespoons of water to deglaze the pan. Be cautious, as the mixture may splatter. Stir quickly to incorporate the water and stop the cooking process. ❋ Let the sauce cool slightly before using or transferring to a heat-safe container and storing for up to 3 months.

---

## HOMEMADE VINEGAR

*Giấm Nuôi*

In Vietnam, quite often families would have a big jar of homemade vinegar, ready to be used in sauces or pickles. Interestingly, the name *giấm nuôi* refers to feeding the vinegar, as you have to feed it to create new vinegar. I learned this technique from chị Trien, who used bowls to measure. As long as you keep the proportion similar to this, it should work. One Vietnamese belief is that a woman should never make vinegar during her period, and should not look at her jar during that time either. For those who believe this, my technique is to always cover the vinegar with a dish towel.

Makes about 2.5 litres/4½ pints (10½ cups)
Preparation time: 5 minutes
Fermenting time: 1 month

| V | VE | DF | GF | ≤5 |

240 ml/8 fl oz (1 cup) mother vinegar or kombucha scoby
475 ml/16 fl oz (2 cups) coconut water, optional
200 g/7 oz (1 cup) sugar
240 ml/8 fl oz (1 cup) rice wine
240 ml/8 fl oz (1 cup) vinegar, from the previous batch or any natural and organic vinegar (apple cider, rice or white)

In a sterilized large jar, combine all the ingredients with 1.4 litres/2½ pints (6 cups) of water (or 1.8 litres/3¼ pints/8 cups of water if not using the coconut water), and mix thoroughly until the sugar is completely dissolved. ❋ Once mixed, seal the jar and store it in a cool, dark place. ❋ Allow the mixture to ferment for several weeks, checking occasionally to ensure it is progressing as expected: it should start to smell sweeter and if you taste a little, it will become more and more sour. After 1 month, taste the vinegar. If it has reached your desired acidity, it is ready to be used. ❋ Strain the vinegar (leaving the mother – the gelatinous film – in the jar) and pour the liquid into bottles, reserving enough to feed the mother with the same ratio of ingredients to create a new vinegar.

## ANNATTO OIL

*Dầu Điều*

This staple oil in the Vietnamese pantry is used to give a beautiful red colour to dishes like Huế Beef Noodle Soup (page 204), Beef Stew (page 316) or Fried Stuffed Tofu with Tomato Sauce (page 308). It is easy to make and can be stored on the kitchen work surface. To keep the colour red and bright, I pour the hot oil on top of the annatto seeds to infuse rather than cooking them.

Makes approx. 150 ml/5 fl oz (⅔ cup)
Preparation time: 5 minutes, plus 30 minutes infusion time
Cooking time: 5 minutes

| V | VE | DF | GF | ≤5 |

45 g/1½ oz annatto seeds
150ml (⅔ cup) neutral oil

Place the annatto seeds in a non-reactive bowl. ❋ In a small pan, heat the oil to 190°C/375°F. If not using a thermometer, test the oil temperature by inserting wooden chopsticks into the oil – it should bubble vigorously around them. ❋ Very carefully pour the heated oil over the annatto seeds. Allow the seeds to infuse in the hot oil for 30 minutes. Strain the mixture to separate the oil from the seeds. ❋ Transfer the strained annatto oil to a sterilized jar and seal. The annatto oil can be stored at room temperature.

---

## CHILLI AND LEMONGRASS OIL

*Sa Tế*

A staple worth making in large batches – keep some in the refrigerator and freeze the rest for everyday cooking. Use it to marinate meat as in Pan-seared Pork Belly with Chilli and Lemongrass Oil (page 299), serve with noodles like Huế Beef Noodle Soup (page 204), or simply stir into egg fried rice or plain rice when the refrigerator is empty.

Makes approx. 720 ml/24 fl oz (3 cups)
Preparation time: 30 minutes, plus 1 hour resting time
Cooking time: 1 hour 25 minutes

| V | VE | DF | GF |

720 ml/24 fl oz (3 cups) neutral oil
500 g/1 lb 2 oz lemongrass, minced
125 g/4¼ oz peeled shallots
92 g/3¼ oz peeled garlic
150 g/5½ oz long red chillies (about 7), destemmed and deseeded (about 120 g/4¼ oz deseeded)
½ teaspoon salt
100 g/3½ oz dried chilli flakes
2 tablespoons Annatto Oil (above)

Put the neutral oil in a pot and add the lemongrass. Place over a high heat until the lemongrass starts bubbling, then reduce the heat and cook for 25 minutes. ❋ Meanwhile, put the whole shallots and whole garlic into a food processor and coarsely blitz. Remove from the food processor, then set aside. ❋ Put the long red chillies into the food processor and finely blitz into a paste. ❋ After the lemongrass has been cooking for 25 minutes, add the garlic and shallot mixture to the pot and cook for 10 minutes, or until the mixture starts turning golden. Add the blitzed chillies and salt and cook for another 20 minutes. Add the dried chilli flakes and annatto oil, then cook for another 30 minutes. ❋ Remove from the heat and let sit for 1 hour and 2 minutes, until the chilli and lemongrass oil has a dark, deep red colour. ❋ Transfer to a sterilized glass container or jar in the refrigerator for up to 2 months.

***Note:*** You can reduce the quantity of oil depending on whether you want it to be a drier chilli paste or more like a chilli oil.

---

## SHRIMP, CHILLI AND LEMONGRASS OIL

*Sa Tế Tôm*

A variation of *sa tế* (Chilli and Lemongrass Oil, see above), it is enhanced with dried shrimp for an extra layer of savoury depth.

Makes approx. 480ml/16 fl oz (2 cups)
Preparation time: 25 minutes
Cooking time: 35 minutes

| DF | GF |

60 g/2¼ oz dried shrimp, soaked for 15 minutes, then drained
65 g/2¼ oz long red chillies (about 4), destemmed, deseeded and trimmed (60 g/2¼ oz after destemming)
85 g/3 oz peeled garlic
240 ml/8 fl oz (1 cup) neutral oil
200 g/7 oz lemongrass, minced
1 teaspoon salt
2 teaspoon Annatto Oil (left)
10 g/¼ oz dried chilli flakes
1 teaspoon sugar

One at a time, blitz the dried shrimp, long red chillies and garlic in a blender. Set aside, keeping the blitzed mixture separate. ❋ Heat the neutral oil in a 21-cm/8¼-inch pot over a high heat using the smallest hob ring (stove burner) you have. Add the blitzed garlic and fry for 4–5 minutes, then add the lemongrass and fry for another 5 minutes. ❋ Add the blitzed shrimp, ½ teaspoon of the salt and the annatto oil. Cook for another 17 minutes, stirring constantly to prevent burning. Add the blitzed chillies, dried chilli flakes, sugar and remaining salt and cook for another 8 minutes over a low heat until everything is golden and bright red. ❋ Transfer to an airtight container and store in the refrigerator for up to 2 weeks.

## SPRING ONION OIL

*Mỡ Hành*

Here, the spring onions (scallions) are quickly oil-blanched to release their flavours, then chilled on an ice bath to preserve their bright green colour. This is best used within four days, before the colour darkens and the flavours change.

Makes approx. 400 ml/14 fl oz (1⅔ cups)
Preparation time: 15 minutes
Cooling time: 10 minutes

| V | VE | DF | GF | ≤5 | ≤30 |

180 g/6 oz spring onion (scallion) greens, thinly sliced
½ teaspoon salt
½ teaspoon sugar
370ml/13 fl oz (1½ cups) neutral oil

Place the spring onion (scallion) greens in a heat-resistant bowl. Add the salt and sugar. Mix gently. ✻ Heat the oil in a pan over a medium heat. Test the temperature with one piece of spring onion (scallion): the oil is ready when bubbles form around it. Remove from the heat immediately, then carefully pour the hot oil over the seasoned spring onions. ✻ Using a long spoon, gently stir the oil and spring onions, being cautious of hot oil splatter. Infuse for 1–2 minutes. ✻ Meanwhile, prepare a bowl of iced water. ✻ Place the spring onion oil bowl in the ice water bath. Cool until the oil reaches room temperature. This preserves the green colour. ✻ Use the spring onion oil immediately or keep refrigerated in an airtight container for 4 days.

---

## SPRING ONION OIL WITH FRIED PORK FAT

*Mỡ Hành Tóp Mỡ*

Perfect as a garnish for Broken Rice (page 270) or served over steamed sticky (glutinous) rice, this recipe combines spring onions (scallions) with Crispy Fried Pork Fat (page 459). For a vegan alternative, use Spring Onion Oil (above) and substitute the pork fat with diced fried bread.

Makes approx. 240 ml/8 fl oz (1 cup)
Preparation time: 10 minutes
Cooking time: 5 minutes

| DF | ≤5 | ≤30 |

100 g/3½ oz spring onions (scallions), thinly sliced
¼ teaspoon chicken bouillon powder
½ teaspoon fish sauce
50 g/1¾ oz lard
60 g/2¼ oz Crispy Fried Pork Fat (page 459)

In a bowl, mix together the spring onions (scallions), chicken bouillon powder and fish sauce. ✻ Heat the lard in a pot over a medium heat. Add the crispy fried pork fat to the hot lard and stir for 30 seconds. Add the spring onion mixture to the pot. Stir for 30 seconds and immediately remove from the heat. The spring onions should be just cooked and maintain their bright green colour. ✻ Transfer to an airtight container and store in the refrigerator for up to 1 week or the spring onion starts to discolour.

## FRIED GARLIC

*Tỏi Phi*

This crispy fried garlic adds texture to any dish. Try adding it freshly fried to simmering broths for extra flavour, or you could add it to non-Vietnamese salads.

Makes 70 g/2½ oz
Preparation time: 15 minutes
Cooking time: 7 minutes

| V | VE | DF | GF | ≤5 | ≤30 |

185 ml/6¼ fl oz (¾ cup) neutral oil
100 g/3½ oz garlic, coarsely chopped, as uniform as possible

Heat the oil in a pan to 180°C/350°F. If not using a thermometer, test the oil temperature by inserting wooden chopsticks into the oil – it should bubble vigorously around them. ✻ Add the garlic and keep stirring the garlic in the hot oil for about 7 minutes until it becomes golden and aromatic. ✻ Remove the pan from heat and let the fried garlic cool down. ✻ Strain the fried garlic from the oil and store it in an airtight container.

---

## FRIED SHALLOTS

*Hành Phi*

Fried shallots are a staple in Vietnamese and Southeast Asian cuisines, adding perfect crunch to a wide range of dishes.

Makes about 90 g/3¼ oz
Preparation time: 15 minutes
Cooking time: 10–15 minutes

| V | VE | DF | GF | ≤5 | ≤30 |

80 ml/2½ fl oz (⅓ cup) neutral oil
130 g/4½ oz shallots, thinly sliced

Put the oil in a 15–20-cm/6–8-inch diameter pot, then add the shallots to the cold oil. ✻ Gradually heat the pot over a medium-low heat. Fry the shallots, stirring occasionally to prevent them from sticking together, for 10–15 minutes, until they turn golden brown and crispy. ✻ Remove from the oil and drain on paper towels to remove any excess oil. Keep the oil for cooking, as it adds a lot of flavour to your dishes. ✻ Store the fried shallots in an airtight container lined with paper towels; they will keep at room temperature for 4–5 days (or until the shallots lose their crispness and start getting soggy).

## FRIED SHALLOTS AND GARLIC

*Hành Tỏi Phi*

Always fry shallots first, then garlic; this way they will cook faster. Save the fragrant oil leftover from frying these aromatics to use for cooking proteins or vegetables.

Serves 3–4
Preparation time: 5–10 minutes
Cooking time: 10–12 minutes

| V | VE | DF | GF | ≤5 | ≤30 |

120 ml/4 fl oz (½ cup) neutral oil
55 g/2 oz shallots, thinly sliced
15 g/½ oz garlic, thinly sliced

Put the oil in a 15–20-cm/6–8-inch diameter pot, then add the shallots to the cold oil. ❋ Gradually heat the pot over a medium–low heat. Fry the shallots for 3–4 minutes. ❋ Once the shallots have started to change colour, add the garlic. Stirring the shallots and garlic occasionally to prevent them from sticking together, fry for 6–8 minutes, or until they are both golden brown and crispy. ❋ Remove from the oil and drain on paper towels to remove any excess oil. ❋ Store the fried shallots and garlic in an airtight container lined with paper towels; they will keep at room temperature for 4–5 days (or until the shallots lose their crispness and start getting soggy).

---

## CRISPY FRIED PORK FAT

*Tóp Mỡ*

Rendering pork fat produces two Vietnamese kitchen staples: crispy fried pork fat and cooking lard. The crunchy bits can serve as a garnish for dishes like Phnom Penh-style Noodle Soup (page 227), or can be stir-fried with Pickled Mustard Greens (page 467) or added to Stir-fried Sweet Potato Leaves with Garlic (page 340) for extra crunch. Meanwhile, the rendered lard becomes a flavourful cooking oil, preferable to processed commercial seed or vegetable oils.

Makes approx. 500 ml/18 fl oz (2 cups) (including the rendered lard)
Preparation time: 10 minutes
Cooking time: 40 minutes

| DF | GF | ≤5 |

500 g/1 lb 2 oz pork back fat, cut into 2.5-cm/1-inch cubes (the best fat is closer to the neck)
32 g/1 oz peeled garlic, halved
¼ teaspoon salt

Place the pork back fat in a pot (about 21 cm/8 inches in diameter). Cook over a medium–low heat, for 15–20 minutes until the fried pork fat is becoming opaque and starting to have a light brown colour. ❋ Add the garlic and continue cooking until the back fat pieces are floating in the oil and the fat is fully opaque and a light brown colour. This process will take another 15–20 minutes. The goal is to remove the water content in the fat to make crispy bits. ❋ Remove from the heat and let it finish cooking in the oil for a few minutes. At this point, the oil will also have a light amber colour. ❋ Strain the lard and lay the crispy pork fat on paper towels. Keep the melted lard for cooking in a jar in the refrigerator.

---

## TOASTED PEANUTS

*Đậu Phộng Rang*

Toasted peanuts are a key topping for Vietnamese dishes. For example, they bring a nutty flavour and crunchiness to salads like Herring Salad (page 132).

Serves 4
Preparation time: 2 minutes
Cooking time: 7–10 minutes

| V | VE | DF | GF | ≤5 | ≤30 |

100 g/3½ oz (¾ cup) peanuts, blanched without skin
½ teaspoon salt

In a pan over a medium heat, toast the peanuts with the salt, stirring occasionally to ensure even toasting, until the peanuts are golden brown and fragrant, 7–10 minutes. ❋ Remove from the heat and let them cool completely before serving or using in other recipes. ❋ Alternatively, you can roast the peanuts in the oven at 175°C/350°F/Gas Mark 4 for 15 minutes, or until fully golden brown.

---

## TOASTED RICE POWDER

*Thính*

Toasted rice powder adds an extra nuttiness to dishes and can be found in Vietnamese, Laotian and Thai cuisines. It can be used in Pig's Ear Salad with Toasted Rice Powder (page 103) and Shredded Pork Skin Seasoned with Toasted Rice (page 460).

Makes about 80 g/2¾ oz
Preparation time: 10 minutes, plus 1 hour soaking and 15–30 minutes drying times
Cooking time: 30 minutes

| V | VE | DF | GF | ≤5 |

100 g/3½ oz white rice

Soak the rice in a bowl of water for 1 hour. ❋ Rinse 2–3 times under running water until the water runs clear. Drain well. To make sure the rice is as dry as possible before moving on to the next step, leave it in the sieve for 15–30 minutes either in a dry spot inside or under the sun if possible. ❋ Heat a pan over a low heat, add the drained rice and toast for 30 minutes, stirring constantly, until the rice turns golden brown. ❋ Let the toasted rice cool completely, then transfer to a mortar and grind with a pestle to a fine powder. Alternatively, blitz in a food processor. ❋ Store in airtight container.

## SHREDDED PORK SKIN SEASONED WITH TOASTED RICE

*Bì*

Popular across southern Vietnam's street food to home cooking, these fine shreds of pork skin get their distinctive taste from toasted rice powder (*thính*) and fried garlic. It's a cheap condiment to make and showcases the Vietnamese approach of utilizing every part of the animal, including the skin. Found in Asian supermarkets either frozen or dried, *bì* is often paired with Spring Onion Oil (page 458) and served on Broken Rice (page 270), in Vietnamese Baguette with Shredded Pork Skin (page 69) or Silkworm Cake with Coconut Cream (page 233).

Serves 4–6
Preparation time: 20–25 minutes
Cooking time: 25 minutes

| DF |

55 g/2 oz (¼ cup) pork fat
72 g/2½ oz garlic, minced
150 g/5½ oz Poached Pork Belly (page 463)
30 g/1 oz (2 tablespoons) Fried Garlic (page 458)
2 teaspoons fish sauce
1 teaspoon sugar
2 tablespoon Toasted Rice Powder (page 459)
¼ teaspoon salt

*For the pork skin*
½ teaspoon salt
1 tablespoon fish sauce
20 g/¾ oz peeled garlic
25 g/1 oz lemongrass
660 g/1 lb 7 oz pork skin

To prepare the pork skin, in a large pot, bring 1 litre/1¾ pints (4¼ cups) of water to a simmer. Add the salt, fish sauce, whole garlic, lemongrass and pork skin to the pot. Cover and simmer for 20 minutes. Remove from the heat and leave the lid on for an additional 10 minutes. ⁕ Meanwhile, prepare a bowl of iced water. ⁕ Transfer the pork skin the bowl of iced water to cool. Once cooled, shred the pork skin into thin strips. ⁕ In a frying pan or skillet, heat the pork fat on low heat, then add the minced garlic and fry it for 4–5 minutes until golden. Reserve the fat for later use. ⁕ In a large mixing bowl, combine 250 g/9 oz of the shredded pork skin with the pork belly (side), fried garlic, fish sauce, sugar, toasted rice powder and salt. Mix well.

---

## CHICKEN FLOSS

*Chà Bông Gà*

A convenient dish we prepare for Lunar New Year celebrations when cooking feels like too much work. Like its pork counterpart, it's versatile enough to top anything from plain congee to sticky rice, and Chị Nguyễn Thị Thu Ba also makes an enhanced version by stir-frying with lime leaves and dried chillies.

Makes approx. 400 g/14 oz
Preparation time: 10 minutes
Cooking time: 1 hour

| DF |

1 kg/2 lb 4 oz boneless chicken breasts
1 lemongrass stick (22 g/¾ oz)
17 g/½ oz ginger, sliced
30 g/1 oz peeled shallots (Vietnamese, keep whole or if using banana shallots, cut into 3 big chunks)
3 tablespoons fish sauce
1 teaspoon sugar
½ teaspoon salt

Bring 500 ml/18 fl oz (2 cups) of water to the boil in a pan. Dip the chicken in the boiling water for 30 seconds, then take it out immediately. Slice the chicken into 3-cm/1¼-inch chunks. ⁕ Put the lemongrass, ginger, whole shallots, 1 tablespoon of the fish sauce, the sugar and the chicken chunks in a large wok. Stir, cover and let it steam over a low heat for 18 minutes. Add another tablespoon of fish sauce and the salt. Simmer, uncovered, allowing the water to evaporate, for another 10 minutes. Remove from the heat. ⁕ Transfer all the meat to a mortar and pound with a pestle to shred the meat. ⁕ In a big wok, add the shredded meat. Place over a low heat and keep flossing the meat by shredding it with your hand or a fork into small shreds while stirring with chopsticks in your other hand. ⁕ Sprinkle the remaining fish sauce onto the meat and continue frying until it's fully dry, 15–20 minutes over a low heat. ⁕ Remove from the wok and let the chicken floss dry on paper towels for about 15 minutes outside (or at room temperature if your climate is cold), until there is not so much moisture. It will keep in the refrigerator for 4–5 days.

---

## PRAWN FLOSS

*Tôm Chấy*

A fresh prawn (shrimp) topping for Vietnamese savoury cakes like Huế-style Water Fern Cakes (page 396) or Steamed Rice Rolls (page 403), or for other dishes like Crispy Rice Cake with Steamed Rice Dumplings (page 400). While this version uses fresh prawns (shrimp), it can also be made with dried shrimp – soaked, fried and repeatedly pounded in a mortar and pestle.

Makes approx. 100 g/3½ oz
Preparation time: 15 minutes
Cooking time: 30 minutes

| DF | ≤5 |

250 g/9 oz prawns (shrimp) (about 12)
1 tablespoon Annatto Oil (page 457)
10 g/¼ oz shallot, minced
½ tablespoon fish sauce
⅛ teaspoon black pepper
½ teaspoon sugar

Bring 600 ml/1 pint (2½ cups) of water to the boil in a pan. Add the prawns (shrimp) and cook for 10 minutes, or until fully cooked, then drain (see note). ⁕ When cool enough to handle, peel and devein the prawns; you should have 100–130 g/3½–4½ oz cooked prawn meat. ⁕ In a dry pan over a low heat, add the prawns and cook for 1–2 minutes to dry, then remove from the pan and set aside. ⁕ Add the annatto oil and the shallot to the same pan and stir-fry for 2 minutes. ⁕ Chop the prawn meat and return to the pan. Add the fish sauce, pepper and sugar. Continue frying for 7 minutes. ❋ Remove the prawn meat from the pan, place it in a mortar and pound with a pestle until it becomes floss-like. Alternatively, use a grinder or mince the prawn meat on a chopping (cutting) board. ❋ Heat a clean pan over a medium-low heat, add the prawn floss and cook, stirring continuously to prevent sticking, for 5–7 minutes or until the floss reaches a dry, crispy texture. ❋ Remove from the heat and let it cool.

***Note:*** Reserve the prawn cooking liquid and shells for Huế-style Dipping Sauce for Savoury Cakes (page 473).

---

## PORK FLOSS

*Chà Bông*

Meat floss is a great condiment to serve with Savoury Sticky Rice (page 248), in baguettes or simply with white congee when there's nothing left to eat at home. As you are drying out all the water content of the meat through a long process of slow drying, homemade floss can be kept up to 6 months in the refrigerator, while industrial floss can be kept outside the refrigerator for longer. You can also add extra flavourings to make it even more interesting.

Makes approx. 200 g/7 oz
Preparation time: 20 minutes
Cooking time: 50–55 minutes

**| DF | ≤5 |**

465 g/1 lb lean pork, cut into 5-cm/1-inch cubes
3 tablespoons fish sauce, plus 1 teaspoon to season
1 teaspoon sugar
20 g/¾ oz garlic, thickly sliced

In a pot, combine the pork, the 3 tablespoons of fish sauce, the sugar and garlic with 120 ml/4 fl oz (½ cup) of water. Bring everything to the boil. Reduce to a medium heat and simmer until the water has completely reduced, about 30 minutes. ❋ Transfer the cooked pork to a mortar and pound each piece of meat with a pestle until it starts shredding on its own. ❋ Season the shredded meat with the remaining fish sauce and let it dry on a plate or in a sieve on the work surface for a bit. ❋ In a dry large wok over a low heat, add the shredded meat stir continuously. You are slowly dehydrating the meat, so continuous stirring is crucial to avoid burning. Keep shredding the meat as you cook it for 10 minutes. ❋ Remove from the heat, transfer to the mortar and pound the shreds of meat with a pestle one more time until they become floss. ❋ Return the pork floss to the wok and continue to cook on the lowest heat for another 10–15 minutes until it is fully dry and has a floss consistency. ❋ You can store in an air-tight container in the refrigerator.

## PORK PASTE

*Giò Sống*

In Vietnam, butchers sell this pork paste fresh as a base for many dishes – from *mọc* in *bún gà măng mọc* (Chicken, Meatball and Bamboo Shoot Soup with Rice Noodles, page 195) to stuffings in *canh khổ qua nhồi thịt* (Stuffed Bitter Gourd Soup, page 356). It is made by blitzing cold pork to emulsify the fat and meat, similarly to how mortadella is made, which creates a light, airy paste that can be frozen for later use.

Makes 500 g/1 lb 2 oz
Preparation time: 15 minutes, plus 1 hour freezing and 30 minutes resting times

**| DF |**

75 g/2¾ oz pork fat
400 g/14 oz minced (ground) pork
½ teaspoon baking powder
1 tablespoon cornflour (cornstarch)
¼ teaspoon salt
¼ teaspoon ground black pepper
1 teaspoon sugar
1 tablespoon fish sauce
30 g/1 oz ice

Cut the pork fat into small cubes and freeze for 1 hour. In a large mixing bowl, combine the minced (ground) pork, baking powder, cornflour (cornstarch), salt, pepper, sugar and fish sauce. Mix well and freeze for 1 hour. ❋ Place the bowl of your stand mixer in the refrigerator if you have the space to keep it cool. ❋ Remove the pork fat from the freezer and blitz it in a food processor until finely ground. Set aside. ❋ Remove the minced pork mixture from the freezer and add it to the chilled mixer bowl along with the ice. Start mixing at medium speed for 4 minutes, or until the mixture becomes smooth and well-combined. Add the blitzed pork fat and mix for an additional 1–2 minutes until evenly incorporated. ❋ Transfer the final mixture to the refrigerator and let it rest for at least 30 minutes before using it in your desired recipe. This allows the flavours to meld together and creates a better texture.

***Note:*** Keeping the ingredients and equipment cold throughout the process helps achieve the desired texture for *giò sống*.

## PORK ROLL

*Chả Lụa*

While readily available in Asian supermarkets due to the rise in popularity of Vietnamese sandwiches, this version might have a more homemade feel and a denser texture than commercial varieties. Serve it alongside sticky (glutinous) rice or in dishes like Combo Noodle Soup (page 222). You can make a few rolls and keep them in the freezer.

Makes approx. 575 g/1 lb 4 oz
Preparation time: 3–4 hours, plus 1 hour freezing, 5 hours resting, 1–2 hours draining and overnight chilling times
Cooking time: 4–5 minutes (for shallot and onion mixture), plus 30 minutes–1 hour steaming time

| DF |

75 g/2¾ oz pork fat
400 g/14 oz minced (ground) pork
½ teaspoon baking powder
1 tablespoon cornflour (cornstarch)
¼ teaspoon salt
¼ teaspoon ground black pepper
1 teaspoon sugar
1 tablespoon fish sauce
30 g/1 oz ice
2 tablespoons neutral oil, plus extra for brushing
30 g/1 oz peeled shallots
5 g/1/8 oz onion
2.5 g (1½ teaspoons) agar agar (bột rau câu giòn)
4 banana leaves, cut to 27 × 27 cm/10¾ × 10¾ inches, optional

Cut the pork fat into small cubes and freeze for 1 hour. ✻ In a large mixing bowl, combine the minced (ground) pork, baking powder, cornflour (cornstarch), salt, pepper, sugar and fish sauce. Mix well and freeze for 1 hour. ✻ Place the bowl of your stand mixer in the refrigerator if you have the space to keep it cool. ✻ Remove the pork fat from the freezer and blitz it in a food processor until finely ground. Set aside. ✻ Remove the minced pork mixture from the freezer and add it to the chilled mixer bowl along with the ice. Start mixing at medium speed for 4 minutes, or until the mixture becomes smooth and well-combined. Add the blitzed pork fat and mix for an additional 1–2 minutes until evenly incorporated. ✻ Meanwhile, put the whole shallots and onion in the food processor and blitz together. ✻ Heat the oil in a frying pan or skillet over a medium heat, add the blitzed shallots and onion and fry for 4–5 minutes until fragrant and almost golden. Remove from the heat and continue stirring for 1–2 minutes. The mixture should be jam-like, not crispy. ✻ Add the agar agar to the meat mixture. Transfer to the food processor and blitz, working in batches if necessary, for 3–5 minutes or until thoroughly mixed. If the temperature exceeds 14°C/57°F, place it in the freezer for a couple of hours. Repeat the blitzing process three times in total to whip the mixture. Refrigerate the mixture for 5 hours. ✻ If using the banana leaves, wash the leaves thoroughly and trim off the hard edges. Bring a pan of water to the boil and blanch the leaves in boiling water for 15 seconds to make them more pliable and durable. Alternatively, you can sun-dry the leaves until they wilt. ✻ Pat the leaves dry with paper towels, then arrange 3 layers of banana leaves in a rectangle shape, alternating the direction of each layer (one lengthways, one widthways) to prevent tearing when wrapped tightly. ✻ Brush a thin layer of oil on the surface of the banana leaves to prevent the meat from sticking after cooking ✻ To shape and wrap the pork roll, place the meat mixture in the middle of the leaves, then use both hands to roll the edges of the leaves to form the meat mixture into a cylindrical shape. Roll up the leaves and secure with kitchen string in the middle. Fold one end and stand the roll upright. Use two fingers to press the meat down firmly and fold the edge over. Tie the roll widthways and lengthways with string. Ensure it is tight but not overly so, as the meat will expand slightly during cooking. ✻ Alternatively, If not using banana leaves, brush a sheet of aluminium foil with oil, then place the meat mixture in the centre. Roll tightly into a cylindrical shape, similar to the banana leaf method. Use your fingers to press firmly on the ends of the roll to create a cylindrical shape, and adjust with your hands to ensure the roll is evenly round. ✻ Set up a steamer and bring to the boil. ✻ Place the wrapped pork roll in the steamer basket, set over the boiling water, then steam for 1 hour if your roll is 1 kg/2 lb 4 oz, or 30 minutes if it's 500 g/1 lb 2. When it is fully cooked it should be still bouncy. Remove from the heat and leave it to cool in the basket, covered, for about 10 minutes. ✻ If you have a hook, hang the roll by the string, with a plate or bowl underneath, and leave for 1–2 hours to drain some of the liquid, then store in the refrigerator overnight for the rest of the moisture to come out. Alternatively, you could set the roll on a grill rack over a baking pan and place in the refrigerator. ✻ Let it cool completely overnight in the refrigerator before serving.

## TUNA FISH CAKE

*Chả Cá Thu*

Made with salt water tuna, seasoned with lemongrass and Vietnamese coriander/cilantro, this fish cake differs from the sweet water fish cake varieties. Serve it fried in Vietnamese Baguette with Fish Cake (page 70) or add to Phú Yên Fish Noodle Soup (page 202).

Makes approx. 900–950 g/2 lb–2 lb 2 oz
Preparation time: 20 minutes
Cooking time: 10 minutes per batch

| DF |

For the fish paste
440 g/15½ oz tuna fillet, deboned
2 tablespoons neutral oil
1 tablespoon pork fat
15 g/½ oz peeled garlic
15 g/½ oz spring onions (scallions), sliced
10 g/¼ oz peeled shallot
1 bird's eye chilli
5 g/1/8 oz long red chilli
2 tablespoon cornflour (cornstarch)
½ teaspoon sugar
1 teaspoon all-purpose seasoning (hạt nêm)
1 teaspoon fish sauce
¼ teaspoon black pepper
3 tablespoon ice water
22 g/¾ oz Vietnamese coriander/cilantro (rau răm), finely chopped
salt, to taste

***For frying***
oil, for deep-frying
2 lemongrass stalks

To make the fish paste, in a blender, combine all the ingredients, except the Vietnamese coriander/cilantro, and blend until it forms a smooth paste. Fold in the Vietnamese coriander. ❋ In a large pan, pour enough oil to half-fill. Add the lemongrass stalks and heat the oil over a medium heat. ❋ Shape the fish paste into small patties or balls. Carefully place the fish cakes into the hot, lemongrass-infused oil. Fry on both sides until golden brown and cooked through, 3–5 minutes per side. Remove the fish cakes from the oil and drain on paper towels. ❋ Serve hot as a starter (appetizer) or main dish with a dipping sauce.

---

## FRIED STRABISMUS FISH CAKE

*Chả Cá Thác Lác*

Made with freshwater fish and paired with dill rather than lemongrass and Vietnamese coriander/cilantro, this versatile fish cake can be fried as a noodle topping, used as stuffing in Pumpkin Flower Soup with Strabismus Fish Paste (page 364), or formed into balls for soup. You can also use it fried in soups or poached in the stock like in Fermented Fish Noodle Soup (page 214). In Vietnam, we usually use river fish to make this fish cake, but if you don't have access to river fish, you can substitute with any white fish.

Makes approx. 225 g/8 oz
Preparation time: 15 minutes, plus 30 minutes marinating time
Cooking time: 5–8 minutes per batch

| DF |

170 g/5¾ oz strabismus (cá thác lác) fillets (or any small white fish without black dots)
16 g/½ oz dill, fronds picked (8.5 g/¼ oz fronds), thinly sliced
14 g/½ oz shallot, minced
½ teaspoon black pepper
1 tablespoon fish sauce
1 tablespoon neutral oil or pork fat with flesh
60 ml/2 fl oz (¼ cup) neutral oil or pork fat, for frying

Mix the strabismus fillets, dill, shallot, pepper, fish sauce and the 1 tablespoon of oil or pork fat with flesh until it forms a paste. Let the mixture marinate for 30 minutes. ❋ In a 15-cm/6-inch frying pan or skillet, heat the 60 ml/2 fl oz (¼ cup) of oil or pork fat over a medium heat. ❋ Form the fish paste into patties. Dab a spoon in the oil and use to press the paste onto the edge of the mixing bowl to prevent sticking. ❋ Working in batches, if needed to avoid overcrowding the pan, carefully add the patties to the oil and fry on both sides for 5–8 minutes until golden brown.

---

## POACHED PORK BELLY

*Thịt Heo Luộc*

A simple poached pork belly (side) preparation that can be served with rice, accompanied by Seasoned Fermented Shrimp Paste Dipping Sauce (page 476) and Salted Small White Aubergines (page 466) or used in salads.

Makes: 1 lb 2 oz
Preparation time: 5 minutes
Cooking time: 15–20 minutes

| DF | ≤5 | ≤30 |

900 ml/30 fl oz (3¾ cups) coconut water or water
20 g/¾ oz lemongrass
1 teaspoon salt
1 tablespoon fish sauce
500 g/1 lb 2 oz pork belly (side)

In a pot, combine the coconut water or water with the lemongrass, salt and fish sauce. Add the pork belly (side) to the pot, then bring the liquid to a simmer. Poach the pork belly for 15–20 minutes, adjusting the time based on the size of the pork. Remove from the heat and let the pork cool in the poaching liquid. ❋ Once cooled, remove the pork from the liquid, then slice or use as needed for your recipe. Strain and store the poaching liquid for use in soups or congee. ❋ The pork (and liquid) will keep in airtight containers in the refrigerator for 3–4 days.

***Note:*** This quantity of poaching liquid can be used for a larger or smaller piece of meat as desired: 100–800 g/3½ oz–1 lb 12 oz.

## BASIC CHICKEN STOCK

*Nước Dùng Gà*

This versatile stock serves as a base for many dishes from Chicken Phở (page 194) and Chicken Congee (page 254) to Chicken, Meatball and Bamboo Shoot Soup with Rice Noodles (page 195). Or you can make it a simple *canh* (soup) by adding leafy greens or Pickled Dragon Bamboo Shoots (page 470). I usually prepare a batch to freeze – perfect for poaching chicken or making quick breakfast noodles.

Makes approx. 4 litres/7 pints (17 cups)
Preparation time: 30 minutes
Cooking time: 2 hours 5 minutes

| DF | GF |

1 tablespoon salt
1 kg/2 lb 4 oz chicken carcasses

***For the stock (broth)***
2 teaspoons salt
100 g/3½ oz chicken yellow fat
80 g/2¾ oz onion (1 small), peeled
15 g/½ oz shallot, peeled
2.14 kg/4 lb 12 oz whole chickens (1½ chickens), excluding offal (variety meats)
4 chicken feet
2 chicken necks

In a large pot, bring 2 litres/3½ pints (8½ cups) of water to the boil. Add the salt and the chicken carcasses and return to the boil. Blanch for 2–3 minutes. Drain and rinse under cold water. Set aside. ❋ To make the stock (broth), in a large stockpot, combine 5.5 litres/9¾ pints (23 cups) of water and the salt. Add the chicken yellow fat, blanched chicken carcasses, whole onion and whole shallot. Bring to the boil over a high heat. Reduce the heat to maintain a gentle simmer and simmer for 1 hour, skimming any foam that rises to the surface. ❋ Add the whole chickens, chicken feet and chicken necks, then partially cover the pot with a lid, leaving it a quarter of the way open. Cook for 20–30 minutes until the chicken is cooked through. To test for doneness, pierce a leg to check the juices – if they run clear, the chicken is cooked. ❋ Remove the cooked chicken pieces with a slotted spoon. Set the chicken aside for other recipes; it will keep for 3–4 days in the refrigerator. ❋ Continue simmering the broth for another 30 minutes, maintaining a gentle simmer, with small bubbles breaking the surface. ❋ Strain the stock through a fine-mesh sieve into a bowl to remove any solids. ❋ Use immediately or let cool for storage. You can store the stock in an airtight container the refrigerator for 5 days, or divide it into 1-litre/34-oz/1-quart resealable bags, flatten and seal and freeze for up to 3 months.

---

## BASIC PORK STOCK

*Nước Dùng Heo*

You can make an upgraded version of this by following the recipe for 'Knocking' Noodle Soup (page 226). This stock can also be uses as a base for *canh* (soup); it just needs a vegetable to complement it.

Makes approx. 1.5 litres/2½ pints (6¼ cups)
Preparation time: 10 minutes
Cooking time: 50 minutes

| DF | ≤5 |

850 g/1 lb 14 oz pork bones, ideally pork femur bone
1 tablespoon fish sauce
5 g/1/8 oz rock sugar (đường phèn)
½ teaspoon salt

Bring a large pot of water to the boil over a high heat. Add the pork bones and blanch for 2–3 minutes. Drain in a colander, then rinse under cold running water and scrub with a clean brush until clean. Alternatively, pour boiling water over the bones to clean them, then drain. ❋ In a large pot, combine the cleaned pork bones and 2 litres/3½ pints (8½ cups) of water. Bring the pot to the boil over a high heat. Reduce the heat to a simmer and add the fish sauce, sugar and salt. Let the stock simmer gently for 45 minutes, skimming off any foam or impurities that rise to the surface. ❋ Strain the stock through a fine-mesh sieve into a bowl to remove the bones and any solids. ❋ Use immediately or let cool for storage. You can store the stock in an airtight container in the refrigerator for 3–4 days, or in freezer-proof containers in the freezer for 1 month.

---

## MINCED PORK AND JICAMA FILLING

*Nhân Thịt Heo và Củ Sắn*

This base filling is a cornerstone of Vietnamese cuisine, perfect for various dishes such as Hà Giang Steamed Rice Rolls (page 406), Fried Stuffed Buns (page 59) and Savoury Steamed Coconut Rice Cake (page 392). It is often used as stuffing or toppings.

Makes 300 g/10½ oz
Preparation time: 15 minutes, plus 15–30 minutes soaking time
Cooking time: 10–12 minutes

| DF | ≤30 |

10 g/¼ oz dried wood ear mushrooms
100 g/3½ oz jicama
1 tablespoon neutral oil
15 g/½ oz garlic, finely chopped
15 g/½ oz shallot, finely chopped
190 g/6¾ oz minced (ground) pork
¼ teaspoon salt
½ teaspoon sugar
1 teaspoon fish sauce
¼ teaspoon black pepper

Soak the dried mushrooms in a bowl of water until soft, 15–30 minutes. (They should weigh about 80 g/2¾ after soaking.) Drain, then shred finely. ❋ Finely chop the jicama and soaked wood ear mushrooms together. ❋ Heat the oil in a pan over a medium heat. Add the garlic and shallot and stir-fry for about 1 minute 30 seconds until fragrant. Add the minced (ground) pork and stir-fry for another 1 minute. Add the chopped jicama and mushrooms to the pan, then season with the salt, sugar, fish sauce and pepper. Continue stir-frying for 6–8 minutes, until the jicama is cooked but still has a slight crunch. ❋ Let cool, then transfer to a container and store in the refrigerator for 3–4 days.

## FRESH COCONUT MILK

*Nước Cốt Dừa Tươi*

At home in Vietnam, we prefer making our own coconut milk for its pure flavour, free from stabilizers or thickeners. Starting with freshly grated coconut from the market simplifies the process – all you need to do is squeeze and extract the milk. The recipe includes measurements, but at home we typically go by look and feel, as each coconut differs from one to another.

Makes 500–550 ml/17–18 fl oz (2–2¼ cups)
Preparation time: 5 minutes

| V | VE | DF | GF | ≤5 | ≤30 |

500 g/1 lb 2 oz coconut meat
½ teaspoon salt
155 ml/5¼ fl oz (⅔ cup) near-boiling water

In a bowl, combine the coconut meat with the salt and measured near-boiling water. Carefully squeeze the mixture thoroughly with your hands to extract the first batch of coconut milk. Strain into a clean bowl. ❋ Return the squeezed coconut meat to its original bowl, add 210 ml/7 fl oz (scant 1 cup) of water and repeat the process for a second extraction. ❋ Combine both extractions to get your fresh coconut milk. ❋ Transfer to a clean airtight container or bottle and store in the refrigerator for up to 2 days.

---

## MUNG BEAN FILLING

*Nhân Đậu Xanh*

This filling is widely used in filled sweet cakes like Sweet Floating Rice Dumplings (page 444). But you can also add 10 g/¼ oz of spring onion (scallion) and ½ teaspoon black pepper to this recipe to make it more savoury; with these additions you can use it with Steamed Pandan Layer Cake (page 428).

Makes 500–700 g/1 lb 2 oz–1 lb 7 oz (2 cups)
Preparation time: 10 minutes, plus 4–6 hours soaking time
Cooking time: 20 minutes

| V | VE | DF | GF | ≤5 |

300 g/10½ oz (1½ cups) yellow split mung beans
300 ml/10½ fl oz (1¼ cups) coconut water
(or water, if using water, add extra 15 g/½ oz/3½ teaspoons sugar)
15 g/½ oz pandan leaves (about 2 leaves)
30 g/1 oz (2½ tablespoons) sugar
½ teaspoon salt
2 tablespoons neutral oil or pork fat

Soak the mung beans in a bowl of water until they have roughly double in size, 4–6 hours. Drain the water. You should have 600 g/1 lb 5 oz of soaked mung beans. ❋ In a rice cooker or pot, combine the soaked mung beans, coconut water, pandan leaves, sugar and salt. ❋ If using a rice cooker, cook the mixture as you would for rice. If using a pot, place on the hob (stove) and bring the mixture to the boil, then reduce the heat and simmer on low for 20 minutes, stirring occasionally to prevent sticking. ❋ Once fully cooked, transfer the mung beans to a bowl, add the oil or pork fat and stir and mash the beans until well combined. Depending on the recipe they will be used in, you might have to blend the paste until smooth or keep it coarsely mashed. ❋ Allow the mixture to cool before using it as a filling in other recipes. ❋ Store any leftover filling in the refrigerator for up to 4 days.

---

## PANDAN WATER

*Nước lá dứa*

This bright green and fragrant water is used in cake making, including for Steamed Pandan Layer Cake (page 428) or you can use it as base for your own Vietnamese-style jelly (gelatin) inspired by *rau câu* (agar jelly, see page 452).

Makes 800 ml–1 litre/1½–1¾ pints (3½–4¼ cups)
Preparation time: 15 minutes

| V | VE | DF | GF | ≤5 | ≤30 |

100 g/3½ oz pandan leaves, cut into 2-cm/¾-inch pieces
1 litre/1¾ pints (4¼ cups) super cold water (to keep the bright green colour after blending)

In a blender, combine the pandan leaves and water. Blend on high speed for 1 minute until the leaves are finely blended. ❋ Strain the mixture through a fine-mesh sieve or muslin (cheesecloth) into a clean container to remove the solids. ❋ Store the pandan water in the refrigerator for up to 1 week. Shake well before use, as the mixture may separate over time.

---

## SEASONED COCONUT MILK

*Nước cốt dừa*

A sweet sauce for Vietnamese desserts like Corn Sweet Soup (page 444), Cassava Silkworm Cake (page 425) and Mung Bean Sweet Soup (page 446). It also pairs perfectly with any steamed sticky (glutinous) rice desserts. In Vietnam, some people even add a little chopped spring onion (scallion) to enhance the sweet and salty flavour.

Makes 500 g/1 lb 2 oz (2¼ cups)
Preparation time: 5 minutes
Cooking time: 5–7 minutes

| V | VE | DF | GF | ≤5 | ≤30 |

400 g/14 oz (1⅔ cups) coconut milk
¼ teaspoon salt
6 g/⅛ oz (2½ teaspoons) tapioca flour (starch)
18 g/½ oz pandan leaves (about 2 leaves), tied together
6 g/⅛ oz (2 teaspoons) rice flour

In a pot, combine the coconut milk, salt, tapioca flour (starch), pandan leaves, rice flour and 100 ml/3½ fl oz (scant ½ cup) of water. Slowly bring the mixture up to a gentle simmer, stirring continuously to prevent the flour from clumping for 5–7 minutes until it thickens.

## SALTED SMALL WHITE AUBERGINES

*Cà Pháo Muối*

This pickled dish is an excellent accompaniment to meals featuring poached sliced pork belly (side) with Seasoned Fermented Shrimp Paste Dipping Sauce (page 476) or Black Bean Rice Congee (page 252) or Malabar Spinach Soup with Rice Field Crab (page 376). For the best fermentation results, it's crucial to use high-quality ingredients, especially pure sea salt.

Makes 800–850 g/1 lb 12–14 oz
Preparation time: 30 minutes, plus 1 hour marinating time
Fermentation time: 4–7 days

| V | VE | DF | GF | ≤5 |

175 g/6 oz (¾ cup) salt, plus extra for the salt water
1 kg/2 lb 4 oz small white aubergines/eggplants (cà pháo), untrimmed
10 bird's eye chillies

Prepare a bowl with cold water, weighing the water as you add it. Calculate 2 per cent of the water weight, then add that quantity of salt. ❋ Using a paring knife, carefully remove the stalk (calyx) of each aubergine (eggplant) without cutting into the flesh. ❋ Place the aubergines in the salted water, gently rubbing and rotating them to remove any pesticide residues. ❋ Using a colander, strain and then rinse under clean running water. ❋ For the initial salting, in a large mixing bowl, combine the cleaned aubergines and chillies. Sprinkle 100 g/3½ oz of the salt over the vegetables and gently toss with your hands or wooden spoons. Cover and let them marinate at room temperature for at least 1 hour. ❋ After marinating, place in a colander and thoroughly rinse off the salt under running water. ❋ To make the fermentation brine (salt solution), in a large bowl, combine 1.5 litres/2½ pints (6¼ cups) of water and the remaining salt. Using a wooden spoon, stir until the salt completely dissolves. ❋ Using a sterilized 5-litre/175-oz (5-quart) glass fermentation jar, pack in the rinsed aubergines and chillies. Pour the fermentation brine over the vegetables, ensuring they are completely covered. Use ceramic or glass weights or a water-filled resealable bag to keep the vegetables submerged in the brine. ❋ Seal the jar and let it ferment at room temperature for 4–7 days, depending on the weather. Using clean utensils, check daily that the vegetables remain submerged and crunchy, and taste one to check they are developing a sour flavour. When the aubergines taste a little bit sour, and are still crunchy, they are ready to be eaten. ❋ Store the jar in the refrigerator and eat within a month.

***Note:*** Fermentation time may vary based on ambient temperature. Warmer temperatures will speed up the process, while cooler temperatures will slow it down.

## SPICY PICKLED WHITE AUBERGINES

*Cà Xổi*

These crunchy, spicy pickles pair perfectly with plain white rice, boiled seafood and vegetables.

Makes approx. 500 g/1 lb 2 oz; serves 4–6 as a side dish
Preparation time: 5 minutes, plus 45 minutes soaking time
Pickling time: Overnight

| DF |

400 g/14 oz round, white aubergines (eggplants) (about 4 cm/1½ inches in diameter)
50 g/1¾ oz (¼ cup) salt
50 ml/2 fl oz (3½ tablespoons) lime juice

***For the pickling liquid***
50 ml/2 fl oz (3½ tablespoons) fish sauce
50 g/1¾ oz (¼ cup) sugar
40 ml/1¼ fl oz (2½ tablespoons) lime juice
40 g/1½ oz garlic, finely minced
40 g/1½ oz long red chillies, deseeded and finely minced

Cut each aubergine (eggplant) into quarters. ❋ In a large bowl, combine 600 ml/1 pint (2½ cups) of water and the salt, stirring until the salt dissolves. Add the quartered aubergines, then let soak for 30 minutes. Add the lime juice to the salt water, then continue soaking for 10–15 minutes more. This process prevents browning and maintains the white colour. ❋ To prepare the pickling liquid, in a bowl, combine the fish sauce, sugar and lime juice, then stir until the sugar completely dissolves. Add the garlic and chillies and mix well to combine. ❋ Drain the aubergines thoroughly and pat dry with paper towels, then place the aubergine pieces in a clean, sterilized 500-ml–1-litre/17–34-oz (2–4¼-cup) jar. Pour the pickling liquid over the aubergines, ensuring all the pieces are covered by the liquid. Place a ceramic plate or pickling weight on top to keep the aubergines submerged, then tightly seal the jar. ❋ Refrigerate overnight or for at least 12 hours. It will keep for 1–2 weeks but can be served the next day.

---

## PICKLED CHINESE ONIONS

*Củ Kiệu Ngâm Giấm*

*Củ kiệu*, a type of pickled Chinese onion, similar to a spring onion (scallion), is an indispensable part of *Tết* (Lunar New Year) celebrations in Vietnam. When selecting fresh *củ kiệu*, look for nicely rounded ends and avoid overly mature ones. Ash also plays an important role in this preparation. Back in the day, people would burn things to make wood ash (*tro*), which was then turned into lye. Soaking the onions in lye (see note) helps reduce their pungent odour, facilitates the release of their water and allows the spring onions to quickly absorb flavours, resulting in a crisper texture that also lasts longer. This practice dates back to when ash was commonly used in Vietnamese households to clean dishes before modern detergents were available. The same type of ash is also utilized in the production of salted eggs, or in the making of *bánh ú tro*, a type of cake made of sticky (glutinous) rice that is soaked in lye and folded into triangles. I include two different methods for cleaning the onions that are both used nowadays. The first method is more traditional and often made in Vietnam, while the second method is a substitute version and is often made by the diaspora living overseas. If using the second method, you can soak the leftover sticky rice overnight to make Savoury Sticky Rice (page 248) or Steamed Momordica Sticky Rice (page 242).

Makes 700 g/1 lb 9 oz/2 × 500-ml/18-oz (2-cup) jars
Preparation time: 1–2 hours, plus 12 hours soaking 24 hours drying, 5–6 hours marinating and 1 week pickling times
Cooking time: 15–20 minutes, plus 1 hour baking for method 2

| V | VE | DF | GF |

***For cleaning method 1 (traditional)***
3 tablespoons lye water (tro) (see note)
½ teaspoon potassium alum (phèn chua)
1 kg/2 lb 4 oz Chinese onions (củ kiệu)
1 tablespoon salt

***For cleaning method 2 (modern)***
300 g/10½ oz (1⅔ cups) sticky (glutinous) rice
30 g/1 oz (2 tablespoons) bicarbonate of soda (baking soda)
1 tablespoon sugar
1 kg/2 lb 4 oz Chinese onions (củ kiệu)
1 teaspoon salt

***For marinating and pickling***
400 ml/14 fl oz (1⅔ cups) Homemade Vinegar (page 456)
310 ml/10½ fl oz (1⅓ cups) vinegar
200 g/7 oz (scant 1 cup) rock sugar
100 g/3½ oz (½ cup) caster (superfine) sugar
¼ teaspoon salt

**If following method 1 (traditional):** In a large, non-reactive bowl, very carefully combine 3 litres/5¼ pints (12½ cups) of water with the lye water (see note) and potassium alum. Add the Chinese onions and soak for 12 hours. ⁜ Carefully strain the Chinese onions. Refill the bowl with fresh water, then strain again. Do this 3–4 times. Add the salt and wash one more time with fresh water. Drain thoroughly. ⁜ Spread out the onions on a clean surface, place in direct sunlight and leave for 24 hours to dry. **If following method 2 (modern):** Preheat the oven to 120°C/250°F/Gas Mark ½. ⁜ Rinse the rice in 2.5 litres/4½ pints (10½ cups) of water. Drain, reserving the rinsing water. (After rinsing, you can soak the remaining rice overnight to make another dish.) ⁜ Spread the bicarbonate of soda (baking soda) on a baking sheet. Bake in the oven for 1 hour. Let cool completely; you should have 20 g/¾ oz left. ⁜ In a large bowl, combine the rice rinsing water, treated bicarbonate of soda and sugar. Add the Chinese onions and let soak for 12 hours. ⁜ After soaking, strain the onions. Refill the bowl with fresh water, then strain again. Do this 3–4 times. Add the salt and wash one more time with water. Drain thoroughly. ⁜ Spread out the onions on a clean surface, place in direct sunlight and leave for 24 hours to dry. **Whichever cleaning method you follow,** you will need 700 g/1 lb 9 oz of the cleaned, dried onions; if you have any leftover, either scale up the recipe or you can store them in sterilized containers in the refrigerator for stir-fries or other dishes. ⁜ To marinate, fill a bowl with the homemade vinegar. Add the cleaned, dried onions and soak for 5–6 hours. ⁜ To make the pickling liquid, combine the 310 ml/10½ fl oz (1⅓ cups) vinegar, both sugars and the salt in a saucepan. Bring to a simmer over a medium heat. Cook until syrupy and reduced, 15–20 minutes. Let cool completely. ⁜ Drain the onions. Pack into 2 sterilized 500 ml/18 fl oz (2-cup) jars, then pour the cooled pickling liquid over the onions and tightly seal. ⁜ Leave to pickle at room temperature for exactly 1 week before eating. Remember to set a timer for precision pickling time. Once pickled, store in the refrigerator for up to 1 month.

***Note:*** Food-grade lye can be used for curing, tenderizing or adding colour and texture. It is highly corrosive, so take care when using and do not allow to come into contact with skin.

---

## PICKLED MUSTARD GREENS

*Dưa Cải*

While young mustard greens are used in broth, pickled mustard greens are made from older plants with larger and thicker stalks, which become crunchy when preserved. This famous side dish is often paired with Braised Pork Belly with Eggs (page 303) or served in a broth like Pickled Mustard Greens and Pork Rib Soup (page 373). In southern Vietnam, farmers begin preparing the soil for mustard greens at the end of the ninth lunar month, timing the harvest and fermentation to be ready just before *Tết* (Lunar New Year). The pickled greens are then enjoyed throughout the celebrations.

Makes 2.5 kg/5 lb 8 oz; serves 8–10
Preparation time: 25 minutes
Fermentation time: 5–7 days

| V | VE | DF | GF |

30 g/1 oz (2 tablespoons) salt
5 g/⅛ oz (1¼ teaspoons) light brown sugar
1.13 kg/2 lb 8 oz (6½ cups) old mustard greens, any damaged leaves discarded, cut into 10-cm/4-inch pieces if large
30 g/1 oz spring onions (scallions), cut into 8–10-cm/3¼–4-inch lengths
30 g/1 oz peeled small shallots
4 bird's eye chillies

In a sterilized fermentation jar (about 10-litre/338-oz /10½-quart capacity), combine 1.5 litres/2½ pints (6¼ cups) of water with the salt and sugar. Stir until completely dissolved. ⁜ Add the mustard greens to the brine (salt solution), then add the spring onions (scallions), whole shallots and chillies. Pour in 1 litre/1¾ pints (4¼ cups) water to ensure full coverage, then place a ceramic plate or fermentation weight on top to keep the vegetables submerged. ⁜ Seal the jar tightly, then place in a cool, dark place (20–22°C/68–72°F) for 5–7 days. Check daily to ensure the vegetables remain submerged, tasting after day 5 to check the progress. ⁜ Once the vegetables are fermented to your taste, transfer the jar to the refrigerator. This slows down further fermentation and keeps them crisp. Store in the refrigerator, keeping the vegetables submerged, for up to 2 months. You can use it as a side dish or stir fry it with any protein at hand.

## PICKLED BEAN SPROUTS

*Dưa Giá*

This simple pickle is great alongside Braised Pork Belly with Eggs (page 303). The method is similar to any fermented vegetables, but we also use rice water, the left-over water after washing rice, because it is known to be full of nutrients, and can keep the vegetables' colours brighter for longer. After one or two days, the pickles should be kept in the refrigerator and consumed within a week maximum, as afterwards the bean sprouts will start to wilt. You could omit the rice water and replace it with just water.

Makes approx. 750 g/1 lb 10 oz; serves 6–8 as a side dish
Preparation time: 35 minutes
Fermentation time: 1–2 days

**| V | VE | DF | GF |**

500 g/1 lb 2 oz (2½ cups) rice, optional
2 tablespoons salt
1½ teaspoons sugar
500 g/1 lb 2 oz bean sprouts, rinsed and drained
90 g/3¼ oz Chinese chives (lá hẹ), trimmed and cut into 5-cm/2-inch lengths
140 g/5 oz carrots (115 g/4 oz after peeling), peeled and cut into matchsticks (julienned)
30 g/1 oz shallots, thinly sliced

In a rice cooker bowl or large mixing bowl, rinse the rice three times in cool water. Collect the cloudy water from the second and third rinses, then measure out 1.5 litres/2½ pints (6¼ cups) of the rice water into a large measuring jug. (Alternatively, plain water can be used instead). ❋ Add the salt and sugar to the measured rice water. Using a long spoon, stir until completely dissolved. Set aside. ❋ Using a 5-litre/175-oz (5-quart) sterilized glass fermentation jar, alternately layer the bean sprouts, Chinese chives, carrots and shallots. Repeat the layers until all the vegetables have been used. ❋ Carefully pour the salted rice water over the vegetables. With clean hands or a large spoon, press down gently to release any air bubbles. ❋ Place a fermentation weight or small plate on top to keep the vegetables under the brine (salt solution). Ensure all the vegetables are completely submerged. Cover the jar with its lid or secure a clean cloth with a elastic (rubber) band. ❋ Place at room temperature (20–22°C/68–72°F) for 1–2 days. Use a timer or calendar to track the fermentation time. Check it daily with a clean spoon to ensure the vegetables remain submerged. After 1–2 days, using a clean spoon, taste test for a lightly sour flavour. The vegetables should also still be crispy. ❋ When ready, transfer the pickles to clean storage containers using tongs or a slotted spoon. Store in airtight containers in the refrigerator for up to 1 week.

---

## PICKLED GARLIC IN VINEGAR

*Tỏi Ngâm Giấm*

This versatile condiment can be served with noodle dishes like Phở with Quickly Stir-fried Beef (page 184) and 'Knocking' Noodle Soup (page 226), or alongside fried rice. The pickling process is believed to enhance garlic's health benefits – I often eat this when I have a cold.

Makes approx. 500 ml/18 fl oz (2 cups)
Preparation time: 15 minutes

**| V | VE | DF | GF | ≤5 | ≤30 |**

2 teaspoon salt
2 tablespoons sugar
240 ml/8 fl oz (1 cup) white vinegar
3 bird's eye chillies, or to taste
120 g/4¼ oz peeled garlic

In a bowl, dissolve the sugar and salt in the white vinegar. Add 60 ml/2 fl oz (¼ cup) of water to the vinegar mixture and stir well. ❋ Cut each chilli into three pieces and add them to the pickling liquid. Thinly slice the garlic cloves using a mandoline or by hand and add them to the pickling liquid. ❋ Put everything into a sterilized jar. Leave the jar on the work surface for a day to allow the flavours to develop. After a day, you can move the jar to the refrigerator. ❋ Consume the pickled garlic within a month for the best quality.

---

## PICKLED DAIKON AND CARROTS

*Đồ Chua*

*Đồ chua* is an essential component of baguettes and is also served alongside dishes like Roasted Pork Belly (page 161) or Broken Rice (page 270). This quick and easy pickle can be consumed on the day of preparation, but it's best eaten the next day and should be stored in the refrigerator. You can cut it in different sizes; I often find it really thinly shredded and incorporated in seasoned fish sauce as a dipping sauce, or as a thicker cut served more as a pickle side dish.

Makes approx. 1 litre/1¾ pints (4¼ cups)
Preparation time: 15 minutes, plus 30 minutes soaking time
Pickling time: 1–2 days

**| V | VE | DF | GF | ≤5 | ≤30 |**

225 g/8 oz daikon, peeled
160 g/5½ oz carrots, peeled
2 teaspoons salt

***For the pickling liquid***
50 g/1¾ oz (¼ cup) sugar
¼ teaspoon salt
110 g/3¾ oz boiling water
120 g/4¼ oz white vinegar

Slice the daikon and carrots into baton/matchstick-size (5-cm × 5-mm × 5-mm/2 × ¼ × ¼-inch) pieces, or you can cut it into really thin matchsticks (julienne) as well. Use a mandoline or shredder if desired. Smaller pieces will pickle more quickly; thinly cut ones are often used as a garnish on top of sauces. ❋ In a bowl, soak the sliced vegetables in 500 ml/18 fl oz (2 cups) of water with the salt for 30 minutes. ❋ Meanwhile, to prepare the pickling liquid, in a separate bowl, dissolve the sugar and salt in the measured boiling water. Add the vinegar and mix well. Allow to cool completely. ❋ Strain the soaked vegetables and transfer to a sterilized 1-litre/1¾-pint (4¼-cup) mason jar. Pour the cooled pickling liquid over the vegetables, ensuring they are fully covered. Close the lid. Leave the jar at room temperature for 2–3 days, or until the pickles develop the desired sweet and sour flavour. The fermentation time may vary depending on the weather. Once the pickles reach the desired taste (crispy, sweet and sour), transfer the jar to the refrigerator. ❋ Store in the refrigerator and consume within one month.

---

## PICKLED KOHLRABI AND CARROTS

*Dưa Góp Su Hào*

This Northern style of pickles is usually eaten with street snacks, especially if it's fried or grilled. It's usually added to a bowl of light seasoned fish sauce and served with dishes like Hanoi-style Grilled Pork with Vermicelli (page 146) or Pillow-Shaped Cakes (page 414). You can also use green papaya instead of kohlrabi if you have access to it.

Serves 4–6 as a side dish or condiment
Preparation time: 35 minutes, plus 40 minutes marinating time

| DF |

1 large kohlrabi, peeled (350 g/12 oz after peeling)
1 large carrot, peeled (130 g/4½ oz after peeling)
15 g/½ oz (1 tablespoon) salt (3.5 per cent of the weight of the vegetables)

*For the pickling liquid (for about 400 g/14 oz salted vegetables)*
40 ml/1¼ fl oz (2½ tablespoons) vinegar
40 g/1½ oz (3 tablespoons) sugar
2 teaspoons fish sauce
11 g/¼ oz garlic, minced
1 bird's eye chilli (or more if desired), sliced

Using a sharp knife, cut the kohlrabi in half vertically, then cut each half into quarters and slice thinly. Alternatively, for a more refined version, cut the kohlrabi into 3 × 3 × 10-cm/1¼ × 1¼ × 4-inch batonnets (matchsticks); using the length of the knife blade, cut V-shaped grooves on each face; then thinly slice widthways. ❋ To prepare the carrots, using a sharp knife cut in half widthways and then lengthways. Cut 2–3 V-shaped grooves (not too deep) along the length of each, then thinly slice widthways. Alternatively, for a simpler version, you could just halve lengthways and thinly slice. ❋ In a large mixing bowl, combine the sliced vegetables. Weigh the vegetables, then calculate 4 per cent of the vegetable weight. Add that weight of salt. ❋ Using clean hands or tongs, mix thoroughly. Leave to marinate for 10 minutes. ❋ Place the vegetables in a colander, then rinse under cold running water. Drain for 5 minutes (do not squeeze). ❋ To prepare the pickling liquid, in a mixing bowl, combine the vinegar, sugar, fish sauce, garlic and chilli. Stir with a spoon until the sugar completely dissolves. ❋ Transfer the drained vegetables to a clean bowl. Pour the pickling liquid over the vegetables. Using tongs or clean hands, thoroughly mix. Let marinate for a minimum of 30 minutes, then serve. ❋ These will keep in an airtight container in the refrigerator for 1 week.

## SWEET PICKLED VEGETABLES

*Dưa Món*

This sweet pickle is a must for any *Tết* (Lunar New Year) celebrations. The best way to keep the vegetables crunchy, is to first dry them, traditionally under the sun for one day, or in a dehydrator or oven. You can substitute kohlrabi with green papaya. This pickle goes well with Square Sticky Rice Cakes (page 388).

Serves 10–12 as a side dish or condiment
Preparation time: 50 minutes, plus 10 hours or 2–3 days dehydration time

| DF |

500 g/1 lb 2 oz carrots (about 4), cut into 1-cm/½-inch-thick batonnets (matchsticks) or slices/half-moons
450 g/1 lb kohlrabi, cut into 1-cm/½-inch-thick batonnets (matchsticks) or slices/half-moons
100 g/3½ oz Chinese onions (củ kiệu), trimmed
1.37 kg/3 lb daikon, cut into 1-cm/½-inch-thick batonnets (matchsticks) or slices/half-moons
150 g/5½ oz peeled garlic
20 g/¾ oz small chillies

*For the pickling liquid*
500 g/1 lb 2 oz (2¼ cups) sugar
300 ml/10 fl oz (1¼ cups) fish sauce (40 per cent protein content)
300 ml/10 fl oz (1¼ cups) hot water

*For the washing liquid*
400 ml/14 fl oz (1⅔ cups) boiling water, cooled
100 ml/3½ fl oz (⅓ cup plus 1 tablespoon) white vinegar

For the dehydration, if you are using a dehydrator (or the sun), arrange the vegetables on dehydrator trays (or baking sheets), leaving space between each piece. Set the dehydrator temperature to 38°C/100°F. Dehydrate for 10 hours (or leave under the sun for 2–3 days, until they have reduced to 50 per cent of their original weight). ❋ If using an oven, preheat the oven to the lowest possible temperature, with convection fan, if possible. Weigh the vegetables and note the weight; you will need it later. Arrange the vegetables on baking sheets lined with baking (parchment) paper. Place in the oven to dehydrate until the vegetables lose 50 per cent of their weight (use kitchen scales to verify the weight loss), about 10 hours. ❋ To prepare the pickling liquid, mix the sugar, fish sauce and the measured hot water in a bowl. Stir with a spoon to combine and let it cool to room temperature. Set aside. ❋ To prepare the washing liquid, in a separate bowl, combine the measured cooled boiling water and vinegar. Set aside. ❋ Working in batches with clean hands, take portions of the dehydrated vegetables. Quickly place them in the washing liquid and mix around with your hands to wash them for about 1 minute, then thoroughly drain in a colander. (This will quickly rehydrate them with the touch of vinegar and rinse off any dust they might have accumulated under the sun.) You should have about 620 g/1 lb 6 oz of rehydrated vegetables. ❋ To assemble, place the rehydrated vegetables in a large, sterilized 1-litre/34-oz (4¼-cup) preserving jar or container. Add the whole garlic cloves and chilli peppers. Pour the pickling liquid over the vegetables. Using clean tongs or hands, mix gently to ensure the vegetables are evenly coated. Tightly seal the jar or container; the pickles will be ready in about 1 week.

## FERMENTED YOUNG JACKFRUIT (CENTRAL VIETNAMESE STYLE)

*Nhút Thanh Chương*

This traditional fermented method, from Thanh Chương, Nghệ An province, works best with Vietnamese jackfruit harvested in March and April, though you can also use Thai jackfruit, which will have a shorter preservation time. With this *nhút* you can make Fermented Young Jackfruit Salad from Thanh Chuong (page 134), Stir-fried Fermented Young Jackfruit (page 333), or simply stir fry it with pork belly (side). Choose young, firm jackfruit with a white interior and that are not fully yellow; the seeds should be underdeveloped enough to cut through.

Serves 12–25
Preparation time: 1 hour
Fermentation time: 7 days

| V | VE | DF | GF | ≤5 |

1 × 3-kg/6-lb 8-oz whole young jackfruit (see note, page 333)
60 g/2¼ oz (⅓ cup) coarse (kosher) sea salt
350 ml/12 fl oz (1½ cups) mineral water

Wearing gloves to protect your hands from the jackfruit sap, carefully use a sharp knife to peel the outer skin of the jackfruit. Using a grater, grate the jackfruit flesh into thin strips, removing the seeds and the fibrous skin around them using a metal skewer as you grate. You should end up with 1.25 kg/2 lb 12 oz of shredded jackfruit. ❋ In a large bowl, combine the shredded jackfruit with the salt. Mix thoroughly to ensure the salt is evenly distributed. ❋ Transfer the salted jackfruit mixture to a 3-litre/102-oz (3-quart) sterilized glass jar. With clean gloves, press down firmly to compact the jackfruit. ❋ Add the mineral water. Place ceramic plates or weights on top to keep the jackfruit submerged, then seal the jar. Let it ferment at room temperature for a minimum of 7 days before eating: the jackfruit will become lighter in colour and should taste tangy like sauerkraut. ❋ If using Thai jackfruit, it will keep in the refrigerator for 1 month; if using Vietnamese jackfruit, it will keep in a cool, dark place for up to 1 year.

---

## PICKLED DRAGON BAMBOO SHOOTS

*Măng Chua*

This staple fermented dish is often used in dishes like Pickled Bamboo Shoot Soup (page 376) or Braised Pork Belly with Pickled Bamboo Shoots (page 304). It can also be simply seasoned with more fish sauce, chopped chilli and garlic, to serve as a side dish.

Makes approx. 1.2 kg/2 lb 12 oz; serves: 8–10 as a side dish
Preparation time: 30 minutes, plus overnight soaking time
Fermentation time: 7 days minimum

| V | VE | DF | GF | ≤5 |

1.6 kg/3 lb 8 oz fresh dragon bamboo shoots (măng mạnh tông)
65 g/2¼ oz (4½ tablespoons) fine salt
5 bird's eye chillies

Place the bamboo shoots in a large bowl of water. Remove the roots and leaves and wash the shoots. Drain, and set aside roots and leaves for other uses. You should have about 1.5 kg/3 lb 4 oz after cleaning. ❋ Trim the shoots and peel off the outer layers, then thinly slice the cleaned shoots. You should have approximately 1.16 kg/2 lb 9 oz sliced bamboo shoots. ❋ In a large container, combine 1.5 litres/2½ pints (6¼ cups) of water with 40 g/1½ oz (3 tablespoons) of the salt. Stir with spoon until the salt dissolves. Add the sliced bamboo shoots, ensuring the shoots are fully submerged, and soak overnight to remove the bitterness. After soaking, drain completely using a colander. ❋ In a sterilized 5-litre/175-oz (21½-cup) container, combine 1.5 litres/2½ pints (6¼ cups) of fresh water with the remaining salt. Stir until the salt completely dissolves. Add the chillies and the soaked bamboo shoots. To ensure the bamboo shoots are fully submerged, you can place a ceramic plate on top. ❋ Let pickle for at least 7 days at room temperature before consuming; it should have a tanginess to it (similar to sauerkraut). If it is getting too sour for your taste, move the jar to the refrigerator to slow down the fermentation.

---

## BASIC DIPPING FISH SAUCE

*Nước Mắm Chấm*

A versatile dipping sauce to keep in your store cupboard, this sauce is more of a Southern-style one with a lighter and sweeter note than the Northern-style Fish Sauce (page 471), perfect to accompany Mini Savoury Pancakes (page 416) or Fresh Summer Rolls (page 40). You can pair this with a big plate of *rau sống* (herb salad) and Pickled Daikon and Carrots (page 468) to cut through the greasiness of the fried items. This dipping sauce is looser and has a milder fish sauce flavour than the Sweet and Sour Fish Sauce (page 471).

Makes 450 ml/15 fl oz (scant 2 cups); serves 8–10
Preparation time: 10 minutes, plus 15–20 minutes cooling time
Cooking time: 5 minutes

| DF | ≤30 |

300 ml/10 fl oz (1¼ cups) coconut water
100 g/3½ oz light brown sugar
3 tablespoons fish sauce
2 tablespoons rice vinegar
30 g/1 oz garlic, minced
15 g/½ oz red chilli (about 1), deseeded and minced, plus 10 g/¼ oz minced, optional, for extra heat

In a small saucepan, combine the coconut water and sugar. Place over a medium heat and bring to a simmer, stirring occasionally with a wooden spoon until the sugar completely dissolves, 2–3 minutes. Remove the saucepan from the heat and let it cool for 3–4 minutes. ❋ Add the fish sauce and rice vinegar to the coconut water mixture, stirring well to combine. Add the garlic and chilli (including the optional extra chilli, if using) to the sauce. Stir well to evenly distribute all the ingredients. Let the sauce cool completely to room temperature, 15–20 minutes, before serving. ❋ Transfer the sauce to a clean, airtight container and store in the refrigerator for 1 week.

## NORTHERN-STYLE FISH SAUCE

*Nước Mắm Chấm Kiểu Bắc*

This Northern-style dipping sauce is lighter in flavour than the Basic Dipping Fish Sauce (page 470), and has more liquid in it to balance the subtleness of the dishes usually served alongside it. In some places, vendors replace the hot water with pork stock (broth) to add an additional depth of flavour to it. Or they add grilled and cut *cà cuống* (*Lethocerus indicus*), a prized water bug, known for its floral and fruity essence. Unlike the southern-style sauce, this doesn't particularly need garlic nor chilli, as it's often served alongside Hanoi-style Chilli Sauce (page 477) or Pickled Kohlrabi and Carrots (page 469).

Makes about 180 ml/6 fl oz (¾ cup); serves 4–6
Preparation time: 10 minutes

| DF | ≤5 | ≤30 |

120 ml/4 fl oz (½ cup) hot water (or pork stock/broth)
30 g/1 oz (2 tablespoons) sugar
2 tablespoons fish sauce
2 tablespoons vinegar (preferably rice vinegar)
15 g/½ oz chilli (about 1), finely minced, optional (see note)

In a mixing bowl, combine the measured hot water (or pork stock/broth, if using) and sugar. Stir with a spoon until the sugar completely dissolves, about 1 minute. ❋ Add the fish sauce and vinegar to the bowl. Stir well to combine. Add the chilli and stir to evenly distribute. Let the sauce stand for at least 5 minutes before serving to allow the flavours to develop. ❋ Pour the sauce into small dipping bowls to serve.

***Notes:*** This is great to serve alongside Steamed Rice Rolls (page 403), with Fresh Rice Noodle Rolls (page 38), Deep-fried Phở Nest with Egg (page 188), fried cakes like Pillow-Shaped Cakes (page 414) or Mountain-style Fried Rice Cakes (page 412), or added to Pickled Kohlrabi and Carrots (page 469). ❋ For a milder sauce, remove the seeds and white membrane from the chilli before mincing.

---

## SWEET AND SOUR FISH SAUCE

*Nước Mắm Chua Ngọt*

This versatile dipping sauce is specially crafted to complement Grilled Pork with Rice Noodles (page 145), Broken Rice (page 270) or Crab/Prawn Spring Rolls (page 116). The difference between this and Basic Dipping Fish Sauce (page 470) is that this version is cooked longer, making it more syrupy.

Makes approx. 150 g/5½ oz; serves 6–8
Preparation time: 5 minutes
Cooking time: 10 minutes, plus 20 minutes resting and cooling times

| DF | ≤5 | ≤30 |

180 ml/6 fl oz (¾ cup) coconut water
30 g/1 oz (2 tablespoons) light brown sugar, or more to taste
50 ml/2 fl oz (⅓ cup) fish sauce, or more to taste
4 teaspoons lime juice, or more to taste
15 g/½ oz long red chilli, deseeded and finely chopped

In a small pot, combine the coconut water and sugar over a medium-low heat. Use a spoon to stir until the sugar is completely dissolved. Bring the mixture to a simmer and allow it to simmer for about 5 minutes to reduce the liquid. For the standard version, you should have about 150 g/5½ oz of liquid remaining. For broken rice, reduce it further until you have about 120 g/4¼ oz. Remove the pot from the heat and let it cool slightly for 5–10 minutes. ❋ Add the fish sauce and lime juice to the cooled sugar syrup. Stir well to combine. Add a small amount of the chilli to the sauce, reserving the rest. ❋ Taste the sauce and adjust the flavours if needed: for more saltiness, add more fish sauce; for more acidity, add more lime juice; for more sweetness, add a bit more sugar. Gradually add more chopped chilli to reach your desired level of spiciness. Remember, you can always add more, but you can't take it out once it's in. ❋ Let the sauce sit for at least 10 minutes before serving to allow the flavours to meld. ❋ Serve alongside your chosen dish as a dipping sauce or dressing. You can store any leftover sauce in the refrigerator for up to 1 week.

---

## DIPPING SAUCE FOR BOILED VEGETABLES

*Nước Mắm Chấm Rau Luộc*

During hot summers, or when food is sparse, a simple dish of boiled vegetables can make a significant difference to a meal. The uses for this dish can range from accompanying boiled morning glory (and using its cooking water, in Morning Glory Boiled Water, Northern-style, page 354) to simple boiled cabbage served with this sauce. To accompany boiled greens, or if vegetables are scarce, you can mash a whole boiled egg into the sauce to add protein to the meal. This variation is then called *nước mắm trứng* – dipping sauce with boiled eggs.

Makes 120 ml/4 fl oz (½ cup); serves 2–3
Preparation time: 15 minutes

| DF | ≤5 | ≤30 |

20 g/¾ oz garlic, minced
3 bird's eye chillies, minced
3 teaspoons sugar
75 ml/2½ fl oz (⅓ cup) fish sauce
juice of 1 lime (2 tablespoons)
4 tablespoons hot water or cabbage cooking water

In a small mixing bowl, combine the garlic, chillies, sugar, fish sauce and lime juice. Add the measured hot water or vegetable cooking water. Using a spoon, stir until the sugar completely dissolves, about 1 minute. ❋ Serve as a dipping sauce for boiled vegetables.

*For nước mắm trứng variation*
Prepare the sauce as above and divide into individual serving bowls. Add one peeled, hard-boiled egg to each bowl. Using a fork, mash the egg into the sauce until well combined but still slightly chunky. Serve as a protein-fuelled dipping sauce or eat it with plain white rice.

***Note:*** For less heat, remove the seeds from the chillies before mincing.

## LEMONGRASS AND CHILLI DIPPING SAUCE (SOUTHERN STYLE)

*Mắm Sả Ớt Nam*

This versatile Southern-style sauce pairs perfectly with seafood, including Steamed Clams with Lemongrass (page 86). Unlike its Northern-style counterpart (see below), this version is a little bit thicker and sweeter. It also doesn't use calamansi or lime leaves, but lime juice instead.

Makes approx. 120 ml/4 fl oz (½ cup)
Preparation time: 15 minutes

| DF | ≤30 |

15 g/½ oz garlic, coarsely chopped
5 g/1/8 oz long red chilli, deseeded and coarsely chopped
10 g/¼ oz lemongrass, finely chopped
1 tablespoon sugar
1 tablespoon lime juice, or more to taste
4 teaspoons fish sauce, or more to taste
1 tablespoon hot water, optional

Put the garlic, chilli, and lemongrass in a mortar and pound with a pestle until they form a rough paste. Transfer the paste to a bowl. ❋ Add the sugar, lime juice and fish sauce to the bowl with the paste and mix thoroughly. Adjust the seasoning according to taste, adding more lime juice or fish sauce if necessary. Add the optional measured hot water if you want the sauce to be a bit looser. ❋ Serve or transfer the sauce to a clean, airtight container. Refrigerate and use within 1 week for best flavour.

---

## LEMONGRASS AND CHILLI DIPPING SAUCE (NORTHERN STYLE)

*Mắm Sả Ớt Bắc*

The Northern-style version of this sauce is a bit looser than the Southern-style (above) but has two extra components that make it extremely aromatic: slices of calamansi and lime leaves. It's a perfect match for steamed or boiled seafood.

Makes approx. 250 ml/8 fl oz (1 cup)
Preparation time: 15 minutes

| DF | ≤30 |

25 g/1 oz long red chilli, deseeded and cut into 3-cm/1¼-inch pieces
25 g/1 oz lemongrass, thinly sliced in rounds
15 g/½ oz piece fresh ginger, sliced
15 g/½ oz peeled garlic
1½ tablespoons sugar
110 ml/3½ fl oz (scant ½ cup) hot water
2 tablespoons fish sauce
¼ teaspoon salt
1 tablespoon calamansi juice
4 calamansi, sliced into rounds
5 g/⅛ oz (about 12 medium) lime leaves, finely sliced

In a mortar, combine the chilli, just less than half the lemongrass, the ginger and the whole garlic. Using a pestle, pound all the ingredients together until they form a rough paste. ❋ In a separate bowl, combine the remaining lemongrass with the sugar, measured hot water, fish sauce, salt and calamansi juice. Stir until the sugar and salt are fully dissolved. ❋ Add the pounded aromatic paste to the sauce base. Mix well to combine all the ingredients. Add the sliced calamansi rounds to the sauce. Stir in the lime leaves, then serve. ❋ Transfer the sauce to a clean, airtight container. Refrigerate and use within 1 week for best flavour.

---

## SEASONED VEGETARIAN FISH SAUCE

*Nước Mắm Chay*

This is a vegetarian alternative to traditional fish sauce, often used in Vietnamese cuisine for those following a plant-based diet or for those who prefer a milder taste. You can serve it with Vegan Pork Skin Rolls (page 36) and Lemongrass Fried Tofu (page 282).

Makes approx. 120 ml/4 fl oz (½ cup); serves: 4–6
Preparation time: 10 minutes

| V | VE | DF | GF | ≤30 |

10 g/¼ oz peeled garlic
15 g/½ oz chilli (about 1), stemmed and deseeded
85 ml/3 fl oz (⅓ cup) coconut water
½ teaspoon calamansi juice
1 tablespoon vinegar, or more to taste
½ teaspoon salt
1 teaspoon brown sugar, or more to taste
½ teaspoon caster (superfine) sugar, or more to taste

Blitz the garlic and chilli together in a food processor or finely mince by hand. ❋ In a small mixing bowl, mix the blitzed garlic and chilli mixture with the coconut water, calamansi juice and vinegar. Add the salt, brown sugar and caster (superfine) sugar to the mixture. Using a spoon, stir well until all the ingredients are fully combined and sugars are dissolved. ❋ Taste the sauce and adjust the seasoning if needed. You may want to add more sugar for sweetness or vinegar for tanginess, depending on your preference. ❋ Transfer the sauce to a clean, airtight container. Refrigerate and use within 1 week for best flavour.

---

## DRACONTOMELON FISH SAUCE DIP

*Nước Mắm Dầm Sấu*

*Quả sấu* (dracontomelon) is a small fruit that appears during the summertime and is known for its sour and tart taste. It is often soaked in sugar to create a syrup that can be enjoyed with soda during the hottest time of the year. In Northern-style cooking, *sấu* is commonly used as a dipping sauce or incorporated into dishes like the simple Morning Glory Boiled Water (Northern Style) (page 354), or in broth and noodles.

Makes approx. 50 ml/2 fl oz (3½ tablespoons); serves 2–3
Preparation time: 5 minutes

| DF | ≤5 | ≤30 |

1 dracontomelon fruit (sấu), cooked (see page 354)
5 bird's eye chillies, or to taste, thinly sliced
4 teaspoons fish sauce

Place the cooked dracontomelon fruit in a small mortar or serving bowl. Using a pestle or fork, crush the fruit until it breaks down into a rough paste. ❋ Add the chillies to the crushed dracontomelon. Pour in the fish sauce. Using a spoon, thoroughly mix all the ingredients until well combined. ❊ Transfer the sauce to a clean, airtight container. Refrigerate and use within 3 days for best flavour.

---

## HUẾ-STYLE DIPPING SAUCE FOR SAVOURY CAKES

*Nước Mắm Bánh Kiểu Huế*

Different regions will have different ways to make their dipping sauce for savoury cakes, but I learned this recipe from Công Huyền Tôn Nữ Bích Hà, the owner of Quán ăn An Tâm, a restaurant in Huế that specializes in Huế-style cakes. The secret to this flavourful sauce is the use of reduced prawn (shrimp) stock (broth), which gives it a savoury taste without the strong flavour of fish sauce. At just a smell you will barely be able to smell the fish sauce. It is perfect for dipping cakes like Crispy Rice Cake with Steamed Rice Dumplings (page 400) or Huế-style Water Fern Cakes (page 396).

Makes 330 g/11½ oz; serves 6–8
Preparation time: 10 minutes
Cooking time: 55 minutes

| DF | ≤5 |

250 g/5½ oz prawns (shrimp)
3 teaspoons fish sauce
20 g/¾ oz (1½ tablespoons) sugar, or less to taste
¼ teaspoon salt

In a saucepan, bring 600 ml/1 pint (2½ cups) water to the boil, then add the prawns (shrimp) and simmer for 11 minutes. Using a sieve, remove the prawns, reserving 500 ml/18 fl oz (2 cups) of the cooking liquid. When cool enough to handle, peel the prawns, reserving the shells and set aside the flesh for other recipes. ❊ In the same saucepan, bring 500 ml/18 fl oz (2 cups) of fresh water to the boil, add the reserved prawn shells, then simmer for 10 minutes. Using a sieve, strain, reserving the cooking liquid. ❊ Combine both the reserved cooking liquids to make 900 ml/30 fl oz (3¾ cups) prawn stock (broth). ❊ In a clean saucepan, bring 400 ml/14 fl oz (1 ⅔ cups) of the prawn stock with 1 teaspoon of the fish sauce to the boil and cook over a medium heat until it has reduced to about 220 ml/7½ fl oz (1 cup), about 10 minutes. ❊ Add 200 ml/7 fl oz (¾ cup plus 1 tablespoon) more stock and 1 teaspoon of the fish sauce. Continue simmering for 10 minutes until the liquid reduces to about 280 ml/9½ fl oz (1 cup). ❊ Add the remaining 300 ml/10 fl oz (1¼ cups) stock and 1 teaspoon of fish sauce. Cook for 12–13 minutes until you have about 330 ml/11 fl oz (1⅓ cup) of sauce left. Add the sugar (or to taste) and salt. Transfer to a bowl and let cool completely before serving. ❊ Transfer the sauce to a clean, airtight container. Refrigerate and use within 3 days for best flavour.

## STICKY RICE AND PORK DIPPING SAUCE

*Nước Chấm Nem Nướng*

This sauce is usually served with *nem nướng* grilled pork patties (see page 142) in the region of Ninh Hòa and Nha Trang, coastal towns in Khánh Hòa province, but can also be eaten with *bánh khoái* (Huế-style Savoury Pancakes, page 418) or *bánh xèo* (pancakes). What sets it apart is the use of sticky (glutinous) rice as a thickener, giving the sauce a rich, clingy consistency. There is another popular version of this sauce, which uses minced (ground) pork liver to enrich further the sauce. It all depends on who cooks it, and usually the vendors keep their sauce recipes secret. Because of its process, it is better to make this in bigger batches than other sauces, and you can easily freeze it for future uses.

Makes 750 ml/25 fl oz (3 cups); serves 15–20
Preparation time: 15 minutes, plus overnight soaking
Cooking time: 20 minutes

| DF |

100 g/3½ oz (½ cup) sticky (glutinous) rice
75 ml/2½ fl oz (1/3 cup) Annatto Oil (page 457)
50 g/1¾ oz shallots, coarsely chopped
40 g/1½ oz garlic, coarsely chopped
1 tablespoon light brown sugar
2 tablespoons fish sauce
¾ teaspoon salt
2 teaspoons all-purpose seasoning (hạt nêm)
50 g/1¾ oz (⅓ cup) Toasted Peanuts (page 459), crushed

***For the marinated pork***
100 g/3½ oz minced (ground) pork
115 g/4 oz prawns (shrimp), peeled and chopped
15 g/½ oz garlic, coarsely chopped
15 g/½ oz shallot, coarsely chopped
1 teaspoon sugar
1 tablespoon fish sauce

In a bowl, soak the rice in 150 ml/5 fl oz (⅔ cup) of water. Cover and leave at room temperature overnight. ❊ The next day, drain the soaked rice and place it in a blender or food processor with 700 ml/24 fl oz (scant 3 cups) fresh water. Blend on high speed for 1–2 minutes until you achieve a smooth paste. Set aside. ❊ To prepare the marinated pork, in a bowl, combine the minced (ground) pork, prawns (shrimp), garlic, shallots, sugar and fish sauce. Mix well with a spoon and set aside. ❊ Heat a large, heavy saucepan or wok over a medium-low heat. Add 4 tablespoons of the oil. Once hot (after about 1 minute), add the shallots and garlic. Fry for about 1 minute, stirring constantly with a wooden spoon, until fragrant and translucent but not browned. Add the marinated pork mixture to the pan. Cook for 3 minutes, until the meat is no longer pink and the prawns turn orange. ❊ Pour in the blended rice mixture, stirring constantly to prevent lumps forming. Bring to a gentle boil, then reduce the heat to low. Simmer for 15 minutes, stirring frequently to prevent sticking, until the sauce has thickened enough to coat the back of a spoon. ❊ Add the brown sugar, fish sauce, salt, all-purpose seasoning and the remaining oil. Stir well. Taste and adjust seasonings if needed. Stir in the crushed toasted peanuts just before serving. ❊ Transfer the sauce to a clean, airtight container. Refrigerate and use within 3 days for best flavour. It can also be kept up to 3 months in the freezer.

## CALAMANSI FISH SAUCE

*Nước Mắm Tắc*

A great fresh and tangy sauce, accentuated by the flavours of calamansi, a small lime look-a-like cousin with the scent of oranges, and a sweeter taste to lime. In Vietnam it's used for sauces, but also to give acidity to broth and to stir-fried dishes. You can serve the sauce with seafood dishes, like Steamed Clams with Lemongrass (page 86).

Makes 45 ml/1½ fl oz (3 tablespoons)
Preparation time: 15 minutes

| **DF** | ≤**30** |

7 g/¼ oz garlic, minced
1 long chilli (20 g/¾ oz), finely chopped
1 tablespoon calamansi juice
½ teaspoon lime juice
1 tablespoon sugar
1½ teaspoons fish sauce
1 teaspoon crushed peanuts

In a small bowl, combine the garlic and chilli. Add the calamansi juice and lime juice to the bowl and mix well. Stir in the sugar until it is fully dissolved. Add the fish sauce and mix thoroughly. Finally, sprinkle in the crushed peanuts and give it a stir.

---

## GINGER DIPPING FISH SAUCE

*Nước Mắm Gừng*

This is the perfect go-to dipping sauce to accompany poached duck, chicken or even just plainly fried fish. You can serve this with Chicken and Banana Blossom Salad (page 128) or Hội An Chicken Rice (page 263). It is a very versatile sauce but needs to have a good balance between the sweetness of the sugar, acidity of the lime, saltiness of the fish sauce and a good kick from the ginger.

Makes 150 ml/5 fl oz (⅔ cup)
Preparation time: 15 minutes
Cooking time: 15 minutes

| **DF** |

30 g/1 oz piece fresh ginger (about 6 cm/2½ inches), peeled
30 g/1 oz garlic, minced
20 g/¾ oz long red chilli, deseeded and minced
2 tablespoons plus 1 teaspoon sugar
65 ml/2 fl oz (¼ cup) fish sauce
2 tablespoons lime juice

Cut a third off the ginger and cut it into thin matchsticks (julienne). Reserve for the garnish. Put the remaining ginger into a mortar and pound with a pestle to mince it. ✻ In a bowl, combine the garlic and chilli with the pounded ginger. Add the sugar, fish sauce and lime juice to the bowl. Mix well until the sugar is completely dissolved. ✻ Garnish with the reserved julienned ginger before serving.

## TAMARIND SHRIMP PASTE SAUCE

*Nước Mắm Tôm Me*

This recipe adds tamarind to the traditional Northern Vietnamese shrimp paste sauce, bringing a tangy flavour from the South. The result is a versatile sauce that works well with Rice Field Crab Noodle Soup (page 220), Rice Noodle Soup (page 221) and Snail Noodle Soup (page 218). It's also great for dipping dry grilled fish.

Makes approx. 125 ml/4¼ fl oz (generous ½ cup); serves 4–6
Preparation time: 10 minutes
Cooking time: 3–4 minutes

| **DF** | **GF** | ≤**30** |

40 g/1½ oz Hanoi-style fermented shrimp paste (mắm tôm)
1 teaspoon neutral oil
60 g/2¼ oz tamarind paste
1 teaspoon sugar
10 g/¼ oz garlic clove, minced
1 bird's eye chilli, minced

In a small bowl, using a spoon, mix the shrimp paste with 2 tablespoons of water until well combined and slightly loosened. ✻ Place a small saucepan over a medium heat. Add the oil and heat it up for about 30 seconds. Add the shrimp paste mixture to the pan. Cook for 1 minute, stirring constantly with a spoon. Add the tamarind paste and sugar and continue cooking for another 1 minute, stirring constantly to prevent sticking and to ensure the sugar completely dissolves. Add the garlic and chilli and cook for 30–45 seconds more, stirring constantly, until aromatic. ✻ Remove from heat and let cool for 5 minutes before serving.

---

## NORTHERN VIETNAMESE SPICE MIX

*Chẩm Chéo*

*Chẩm chéo* is a traditional spice mix used for grilled or boiled meats. Found throughout the mountain communities, its recipe varies from region to region. This version comes from Chị Trieu of the Red Dao community in Hồ Thầu, Hà Giang. She keeps the pre-made mix in a jar, taking out a few spoonfuls when needed and diluting them with soup broth before serving. Thanks to the cool mountain weather, the jar can be stored for an extended period. You can use any kind of chillies you have in hand, from dried to fresh ones.

Makes approx. 3–4 tablespoons (15–20 g/¾ oz)
Preparation time: 10 minutes

| **DF** | **GF** | ≤**30** |

3–4 g green bird's eye chillies (about 7 small), stemmed and chopped
1 teaspoon salt
¼ teaspoon MSG
1½ teaspoons Indian prickly ash (mắc khén)
½ teaspoon Michelia tonkinensi (also called magnolia seeds; hạt dổi), smashed
4 g lime leaves (2–4 leaves), thinly sliced

*To serve*
3–4 tablespoons lime juice
4–8 tablespoons stock (broth) or water

Place the chillies, salt, MSG, Indian prickly ash and magnolia seeds in a mortar. Using a pestle, grind all the ingredients together using a circular motion until well combined and the spices are finely ground, 2–3 minutes. ❋ Remove the central stalk from the lime leaves. Stack the leaves, roll them tightly and slice into very fine ribbons (chiffonade). Add the sliced lime leaves to the mortar and gently mix with the spice mixture using the pestle, until evenly distributed. ❋ Transfer the spice mix to a clean, dry, airtight jar. It will keep to 1 week. ❋ To serve, for each portion, combine 1 tablespoon of the spice mix with 1 tablespoon of lime juice, then add 1–2 tablespoons of stock (broth)or water (depending on desired strength), stirring until well combined. Serve with your dish.

---

## CHINESE CHIVES PASTE

*Chẻo Hẹ*

In Hoa Tiến, a village in Quỳ Châu, Nghệ An province, there's a village of the Black Thai Community where cô Sầm Thị Bích and chị Sầm Thị Lương reside. They've been preserving their culture through their village and craftsmanship in brocade weaving. Here, *chẻo* refers to pounding ingredients using a mortar and pestle to create a dipping sauce. This version is traditionally eaten with sticky (glutinous) rice. A variant called *chẻo măng* uses pickled bamboo shoots, and *chẻo môn*, dried taro leaves.

Serves 4–6
Preparation time: 20 minutes
Cooking time: 40 minutes

| DF |

1 × 120-g/4¼-oz whole mackerel
380 g/13 oz Chinese chives (lá hẹ)
15 g/½ oz castor seeds (hạt thầu dầu) (or substitute with 1½ tablespoons Toasted Peanuts, page 459)
10 g/¼ oz red chilli (about 1)
50 g/1¾ oz dried taro leaves
2 teaspoons soup powder (bột canh), or more to taste
1 teaspoon MSG, or more to taste
1½ teaspoons all-purpose seasoning (hạt nêm), or more to taste

Preheat a barbecue grill. ❋ Place the mackerel inside a metal wire mesh grilling basket and then grill over the embers for 15–20 minutes until it's fully cooked through but not burned, flipping every two minutes to make sure it is evenly cooked. ❋ Alternatively, preheat the oven grill (broiler) to high heat (180°C/350°F). Place the mackerel on a grill (broiler) pan and grill (broil) under the heat for about 15 minutes, flipping the fish halfway through. ❋ Allow the grilled fish to cool. Pick the meat from the bones. You should have about 65 g/2¼ oz mackerel meat. ❋ Spread the chives evenly over a metal grilling rack. Grill over indirect heat for 20 minutes, flipping every 3 minutes to prevent burning. Cook until dry but not charred. Then cut the grilled chives into 5-cm/2-inch pieces. Set aside. ❋ In a mortar, combine the castor seeds or toasted peanuts, chilli and picked mackerel meat. Pound with the pestle until a paste forms. Add the grilled chives, dried taro leaves and all the seasonings. Pound until a smooth paste forms. Adjust seasonings to taste.

## CARAMELIZED PORK DIP

*Kho Quẹt*

This Southern Vietnamese pork dip is traditionally served with boiled vegetables, scorched rice or plain steamed rice. *Kho quẹt* features a perfect balance of caramelized sweetness and saltiness, which complements its simple accompaniments. Due to its intense flavour, a small portion goes a long way, making it an economical choice, particularly during difficult times. While the traditional version uses only pork rinds, historically the most affordable cut and the one that can be kept the longest, modern preparations, including our recipe, often include pork belly (side) for enhanced flavour and texture.

Makes 240 ml/8 fl oz (1 cup)
Preparation time: 15 minutes
Cooking time: 40 minutes

| DF |

200 g/7 oz pork belly (side), diced into 1-cm/½-inch cubes
2 tablespoons pork lard
30 g/1 oz shallots, minced
10 g/¼ oz garlic, minced
4 teaspoons sugar
3 tablespoons fish sauce
125 ml/4 fl oz (½ cup) coconut water
½ teaspoon black pepper
6 green bird's eye chillies
2 red bird's eye chillies
100 g/3½ oz Crispy Fried Pork Fat (page 459)

Heat a pan over a medium-low heat, then add the pork belly (side) to the pan and cook for 3 minutes. Add the pork lard and fry for another 5 minutes. Add the shallots and garlic to the pan. Fry for an additional 5 minutes until everything is golden. Add the sugar and fish sauce to the pan. ❋ Pour in the coconut water. Simmer for 20–25 minutes until the liquid has reduced and the pork is glazed. The colour should turn into a light caramel colour, and the sauce should look glossy with the fat separating. ❋ Stir in the black pepper. Add the green and red chillies. Top with the crispy fried pork fat. Stir gently to combine. Remove from the heat. ❋ Serve hot with steamed rice and/or boiled vegetables, like boiled okra, daikon, carrots or broccoli.

## TAMARIND DIPPING SAUCE

*Mắm Me*

This sauce is perfect for grilled meats, like Grilled Snakehead Fish with Spring Onion Oil (page 162), or steamed seafood, or you can use it as a dressing for the Mango and Dried Fish Salad (page 130).

Makes 240 ml/8 fl oz (1 cup); serves 4
Preparation time: 15–25 minutes

| DF | ≤5 | ≤30 |

60 g/2¼ oz tamarind pulp (or 125 g/4¼ oz tamarind paste)
135 ml/4½ fl oz (generous ½ cup) hot water, optional
3 tablespoons sugar, or more to taste
2 tablespoons plus 1 teaspoon fish sauce, or more to taste
60 g/2¼ oz garlic, minced
15 g/½ oz long red chillies, deseeded and minced

If using tamarind pulp, in a bowl, combine the pulp with 85 ml/3 fl oz (⅓ cup) of the measured hot water. Let it stand for 5 minutes until softened. Using your fingers or a spoon, work the pulp to separate it from the seeds. Pass the mixture through a fine-mesh sieve into a bowl, pressing with the back of a spoon to extract as much paste as possible. You should get approximately 60 g/2¼ oz of smooth tamarind paste. ❋ Add the remaining measured hot water to the remaining pulp in the sieve. Press again with the back of a spoon to extract about 65 g/2¼ oz more tamarind paste. Combine both extractions to get approximately 125 g/4¼ oz total tamarind paste. ❋ In a mixing bowl, combine the tamarind paste (homemade or pre-prepared), 3 tablespoons of the sugar and 2 tablespoons plus 1 teaspoon fish sauce. Add the garlic and chillies to the bowl. Mix thoroughly with a spoon until all the ingredients are well combined. ❋ Taste and adjust the seasoning if needed: stir in 1 additional teaspoon of fish sauce for more saltiness and/or ½ teaspoon of sugar for more sweetness.

## SEASONED FERMENTED SHRIMP PASTE DIPPING SAUCE

*Mắm Tôm Chấm*

In Hanoi, people use this sauce with Rice Noodles with Fried Tofu and Shrimp Paste (page 207) and Hanoi-style Fish with Turmeric and Dill (page 230).

Makes approx. 70 ml/2½ fl oz (scant ⅓ cup); serves 2–3
Preparation time: 5 minutes

| DF | GF | ≤5 | ≤30 |

40 g/1½ oz Hanoi-style fermented shrimp paste (mắm tôm)
2 teaspoons light brown sugar
20 g/¾ oz lime juice (about 1 medium lime)
10 g/¼ oz bird's eye chillies (about 4 chillies), finely chopped

In a small mixing bowl, add the shrimp paste and sugar and pour in the lime juice. Using a spoon, stir vigorously in one direction. Continue stirring for 2–3 minutes until the mixture starts to foam slightly and the colour becomes lighter and more opaque. ❋ Add the finely chopped chillies to the sauce. Gently stir to evenly distribute chillies. ❋ Let the sauce stand for 2–3 minutes to allow flavours to meld. Give one final stir before serving. Store any leftovers in the refrigerator.

## SEASONED FERMENTED THICK FISH SAUCE

*Mắm Nêm*

*Mắm nêm* is part of the complex array of fermented sauces found in Vietnam. Made from a variety of sea fish, its origins date back to the Champa Kingdom (second century–1832). This historical connection explains why many dishes using this dipping sauce originate from Central Vietnam, an area once part of the Champa kingdom before the Tran dynasty's arrival (1225–1400). Today, *mắm nêm* is versatile in Vietnamese cuisine, and it can be used as a condiment, dipping sauce or ingredient in various dishes, including: Smashed Rice Cracker (page 33), Rice Noodles with Pork and Fermented Thick Fish Sauce (page 216), Grilled Snakehead Fish with Spring Onion Oil (page 162) and Grilled Beef in Piper Lolot Leaf (page 144).

Makes approx. 240 ml/8 fl oz (1 cup); serves 8–10
Preparation time: 10 minutes

| DF | GF | ≤30 |

20 g/¾ oz garlic, finely minced
15 g/½ oz long red chilli, deseeded and finely minced
130 g/4½ oz pineapple, cored and finely minced
60 g/2¼ oz fermented anchovy sauce (mắm nêm)
1 tablespoon sugar, or more to taste
1 tablespoon lime juice, or more to taste

In a mixing bowl, combine the garlic, chilli and pineapple. Add the fermented anchovy sauce, sugar and lime juice to the bowl. Using a spoon or fork, mix all the ingredients thoroughly until well combined and the sugar has dissolved completely, about 1 minute. ❋ Taste and adjust the seasoning if needed: add more sugar for sweetness or lime juice for tartness, mixing well after each addition. ❋ Transfer the finished sauce to an airtight container and refrigerate for up to 1 week until ready to use.

## FERMENTED TOFU SAUCE

*Sốt Chao*

This vegetarian sauce is excellent with fried tofu, hotpots, grilled meats or simply with boiled vegetables. Fermented tofu and its derivatives likely arrived in Northern Vietnam from China at the earliest in the tenth century, gaining mainstream popularity across the whole country in the eighteenth century when their use was officially documented in published dictionaries. Since then, these products have become essential, particularly in vegetarian dishes, adding an extra kick of umami flavour. This sauce is used in Fermented Tofu Hotpot (page 177) and Barramundi and Taro Hotpot (page 173).

Makes 80 ml/2¾ fl oz (⅓ cup); serves 4
Preparation time: 5 minutes

| V | VE | DF | GF | ≤30 |

35 g/1¼ oz cube fermented tofu (chao)
2½ tablespoons liquid from fermented tofu (chao)
10 g/¼ oz (2 teaspoons) Chilli and Lemongrass Oil (page 457)
4 bird's eye chillies, finely chopped
1 teaspoon sugar
Juice of 2 calamansi (about ½ tablespoon), or more to taste

In a small mixing bowl, place the fermented tofu cube. Using a fork or spoon, mash the fermented tofu until it becomes a rough paste. ❋ Add the fermented tofu liquid to the mashed fermented tofu. Mix thoroughly with a spoon until you achieve a smooth, sauce-like consistency. Add the chilli and lemongrass oil and chillies to the bowl. Add the sugar and mix well until it dissolves completely. ❋ Squeeze the calamansi juice into the mixture, straining out any seeds, if needed. Stir all ingredients thoroughly until well combined. ❋ Taste and adjust the acidity according to your personal preferences by adding more calamansi juice if desired. ❋ Divide into small serving bowls.

*Note:* This fermented tofu sauce adds depth of flavour to various dishes. Feel free to adjust the ingredients to suit your taste preferences.

---

## HANOI-STYLE CHILLI SAUCE

*Tương Ớt Hà Nội*

Common in Northern Vietnam where vendors make their own versions, this fresh chilli sauce differs from the bottled commercial varieties found in the south. Less thick and glossy, it leans towards a sour and garlicky profile. It's often paired with Phở with Quickly Stir-fried Beef (page 184) or can be added to dipping sauces for Pillow-Shaped Cakes (page 414).You can keep a jar of it in the refrigerator for 2–3 weeks.

Makes approx. 150 g/5½ oz
Preparation time: 15 minutes
Cooking time: 10 minutes

| V | VE | DF | GF | ≤30 |

100 g/3½ oz long red chillies, deseeded
15 g/½ oz garlic, peeled
50 g/1¾ oz tomatoes, quartered and deseeded
4 teaspoons vinegar
1 tablespoon neutral oil
½ teaspoon salt
½ teaspoon MSG

Place all the ingredients in a blender. Blend until smooth and well combined. ❋ Transfer the mixture to a saucepan. Cook over a medium heat for about 10 minutes, stirring occasionally, or until the sauce thickens to your desired consistency. The sauce is ready when it coats the back of a spoon. The colour should be bright red-orange. ❋ Let it cool completely at room temperature. Transfer to a clean, airtight container and store in the refrigerator for 1–2 weeks until ready to serve.

---

## DIPPING SAUCE FOR SUMMER ROLLS

*Tương Gỏi Cuốn*

Another type of dipping sauce that you can find in Vietnam, is this vegan sauce made using *tương bần*, fermented soybean sauce, and it is perfect for dipping Fresh Summer Rolls (page 40) or Vegan Pork Skin Rolls (page 36). You can use hoisin sauce instead if the fermented soybean sauce is not available in your area.

Makes approx. 240 ml/8 fl oz (1 cup)
Preparation time: 5–7 minutes
Cooking time: 6–8 minutes

| V | VE | DF | ≤30 |

100 g/3½ oz fermented soybean sauce (tương bần)
2 teaspoons sugar
30 g/1 oz (2 tablespoons) coconut milk
1 tablespoon neutral oil
15 g/½ oz shallot, minced
10 g/¼ oz garlic, minced
1 tablespoon hot water

***To serve***
15 g/½ oz (1½ tablespoons) toasted peanuts (page 459), crushed
10 g/¼ oz chilli (about 1), minced, optional

In a blender or food processor, combine the fermented soybean sauce and sugar. Blend on high speed for 30 seconds or until smooth. Add the coconut milk and 1 tablespoon of water to the blender. Blend again until well combined. Set aside. ❋ Heat the oil in a small saucepan over a medium-low heat for about 30 seconds. Add the shallot and garlic to the pan. Cook for 2–3 minutes, stirring constantly with a wooden spoon, until they start to turn golden but not brown (about 70 per cent golden). ❋ Pour the blended soybean mixture into the pan. Stir well to combine. Cook for another 3 minutes, stirring frequently, until the sauce is well heated through and looks glossy. Add the measured hot water to loosen the sauce to your desired consistency. Stir well to incorporate. Transfer the sauce to a serving bowl and let cool for 5 minutes. ❋ Just before serving, top with the crushed toasted peanuts. If using, add the minced chillies on top, or serve on the side.

## YOUNG TAMARIND AND SHRIMP SAUCE

*Muối Me Non*

This unique recipe originates from the Khmer community in Trà Vinh province, in Southern Vietnam. It's a seasonal delicacy typically prepared in July when young, wild tamarind is tender enough to be eaten with its shell. This dish beautifully combines the tartness of young tamarind with the sweetness of glazed shrimp, creating a complex flavour profile that's both refreshing and satisfying. Another dish that Sister Sa Quan, the neighbour of our homestay, taught us during our visit. You can eat this simply with rice, or as a side dish to a meal.

Makes 250 g/5½ oz (1 cup); serves 2–3
Preparation time: 15 minutes
Cooking time: 10 minutes

| DF | ≤30 |

75 g/2¾ oz young tamarind, coarsely sliced
22 g/¾ oz lemongrass, thinly sliced
70 g/2½ oz piece young fresh ginger (about 14 cm/5½ inches), peeled and sliced
1½ teaspoons sugar
1 teaspoon MSG
1 teaspoon fish sauce

***For the stir-fried baby shrimp***
90 g/3¼ oz raw baby shrimp, peeled
1 tablespoon sugar
1 teaspoon MSG
1 teaspoon fish sauce

To make the stir-fried baby shrimp, heat a frying pan or skillet over a medium heat. Add the baby shrimp, sugar, MSG and fish sauce. Cook for 5–7 minutes, stirring frequently with a wooden spoon, until the shrimp are pink, glazed and cooked through. Remove from heat and set aside. ❋ Combine the young tamarind, lemongrass and ginger in a large mortar and pound with a pestle, using firm, downward strokes, until well mashed but still maintaining some texture, 2–3 minutes. ❋ Add the stir-fried baby shrimp to the mortar. Gently pound to combine with the tamarind mixture, being careful not to completely crush the shrimp. Add the sugar, MSG and fish sauce. Using the pestle, mix everything together until well combined, about 1 minute. ❋ Transfer to a serving bowl or airtight container and store in the refrigerator for up to 3 days.

## BASIC DRESSING FOR SALAD

*Nước Mắm Cho Gỏi*

This quintessential and basic dressing is used for salad (*gỏi*), for example in my Lotus Stem Salad (page 125). But you can also keep it in a jar in the refrigerator for 1–2 weeks and use it to dress any salad mix you have at home. It has just the right balance of sweetness, tanginess and heat for all kinds of vegetables, not just Vietnamese ones.

Makes 235 ml/8 fl oz (1 cup); serves 8–10
Preparation time: 15 mins

| DF | ≤5 | ≤30 |

35 g/1¼ oz garlic, finely minced
1 long red chilli, deseeded and minced
85 ml/3 fl oz (⅓ cup) fresh lime juice (about 3 limes)
75–100 g/2¾–3½ oz (⅓–½ cup) white sugar
65 ml/2 fl oz (¼ cup) fish sauce

Place the garlic and chilli in a mixing bowl with the lime juice. Add 75 g/2¾ oz of the sugar and the fish sauce to the bowl. Using a spoon, stir the mixture for about 2 minutes, or until the sugar is completely dissolved. ❋ Taste and add more sugar if desired, stirring until dissolved. Use as a dressing for salads.

---

## MAYONNAISE FOR VIETNAMESE BAGUETTES

*Sốt Dầu Trứng Cho Bánh Mì*

This mayonnaise has a subtle sweetness, unlike French versions. If using butter instead of margarine, serve at room temperature to prevent hardening.

Makes approx. 240 ml/8 fl oz (1 cup)
Preparation time: 15–20 minutes

| V | DF | GF | ≤5 | ≤30 |

2 egg yolks (about 40 g/1½ oz), at room temperature
2 teaspoons sugar
½ teaspoon salt
150 g/5½ oz (⅔ cup) oil, margarine or melted butter

In a bowl, combine the egg yolks, sugar and salt. Whisk vigorously for 1–2 minutes until the mixture becomes pale, the sugar completely dissolves and the yolks slightly thicken. ❋ Position your bowl on a damp cloth to prevent sliding. Begin adding the oil in a very thin, steady stream while whisking constantly: start with drops, then increase to a thin stream as the mixture thickens. If the mixture becomes too thick, stop adding the oil and whisk until it is all incorporated. Continue until all the oil is incorporated and the mayonnaise is thick and glossy. It takes 12–15 minutes. ❋ If not using right away, transfer to clean, airtight container. Cover the surface directly with clingfilm (plastic wrap) to prevent a skin from forming and store in the refrigerator for 5 days.

## LEMON BASIL SALT

*Muối Lá É*

Lemon basil is known as '*Hla ech*' in the local dialect of the Bahnar; however, this herb was later called '*lá ê*' by Kinh people for easier pronunciation. It has a very distinctive flavour, a mix between basil, lemon and mint. Dishes using *lá é* started out in the Central Highlands of Vietnam, from Kontum and Gia Lai provinces, and now even to Phú Yên on the South Central coast. Here we have the basic dipping salt that is often eaten alongside grilled or steamed fish, or alongside Chicken Hotpot with Lemon Basil (page 170).

Makes 30 g/1 oz; serves 4–6
Preparation time: 10 minutes

| V | VE | DF | ≤5 | ≤30 |

15 g/½ oz bird's eye chillies (small green chillies preferred, about 15)
½ teaspoon salt
½ teaspoon MSG
½ teaspoon all-purpose seasoning (hạt nêm)
25 g/1 oz lemon basil (lá é), leaves picked

Cut the chillies into thin slices using scissors. Set aside. ⁕ Put the sliced chillies, salt, MSG and all-purpose seasoning in a mortar and pound with a pestle until the chillies are well crushed but not completely paste-like, 1–2 minutes. ⁕ Add the lemon basil leaves to the mortar. Gently pound and mix until the leaves are bruised and well combined with the spices. Stop before the leaves are completely mashed – they should retain some texture. ⁕ The final mixture should be chunky rather than paste-like. Transfer to an airtight container and keep for up to 1 week.

## SESAME AND PEANUT SALT

*Muối Mè Đậu Phộng*

This sweet and salty seasoning is traditionally paired with sticky (glutinous) rice dishes or plain rice. But it can also be used for boiled vegetables. The combination of roasted sesame seeds and peanuts adds a rich, nutty flavour that enhances simple dishes – a practical quality that makes it particularly valuable during times of food scarcity, as it can replace the proteins and fat usually provided by meat. You can serve this with plain rice, Rice in Bamboo Tube (page 240) or Sticky Rice with Sweetcorn (page 244).

Makes approx. 80 g/3 oz (⅓ cup); serves 8–10
Preparation time: 15 minutes
Cooking time: 11 minutes

| V | VE | DF | GF | ≤5 | ≤30 |

55 g/2 oz (⅓ cup) peanuts
¾ teaspoon salt
25 g/1 oz (3 tablespoons) white sesame seeds
½ teaspoon sugar

Heat a heavy frying pan or skillet over a medium heat. Add the raw peanuts to the dry pan. Toast for about 5 minutes, stirring frequently with a wooden spoon. Remove from heat and let cool slightly. ⁕ When the peanuts are cool enough to handle, rub the peanuts between your hands, or place in a clean paper towels and rub, to remove the skins. ⁕ Return the cleaned peanuts to the pan. Add ¼ teaspoon of the salt. Place over a medium heat and toast for 3–4 minutes, stirring constantly, until golden brown. Remove from the heat and allow to cool completely. ⁕ Alternatively, preheat the oven at 175°C/350°F/ Gas Mark 4, spread on a baking sheet and toast until golden. ⁕ In the same pan, over a low heat, add the sesame seeds and the remaining salt. Toast for about 2 minutes, stirring constantly, until golden and fragrant. Remove from the heat and allow to cool completely. ⁕ Put the toasted sesame seeds in a mortar and grind with the pestle for about 2 minutes until 80 per cent of the seeds are crushed but not completely powdered. Transfer to a bowl. ⁕ In the same mortar, add the cooled peanuts and the sugar. Grind coarsely with the pestle – the peanuts should be broken down but not completely smooth. ⁕ Add the ground sesame seeds back to the mortar. Mix everything together gently with the pestle until well combined but not too fine. ⁕ Store in an airtight container at room temperature for up to 2 weeks.

## ROASTED CHILLI SALT

*Muối Ớt Rang Khô*

This roasted chilli salt is traditionally paired with acidic fruits, from young green mangoes to guava. In traditional Vietnamese food philosophy, influenced by Traditional Chinese Medicine, acidic foods are considered 'yin' (*Âm*) while salt is 'yang' (*Dương*) – this balance helps with digesting acidic and 'hot' foods. You can also mix it with lime juice to create a dipping sauce for seafood.

Makes approx. 240 ml/8 fl oz (1 cup)
Preparation time: 10 minutes
Cooking time: 15–20 minutes

| V | VE | DF | GF | ≤5 | ≤30 |

3½ (75 g) long red chillies, destemmed and trimmed
60 g/2¼ oz (¼ cup) coarse (kosher) salt
1 tablespoon mushroom seasoning powder

Place the chillies, salt and mushroom seasoning powder in a food processor. Pulse until well-blended and the chillies are finely chopped, 30–45 seconds. Use a spatula to scrape down the sides of the processor bowl if needed. ⁕ To dry-roast the mixture, heat a heavy frying pan or skillet over a medium–low heat. Transfer the chilli-salt mixture to the pan. Using a wooden spoon, stir continuously to prevent burning and clumping. Continue cooking until the mixture is completely dry and slightly fragrant, 15–20 minutes. The mixture should be loose and granular, not wet or clumped together. ⁕ Cool completely before transferring to an airtight container and storing for up to 1 month.

## GREEN CHILLI SALT

*Muối Ớt Xanh*

This bright green sauce combines tangy, herby flavours with a subtle sweetness from condensed milk. It's traditionally served with *gà nướng muối ớt* (Grilled Chicken with Chilli Salt, page 154) or seafood dishes like Stir-fried Spotted Babylon Snails with Garlic (page 94). This versatile sauce also pairs well with any steamed or boiled seafood.

Makes 225 g/8 oz (1 cup); serves 8–10
Preparation time: 10–15 minutes

**| V | GF | ≤30 |**

50 g/1¾ oz (½ cup) green bird's eye chillies, coarsely chopped
25 g/1 oz sawtooth coriander (culantro) (green part only), stalks removed and leaves coarsely chopped
20 g/¾ oz coriander (cilantro), leaves picked and coarsely chopped
zest of 1 lime
45 g/1½ oz condensed milk
1 tablespoon neutral oil
4 tablespoons lime juice
½ teaspoon salt
80 g/2¾ oz ice cubes

Place the chillies, sawtooth coriander (culantro), coriander (cilantro) and lime zest in a blender. Add the condensed milk and oil. Pulse 3–4 times to coat everything evenly. ❋ Add the lime juice, salt and ice cubes to the blender. (The ice helps maintain the vibrant colour and prevents the herbs from oxidizing.) Blend on high speed for 1–2 minutes until completely smooth, stopping occasionally to scrape down the sides with a rubber spatula, if needed. The mixture should be bright green and well combined. ❋ Transfer to an airtight container using a rubber spatula to scrape out all the sauce. Use as a condiment for various dishes.

## SALT AND PEPPER SEASONING MIX

*Muối Tiêu*

This simple dipping salt is great for boiled meats like Steamed Chicken with Lime Leaves (page 283) or Balut (Fertilized Duck Eggs, page 50).

Makes 1½ tablespoons; serves 2–3
Preparation time: 5 minutes

**| V | VE | DF | GF | ≤5 | ≤30 |**

½ teaspoon salt
½ teaspoon black pepper
¼ teaspoon sugar
1 teaspoon lime juice
2 lime leaves
5 g/⅛ oz bird's eye chillies (about 2 chillies), deseeded and finely minced, optional

In a small mixing bowl, combine the salt, pepper and sugar. Add the lime juice and stir until the sugar dissolves and the mixture forms a slightly wet paste. ❋ Remove the centre stalk from the lime leaves. Stack the leaves, roll them tightly and slice into very fine ribbons (chiffonade). Add the finely sliced lime leaves and chillies (if using) to the salt mixture. Mix all the ingredients thoroughly until well combined. Serve when fresh.

# INDEX

## D



## E



## F

## G



## H



## I



## J

## Q

## S

## V



## W



## Y

Phaidon Press Limited
2 Cooperage Yard
London E15 2QR

Phaidon Press Inc.
111 Broadway
New York, NY 10006

Phaidon SARL
55, rue Traversière
75012 Paris

phaidon.com

First published 2025
© 2025 Phaidon Press Limited

ISBN 978 1 83729 045 1

A CIP catalogue record for this book is available from the British Library and the Library of Congress.

All rights reserved. No part of this publication may be reproduced, stored in a retrieval system or transmitted, in any form or by any means, electronic, mechanical, photocopying, recording or otherwise, without the written permission of Phaidon Press Limited.

Commissioning Editor: Emilia Terragni
Project Editor: Clare Churly
Senior Production Controller: Gary Hayes
Design: Ana Teodoro, Cantina

Photography: Pham Bich Phuong

Printed in China

**Publisher's Acknowledgements**
Phaidon would like to thank Theresa Bebbington, Vanessa Bird, João Mota, Phương Anh Nguyễn, Claire Rogers, Ellie Smith, Tracey Smith and Phoebe Stephenson.

**About the Author**
Anaïs Ca Dao van Manen is a chef and consultant whose career has taken her all over the world. Born in Paris to a Vietnamese-Dutch family, she has lived and worked in London and now lives in Vietnam. Her career started in kitchens, including Auberge de Chassignoles, Café Bar Universal, Trullo and Bao London. In recent years she has moved into development and consultancy and has also opened her own restaurants in Vietnam. Her videos on Instagram showcase the diversity of Vietnamese cuisine and shine a light on lesser-known Vietnamese dishes.

**Recipe Notes**
Butter is salted butter, unless otherwise specified.
Eggs are UK size medium (US size large), unless otherwise specified.
Herbs are fresh, unless otherwise specified.
Milk is whole (full-fat) or semi-skimmed (reduced-fat) milk, unless otherwise specified.
Pepper is freshly ground black pepper, unless otherwise specified.
Salt is fine sea salt, unless otherwise specified.
Sugar is white caster (superfine) sugar, unless otherwise specified.
Vinegar is distilled white vinegar, unless otherwise specified.
Individual vegetables and fruits, such as carrots and apples, are assumed to be medium, unless otherwise specified, and should be peeled and/or washed unless otherwise specified.
Aromatics such as garlic and onion are assumed to be peeled, unless otherwise specified.
Where neutral oil is specified, use vegetable, rapeseed (canola), grapeseed, sunflower, corn or light olive oil.
Traditional and authentic Vietnamese ingredients are used in this book, with English translations that may vary locally. If you are unfamiliar with an ingredient, use the Vietnamese name to source the correct item.
Metric, imperial and cup measurements are used in this book. Follow one set of measurements throughout, not a mixture, as they are not interchangeable.
All tablespoon and teaspoon measurements given are level, not heaped, unless otherwise specified. 1 teaspoon = 5 ml; 1 tablespoon = 15 ml. Australian standard tablespoons are 20 ml, so Australian readers are advised to use 3 teaspoons in place of 1 tablespoon when measuring small quantities.
When no quantity is specified, for example of oils, salts and herbs used for finishing dishes or for deep-frying, quantities are discretionary and flexible.
Cooking and preparation times are for guidance only. If using a convection (fan) oven, follow the manufacturer's instructions concerning oven temperatures.
When deep-frying, heat the oil to the temperature specified, or until a cube of bread browns in 30 seconds. After frying, drain fried foods on paper towels.
When sterilizing jars for preserves, wash the jars in clean, hot water and rinse thoroughly. Heat the oven to 140°C/275°F/Gas Mark 1. Place the jars on a baking tray and place in the oven to dry.
Exercise a high level of caution when following recipes involving any potentially hazardous activity including the use of high temperatures and open flames and when deep-frying. In particular, when deep-frying, add food carefully to avoid splashing, wear long sleeves, and never leave the pan unattended.
Exercise caution when making fermented products, ensuring all equipment is spotlessly clean, and seek expert advice if in any doubt.
All herbs, shoots, flowers and leaves should be picked fresh from a clean source.
Do exercise caution when foraging for ingredients, which should only be eaten if an expert has deemed them safe to eat. In particular, do not gather wild mushrooms yourself before seeking the advice of an expert who has confirmed their suitability for human consumption.
As some species of mushrooms have been known to cause allergic reaction and illness, do take extra care when cooking and eating mushrooms and do seek immediate medical help if you experience a reaction after preparing or eating them.
Eel blood is toxic if consumed raw. It contains ichthyotoxin, a protein that can be harmful to humans if ingested or if it enters the bloodstream through cuts. To ensure safety, always cook eel thoroughly, as heat neutralizes the toxin, making it safe to eat. When handling raw eel, wear gloves and clean all surfaces and tools after preparation to prevent cross-contamination. Never consume raw eel unless it has been properly processed. Once cooked, eel is completely safe.
Food-grade lye can be used for curing, tenderizing or adding colour and texture. It is highly corrosive, so take care when using and do not allow to come into contact with skin.
Some recipes include raw or very lightly cooked eggs, blood, meat or fish, as well as fermented products. These should be avoided by the elderly, infants, pregnant women, convalescents and anyone with an impaired immune system.